THE
SOCIAL AND ECONOMIC
HISTORY OF THE
HELLENISTIC
WORLD

THE
SOCIAL & ECONOMIC HISTORY OF THE HELLENISTIC WORLD

By

M. ROSTOVTZEFF

Hon. D.Litt., Hon. Litt.D. (*Cambridge*)
Hon. Litt.D. (*Harvard*), Hon. Litt.D. (*Wisconsin*)
Professor of Ancient History in Yale University

VOLUME II

OXFORD
AT THE CLARENDON PRESS

Oxford University Press, Ely House, London W. 1

GLASGOW NEW YORK TORONTO MELBOURNE WELLINGTON
CAPE TOWN SALISBURY IBADAN NAIROBI LUSAKA ADDIS ABABA
BOMBAY CALCUTTA MADRAS KARACHI LAHORE DACCA
KUALA LUMPUR HONG KONG TOKYO

FIRST EDITION 1941
REPRINTED LITHOGRAPHICALLY IN GREAT BRITAIN
AT THE UNIVERSITY PRESS, OXFORD
FROM CORRECTED SHEETS OF THE FIRST EDITION
1953, 1959, 1964, 1967

3920

CONTENTS

FIGURES IN THE TEXT

LIST OF PLATES

V

DISINTEGRATION OF THE BALANCE OF POWER AND ROMAN INTERVENTION

A NEW situation was created in the Hellenistic world by the events of the end of the third and of the early second century B.C. (down to the Third Macedonian War). I have already dealt with the political aspect of this situation, but I may recall certain outstanding events. In the first place two young and ambitious rulers, Antiochus III in Syria and Philip V in Macedonia, undermined the balance of power by their efforts to put an end to the hegemony of Egypt and to restore the past glory of their respective monarchies. Later, Antiochus, by his restless activity in the East, and Philip, by his similar activity in the Aegean and Adriatic, aroused the suspicion of Rome, and impelled her to interfere in the politics of the Hellenistic world. The most important results of these political events from the economic point of view were: the loss by Egypt of her dominions both in Syria and in the Aegean, her almost complete withdrawal from the Aegean, and her growing political isolation; the political isolation of Macedonia; the bestowal on Greece of a freedom which brought with it political anarchy; the political isolation likewise of Syria, which was now separated from the Aegean world by the barrier of the Pergamene kingdom and of other kingdoms in Asia Minor; and finally the growing political importance of Rhodes and Pergamon.

I. GREECE

During this period Greece was once more the theatre of continuous war. It was conducted on much the same lines as in the past, but all our authorities for the period are agreed in emphasizing the fact that the seed of savagery in the third century yielded a rich harvest in the second. War was now carried on with an unnecessary cruelty and a lawlessness previously unheard of. The Aetolians and Philip, especially after Philip's 'change of heart' (μεταβολή), set the example.

3261·2   B

PLATE LXIX

1. Æ Aetolian league. B.C. 279–168. Obv. Head of Aetolos, wearing kausia. Rev. ΑΙΤΩΛΩΝ. Boar and spear head.

2. Æ Achaean league. B.C. 280–146 (Sicyon). Obv. Head of Zeus Amarios. Rev. Achaean monogram in wreath, beneath, ΣΙ.

3. Æ Tetradrachm of Antigonus Gonatas (or Doson?), Macedonia. Obv. Head of Pan in centre of Macedonian shield. Rev. ΒΑΣΙΛΕΩΣ ΑΝΤΙΓΟΝΟΥ. Athena Alkis in archaistic style.

4. Æ Tetradrachm 'New Style', Athens, c. B.C. 229–197. Obv. Head of Athena. Rev. ΑΘΕ. Owl on amphora in wreath.

5. Æ Tetradrachm of Seleucus IV, Syria. Obv. Head of Seleucus IV, wearing diadem. Rev. ΒΑΣΙΛΕΩΣ ΣΕΛΕΥΚΟΥ. Apollo seated on omphalos.

6. N Octodrachm of Ptolemy IV, Egypt. Obv. Bust of Ptolemy IV. Rev. ΠΤΟΛΕΜΑΙΟΥ ΦΙΛΟΠΑΤΟΡΟΣ. Eagle on fulmen.

7. N Octodrachm of Ptolemy V, Egypt. Obv. Bust of Ptolemy V. Rev. ΒΑΣΙΛΕΩΣ ΠΤΟΛΕΜΑΙΟΥ. Eagle on fulmen.

8. Æ Tetradrachm of Demetrius of Bactria. Obv. Bust of the king wearing diadem and elephant hide. Rev. ΒΑΣΙΛΕΩΣ ΔΗΜΗΤΡΙΟΥ. Heracles crowning himself.

9. Æ Tetradrachm of Philip V of Macedonia. Obv. Head of Philip. Rev. ΒΑΣΙΛΕΩΣ ΦΙΛΙΠΠΟΥ. Athena Alkis hurling fulmen.

10. Æ Tetradrachm of Perseus of Macedonia. Obv. Head of Perseus. Rev. ΒΑΣΙΛΕΩΣ ΠΕΡΣΕΩΣ. Eagle on fulmen, all in wreath.

The coins of this plate illustrate the leading currencies at the time of Roman intervention in the affairs of the Hellenistic world: for the mainland of Greece the still important issues of Athenian owls and those of the two leading Leagues (the Achaean and Aetolian); and parallel to them the abundant issues of the Macedonian kings: Antigonus Gonatas and Doson, Philip V, and Perseus. The East is represented by the coinage of Syria (Seleucus IV) and Egypt (Ptolemy IV and Ptolemy V), and the further East by that of Demetrius of Bactria, the creator of the Bactro-Indian Empire (above, pl. VII, 3). I may note that the issue illustrated by no. 3 is ascribed by H. Gaebler, *Die antiken Münzen von Makedonia und Paionia*, 1935, to Antigonus Gonatas, though he admits that the coinage of Gonatas was probably continued without change by Doson.

PLATE LXIX

COINS OF THE LATE THIRD AND EARLY SECOND CENTURIES B.C.
PERIOD OF ROMAN INTERVENTION

They found apt pupils in the Achaeans, and they were soon outdone by Nabis in Sparta and still more by the Romans. I have drawn attention in an earlier chapter (see above, pp. 200 ff.) to some characteristic examples of the methods of the Aetolians and of Philip during the Social War, especially to the acts of ἱεροσυλία, which produced so deep an impression on the whole of Greece. I may quote here two general statements on the subject, one relating to Philip ascribed by Polybius to Alexander Isius, an Aetolian, the richest man in Greece; the other made by Philip himself with regard to the Aetolians. The two statements occur in speeches delivered by Alexander and Philip before Flamininus at the peace conference of 198 B.C. at Nicaea in Locris. The former* contrasts the methods of Philip with those of Alexander and Antigonus and their successors down to the time of Pyrrhus and adds: 'for he avoided meeting his enemies face to face and, as he fled before them, burned and sacked the cities.'† He adduces in support of his statement the fate of many Thessalian cities which Philip devastated, 'though he was their friend and ally' (φίλος ὢν καὶ σύμμαχος). In his reply Philip describes with bitter sarcasm the Aetolian procedure. He begins by stating that he himself and Greece have repeatedly asked the Aetolians to abolish the law which gave them the right 'to get spoil from spoil'. The reply was: 'You would rather remove Aetolia from Aetolia than this law.'‡¹ At the request of Flamininus Philip then gives further details about this law and says that the Aetolians have a special habit of pillaging not only the countries of their enemies, 'but if any other peoples are at war with each other who are friends and allies of theirs, it is none the less permissible to the Aetolians without a decree of the people to help both belligerents and pillage the territory of both'.§ Neither Philip nor the Aetolians ever changed their method of carrying on war. I may quote, for instance, as regards

* Polyb. xviii. 3. 3.

† ἀφέντα γὰρ τοῦ κατὰ πρόσωπον ἀπαντᾶν τοῖς πολεμίοις, φεύγοντα τὰς πόλεις ἐμπιμπράναι καὶ διαρπάζειν.

‡ ἄγειν λάφυρον ἀπὸ λαφύρου.—πρότερον . . . τὴν Αἰτωλίαν ἐκ τῆς Αἰτωλίας ἀρεῖν ἢ τοῦτον τὸν νόμον. Id. xviii. 4. 8.

§ ἀλλὰ κἂν ἕτεροί τινες πολεμῶσι πρὸς ἀλλήλους, ὄντες Αἰτωλῶν φίλοι καὶ σύμμαχοι, μηδὲν ἧττον ἐξεῖναι τοῖς Αἰτωλοῖς ἄνευ κοινοῦ δόγματος καὶ παραβοηθεῖν ἀμφοτέροις τοῖς πολεμοῦσι καὶ τὴν χώραν ἄγειν τὴν ἀμφοτέρων. Id. xviii. 5. 2.

the former the famous case of his treatment of the cities of Cius, Myrleia, and Thasos in his Asiatic war: the whole or the greater part of the population of these cities was sold into slavery. I may remind the reader that his procedure was exactly the same as in 217 B.C., when Phthiotic Thebes was annihilated in the same way.[2]

The Roman method of conducting war is illustrated by a number of well-known texts. In their treaty with the Aetolians at the beginning of the First Macedonian War the Romans did not conceal the fact that one of their principal objects in embarking upon a war in Greece was to enrich themselves and their armies. While they left all conquered territory to the Aetolians they reserved for themselves the booty, whether consisting of men or goods, and undertook to carry on the war in such a way as to leave nothing but the 'bare ground, roofs, and walls'.[3]

Their proceedings in Aegina were outrageous and aroused general indignation in Greece.[4] The methods of Valerius Laevinus inspired the Greeks with horror and indignation. The eloquent words of Carcopino sum up concisely the many passages in Polybius and Livy. 'Il ne négocie point,' says Carcopino of Laevinus, 'il ne gradue pas ses coups. Il a besoin d'esclaves, de matériaux et d'argent. Il cogne, pille et massacre, sans exception ni tempérament, avec une exécrable monotonie de sanglantes dévastations qui propagent jusqu'en Egypte et sur les rivages d'Asie l'horreur des Barbares d'Italie.'[5]

Nor can I give a better summary of what the great war of liberation cost the Greeks than the following words of Holleaux, the best authority on the subject (the quotations from ancient authors would be endless).[6] 'They (the Romans) declared that they had come to Greece only to bring it freedom, and they had in fact brought also, and for the second time, war of the brutal Roman sort. Oreus, in 199 as in 208, had seen its people enslaved; the "liberator" Flamininus had spread cruel havoc throughout Thessaly, Phocis, Euboea, Acarnania and, later, Laconia; besides, three years of occupation with its train of requisitions and exactions, and the great mobilization against Nabis, had produced widespread exhaustion. Flamininus had, it is true, restored their property to the Chyretians, but he had freighted his ships deep not only with heaps of coin but also with works of art carried off from many cities which, like Andros and Eretria, had obeyed Philip against their will. The price of Greek "freedom" was that Greece lay bruised, ruined, and despoiled.'

One of the principal features of the warfare of the period was the active part taken in it by pirates and freebooters of all kinds. I need not repeat what I have already said about the prominence of piracy in the life and in the wars of the Hellenistic period. It was natural that almost all the States at war in the period we are now concerned with should make extensive use of pirates, especially for raiding and sacking neutral cities. For this purpose they employed adventurers who professed to be acting at their own risk and on their own account, but were in fact the agents of one of the great powers of the time. The Aetolians commonly adopted this practice, and Philip did the same after the peace of Phoenice, when he was in urgent need of money. The Achaeans probably did likewise, and the same device was freely used by Nabis.[7] Professional piracy on a large scale was carried on by the Cretans.[8] All sorts of methods were adopted in order to put an end to their activity, but none succeeded. The Cretans would not renounce their raids, and all the efforts of the Rhodians to force them into submission were fruitless. Philip, who controlled a large group of Cretan cities and in 216 nearly established his protectorate over the whole of Crete, had no desire to help the Rhodians in their almost constant struggle with the Cretans. On the contrary, he supported the Cretans against the Rhodians and was to a large extent responsible for what is known as the Cretan War (Κρητικὸς πόλεμος) which lasted for several years (204–201 B.C.), and was a terrible scourge to all the islands of the Aegean. Many inscriptions mention this war and the subsequent war between Philip and the Rhodians (the συνεστακὼς πόλεμος, as they call it), in which the same methods were used. None are more explicit than the group of inscriptions from Cos and Calymna, some of them recently published and discussed.[9] In all probability Philip was glad to see Rhodes engaged in this troublesome war while he was preparing and carrying out his own conquests in Asia Minor, and it is natural to suppose that in return for the protection and support he gave to the Cretans he would receive some share of their booty.

The chief victims of the Cretans were inevitably the islands of the Aegean. But the pirates in the service of Philip did not abstain from plundering the Greek coastal territory, and the use of specially trained land robbers seems to have been one of the most effective inventions of Nabis. Livy says, for instance, that at the beginning of the Second Macedonian War pirate ships in the service of Philip, using Chalcis as their base, infested the sea and pillaged the Attic littoral;* the same situation as we have seen when the Aetolians were pillaging the Attic territory, carrying off the people and selling them in Crete (above, p. 199).† Nor was the system followed by Nabis very different. A decree of Mycenae in honour of Protimus, citizen of Gortyn, praises him for having rescued some ephebes who had been abducted by Nabis and probably brought to Crete.[10] I need hardly remind the reader of the famous statement of Polybius‡ concerning Nabis: 'He participated in the piracy of the Cretans. Through the whole of the Peloponnese he had robbers of temples, highwaymen, and assassins, whose profits he shared and whom he allowed to make Sparta their base and their refuge.'

The years preceding the Syrian War and the period of the war itself were stirring and prosperous times for the pirates alike in the Aegean, the Black Sea, and in the Western seas, as some outstanding facts will testify.

We must not forget that the success of the treacherous attack of Polyxenidas, the Rhodian admiral of Antiochus, on Pausistratus, the Rhodian commander, was due in part to the co-operation of the arch-pirate Nicandrus.§ An interesting episode reported in a Delphian inscription appears to point to a somewhat similar activity of pirates in the Black Sea. Delphian *theoroi* who sailed in 194 B.C. to the Crimea were captured by pirates and redeemed by Chersonesus. This, it is true, suggests the Taurians, the professional sea-robbers of the

---

* Liv. xxxi. 22. 7, cf. Diod. xxviii, 1.

† Decree for Eumaridas, *S.I.G.*³ 535; *I.G.* ii. 2nd ed. 844. = *I.G.* ii, 5 no. 385 c.

‡ xiii. 8. 1.   § Liv. xxxvii. 11. 6.

Crimea. But since the incident occurred when Antiochus III
was trying to establish his supremacy in Asia Minor, on the
Thracian coast, and in the Straits, one may think that those
responsible for the capture of the Delphian envoys were Tauric
pirates in the service of Antiochus who were engaged in the
Black Sea in preventing the king's enemies from drawing
supplies from that region.[11]

Nor was it different in the West. Here the sea as late as
190 B.C. was still in the hands of Cephallonian pirates led by
Hybristas, whom Livy calls a Lacaedemonian, but who may
have been an Aetolian.*[12]

I may note in this connexion that the Aetolians, the former
allies of Antiochus, who were active at sea and employed pirate
forces, did the same on land even after the war. Their
proceedings in this respect led the Delphians to send an
embassy to Rome in 189 B.C., in order to request for the
sanctuary and the city inviolability, freedom, and exemption
from taxation (ἀσυλία, ἐλευθερία, ἀνεισφορία), a measure
certainly directed mainly against the Aetolians. We are not
surprised therefore to learn that their ambassadors, while
returning with this request granted, were assassinated probably
by pirates, and perhaps by pirates not unconnected with the
Aetolians. Another embassy was sent to Rome by the Delphians, ostensibly to announce the organization of an *agon*
and sacrifices in honour of Rome, but in fact to complain of the
assassination of their ambassadors, of the continued robberies
of the Aetolians, and of troubles created at Delphi by 'undesirable foreigners', probably in the main Aetolians. The
reply of C. Livius Salinator was favourable: M. Fulvius
Nobilior was commissioned after the siege of Same to investigate the assassination, the Aetolians were advised to restore
to the Delphians all the property that had been taken (τὰ
ἀπηγμένα ἄπαντα), and to desist from their misdeeds (ἀδική-
ματα), and the Delphians were permitted to remove all undesirable residents from the city and to allow only such as were
agreeable to them to remain there (εὐαρεστοῦντας τῶι κοινῶι τῶν
Δελφῶν).[13]

---

* Liv. xxxvii. 13, 12. An Aetolian *strategos* of this name is mentioned
165/4 B.C., *I.G.* ix. 2nd ed. i, p. lii.

These facts show that the end of the Syrian War and the establishment of a Roman protectorate over Macedonia and Greece had not changed the situation. The pirates had lost good employers in the persons of Philip and Antiochus, but they still had the Aetolians and Nabis for a time, and they were still able to resist the Rhodians and Eumenes II. Both Rhodes and Pergamon, which after the two great victories of Rome enjoyed temporarily her full confidence, took seriously their task of putting an end to piracy in the Aegean. To bring the Cretan cities to reason they tried the method of individual alliances with them, either singly or in groups, hoping thereby to put an end to their depredations without having recourse to acts of war.* The method was judicious and its final success probable, had it not been for the war of Perseus with Rome, in which, it may be noted, the pirates took an active part on both sides. It was during this war that Rhodes took a decisive step towards the pacification of the Aegean. She invited the Cretans to form an alliance with her. Unfortunately her abortive mediation between Rome and Perseus defeated her attempt to extinguish piracy.

Such was the situation in Greece in the late third and early second century B.C., a miserable time in her not very happy history. It is not surprising that, downtrodden and humiliated, robbed and pillaged, having lost faith in gods and men, the country was more than ever distracted by political and social unrest.

In the atmosphere of war, of organized brigandage and common rapine, of confiscations and requisitions, life in Greece was utterly disorganized. Demoralization seized upon both the upper and the lower classes, and social unrest, disturbances, and revolutions were of ordinary occurrence. Demoralization and class antagonism made extremely acute by the impoverishment and proletarian condition of the working class provided favourable conditions for the manœuvres of unscrupulous politicians. These conditions prevailed at the time of the 'Social War' and they persisted during the First and Second Macedonian Wars and the interval between them. I may recall certain well-known facts in connexion with the early

* *S.I.G.*³ 581 and 627 (200–197 B.C., and 183 B.C. respectively).

part of this period. Philip, both in his struggle with the Romans and Aetolians, and later, appeared for a while as a champion of the oppressed masses and acted accordingly. The opposition of the upper classes to his political aspirations provoked his anger, and he wanted to frighten them. The support of Nabis gave lasting success to the social revolution in Sparta. With the help of Cretans and mercenaries he seized the crown and 'applied the extremist programme in its entirety—spoliation, proscription, systematic destruction of the upper classes, confiscation of private fortunes (ostensibly for the State). Moreover, he enfranchised many Helots, who were made citizens, assigned land to these same Helots and to the poor, and distributed among mob-leaders and mercenaries the goods and even the wives and daughters of the proscribed' (Holleaux).

Nor was the situation better in Aetolia. Polybius* gives a striking account of it. Here the role of Nabis was played by Scopas and Dorimachus. Troubles between debtors and creditors, arising out of wars and the luxurious mode of life, enabled these men to get themselves elected 'lawgivers' (*nomographoi*), and in this capacity Scopas suggested radical measures. He was, however, defeated by the leader of the conservatives, Alexander Isius.†

The conditions remained the same after the Second Macedonian and the Syrian wars. Polybius describes the social and political demoralization, the unsettled conditions, the spoliations and depredations, the mob-rule under the leadership of unscrupulous and selfish politicians, that prevailed in Boeotia in the early second century B.C. These passages‡ are familiar to every student of ancient history and have been frequently discussed. I will, however, summarize them, since they give a picture unsurpassed in its poignancy. It appears from them that class antagonism reached its highest pitch in Boeotia at that time. The mob was at the helm. It was represented by the *strategoi* who carried out one measure after another in the interest of the proletariat, and were naturally re-elected from year to year. One of these measures was the *de facto* suspension

* xiii. 1, cf. iv. 3. 1.   † Polyb. xiii. 1. 1ᵃ.
‡ xx. 6, and xxii. 4.

3920

of the lawcourts for about 25 years.* By this means the lower classes evaded responsibility for their crimes and for their debts. From the economic point of view the measure was almost equivalent to a general 'abolition of debts' (χρεῶν ἀποκοπή). Another still more radical measure carried out by the *strategoi* was payment of a regular salary out of the public funds to all poor, that is to say, unemployed citizens. This last measure was of course extreme, but entirely in the spirit of radical Greek democracy. Even wise aristocratic governments resorted to it to avoid class war. I may remind the reader of Rhodes and her solution of the social problem (below, p. 684). The insecurity of life and the unsettled conditions demoralized not only the lower but also the upper classes. Family life was broken up. Dissipated club life flourished and produced a general lowering of moral tone.

The conditions described by Polybius as prevailing in 192 B.C. endured for a long time and led to repeated conflicts. These drew the attention of the Romans, who ordered the Aetolians and Achaeans to carry out a punitive expedition against Boeotia. Nothing resulted from this, though the Achaeans, impatient for a settlement of their claims against the Boeotians, forcibly seized some Boeotian cattle by way of reprisals (ῥύσια), thereby nearly bringing about a war between Achaea and Boeotia.

The conditions in Boeotia were not exceptional. They existed likewise, according to Polybius, among the Achaeans and Thessalians, and similar occurrences were not temporary but enduring phenomena in the history of Greece. I may quote, for example the renewal of social and economic troubles in Aetolia in 174/3 B.C.† The Romans never seriously interfered. Indeed, in many cases they were ready, as Philip had been in the past, to support the proletarians against the richer classes, whom they did not trust.[14]

Never was the prospect of a general social revolution more threatening in Greece than in the period under consideration down to the Achaean war. But the efforts of the proletariat

* Similar phenomena in the history of Thebes are mentioned by Ps.-Heracleides Criticus, 16, in his description of Boeotia, above, p. 211.

† Liv. xli. 25. 1–6; xlii. 4. 5; 5. 10–12; 6, 1.

were chaotic and sporadic, the resistance of the bourgeoisie staunch, and the aims of the leaders and supporters of the proletariat selfish and mostly political, the proletariat being for them a pawn in their political game. The social unrest in Greece therefore remained sterile and destructive, shifting from one place to another and never achieving more or less lasting and positive results.

An illustration of the disorganization that reigned at this time in Greece, both a cause and the result of discontent and economic instability, is to be seen in the enormous number of lawsuits pending between citizens of a particular city, between citizens and foreigners, and between city and city. The corruption and inefficiency of the regular city lawcourts were so evident that all confidence in them was lost. As a remedy the cities had recourse to an expedient which was never so popular in Greece as in the second century B.C., the bringing in of foreign judges not only to act as arbiters between two cities, but also and chiefly to carry on the ordinary work of the lawcourts of a particular city, either because the courts were unable to cope with the arrears of litigation (τῶν ἐγκλημάτων εἰλκυμένων ἐκ πλειόνων χρόνων), or were prevented from functioning by social troubles, or were rejected by the parties as biased and not impartial. We have scores of inscriptions referring to foreign judges, most of them decrees in their honour. The list of them is too long to be given here. Robert, in his masterly article on the subject, quotes as places in northern Greece where foreign judges adjudicated in the second century, apart from Delphi of which I shall speak below, Gonnoi, Demetrias, and the Magnetes, the Thessalian confederation, the Ainianes, Crannon, and Thespiae.[15]

A good example of the vicissitudes of the Greek cities in this period is offered by the history of Delphi, which has recently been studied by M. Holleaux, P. Roussel, R. Flacelière, and G. Daux. After a period of quiet and prosperity under the Aetolian rule, the city encountered difficulties in the times of Philip V and of his struggle with the Aetolians. Philip was now its near neighbour and its frontiers were not secure. The people, foreseeing the downfall of their temporary masters, were restless and agitated. The prevalence of war in Greece had an unfavourable effect on the economic situation of the sanctuary and the city. It is not surprising that the Aetolians appointed special curators (*epimeletai*), probably military and civil officials, charged with the duty of protecting the city and temple and keeping the peace.

Soon, however, the Aetolians were ousted from Delphi by the Romans. Delphi recovered its liberty, but not its tranquillity and prosperity. The population had always consisted of many foreigners and a comparatively small number of Delphians. Most of the 'foreign' settlers there were members of the Aetolian League. Such of them as were said to have acquired property in Delphi without special authorization forfeited their houses and land, which were 'restored' by the Romans to the city and temple. We still possess a list of these properties appended to an official letter of the 'restorer', Acilius Glabrio. Twenty-seven κτήματα and forty houses are enumerated as gifts of the Romans to Delphi. The practical effects of this confiscation may be imagined: endless litigation, hatred and hostility not only between 'foreigners' and 'natives', but among the 'natives' themselves. Some of the 'natives' suffered as much by the Roman donations as did those whose property was confiscated, for loans, mortgages, dowries, &c., were involved. It was in vain that those who profited appealed to the Roman masters and obtained their confirmation of the donations: Greek law was complicated and Greek lawyers were cunning and experienced. It is no wonder that lawsuits accumulated in the Delphian courts and that the city repeatedly had recourse to foreign judges. We still possess a notable series of decrees in honour of these foreign judges, most of them dating from the early and middle second century B.C.

Further complications arose from the authority given to the Delphians to exile 'undesirable' inhabitants, and to grant permission of residence only to persons acceptable to the rulers of the day. Anyone who knows the extent to which bribery and corruption permeated a Greek democracy can realize what this measure meant in practice.

Finally, a reorganization of the Amphictiony became imperative after the withdrawal of the Aetolians. In reality it was an obsolete institution, without influence or importance. Nevertheless, the competition for the seats that became vacant

was very keen, while the Delphians showed the liveliest dread
of any new ascendancy on the council, whether Thessalian or
any other, and of the intrigues of their former masters, the
Macedonians and the Aetolians.

All these factors contributed to a general feeling of insecurity
and instability. No one felt that even his life was safe, while
the violent changes could not be other than detrimental to the
economic prosperity of the community as a whole.[16]

The dominating factor in the life of Greece at this time was
the increase of poverty and distress. Its causes are evident.
War and social unrest were among them. But there were other
reasons for it which were less evident to contemporaries than
they are to us, reasons connected, not with the political and
social conditions of the moment, but with the general economic
trend of the period. I have explained how the new markets
opened to Greek industry by Alexander and the successors
gradually emancipated themselves from dependence on Greece.
I have shown how the new monarchies of the East strove to
become self-sufficient, how they increased their agricultural
and industrial production and aimed at exporting as much and
importing as little as possible. For Greece this meant a decrease
of exports, an increase of imports, and a condition of growing
economic stress. The process was slow but uninterrupted. In
Greece itself economic production became more and more dispersed, each city trying to supply its own requirements. This
dispersion is noticeable chiefly in the field of industry.

I have already spoken of this evolution and I shall return to
it later in this chapter and in the next, but a few illustrations
may be given here. Our material is scanty and has been little
studied, but we see an example of the process in question in
the manufacture of pottery, of what are known, for instance,
as Megarian bowls. I have dealt with this typically Hellenistic
branch of pottery above, and I have mentioned that in early
Hellenistic times its production was begun perhaps in two
centres simultaneously: in northern Greece, Boeotia, and
Athens on the one hand, and in Alexandria on the other. It
very soon became decentralized. It was not long before Syria,
South Italy, and South Russia began to compete with Greece
and Alexandria, and satisfied their own needs by their own

output. Later the manufacture of Megarian bowls spread still more widely. Sparta and Macedonia, Pergamon, perhaps Delos, and certainly many more cities in Greece and in the Hellenistic world had their own local brands. Further archaeological exploration will probably show that there was hardly any place in the Hellenistic world which had not its own Megarian bowls. This sketch of their evolution is, of course, tentative and hypothetical. A closer and more thorough study of the clay of which Megarian bowls were made and of their shapes and ornamentation will add precision to our knowledge of their history. However, its general trend is certain.

The development of the production of other varieties of pottery was similar. Such interesting examples as the well-known *lagynoi* and the other Hellenistic varieties of painted pottery are found in all parts of the Hellenistic world and many of the specimens were certainly produced locally. Nor was it otherwise with such products of ceramic industry as the censers (small portable altars adorned with reliefs), the portable charcoal ovens (*réchauds*), and the lamps, but especially the clay figurines. The material at our disposal allows us to recognize several centres of terracotta production, some in large and flourishing cities, others in quite insignificant places. Alongside of Alexandria, Antioch, Pergamon, Smyrna, Tarentum and other cities in South Italy, we know of the existence of local factories of clay figurines in such widely separated places as Seleuceia on the Tigris, South Russia, Cyrene, Amisus in Pontus, Tarsus in Cilicia, and such minor centres as several cities in the Troad, Myrina in Aeolis, Priene. All these local factories started by reproducing and imitating the Greek and perhaps South Italian types of terracotta figurines, but gradually created their own types and style. The second and first centuries B.C. were the best period of Myrina.[17]

We have no means of estimating the material losses of Greece in the period immediately before and during the establishment of the Roman protectorate. Those which were caused by the Roman wars are partially reflected in the figures of the booty captured and of the money exacted as indemnities by the victors, which were carried to Rome from Greece after the wars and were displayed in the triumphs of the Roman generals. The amount of this booty and indemnity money was carefully recorded by the historians of the time, and the figures which they give were certainly drawn from official sources and are on the whole reliable. They have been often collected and tabulated by modern scholars. It is unnecessary to repeat these tabulations here.

The amounts recorded by the Roman annalists represent, however, only a fraction, and probably not a very large one, of the material damage done to Greece and Macedonia during the Roman wars. The private booty that Roman officers and soldiers took with them to Italy or sold in Greece was in all probability very large. But no exact or even approximate figures are available. Nor do we know what was the equivalent in money of the loss suffered by Greece and Macedonia through the destruction of houses and public buildings in the cities, and of farms, crops, vines, olive-trees, and orchards in the country. Nor again can we estimate the effect on the prosperity of the cities and the individual citizens of the political and social revolutions which were endemic in Greece in this period. Therefore, although we know that the booty of Flamininus amounted to 6,061,530 denarii, this knowledge gives us a very vague idea of what the war of 'liberation' meant for Greece and Macedonia.

The wars and revolutions naturally did not affect all parts of Greece and Macedonia to the same degree. Some suffered more, others less. But it would be a mistake to suppose that the wars and revolutions did not contribute substantially to the gradual economic decay of Greece and Macedonia.[18]

Certain more general phenomena in the life of Greece at this time, which have been little noticed by modern scholars, perhaps reflect the gradual impoverishment of the country better than do the figures of the Roman spoils. Though they cannot be expressed statistically, they are important and deserve mention in this connexion.

I have shown above how, under the influence of the new economic conditions created by Alexander and his successors, Greece recovered from the temporary economic depression of the end of the fourth century. The main wealth of Greece was in the hands of her middle class, and it was not so much the wealthy few as this middle class who profited from the new economic opportunities.

A change for the worse had already begun, and it became increasingly manifest in the period we are considering. It was the *bourgeoisie* or middle class in the Greek cities that chiefly suffered in the turmoil of the late third and the early second century B.C. The few rich people were much more favourably situated, and indeed rather profited by the decay of the middle class. We have evidence here and there of the rapid concentration of wealth in this period in a few hands, for instance at Athens,[19] in Boeotia,* and in Sparta after Cleomenes and before Nabis. Alexander Isius of Aetolia and Protogenes of Olbia were early examples of a class of men which later became typical in the Greek world.

We may form an idea of the gradual and steady decline of the middle class if we study the material conditions of life in most of the cities of Greece and the measures taken by these to maintain themselves amid the difficulties of the time.

To begin with, the problem of the daily food supply, which was always prominent in the life of the Greek cities, now became more acute than ever, as in the circumstances was natural. Even the few cities that were self-sufficient in this respect in normal times were no longer secure, much less those which had always depended on imports for their subsistence . Now, there was no general scarcity of foodstuffs. There were many productive countries with abundance of grain, fish, and other foods to export. Though Egypt's output was declining, it was doing so gradually, not catastrophically (see below), and the position was the same in Thrace and South Russia. The decline was not so great that these countries had nothing to export. The relations of Rhodes with Egypt, the commercial connexions between Delos, Delphi, Miletus, Rhodes on the one hand and the Bosporan kingdom and the Tauric Chersonese on the other, show that Egypt and South Russia were still important centres of export. Moreover, we shall see later that Asia Minor was rapidly developing its agriculture, and that Syria and Phoenicia did not lag behind. Finally it was in these times,

* Pol. xx. 6. i.

after the Second Punic War, that the Greek market saw the reappearance of African grain, brought from Numidia and Carthage.[20]

Nor are we entitled to say that, though there was plenty of food in existence, the available supply was scanty because trade relations were disorganized when the Ptolemies disappeared from the Aegean. This may be true for the late third century B.C. But even then and especially in the early second century the task of policing the sea, abandoned by Egypt, was not left entirely neglected. We shall see presently that Rhodes took up this task and, when not handicapped by wars, succeeded in establishing a relative safety of commerce in the Aegean and in giving the merchants a fair measure of protection against piracy and the selfish measures taken by some of the Greek city-states. It should be observed that after Magnesia there was for a time no further fighting in Aegean waters, except such as was occasioned by the acts of the Cretan pirates. The price of grain was certainly rising and unsteady, but the supply was still abundant.

Yet never had the cities of Greece and of some of the islands been in a worse plight in respect of the regular supply of food. The problem of daily sustenance haunted every one; it confronted the individual as well as the city. This is proved by scores of inscriptions which speak of food shortage, famine, and so forth. The chief cause of this state of things is undoubtedly to be found in the financial difficulties of most of the Greek cities and in their deficient purchasing capacity, a proof of the impoverishment of their citizens in this period.[21]

Politically impotent and financially drained, the Greek cities tried various methods of solving the food problem. Help was implored from the kings, rich foreigners were humbly asked for donations. But these were mere palliatives. The only effective solution was to draw on the cities' own resources. Their needs could not be met by regular taxation. We have seen the variety and oppressive character of the taxes in most of the cities, especially in the second century B.C., and how little they yielded. Failing taxation, the only means of securing the necessary foodstuffs was to have recourse to what were known as liturgies, in other words, to the private resources of the citizens and other residents in the city, a measure which affected only the well-to-do members of the communities.

A satisfactory history of liturgies in Greece in Classical and Hellenistic times has never been written, and the abundant material bearing on it has never been collected. It seems to me evident that the liturgy, at first an emergency measure, gradually became, especially in the Hellenistic period, an almost regular form of taxation, burdensome and ruinous for the well-to-do classes and extremely unpopular with them. That this may be better understood, I may cite the vivid description of the feelings, on this subject, of a well-to-do Athenian citizen of the late fourth century as given by Antiphanes in his 'The Soldier or Tychon'.* Since the situation in the Hellenistic period did not improve, but rather became worse, it may serve equally as an illustration of the feelings of an average citizen of that period. 'Any human being', says Antiphanes, 'who counts on having anything he owns secure for life is very much mistaken. For either an extraordinary tax snatches away all his fortune, or he becomes involved in a lawsuit and loses all, or as a former commander he is mulcted in the surplus expense,† or, chosen to finance a play, he has to wear rags himself after supplying golden costumes for the chorus, or having been appointed trierarch he hangs himself, or sailing his ship somewhere he is captured [presumably by enemies or pirates], or in walking or sleeping he is murdered by his slaves. No, nothing is certain . . . .'

It was this new form of taxation that was extensively used by the cities of Greece to help them out of their financial difficulties and especially to solve the food problem. To the series of liturgies in the strict sense of this word were added many offices which were created as regular ἀρχαί, liturgical magistracies as it were. The most burdensome were those which dealt with the supply of food, particularly with the corn supply, the *sitonia*, the obligation of richer citizens to buy corn for the city. They did not, it is true, pay for the corn with their

---

* Kock, ii, p. 98, no. 204.

† Prof. C. B. Welles suggests as an alternative translation of this difficult passage: 'having served as general he is brought to trial and fined'.

own money, at least as a rule. But they spent their time and their energy and were responsible for the operation. In the Greek cities the management of public funds was a very difficult, delicate, and dangerous matter.

Next came the *agoranomia*, another liturgical magistracy which was supposed to have charge of the market and to look after it, especially as regards sufficiency of supply and reasonable prices. The office was very important, as is shown, for example, by the group of inscriptions to which I have already referred (above, p. 193) and in which certain *agoranomoi* receive high praise for having secured 'abundance' in the city during their term of magistracy. The burden of these liturgical magistracies, added to the other traditional liturgies, weighed heavily on the city *bourgeoisie*, the well-to-do class, whose individual prosperity suffered as much as the collective prosperity in the difficult times of wars and revolutions.

But it often happened that the city had no funds to advance to its liturgical magistrates. In such cases the funds for the purchase of corn, olive-oil, and fish were provided by emergency measures, by subscriptions (*epidoseis*) or by loans, voluntary *de jure*, but compulsory *de facto*. Many inscriptions mention them, with especial frequency during this period . The richer people, the members of the well-to-do class, were naturally expected to be the chief subscribers.

If these measures failed, many other devices were resorted to. Individual gifts and foundations were suggested to men of wealth. The city franchise was granted to foreigners against payment. Priesthoods were sold to the highest bidders (probably in Asia Minor only), and so on. I quote these expedients, not because they directly affected the well-to-do, but because they show in what difficulties the cities were involved and how heavy in all probability was the pressure on the richer citizens and other residents.

Nevertheless, in spite of all these ingenious and oppressive devices, the problem of food-supply was never solved by the Greek cities. The measures described above undermined the welfare of the *bourgeoisie*, intensified their feeling of economic instability, weakened their energy, and made their financial situation difficult, without succeeding in removing the spectre of famine. The main source of trouble remained, the low purchasing power of the people.

The question of food-supply, though fundamental and all-important, was only one of the many problems with which the Greek cities were confronted. The Greeks were used to a comfortable and civilized mode of life, which required that old public and religious buildings should be repaired and new ones built, that water should be supplied and the streets kept clean, that cults and shows should be maintained, and that the education of the young should be organized. Since here again taxation did not yield enough to meet requirements, the cities resorted to various forms of liturgies and to liturgical magistracies.[22]

I must not be understood as affirming that everything that a well-to-do Greek did for his city or for some association to which he belonged was done under constraint. Many gifts were real gifts. The Greeks were not illiberal by nature and they had a genuine love of their respective cities. But, very often, gifts were made under pressure. This did not always take a legal form, such as a law, a decree of the popular assembly and of the βουλή, or the action of a magistrate. There was another form of constraint, perhaps more effective than legal obligation— social and moral compulsion, the pressure of public opinion from which there was no escape. To this may be added the fear of some violent outburst on the part of the ever-increasing proletariat of the cities.

This sketch of the conditions prevailing at this time in an average Greek city, brief and incomplete as it is (cf. below, ch. VIII), shows that we cannot attribute the difficult and sometimes desperate situation of the cities to the inefficiency of their government alone. The Greek *politeia* was not the best possible form of government nor was it well adapted to the management of the economic affairs of a community, especially in troublous times. Very few cities (Rhodes was one of these rare exceptions) succeeded in combining democratic institutions with efficient administration and sound social policy.* But defects in this sphere were evidently not the chief cause of the economic distress of the cities at this time. This cause is to be sought in the hard pressure of circumstances,

* Strabo xiv. 2. 5, p. 653.

and more particularly in the declining prosperity of the citizens and especially of the well-to-do *bourgeoisie*. It was not liturgies and liturgical magistracies that were the main cause of this impoverishment of the Greeks. They were a sign of the existence of the disease, for which they were designed as remedies, but they only aggravated the condition of the patient.

One result of the economic situation of most of the Greeks, of their impoverishment and concomitant despondency, was that depopulation of Greece and that desertion of her cities and countryside which Polybius has so vividly and convincingly described.* According to him it was the result not of wars and epidemics but of race suicide, the inhabitants being reluctant to contract marriages or, if they did marry, to rear more than one or two children. His vivid picture is confirmed by data derived from contemporary epigraphical documents, which show that a normal family in Greece of the late third and early second centuries B.C. consisted of one or two boys and not more than one girl. Polybius was not alone among Greeks in viewing with anxiety the catastrophic decline of the population and in condemning the means adopted to bring it about (abortion, exposure of children, &c.). But circumstances were more powerful than the feelings of the people. Race suicide came to Greece to stay and continued with some interruptions far into the Roman period. [23]

Abortion, exposure of children, and the like were not new phenomena in Greece (above, ch. III, p. 96). But it was certainly the first time in its history that they assumed such disastrous proportions and led to a gradual depopulation. The poor had often before restricted their families by these means, and so did occasionally the rich. We know from certain passages in Menander and Poseidippus that they acted in this way in the time of Alexander and the Successors.[24] The loss, however, was compensated by the gradual though slow growth of the well-to-do classes and by the increase in the number of foreigners (κατοικοῦντες and μέτοικοι) and of the slaves employed by the *bourgeoisie*, some of whom were manumitted. The widespread development of the practice in the time of Polybius was the result not of an occasional and partial race

* xxxvi. 17 (xxxvii. 4.)

suicide spread chiefly among the proletarians, but of its rapid growth among that class and by its growing use by the well-to-do, the middle and upper classes of the population. Polybius is explicit on this point. Speaking of the selfish reasons which led the Greeks to restrict the number of their children, he says their motive was 'to leave them in affluence and bring them up in luxury'.* When Poseidippus and Menander refer to the same phenomenon among the proletariat, they emphasize not the desire to keep the children rich but the impossibility of feeding them.

Polybius attributes the rapid depopulation of Greece to the passion for show (ἀλαζονεία), for money (φιλοχρηματοσύνη), and for a life of ease (ῥᾳθυμία), which seized upon his contemporaries in Greece, that is to say, he finds the explanation of the phenomenon in psychological causes. Modern scholars prefer to find it in material causes, which Polybius emphatically rejects. They draw attention to the poverty of the Greek soil, which was unable to support a large and steadily increasing population, and to the difficulty experienced by the Greeks, owing to political and economic circumstances, in finding an outlet for the surplus population in emigration.[25]

There is truth in both explanations. The reasons for race suicide were in the main psychological. But the mood of the people, the gradual demoralization of the inhabitants of Greece, was not due to their moral deficiencies, but to the unsound political and economic conditions in which they lived and for which they were unable to discover a remedy.

Among these conditions the infertility of the land and the impossibility of emigration were not the most important. The soil of Greece had always been infertile; nevertheless Greece had succeeded in the past in supporting its population by importing food from abroad. We require to know why it was no longer possible to do this. On the other hand, it is an exaggeration to say that the Greeks had at this time no opportunity of emigrating to the East. The Hellenistic armies still needed large numbers of mercenaries. The two armies, for instance, at the battle of Raphia included large numbers of

* χάριν τοῦ πλουσίους τούτους (the children) καταλιπεῖν καὶ σπαταλῶντας θρέψαι.

mercenaries, some of them Greek. Nor did conditions change in the second century. It is true that Rome forbade Antiochus III after Magnesia to recruit beyond the Taurus. But this prohibition did not prevent later monarchs of Syria from engaging mercenaries from beyond that limit. No restrictions of this kind were ever imposed on Egypt, Pergamon, or the other Hellenistic monarchies of the second century. Though we have no figures, it is probable that in that century fewer mercenaries were recruited in Greece, and more in Thrace, Asia Minor, and the East. But it is certain that a well-trained Greek could at that time easily find military employment in the East. Nor did civil emigration completely cease in the second century. No doubt the East no longer presented the same opportunities to Greek emigrants as in the past. Conditions for emigrants were not so attractive in Egypt as they had been. But Antiochus IV was making efforts to strengthen the Greek element in the population of his kingdom probably by reinforcing the cities with new settlers and certainly by creating new centres of Greek life in Syria and Mesopotamia. There were also good opportunities for Greek settlers in Asia Minor, not only in the Anatolian monarchies, but also in the ancient semi-independent Greek cities.[26] Greeks were in demand, but apparently the supply was small.

Thus it was not the two elemental causes—poverty of soil and over-population—that led Greece to adopt the course of race suicide. The reason of her loss of nerve is to be found in the conditions amid which her inhabitants were living at this time.

I have already described these conditions. Most prominent among them was the uncertainty of life. This was the result of many factors. One was incessant war and revolution. For the average citizen this meant the likelihood either of being killed, or—what was worse—of retaining his life but losing his property and his individual freedom, in other words, of becoming a pauper, a proletarian, or, worst of all, a slave. War, revolution, and piracy were all contributing to throw on the market ever larger numbers of slaves, of whom some were not 'barbarians' but pure-blooded Greeks. Every one knew this and no one regarded himself as safe. The fact is attested, not only by the evidence adduced above (pp. 604 ff.), but also, for example, by the Delphian manumissions. From 201 to 140 B.C. at Delphi, in a small and not very rich community, where there was neither commerce nor industry, no fewer than 8 or 9 slaves (and probably more, for our evidence is incomplete) were manumitted yearly on the average by their masters. Some of these slaves were of Greek origin.[27]

Second in importance was the impoverishment of Greece as I have described it. People who had been well-to-do saw their fortunes gradually reduced, undermined as they were by the general economic conditions, by devastations, confiscations, and requisitions during the wars, and by the pressure of the city government, which required from them more than they could give. It was natural that, not wishing their children to share their lot, they should either have no children at all or closely restrict their number. This may be called with Polybius selfishness or lack of patriotism; I prefer to call it self-preservation, in some cases despair. Pure selfishness it was not. At Athens, for instance, no later than the period following 166 B.C. when the economic conditions of the city improved, the well-to-do classes began once more to rear children and to have at least medium-sized families.[28]

This picture of the poverty of Greece in the period we are considering conflicts to some extent with the views of certain competent scholars, particularly W. W. Tarn, as set forth in his excellent sketches of the social and economic conditions of the Greek cities of the Hellenistic period.* In his opinion, 'prior to Sulla, and with local fluctuations, [the Hellenistic period] was without question a prosperous time for the upper classes'. The facts quoted above do not support this statement so far as it relates to Greece and some of the islands in the late third and early second centuries. I am unable to find any support for his contention, for example, that some parts of Greece experienced during the Hellenistic period a continuous 'rising tide' of prosperity. I doubt whether Corinth in the late third and the early second century was becoming more prosperous than before, and whether Demetrias, which had suffered severely in the Second Macedonian and the Syrian wars, retained in the first half of the

* e.g. *Hell. Civ.*, 2nd ed., pp. 102 ff. (3rd ed., pp. 111 ff.)

second century the prosperity that it had enjoyed in the third. Nor do I believe that the prosperity of Aetolia was increasing during the rule of Philip and especially during the wars of Rome with Philip and Antiochus III.[29] Nor do I see any convincing proof that northern Greece in general escaped the general economic decline of this period. The proof of the supposed prosperity of northern Greece lies, in Tarn's opinion, in the comparatively large numbers of slaves owned at this time by citizens of Delphi and Buttos (near Naupactus), as shown by the manumission documents. I am inclined to believe that this increase in the number of slaves, if increase there was, was a general not a local phenomenon (see above, p. 626) and was due to wars and piracy which temporarily augmented the supply of slaves and reduced their price. Very soon, however, the number of slaves in all parts of Greece began to decrease again.[30]

No one will deny that life in the Hellenistic world, especially in its richer centres, was more luxurious and more refined than in the previous period. In the times of prosperity, that is to say, in the days of Alexander and in the first half of the third century, the upper classes in the chief commercial and industrial cities became very exacting in matters affecting their comfort, such as town planning, the construction of private houses, the organization of games and sacrifices, and the formation of clubs and all kinds of associations, more refinements in their daily life and diet, &c. And so they remained, when circumstances permitted, to the end of the Hellenistic period. But the evidence, which is meagre and most of it undated, does not allow us to follow the changes in this respect that occurred from time to time and in various places. I have not found any dated evidence which would show that the standard of life in Greece in the late third and the early second century was very high, higher than, or even as high as, in an earlier period. Some new games were organized at this time even in Greece, but the organization of games was a profitable business and might bring with it the much coveted *asylia* or immunity from attack. Some *thiasoi* and other associations, especially on the islands, may have been fairly prosperous. But associations were not a characteristic feature of Greece proper (except Athens), and as for the islands, our material is not sufficient to enable us to follow the vicissitudes of their collegial foundations.[31]   A similar impression is derived from a study of the prices of the most important commodities. Evidence from Delos shows that in the early second century B.C. prices in general were rising, with one short interruption which it is difficult to explain satisfactorily. It has been shown, however, that while the price of grain—a commodity which Greece imported—was high, the price of those commodities (olive-oil and wine) which were produced in Greece and in part exported was very low, much lower than in the third century. From this we may infer that in general the economic situation of Greece was deteriorating, the balance of trade being in all probability not in her favour.[32]   Reviewing all the evidence, I see many signs of economic decline in Greece in the late third and the early second century and none of increasing prosperity.

The conditions of life, which, as I have shown, had been intolerable during Philip's Greek wars and the Second Macedonian and the Syrian wars, improved to a certain extent in the period that followed the two Roman wars. Frequent and devastating as they were, the local Greek wars of this period were conducted on a much smaller scale than before. On the sea peace reigned for a time. The pirates were held in check by the Rhodians, who successfully policed the sea without, however, being able to suppress piracy altogether.

We may interpret as a sign of recovery, for example, the large issue of currency made by the Achaean League after the Second Macedonian War. But it must be remembered that it probably replaced the abundant coinage of the individual members of that League, especially Sicyon and Corinth, and that after 192 B.C. certain important States—Elis, Messene, and Sparta— were forced to become members of the League. Nevertheless this issue of currency is significant, especially for the period subsequent to 168 B.C.*   In 146 B.C. it came to an end.[33]

The most typical example, however, of the recovery of certain parts of Greece after the Syrian war is Athens. It would be superfluous to set out here the condition of that city in the difficult times of the late third and early second centuries, which W. S. Ferguson has so admirably described. I will confine

* Exact dating of the various issues of Achaean coins is very difficult.

myself to quoting two recently discovered documents which illuminate this period in her history. One is a good illustration of the danger to which the city was exposed during the rule of Antigonus Doson. It is a decree in honour of the well-known Peripatetic philosopher Prytanis of Carystus, who went to Antigonus on behalf of Athens, incurred many hardships, spent a large sum of money, and finally reported at Athens on the results of his mission.

Even more illuminating in respect of the succeeding period, that of Philip's attacks on Athens, is a decree of 196/5 B.C. in honour of the great anti-Macedonian Athenian leader Cephisodorus, of whose career Pausanias, when describing his funeral monument,* has given a sketch, probably based in part on a similar decree in his honour. Among his services to the city I may refer to what he had done for Athens in the critical year 203/2 B.C. Athens, it seems, was financially ruined and on the verge of starvation. Cephisodorus did not hesitate to become treasurer of the military funds (ταμίας στρατιωτικῶν) and at the same time treasurer of the grain-fund (ταμίας σιτωνικῶν). He suggested certain financial reforms and in addition made various gifts to the city in money and in grain.[34]

But after these hard times and in the more peaceful atmosphere that prevailed after Magnesia, Athens—the faithful friend and supporter of Rome—enjoyed a period of comparative ease. We may say more than that. Many facts, known to most modern scholars but in my opinion not correctly interpreted by them, show that the years subsequent to the liberation of Athens from Macedonia and especially those following the Macedonian and Syrian wars, were a time of slow but steady recovery, of a real economic renascence. Most of the modern scholars date this renascence after the war of Perseus with Rome, but I am convinced that the recovery of Athens began much earlier, immediately after her liberation and especially after Cynoscephalae and Magnesia.

Many facts show that it was at this time that Athens resumed her important role in trade, and especially in the grain trade. When the war with Perseus broke out, her part in this trade had probably become very important indeed. Livy†

* Paus. i. 36. 5.   † xliii. 6. 2–3.

states that in 171 B.C. the Romans demanded from Athens the delivery of 100,000 *medimni* of corn. The Athenians tried to excuse themselves, but finally yielded. Now the Romans were too intelligent to demand this quantity of grain from a poverty-stricken city, hardly able to feed its own population. They certainly knew that large amounts of grain were stored at the Piraeus and that the control of the grain trade rested in part with the merchants of Athens.

This interpretation of the passage in Livy is supported by many facts. It is well known that Athens in the first half of the second century B.C. both before and after the war with Perseus, entertained very close relations with many of the chief powers of the time, notably with those concerned in the grain trade and most of all with the Ptolemies, Epiphanes and Philometor in particular. It may be noticed that in the same period many Alexandrians became *proxenoi* of Athens (in 188, 184, and about 170) and that, on the other hand, many Athenians appeared in Alexandria and in the island of Cyprus. There were also very cordial relations between Athens and Pergamon (see below, p. 641, cf. above, p. 565). It must be remembered that it was about this time that Pergamon was rapidly developing its resources and was beginning to produce in its territory large quantities of grain (below, p. 649). Not less significant of Athens' commercial relations are the honours conferred by her on Antiochus IV, Ariarathes of Cappadocia, and above all Pharnaces of Pontus, and the gifts received by her from them. The last of these, it is to be borne in mind, became about this time master of the two greatest commercial ports on the southern coast of the Euxine, Amisus and Sinope, both very important centres of the grain trade, and both closely connected with Athens in the past. We have, moreover, the fact that the royal corn-grower, Massinissa, whose grain now appeared in abundance on the Aegean market, was one of the victors at the Panathenaea, and that many citizens of Heraclea Pontica, another great centre of the grain trade, the successful rival and partner of Panticapaeum and Chersonesus, took up their residence at Athens about this time.[35] It is interesting to observe that all the powers that played so important a part in the affairs of Athens in the early second century, as friends and business partners, and who were at the same time the largest producers of grain, had a little earlier (225 B.C.) come to the assistance of Rhodes after the disaster of the famous earthquake.* They had certainly not done this solely from philhellenic feelings, but had also been influenced by the desire to keep on good terms with the republic that had gradually become the mistress of the Aegean. They were actuated by the same motives in their relations with Athens. The high regard paid by the leading powers to that city cannot be explained exclusively as the tribute of the Hellenistic world to her great past and as the outcome of a wish for good relations with the influential friend of Rome. Such an explanation is too narrow. It does not account for the out-burst of sympathy at the very moment when the conditions were especially propitious for the economic revival of Athens. Moreover, all numismatists and historians of this period are familiar with the fact that about 229 B.C. Athens began to emit her new 'Owls', which were soon imitated by some of the Cretan and Ionian cities, and that after 180 B.C. there was a distinct change in her procedure in respect of this coinage. She began to issue much larger quantities of currency and made the issues monthly. Some scholars, especially Sundwall, who was the first to point out this new development of the Athenian coinage, endeavoured to explain it by the conjectural annexation of Delos, Lemnos, Scyros, and Imbros to Athens immediately after Cynoscephalae. But this contention, based on an erroneous statement of Valerius Antias, conflicts with all the known facts of the history of Delos and Athens. There is no doubt that the restitution of the cleruchies to Athens did not take place before 167/6 B.C. The extraordinary increase in the Athenian coinage, the masses of 'Owls' of the new style which appeared on the market, were due, not to the imaginary partial restoration of the Athenian Empire, but to the growing importance of Athens and the Piraeus in the trade of the time.[36]

In view of all these considerations, it appears probable that Athens, after the breakdown of the Macedonian hegemony in the Aegean, rapidly recovered her wealth and became once more, particularly as regards the trade in grain with the North,

* Polyb. v. 88.

a rival of Rhodes, and to a certain extent the successor of Delos, which had been the Macedonian agent for the grain trade of the Aegean since the battles of Cos and Andros.

II. THE MONARCHIES

A. *MACEDONIA*

While Greece suffered heavily and her prosperity rapidly declined, the resources of Macedonia during the reigns both of Philip and Perseus were still large. Both rulers did their best to develop them and derived an ample revenue from the country wherewith to carry out their ambitious foreign policy.

Many documents discovered in Macedonia and elsewhere testify to the feverish activity of Philip in every branch of public affairs, and especially in matters connected with the army. The military system, including the supply service, was carefully regulated by special orders of the king (διαγράμματα), which were published in the most important strongholds of the kingdom. The same care and activity were displayed in prescribing the relations of the king with the cities of his kingdom. Here again much use was made of letters and orders (διαγράμματα). Thessalonice, the great seaport of the Antigonids, played an increasingly prominent part in the life of the country, and Demetrias also was of considerable importance.[37]

Of the economic policy of Philip and Perseus we know little. We are told in certain passages of Livy and Polybius* that after the end of the Syrian war Philip, finding himself badly cheated by the Romans, took various measures to improve the economic situation of his kingdom. One of the most alarming phenomena was the gradual depopulation of Macedonia and Thessaly, caused mainly by the incessant wars. He tried to check this process by various means. I have mentioned his letters to Larissa in which he recommended a more liberal policy in the matter of granting the city franchise. To meet the depopulation of Macedonia proper, which increased to an alarming extent both in town and country, he had recourse to the traditional policy of his predecessors: he brought in large

---

* Liv. xxxix. 24; cf. Polyb. xxiii. 10.

numbers of Thracians, probably settling them not only in the
cities but also in the rural districts.[38] As regards his revenues,
he increased the taxes from cultivated land (which certainly
means that he attended to the agricultural development of his
kingdom), looked after the cultivation of his large estates
(*praedia*),[39] raised the import and export duties (which shows
that he interested himself in the development of Macedonian
trade, especially in grain and in timber), and finally resumed the
working of certain neglected mines and opened some new ones.
I feel convinced that this was in no respect a new policy, but
that he had adopted it from the very beginning of his reign.
No doubt, at first, when the resources of his country had not
yet been undermined by a long and ruinous war, his activity
had been less feverish.

Philip managed the currency of his kingdom in accordance
with this general economic policy. The coinage that he himself
issued was abundant and reliable. Not satisfied with this,
soon after the conference at Tempe in 187 B.C., he went to
Thessalonice and there conceded the right of issue to the most
important cities of his kingdom, Thessalonice, Pella, and
Amphipolis, a concession which he soon extended to the five
districts of Macedonia that were closely connected with the
mining regions. This he did primarily to gain the goodwill of
these cities and districts, but certainly also in order to obtain
their help in promoting the exploitation of the mines and in
increasing the volume of the currency. His policy was in its
general lines the same as that of Eumenes II and Antiochus IV
(see below, pp. 654 ff.), and was undoubtedly carried on and
developed by his successor Perseus.[40]

The economic policy of Philip and Perseus was successful.
It was not lack of money or men that were the decisive factors
in the final failure of Perseus to win back the political independence of his kingdom. Some facts concerning the Persean War
reported by Livy, Polybius, and Plutarch show that Perseus
began it well-provided with men,* money, and supplies. His
army was large and well-trained, his strongholds were stocked
with provisions (we have already seen the activity of Philip in

* We learn from Livy (xlii. 12. 8–10) that in addition to Macedonians he
recruited soldiers in Thrace.

this respect; Perseus, without doubt, continued his work), and he accumulated a great amount of money; of this we have evidence in the 6,000 talents of silver and gold found by the Romans in his treasuries, and in the magnitude of the spoils brought to Rome by Aemilius Paulus.[41]

All this produces the impression that Philip and Perseus succeeded in restoring the prosperity of the State. How far and in what way their policy affected the population we do not know.

B. *ASIA MINOR, THE EUXINE, RHODES, AND DELOS*

In Asia Minor the period we are considering must be divided into two parts: a time of continuous and prolonged fighting which brought much suffering on the population and ended with the battle of Magnesia, and the more peaceful time that followed, when Asia Minor, except the northern monarchies, was practically ruled by the two friends and allies of Rome, Eumenes II and Rhodes.[42]

The condition of Asia Minor prior to Magnesia and Apamea can be described in a few lines. Philip's treatment of the cities of which he took possession after the First Macedonian War was harsh, as has already been mentioned, for his seizure of Asia Minor was dictated chiefly by his desire to improve his economic situation. He was followed by Antiochus III, who, during and after the Second Macedonian War endeavoured to restore the empire of Seleucus in the West. Amid the resulting confusion and political unsettlement, some of the chief cities of Asia Minor, especially those nominally subject to Egypt, now enjoying practical independence, indulged in their own private wars. It is by chance that we know much of such a war between Miletus and Magnesia on the Maeander, which lasted for many years, led to the repeated pillaging of their territories, and yielded many captives to the belligerents. The war was terminated in 196 B.C. by the intervention of Rhodes, and the terms of the peace conformed to the rules of the international law then prevailing.*[43]

We possess some information on the treatment to which Antiochus III subjected the cities that he reconquered and

* *S.I.G.*³ 588.

incorporated in his kingdom. To those cities which surrendered to him and remained loyal he showed high regard. They were granted 'autonomy' and the burden of their payments to the king was not very heavy. It is, however, probable that he showed no tenderness to those which had not been on his side and had not opened their gates at his first summons. There is good reason for thinking that an important inscription copied at Brûssa (Prusa) but probably found in one of the Greek cities near it, perhaps Apollonia ad Rhyndacum—a decree in honour of Corragus, the governor (probably for Eumenes II) of Hellespontine Phrygia—belongs to the time after the defeat of Antiochus. I cannot deal at length with this inscription. The point of interest here is that the city was handed over to the new governor (who acted in the name of his master) after a long and ruinous war, and that the new ruler of the city restored all sorts of rights and privileges which had been taken from it by its former master, the most important being its ancestral constitution and laws (πάτριος πολιτεία and νόμοι). As I am convinced that this former master was Antiochus III, the treatment accorded in this instance shows that ruler's method of dealing with the recalcitrant cities of his kingdom. Similar penalties (loss of *autonomia*) were incurred at the time of a disastrous war by another city whose name is lost, probably in the reign of Antiochus III. The date of the document which sets forth the misfortunes of the city during the war and the important concessions which it subsequently received is unfortunately uncertain. It may refer to the war of Antiochus with the Romans or to an earlier one.[44]

After Magnesia Asia Minor was ruled *de facto* by Eumenes II, the super-arbiter of Anatolian affairs, and in part by Rhodes.[*] It was not, however, a time of complete rest and peace for the population. The expedition that Manlius Vulso now conducted against the Galatians, cruel as it was, and the subordination of the Galatians to Pergamon, did not break the spirit of that people. They tried repeatedly to recover their liberty of pillaging Anatolia. Moreover, the kingdoms of northern Anatolia were not disposed to recognize the position of Eumenes II and more than once tried to enlarge their territory

[*] On Rhodes and her possessions on the mainland see below, p. 679.

at his expense. This led to long and renewed wars, which are little known to us, but gave northern Anatolia no rest for many years. From 186 to 183 Eumenes was fighting against Prusias I, who received help from Macedonia and from the Galatians under Ortiagon. The impression produced by this war is reflected in a decree recently discovered at Telmessus, and it is possible that, as a result of his great victory, Eumenes received the title of Soter.[45] A little later a great war was raging throughout this same region. It was the Pontic war of 183–179, in which Pharnaces I, allied with the Galatians, fought against a coalition of Pergamon, Bithynia, Paphlagonia, and Cappadocia. Rome made several attempts to end the war, but without success. She was not prepared for military intervention and her diplomatic efforts, unsupported by force, were fruitless and only aggravated the situation—which perhaps was not unwelcome to her.[46]

And yet the sufferings of Asia Minor and especially of the Greek cities of Anatolia at this time cannot be compared with those of continental Greece. Though our information is inadequate, certain facts stand out and may be relied upon. Eumenes II in his lifetime was in truth a great benefactor of Asia Minor, and so were his successors. I shall speak of his economic policy presently. A large part of Asia Minor was not affected at all by the wars I have referred to. The rest suffered from them severely, but not to the same extent as Greece suffered from the wars of 'liberation'. The Anatolian kings were fighting in their own countries, which provided their only resources, and to acquire territory which they wished to add to their kingdoms. Their methods of warfare therefore would hardly resemble those adopted by the combatants in the West. The only exception were the Galatians. It is significant of the attitude of Asia Minor that Eumenes II gained great popularity by putting an end to their barbarities, and was regarded as the saviour of Hellenism in that country. Being more or less merciful to their enemies, the Anatolian kings were not very hard on their own subjects, on whose moral and material support they knew well that their success depended.

The welfare of Asia Minor was consequently not seriously affected by the wars waged within its boundaries. Indeed it enjoyed, after Magnesia, a period of prosperity, which endured until the end of the Pergamene dynasty. Though harassed and controlled by the Romans in their foreign policy, the Attalids were left by their suzerains free to manage the internal affairs of their kingdom as they pleased. A few remarks, therefore, on their social and economic policy at this time will not be inappropriate.

I have already (pp. 553 ff.) spoken of the period of the Attalid *dynasteia* of PERGAMON, when these rulers, by their ceaseless efforts, organized their little State and made Pergamon one òf the richest countries of the day. With Attalus I the policy of the early dynasts was fundamentally changed. His aim was to build up, on the foundations laid by his predecessors and himself, a Pan-Anatolian State, which should be the equal and the rival of the great Macedonian monarchies. Despite some brilliant successes he failed in his endeavour. Philip V and Antiochus III were too strong for him and for his allies and supporters, the Ptolemies and, since 201 B.C., Rhodes. Instead of giving up their ambitious programme, Attalus I and Eumenes II sought to achieve it in another way, by throwing in their lot with Rome, the new foreign power that had appeared on the horizon of the Hellenistic world and was interfering in its affairs. With the help of this foreign ally the Attalids attained their principal end, and became the rulers of the greater part of Asia Minor. But they paid a heavy price for their success, for they ruled over that country, not as independent kings, but as the vassals and political agents of Rome. It is idle to speculate whether Attalus I and Eumenes II foresaw this when they first embarked upon their imperialistic policy.

Rulers of a large territory, the Attalids were confronted with the problem of its organization. I have already described the economic and social structure of the old *dynasteia*, and expressed the opinion that the later Attalids made very little change therein. Like Egypt in its relation to the Ptolemaic Empire, the old *dynasteia* became the centre of the Attalid realm or empire, its base and foundation, while the remainder of their dominions took to some extent the character of foreign provinces.

Very little is known of the system of government that the

PLATE LXX

1. I reproduce here, with the permission of the authorities of the Pergamon Museum in Berlin, two models showing parts of the restored Acra of Pergamon. These models, made by Dr. H. Schleif, are exhibited in the Pergamon Museum in Berlin. Though somewhat antiquated in details, they give a good idea of the general aspect of these portions of the Acra. In the centre of the first model is seen the temple of Athena Nikephoros, the protector of the pre-Attalid Greek city of Pergamon, adopted by the Attalids. The temple was built at the end of the fourth century B.C. In the time of Eumenes II it was surrounded on three sides by two-storied porticos with a monumental entrance. The portico behind the temple (north wing) formed the front of the famous Library, first built probably by Attalus I and later enlarged and rebuilt by Eumenes II. This central part of the Acra was an eloquent exponent of the leading ideas of the Attalids. The temple, the Library, and the statue of Athena before the entrance to the Library, a reproduction of the statue of Phidias, linked Pergamon with Athens and all that it meant for the Greek world. Pergamon aspired to be an Anatolian Athens. On the other hand the votive bronze statues in the court (pls. LXIII, 2, and LXVI) dedicated by Attalus I, and the bas-reliefs of the parapet of the second story of the portico, showing the pieces of military equipment captured from the enemies of Pergamon by the Attalids, symbolized the military strength and splendid achievements of those kings in defending their independence and protecting Asia Minor from barbarism. The fragments of the carved parapet, I may add, are an exceptionally rich source of information about the military equipment of the Galatians and of the Macedonian armies and navies (including those of the Seleucids). Before the sacred precinct of Athene is seen the beginning of the cavea of the impressive theatre of Pergamon, another link with Athens and Greece, and behind it the spacious and comfortable but modest palaces of the kings.

2. To this centre Eumenes II added his famous majestic altar, or rather monumental temenos surrounding an impressive altar. Parts of this 'altar' are now restored in the Pergamon Museum in Berlin. Figure 2 reproduces a restored model of the altar precinct and the adjoining parts of the Acra, the most important being the market-place. The altar of Pergamon is well-known to students of antiquity and need not be described here. Its sculptural decoration emphasized once more the two leading ideas of the Attalids: the intimate connexion of Pergamon and its kings with Greece and its mythical past (the Telephus' frieze illustrating the story of Telephus, son of Heracles, the founder of Pergamon and of the Attalid dynasty) and the great service rendered by the kings to Hellenism by their victorious struggle with barbarism (the famous frieze of Gods fighting the Giants). For a fuller description of the Acra see the books quoted above, Ch. IV, n. 321, and in this Ch., n. 72. More complete bibliographical references and a short well-illustrated description of the Acra will be found in W. von Massow, *Führer durch das Pergamon Museum*, 2nd ed., 1936. On the altar, H. Kähler, *Funde u. Forsch.* XV (1939), pp. 294 ff.

PLATE LXX

1. Restoration of the temple of Athena and adjoining buildings

2. Restoration of the great altar and of the market-place

THE ACRA OF PERGAMON IN THE TIME OF EUMENES II

PLATE LXXI

1. Restoration of the royal arsenal and barracks of Pergamon

2. Stone bullets used for ancient artillery

THE ACRA OF PERGAMON. MILITARY BUILDINGS

PLATE LXXI

The northern spur of the Acra plateau of Pergamon and part of the adjacent area were occupied by buildings of a military character: a group of storehouses and close to them spacious barracks for the garrison of the Acra (*O.G.I.* 338, 1, 14: καὶ τῶν στρατιωτῶν τοῖς κα[το]ικοῦσιν [τὴμ πό]λιγ). The earliest buildings in this area were erected by Philetaerus. In later times several new ones were added. Both corn and other foodstuffs and war material were kept in the storehouses. The stone bullets reproduced in Fig. 2, like the ruins of the arsenals and barracks, must be assigned to the Hellenistic period. They are of different sizes and weights. Similar stone bullets have been found in many ancient cities, the latest (to my knowledge) being those of Dura on the Euphrates (used during the siege of the city in 256 A.D. or soon after; scores if not hundreds of them were found on and near the desert wall of the city). Fig. 1 is reproduced from a photograph supplied by the authorities of the Pergamon Museum, while Fig. 2 is from a photograph supplied by Prof. E. Boehringer. For a detailed report on the excavation of this part of the Acra and a study of the ruins and finds made in them see Askos von Szalay and E. Boehringer, 'Die hellenistischen Arsenale', *A. v. P.* x, 1937, cf. n. 72 to this chapter. Cf. (on the stone bullets found at Rhodes) L. Laurenzi, 'Projettili dell'artiglieria antica scoperti a Rodi', *Mem. FERT.* ii (1938), pp. 31 ff.

later Attalids established for these new accessions. It is certain
that the Hellespont and Thrace were organized as satrapies or
strategiai, one called that 'of the Chersonese and the Thracian
districts' (Χερσονήσου καὶ τῶν κατὰ Θράκην τόπων), the other
that 'of the Hellespontine districts' (τῶν καθ᾽ Ἑλλήσποντον τόπων)
or of 'Phrygia on the Hellespont' (Φρυγία ἡ ἐφ᾽ Ἑλλησπόντῳ), and
that these were governed in the Seleucid and Ptolemaic fashion
by *strategoi*. A similar status was held by Aegina. Whether the
rest of the new accessions were likewise divided into satrapies
or *strategiai* with subdivision into hyparchies, again in the
Seleucid and Ptolemaic fashion, there is no evidence to show.
The financial administration may have been organized in this
way. It is strange, however, that the epigraphical evidence,
which of course, except for the Hellespont and Thrace, is very
meagre, contains no explicit mention of *strategoi* or *hyparchoi*.
In some cases the kings appear to have dealt direct with the
cities.[47]

The new acquisitions of the Attalids were inherited by them
from the Seleucids. The relations of these cities and regions to
their former rulers had been established by many years of practice, and evidently, once established, they would not be
radically changed by the new rulers. We know, however, very
little either of the old or of the new status of these localities,
and therefore cannot discriminate between the two.[48] I will
confine myself accordingly to such evidence as we have relating
to the position under the Attalids, without attempting to consider what changes were introduced by the latter.

Our information regarding the status of the new accessions
to the Pergamene kingdom is based mainly on the terms of the
Roman settlement of Asia Minor after Magnesia, as stated by
Polybius and Livy,* and as illustrated by some inscriptions.
The Romans in dealing with the land taken from Antiochus III
distinguished sharply between the 'country' (specified as
castella, vici, agri, silvae, and *oppida non libera*) and the Greek
cities. The country and some of the Greek cities (Tralles,
Ephesus, Telmessus) they gave to Eumenes II as gifts (δωρεαί).
A little later that king was very desirous of obtaining on the
same conditions the cities of Aenus and Maronea in Thrace,

* Liv. xxxvii. 55–6, and xxxviii. 38–9; and Polyb. xxi. 24 and 42.

besides Lysimacheia and its territory. Those Greek cities which were not handed over as gifts to him were divided into two classes: the cities which had sided with the Romans and had not helped Antiochus III were declared *liberae et immunes*, that is, non-tributary to Eumenes II; on the other hand, those which had sided with the enemies of Rome were now to pay tribute to Eumenes II, in other words, were made subject to him. The fate of those cities which transferred their allegiance from Antiochus III to Rome late in the war was decided individually.[49]

With the cities that remained free the Attalids sought to maintain the best relations. Of this I may quote a few examples without attempting to present all the evidence. They made gifts to the city of Miletus and to the Ionian League, and granted loans or gifts to Chios; they gave privileges to Cyzicus, and they appear in friendly and close relations with Colophon and Iasus. They adopted in fact the same policy towards them as towards the cities of Greece and the islands, a policy of conciliation or bribery on a large scale.[50]

The subject cities[51] were dealt with in a different way. Doubtless there were some general principles which were applied to all of these, and certainly there was a strict control of finance, as in the city of Pergamon. In this the policy of the Attalids resembles that of the Ptolemies. But this policy probably admitted of variation in practice.

How far the Attalids changed the constitutions of the cities we cannot say. There is some evidence of an attempt to introduce *strategoi* in many of them and to give to these magistrates a dominating position in their affairs. There is, however, no absolute proof that this policy was applied to all, or even to the majority of the Greek cities. It is known that the orders of the kings were regarded as laws by the subject cities, and that some of these orders were incorporated in the city laws by a special direction of the king; and this prerogative of the crown must, in varying degrees, have replaced the right of the cities to legislate for their own affairs.[52] It is equally natural that the kings should appear as arbiters in territorial disputes between neighbouring cities and should send their surveyors to settle the disputes more or less authoritatively.[53]

But the chief concern of the kings was the orderly administration of the finances of the cities. The inhabitants of most of these paid various and probably heavy royal taxes, perhaps in addition to their regular tribute—a continuation of the practice established by the Seleucids. This can be gathered from some recently discovered documents. Of these the most important is an inscription* set up by an unknown city in honour of Corragus, the governor of Hellespontine Phrygia probably during the reign of Eumenes II. In this document (referred to above, p. 635) we find the city just taken over by the Pergamene governor after a ruinous war, probably that of Antiochus III. It has forfeited all its privileges in this war— liberty, autonomy, and the rest—and is at the mercy of its new ruler. He takes no advantage of this situation and restores its former privileges; but the city is not *immunis*: the citizens pay taxes (πρόσοδοι) to the king. Since, however, they are in financial straits, they receive a remission of taxation for three years, increased by the governor to five. It is possible that a similar remission was granted by Eumenes II to all the cities that had suffered at the hands of Antiochus III, of which the former now became the overlord.

This possibility is suggested by the fate of another city whose name begins with T (Temnos or Tmolos?). Its sufferings are described in the first lines of the fragmentary document, very difficult to restore (above, note 44 and below note 55): mention is made of Antiochus (apparently the Third), of 'the rule which they endured', and of the fact 'that their city had been burnt and [laid waste] in the war, that most of the citizens had lost their property and had perished, and that altogether but few of them [still survived]'. The citizens had therefore asked through their envoy for the restoration of their constitution, for remission of debts (ἄφεσις χρημάτων) (?), for release from the tribute (ἀπόλυσις φόρων), and for the admission of new settlers to the city. Their requests were granted: αὐτονομία, remission of all payments for seven years, and thereafter the payment of a lump sum in three instalments, the amount—20 minae —to be taken from their revenues (πρόσοδοι), no other taxes to be paid, no garrison in the city, no oppression (?), no liturgies,

* *S.E.G.* ii. 663.

and some further remissions (the document is incomplete). The picture of the relations between the city and the king is very similar to that given in the Corragus decree.

Not very different was the situation many years later in the Pisidian and only slightly hellenized frontier-city of Amlada (or Amblada).* In the time of Eumenes II the city was required to pay a regular tribute (φόρος and τέλεσμα) of two talents a year and in addition probably an εἰσφορά imposed on it during the Galatian war of that ruler (see below, Ch. VI, p. 800). It suffered heavily during the war of Attalus II with Selge (below, Ch. VI, p. 801), in which it temporarily sided with Selge, and asked Attalus II and his co-ruler, the later Attalus III, for partial remission (κουφίζειν) of the tribute and for full remission of the unpaid balance of the εἰσφορά. These remissions Attalus II graciously granted to the city.

Finally, in an inscription from Teos,† the city grants to the Dionysiac artistes (*technitai*) a piece of land, a *ktema*, 'exempt from the taxes imposed by the city'.‡ This means that alongside of the city taxes (τέλη πολιτικά) there were other taxes which the citizens had to pay, in all probability royal taxes.[54]

The financial system to be inferred from the examples I have quoted is not quite clear. It was probably not very different from that of the Seleucids (above, pp. 464 ff.). It appears that many if not all, the subject cities paid a yearly tribute (φόρος), a lump sum which represented a part of their own revenue (πρόσοδοι). This is what our literary sources mean when they refer to φόροι. In addition, however, the inhabitants of the city paid various taxes, for the collection of which the city may have been responsible, apparently royal taxes of a general character. Whether these taxes were identical with those collected by the Seleucids we do not exactly know. A passage in the inscription of Corragus suggests that one of them was a tax on olive-oil or on olive-groves or on both, perhaps a kind of partial monopoly of the king. Furthermore, the cities were subject to requisitions in time of war and to all sorts of extraordinary services

---

* *O.G.I.* 751; Welles, *R.C.* 54; H. Swoboda, J. Keil, F. Knoll, *Denkmäler aus Lykaonien*, &c, 1935, nos. 74–5.

† *S.E.G.* ii. 580.

‡ l. 9. ὃν ἀτελὲς ὢν ἡ πόλις ἐπιβάλλει τελῶν.

(λειτουργίαι). The citizens and other inhabitants of the Greek cities therefore were expected in the first place to pay their regular taxes into the treasury of their respective cities. Out of the proceeds of these taxes and the other revenues of the city (from land, buildings in the city, such as shops, &c.) the tribute was paid to the king. The inhabitants were further liable to various royal taxes in addition to the city taxes, and bore their share in the requisitions and liturgies imposed on the cities, the heaviest being the obligation to provide food and quarters for the royal garrison.[55]

It is, however, curious that while the kings laid heavy burdens on the population of the subject cities, they at the same time paid certain regular subsidies in money and in kind, both to the cities and temples, and to the associations of young men (probably to the gymnasia). In the inscription in honour of Corragus this payment is described as made 'for the management (or administration)' (εἰς διοίκησιν) of the city. Since references to such a payment recur in inscriptions concerning Teos* and Temnus,† the practice seems to have been common. We may assume that in acting thus the kings satisfied on the one hand their desire to control the finances of the cities, and on the other assumed the character of benefactors of the community, which, in consequence of the heavy royal taxation, was unable to raise sufficient municipal revenue to defray the expense of civic administration and the maintenance of temples and gymnasia.

The situation of Aegina, which Attalus I acquired by purchase from the Aetolians in 210 B.C., was similar to that of the subject cities and of the cities granted to the Pergamene kings. Though the city retained its constitution and its magistrates (we know of the existence of *strategoi*), there was a royal governor, and the life of the citizens was regulated mainly by the laws and orders of the king. The governor was *de facto*, if not *de jure*, supreme judge in disputes between citizens.[56] The island of Andros may have been similarly treated, but we have no precise evidence on the point.[57]

It is difficult to say how much the Attalids contributed to the urbanization of their kingdom. I have dealt above with the

* *S.E.G.* ii. 580.   † *Inschr. v. Perg.* 157; Welles, *R.C.* 48.

old territory. In the new territory the Attalids inherited about a score of Macedonian settlements founded by the Seleucids. How many new colonies they themselves established is uncertain. One (Apollonis) is beyond doubt; others are probable (for instance, Eumeneia and Dionysopolis in Phrygia, Philadelpheia in Lydia, and Attaleia in Pamphylia); others again are quite conjectural. In Apollonis the Attalids no doubt intended to create a new city, and this was done by a synoecism of various pre-Attalid (that is to say Seleucid) Macedonian village-like settlements. The new community is definitely spoken of as a *polis*. In certain other colonies there are traces of city life both under the Seleucids and under the Attalids. Most of them, however, did not develop into regular cities until the period of Roman domination.[58]

As regards the military colonies which did not attain to the status and constitution of a city, we must sharply discriminate between those established by the predecessors of Eumenes II in the territory of the old *dynasteia* and those which Eumenes II inherited from the Seleucids. There may have been in addition some new κατοικίαι created by Eumenes II and his successors outside the old *dynasteia*. Some of their foundations mentioned above may have been not cities but village-like communities of settled soldiers.

Of the ancient Attalid κατοικίαι we hear occasionally. Philetaireia, for example, is mentioned in an inscription of uncertain date* as administered by a military governor. Of the new ones we know practically nothing. Especially interesting, however, are the κατοικίαι inherited by Eumenes II from the Seleucids. Of their vicissitudes and organization in the Attalid time we know very little. We hear for example that Akrasos† in the time of Eumenes II had its own magistrates, probably appointed by the king. However, Akrasos may have been, not a Seleucid, but an Attalid κατοικία.

Some light is shed on this problem by a recently discovered inscription, a fragmentary dossier which contains a complete letter of Eumenes II of 181 B.C. to his official in the region of Telmessus, written in answer to a petition (εἰσγραφή) of the 'residents of the village of the Cardaces' (κατοικοῦντες ἐν

* O.G.I. 336.   † L. Robert, *Les Villes*, &c., p. 75.

Καρδάκων κώμη). It is followed on the stone by a fragment of another document, dated in the reign of Antiochus III (193 B.C.), which perhaps was a sale of land.[59]

In order better to understand this important document I must return to the history of the region of Telmessus (above, p. 336); we are able to reconstruct this with great probability from the letter of Eumenes II just mentioned, from several other inscriptions, and from some literary texts.[60]

I have stated that Telmessus and its region were constituted by Euergetes I a kind of small *dynasteia* ruled by his relative Ptolemy, son of King Lysimachus. This ruler was succeeded, in all probability, by his son Lysimachus. We know of his existence from a decree of the city of Telmessus published by M. Segre.* Lysimachus was probably still dependent on the successor of Euergetes I, Ptolemy Philopator, but maintained cordial relations with Antiochus III, whose star was rising.† Some time after 204 Lysimachus was succeeded by his son Ptolemy. This we may infer from the letter of Eumenes quoted above, in which this Ptolemy is mentioned, and from some dedications by Ptolemy found at Delos (188 B.C.).

In 197 the whole of Lycia and with it Telmessus and its region were undoubtedly occupied by Antiochus III, and Ptolemy apparently lost his *dynasteia*. After the occupation, Antiochus III colonized the region of Telmessus in the same way as he had colonized Lydia and Phrygia, that is to say, by means of military colonies. Jews were settled in Lydia and Phrygia (above, p. 492), while land was assigned to certain barbarians near Telmessus, in the neighbourhood of the Rhodian sphere of influence. This we infer from the above-mentioned letter of Eumenes, which indicates that in 181 B.C. a settlement of Cardaces (barbarian mercenary soldiers whom we know to have formed part of Antiochus' army at Raphia) was in existence in the region of Telmessus, and it is very probable that this settlement was established there not by Eumenes II but by Antiochus. Some time before 181 B.C.,

---

* *Atti IV Congr. Pap.*, 1936, pp. 359 ff.; *Clara Rhodos* ix (1938), p. 183.

† Antiochus III appointed Berenice, the sister (?) of Lysimachus, chief priestess of Antiochus' queen Laodice in 204 B.C. (*O.G.I.* 224; Welles, *R.C.* 36, 37).

according to the same inscription, the settlers, not satisfied with their allotments, bought an additional piece of land from Ptolemy, the son of Lysimachus. This shows that Ptolemy, though no longer dynast of Telmessus, retained for a while his ancestral *dorea*. In 188, however, as appears from a special paragraph in the treaty of Apamea* the *agri Ptolemaei Telmessii* passed into the hands of the Romans. While Telmessus and its region were assigned by the treaty to Eumenes, the *dorea* of Ptolemy was exempted and was probably restored to Ptolemy, who was still alive, as is proved by his dedications at Delos. It would seem therefore that the *dorea* was taken from Ptolemy by Antiochus and was returned to him by the Romans. Ptolemy probably sided with the Romans during their war with Antiochus and rendered them valuable services.

Eumenes thus inherited the region of Telmessus from Antiochus and with it his military κατοικίαι. How did he deal with them? His letter gives us some insight into his policy in this respect. The settlers, as they explained in their petition, were in evil plight: the yield of their fruit trees was meagre, the land was in a wretched condition, many inhabitants of the village had left, the little fortress (πυργίον) which protected the village from robbers was in ruins. Moreover, they had no money to pay for the land which they had acquired from Ptolemy, and they were hardly able to pay the poll-tax of four Rhodian drachmae and one obol a head imposed on them. Eumenes in order to retain them in the village and, if possible, to increase its population grants them their requests. He remits the price of the land bought from Ptolemy and the arrears of poll-tax, and lowers the poll-tax for the future to one drachma and one obol; he permits the restoration of the fortress and sends an architect of his own to give assistance; and finally, he promises immunity from taxes for three years to new settlers and of two years to such inhabitants as had left the village (τοῖς ἐκχωρήσασι; cf. the ἀναχωρήσεις and ἐκχωρήσεις of Egypt) and were willing to return.

The measures taken by Eumenes II are highly interesting. They show how anxious he was to revive agricultural life in his kingdom, to resettle the rural communities, to protect them

* Liv. xxxvii. 56, 4–5.

against marauding bands. It appears, however, from the inscription that the former military colony became a simple village and the former κάτοικοι plain *laoi*. There is no word in the letter of Eumenes of any military obligations imposed on the Cardaces. Moreover, they were supposed to pay a poll-tax (σύνταξις), which in the Seleucid kingdom was hardly paid by members of privileged classes and in the tax system of the Ptolemies (and perhaps of the Seleucids also) was perhaps restricted to the *laoi*. Apparently Eumenes had no confidence in the loyalty of the former Seleucid κάτοικοι, who had always shown great fidelity to their masters and suzerains and formed the backbone of their kingdom. It is possible, however, that the Cardaces were treated in this way by Eumenes because they were barbarians. He would perhaps act differently towards Macedonians.[61]

Next in importance to the cities and the military and civil colonies were the large and wealthy temples, some of which were attached to a city, while others were the central points of rural districts. The former were administered by their respective cities, as at Ephesus, Clarus, and Sardis. Since some of them were very rich and played an important part in the economy of the country as centres of banking and industry, the Attalids had every inducement to claim a measure of control over their finances and the right to dispose of their income and landed property. This right of control they exercised by appointing financial managers of the temples (*neokoroi*), as, for instance, at the temple of Sardis. Their claim in respect of temple revenues was forcibly shown when one of them confiscated the income derived by the temple of Ephesus from fisheries. Their relations with the temples that were not attached to any city were probably similar. Like the subject cities, these temples paid taxes on their property, and there was nothing to prevent the king from appointing a manager of their finances or seizing some of their land or other sources of income. At Aezani in Phrygia the kings, both Seleucid and Attalid, exercised this right of partial confiscation.* The relations of certain temples, as of certain Greek cities, to the Attalids were rather those of alliance or vassalage than of subjec-

* *O.G.I.* 502.

tion. This was true of the important temple of Pessinus with its hereditary king-priests. A series of letters of Eumenes II and of Attalus II to these priests give us a vivid idea of their mutual relations.* It must be borne in mind, however, that Galatia was never a regular Pergamene province and that Pessinus succeeded in keeping its semi-independence even in respect to Galatian rulers. It is, moreover, to be remembered that, from the time of Attalus I, the priests of Pessinus had maintained cordial relations with Pergamon.[62]

In the new acquisitions of the Attalids, besides Greek cities, colonies created by the Seleucids, and temples, all of them with their territories studded with villages, there were large stretches of land inhabited by semi-independent tribes which were also full of villages, groups of villages, and fortified refuges, and in addition many forests, mines, quarries, lakes, &c. It seems beyond doubt that all the land other than that in the possession of the Greek cities and perhaps of some of the colonies, and all the mines, quarries, forests, pastures, lakes, &c., were deemed, as in the past, the private property of the kings. Out of this property important parcels of cultivable land were given by the new rulers, in continuation of the policy of their predecessors, to court dignitaries and high officers and officials, to citizens of Greek subject cities, and to soldiers of the territorial army. Corragus, for instance (as is shown by the inscription quoted in note 44), was in possession of a large estate in the neighbourhood of the city from which he was able to draw cattle and present them to the city for sacrifices. In the same inscription we find the king assigning plots of land from the royal property to citizens who had none. These landless citizens were probably new colonists to whom land had not yet been assigned. As regards the military settlers, interesting evidence is afforded by certain inscriptions: one of Pergamon dealt with above (p. 562), those dealing with the synoecism of Apollonis, and those of Aezani.

The system of exploitation of this ' royal land' had probably not changed very much in the Attalid period. I shall return to this question in the next chapter.[63]

The new accessions to the Pergamene kingdom naturally

* *O.G.I.* 315; Welles, *R.C.* 55-61.

yielded a large and regular revenue to the kings. Added to the revenue from the old territory it made the Attalids the richest sovereigns of their time. None the less the later Attalids, thrifty business men, never neglected the kernel of their kingdom, but developed extensively the economic policy of their predecessors both in the old and in the new territories.

The inadequacy of our information makes it difficult to distinguish in the economic measures of these later kings between the intensified use of old methods and the introduction of new ones. Without doubt the improvement of agriculture and pasturage, of which I have already spoken, remained their chief preoccupation. In the field of industry we may notice some new developments.

Our information about the industrial development of the Pergamene kingdom in this period is based almost exclusively on the archaeological material yielded by the systematic excavations of various important industrial centres of Asia Minor, such as Pergamon, Priene, Miletus, Ephesus, Myrina, Cyme, Sardis, Tarsus. The minor finds made in these cities may, when properly collected, published, classified, and studied, shed some much needed light on the problem under discussion. As things stand, only preliminary and tentative statements are possible.[64]

Many Anatolian cities which were either incorporated in the Pergamene kingdom or were closely connected with it had in the Archaic and Classical periods been important centres of metal industry. I may mention Lesbos, Samos, Chios, Cyzicus, Sardis, and Miletus. It is only natural that the ancient traditions should have stimulated metal industry in Pergamon itself and in some other cities of the Pergamene kingdom. Certain specimens of silver ware found in Pergamon and in its immediate vicinity which stylistically show great affinities with the development of plastic arts in Pergamon, and some Pergamene products of ceramic art reproducing metal originals in clay (see below), make it appear very probable that Pergamon in the third and especially in the second century B.C. created a special and peculiar school of toreutic artists. These artists certainly did not work exclusively for the local Pergamene and for the Anatolian market. Some works of toreutic art found in

South Russia are Pergamene in style and were probably imported to South Russia from Pergamon. On the other hand we
have probable evidence of export to Italy in the influence,
demonstrated by Pagenstecher, of Pergamene models on the
Calenian relief ceramic, and in the Pergamene character of some
pieces of silver ware made in Italy in the later Republican and
early Imperial periods. I cannot here enter into details, and
the question has been very little studied. I may add that
Anatolian silver ware was apparently copied and imitated in
the many much later vases treated with green and brown glaze,
which were probably manufactured in Asia Minor (see Chapter
VII, note 130).

No less important than the metal ware was probably a new
type of pottery, which may have originated in Asia Minor, one
of the centres of its production being probably Pergamon.
I refer to the red-glazed, light-bodied, plain dishes and cups.
On this brand of pottery potter's marks are comparatively
common. The history, the place of origin, and the development of this pottery are subjects of keen debate. It came into
widespread use. Pottery of this type was the most popular
ware of the second and first centuries B.C. all over Syria, Palestine, and Mesopotamia (at Antioch on the Orontes, Seleuceia
in Pieria and in other places in Syria, at Samaria, Gezer, Beth-
shan, Beth-Zur, and in many other places in Palestine, at Dura
on the Euphrates and Seleuceia on the Tigris in Mesopotamia),
in Asia Minor (e.g. Ephesus, Priene, Tarsus, and several other
places, not to speak of Pergamon), on the Greek islands (for
example Delos), in Greece (for example Athens), in South
Russia, in Egypt (Alexandria) and perhaps in Italy (the well-
known term *vasa Samia* in Roman literary texts and Pliny's
praise of goblets from Pergamon and Tralles* have been
connected with this pottery).

The problem of its place of origin is difficult and cannot be
discussed here. It was for a long time thought to be Asia Minor
and especially Pergamon. Recent finds and observations have
gradually undermined this theory, and Syria has been suggested as an alternative. There is no doubt that the production of this type of pottery in the late second and in the first

* *N.H.* xxxv. 160.

PLATE LXXII

The two silver *emblemata* of silver vessels reproduced in this plate were found at Miletopolis near Pergamon. I have mentioned them in n. 65 to this chapter (with bibliography). Similar *emblemata* probably served as originals for Anatolian and Syrian potters who often adorned the bottoms of the red-glazed vases of different forms made by them with portrait heads (see pl. LXXIII). These heads represent either celebrities in the literary history of the past (Demosthenes, Euripides, Aeschines, and a half figure of Diogenes?), or contemporary rulers, see description of pl. LXXIII. Since the earliest specimens of this type of Eastern *terra sigillata* must be assigned to the middle of the second century B.C., and the head of Silenus in the *emblema* of Miletopolis shows striking similarities of style to the heads of the Giants of the Pergamene altar, we may safely assign the two *emblemata* to the middle of the second century B.C. and regard them as products of the Pergamene school of toreutic artists. Photographs supplied by the authorities of the Berlin Museum.

PLATE LXXII

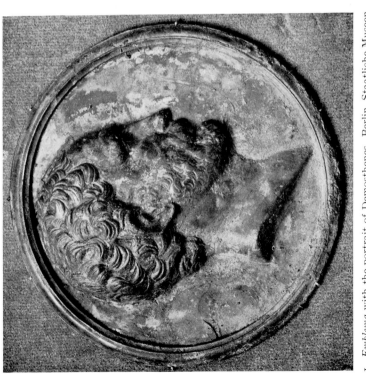

1. *Emblema* with the portrait of Demosthenes. Berlin, Staatliche Museen   2. *Emblema* with the head of a Silenus. Berlin, Staatliche Museen

PERGAMENE METALWORK

PLATE LXXIII

1. Berlin, Staatliche Museen

2. British Museum

3. Berlin, Staatliche Museen

4. Berlin, Staatliche Museen

PERGAMENE POTTERY

PLATE LXXIII

1. Red-glazed beaker with appliqué figures of Maenads.
A. Furtwängler, *J.D.A.I.* x (1895), Anz., p. 43, fig. 61, cf. a similar beaker found at Delos; F. Courby, 'Vases avec reliefs appliqués du Musée de Délos', *B.C.H.* xxxvii (1913), p. 422, no. 716, fig. 5. Photograph supplied by the authorities of the Staatliche Museen, Berlin.

2. Similar beaker of finer workmanship found at Laodicea. The appliqué decoration consists of ivy leaves and 'corymboi'. Several sherds with exactly the same decoration have been found at Pergamon.
Frequently published and discussed: H. B. Walters, *Br. Mus. Cat., Rom. Pott.*, p. 17, no. L 35; E. Courby, *Les vases grecs à reliefs*, 1922, p. 454, and passim, fig. 98; C. W. Lunsingh Scheurleer, *Grieksche Ceramiek*, 1936, pp. 165 ff., pl. lii, fig. 156; O. Deubner, *J.D.A.I.* liv (1939), Anz., col. 342, fig. 5, cf. figs. 4 and 6. Photograph supplied by the authorities of the British Museum.

3. Fragmentary red-glazed clay medallion found in South Russia, showing the portrait head of a Hellenistic ruler. The identity of the portrait is disputed. Most students suggest Orophernes Nikephoros, the well-known ruler of Cappadocia (about 158/7 B.C.), though the head on the sherd does not appear to be exactly like that which we find on the coins of Orophernes (e.g. M. Schede, *Die Ruinen von Priene*, 1934, p. 9, fig. 9).
First published and discussed by H. Winnefeld, 'Hellenistische Silberreliefs im Antiquarium der Kön. Mus.', *Winckelmannspr.*, lxxxvi (1908), p. 18, pl. iii, 2, cf. O. Deubner, loc. cit., col. 349. Deubner quotes other similar sherds with portraits of Hellenistic rulers; cf. Lunsingh Scheurleer, loc. cit., p. 157, fig. 157 (portrait of a philosopher?). Photograph supplied by the authorities of the Staatliche Museen, Berlin.

4. Red-glazed drinking cup (skyphos) with appliqué ornaments (ivy leaves). A similar intact cup and several fragments were found at Delos. Photograph supplied by the authorities of the Staatliche Museen, Berlin.
F. Courby, *B.C.H.* xxxvii (1913), p. 419 f., no. 687, fig. 1; *Les vases grecs à reliefs*, pl. xvi a.
It is evident that the type of red-glazed pottery with appliqué reliefs represented in Figs. 1, 2, and 4 must be regarded as created by Pergamene potters. Many of these vases have been found at Pergamon. This fine Pergamene pottery was exported, though not in very large quantities. The best buyers were the cities of Asia Minor and Delos (see the memoir by F. Courby quoted above), next came South Russia, where this type of vases is quite common, and probably the cities of the north-western coast of the Black Sea. Where red-glazed vases with portrait medallions were produced is more doubtful. I am inclined to assign them to eastern Anatolia and Syria rather than to Pergamon. It is striking that not a single Pergamene ruler appears among those whose portrait heads adorn these vases. Besides the problematic Orophernes, who may be one of the later Seleucids, we find Nicomedes II of Bithynia, Ariobarzanes I, and Brutus. The basic studies of this pottery are those of F. Courby and O. Deubner quoted above. On the Eastern red-glazed pottery, with and without ornaments, in general see p. 651 f. and n. 66. Vessels of other types than those reproduced in this plate may have occasionally been made at Pergamon, but Syria has a better claim to be the place of origin of red-glazed pottery in general. See Excursus IV by F. O. Waagé at the end of this book.

century was not confined to one place and to one region. Further study of it may bring more precision and help to clarify its history.

Besides the plain dishes and cups, finer examples of this type of pottery were produced in various places, such as, in particular, the red-glazed vases adorned with bas-reliefs. These bas-reliefs were often made in special moulds and pasted on the body of the vases. Some striking specimens of this style, together with a special brand of Megarian bowls and other types of relief pottery, were certainly made in Pergamon, where not only moulds for the appliqué ornaments, but entire vases of the type have been found in considerable quantities. This ornamental ware produced at Pergamon was exported to various places: many specimens of it have been discovered at Delos, in South Russia, and in Italy.[66]

The relations between the eastern, especially Pergamene, relief pottery and the early *terra sigillata* of Italy cannot be discussed here. It is, however, certain that the early Arretine pottery must be connected in one way or another with the East —with Asia Minor or Syria.[67]

The increase in agricultural production and the popularity of certain products of Anatolian industry in the Aegean, in Syria, in Italy, and in South Russia, are proof that the Pergamene kingdom carried on a flourishing trade. It is, however, difficult to say whether the products were exported by Pergamene merchants or by intermediaries, merchants of the large trading cities—Miletus, Ephesus, and especially Rhodes and Delos.[68]

In connexion with the development of Pergamene trade with the Greek world, the Seleucid monarchy, and Italy, we may notice an interesting feature in the economic policy of the late Attalids. There is good reason for thinking that they sought to maintain the economic unity of at least part of the Hellenistic world, established (as we have seen) by the Seleucids in agreement with the minor Anatolian monarchies, a unity which had now suffered severely from the Roman policy of liberation. There is evidence of this design in their monetary system and their monetary policy.

It is well known that the Romans, when they restored freedom to certain Greek cities after Cynoscephalae and Magnesia, automatically restored at the same time the local urban mints which had in a large measure been idle under Alexander and the early Hellenistic rulers. Yet despite the revival of what appeared at first sight to be monetary anarchy, similar to that which had been characteristic of Greece and Asia Minor before Alexander, no such monetary anarchy in fact resulted. It is interesting to note that the majority of the restored mints adopted, especially for heavy silver, the Attic standard, which had been the predominant standard of the Syrian and Anatolian mints in the previous period, and struck exact copies of the Lysimachian and Alexandrian coins, with the addition of the names of the cities that issued them. According to Regling, more than forty cities in Asia Minor, in the islands, in the Peloponnese, and in Crete, were at that time using the Attic standard exclusively for their coinage.[69]

It was the same desire for unity that led the Pergamene kings about the same time to issue in Asia Minor, alongside of their own royal coinage, a new type of coins, known as *cistophori*, which were intended to become the common currency of western Asia Minor. It is well known that the Pergamene policy was adopted by the Romans and that in the course of Roman rule the *cistophori* became for a time the standard currency of Asia Minor.[70]

These developments, which took place in Asia Minor and Greece and were probably the result, at least in part, of the economic policy of the Attalids, had their counterpart in the contemporary monetary and economic policy of the Seleucids. I propose to discuss this subject here, and not in the section dealing with the Seleucid Empire, because the monetary policy of the Seleucids after Antiochus III was apparently devised in concert with Eumenes II and his successors. The Seleucids at this time maintained their policy of monetary unity with the Anatolian and Greek world of which I have spoken. We have evidence of this in the coin hoards of the period subsequent to Antiochus III, which in their general aspect resemble earlier hoards, but present at the same time some characteristic peculiarities. These hoards are very numerous. Four of them have been recorded and described by Regling. Many more have appeared on the coin market since 1928. All these hoards may be accurately dated in the period extending from the late years of Antiochus III to the end of the rule of the Pergamene dynasty in Asia Minor.[71]

The main characteristic features of these hoards are as follows: (1) They consist predominantly, as before, of posthumous silver tetradrachms and drachms of Alexander and Lysimachus, some of them bearing a Seleucid countermark (anchor, head of Helios, and under Tryphon his own badge—the Macedonian helmet). Many of them were struck in mints of various cities, mostly Anatolian. (2) Next to the Alexanders and Lysimachi we find coins, mostly tetradrachms, of various cities of Asia Minor, some of them bearing Seleucid countermarks. (3) Alongside of these two groups appear occasionally coins of various cities of Greece and of the Greek islands, some with Seleucid countermarks. (4) Besides these coins we find large quantities of dynastic coins: Seleucid coins of course prevail, but by their side we notice ever-increasing numbers of Attalid coins (especially of Eumenes II and Attalus II) and occasionally coins of the kings of Pontus and Bithynia. (5) It is worthy of note that, while Anatolian dynastic and city coins appear in large numbers, the early *cistophori* are absent. (6) Most of the coins found in these hoards are much worn and had apparently been in circulation for a long time. (7) All the coins in these hoards are of the Attic standard. No coins of the Ptolemies appear among them.

The coin hoards, whose characteristics I have thus described, are highly interesting. In general, they do not differ very much from the hoards of the preceding period. They show the same international character and the same prevalence of foreign over Seleucid coins.

There are, however, some new features. One is the fact that the coinage which circulated in Syria issued mainly, and almost exclusively, from the mints of Asia Minor, not from the royal but from the city mints, mints of cities in part belonging to the Pergamene kingdom or to the sphere of Pergamene political and economic influence. The other is a fact known to numismatists from the time of H. P. Borrell, viz. that the Anatolian tetradrachms had almost no circulation in Asia Minor itself, but were distributed far and wide over the whole of Syria and were there regarded as legal currency. In fact I know of only one hoard found in Asia Minor that is somewhat similar to the Syrian hoards.* Moreover it is very probable that the coins minted in the above-mentioned cities were not admitted to circulation in other cities of Asia Minor without the special permission of the urban authorities testified by appropriate countermarks. Thus we find tetradrachms of Temnus with a countermark of Priene, and many tetradrachms of Side bear countermarks of various cities of Asia Minor that minted *cistophori*. I draw attention to the fact already stated that the *cistophori* never appear in the hoards or among the occasional finds in Syria.

How are we to explain the two phenomena described above, viz. the municipal character of the Anatolian silver currency so widely used in the Seleucid realm and the apparent connexion of this currency with the Pergamene kingdom? They cannot be interpreted as a natural development of the conditions of the third century.

We see an economic policy behind it, a kind of *entente cordiale* between the Seleucids on the one hand and the Attalids and the independent cities of Asia Minor on the other. I cannot help thinking that the Attalids were the moving force behind the phenomena that I have described. It was probably under their influence and with their support that the international silver coinage (Alexanders and Lysimachi) of Asia Minor was intensified and that a uniform character was given to it. Though most of the places where this coinage was minted were free cities, they lay either within the territories of the Attalid kings or in the sphere of their political influence.

Their principal motives may have been as follows. They looked for a good market for their silver. Masters of most of the silver mines in Asia Minor, they certainly intensified the production of these mines and were eager to dispose profitably of the output. It was probably not without their encouragement that, not only large commercial cities, but many small and insignificant towns of the Aeolis and Lydia, of the Troas, of Caria and Paphlagonia, embarked on the minting of silver.

*Noe², 926, Sardis, cp. for Pontus, Noe², 40, Amasia.

It should be noticed that all these groups of towns were well situated geographically both for obtaining the raw material and for forwarding currency to Syria. We can hardly suppose that the minting cities—important or unimportant—owned silver mines. It is more than likely that the metal was supplied to them by the kings who, in all probability, were the owners of the mines. Why the Attalids had recourse to the good offices of the cities is hard to say. It would have been much more natural for them to increase their own royal coinage. However, they preferred the other course.

The leading reason may have been, as Prof. C. B. Welles has suggested, the desire not to hurt the feelings of the Seleucids by offering them as a supplement to their currency the Attalids' own coinage, but to create for their needs a kind of 'neutral' impersonal international coinage. It may be noted that they adopted the same course, at about the same time with regard to the *cistophori*. Other rulers, it should be observed, namely Antiochus IV and the Macedonian kings, acted in a similar way in respect of several cities in their kingdoms. Whether this was done in order to spread the risk of the new venture, and whether the kings derived some substantial profit from the minting operations of the cities, it is impossible to say.

Be this as it may, it is certain that the output of coined money of a special type, especially silver, was substantially increased in Asia Minor at the time of Eumenes II and Attalus II, and that this was done in agreement with the Seleucids. The object was of course to serve the commercial policy of the two kingdoms; in other words there was a commercial policy behind this monetary policy. The main lines of this commercial policy may have been as follows. After the occupation of Palestine, Phoenicia, and Coelesyria the Seleucids were in control of most of the Arabian, Indian, and Chinese caravan trade. Very little of it was left in the hands of the Ptolemies. The development of the caravan trade required a rapid expansion of the currency. The abundant Ptolemaic coins disappeared from Syria and were no longer available as a medium of the Palestinian, Phoenician, and Syrian trade. There was bitter hostility and commercial competition between the Seleucids and the Ptolemies. The only way by which the Seleucids could increase the volume of their silver currency and so replace the Ptolemaic silver, was to have recourse to the Attalids, who were masters of the main silver supply of the Near East. And the Attalids were ready to help, provided that the Seleucids directed their trade not to Alexandria or to Rhodes and Delos, but to the harbours of the Attalid Empire. The best and safest way of doing this was to make use of the land route. The sea route was not entirely out of the question, but resort to it meant almost necessarily that the lion's share of the trade would be diverted from the Attalids by Rhodes and Delos.

The period of the *entente cordiale* between Pergamon and Syria and of their common monetary and commercial policy did not last very long. The city coins of Anatolia and the Alexanders and Lysimachi of the Anatolian mints soon disappeared from circulation. They are hardly ever found in the Syrian hoards of the late second and of the first century B.C. The coins of the Attalids similarly disappeared. Seleucid coins prevail in the hoards of this period. Besides them we find some foreign dynastic (but not Attalid) coins, and many coins of the now autonomous cities of Syria, Phoenicia, and Palestine. It is significant that in several hoards we have comparatively large numbers of Athenian coins of the new style and that Arabian dynasts begin (after 115 B.C.) to imitate the new Athenian 'Owls',* whereas previously only some minor kings, neighbours of the Seleucids, had issued imitations of the chief currency of the time—the coins of Alexander.

The monetary policy of the Attalids that I have described, and the policy of commercial expansion that probably stood behind it, form another trait in the picture of the rapid economic growth and increasing wealth of the Pergamene kingdom to which I have repeatedly referred. The best illustration of this wealth and of the political and cultural aspirations and achievements of Eumenes II and his successor Attalus II is furnished by the city of Pergamon. I have already described its general disposition. I may here add a few words about the changes that the city and especially its *acra* underwent at the hands of these two ambitious rulers. It was they who made

* G. F. Hill, *B.M.C. Arabia*, &c., 1922, pp. liv ff.

PLATE LXXIV

The mosaic was found in situ in one of the οἶκοι of the largest unit in the group of buildings which formed the royal palace of the Attalids. It belongs certainly to the time of Eumenes II. The patterns used in the mosaic are those typical of the mosaics of the Hellenistic period, as we find them in Alexandria (above, pl. xxxv), Delos (pl. lxxxix) and Pompeii. The most beautiful part of the mosaic is the vine and acanthus scroll on black background. The scroll is enlivened by figures of grasshoppers, butterflies, and little boys playing with the leaves of the scroll or catching the butterflies. Unfortunately the central part, the *emblema* of the mosaic, is not preserved. It was removed, probably in Roman times. What is left of the central part is the signature of the artist: Ἡφαιστίων ἐποίει, as if written on a piece of paper pinned to the mosaic with one corner loose. The mosaic, like the other mosaics of which fragments were found in the palace, was certainly laid in Pergamon. The artists may have come to Pergamon from abroad (the mosaic with the *emblema* of an Indian parrot may have been made by a Syrian mosaicist).

G. Kawerau and Th. Wiegand, 'Die Paläste der Hochburg', *A. v. P.* v, 1 (1930), pp. 63 ff.; cf. on the later (Augustan period) mosaics of the 'house of Attalus' found at Pergamon E. Pernice, 'Pavimente und figürliche Mosaiken', *Die hellenistische Kunst in Pompeji*, 1938, p. 31 f. 1 and 2 from A. Kawerau and Th. Wiegand, op. cit. Photograph of 3 supplied by the authorities of the Staatliche Museen, Berlin.

PLATE LXXIV

1

2

3

MOSAIC IN THE ROYAL PALACE AT PERGAMON
Berlin, Staatliche Museen

Pergamon one of the most beautiful cities in the Greek world, a rival of Athens, Alexandria, and Antioch. We hear it said of Attalus II that he found a city of trachyte and 'marmoream reliquit'.

The main outlines of the *acra* were not changed. But its area was enlarged by the inclusion of a stretch of land on the slope adjoining the fortified city of Philetaerus and Attalus I. Here arose many public buildings. We know several of them: a spacious second *agora*, a magnificent gymnasium on three terraces, a new temple of Hera, and a reconstructed temple of Demeter. But the main activity of Eumenes II was devoted to rebuilding, enlarging, and beautifying almost all the surviving buildings of the original *acra* and to adding various new ones. There was hardly a single earlier building that was not remodelled by Eumenes II and Attalus II, and several new ones were added. The Hellenistic *acra* as revealed by excavation is Eumenian and Attalian: the palaces with their gardens, no longer so modest as they had originally been; the new *heroon*-like building, perhaps for the dynastic cult; the impressive *horrea* with their spacious store-rooms for grain and arms, a marvel of technical achievement; the theatre with its terrace on which stood a temple, perhaps of Dionysus Kathegemon, and an Attaleion where the Dionysiac artistes met; the temple of Athena with the new building for housing the library created or enlarged by Eumenes; the great altar with the famous sculptures, probably another addition of Eumenes; and the early upper market-place (*agora*) with a temple of Dionysus at the foot of it.

The *acra* remained what it had previously been, the capital and the stronghold of the kings. But in the Eumenian and Attalian capital another idea received an increased emphasis— the idea that this royal capital was at the same time a bulwark of Hellenism, a beautiful symbol not only of the political but also of the cultural mission of Pergamon. Pergamon now claimed to be as much a leader of Hellenism in its cultural aspect as were Athens, Alexandria, and Antioch.[72]

The 'municipal' issues of currency mentioned above afford eloquent testimony to the participation of the larger and smaller cities of Asia Minor in the prosperity of the Pergamene kingdom. The impression produced by these monetary issues is confirmed by the fragmentary information we possess regarding some of the cities of the kingdom, among them, for example, Myrina. We know little of its history. But its necropolis, carefully excavated by E. Pottier and S. Reinach, shows that it reached the zenith of its prosperity in the second century B.C., for it is to this period that most of the graves, full of exquisite terracottas and interesting pottery, are to be attributed. The same impression is conveyed by some of the inscriptions from Teos, especially those concerned with the relations between the city and the Dionysiac artistes who resided for a time in it.[73]

I have stated that the culminating point in the history of BITHYNIA coincides approximately with the most brilliant period in that of Pergamon, and the same may be said of Pontus. All these kingdoms, amid the turmoil of the great Roman wars, succeeded by clever policy in enlarging their territories and in consolidating their power. They no longer felt the menace of the great Seleucids and the ambitious Antigonids. Thus it came about that at the moment of the downfall of the great Macedonian monarchies, the more or less hellenized non-Macedonian monarchies aspired to take their place. For a time Rome did not appear to oppose their aspirations. She had many other matters to occupy her and had no objection to the temporary establishment of a new balance of power in the East.[74]

Prusias I (about 235–182? B.C.), the successor of Ziaëlas, inherited from his predecessors a large and well-organized kingdom, and he carried on their work with great energy and skill. An ally of Philip V (whose sister Apama he married), he helped him in the First Macedonian War. As a reward he received from him the ruins of Cios and took possession of Calchedon. Myrlea also succumbed to him. During the Second Macedonian war, however, though he did not assist the Romans, he was wise enough not to succour Philip. In the prevailing confusion he strove hard to achieve his principal aims. A successful war against Attalus I enlarged for a time the territory of Bithynia at the expense of Pergamon. But his main efforts were directed against the proud and powerful city of Heraclea, which had been a thorn in his side. He seized its dependencies, Cierus and Tius, and besieged the city itself; and, but for an accident, would have captured it. He retained the bulk of his conquests and almost entirely occupied the rich and fertile territory of Heraclea. In the war of Antiochus with Rome he sided with the latter. But the support he gave brought him no substantial addition of territory. Disappointed, he waged a war against Pergamon with little success.

The most notable feature of his reign was the completion of the work begun by his predecessor, the establishment of a continuous Greek front on the sea-coast of his kingdom. He has the reputation of having been a great urbanizer of his dominion. This is not quite exact. What he did was to rebuild the Greek cities of his kingdom, to refound them under new names, and probably to organize them on new lines. Cius, destroyed by Philip, he refounded under the name of Prusias-on-the-Sea. Myrlea was not neglected, but its re-founding under the name of Apamea appears to have been of a later date. Cierus, taken from Heraclea, entered on a new phase of its history under the name of Prusias-on-the-Hypius. Finally, at the suggestion of Hannibal, he founded a third city named after himself, Prusa, near Mount Olympus.[75]

In his economic policy he showed the same tendencies as his predecessors. He was now a factor in the balance of commercial power which then obtained. In this capacity he helped Rhodes after the earthquake, and sided with the Rhodians in their war against Byzantium for the freedom of the Straits. He left to his successor a kingdom strong and outwardly hellenized, and hoped that it would thrive and grow. This hope, however, was not to be fulfilled.

More spectacular, almost as spectacular as the successes of Eumenes II, were the achievements of Pharnaces I of PONTUS, the great predecessor of Mithridates VI. We know very little of him, but what we do know shows his ability and the great contribution he made to the prestige of his kingdom. His most striking success was the capture and retention of Sinope and of its territory, which had been saved from the same fate a few years earlier by the intervention of Rhodes (in 220 B.C.; below, p. 674). This happened in the course of the long war previously referred to, in which many of the principal powers

PLATE LXXV

Model of a part of the city of Miletus. I owe the following description of this model (translated by myself from the German) to the kindness of Prof. A. von Gerkan, who took a leading part in the excavation of the city.

'The part-model made by Dr. H. Schleif represents the harbour region of Miletus on the Lions' bay, seen from the north. Cf. *Milet. Erg. d. Ausgr.* i, 6, plan, fig. 1. To the left in the foreground are seen the Roman *thermae* on Humei-tepe, then beyond them the Delphinion and the Roman harbour-gate. Further on runs the wide parade street, on its left side stand the thermae of Capito and the Gymnasium, with the long Ionian portico in front of them. Still further is seen the Nymphaeum, and finally the market-gate. Of the south market only the north portico is included in the model. To the right stands the group of buildings which form the north market, and before them on the shore the Tripod and the Grattius monuments. Behind the north market appears the little Roman temple and the Bouleuterion. To the right of the north market are seen: the northern part of the long corn stoa, in the middle background the Hellenistic temple beneath the later basilica of St. Michael, and as the last building on the extreme right the Mausoleum in the little peristyle-court. The model is not quite exact as regards the entrance to the Lions' harbour, which is made too wide, and the flatness of the ground to the right and left: actually the ground rises towards the heights of Humei-tepe and Kaleh-tepe. There is also no evidence for the trees on the shore of the bay.'

Photograph of the model supplied by the authorities of the Pergamon Museum, where the model is exhibited.

PLATE LXXV

PART OF THE CITY OF MILETUS

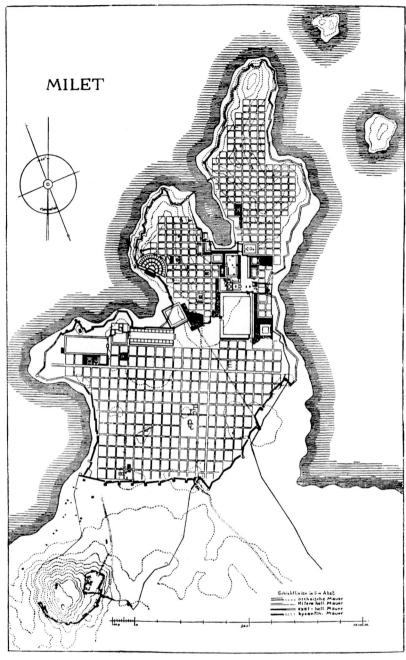

FIG. 5. Plan of Miletus. By permission of the German State
Archaeological Institute.

of the time were involved, the protagonists being Pharnaces I and Eumenes II. It is significant that, although the war ended with the humiliation of Pharnaces, he nevertheless kept Sinope and retained his influence over such distant Greek cities as Odessus on the north-western shore of the Black Sea and Chersonesus in the Crimea; it must be remembered that the cities of the 'left' Euxine and the Crimea were connected by many ties with the great trading cities of the Pontic coast, especially Sinope and Heraclea. It is not less significant that, as master of Sinope, he became also master of its colonies. We hear that he annexed Cerasus and Cotyora and transported their population to a new city named Pharnacia after himself. The few isolated facts mentioned above and his cordial relations with Athens show that he did for his kingdom what Prusias did for Bithynia and probably more. The Greek front of his kingdom was now in his hands, and his capital was no longer the Pontic Amasia but the splendid Greek city of Sinope. As king of a Hellenistic kingdom and with the great wealth of Sinope in his possession he had the goodwill of Athens. His dream of creating an Euxine Empire, inherited by him from the Bosporan Eumelus, was smashed by his rivals and enemies. But by keeping close relations with the Greek cities of the Euxine he prepared the ground for the revival of his dream by his late successor Mithridates VI Eupator [75a]).

The prosperity of the chief kingdoms of Asia Minor was shared by the most important GREEK CITIES of Anatolia, which before and even after Magnesia retained a good deal of political and economic independence. Our information about these cities is, as I have already shown, meagre and unevenly distributed. It is only those Greek cities of Asia Minor which have been systematically excavated whose history can be traced with some approach to accuracy. Such are Miletus, Priene, Magnesia on the Maeander, and to some extent Ephesus.

The best known and most thoroughly studied of these four cities is undoubtedly MILETUS. Its political history and its economic and social structure in the late third and early second centuries B.C. are illustrated by several substantial inscriptions found mostly in the sanctuary (*temenos*) dedicated to Apollo and called Delphinion, and also by the ruins of the city, which have been so carefully and methodically excavated. The most notable of the inscriptions are the great Cretan 'dossier', the peace treaties with Magnesia and Heraclea, the sympolity with Pidasa, the inscription of Eudemus and that relating to the war-loan. I think that Miletus may be taken as a typical example of all the larger Greek cities of the western coast of Asia Minor. It will therefore be appropriate to set forth what is known of the economic conditions prevailing there at this time.

In the last two decades of the third and in the first decade of the second century B.C. Miletus was certainly not a poor city. Of this there are many indications. One of the most important is its foreign policy. In the late third century Miletus, though politically dependent on Egypt in name, acted in practice as an independent city and developed an aggressive policy towards its nearest neighbours. Supported by an alliance with Tralles and Mylasa (212/11 and 209/8 B.C.), it engaged in a long war with Magnesia and in another with Priene. The war with Magnesia lasted until 196 B.C. (above, p. 634).

In the course of these and earlier wars Miletus had frequent resort to mercenary troops. We hear for example of a considerable number of Cretans, descendants of Milesian ancestors, hired for one of the wars of the time of Doson or Philip V. In order to increase its man-power the city settled these Cretan mercenaries (more than a thousand in number) in Myus, which at that time was subject to it. With the same object Miletus opened its gates to other foreigners and freely granted them franchise. Some of them settled in the city itself, others probably in the country. Thus, it appears, was founded in the early second century B.C. Ἰωνία πόλις or Ionopolis, a small harbour city on the Latmian Gulf and an ideal site for a regular ferry service connecting Miletus with the other side of that Gulf.*

Another unmistakable sign of vitality and comparative prosperity is the flourishing condition of the sanctuary of Didyma; it appears to have attracted large numbers of pilgrims, who filled the treasury of the temple with their gifts. To make Didyma still more attractive to pilgrims and at the

* Rehm, *Milet, Erg. d. Ausgr.* i. 3, 150, l. 99 f.; *S.I.G.*[3] 633.

same time to compete with the growing fame of Artemis Leukophryene of Magnesia, Miletus organized new games, the Didymeia, and celebrated them with much splendour.

Finally, we have evidence of the prosperity of the citizens of Miletus in the fact that at a time of stress (200–199 B.C.) one of them (and he was certainly not an exception), the famous Eudemus, gave an important donation for the education of children of his fellow citizens; while some of the well-to-do Milesians were prepared to lend money to the city (a war loan?) on easy terms.

All these disconnected facts are no doubt susceptible of various interpretations, but they appear to point to the conclusion that I have drawn.

Miletus suffered no decline after Magnesia. It still pursued, as a practically independent city, a policy of expansion. Thus the incorporation of the small Carian city of Pidasa in the territory of Miletus, which took the form of a treaty of *sympoliteia* (176/5 B.C.) perhaps imposed upon Pidasa, led to an acute conflict with Heraclea-under-Latinus, a conflict ended by a detailed treaty (173/2 B.C.). This incorporation increased the number of Milesian citizens and the taxes paid by the citizens of Pidasa went to swell the Milesian revenue.

No doubt during the war between Rome and Antiochus III and later when the Galatians renewed their inroads, the city from time to time felt the economic pinch: no candidates appeared for the expensive *stephanephoria*, and Apollo, son of Zeus, had to fill the gap. Nevertheless, the city was able to erect some important public buildings (for example the *bouleuterion*) and to rebuild one of its markets (the north market)* ; it could also afford to continue work on the temple of Didyma, which remained in a hopelessly unfinished state.

The main source of its affluence was still its flourishing trade, as is shown by the donations and endowments given by those who participated in that trade—the Bithynian king Prusias, the Bosporan king and queen (Paerisades and Camasarye), and various cities. The devotion of the native Milesians to their own city and the general renown of the city are attested by the lavish gift to the city of a fine new *bouleuterion* by

* See below, note 78.

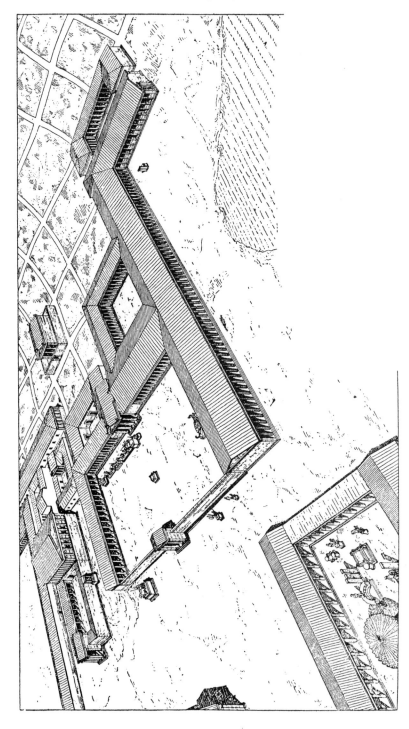

FIG. 6. Miletus. Reconstruction of the North Market as it was at the end of the Hellenistic period. From A. von Gerkan, *Milet: Erg. d. Ausgr.*, i. 6, pl. xxvii, by permission of the German State Archaeological Institute.

Timarchus and Heracleides, the two well-known fabulously rich Milesians, chief assistants of Antiochus IV, the building being erected for the safety of the king certainly with his knowledge and approval; while its political and economic importance is shown by the donations and endowments of Eumenes II after he had protected the city against the Galatians. All this makes it certain that Miletus enjoyed prosperity in the first half of the second century, a prosperity reflected incidentally in its abundant coinage.[76]

The impression of prosperity and of efficient organization is supported moreover by what we know of its military, financial, social, and economic life at this time. Miletus in the late third and early second centuries B.C. was in possession of a large and fertile territory, well fortified and closely guarded by detachments of the Milesian army stationed in small fortresses and in subject cities.* To watch the frontiers, the magistrates and tax-farmers of the city had at their disposal a strong force of police and gendarmerie (ὁροφύλακες), some of them mounted, under the command of a *paraphylax*.† The *horophylakes* certainly had not only administrative but also financial functions. We may compare them with the ἐρημοφύλακες of Egypt. While in Egypt the tax ἐρημοφυλακία, that is to say, the tax for the support of the desert gendarmes, was collected by the tax-farmers in addition to the customs duties, in Miletus the ὁροφυλακικὸν τέλος may have been a combination of a gendarme tax and the customs duties, levied on the frontiers of the Milesian territory.[76a] The system of taxation was, as usual in the Greek cities (above, pp. 619 f.), very elaborate and probably very oppressive. We have information regarding some of the taxes in the treaty of sympolity made by Miletus with Pidasa in 176/5 B.C. It was stipulated in this treaty that the Pidaseans should enjoy temporary exemption from certain taxes.‡ Nor was the system of liturgies less elaborate or less onerous.§ The

---

* Rehm, *Milet: Erg. d. Ausgr.* i. 3., nos. 37c, 43; 37d, 65, and 37e, 85 ff.; 143, 30; 146, 39; 149, 15 ff.; 150, 51.

† Rehm, loc. cit., no. 150, paragraph 11; *S.I.G³* 633, cf. Rehm, loc. cit., p. 363, and the inscription *B.C.H.*, xxxii (1908), pp. 499 ff.

‡ Rehm, loc. cit., no 149, paragraph 4, cf. 150, 100 ff. (*S.I.G.³* 633).

§ Rehm, loc. cit., 37 d, 66; 149, 35 ff. and 45 ff.

city bank of Miletus, first organized probably about 200 B.C., was well managed. It had charge of the city funds and, under the control of the city administration, carried out various business transactions, such as the granting of trade loans (δάνεια ἐμπορικά).[77] The industrial and commercial character of the city is attested, not only by the evidence cited above, but also by its spacious market-places—the larger south and the smaller north market—and by the care taken of them as well as of the harbours and the roads.[78] Slave labour was extensively used both by the city and by private citizens. Some of the slaves are described in the inscriptions as οἰκετικὰ σώματα, which probably means private slaves, that is, slaves belonging to private households (as opposed to δημόσιοι, city slaves), and does not imply that these slaves were exclusively employed in domestic service. The number of slaves in Heraclea under Mt. Latmus was also large.[79]

The records of the other cities in the valley of the Maeander which have been excavated in modern times are far less ample and trustworthy than those of Miletus. And yet even the meagre evidence that we possess regarding PRIENE, MAGNESIA, and HERACLEA AD LATMUM is eloquent of their condition. Priene, though its brilliant period was that of Alexander and the Successors, was still strong enough in the last years of the third century to make war against Miletus and sufficiently confident in itself in the middle of the second century to grant asylum to the fugitive Orophernes. Though devastated by Ariarathes V and Attalus II, it ultimately profited by this act of political hospitality. Apart from the edifices that Orophernes bestowed on the city, it is more than probable that it was his money that enabled Priene to carry out an ambitious building programme in the late second century.[80] Priene's neighbour Magnesia was able about 220 B.C. to plan the construction of an imposing temple for its goddess and later to carry out the project, at least partially, while at the same time indulging in a ruinous though victorious war against Miletus.

While our information on the larger cities of Ionia and Caria, except Miletus, is poor, some epigraphical texts allow us to form an idea of the economic life of certain minor cities and settlements in this part of Asia Minor. Illuminating in this respect is the above-named treaty of 176/5 B.C. between Miletus and Pidasa.* PIDASA was a small Carian city. Its life, as revealed by the settlement of its financial obligations to Miletus after its incorporation, was purely rural, based on the exploitation of its fertile land. The land belonged partly to the city (γῆ δημοσία) and to the temples (γῆ ἱερά), but most of it was owned by the citizens. The main income was derived from the olive groves; next came cattle and bee-keeping, the last a speciality of Caria, known to have been practised also at Theangela, another Carian city. Corn was probably produced mostly on the mountain slopes; this at least we find stated in the case of the land owned by the temples.† The yield of these cornfields was probably small and consequently the tax paid for this land was low (1 per cent., ἑκατοστή). In addition to land in the territory of the city the citizens of Pidasa owned vineyards in the territory of the city of Euromus. The estates (κτήματα) were large: some of them produced more than one thousand *metretai*. The wine was probably of excellent quality, since the Milesians endeavoured, by lowering the customs duties (ἐλλιμένιον), to attract it to the market of their own city. Not all the agricultural goods produced in the territory of Pidasa were consumed locally: there is no doubt that a considerable proportion was exported. Before the annexation this went in all probability to the Carian harbours, especially Iasus. After the annexation the Milesians endeavoured to divert the exports from Pidasa and Euromus to their own market and harbour. It was with this object that they built the road previously mentioned from Pidasa to Ionopolis, the construction of a road from Pidasa direct to Miletus being rendered difficult and expensive by Mount Grion. How far and for how long they succeeded in changing the direction of the Carian export trade we do not know.

The document on which the above inferences are based, the treaty between Pidasa and Miletus, allows no conclusions to be drawn *ex silentio*. What we possess is probably not the full treaty but corrections and amendments of it. It is interesting

---

* Rehm, loc. cit., no. 149.

† 'corn . . . produced in the sacred mountains'—τοῦ δὲ ἐν τοῖς ἱεροῖς ὄρεσιν . . . γινομένο[υ] σίτου.

to note, however, that industrial taxes do not figure in the list of taxes paid by the Pidaseans and that the document makes no mention of slaves, though slaves were so numerous at Heraclea and Miletus (above, p. 670). Silence on the latter point may be an accident, on the former probably not.[81]

That two other cities of Caria—the large and powerful city of MYLASA and the obscure OLYMUS—were likewise rural communities living chiefly on the income derived by the city, the temples, and private individuals from the exploitation of the land, is attested by the well-known set of inscriptions of the second and first centuries B.C. found in this region. The documents of Mylasa and Olymus are concerned mostly with the lease of lands owned by the temples or with the purchase of lands by the temples and their subsequent lease. They are of great importance from the juridical point of view and illuminate at the same time certain problems connected with land economy and money-lending. Like the treaty of Miletus with Pidasa and several other documents of Asia Minor, they show the important role that temples played in the economic life of the time. The temples—even the temples connected with minor cities—appear to have been not merely large agricultural establishments, but at the same time important banking institutions. Their operations were mostly connected with rural economy. This was the case at Olymus and Mylasa, and the financial operations carried out a little earlier by the temple of Artemis at Sardis (above, ch. IV, p. 495) are known to have been of the same character. But in larger cities, for example at Ephesus, it may have been otherwise. Here the temple banking had a larger scope and business transactions may have been more diversified.[82]

We have much less evidence regarding the rest of Asia Minor. We should certainly wish to know more of Ephesus, of Smyrna, and of the great islands off the coast, Samos, Chios, and Lesbos. EPHESUS in all probability remained in the second century what it had been in the third—a great centre of trade, especially with Syria, and of banking.[83] And so it was probably with SMYRNA.

The situation of SAMOS appears to have been far from brilliant about 200 B.C.;* nor did it improve later, as is shown by

* G. Klaffenbach, *Ath. Mitt.* li (1926), pp. 26 ff., inscr. no. 2.

its famous grain regulations.* But such isolated fragments of evidence hardly justify any general inferences.

We may, however, affirm with certainty that such great commercial cities of the Propontis and the Straits as CYZICUS, LAMPSACUS, and BYZANTIUM (above, pp. 587 ff.) continued to lead more or less the same kind of prosperous existence as before. As regards Cyzicus we have proof of this in the famous description of the city by Strabo already quoted. That Byzantium was thriving we have evidence in the fact that, although hard pressed by its Celtic and Thracian neighbours, it challenged the rest of the commercial world, and Rhodes in particular, by imposing about 220 B.C. a tax on ships passing through the Bosporus, a challenge that was followed by a protracted war. We have further evidence in the heavy tribute (eighty talents) that the city was paying (though not without difficulty) to its suzerains and neighbours, the Celtic kings. It may be, no doubt, that the tax on shipping was a measure concerted between Byzantium and the Celtic ruler Cavarus, in order to enable the city to pay the onerous tribute to the king. After the war Byzantium lost none of its importance. Cordial relations with Rhodes were soon re-established, and about 200 B.C. the city gave active help to Rhodes and Attalus in their struggle with Philip. About this time a Byzantine squadron visited the Piraeus and its commanders were received by Athens with high honours.[84]

Finally, the importance and wealth of Lampsacus are shown by the active part it took in the politics of the early second century, by its embassy to Massilia and Rome in 196 B.C.† and the prominent part it played on the eve of the great war between Antiochus III and Rome.[85]

The same may be said of HERACLEA PONTICA and SINOPE, which have already been spoken of. Heraclea, it is true, lived through difficult times, its liberty constantly threatened by the Bithynian kings. The attack of Prusias I which brought upon it the loss of its dependencies and subject territory,‡ has already been mentioned. However, its role as a great commercial city was not concluded, as we learn from the treaty between Pharnaces on the one side and Eumenes, Prusias, and Ariarathes on the other, which put an end to the war of 183–179 B.C. In

---

* *S.I.G.*³ 976, after 188 B.C.   † *S.I.G.*³ 591.   ‡ Memnon 27.

the treaty were included (περιελήφθησαν) some of the great cities of the Euxine and Propontis, probably those which in some way had taken part in the war. They were Heraclea, Mesembria on the Thracian coast, Chersonesus in the Crimea, and Cyzicus.*

Sinope, even after its annexation (in 183 B.C.) by Pharnaces I, retained its importance as a commercial and industrial city. I have already referred to the cordial relations that existed between Rhodes and Sinope, and I shall return presently to the subject. They were strikingly manifested by the action of Rhodes, first in affording substantial help to Sinope when it was besieged by Mithridates III of Pontus,† and then in attempting to preserve the liberty of that city when it was annexed by Pharnaces I.‡

Our information regarding the cities of the western coast of the EUXINE, APOLLONIA, MESEMBRIA, CALLATIS, TOMI, DIONYSOPOLIS, and ISTRUS for this period is somewhat better than for the third century. We possess some inscriptions, which all speak of severe hardships, of attacks by Celtic and Thracian kings and tribes, of famine and misery. Unfortunately none of these inscriptions is dated, and we have to rely on the form of the letters, a very insecure basis of inference.

Since no exact dates can be assigned to these inscriptions and they may belong to the next period, dealt with in Ch. VI, I prefer to deal with all of them at once and refer the reader to that chapter for more detailed information. The situation of the Euxine cities was approximately the same in the two periods.

One result of this situation was the fact mentioned by Polybius,§ that the Pontic cities of his time, though still actively exporting a variety of commodities to Greece, no longer possessed such abundance of grain as in the past. They would, in fact, sometimes export grain and at other times import it. This was certainly due to the spasmodic character of the production in their own territories and in their hinterland. The testimony of Polybius, however, relates to the cities on the

* Polyb. xxvi. 6. 2 (xxv. 2, Loeb).
† Polyb. iv. 56 is our main source, cf. below, p. 677.
‡ Polyb. xxiv. 10 (xxiii. 9. 2, Loeb).   § iv. 38.

northern and western coasts of the Black Sea, but not to the Bosporus. His statement is supported by the inscription from Istrus (perhaps of a slightly later date) which I have quoted and which speaks of a shortage of grain and of services rendered in this respect by a Carthaginian merchant, who imported grain into the city.*[86]

While conditions were constantly deteriorating in the cities of the west coast of the Euxine, the Crimea and especially the BOSPORAN KINGDOM, after a short period of decline and anarchy, were once more prosperous. This is shown by the archaeological evidence and by some isolated documents referring to the commercial relations between Bosporus and the Greek world. Rhodes steadily developed its commerce with the Crimea. We have proof of this in the abundance of Rhodian stamped jars in South Russia in general, and by some inscriptions found at Panticapaeum,† at Chersonesus,‡ and at Olbia,§ all dating from the third century B.C. It is worthy of note that Scilurus, the powerful king of the Crimean Scythians and the suzerain of Olbia in the early and middle second century B.C., entertained close commercial relations with Rhodes, his agent in Olbia, Posideus, being one of the richest and most influential citizens of that city. This man was a wealthy merchant and the active enemy of the Satarchaeans, a group of Pontic pirates, from whom he freed the island of Leuce.‖ Posideus at Olbia stood in the same relation to Scilurus as did Acornion of Dionysopolis at a later time to Byrebista.¶ Finally, I may refer to the presence of many Pontic slaves at Rhodes: Scythians, Sarmatians, and Maeotians. Alongside of them we find an Olbian (Borysthenite) and a Bosporan, probably not slaves but free men. The inscriptions are not dated, but some of them may belong to the second century, while some are a little later.[87]

There were likewise active relations between Panticapaeum and Chersonesus on the one hand, and Delphi on the other. The well-known Delphian list of *proxenoi* gives evidence of

---

* S. Lambrino, *Dacia*, 3–4 (1927–32), pp. 400 ff.

† *I.O.S.P.E.* ii. 35.   ‡ *Ibid.* i, 2nd ed., 340.

§ *Ibid.* i, 2nd ed., 30.   ‖ *Ibid.* i, 2nd ed., 672; *S.E.G.* iii. 606.

¶ *S.I.G.*³ 762.

these relations in 195/4 and again in 192/1. The *proxenoi* of 192/1 are met with again in a decree of the same year,* to which I have already referred. It describes the capture (perhaps by pirates) of the Delphian *theoroi* and their rescue (λελυτρωμένοι) by the city of Chersonesus. It shows that the Chersonesites carefully watched the Tauric pirates, who probably were the captors of the Delphian envoys, and that they were well informed about them. A Chersonesite from the Euxine (ἐκ τοῦ Πόντου) was honoured at about the same time by the city of Oropus (?).† The cordial relations between continental Greece and the Bosporan kingdom were maintained later, after 168 B.C., as we may infer from the honours paid to king Paerisades and his queen Camasarye at Delphi. The royal couple dedicated a gift at the Didymeion of Miletus at the same time.[88]

It is interesting to note that, while the Bosporan kingdom, Olbia, and Chersonesus were thus closely connected with Rhodes and continental Greece (probably through Athens), there is no sign of the maintenance of the former close commercial relations with Delos. The time had passed when Delos played a prominent part in the grain trade, for this trade was now controlled by Rhodes and Athens.[89]

Very active also were the commercial relations between Bosporus and Pergamon, as is shown by pottery of Anatolian origin and metal ware of Pergamene style found in the Bosporan kingdom, and between Bosporus and Ptolemaic Egypt (Egyptian glass and faience have been found in South Russia). Closer investigation of the minor objects found in the Greek cities of South Russia and in the graves of the Scytho-Sarmatian steppes will probably reveal business relations between Bosporus and other important Hellenistic centres of industry and commerce. Finds of metal horse-trappings of a peculiar style, for example, show that trade connexions with Bactria and India were not broken off as a consequence of the political changes that occurred both in South Russia and in Bactria and India.[90]

RHODES, which had already been wealthy and important in the period of the balance of power, now became the richest and

* *S.I.G.*[3] 604. † *S.E.G.* i. 106.

most influential city of the Hellenistic world.[91] I have previously described how in the late fourth century and in the
early Hellenistic period Rhodes became a rival of Athens. We
have seen it asserting its liberty against Antigonus and
Demetrius, and later against Ptolemy Philadelphus. But it was
not until the downfall of the Ptolemaic hegemony in the
Aegean that it reached its zenith. I have shown how, in the
last two or three decades of the third century, this island State
became the recognized leader of the Aegean Greeks, the
defender of Greek liberty and of the freedom of Aegean commerce, and the active enemy of professional pirates.

Two exceedingly interesting episodes in this period of its history are well known to us. One is the help that it gave to the city
of Sinope when attacked (about 220 B.C.) by the king of Pontus,
Mithridates III. An embassy from Sinope came to Rhodes to
ask for assistance. Military intervention was of course out of
question, but Rhodes readily granted a loan of 140,000 Rhodian
drachmas, which sum was applied to the purchase of wine
(10,000 κεράμια), war material (hair and sinews for the manufacture of engines of war), arms and weapons (1,000 panoplies),
two catapults (λιθοφόροι), and operators (ἀφέται) for them.
Three thousand gold staters were also given, whether as a loan
or a gift is not clear. All this was sent to Sinope, probably
under Rhodian military escort. The detailed description of this
episode by Polybius is invaluable, for it gives an idea of the
political and economic importance of Rhodes at this time and
of the resources at its command.[93] It shows that in 220 B.C.
Rhodes was the greatest centre of banking and credit in the
Greek world, and carried on extensive financial operations; and
this conclusion is supported by other fragments of evidence.
At the same time we learn from the narrative of Polybius that
the staple article of Rhodian trade was wine, which the island
produced and exported in large quantities (see below on the
stamped amphora handles of Rhodes). We may also infer from
the same source that Rhodes carried on a flourishing trade in
war material. The siege of Demetrius Poliorcetes shows how
highly military technique was developed there.[92]

The second episode relates to the city of Byzantium (above,
p. 673). The assistance given by Rhodes to Sinope demonstrates

PLATE LXXVI

1. The air view of the modern city of Rhodes and of its harbours printed in Fig. 1 has not hitherto been published. It was made at my request by order of His Excellency the Governor of Rhodes, by whose kind permission it is reproduced. I cannot discuss here the two (or perhaps three) ancient harbours of Rhodes which were regarded as stupendous creations of human genius and are impressively described by Strabo, (xiv, 2, 5, p. 652 f.); Dio Chrysostom (xxxi. 146), and Aristeides (xxv, p. 810 D.). The ancient remains of these harbours have not been, to my knowledge, recently studied and illustrated. Such a study is not an easy one, for the harbours of Rhodes have never been out of use from ancient times. It is more than probable, however, that the general aspect of Rhodes in those times was *mutatis mutandis* the same as it is now. The reader who wishes to know more of its ancient harbours and of the general aspect of the city may read the ancient descriptions of them cited above, and supplement these by what has been written in modern times on the subject. The best modern general description will be found in H. van Gelder, *Geschichte der alten Rhodier*, 1900, pp. 5 ff. (on the harbours pp. 8 ff.); cf. K. Lehmann-Hartleben, 'Die antiken Hafenanlagen des Mittelmeeres', *Klio*, Beih. xiv (N.F. i), 1923, pp. 128 ff., with bibliography; a good plan will be found in C. Merckel, *Die Ingenieurtechnik im Altertum*, 1899, pp. 340 ff.

2. Figure 2 of this plate is from a photograph placed at my disposal by Prof. L. Laurenzi, then Director of the Archaeological Exploration of Rhodes and the Dodecanese. It shows the general aspect of the beautiful city of Lindus, which has recently been excavated by a Danish Expedition and is now in process of restoration by the Archaeological Service of Rhodes. On the two harbours of Lindus, lying on opposite sides of the Acropolis (which was built on a promontory), see K. Lehmann-Hartleben, loc. cit., p. 20 and pl. i. The restorations of the buildings of the Acropolis are discussed by L. Laurenzi, *Mem. FERT.* ii (1938), pp. 9 ff. and iii (1938), pp. 27 ff.

PLATE LXXVI

1

2

RHODES AND LINDUS

the important part played by the city at this time in the Pontic trade. I have shown that we have evidence of the close commercial relations of Rhodes with Olbia, Chersonesus, and the Bosporan kingdom. It had similar relations with Greek colonies of the western coast of the Black Sea. Rhodian stamped jar-handles are as abundant in Apollonia, Callatis, Istrus, &c., and their respective spheres of commercial intercourse, as at Olbia and in the Bosporan kingdom.*⁹³ It was consequently natural that Rhodes should resist the imposition by Byzantium of a transit toll in the Thracian Bosporus, however vital the measure might be for that city, threatened as she was in her very existence by her Thracian and Celtic neighbours. The resulting war of 220 B.C. between the two States, in which Prusias I of Bithynia took an active part as the ally of Rhodes, has been referred to above. The student of economic history will find pleasure in reading the detailed and lucid account of it given by Polybius.

We find Rhodes at a later date pursuing the same vigorous policy in regard to Aegean affairs and guided thereby in its attitude towards Philip V. Challenged by the latter, Rhodes, allied with Pergamon and Byzantium, successfully combated his aspiration to revive the hegemony of Antigonus Gonatas in the Aegean.⁹⁴ Its hostility to Philip made the island State an efficient ally of Rome in her war with Philip, and its fear of the ambition of Antiochus to dominate the Aegean explains (in part) its active share in the war of Rome with that ruler.

After Cynoscephalae and Magnesia, Rhodes, the friend of Rome, shared with Pergamon the spoils of the two wars. It was now the official president and the actual leader of the Island League, which it reconstituted. It ruled over large and fertile territories in southern Asia Minor. Through this new political role it considerably increased its wealth. It knew how to extract large sums of money from its dominions, probably by an elaborate and perhaps oppressive taxation. It required its allies, the islands of the Aegean, to contribute substantial sums as their share in the common policing of the sea, and may have obliged them to meet the cost of this by developing their

* A careful collection and publication of this evidence would be of great service to students of the economic history of the ancient world.

own system of taxation. But the bulk of the revenue of Rhodes was derived from the part it took in the commercial life of the civilized world at this time. Rhodes certainly now became what Athens had been in the fourth century and what Alexandria endeavoured to be after Athens—the chief clearing-house for Mediterranean commerce, especially for the grain trade, and the most important centre of banking in the Hellenistic world. Even the scanty evidence we possess is sufficient to establish this.[95]

We know little of the organization and volume of the trade of Rhodes. It may have attained a yearly value of 50 million Rhodian drachmas. In any case the revenue from its commerce and banking and from its dominions was suffiicient to enable it to maintain a large army in its dominions and a strong navy in the Aegean, in constant readiness to engage the pirates. Confident of its strength, Rhodes never shrank from actual war if driven to it.[96]

The guiding principle in the policy of Rhodes was without doubt the unity of the Greek world, at least in its economic and commercial aspect. This is shown by the history of the Rhodian currency, which spread far and wide over the Aegean and both rivalled and supplemented the monetary unity promoted by Pergamon and Syria as previously described. It is shown also by the attempt of Rhodes to set up and obtain general acceptance for a maritime code, known as the *lex Rhodia*, about which we have little information. This code of regulations governing trade by sea was tacitly accepted by all merchants of the Mediterranean as soon as it was formulated, and remained for a long time the standard maritime law of antiquity.

The success of Rhodes was amazing. Its commercial relations were of wide extent. Rhodian ships frequented all parts of the Mediterranean. Jars with Rhodian stamps are found in every important commercial centre of the Hellenistic world; in Greece and Asia Minor, in Egypt, in Syria and Palestine, as far east as Seleuceia on the Tigris and Susa on the Eulaeus, in Carthage, southern Italy and Sicily, in South Russia and the western Pontic harbours, and as far north as the slopes of the Carpathian mountains.[97]

We may now pause to consider the peculiar features of the

social and economic life of Rhodes. Our information is no doubt defective. but the archaeological exploration of the city is proceeding rapidly and every day brings to light fresh information of importance.

It was the common opinion of the Greeks that Rhodes was the most beautiful city of the Greek world, a rival of Athens, Alexandria, and Pergamon, and one of the most important centres of Greek civilization and art. The best descriptions of it are those of Strabo,* Diodorus,† and Dio Chrysostomus.‡ They cannot be verified by the remains of the ancient city, for these are hidden under the medieval and modern city. To form an idea of ancient Rhodes, we must therefore rely upon the above trustworthy and well-informed guides.[98]

They show us the three harbours of Rhodes, all of them the work of man, the city descending to them from the hills, fan-like or theatre-like, the city walls surrounding the city even on the sea side, and the famous *deigma* where the merchandise of all the nations was displayed. They mention the great short-lived 'colossus', the squares around the *deigma*, and, last but not least, the pride of the Rhodians, the famous docks. We hear also of the acropolis with its open spaces and groves, of the temples of Helios, of Apollo Pythius and of Zeus Atabyrios, but we are unable to determine their sites. The story that the famous Hippodamus of Miletus was the builder of Rhodes is no doubt an invention. It is significant, however, of the high renown of the city that its construction should be attributed to the greatest town-planner of the ancient world.

The city, our authorities tell us, was full of statues and pictures. Of the last we have no remains. But the fragments of sculpture found in the subsoil of the modern city and in the island of Cos are numerous, and some of them of a certain artistic value. They afford a good illustration of the artistic currents that prevailed in the city, and convey some idea of the leading traits of the Rhodian school of sculpture, of which, however, our knowledge is principally derived from statues and groups of statues exported in one way or another from Rhodes, mostly to Italy. The flourishing state of the plastic arts in Rhodes is further attested by the frequent mention in

---

* xiv. 2. 5 ff., pp. 652 ff.   † xix. 45, and xx. 85.   ‡ *Or.* xxxi. 162.

PLATE LXXVII

Rock-cut bas-relief of a Rhodian τριημιολία. It still stands in all its impressive beauty, as excavated by the Danish Expedition, near the ancient stairs which led to the Acropolis of Lindus. The bas-relief, which represents the stern of a Rhodian war ship, was carved to serve as the base for the bronze statue of a Rhodian naval officer. This is stated explicitly in the inscription engraved on the side of the ship just below the place where stood the statue of the officer: Λίν]διοι | ἐτίμασαν | ['Αγή]σανδρον Μικίωνος | χ[ρυ]σέωι στεφάνωι, | εἰκόνι, προεδρίαι ἐ[ν] τοῖς ἀγῶσι ἀρετᾶς ἔνεκα καὶ | εὐνοίας ἂν ἔχων διατελεῖ | περὶ τὸ πλῆθος τὸ Λινδίων· | Πυθόκριτος Τιμοχάριος 'Ρόδιος ἐπόησε. The family of the officer is known from the inscriptions of Lindus. His grandfather was priest of Poseidon Hippius in 239 B.C. The officer's career must therefore be assigned to the early second century B.C., and the erection of the statue to about 180 B.C. This accords with the dates assigned to the sculptor of the statue, who was probably responsible for its base also. We may suppose that the honour was bestowed on Hagesandrus on account of his military achievements, probably a successful expedition against the pirates or the neighbours and enemies of the Rhodians—the Lycians. The bas-relief has been several times published and discussed, the last detailed study being that of Chr. Blinkenberg, 'Triemiolia', Lindiaka VII, Det Kgl. Danske Videnskabernes Selskab, Arch.-Kunsth. Medd. ii, 3 (1938), pp. 22 ff., where the reader will find a complete bibliography and excellent illustrations. Here reproduced from a photograph supplied by Prof. Blinkenberg and from a drawing made by Mrs. Kinch and placed at my disposal by the former.

PLATE LXXVII

1

2

THE RHODIAN NAVY

PLATE LXXVIII

2. Pompeian painting. Naples Museum

RHODES, LIFE AND MYTH

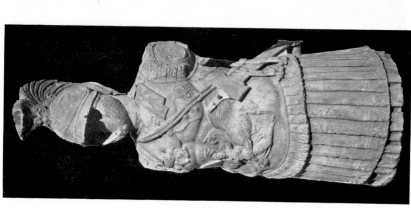

1. Panoply. Rhodes Museum

PLATE LXXVIII

1. A marble panoply which formed part of a funeral monument of a Rhodian officer who in his lifetime had served in the navy or the army. It consists of a fine cuirass adorned with figures in repousse work, a helmet with elaborate crest, likewise adorned with figures, visor, cheek- and back-pieces, and a sword suspended from a baldric. The specimen reproduced here is the best preserved of the funeral monuments of this type, not uncommon at Rhodes. It may be assigned to the first century, B.C. For a more detailed description see A. Maiuri, *Clara Rhodos*, ii (1932), pp. 57 ff. and figs. 28–30; G. Jacopi, *L'Ospedale dei Cavalieri e il Museo Archeologico di Rodi, 1932*, p. 52.

2. A fragmentary mythological painting from Pompeii found in the Casa dei Capitelli Colorati (vii, 4, 51). The picture shows Apollo-Helios, his head encircled by a radiate crown, seated on a rock near a young girl who is weaving a crown of flowers. The painting has been interpreted as representing Apollo-Helios the patron of Rhodes and his daughter, Rhodes. It may go back to a Hellenistic Rhodian original. For a short description and bibliography see O. Elia, *Pitture murali e mosaici nel Museo Nazionale di Napoli*, 1932, p. 83, no. 192, fig. 26.

Photographs for no. 1 supplied by the authorities of the Rhodes Museum, for no. 2 by Alinari.

our literary texts of Rhodian artists of the Hellenistic period and by their many extant signatures. The signatures found in Rhodes itself belong not only to Rhodian but also to foreign artists and vividly reflect the international character of the city's life. We may notice in particular the many Athenians among them.

It is surprising that we know so little of the world-famous colossus. We believe its face is reproduced on coins, but of the general appearance of the Apollo of the Rhodian harbour, figured as a sun-god, we remain ignorant.*[99]

We have better knowledge of the constitution of the city in the Hellenistic period. The Rhodians were celebrated for their *eunomia*. The city had the reputation not only of having an excellent constitution but also of having found (in a compromise) a satisfactory solution of the crucial problem with which Greek cities were perpetually confronted, the maintenance of peaceful relations between the rich and the poor. 'The Rhodians', says Strabo,† 'care for the *demos*, though they are not ruled by it; still, they desire to sustain the masses of the poor. The people are accordingly supplied with corn, and the well-to-do support those in need according to ancestral practice (and there are also liturgies for the provision of food). Thus the poor have the means to live and at the same time the city has its needs amply supplied, especially as regards its shipping.'

This is not the place to describe the peculiar constitution of the city and island of Rhodes and that of the Rhodian territory outside it, that is to say, its territory on the mainland and the subject islands. Suffice it to say as regards the last that the provinces of Rhodes, its possessions in Caria and Lycia, were not regarded as Rhodian soil, and were not divided into *demoi*. They were treated as foreign dominions and yielded an important revenue to the State. The yearly revenue from two cities alone, Stratonicea and Caunus, amounted to 120 talents.

What we are concerned with is the social and economic structure of Rhodes. We should like to be better informed regarding the method by which the State provided for the poor

* *C.A.H.* vol. of pls. III, 14 *g.*
† xiv. 2. 5 ff., pp. 652 ff., probably following Panaetius and Posidonius.

and avoided revolutions; but we have no documents to throw light upon this point. Since Rhodes probably depended largely on imported corn, the problem of a regular supply of corn alone required careful attention and an unusual amount of intelligent organization.

The task of the government was no doubt made easier than in other cities by the steadily growing prosperity that accompanied the social and economic progress of the State. This prosperity depended not only on the peaceful activity of the Rhodian citizens and other residents but more especially on the skilful management of foreign relations, diplomatic activity being supported by a rational and efficient organization of the naval and military forces. The navy of the Rhodians played so important and peculiar a part in their affairs that we shall be justified in setting out the little information we have about its organization.[100]

It is certain, to begin with, that the Rhodians devoted great attention to the technique of shipbuilding. The ancients greatly admired their achievements. Strabo tells us* that the Rhodians kept some of their docks strictly closed and that no stranger was admitted to them. This precaution was taken both on account of the danger of damage by agents of some foreign power (such as Philip's emissary Heracleides), and also probably because they had certain devices which they wished to keep secret.

The navy of Rhodes was highly organized and consisted of all kinds of craft from quinqueremes downwards, with a hierarchy of officers and skilled seamen and marines. Some few inscriptions found both at Rhodes and in other places give us an excellent idea of the composition of the crew of a Rhodian man-of-war. These inscriptions are dedications by crews of ships; they give lists of names of the crew with their respective functions in hierarchic order. The most complete of them, recently found at Rhodes in good preservation, may serve as example.† The man whose statue was dedicated by the crew of a ship was not of very high rank. He began his career as a marine (στρατευσάμενος ἐν ταῖς τριημολίαις καὶ ἐν ταῖς καταφράκτοις

---

* xiv. 2. 5, p. 653.
† M. Segre, *Clara Rhodos*, viii (1936), pp. 228 ff.

ναυσί), then became chief engineer, the head of the technical service of a ship (ἀγησάμενος τῶν ἔργων), and was finally second officer during the (Mithridatic) war, in charge of the helm on several ships in succession (πρωρατεύσας τριημιολιᾶν καὶ τετρήρευς κατὰ πόλεμον). The list of the dedicants is headed by officers of various classes, among whom the technical service officers are prominent. Next in the list after the helmsman (κυβερνήτης) come the building inspector or carpenter (ναυπαγός); the steersman (παδαλιοῦχος), who was a Samian, that is, a foreigner; the man responsible for oiling or greasing the machines and oars (ἐλαιοχρηίστας); the ship's doctor (ἰατρός), who was a μέτοικος from Tripoli in Syria; and the man in charge of the oars (κωποδέτας). Then follow the members of the crew: the technical hands (ἐργαζόμενοι ἐν πρώρᾳ and ἐν πρύμναι), ten in number; and the men-at-arms: two artillerymen (καταπελταφέται), six bowmen (τοξόται), and nineteen marines (ἐπιβάται).

There are three more similar lists and the same ratings are mentioned in them. In one of them* we have again the ναυπαγός and six ἐργαζόμενοι, all Rhodian citizens. In another,† besides a κωποδέτας, we find one ἀρχιναυφύλαξ and one [φ]ύλαξ. It is curious to find such guards on a ship. One would be disposed to see in these guards members of the police force of the docks; but the κωποδέτας and the παρακαθήμενοι of the same inscription tell against this interpretation.[101] I may suggest therefore that special guards, a kind of naval police, were responsible for keeping watch over the rowers of the ships.

The above lists show that the crews of the Rhodian men-of-war consisted, with a few exceptions in the technical service, of Rhodian citizens exclusively. Whether naval service was compulsory or voluntary for them we do not know, nor how long it lasted, nor how often a Rhodian might be called upon to serve. Most of the ships were built by rich citizens, the trierarchs, who in time of war provided pay for the crews, but on the understanding that the State would reimburse them. The emulation of the trierarchs was kept up by competitions between the ships, and a victory in such an *agon* was accounted

* G.D.I. 4335; A. Maiuri, N.S., 5.

† M. Chaviaras, 'Αρχ. 'Εφ., 1915, p. 128, no. 1; A. Maiuri, Ann. Sc. It. ii (1916), p. 136, no. 2.

a very high distinction.[102] The Rhodian sailors, whether in the navy or the merchant fleet, enjoyed a high reputation among all the Greeks for bravery and skill. Time has spared us one glimpse of their lives in a Rhodian sailor's song recently found in Egypt.*

About the Rhodian army less is known. It was in the main an army of mercenaries, though recruited in part in the Peraea.[103] Service in the army was apparently held in less esteem than service in the navy. While well-born Rhodians never fail to mention in their *cursus honorum* that they began their public life by serving in the navy as marines, they never mention service in the ranks of the army. It was probably considered that service in the army, except as an officer, was no occupation for a respectable Rhodian. War service in general, however, was very highly thought of in Rhodes, as is shown by the beautiful monuments, in the form of a ship's stern or of a panoply or trophy, erected to the honour or memory of heroes on sea or land.[104]

It is remarkable, indeed, how developed was the spirit of comradeship in the Rhodian navy. This spirit was, no doubt, characteristic of all Hellenistic armies, as is shown by military dedications in which officers and men appear together. But in Rhodes alone do we find associations of men who had served on the same ship. The ties of comradeship formed during service were made permanent, and officers and men became members of the same associations of ex-service men (οἱ στρατευσάμενοι), which beyond doubt did much to keep alive in many a Rhodian citizen the spirit of military valour, of patriotism, and of good fellowship.

And yet Rhodes was not a democracy. The traditions of the State were maintained by a group of families of the old stock. But although the highest offices, both civil and military, and the most prominent priesthoods were, in practice at least, the monopoly of an aristocracy of birth, wealth, and State service, even the noblest Rhodians began their career as common sailors in the fleet. After that their advancement followed.[105]

Behind the navy and the army we see in dim outline the classes that formed the economic backbone of the State—the

* *Oxyr.* 1383; A. Körte, *Arch. Pap.* vii (1924), p. 141.

merchants, the bankers, the business men, the workmen in the shipyards, the owners of shops, the landowners, and so forth. We have already met Rhodians abroad—as commanders and officers of the Rhodian navy, as diplomatic envoys, as rich merchants and bankers. In Rhodes itself we know the names of many an ordinary Rhodian, either as an individual citizen or as a member of some association. But the Rhodians very seldom mentioned their profession, even in their funeral inscriptions, differing in this from the inhabitants of other parts of Greece, not to speak of Italy and the West. It is therefore significant that one of the few exceptions is a banker. In his epitaph he modestly says 'for three decades he kept on deposit gold for foreigners and citizens alike, with purest honesty'.* This recalls the well-known epigram of Theocritus on the banker Caecus, who paid the same interest to natives and foreigners and kept his bank open even at night.†[106]

One of the most lasting achievements of the Rhodians in the sphere of business, law, and navigation was without doubt the famous 'Rhodian Law', which I have already mentioned. It is characteristic of the state of our information that our only evidence regarding it consists of a fragment of the Roman jurist Paulus,‡ who mentions the *lex Rhodia de iactu*. Appended to this fragment§ is a statement by Volusius Maecianus who refers to a *decretum* of an emperor Antoninus (Antoninus Pius or M. Aurelius) in which the latter directs that in naval suits regard should be had to the 'law of the Rhodians' so far as it does not conflict with Roman law. From these references is derived the description of the law in Isidore of Seville.‖ The quasi-historical evidence which is contained in the title of and the introduction to the so-called *lex Rhodia* of the Byzantine period has no value, these having been added in the twelfth century. Meagre as our evidence is, it shows that the current maritime law of the Mediterranean, the rules which were known to every seaman and of which the Roman administration and the Roman jurists had to take account in building up their own maritime law, was commonly called in the Mediterranean the

* A. Maiuri, *N.S.* 19, about 200 B.C.
† Theocr. *Ep.* 14; *Anth. Pal.* ix. 435.
‡ *Dig.* 14. 2. 1, cf. *Sent.* 2, 7, 1.   § 1. 9.   ‖ *Orig.* 5. 17.

law of the Rhodians. This implies that the Rhodians, in the period of their rule, enforced on the seas a body of rules which probably attempted to sum up and perhaps to codify all that the Greeks had previously achieved in this field, a law which was thus acceptable to all who followed the sea. It should, however, be noted that we have no proof of the existence of a written code of maritime law compiled by the Rhodians.[107]

The size of the population of Rhodes and of the State as a whole is unknown. No ancient statistics are available and modern conditions are misleading, for Rhodes is nowadays an agricultural, not a commercial community. Nor do we know what was the proportion of citizens, slaves, and foreigners. If, however, we analyse the population of Rhodes according to the political rights and social standing of its members, we find it highly differentiated. The full citizens were those who belonged to one of the old cities of Rhodes. They appended to their names those of their fathers and of the *damos* to which they belonged. Next to the full citizens stood those who had the right of naming their father but did not belong to a *damos*. As will be seen later, there were great numbers of foreigners in Rhodes, and it is not surprising that many of them tried to become, by some method, Rhodian citizens. This was not easy. Foreigners first received the right of residence, the *epidamia*, and later might be advanced to the standing of a 'Rhodian', a kind of minor franchise. But no example is known of a foreigner who became a full citizen. On the other hand, those who had only one Rhodian parent became a kind of political half-caste known as *matroxenos*, i.e. born of a foreign mother. The constitution of such a mixed family is well illustrated by an inscription of about 200 B.C.* In a certain well-to-do Rhodian family of prosperous bankers the grandfather had been a regular Rhodian citizen. He married a foreign woman, and his son was therefore a Rhodian, but only a *matroxenos*. His grandson, perhaps in turn born of a foreign mother, was not reckoned as a citizen but as a foreigner, a Samian with the right of residence.

A special class was that of the *paroikoi* and *katoikoi*. Their status is puzzling. We have two references to a special group

* A. Maiuri, *N.S.* 19.

of residents in the city of Lindus, 'resident and holding land'.*
In the first of these they are called aliens (ξένοι), and yet they
are permanent residents and landowners and apparently well-
to-do people, since the city of Lindus decrees that they shall
take part in the provision of choruses (similar was the position
in this respect of the metics at Athens). Parallels from Asia
Minor suggest that these *katoikoi* were natives of Rhodes, but
belonged to the pre-Hellenic population of the island. It is
possible that this class was also numerous in the Peraea, and
formed there the population of the 'country'.

Our scanty evidence conveys the impression that the
Rhodian citizens in general, or at least the group of aristocratic
families, were a strictly exclusive body. They had their own
associations of an archaic character, based on a combination
of religious and family ties. No foreigner was admitted to these
associations, and, on the other hand, no good Rhodian would
take an active part in the associations reserved for foreigners.
Families were kept alive by adoption, a practice as frequent at
Rhodes as at Rome. Lastly, the gymnasia in which Rhodians
educated their children and took their exercise were strictly
reserved for Rhodian citizens.†

If we consider the extent of the services that the citizens
were expected to render to the State in the navy, in the docks,
as public officers, and as members of the council, we shall not be
surprised that the economy of Rhodes was based, not on the
work of its citizens, but on that of foreigners and slaves.

Among the foreigners, likewise, we may distinguish various
classes. The right of residence appears to have been a kind of
distinction carrying with it the right to the description *metoikos*‡
and differentiating its possessors from 'aliens'. It is possible
that some *metoikoi* were freedmen, as at Athens.§ Foreigners
and freedmen formed the most active and the most numerous
body among the free inhabitants of Rhodes. In their epitaphs
and in the inscriptions relating to their associations—the only
evidence that we have about them—their avocations are hardly
ever mentioned. Many of them, however, were very rich. They
took a share in the liturgies of the State, and they were liberal

---

* κατοικεῦντες καὶ γεωργεῦντες, *I.G.* xii. I. 762.
† *I.G.* xii. I. 46.   ‡ *I.G.* xii. I. 382.   § *I.G.* xii. I. 383.

benefactors of the associations to which they belonged. They evidently became rich by productive work—no doubt by commerce, banking, and industry. Their countries of origin support this suggestion. Most of them came from regions which had active commercial relations with Rhodes. The majority were natives of Asia Minor, the Greek islands, Syria and Phoenicia, and Egypt. Very few Greeks from southern Italy and Sicily are found among them, nor very many from Greece itself or from the Black Sea region. It is remarkable that there were no Romans or romanized Italians. These were, perhaps, too proud to settle on an island where they would have such restricted rights.

Excluded from public life and from the aristocratic associations of the citizens, the foreigners developed a life of their own in the scores of associations which they formed all over the island. All these associations were religious; some, if not all of them, provided for the burial of their members.* None of them were strictly national or vocational. In all of them we find a mixture of men of various countries of origin and probably of different professions. Thus in one inscription† the great benefactor of the association is a man from Selge. In the same document three other foreigners are mentioned, one from Phaselis, another a Galatian, and the third an Arab. Some associations admitted slaves. Otherwise slaves, especially public slaves, had their own associations.‡

The slave population appears to have been very large. The public slaves formed the upper class of it and intermarried with foreigners. Next came the class of slaves born in Rhodes, corresponding to the home-bred slaves of other cities, and finally a multitude of those who had been bought in the slave-market and who are designated in their short epitaphs by the name of their country of origin. Most of them came from Asia—Lydians, Phrygians, Cilicians, Cappadocians, Galatians, Syrians, Armenians, Medians. There are very few from Thrace, some from South Russia—Scythians, Sarmatians, and Maeotians (see note 87).

---

* See especially A. Maiuri, *Ann. Sc. Ital.* iv–v (1924), pp. 223 ff.; *S.E.G.* iii. 674.

† *S.E.G.* iii. 674.   ‡ *I.G.* xii. 1. 31.

Under the protection of Rhodes some of the islands fared very well. DELOS certainly came at this time into still closer relations with and greater dependence on Rhodes than before. There is ground for thinking that the leading part it had played in the grain trade at the time of the Macedonian domination was coming to an end. Rhodes appears to have now been the dominant factor in this important branch of the trade of the Aegean, and second to Rhodes, as we have seen, came Athens, not Delos. I have mentioned how close the links between Rhodes and South Russia now were, while Delos lost its connexion with that region. I have also pointed out that it was through Rhodes, and not directly, that Delos had dealings with Massinissa, king of Numidia, the great new purveyor of corn to the ancient world. Between Delos and Egypt in the last years of Philopator and during the reign of Epiphanes relations were friendly, but not so close as earlier and later, whereas those between Rhodes and Egypt were very intimate. In view of these facts we may suppose that the temporary leadership of Delos in the grain trade with the North had come to an end and that Rhodes was now dominant both in the North-East and the West, Delos acting now as a market subsidiary to that of Rhodes.[108] The dependence of Delos on Rhodes is reflected also in the prominence of Rhodian and Cnidian stamped jar-handles among those found at Delos. Ninety-five per cent. of them are either Cnidian (70 per cent.) or Rhodian (25 per cent.). Cnidus, it may be recalled, was in the second century B.C. a dependency of Rhodes, and a very large proportion of the stamped jar-handles must be assigned to that century.[109] No wonder that the price of corn was steadily rising in Delos in the early second century, and that rents were falling.[110]

There was, however, a notable change at the very end of the third century as regards rents. While the price of grain was fluctuating with a general upward tendency, rents were rising almost steadily. This is perhaps to be explained, at least in part, by the closer relations established between Syria and Delos. It is not, I think, an accident that the first foreign association in Delos, that of the ἐγδοχεῖς and ναύκληροι of Phoenician Laodicea, appears to be first recorded in 178 B.C., under Seleucus IV, the successor of Antiochus III,* or that Delos developed such close ties with Syria from the time of Antiochus III as are indicated by the honours that it paid to the Syrian kings. I think it probable that the latter, for reasons unknown to us, reasons perhaps of a political character, gradually transferred their dealings from Rhodes to Delos and finally made Delos the clearing-house for at least a considerable part of their trade. To this trade with Syria Delos owed the gradual increase of its foreign population, and, in consequence, the rise of rents.[111]

In friendly relations with Rhodes, but not in practical subjection to it, like the members of the Rhodian League,† were certain islands in the North, especially THASOS. The results of the recent French excavations in this island have not all yet been published. But it may be inferred from the material carefully collected by Hiller von Gaertringen that Thasos, hard pressed by Philip, began to recover after the Roman victory and to renew its foreign connexions. However, its great days came later, after the war with Perseus.[112]

Of the other islands we are exceptionally well informed about COS and THERA. The glorious days of Cos, the time of the Ptolemaic domination so vividly depicted in some of the mimiambs of Herondas, were over. The island was now a dependency of Rhodes. The well-known Coan inscription, which gives so detailed a picture of its oppressive and highly differentiated taxation, does not convey the idea of any great degree of prosperity. Moreover the island, with its famous sanctuary and glorious past, was exposed to frequent attacks by pirates and suffered heavily in consequence. But no final judgement can be formed so long as the material collected by R. Herzog in his excavations remains in large part unpublished and the systematic exploration of the island by the Italians is not completed.[113]

The situation as regards Thera is different. Since the thorough excavations of Hiller von Gaertringen little new material, if any, has been discovered. The abundant evidence that he brought to light and summarized leads to the conclusion that Thera was fairly prosperous under the long rule of the

* *I.G.* xi. 4, 1114; Durrbach, *Choix*, 72.
† Our information regarding these is exceptionally good for Tenos.

PLATE LXXIX

1. Æ Panticapaeum, *c.* B.C. 300–200 and later. Obv. Head of young Dionysos. Rev. ΠΑΝΤΙΚΑΠΑΙΤΩΝ within wreath.

2. *N* Stater of Paerisades, one of the later kings so named of the Cimmerian Bosporus. Obv. Head of king. Rev. ΒΑΣΙΛΕΩΣ ΠΑΙΡΙΣΑΔΟΥ, Athena. Imitated from stater of Lysimachus.

3. Æ Drachm, Himyarite. Imitation of Athenian coin, *c.* B.C. 300–100. Obv. Head of Athena, Ν (Sabaean letter) on cheek. Rev. Owl.

4. Æ Drachm of Ariarathes IV, Cappadocia. Obv. Head of Ariarathes IV. Rev. ΒΑΣΙΛΕΩΣ ΑΡΙΑΡΑΘΟΥ ΕΥΣΕΒΟΥΣ. Athena holding Nike.

5. Æ Antiochus IV, Edessa in Osrhoene. Obv. Head of Antiochus IV, radiate. Rev. ΑΝΤΙΟΧΕΩΝ ΤΩΝ ΕΠΙ ΚΑΛΛΙΡΟΗΙ. Zeus holding eagle.

6. Æ Antiochus IV, Tyre. Obv. Head of Antiochus IV, diademed. Rev. ΒΑΣΙΛΕΩΣ ΑΝΤΙΟΧΟΥ ΤΥΡΙΩΝ above prow of galley; below, in Phoenician letters, 'Tyre metropolis of the Sidonians'.

7. Æ Tetradrachm of Antiochus IV, Antioch. Obv. Head of Antiochus IV wearing diadem. Rev. ΒΑΣΙΛΕΩΣ ΑΝΤΙΟΧΟΥ ΘΕΟΥ ΕΠΙΦΑΝΟΥΣ. Zeus Nikephoros.

8. Æ Tetradrachm of Antiochus IV, Athens. Obv. Helmeted head of Athena. Rev. ΑΘΕ ΑΝΤΙΟΧΟΣ ΝΙΚΟΓ ΑΝΤΙΛΟΧ. Owl on amphora; in field, elephant; whole in olive wreath.

9. Æ Antiochus IV, Seleuceia Pieria. Obv. Radiate head of Antiochus IV. Rev. ΣΕΛΕΥΚΕΩΝ ΤΩΝ ΕΜ ΠΙΕΡΙΑΙ. Fulmen. All in wreath.

10. Æ Tetradrachm, 'cistophorus', Pergamon, *c.* 200–133 B.C. Obv. Cista mystica with half-open lid from which a serpent issues; whole in ivy wreath. Rev. Two coiled serpents, between them bow-case. Monogram ΠΕΡ.

11. Æ Tetradrachm of Eumenes II, Thyatira. Cistophorus as above, but in left field of reverse ΘΥΑ.

12. Æ Drachm of Aradus in alliance with Ephesus, *c.* B.C. 174–110. Obv. Bee and date Ϙ, 167/6 B.C. Rev. ΑΡΑΔΙΩΝ. Stag and palm tree.

13. Æ Double Victoriatus, Thessalian League, *c.* B.C. 196–146. Obv. Head of Zeus crowned with oak. Rev. ΘΕΣΣΑΛΩΝ. The Thessalian Athena Itonia in fighting attitude, and two magistrates' names.

The coins reproduced on this plate require no special comments. They represent some popular issues of the period considered in this chapter in the various parts of the Hellenistic world—from Arabia to Panticapaeum. I may, however, draw attention to the peculiar alliance coins of Aradus–Ephesus (no. 12). According to Mr. E. T. Newell, whom I have consulted on this point, the abundant issues of these drachms must be assigned to *c.* 189–133 B.C., that is to say, they are contemporary with the Alexandrian and other tetradrachms minted by the Anatolian cities to satisfy the need of the Seleucid kingdom for coined silver under and after Antiochus III (discussed in the text of this chapter, pp. 655 ff.). In my opinion the alliance coins of Aradus and Ephesus must be interpreted in the same way. Like the large issues of Alexanders by the Anatolian cities (and among them by Ephesus) they testify to a lively commerce between Syria and Asia Minor in the early and middle second century B.C. On no. 6 of this plate see E. T. Newell, *The Seleucid coinages of Tyre*, p. 14, no. 39a (pl. III, 4).

PLATE LXXIX

COINS OF THE SECOND CENTURY B.C.

Ptolemies, which continued here until the last decades of the second century. It was a rich agricultural island and depended very little on exports and imports. The natives had good customers for their produce in the Ptolemaic garrison. Some of the richer Ptolemaic soldiers settled in the island and spent part of their wealth on benefactions for the people. And, finally, the famous foundation of Epicteta shows that the old aristocracy of Thera was still well-to-do in the second century and kept apart from the foreigners.[114]

C. *THE SELEUCID EMPIRE*

The prosperity of Asia Minor was equalled if not surpassed by that of Syria. No doubt the defeat of Antiochus III by the Romans and the heavy contribution imposed on him and on his successors by the treaty of Apamea on the one hand, and the loss of the Anatolian satrapies on the other, created temporarily a difficult situation for that ruler and for his immediate successors, especially at times when they were engaged on ambitious and costly political and military enterprises. It is not surprising that from time to time they had recourse to violent methods. For example, as representatives of God on earth, as 'the Lord's anointed', and thus entitled to use the resources of the gods worshipped in various parts of their empire, they demanded heavy contributions from the wealthy temples of their kingdom and never hesitated to resort to compulsion if the priests did not comply with their demands. Our historical texts, hostile to Antiochus III and Antiochus IV, represent these acts as the unlawful and sacrilegious pillage of the temples. And this they appeared to be in the eyes of the natives. Such was the 'pillage' of a temple of Bel in Elam by Antiochus III in 187 B.C., when the king lost his life; such was also the treatment by Seleucus IV and Antiochus IV of the temple-state of Judaea and especially the famous sack of the temple in 169 B.C. (with the consent of the high priest Menelaus) before the great Egyptian expedition.

Similar in all probability was the action taken by Antiochus IV in regard to the temple of Nanaia in the Elymais during his great expedition to the East. The temple in question was no doubt that of Nanaia at Susa, the large, rich, and influential temple of which we read in several inscriptions found in the ruins of Susa by the French expedition. The story is variously reported in our meagre historical documents. Polybius,* our most reliable source, implies in his brief statement that Antiochus, while in Susa, demanded from the natives (i.e. from the priests) a contribution from the funds of the goddess. The priests refused, regarding the demand as a παρανομία. What happened afterwards is not clear. Polybius appears to think that Antiochus did not insist. Appian,† on the contrary, states that he sacked the temple. The other sources are not trustworthy. In any case it is evident that Antiochus acted at Susa in the same way and on the same grounds as Antiochus III had acted in respect of the temple of Bel, and as Seleucus IV and he himself had acted in respect of the temple of Jerusalem.[115]

However, despite the losses of the Seleucid kingdom after Apamea and its later political misfortunes, despite, in particular, the failure of Antiochus IV in his attempt to annex Egypt, and the dynastic troubles that followed his death (which last were the main cause of the ultimate loss of Palestine), Syria, it is evident, was not ruined, nor was its prosperity even seriously undermined.

The territorial losses were amply compensated by the great advantages acquired by Antiochus III and retained by his successors—the re-establishment of Seleucid authority in the East and the annexation to the Syrian kingdom of the Ptolemaic dominions of southern Syria and Palestine. These two achievements had the effect of making the Seleucids practically sole masters of the most important caravan routes connecting the Greco-Italian world with Arabia, India, and China. It is true that the Nabataeans in the west and the Gerrhaeans in the east of northern Arabia never became subjects of these kings, notwithstanding the efforts of Antiochus III and Antiochus IV to bring them under control. Moreover, the unsettled condition of Palestine during and after the reign of Antiochus IV disturbed to some extent the regular commercial relations of Syria with the Nabataeans and southern Arabia. Nevertheless it is certain that most of the trade from the latter now passed, not through

* xxxi. 9 (11).   † *Syr.* 66.

Gaza and Alexandria, but through Syria, and enriched the great
commercial cities of the Seleucid kingdom both along the
Euphrates route (especially Seleuceia on the Tigris, the cities of
northern Mesopotamia, and Antioch with its harbours) and
along the western Arabian route (some of the cities of Transjordan, Damascus, and the ports of Palestine and Phoenicia).
Of the Chinese 'silk route', so far as it was in use at that time
(see below, Ch. VI), and of the land routes of the Indian
trade the Seleucids were the undisputed masters—a position
which they retained until the great advance of the Parthians and
their conquest of Babylonia and Mesopotamia. Indeed, even
after the Parthian conquest the new rulers of these territories
depended in respect of this trade largely on the goodwill of the
Seleucids and on their caravan roads; for the only other route
open to the Parthians was that through the Caucasus, which
was unsafe and expensive, and was therefore regarded with disfavour by the merchants.[116]

Moreover, Syria itself, especially after the annexation of
Phoenicia, southern Syria, and Palestine, was now producing
in good quantity a great variety of commodities. A century of
efforts by the early Seleucids had brought agriculture to a
flourishing condition all over Syria and Mesopotamia. The
agricultural produce of Syria in the late third and early second
centuries was without doubt sufficient for the needs of the
country, with a large surplus for export. We may notice, for
instance, the intensive cultivation of the territory of Dura in
the Hellenistic period and the prosperous state of Susa on the
Eulaeus. Vineyards in the Khabur region, which depended on
Dura, noticed by Xenophon were certainly not neglected by
Macedonians settled in that region. I need hardly mention the
luxuriance of the valley of the Orontes, of the valleys of southern
Syria, and of the plains of Phoenicia, regions that had always
been celebrated for their agricultural wealth. We need not
wonder that Posidonius speaks of Syria at the end of the
second century as an exceedingly rich and fertile country:
'and all the people of Syria because of the great plenty which
their land afforded were relieved of any distress regarding the
necessaries of life' and therefore lived as in a continuous feast.*

* Athen. v. 210 e–f; and xii. 527 e–f; *F. Gr. Hist.* 87, Fr. 10.

Besides its wealth in agricultural produce Syria was at the same time an industrial country. It is scarcely necessary to remind the reader of the immemorial industries of Babylonia, especially its textiles, and of the flourishing manufactures of the Phoenician cities, notably the purple-dyed stuffs and the glass of Sidon and Tyre. It is certain that even before the invention of blown glass (late first century B.C., another testimony to the keen industrial spirit of Syria) the Phoenician cities produced vessels of cast glass both for local use and for export (see above, p. 539). The subject merits some further remarks.

When discussing the Egyptian glass industry (Chapter IV, note 164), I spoke of the beautiful cast and chiselled glass vases made in imitation of metal ware, and sometimes mounted in gold inset with precious stones, that are found mostly in South Russia, especially in the Kuban region. They certainly belong to the Hellenistic period. I pointed out that in the opinion of most modern scholars they had been imported from Egypt. But their exclusively Egyptian origin is not beyond doubt. Nothing similar to them has ever been found in Egypt. There is certainly good reason to think that the Syrian glass-makers also produced glass of this kind and especially that they combined the art of glass-making with the arts of jewellery and toreutic. I have mentioned above (Chapter III, note 40) that the λιθοκόλλητα and διάλιθα became fashionable in the days of Alexander and the Successors. The fashion persisted during the whole of the Hellenistic period, and came certainly from the East, rather than from Egypt. The glass vases under review belong to this class. It is therefore not improbable that the combination of cast glass imitating crystal with jewellery may be regarded as a Syrian innovation, vessels of cast glass being produced both in Egypt and in Syria. Their importation into the Kuban valley from Syria direct or in later times through Parthia is easily explained. Metal ware of types used in Parthia and Parthian coins have often been found in the Caucasus and in South Russia generally.[117]

Nor was Syria backward in the toreutic art, a subject to which I have already referred (above, p. 539 f.). A few remarks will show how brilliantly the art developed in this country in the period we are considering. Every student of antiquity remembers the striking description of the famous *pompe* of Antiochus IV, his retort to the Roman triumphs over the humiliated Hellenistic world. The display of gold and silver ware on this occasion was fabulous. A thousand slaves of Dionysius, the *epistolographos*, a friend of Epiphanes, figured in the procession, carrying silver vessels in their hands. Each of the vessels weighed not less than one thousand drachmas. The king himself contributed to the procession 600 'royal pages' (βασιλικοὶ παῖδες) bearing vessels of gold and 200 women carrying golden vessels for unguents. Nor will students have forgotten the sarcastic words of Polybius with regard to Epiphanes. He describes Antiochus as a toreutic amateur, frequently to be seen in the shops of the goldsmiths and silver-smiths in Antioch. There is not the slightest doubt that the toreutic art was no less flourishing in Syria in the time of Epiphanes than it had been previously.[118]

The abundance of all kinds of scented oils and perfumes in Syria, some of them produced in Babylon and others in various Syrian cities, is shown *inter alia* by the lavish use of them made by the Syrian kings on divers occasions. As examples taken at random I may mention the extravagant quantities of scented oils expended by Antiochus IV in and after his Daphne pageant,* and the story of the same king and the poor man in the bath;† the public entertainments of Antiochus Sidetes in his Parthian expedition, on which occasions wreaths of myrrh and frankincense were distributed,‡ and the *symposia* of Antiochus Grypus with their profusion of crowns and Babylonian scents.§[119]

I may finally say a few words on the pottery. It was for a long time accepted that the type of pottery which predominated in the whole of Mesopotamia and is occasionally found in parts of Syria in Parthian and Roman times, a type which had a long life and a deep influence, viz. the blue-green glazed Mesopotamian faience, ancestor of the famous Raqqa pottery, was first developed in the Parthian kingdom in the late first century B.C. A recent discovery at Susa in Elam

---

* Athen. v. 195 b–c.   † Athen. v. 194 b.
‡ Posidonius *apud* Athen. xii. 540 c; *F. Gr. Hist.* 87, Fr. 9.
§ Posidonius *apud* Athen. xv. 692 c–d; *F. Gr. Hist.* 87, Fr. 20.

PLATE LXXX

1, 2. Two amphorae of greenish-blue faience found in Dura-Europus. No. 1 must be assigned to the first century B.C. and no. 2 to the first century A.D.

3. Faience amphora with green glaze, found at Salemiyeh, near Hama in Syria. First century B.C.–first century A.D. It is decorated with reliefs showing ornamental figures of Erotes and other, probably mythological, beings.

G. M. A. Richter, *Bull. Metr. Mus.* xix (1924), p. 94; *Handb. of the Class. Coll.* 1927, p. 316, fig. 223; *Guide to the Collections*, 1934, pt. i, p. 41. Medallions made from the same moulds were used to decorate an amphora of a different shape said to have been found at Hama, now in the Metropolitan Museum. G. M. A. Richter, *Bull. Metr. Mus.* xxxiii (1938), p. 240 f., fig. 1. Photograph supplied by the authorities of the Metropolitan Museum of Art, New York.

4. Faience amphora with green glaze, said to have been found at Homs in Syria. Rich ornamental decoration. The only figured reliefs are at the handles—the upper part of an Eros, four times repeated. Photograph supplied by the authorities of the Metropolitan Museum of Art, New York.

I have discussed in this chapter, p. 700 f. and n. 120, and below in ch. VIII, the peculiar Mesopotamian and Syrian faience ware which, having first appeared in the early second century B.C., became the leading pottery of Mesopotamia and part of Syria in late Hellenistic and Roman times. To the bibliographical references given there add my *Dura and the problem of Parthian art*, 1935, p. 219; N. C. Debevoise, *Berytus*, ii (1935), pp. 1 ff.; R. Ettinghausen in A. U. Pope, *A Survey of Persian Art*, i, 1938, pp. 646 ff., pls. 181–3; G. M. A. Richter, *Bull. Metr. Mus.* xxxiii (1938), pp. 240 ff.; cf. n. 117 to this chapter, where I have pointed out that Mesopotamian faience was exported to South Russia.

PLATE LXXX

1. New Haven, Yale Gallery of Fine Arts

2. New Haven, Yale Gallery of Fine Arts

3. New York, Metropolitan Museum of Art

4. New York, Metropolitan Museum of Art

MESOPOTAMIAN AND SYRIAN GLAZED POTTERY

proves this assumption to be inexact. In the ruins of the city was found a hoard of coins in a small pot coated (inside and out) with greyish-blue glaze and having two handles, the shape and glaze being almost identical with those of the later pottery of the same type. The hoard was buried certainly not later than 144 B.C., as is shown by the coins of which it consisted (almost all Seleucid, the latest being coins of Demetrius II). This proves with certainty that the Mesopotamian faience was in common use in Seleuceia on the Tigris in Seleucid times.[120]

The wealth of Syria, notwithstanding its political isolation, gave it a marked and ever increasing importance in the international trade of the time. It is interesting to observe how close and cordial were the political and commercial relations between Rhodes and Syria. I may recall, for instance, the naval escort provided by Rhodes for the daughter of Seleucus IV, bride of Perseus. I have already mentioned the large number of Rhodian stamped jars found all over Syria, Phoenicia, and Palestine, and as far east as Seleuceia on the Tigris and Susa on the Eulaeus. Many Syrians took up their abode at Rhodes, where they were certainly engaged in commerce. We may conclude therefore that Rhodes was used for a time concurrently with Ephesus and Miletus as an important clearing-house for Syrian commerce with Greece and especially with the Italian West.[121]

Syria had also active commercial relations both with the independent cities of Asia Minor and with the Pergamene kingdom. The gift of the two chief assistants of Antiochus IV mentioned above was made by them not only because of their devotion to their native city but probably also to serve the end of political and commercial propaganda. The help given by Eumenes II to Antiochus IV, when he returned to his own country to become its king, must not be attributed solely to political motives. As regards the activity of trade between Syria and the Pergamene kingdom, I have already adduced the evidence of presumably Anatolian pottery found in Syria, Phoenicia, Palestine, and Mesopotamia (or *vice versa*); also that furnished by the circulation of Seleucid coins in the West and by the large proportion of Anatolian city coins found in hoards in all parts of Syria and as far away as Babylon. I may remind the reader of one significant fact, that most of the tetradrachms issued by cities of Asia Minor were coined with the special purpose of being circulated in Syria.[122]

We come lastly to Delos. I have explained how the island became in the early second century perhaps the most important clearing-house for Syrian trade. Later, especially after 166 B.C. and still more after 130 B.C., Syrian merchants played in the commercial affairs of Delos a part of constantly increasing importance, second only to that of the Italians. Relations between Syria and Delos were not only of a commercial character. In the second century Syrian craftsmen were employed at Delos adorning with fine mosaics the larger and richer houses of the Syrian Delians. Greco-Syrians form the majority in a list of *epheboi* of the late second century found at Delos. Sanctuaries of the gods of the various parts of the Syrian kingdom arose one after another on the sacred island. The earliest was that of the Tyrian Melqart (Heracles), next came that of the North Syrian Hadad and Atargatis, then those of Astarte, of the gods of Ascalon, and finally those of certain South Arabian gods. In these sanctuaries foreign languages (e.g. Sabaean, Minaean, and Phoenician) were used alongside of Greek.[123]

I may note in this connexion that in the same century several Arabian and Asiatic merchants first appeared in Delos and in other centres of international trade (Rhodes, Tenos, Puteoli). Among these, the Arabs, that is the Petraeans, were the most important. Second to them were the Gerrhaeans (Temallatus, the Gerrhaean, was very prominent at Delos; another was Aulus). Then came Minaeans, Sabaeans, and Bactrians. It is evident that these merchants could hardly establish direct relations with the northern markets. Their *funduqs* (commercial settlements) in the North were probably branches of those that existed in the ports of the Seleucid kingdom. These Orientals were certainly familiar figures in the great commercial cities of the Seleucid Empire. Towards the end of the second century, when the Nabataean Kingdom became more important than what remained of the Seleucid Empire, the Nabataean kings may have established direct relations with the North.[124]

The Seleucids who succeeded Antiochus III, though they were unsuccessful in their political ventures, were still enormously wealthy, probably more so than their Egyptian rivals. Antiochus III and Seleucus IV were able to pay the heavy contribution to Rome, Antiochus IV was rich enough to bestow large gifts on various Greek cities, to maintain a large and well-equipped army, to finance the expensive expeditions to Egypt, and to display enormous wealth in his pageant at Daphne, which was intended to outshine the triumph of Aemilius Paulus. Antiochus Sidetes made a similar ostentatious display in his ill-fated expedition against the Parthians (131/0 B.C.), which has been so vividly described by Posidonius and Pompeius Trogus.* Nor was Antiochus Grypus poor in resources; he impressed his contemporaries by his lavish feasts and banquets.†

It is not surprising that in these circumstances the Syria of the time of Antiochus III, Seleucus IV, and Antiochus IV never gave up her political aspirations or her hopes of political recovery and consolidation. It would not be appropriate here to discuss this topic at length. But I may touch upon one keenly debated feature of the activity of Antiochus IV. Even our scanty information shows how zealous he was in his endeavours to enlarge and consolidate his still extensive empire. We learn that he made a new attempt to carry on the policy of 'colonization' pursued by his great predecessors Seleucus I and Antiochus I. Many new Greek *poleis* bearing the dynastic name of Antioch appeared during his rule. In many cases it was not a renaming of already existing Macedonian colonies but a transformation of oriental towns into Greek *poleis* with a Greek constitution and the Greek mode of life. The most famous case is that of Jerusalem, though this was no exception. The underlying principle of the policy of Epiphanes was not to hellenize the oriental towns by force, but to legalize a process of amalgamation between Orientals and Greeks which had apparently made great progress both in the early Macedonian colonies and in many native towns. The existence of Greco-Semites, either hellenized Semites or orientalized Greeks, was

---

* Posidonius, *F. Gr. Hist.* 87, Fr. 9; Just. 38. 10. 1–4; Oros. v. 10. 8.
† Posidonius, *F. Gr. Hist.* 87, Fr. 20 and 21.

a fact, and Epiphanes endeavoured to make use of it for the consolidation and unification of his empire. His aim was to transform his realm, on lines partly devised by the Romans, into a network of cities with Greek organization and a Greek mentality and mode of life, by utilizing for this purpose the interpenetration of Greek and Semitic life all over his kingdom, especially among the higher and richer classes of the population.

One of the devices contributing to this policy of amalgamation, of merging into one ruling class all the elements of his kingdom that were ready for it, was his zeal for the cult of Zeus Olympius and the introduction of this cult into his new *poleis*. We have here the most interesting feature of his religious system. It is probable that his Zeus Olympius was a counterpart of the Ptolemaic Sarapis, a synthesis of the leading religious ideas of his empire. Bearing a Greek name, Zeus Olympius was worshipped in semi-oriental temples, was represented in a semi-oriental dress and with semi-oriental attributes, and was as much the Pansemitic Baalshamin as the Greek Zeus, the symbol as it were of the growing Syrian solar henotheism. The new cult was closely connected with the dynastic cult, inasmuch as the Great God of Epiphanes was the God of Alexander and Seleucus and the great protector, nay the chief god, of most of the Macedonian colonies of Seleucus I and now of the new cities of their great *ktistes* Epiphanes. In this character Zeus Olympius appears, for example, on a cult bas-relief of the temple of the Gaddé at Dura, where he, as the Gad of Dura, is being crowned by its founder Seleucus I. I have no doubt that the bas-relief of Dura reflects similar statuary groups of the time of Epiphanes erected in his several sanctuaries of Zeus Olympius, the role of Seleucus I being played, in the cities founded by Epiphanes, by that ruler as the founder, the *ktistes*. It is very probable that such a group stood in the ἄλσος or τέμενος of Zeus Olympius which replaced the temple of Zerubbabel on Mt. Zion.

The amalgamating tendencies of Epiphanes had many adherents in the empire and his policy was very popular with the hellenized and hellenizing strata of most of its Semitic cities. Thus it was in Jerusalem. It was not the fault of Epiphanes that, by pursuing this policy and by supporting the efforts of those who approved it among the higher classes of the population of Judaea, he encountered the fierce resistance of Judas and of his followers, who were ready to die for the old traditions and for their monotheistic religious seclusion. In fact Judas represented the ideals and the dreams of the large masses of the natives, a class neglected by the government and exploited by the city *bourgeoisie*. The revolt of Judas was directed more against the ruling classes than against the central government. We may assume similar aspirations in other parts of the territories of Epiphanes, especially where the Greek settlers were few and the ancient tribal organization was still alive and vigorous. This tribal reaction, both religious and social, took shape later in the troubled times that followed the death of Epiphanes; it resulted in the creation of many local tyrannies in the border districts of the Seleucid Empire, where the local religious traditions were much stronger than in Syria proper.

Undisturbed by the miscarriage of his project to unite under his rule the two great focuses of Hellenism that were still independent, rich, and vigorous—Egypt and Syria—Antiochus after his return to Syria resumed his former activity. He pursued his policy of amalgamation and turned his attention to the Far East in his endeavour to restore the great empire of his glorious predecessors. His oriental expedition, directed against the Parthians, which was probably connected with the events in Bactria—the war between Demetrius and Eucratides, the last being, if not an agent of Epiphanes, at least his ally—bears eloquent testimony to his unbroken spirit, even after the brutal 'Roman circle' of Popillius Laenas.

The untimely death of Antiochus was a great calamity for Eastern Hellenism, which might have experienced a new renascence had he survived and been successful in his oriental expedition.[125]

D. *EGYPT*

In discussing the social and economic conditions of Egypt under Philopator (221–203 B.C.), Epiphanes (203–181), and Philometor (181–145) we must keep in mind one basic fact. As for the preceding period, our information is derived from literary texts, papyri, inscriptions, and coins, but it is much more meagre. The literary evidence is limited mostly to fragments of the historical work of Polybius. Papyri and inscriptions are much less numerous than for the third century. This, however, may be an accident. For example, among the papyri of Tebtunis recently published (vol. iii) there are some valuable documents of this period which add a good deal to our information, and the recently discovered fragments of a priestly decree of the reign of Philopator are as valuable as the Rosetta stone of the time of Epiphanes. The interesting and abundant series of coins are no less important than those of the third century.

In dealing with this period we must therefore be very careful and make the least possible use of *argumenta ex silentio*. For instance, if we have evidence that a certain office existed in the third century, but none of its survival in the second, it does not necessarily follow that it had by then disappeared. And *vice versa*, if some important feature of social and economic life is never mentioned in the documents of the third century and first appears in those of the second, this may also be an accident: our information regarding the third century, good as it is, is not complete. It is therefore only with great caution that we can declare any social or economic phenomenon to be typical of the late third and the second century and of that century only.

We may, however, regard certain features of this kind as new developments at this time, either with certainty or with great probability. It is certain that under Philopator, Epiphanes, and Philometor Egypt passed through a critical period of its history. Two tendencies, which were not entirely new, became increasingly prominent in the policy of the Ptolemies. The first relates to the king's treatment of the natives. I have described the policy of the early Ptolemies towards the natives and the ' Greeks '. It was in the main one of benevolent domination. The king, master of the land, shared his domination over the country and especially over the natives with the members of his household (οἶκος), his associates and assistants in military and civil affairs, the great majority of whom were 'Greeks'. Under Philopator a different policy was tentatively adopted. Association took the place of domination as the guiding principle. This entailed extensive concessions in the sphere of military and religious organization to the most prominent among the natives, in order to win their sympathy and support.

The second tendency relates to the foreign policy of the Ptolemies. Concurrently with the changed system of internal administration came a change in the management of foreign affairs. I have shown how the first Ptolemies directed their efforts at home and abroad to two principal objects: the first, complete independence and self-sufficiency (*autarchia* and *autarkeia*) both economic and political; and the second, to which the first was to contribute, the greatest possible degree of hegemony in the affairs of the civilized world. Both of these they succeeded in attaining. Egypt became almost self-sufficient both economically and politically, and secured for itself, in a considerable measure, a position of hegemony. Of these two objects of Ptolemaic policy, which the early members of the dynasty kept in even balance, Philopator and his successors endeavoured to maintain the first—political and economic self-sufficiency. The second object—hegemony—they gradually abandoned under the pressure of circumstances.

Of the reign of PHILOPATOR, beyond what we learn from literary sources regarding his foreign policy and his family and court life, very little is known. Exactly dated documents of this short period are few and mostly of little value. And yet his rule and the activity of his prime minister Sosibius appear to have had greater influence on the evolution of Egypt in general than the literary evidence would suggest.[126]

It is highly probable that in the years of feverish preparation for the war with Antiochus III, and again, after this was ended, at the time of the civil war, Philopator and Sosibius, in order to meet the heavy cost of the two wars, carried out some changes in the financial and administrative organization of Egypt. Certain taxes and especially the land rents—ἐκφόρια —may have been increased and new taxes may have been imposed. It has been suggested recently, with some probability, that the poll-tax (σύνταξις), unknown in the third century and of which we have evidence (and that very meagre, it must be confessed) only in late Ptolemaic times, was first instituted by Philopator.[127] It is also probable that recourse was had to a stricter collection of rents, taxes, and arrears, and to the frequent use of extraordinary contributions and requisitions, as would be natural at a time of dangerous war. This practice may have led to reforms in the bureaucratic machinery. It is well known that in the second century B.C. some important changes may be observed in the financial administration: the bureaucratic element, for instance, was strengthened and the relations between the officials in charge of and materially responsible for the collection of taxes were more strictly defined. It is tempting to suppose that this reform was carried out by Philopator. Since a more stringent collection of the taxes and a more rigorous enforcement of the material responsibility of the officials, tax-farmers, and their sureties naturally led to frequent confiscations of property, the resulting accumulation of the property confiscated would naturally suggest the creation of a special department to take charge of it. If therefore we find evidence from 179 B.C. onwards of an apparently new department of financial administration, with the name ἴδιος λόγος, which later in Roman times was concerned with ownerless (ἀδέσποτα) and confiscated property (τὰ εἰς τὸν Καίσαρα πίπτειν ὀφείλοντα), we have ground for thinking that this department may have been first organized or given increased importance under Philopator. No doubt these are no more than possibilities, which the discovery of new evidence may hereafter disprove.[128]

However, the main and most important reform of Philopator—and of this we have satisfactory evidence—was the transition from a policy of domination over the natives to one of association with them. It is familiar to students of Hellenistic history, and has been frequently brought to notice and discussed. A few words on the subject will therefore suffice. It is well known that Philopator, for the purpose of his struggle with Antiochus III, increased his army not only by mobilizing his cleruchs and hiring new mercenaries, but also by appealing to the Egyptians and by forming a regular phalanx, trained in the Macedonian fashion, from the native militia (μάχιμοι), which before his time had taken part in military expeditions as auxiliary corps. This was a novel policy, involving a radical change. In adopting it Philopator was no doubt actuated by various motives, of which one in particular deserves mention. It was not merely for economic reasons or because of a scarcity of mercenaries that Philopator and Sosibius decided to place Egyptians and Macedonians on a footing of equality in the army. The measure was probably dictated by a political emergency. The revolt of the natives during the Syrian war of Euergetes I had taught the Egyptian government a severe lesson. To avoid a repetition of this incident Philopator endeavoured, by mobilizing the μάχιμοι as part of his fighting force, to make the war against Antiochus a national affair and so to safeguard his rear from a native revolt.

Philopator's innovation, though successful during the war, proved disastrous as soon as the war was over. Forced by insubordination among his generals to make a hasty peace with his Syrian rival, Philopator returned in triumph. But as soon as he reached home he had to take up arms again, this time against his own subjects, the natives. Of this war and of the reasons that led the natives to begin it little is known. Polybius, our chief authority, gives a short description of the war (v. 107, and xiv. 12), the character of which filled him with disgust. He explains it as a national revolt of the natives, proud of their victory, against foreign domination. The little we know of this conflict from other sources shows that it was not a regular war, but a chaotic rebellion of the natives all over Egypt, an outbreak of despair and pillage directed not only against the foreign rulers but against all the oppressors of the people, including some of the temples.[129]

In my opinion the rebellion under Philopator did not differ much in character from that under Euergetes or from the rebellions of later times. It was more dangerous for the government than that under Euergetes because some of the natives were now better armed and had received a good military training. They had, moreover, seen during the Syrian campaign that on the field of battle the Macedonians and Greeks were not much better men than themselves.

While the character of the war is more or less known, its causes are less clear and have been frequently discussed. An outburst of national feeling and of religious fanaticism aroused by the priests, hatred of the foreign oppressors, have been suggested by many writers since Polybius as the chief motives of the war. There may be a certain measure of truth in this view, but it does not explain why the revolt broke out immediately after a victorious war. In my view the rebellion of the natives must be attributed to the general conditions of the time. The war against Antiochus III had involved heavy expenditure. This is recognized by Philopator himself in the proclamation that he made after the war, a proclamation extensively used and quoted by the priests in the decree (still in part extant) published by them at Memphis. The cost of the war, of the lavish bonus distributed by the king to the army after Raphia, and of the various gifts bestowed on the temples, was not covered by the booty referred to by the king in his proclamation and by the priests in their Memphis decree. I must confess I regard this booty with some scepticism. The bulk of the expenditure was certainly met out of the regular revenue that Philopator derived from Egypt. There is no doubt that the burden of rents and taxes on the population before, during, and after the war was very heavy, and that this burden rested with especial weight on the shoulders of the *laoi*.[130]

When, therefore, the native soldiers after their victory returned to their villages and took up again the routine of their everyday life, the consciousness of their inferior position became more bitter, and they resented more keenly than before the hardships to which they were subjected through the increasing pressure of taxation and the system of planned economy in general. If on their return to their villages, elated with victory and faced with poverty and oppression, they took up arms and started a bloody revolt, there is little occasion for surprise.

One of the chief centres of revolt was the Thebaid. Here it took the form of secession, and this secession was a source of additional danger. Under Nubian rulers—Armachis and then Anmachis—the Thebaid, supported without doubt to some extent by the Ethiopians and probably an instrument in their hands, engaged in a bitter struggle with Philopator, and this struggle was inherited by Epiphanes. It appears from the evidence that in all probability the Thebaid was ruled by the two Nubian kings named above for almost a complete period of twenty years (from 206 to 185 B.C.).

The second change that I have mentioned, the political isolation of Egypt, is again an ascertained fact. It was slow to develop. The empire of the Ptolemies remained intact until the end of the rule of Philopator, and the prestige of the dynasty in the eyes of the Greeks remained very high, based as it was on the reputation of the Ptolemies as the wealthiest rulers of the time. Nevertheless this growing isolation cannot be questioned; it was noted and described by so acute an observer as Polybius.* The increasing indifference of the Egyptian government to foreign policy and commercial hegemony is thus an indisputable fact. It is attested, for instance, by the steady development of the political and commercial importance of Rhodes in the Aegean.

The phenomenon in question is generally explained by the personal character of Philopator, his neglect of public affairs in general and his love of pleasure and an easy life. I am not certain that this is the true explanation. We know very little of the native revolt in Egypt described above. Polybius dismisses it in a few words, and it is illustrated by only a few documents.† Nevertheless it certainly was a dangerous affair, which required a great concentration of military effort and proved very costly, for it drained Egypt of labour and disorganized agriculture and industry in two areas, the Delta and Upper Egypt. Moreover, the disorders and civil war in Upper Egypt may have had a detrimental influence on the country's supply of gold (which came from the South) and on the commercial relations between Egypt and Nubia, and between Egypt and Somaliland. With its attention concentrated on internal affairs, the Alexandrian government scarcely had either time or energy to devote to an active policy in the Aegean or to the preservation, as carefully as in the past, of the safety of the seas.

This neglect of foreign relations certainly deprived Egypt of its leading position in the commercial life of the Aegean, especially amid the troubles through which that region passed in the last years of the third century, and it consequently

* v. 34.   † e.g. *B.G.U.* 1215.

diminished the revenue that the State derived from its Aegean trade. Further, the Second Punic War was raging in the West and spoiling the best markets of Egypt in that quarter—southern Italy, Sicily, and Carthage. It must be remembered how important these markets were for Egypt in the times of Philadelphus and Euergetes (above, pp. 394 ff.). It would, however, be an exaggeration to say that the general prosperity of Egypt was undermined by all these circumstances. Egypt, and especially the king, were still rich, and Philopator never failed to call attention to his wealth by spectacular acts calculated to impress the Greek world, such as, for instance, the building of the largest sea-going ship and of his floating palace on the Nile. And yet it must be realized that Egyptian prosperity was beginning to decline. The decline was gradual and not catastrophic. It was manifested, for instance, by the scarcity of silver, which Egypt derived chiefly from its trade with Greece and Carthage. This scarcity and the urgent need that the government had of the metal, coupled with a desire to make another concession to the Egyptian population and the temples, led Philopator, some time after 210 B.C., to introduce the copper standard into Egypt, in other words to recognize the copper drachma as the standard coin for internal circulation. The ratio of silver to copper was fixed at 1 to 60. The difficulty experienced by the government in securing a sufficient supply of silver may also have led it to debase its silver coinage now and then (not systematically) and on a small scale. The danger of inflation was not remote.[131]

The situation of Egypt was even more difficult during the short reign of Philopator's son and successor EPIPHANES.[132] The central government was disorganized, one regent following another during the minority of the king and most of them pursuing their own selfish interests. Civil war, inherited from the reign of Philopator, was raging both in Lower Egypt, where the city of Lycopolis was one of the centres of the struggle, and in the south, which was still independent under its king Anmachis. Whether it was at this time or later, in the reign of Philometor, that a native (Nubian) king ruled at Abydos and inflicted a defeat on the royal army, cannot be determined. In any case peasants and native soldiery, in ever increasing numbers, took up arms in the civil war. Many of them dreamt of the restoration of the National Egyptian State. Antiochus III, well aware of the internal difficulties with which the new and inexperienced king was confronted, renewed his attack on Egypt and after the battle of Panion deprived Epiphanes of almost all his possessions in Syria, Asia Minor, and Thrace.

A rapid decline in Egypt's economic resources naturally followed. The caravan trade of Syria was now in the hands of the Seleucids, the trade with Trogodytike and Somaliland was disorganized, the Aegean market was lost, and the Western market not yet recovered. The revenue from the international trade and from the foreign dominions of Egypt became in consequence insignificant.

Nor was the situation of Egypt itself better. We derive some valuable information regarding it from an inestimable document of 196 B.C., the famous Rosetta stone, a decree of priests in honour of Epiphanes. Like the similar decree above referred to, which was published after Raphia, it was based on a proclamation of the king and contains several quotations from it. The contents of this proclamation of Epiphanes closely resembled those of the proclamation of Philopator, and at the same time were almost identical with the principal provisions of the later so-called peace proclamations or amnesty decrees of which I shall speak in greater detail in the next chapter.[133]

The proclamation of Epiphanes has been very little studied. The priests, in my opinion, based their decree not on one but on two proclamations of the king: an earlier one, which had been issued before the capture of Lycopolis (1. 10 ff.), and a later one, published after this event (1. 20 ff.). The first was a general proclamation addressed to the whole of Egypt, probably after the death of Philopator, in the hope of putting an end to the disturbances that prevailed there. It announced a general amnesty (especially to the μάχιμοι) and a number of benefactions to the army, to the temples, and to the population at large. The benefactions to the army are not specified in the Rosetta stone. The *laoi* and the rest of the population of Egypt received a remission or a reduction (κουφισμός) of certain taxes and rents, and a remission of arrears. Moreover, certain classes of prisoners were pardoned (probably political offenders, criminals, and public and private debtors). The benefactions to the temples were various and important. Besides granting them lavish gifts, the king confirmed some of their basic rights, especially those relating to their most important sources of income—their remuneration in kind and money ($\sigma\acute{v}\nu\tau\alpha\xi\iota s$), their share of the *apomoira* and other dues. They were exempted, moreover, from certain taxes and 'liturgies' (one of them was service in the navy), and their deliveries of *byssos* to the crown were regulated.

The second proclamation was of a more special character. It was published at Memphis on the occasion of the coronation ceremony ($\pi\alpha\rho\acute{\alpha}\lambda\eta\psi\iota s$ $\tau\hat{\eta}s$ $\beta\alpha\sigma\iota\lambda\epsilon\acute{\iota}\alpha s$). It gave, in an introduction, similar in this respect to the proclamation of Philopator, an account of the capture of Lycopolis, and proceeded to announce a number of $\phi\iota\lambda\acute{\alpha}\nu\theta\rho\omega\pi\alpha$. The benefactions this time were confined to priests. They consisted of two groups, (1) remission of arrears and two important changes as regards the $\gamma\hat{\eta}$ $\iota\epsilon\rho\acute{\alpha}$. (2) remission of the artaba-tax for the sown land, and of the ceramion-tax for the vineyards. It should be noticed that in the last two measures we meet for the first time with concessions to the priests that were not of a temporary or confirmatory and emendatory character, but were grants which, though in themselves not very important, were basic and enduring, grants entailing a permanent diminution of the royal revenue.

A study of the Rosetta stone reveals a pitiful picture of the conditions that prevailed in Egypt in the last years of Philopator and the early years of Epiphanes. Behind the $\phi\iota\lambda\acute{\alpha}\nu\theta\rho\omega\pi\alpha$, the grants and concessions of the king, we see the phenomena that made them imperative: pressure of taxes, rapid accumulation of arrears and the concomitant confiscations, prisons full of criminals and public and private debtors, many fugitives scattered all over the country and living by robbery, compulsion applied in every sphere of life, including recruitment for the army and navy. The natural results were scarcity of labour, a gradual depopulation of villages, abandonment of fields, deterioration of land, neglect of dikes and canals; and these evils developed rapidly in the atmosphere of war and unrest.

The 'proclamation of peace' made by Epiphanes did not put

an end to the civil war. Although he gained some successes, it persisted in the south at least until 184–3 and probably later. Nor did the general situation of Egypt improve after 196 B.C., a fact of which we have evidence here and there. I may mention, without aiming at completeness, some of the documents which throw a vivid light on various aspects of the social and economic conditions of this period.

Between 196 and 181 B.C. life was far from secure. Fragments of two documents,* unfortunately not exactly dated, but probably of the last years of Epiphanes or the early years of Philometor,† refer apparently to uprisings and robbery. The first mentions a leader ($\dot{\eta}\gamma\epsilon\mu\dot{\omega}\nu$), $\dot{o}\rho\kappa\omega\mu\dot{o}\sigma\iota\alpha$, the siege of a city, a ship bringing corn; the second speaks of robberies ($\lambda\eta\sigma\tau\dot{\eta}\rho\iota\sigma\nu$), of some people saved and others dead.

The same uncertainty of life is reflected in the little we know of the state of communications at this time. The regular river police was apparently unable to guarantee the safety of river transport. In 187 B.C. Comanus, a person of influence, *strategos* of the Arsinoites, has an army officer, probably accompanied by a detachment of soldiers, to guard a ship which is transporting his goods. We hear further that some time during the reign of Philopator or Epiphanes a special group of $\mu\dot{\alpha}\chi\iota\mu\sigma\iota$ was organized to man the police ships on the river. They received the special name $\nu\alpha\nu\kappa\lambda\eta\rho\sigma\mu\dot{\alpha}\chi\iota\mu\sigma\iota$, which characterizes their function—native soldiers guarding the $\nu\alpha\dot{\nu}\kappa\lambda\eta\rho\sigma\iota$. I shall return to these presently. They were probably numerous and part of them was stationed at Alexandria. Finally in the late years of the reign of Epiphanes we come upon the first mention in our documents of ships of the royal navy on the Nile, with their trierarchs and crews, placed at the disposal of the *dioecetes* and probably other high officers, for the purpose of assuring the safety of communications on the river and the canals.[134]

A group of documents recently published, which at first sight have scarcely any bearing on the civil war and its consequences (the civil war is never mentioned in them), illuminate, in my opinion, the general conditions of the time no less clearly than do the Rosetta stone and the other documents quoted above.

* *Teb.* 919 and 920.

† *Teb.* 920 mentions an *epistrategos*, probably Hippalus; see below.

I refer to the dossier of the lawsuit between two members of the family of a priest of Siut in Upper Egypt, Petetum by name. The period covered by the evidence produced by the parties in support of their respective claims extends from the last years of Philopator to the first years of Philometor. Two of the documents, which give the inventory of the belongings of Petetum as divided between his two sons, play a decisive part in the suit. We find this inventory in two versions: one (in several copies) dated in the year 25 of Epiphanes, 181/0 B.C.; the other in the year 8 of Philometor, 174/3 B.C. These two documents are separated by only a few years, and years apparently undisturbed by any war (the rebellion in the south was suppressed in 184/3 B.C.). And yet we find that many premises which were in excellent condition in 181/0 B.C. are in ruins and lying waste in 174/3 B.C.; a storehouse, new in 181, is in ruins in 174 (item 4); the same is true of item 6 (a house in the necropolis) and of items 10, 11, 12 (houses and gardens), that is, five items out of a total of eighteen. Is the explanation perhaps that our scanty evidence regarding the war in the south is misleading, that the war dragged on after 184, and that the houses were destroyed during the trouble? Or was their decay due to neglect, a consequence of the general impoverishment in the south? It is impossible to say. I may add that this group of documents as a whole affords an excellent illustration of the sources of income of the members of a numerous and important class of the population of Egypt, the priests of the innumerable temples.[135]

Another corner of the picture is illuminated by a set of royal letters of 184/3 B.C. addressed to the police force of the kingdom, which survive only in fragments. The principal letter contains the instructions of the king to a certain Synnomus; these refer to royal διαγράμματα and προστάγματα—his own, those of his father and of his ancestors (πρόγονοι)—and are styled χρηματισμοί.* One paragraph of the letter only is more or less intact. It deals with informers. After the turmoil of the civil war their profession was apparently thriving. Persons molested by them no doubt appealed repeatedly to the king. His instructions to the police were in all probability his

* Cf. *Teb.* 703.

answer to the complaints. He does not countenance informers. The authors of foolish but harmless denunciations are to be rebuked. Those, however, who denounce with the intention of blackmailing and creating strife (διαφορᾶς ἢ σεισμοῦ χάριν) are to be immediately handed over to the king.[136]

A passage in a later document which will be discussed presently* brings to light another aspect of the situation. It shows the effect of the turmoil of civil war upon the condition of agriculture in the royal domains. Herodes, Philometor's minister of finance and economy, in his detailed instructions (ἐντολαί) to his subordinates mentions a certain Hippalus, a high functionary of the past, 'who at that time stood at the head of the country' (ὁ τότε προκαθήμενος τῆς χώρας), and in similar conditions was confronted with the same difficulties. This Hippalus was a well-known man in the reign of Epiphanes and Philometor. He figures in several Demotic documents (from 185 to 169 B.C.) as high priest of Ptolemy Soter in Ptolemais and is styled ἐπιστράτηγος (governor-general), apparently of the whole of Egypt, in an inscription of Ptolemais† and in a petition from Tebtunis.‡ As such he may well be described by Herodes as chief governor of the country, and may in this capacity have taken the measures detailed below. The office he held was a new one, probably created by Epiphanes to counteract the effects of the civil war and to reorganize the life of the country. One of his measures in this connexion was mentioned by Herodes. During the civil war many areas that had been formerly cultivated lay waste, having been abandoned by their cultivators. Hippalus appealed to the richer and patriotically minded groups of the population of Egypt—the wealthier royal peasants, landowners, and officials of the crown—and succeeded, by gentle pressure, in influencing them to accept the responsibility for the payments due on the waste land, in other words to cultivate it at their own risk. It seems to be one of the earliest, if not the earliest, instance of the ἐπιβολή of waste land, that is to say, its compulsory cultivation in case of emergency by members of the well-to-do classes, an institution which was destined to become a dominating factor in the

* *U.P.Z.* 110.   † *O.G.I.* 103.
‡ *Teb.* 778, republished in full *Teb.* 895.

agricultural system of the country during the following centuries.[137]

Hippalus' measure was of course an emergency one dictated by necessity. But the phenomenon behind it was a lasting one. It was the scarcity of labour and the corresponding reduction of the cultivated area that undermined the foundations of the royal economy. I have mentioned this phenomenon in speaking of the 'amnesty decree' of Epiphanes. After the proclamation the situation did not improve. A report on crops of the second year of Philometor contains some items characteristic in this respect.* A plot of land† had formerly been rented for a certain ἐκφόριον. At some previous time, by a special concession or contract made by an official, the rate of the rent had been changed (reduced?). In 180/79 B.C. no tenants were found who were willing to rent the land on these conditions. By a new arrangement the land was rented κατὰ τὴν ἀρετήν, that is to say; according to its actual condition (the later *terminus technicus* is ἐξ ἀξίας, see below) and perhaps for an indefinite term. Another document of about the same time illustrates the same situation. In the former *dorea* of Apollonius, probably the once flourishing *dorea* of which I have spoken above, there was a large area of waste land.‡ The government desired to have this land reclaimed and offered it to applicants on very favourable emphyteutic conditions: 10 years without payment (ἀφορί), and subsequently at a nominal rent of one drachma per *aroura*. We may perhaps connect with this process of abandonment of land by tenants followed by its reclamation several features of the land policy of the later Ptolemaic times, of which I shall speak more fully hereafter: assignment of *kleroi* to new soldier-settlers, mostly from land under reclamation; lease of the same land in large parcels to the temples; and finally perhaps the revival of the *doreai*.[138]

I have mentioned that the difficult economic situation in the reigns of Philopator and Epiphanes opened the door to inflation. A recently published document,§ the bearing of which on the monetary policy of the king has recently been brought to notice by C. B. Welles, shows that inflation developed rapidly

* *Teb.* 829. † ll. 19 ff.
‡ *Teb.* 918. § *Mich.* iii. 182, of 182 B.C.

in Egypt as early as the reign of Epiphanes. In a contract of 182 B.C., which relates to a payment of 48 copper talents, the penalty for non-performance, which usually amounts to one and a half times the sum involved, is fixed at one thousand drachmas of silver of the old Ptolemaic standard (ἀργυρίου τοῦ παλαιοῦ Πτολεμαϊκοῦ). The definition Πτολεμαϊκοῦ is surprising, and raises the question whether silver other than Ptolemaic was at that time circulating in Egypt. But the point of most importance is the ratio. In 182 B.C. the silver drachma was worth about 432 copper drachmas, almost the same rate as later in the reign of Philometor (see below).[139]

Political conditions in Egypt improved slightly in the last years of Epiphanes' reign. His sudden death at the age of 28 was a severe blow to the country. A minor—PHILOMETOR—was once more king. The unscrupulous adventurers Eulaeus and Lenaeus, greedy, dishonest, and incompetent, acted as regents and demoralized the government. The situation was aggravated by a new war with Syria, which led to the temporary occupation of Egypt by Antiochus IV and to widespread devastation.[140]

Soon after the termination of this war a fresh native revolt broke out, perhaps connected with the dynastic strife between Philometor and Euergetes II. It began about 165/4 B.C. under the leadership of a certain Dionysius Petosarapis. It spread far into the south and the gravity of the situation was perhaps increased by a war with Nubia.[141]

The conditions that prevailed in Egypt during the reign of Philometor and, in particular, the consequences of the revolt of Petosarapis are clearly revealed to us by several documents. The longest and the most illuminating of these is one of 164 B.C. (above, p. 717) relating to an order of the king which dealt with the agricultural situation, especially with the cultivation of the land (πρόσταγμα περὶ γεωργίας). The revolt under Epiphanes and the war of Antiochus IV had utterly disorganized the normal cultivation of the land. But at that time it was still possible to restore order by mild measures and gentle pressure on the cultivators. Then came the revolt of Petosarapis, which was certainly a serious affair. Large numbers of natives took part in it and either perished in the many battles, or were executed after the suppression of the revolt, or remained in hiding in the swamps, living the life of robbers. Their lands lay abandoned and desolate. There·was a scarcity of labour throughout Egypt and in addition a scarcity of draught cattle. The document in question speaks of the revolt as an immense calamity (καταφθορά). The year immediately following the end of the rebellion threatened to be disastrous. A dearth of grain and perhaps famine were imminent. To appeal to the patriotism and self-sacrifice of the well-to-do classes, as had been done successfully before, was now useless as a means of salvation. The government resorted to compulsion. The king ordered that every one (πάντες) should take a share in the cultivation of the abandoned land. Parcels of it were ordered to be assigned (ἐπιγραφή) to such as were supposed to be capable of undertaking the charge. To make the burden less heavy a reduction of rent technically called (κουφισμός) was granted to the prospective cultivators and government loans were promised.

The results of this measure were deplorable. The local officials set about giving effect to the royal order with zeal and enthusiasm. 'Every one' (πάντες) in the order was interpreted literally. But rich and influential people probably found means of escaping the liability by bribes and pressure on the officials. The sufferers were smaller folk, who had neither means of bribery nor influence. Such were the 'royal peasants' (especially the poorer among them), those employed in various royal enterprises (ἐπιπεπλεγμένοι ταῖς προσόδοις), employees of the government in the cities, and above all the soldiers of the army, especially the native soldiers, the μάχιμοι, whose *cleroi* were very small (8, 7, or 5 *arourae*), hardly sufficient to support the holders and their families. The pressure of the officials was exerted both on such of the soldiers as had not been mobilized and on the families (ἀποσκευαί) of those who were on active service.

The situation was critical. It must be remembered that the revolt of Petosarapis was apparently connected with the dynastic strife between Philometor and his brother Ptolemy the Younger (νεώτερος, the later Euergetes II). The document above referred to and some others of the time show that the number of settled μάχιμοι, mostly native mercenary soldiers, had increased rapidly and that after Raphia these μάχιμοι occupied an important position in the royal army. These men were infuriated, and they knew their strength. Some of them were stationed at Alexandria as a kind of royal body-guard. The first step that they took, jointly with their comrades, the river-soldiers (ναυκληρομάχιμοι), who were responsible for the protection of traffic on the Nile and canals, was to send a petition to the king.* The king and his advisers were alarmed. Philometor gave orders to his 'minister of royal economy', the *dioecetes,* to take appropriate measures to satisfy the just demands of the *machimoi* and of the lower, especially the native, classes of the population in general. The *dioecetes* Herodes gave vent to his anger in fresh instructions to his local subordinates, in which he fulminated against their stupidity and dishonesty. They had utterly misunderstood him. By πάντες he meant not 'every one', but those who were capable of supporting the burden, the richer and the well-to-do, the *bourgeoisie,* not the working classes. We have no means of estimating the degree of success attained by his injunctions (ἐντολαί). They contain very vague remarks about the 'capable' and 'incapable' (δυνατοί and ἀδυνατοῦντες) and no clear definition of who were the one and who the other. Compulsion always leads to oppression, and compulsion was the only resource of a government that regarded itself as the sole ruling force in economic life. However this may have been, we have in the order of Philometor the first known example of the compulsory cultivation of land on a large scale by all the members of the richer classes, though the principle itself was not new. The members of the new oppressed class naturally endeavoured to escape the burden imposed upon them. One of their subterfuges was to enter the ranks of that class which was really privileged, the military forces of the kingdom. This was known to the government, and measures were taken to defeat it in the document in question.[142]

The injunctions of Herodes and the situation of Egypt during and after the wars of Antiochus IV and Petosarapis are illustrated by several other documents. Two of them throw light

---

* It is stated explicitly in the document that this was done by οἱ παρεδρεύοντες ἐν ᾿Αλεξανδρείᾳ ἐπίλεκτοι (μάχιμοι); (native) guards of the king, that is to say, the μάχιμοι and the ναυκληρομάχιμοι.

on the attitude of the Egyptian population and especially on that of the priests. We may infer from them and from the presence, referred to above, of native soldiers in Alexandria that the Egyptians were divided among themselves during the revolt of Petosarapis, some of them supporting him, others the king. It is in this sense that I am inclined to interpret *Teb.* 781, a fragmentary petition of an overseer of the Ammonion of Moeris (near Arsinoe-Crocodilopolis) of about 164 B.C., in which the story of his sanctuary is told. The sanctuary was first destroyed by Antiochus IV and subsequently restored by Philometor. It was this benefaction of the king and probably the loyal attitude of the priests towards him at the time of Petosarapis' revolt, and also perhaps the fact that the sanctuary was that of the cleruchs ($\tau\epsilon\sigma\sigma\alpha\rho\alpha\kappa\sigma\nu\tau\alpha\pi\epsilon\nu\tau\acute\alpha\rho\sigma\nu\rho\sigma\iota$) settled in Moeris, that roused the ire of Petosarapis against the temple and led to its utter destruction by his supporters.

The situation at Socnopaiou Nesos was probably similar.* Before the war a certain Marres, a priest, had bought a house from a relative of Thembos, a priestess. The contract of sale was deposited with a certain Condylus, a fisherman, who acted probably in the capacity of a 'document-keeper' ($\sigma\nu\gamma\gamma\rho\alpha\phi\sigma$-$\phi\acute\nu\lambda\alpha\xi$) and resided in the 'city'. When the 'city' was captured by the rebels, the contract was taken from him and burnt. Thembos seized this opportunity to occupy the house. Such burning of contracts is a typical feature of social revolutions in general (cf. the case of Dyme in Achaia in 115 B.C., below, Ch. VI). In this case it may have been done at the instigation of certain priests, partisans of Petosarapis, and directed against loyal priests. Thembos may have had a hand in the affair.[143]

Another document illustrates the economic chaos which the 'disturbance' ($\tau\alpha\rho\alpha\chi\acute\eta$) created in the Thebaid. It is a petition (undated), recently discovered at Deir el Bahari on the west bank of the Nile, submitted by a certain Petearoeris to the *strategos* of Perithebas against a certain Pemsais. The latter had partly bought, partly seized, a piece of land of 80 *arourae* which belonged to the wife of Petearoeris and had 'in the disturbance' ($\dot\epsilon\nu\ \tau\hat\eta\iota\ \gamma\epsilon\nu\sigma\mu\acute\epsilon\nu\eta\iota\ \tau\alpha\rho\alpha\chi\hat\eta\iota$) been declared 'ownerless land' ($\dot\epsilon\nu$ $\tau\sigma\hat\iota\varsigma\ \dot\alpha\delta\epsilon\sigma\pi\acute\sigma\tau\sigma\iota\varsigma$). The wife of Petearoeris and probably he him-

* *P. Amh.* 30; Wilcken, *Chrest.* 9.

self were at that time ἐν τοῖς κάτω τόποις, that is to say, had
fled from the south to the north, where they remained for a
certain time, long enough for her belongings to be declared
ἀδέσποτα and sold. One sees to what difficulties the 'disturbance' gave rise. We do not know what part Petearoeris played
in the revolt. He may have been one of those who fled from the
rebels. In any case the picture called up by the petitioner is
characteristic of the conditions of the time.[144]

The same 'disturbance' affected various other persons. We
know by chance the history of the family of Ptolemy, the
famous recluse (ἐγκάτοχος) of the Sarapeum of Memphis.
Ptolemy had betaken himself to the Sarapeum long before
165/4, the date of the revolution of Petosarapis. He may have
chosen the Sarapeum as his abode from personal devotion and
religious enthusiasm. It is, however, not improbable that the
troubled state of Egypt had something to do with his decision.
It must be remembered that the rebellion in southern Egypt
had just been suppressed and that the danger of a war with
Syria was in the air. Ptolemy was the son of a κάτοικος and
probably liable to military service. He may have preferred the
more or less quiet life of a holy recluse in the Sarapeum, under
the protection of the god and the king, to the trials of a soldier's
life and to the dangers that would attend residence in his native
Psichis among hostile Egyptians. His father Glaucias was in
fact killed at Psichis, probably by the rebels, at the very end,
or soon after the official end, of the revolt (164 B.C.). Ptolemy
himself, in his retreat, was molested during and soon after the
rebellion by the Egyptian priests because, as he states in his
complaint on the subject, he was a Greek.[145]

The suppression of the revolt did not mean the end of
troubles in Egypt. Soon after his return from Rome and his
diplomatic victory over his rebellious brother, Philometor was
forced, in order to pacify Egypt, to proclaim in 163 B.C. a
general amnesty, extending probably to all who were in hiding
or had been denounced (compare the similar situation under
Epiphanes) as participators in the revolt.[146] But even after the
amnesty quiet was not restored in Egypt. It is characteristic
of the conditions of the time that bands of robbers were active
in the immediate neighbourhood of the Sarapeum of Memphis

in 157 B.C.* and in 152 B.C.† The robbers (λῃσταί) here referred
to were in all probability men who had been excluded from the
amnesty. We hear occasionally that about 157 B.C. there were
many 'royal peasants' (βασιλικοὶ γεωργοί) who were under trial
on charges of pillage and other crimes (ἐνεσχημένοι λείαις καὶ
ἄλλαις αἰτίαις) and whose landholdings were probably confiscated.‡ We need not wonder that the frontiers of Egypt were
jealously guarded. We hear that in 143 B.C. regular soldiers
and Arab gendarmes were keeping watch on the desert frontier
of the Fayûm near the famous Labyrinth.§ This may have
been an emergency measure taken by Euergetes II in the first
years of his reign, but it may on the other hand have been a
regular institution for the arrest of undesirable, homeless people
who might be leaving or entering Egypt.[147]

All the documents quoted above show how rapidly the
situation of Egypt deteriorated under Philometor and how
alarmingly the discontent of the population increased. Something had to be done. Various measures whereby the situation
might be improved were open to the government: they had all
been adopted from time to time in the past, even in the great
days of peace, order, and prosperity of the third century.
I have referred to some of them in connexion with Philopator
and Epiphanes. The evidence is more abundant for the time
of Philometor. The most disturbing fact confronting the
government was the decline of the revenue, due to difficulties
in the collection of the taxes and the accumulation of arrears.
To counteract this, the most natural course for the government
was to resort to force and compulsion. The king wished taxes
and rents to be collected in full. He exercised pressure on the
dioecetes, the *dioecetes* on his subordinates, and so on. The
officials of the crown, since they were all responsible in person
and property to the king, were alarmed, and transmitted the
pressure to the population by applying all the means of compulsion at their disposal.

Illustrations of this system of compulsion and of its results
in the field of tax and rent collection are presented by many
documents of the time of Philometor. None is more eloquent

* *U.P.Z.* 122, 9.   † *U.P.Z.* 71, 7.
‡ *Teb.* 742, 26 f., and 32 f.   § *Teb.* 736.

and typical than one of the Sarapeum papyri of 156 B.C.*
Many of the royal revenues, as I have explained, were collected
through the agency of tax-farmers (τελῶναι), who were not
actually tax-collectors but were responsible for the collection
of the tax in full. In this document we see how the tax-farmers,
being hard pressed themselves, transferred the pressure to the
tax-payers. Compulsory exactions (διασεισμοί), trickery (παρα-
λογεῖαι), and denunciations (συκοφαντεῖαι) of tax-payers alleged
to be recalcitrant and dishonest, were of common occurrence.
Complaints to the local administration proved ineffective. The
taxpayers in their sorry plight had recourse to the king and to
his *dioecetes*, setting forth their grievances against the local
administration and the tax-farmers. Alexandria was full of
these petitioners. To stop this flow of malcontents the *dioecetes*
Dioscurides sent a circular letter to his subordinates in the χώρα
reminding them of the desire of the king and queen that justice
should be done and of his own policy directed to the same end,
and forbidding acts of oppression and denunciation. The intentions of the king and his *dioecetes* were excellent, their principles
of government benevolent and humane, but I doubt very much
whether any positive improvement resulted from the letter.
The tax-farmers were still subjected to heavy pressure, for the
government was in urgent need of money, and this pressure was
automatically transmitted by the tax-farmers to the taxpayers.[148]

Compulsion was of course not the only means at the disposal
of the government nor the only one adopted. It was a dangerous weapon. The reactions of the population to it were many
and various. Bitter complaints were only one of them, and the
most harmless. More dangerous were the strikes, secessions
(ἀναχωρήσεις), of which I have already spoken and which I shall
discuss more fully in the next chapter. The secessions were
mostly collective but often individual. A man hard pressed
would simply disappear from his home (ἰδία) and vanish.
Finally, behind the secession stood the perpetual spectre of
armed revolt, of civil war.

It was natural that in these circumstances the king should
not always resort to compulsion and violence, but should try

* *U.P.Z.* 113.

more peaceful means: mutual understanding, compromise, concessions. We find examples of this method principally in the administration of the crown or royal land, from which a large revenue was derived by the king. I have mentioned some of the measures adopted by the government to check the depopulation of the royal villages and the abandonment of the land, which led to a decrease of the cultivated area. On the one hand compulsion, mitigated or unmitigated, was applied: I have described the early stages of the ἐπιγραφή or ἐπιβολή when speaking of Hippalus and Herodes. Even here, of course, the government preferred persuasion to compulsion. On the other hand, conciliatory measures were resorted to: reduction of rents (κουφισμός); privileges granted to farmers in consideration of their reclaiming waste and abandoned land—total exemption from rent for the first ten or five years, followed by a nominal and finally a full rent (emphyteutic contracts); assessment of the rent of certain parcels of land not according to their nominal value (i.e. the class to which they belonged in the land registers) but to their actual value (κατὰ τὴν ἀρετήν, ἐξ ἀξίας), and that sometimes for a long or even an indefinite term. In some documents we find combinations of several of these methods. The results were sometimes satisfactory. In the land registers and other documents we find instances of land reclaimed and restored to its former status. But such cases are rare. In general the measures described above did not arrest the gradual, sometimes rapid growth of the area of uncultivated land (ὑπόλογος) which produced no revenue for the king.[149]

Though well meant and sometimes useful, the concessions made by the government never satisfied the people, and it is not surprising that certain classes of the population attempted to obtain what they chiefly desired by other means, by a constant pressure from below which should finally force the government to recognize and legalize, as *faits accomplis*, certain changes in the economic and social system of the country. Chief among these classes, as might be expected, were those which had enjoyed a privileged position in Ptolemaic Egypt and which strove to obtain the extension and legalization of such privileges as they possessed. They were the priests, the soldiers settled on the land, and the landowning *bourgeoisie*, most of the last two groups of foreign origin.

As regards the temples and priests I have already shown how successful they were in wresting from the government some partial concessions. Their endeavours were directed principally to securing for themselves more freedom in the management of the γῆ ἱερά and the completely free management of the γῆ ἀνιερωμένη, the numerous grants of land made to the temples and priests by the kings themselves and by other donors. If these efforts were successful (about the management of this category of land under Philometor we know very little), they would have led directly to the creation of an enclave under private management in the otherwise continuous tract that was under the control of the government.

Another development of the same kind related to the γῆ κληρουχική. We must notice in the first place the claim of the cleruchs to be recognized, not as temporary holders of their *cleroi*, but as their actual owners, with the right of transferring them, subject to certain slight formalities, to their heirs—to their sons (and perhaps other relatives)—who would take their place in the ranks of the army. Some time before Raphia this claim was recognized by the government.* Even more important was another feature in the army system. I have already described how political and military considerations forced Philopator to reorganize his army. The soldiers settled on the land whom he had inherited from his predecessors were few in number, insufficient to guarantee Egypt against external aggression and internal disorder. To supplement the army exclusively by mercenaries, by large detachments of foreign soldiers on temporary service, would have been both dangerous and expensive. The only way in which the size of the army could be increased and its trustworthiness and efficiency at the same time maintained was to develop it on the lines devised by the early Ptolemies, that is, by adding to the number of the settled cleruchs and so enlarging the territorial force. This reinforcement could no doubt be effected, in strict adherence to the traditions of the early Ptolemies, by bringing in large bodies of mercenaries from abroad and settling them on the

* *P. Lille* 4; *Chrest.* 336, 218/17 B.C.

land. Such a course was possible, for mercenaries could be obtained abroad in ample numbers, and the method was applied.

But this course was open to serious objections. The *cleroi* assigned to the early cleruchs were large and their creation had been a costly measure. On the other hand smaller *cleroi*, especially of land that was not under cultivation, would hardly satisfy mercenaries of a good class and trustworthy character. Moreover, the area of cultivable and cultivated, or if not cultivated easily reclaimed, land at the disposal of the government was no longer so large as it had been in the times of Soter and Philadelphus. To increase it by drainage and irrigation was an expensive process and to deprive natives of their land in order to provide for new settlers would be highly dangerous.

While it was not very probable that large numbers of foreign mercenaries would be content with small plots of land under reclamation as remuneration for their service (this was how the Ptolemies of the second century B.C. provided for the new military settlers), there was a better prospect of satisfying natives in this way, and natives might after all, in case of necessity, be pressed into military service. Besides, the introduction into Egypt of large numbers of foreigners was fraught with peril from a political standpoint. The Ptolemies were certainly aware, after the revolt that had occurred during the last years of Euergetes, of the dangers inherent in a course which would intensify in Egypt the social and political antinomy which I have described in detail in an earlier chapter.

In these circumstances Philopator and his successors decided to resort to a compromise, to open wide the doors of the territorial army to the natives, in other words to organize the μάχιμοι of the past on new lines and to increase their number. A new body of cleruchs was called into being, composed of the various corps of μάχιμοι. First created by Philopator before Raphia, these native military units became part of the territorial army. The soldiers forming this new military contingent received *cleroi* probably on the same conditions on which they had been granted in the time of Philadelphus, with some modifications (smaller size of the plots, the use for this purpose of land under reclamation and not land under cultivation, subjection to liturgies, and a higher rate of *apomoira*—one-sixth instead of one-tenth).

It seemed as if a new national army had been created, in which Hellenes and natives were equally represented. But this was not the result. In fact the ancient cleruchs became a kind of military aristocracy, a position shared by the mercenaries, while the mass of native soldiers were inferior to them both in rank and remuneration. In order to distinguish between the two groups, the older group was no longer known as κληροῦχοι but as κάτοικοι.

The reform, though neither complete nor radical, had important consequences for the country. The status of many of the λαοί was changed by it. They were now no longer λαοί but cleruchs, and were treated in almost all respects like the Greek cleruchs of the past. They enjoyed much greater freedom in their economic pursuits. Their *cleroi* were small and required attention and work, but they could be easily ameliorated and enlarged by the purchase of more land or by emphyteusis. And, last but not least, they were assured of leaving their holdings to their male heirs. It is no wonder that some λαοί tried surreptitiously to get themselves included among the μάχιμοι, and that whenever the Ptolemies wished to increase their territorial army, there was probably no lack of recruits. Nor is it surprising that even some of the foreign mercenaries should be willing to accept the same conditions of service and to become settled μάχιμοι, a fact of which we have evidence not only in the first but also in the early second century B.C.

The course thus adopted by the rulers of Egypt was naturally not free from danger, as was shown by the revolts under Philopator, Epiphanes, and Philometor. But the fact that the kings were successful in suppressing these revolts proves that the majority of the μάχιμοι remained loyal, though many of them joined the ranks of the rebels. The Rosetta stone and perhaps *Teb.* 703 (if it belongs to the time of Philopator) furnish evidence of this.

The position may be summed up as follows. As in respect of the temples, so in respect of the rest of the population, the Ptolemies found themselves forced by circumstances to permit a wide breach to be made in their system of State control. The

PLATE LXXXI

No. 2 of this plate forms part of the find of Mit-Rahineh (above, pls. XLV and XLVIII). It is a plaster model of a bronze plaquette displaying the head of Ptolemy Soter. See G. Roeder and A. Ippel, *Die Denkmäler des Pelizaeus-Museums*, 1921, p. 141, no. 1120 and figs. 56 (plaster original) and 57 (restored modern bronze cast of the model). It is reproduced here and not among the illustrations to Ch. IV in order to show the stylistic differences between bronze works of the third and the second centuries B.C.

The other three bronze objects reproduced in this plate form part of the find of Galjûb (north-east of Cairo, see above, Ch. IV, p. 375, n. 173). Here were found in a clay pot more than one hundred bronze objects and the tools of the artisan who made them. The bronzes are reproductions of wax models used for casting bronze objects, before these models were completely ready. They served as specimens displayed to customers in the shop of a Greek gold- or silver-smith. Included in the find were statuettes of a decorative character, plaques with sketches of bas-reliefs, and medallions.

1. Bust of youthful Heracles with club and lion skin. The fine head looks like a portrait, perhaps of one of the later Hellenistic rulers. A. Ippel, *Der Bronzefund von Galjûb*, 1922, p. 64 f., no. 73, pl. vii, cf. *Denkm. Pelizaeus-Mus.* p. 156, no. 2284, fig. 64. Ippel suggests Antiochus IV as the ruler represented on the medallion.

3. Statuette of Attis on a lion's back. A. Ippel, loc. cit., p. 27, no. 6, pl. I.

4. Head of a hairpin representing Aphrodite dressing her hair. A. Ippel, loc. cit., p. 28, no. 7, pl. iii; *Denkm. Pel.-Mus.* p. 154, no. 2273, fig. 63.

The find, excellently illustrated by Ippel, provides invaluable material for the study of the technique of metal-working in Hellenistic times.

PLATE LXXXI

1

2

3

4

BRONZE INDUSTRY IN EGYPT

Pelizaeus-Museum at Hildesheim

number of those who enjoyed a certain amount of economic freedom had to be increased, those admitted to the privileged position being mainly native farmers (λαοὶ βασιλικοί).[150]

There was probably likewise an increase in the number of those who were more or less exempt from governmental control as being owners or holders of other privileged classes of land. Our information regarding the history of the royal grants (*doreai*) is defective (see above, p. 420, cf. 415). It appears from the meagre evidence that some *doreai* of the past 'returned to the crown' and were managed by agents of the kings (such was probably the fate of the *dorea* of Apollonius, *Teb.* 918). New *doreai*, on the other hand, were granted and apparently in no small number to the personages freshly risen to prominence at Alexandria. To the evidence cited above I may add some further indications derived mostly from the new volume of the Tebtunis papyri. In the official documents of the late third century B.C. (209 B.C.) the γῆ ἐν δωρεᾷ appears as an important class of land.* We know, moreover, from a document of the late third century of the existence of a *dorea* near Sebennytus† and from a later document (171 B.C.) of another near Psinteo.‡ Unfortunately the names of the holders of both these *doreai* are unknown. Still more interesting is the mention in an account of receipts in kind and in money of 138 B.C.§ of a *dorea* of Sosibius, probably the prime minister of Philopator. In 138 B.C. this *dorea* was probably in the hands of the royal administration, though it kept, like the *dorea* of Apollonius, its ancient name. The same was true of the *dorea* of Comanus,‖ a prominent man of the time of Epiphanes and Philometor, probably the temporary ruler of Egypt after the death of Eulaeus and Lenaeus.

It is evident that the system of granting gift estates to prominent persons was still in vogue, or perhaps again in vogue, in the second century B.C., and was not replaced by the equally ancient system of *doreai* consisting of the revenue of certain taxes or monopolies.¶ The reason for the adoption of

---

* *Teb.* 705.   † Ibid. 773.
‡ Ibid. 780.   § Ibid. 860.
‖ *P. Ryl.* 207 (a), 4, cf. W. L. Westermann, *Arch. Pap.* xiii (1938), pp. 1 ff.
¶ Diod. i. 52. 5, mentions the grant by Philadelphus to his wife of the income from Lake Moeris.

this policy by the kings of the second century may have been the same—*mutatis mutandis*—as that which influenced Soter, Philadelphus, and Euergetes, that is to say, the desire not only to remunerate loyalty and faithful service but also to attract capital and energy to the difficult task of reclaiming uncultivated land. In the second century, however, this land was as a rule not new land wrested by the efforts of the king and his officials from the desert and the swamps, but land which had once been productive but now lay abandoned and waste.[150a]

There was no reason why the members of the royal family should not have their part in this work. We may connect with the γῆ ἐν δωρεᾷ two enigmatic classes of land described as 'appanage of the royal children' (ἐν προσόδῳ τῶν τέκνων τοῦ βασιλέως)* and as 'separate income' (κεχωρισμένη πρόσοδος).†

Side by side with the *doreai* we meet more often than before holders of 'privately owned land' (γῆ ἰδιόκτητος, see above, pp. 289 ff.). We may perhaps class with this group the γεοῦχοι, who appear, numerous and well organized, in several nomes of lower Egypt (near Alexandria), the nomes of Berenice, of Ptolemaeus, and the Menelaite. Two inscriptions—one of the reign of Epiphanes (or Philometor or Euergetes II ?), another of 5 B.C.—give us substantial information about the corporative life of two very similar clubs or associations of such landowners, framed on a Greek model. One group calls itself 'holders of land in the neighbourhood of Psenamosis of the Berenicean nome' (συγγέωργοι ἔχοντες δὲ κτήσεις περὶ Ψενάμωσιν τοῦ Βερενίκης νομοῦ), the other 'landowners of Psenemphaia of the Ptolemaean nome' (γεοῦχοι οἱ ἀπὸ Ψενεμφαίας τοῦ Πτολεμαίου νομοῦ). A third inscription of the second century B.C. refers to 'landowners from the city' (οἱ ἀπὸ πόλεως γεοῦχοι). The members of these three clubs or associations were apparently Greeks and almost certainly, at least in part, residents in Alexandria: the club recorded in the first inscription adopted a formal resolution to buy a piece of land for the construction of a gymnasium. It is evident that Egyptian *laoi* would not and could not do such a thing.

It is a pity that we know so little of the γεοῦχοι, especially of the character of their land-holdings and of their relations to

* *Petr.* iii. 97, p. 237.   † See my *Kolonat*, pp. 44 ff.

the government. Their corporative activities suggest that they were not modest peasants but rather well-to-do landowners, and the term used to describe their land-holdings (κτήσεις) and certain allusions in the text of the first inscription may indicate that their estates consisted, at least partly, of vineyards and that they were producers of the famous Mareotic wine. Our evidence regarding them belongs to the second and first centuries B.C. Are we to suppose that they represent a new phenomenon in the life of Egypt in general or at least in the life of the three suburban nomes of Alexandria (see above, Ch. IV, n. 87)—in other words, that their existence and organization testify to the growth of private property at this time? Or are we to think that the late date of the evidence is an accident and that it reflects a peculiar evolution of land-holding in the neighbourhood of Alexandria from the early times of the Ptolemaic rule in Egypt, a continuation perhaps of institutions of the Saitic and Persian periods? In any case the γεοῦχοι of the Delta in the second and first centuries B.C. represent a class of landholders quite different from that of the βασιλικοὶ γεωργοί, much more free in its economic pursuits, more like the landowners of the city territories of Greece. Moreover it is clear that this class was not decaying or moribund.

Their associations (σύνοδοι) were not professional corporations or corporative units of an administrative character, like the villages of the βασιλικοὶ γεωργοί and the Egyptian villages and cities in general. They certainly were 'clubs' of the Greek type, associations formed for entertainment and common cult; but we must not forget that these associations consisted of men of one and the same class and of one and the same profession. In this respect they may be compared with similar associations of the κάτοικοι.*151

The preceding remarks point to one general conclusion, the gradual disintegration of the system of royal economy created by the early Ptolemies. The king, under the pressure of circumstances, was forced to make concessions to the population and these concessions have all one and the same character —the emancipation of private initiative from the heavy burden of State control.

* e.g. *Teb.* 119, of 105–101 B.C.; cf. *B.G.U.* 1188.

Such partial concessions were, of course, incapable of arresting the process of impoverishment either of the government or of the people of Egypt. The most striking proof of this impoverishment is to be seen in the monetary crisis which, as I have already shown, had begun early in the period with which we are dealing. Inflation was rapidly developing and becoming a permanent feature of the situation. Its character is little known and not easy to explain. It is, however, certain that the relative value of silver coins was increasing and that these were gradually disappearing from circulation, being treated as mere bullion: 500 and more copper drachmas to the silver drachma became the common ratio of exchange. Simultaneously the tendency of the prices of foodstuffs, manufactured goods, and labour was consistently upward, though the rise was somewhat spasmodic. The government profited from the inflation by discharging its obligations to those in its employ (including the military) in debased currency at a rate of exchange which did not correspond with the real value of copper money.[152]

I may conclude this brief and incomplete survey of the social and economic situation of Egypt at this time by a sketch of the conditions prevailing in one of its temples, derived from the correspondence of Ptolemy, the recluse in the Memphitic Sarapeum. It will enable us to understand the state of the country during the troubled times that followed the reign of Philopator, especially during the rule of Philometor.

The great temple of Sarapis near Memphis stood like a quiet island in the midst of a stormy sea. Political disturbances appear not to have affected its prosperity or the routine of its life. There was no diminution in the number of its priests, nor in the concourse of visitors and pilgrims, including the king himself,* whom it received. Nor was its lay population declining. The temple was one of the few *asyla* recognized by the government, and many sought its shelter from the hardships of life. We hear occasionally of some of them: the famous twin girls,† who, persecuted by their mother after the flight and death of their father, found refuge and later employment in the sanctuary under the protection of the recluse Ptolemy; a girl Heracleia,‡ who tried in vain to save herself from slavery under

* *U.P.Z.* 41. 4.   † Ibid. 17–58.   ‡ Ibid. 3 and 4.

the protection of Sarapis and of the same Ptolemy; perhaps another girl of the name Tathemis,* who earned her living as a temple beggar; the workmen in the kiki mills,† who were in danger of crucifixion either for something they had done in the mills, or for having fled from them; 'criminals' who had escaped from prison‡; and others.

The ἐγκάτοχοι to whom I have referred were likewise, in my opinion, seeking escape from their troubles. They were not refugees in the technical sense of the word. They did not come to the temple as suppliants (ἰκέται) to obtain protection. But their conversion and their withdrawal into retirement testify to a crisis in their lives which may have been purely personal and spiritual, but may on the other hand have been, as I suggest, the result of their hard experience. The case of Ptolemy was perhaps of this kind. The episode of Hephaistion, Conon, and their companions was similar. They were Macedonians like Ptolemy, probably soldiers of Philometor in the war with Antiochus. In 168 B.C. they were returning to their *polis*, but stopped on the way at the Sarapeum, probably to give thanks to the god for having saved them from great dangers. They were 'seized' by the god and stayed for a time in the sanctuary as temporary ἐγκάτοχοι.. Most of them eventually found their way home, but one—Hephaistion—hesitated, tempted to remain in that quiet spot where, like Ptolemy, one could earn money. Hephaistion knew that the life of the recluse was not an easy one, as is repeatedly stated by Ptolemy. From time to time he was hard pressed and became despondent.§ But conditions at home, as he knew, were much worse, for they were fully described to him by his wife Isias and his brother Dionysius.‖ Here are some lines from the touching letter of his wife, who had heard with despair that Hephaistion was still in the Sarapeum after his comrades had all returned home: 'But about your not coming home ... I am ill-pleased, because, after having piloted myself and your child through such bad times and having been driven to every extremity owing to the price of corn, I thought that, with you at home, I should enjoy

---

* *U.P.Z.* 2.   † Ibid. 119 and 120.
‡ Ibid. 64.   § Ibid. 63.
‖ Ibid. 59 and 60; Hunt–Edgar, *Select Pap.* i. no. 97.

some respite', and again: 'Remembering how I was in want of everything while you were still here, not to mention the long lapse of time and these critical days during which you have sent us nothing'. It should be remembered that Hephaistion and his wife were Greeks, that is members of the privileged class, Hephaistion being certainly a κληροῦχος. Whether Hephaistion listened to the prayers of his wife and brother or remained in the temple we do not know. Most of his companions did return to their homes; whether this turned out to their advantage or not is matter of conjecture, for the revolt of Petosarapis was at hand.

The case of Hephaistion may perhaps be thought exceptional. But the tone of the two letters, the mood that it reflects, lead me rather to regard it as typical.

Such were the conditions in Egypt in the period with which we are concerned. We shall see later that they did not improve until the end of the rule of the Ptolemaic dynasty.

Considered in all its aspects, this period, comprising the end of the third and the beginning of the second century B.C., was not an unfavourable one for the Hellenistic world. What Egypt and Greece lost, Syria, Pergamon, Rhodes, and Delos gained. The economic centre of gravity shifted a little, but production remained abundant and trade was active. These general conditions are reflected in the coinage and prices. None of the leading States except Egypt had recourse to any sort of inflation, and prices, again with the exception of Egypt, were not subject, so far as we know, to violent fluctuations. Their general tendency appears to have been to rise steadily, which may have been due in part to a larger demand for commodities of all sorts both in the East and in the West.

VI

THE ROMAN PROTECTORATE AND THE FIRST STAGE OF ROMAN DOMINATION

THE principal features in the economic aspect of the Hellenistic world before and during the Third Macedonian war were, first, the economic recovery or increasing prosperity of certain parts of this world and, second, the attempt of certain leading Powers to restore its economic unity, which political disintegration and Roman intervention had greatly impaired. This second element we see manifested in the efforts made by these States to prevent the complete subjugation of Macedonia by Rome and so to maintain the Hellenistic balance of power. Behind this movement stood an increasing hatred of the Romans.

Rome was well aware of all these developments. In economic prosperity and the restoration of economic unity, combined with national self-consciousness, she saw the possibility of a political renascence of the Hellenistic world under the leadership of one of its stronger States, and renascence might mean a war of revenge. Rome was determined to prevent such possibilities and struck hard.

Her first victims were the most powerful of these States, her enemies of the past—Macedonia and Syria. The former after the Persean war ceased to exist as an independent and united country. Its economic and possibly political recovery was forestalled by certain economic sanctions: the Macedonians were forbidden to exploit their two main sources of wealth and military strength, their mines and forests. About the same time Antiochus IV was forced out of Egypt by insolent diplomatic action and thus prevented from uniting the whole of the Near East under his rule. Moreover Syria was weakened by the support given by Rome to the separatist tendencies which were developing within the Seleucid Empire, especially among the Jews. Nevertheless Antiochus IV in the last years of his life made another resolute attempt to strengthen and consolidate his still great and powerful empire. This is attested by his activity in Palestine, his reorganization of his Syrian kingdom, and his expedition to the East. The Romans did not interfere: they were afraid of his still considerable resources and of his well-organized army, and were satisfied with the success they had gained over him in Egypt. Unfortunately the effort of Antiochus was defeated by his untimely death. With him the last great Seleucid passed away, and Syria entered on a period of rapid political decay and disintegration. His successors were no longer able to discharge their principal mission, that of checking the Oriental tide which was advancing rapidly from the Iranian regions in the East and of stopping at the same time the disintegration of Syria from within.

Next came Rome's friends and allies—Pergamon and Rhodes. They became too strong and too self-confident for Rome, too popular with the Greeks all over the Hellenistic world as supporters of Hellenism. Their efforts to put an end to the Persean war by diplomatic intervention were interpreted as treason. In the case of Pergamon, Rome limited herself to withdrawing her active support from Eumenes II and to humiliating him diplomatically and politically. Rhodes, more active and more popular, was punished by harsh economic sanctions. Its dominions on the mainland of Asia Minor—of which the richest had come into its possession (by purchase or diplomatic action) before the war with Antiochus III—were taken from it and the revenue that it derived from the transit trade between the East and the West was reduced by making Delos, now once more a cleruchy of Athens, a free port. Rhodes was no longer able to keep up as strong a navy as in the past and therefore gradually lost its reputation as protector of the freedom of trade in the Aegean. Finally, as soon as Corinth and the rest of Greece began to recover their prosperity and self-confidence in the atmosphere of peace which followed the battle of Pydna, Corinth was ruthlessly destroyed and part of Greece was devastated and humiliated.

What were the economic consequences of these political measures? Did they lead to a rapid economic decay of the Hellenistic world? The new political configuration of that world, the Roman protectorate which henceforth was heavily felt by all its 'independent' States and gradually developed into Roman domination, and more especially the rapid and

brilliant evolution of Italy (see below), were of course important factors in the economic history of the age and considerably
changed the aspect of economic life in the Hellenistic countries.
The changes were, however, not the same in all of them. No
general picture can be drawn nor can any general statement be
made regarding them. Each part of the Hellenistic world must
be dealt with separately.

I. GREECE, MACEDONIA, AND THE EUXINE

To begin with continental Greece. The war with Perseus was
a great calamity for Greece. The Romans did not humanize
their methods of warfare, but on the contrary showed themselves more cruel and ruthless than before. Destruction of cities,
enslavement of the population, requisitions, confiscations, were
of constant occurrence.[1] A single example will suffice, the
treatment of Epirus by Aemilius Paulus after the Macedonian
war. After the settlement of Macedonian affairs Aemilus Paulus
marched against Epirus. The Senate had ordered him to deliver
Epirus to be pillaged by the soldiers who had fought under him
against Perseus, as a punishment for its having sided with
Perseus since 170 B.C. Aemilius Paulus carried out his instructions with efficiency. By a clever and treacherous device he
succeeded in placing detachments of Roman soldiers in all the
cities of Epirus at the same time, without awakening the sus-
picions of the inhabitants. When the word was given, wholesale
pillage began in all the cities. 'When the day came', says
Plutarch, 'these [the soldiers] all started at the same time and
began the raiding and pillaging of the cities, so that in a single
hour 150,000 men were enslaved and seventy cities were sacked.
And yet from all this destruction and ruin each soldier got no
more than eleven drachmae as his share.'[2]

It is unnecessary to supplement this incident by the lamentable story of the devastation of Achaea during the last
Achaean war and the subsequent destruction of Corinth.[3]
We may interpret these proceedings as a political and social
measure intended to effect the pacification of the whole of
Greece, to put an end to social and economic revolutions, and
to prevent further acts of insubordination; nevertheless the
cruelty and ruthlessness with which they were carried out

PLATE LXXXII

The monument here reproduced (mentioned by Plut. *Aem. Paul.* 28. 4, cf. Polyb. xxx. 10. 2 and Liv. xlv. 27) once stood in the sacred precinct of Delphi somewhere near the south-east corner of the great temple (exact location apparently unknown). It was found in fragments and restored in the Museum of Delphi. It had the form of a rectangular pillar on a rectangular base covered with slabs of Pentelic marble (h. of the pillar and base 8·20 m.). The pillar was probably first erected in honour of the Macedonian king Perseus. After the battle of Pydna Aemilius Paullus used it to commemorate his victory over the Macedonian king. On the top stood the equestrian bronze statue of Aemilius. The base of the statue, i.e. the top of the pillar, was adorned with a carved frieze (in part extant) showing the most remarkable and decisive episodes of the battle of Pydna, recorded in our literary evidence. On the base of the pillar was engraved the still extant inscription reproduced in the plate: *L. Aimilius L. f. inperator de rege Perse Macedonibusque cepet.* Later, several other documents were engraved on the pillar, among them the law of about 100 B.C. concerning the pirates, mentioned in the text of this chapter.

The monument has been published and discussed several times. The best study from the point of view of architecture is that of F. Courby, *F. D.* ii. 2, 1927 (see the restoration p. 303, fig. 250). The inscriptions engraved on the monument will be found in G. Colin, ibid. iii. 4, 1932. On the other monuments erected at Delphi in honour of prominent Romans, G. Daux, *Delphes au II⁰ et au I⁰ʳ siècle* pp. 584 ff. Cf. M. Guarducci, 'Le offerte dei conquistatori Romani ai santuari della Grecia', *Rend. Pontif. Acc. Rom. Arch.* xiii (1938), pp. 49 ff. The monument of Aemilius is here reproduced from a plastic restoration of it which was exhibited in the Mostra Augustea at Rome in 1938. Photographs of this model and of a cast of the inscription have been supplied by the authorities of the Mostra. Cf. *Mostra Augustea di Romanità. Catalogo*, ii, p. 37 (room iv, 43–5).

PLATE LXXXII

1

2

THE END OF MACEDONIAN INDEPENDENCE. MONUMENT COMMEMORATING THE
VICTORY OF PYDNA ERECTED AT DELPHI

made a lasting impression on the civilized world of that time.[4] I may add that, apart from the destruction of Corinth, the Greeks paid for the loss of liberty a price as heavy as that which they had paid to obtain it. Again a substantial part of Greece lay prostrate, humiliated, and miserably poor.

It must be observed, however, that all parts of Greece did not suffer heavily during the Persean and later during the Achaean war. Large areas were not involved in these wars at all, while the pacification after Pydna and Corinth did not fail to exercise a beneficent influence on certain regions at least.

We have seen that ATHENS was rapidly developing in the preceding period, and in all probability had recovered its industrial and commercial importance, sharing with Rhodes, Corinth, and Delos the advantage of being a clearing-house for Aegean trade. Its population increased rapidly. Foreigners in large numbers settled once more in the city and took an active part in its economic life.

The settlement of Greek affairs after the Persean war appears to have brought great profit to Athens, the only faithful friend of Rome in Greece. It is well known that some of its cleruchies were restored to it: Lemnos and later Imbros and Scyros. To these cleruchies was added the territory of the Boeotian city of Haliartus. This meant for Athens no more than a certain increase in territory and in international prestige. More important was the recovery of Delos and the establishment of an Athenian cleruchy on the island in place of the native population, which was removed to Achaea.[5]

Polybius (xxx. 20. 8) does not regard the Roman gifts to Athens as an unmixed blessing, and to some extent he may be right. It is evident that the possession of Delos (to confine ourselves to this point) contributed to the prosperity of Athens and of many Athenian citizens. Some of the poorer Athenians settled in the island and received plots of land and houses. Among these may have been some who enriched themselves by selling or renting their property to foreign merchants. Some of the richer Athenians probably took an active part in the international trade which developed so brilliantly in the new *porto franco*: the merchants of the Piraeus, in particular, certainly did not fail to invest their money in the Delian ventures in competition or in association with their Eastern and Italian fellow-traders. A few instances of this are known to us. It is highly probable also that certain of the more refined products of Athenian agriculture and kindred industries (especially olive-oil and honey) found a good market in Delos, where there was practically no cultivated land, and it may have been the same with some articles of Athenian manufacture, though archaeological evidence does not support this view (the pottery, for example, used in Delos, 'Megarian' bowls, incense-burners, portable ovens, was not imported from Athens). Athenian artists must have settled in Delos and found a rich and numerous *clientèle* in the mixed population of the island.

But while it is evident that some Athenian citizens profited by the close connexion now established with Delos, it is more difficult to say whether the Athenian State was enriched by it. We know that no customs duties were levied by Athens in the port of Delos. Harbour dues of various kinds were probably still paid by the ships that anchored there, and Athens may have owned storehouses in the harbour and houses in the city which it rented to the ναύκληροι and ἐγδοχεῖς. Other minor duties may have been collected from Athenian and foreign merchants. But the upkeep and administration of the harbour and the management of the cleruchy were a source of much expense, and in general Athens incurred a heavy responsibility to its own cleruchy and to the business community.[6]

Moreover, it is natural to suppose that if the free port of Delos had so detrimental an influence on the trade of Rhodes, it must have had a similar effect on that of Athens. But of this the scanty evidence available offers no indication.

And yet there are some signs of the growing prosperity of Athens not directly connected with its possession of Delos. One of these signs is the history of Athenian currency. Athenian currency was as abundant and as trustworthy after 167 as in the earlier period. In fact after 146 B.C. Athens was the only Greek State which was allowed by the Romans to coin its own silver money. This may be explained in part by the use made of Athenian currency by the Delian merchants. The circulation of various currencies seems to have been more or less unrestricted at Delos. Though the savings of the Delian population consisted almost exclusively of Athenian silver coins, as is shown by several hoards of this period found in the island, and although the government of Delos used exclusively Athenian coins, nevertheless even after 167 B.C. many other currencies also circulated there.[7] Athenian 'Owls', however, were in all probability the principal medium of exchange employed in Delian trade after that date, especially at the end of the second and in the early part of the first century B.C., as appears from a careful study of the coin hoards of Syria, a country closely connected with Delos. At the end of the second century B.C., after the annexation of the Pergamene kingdom by the Romans, the main currency of the previous period—the tetradrachms of Alexander minted by several cities of Asia Minor—gradually disappear from the Syrian hoards and are replaced either by Seleucid coins or by Athenian 'Owls'. On the other hand the dynasts of caravan cities ceased to issue imitations of Alexanders and substituted imitations of late Athenian coins.[8]

Thus Delos and the East absorbed a large part of the silver minted at Athens. But it was not from Delos alone that Athenian currency spread over the Hellenistic world. Such facts as the imitation of Athenian coins of the new style in Ionia, Thessaly, and Crete, and the discovery of several hoards of Athenian coins in various parts of Greece and in the northern part of the Balkan peninsula, testify to the prevalence, not of Delian, but of Athenian trade in Greece, Asia Minor, and the Balkans.

The most striking proof of the importance of Athenian trade in Greece, especially in Central Greece, is afforded by the promulgation of the well-known Amphictionic law of the end of the second century B.C. which was intended to confirm the preponderance of Athenian currency in Greece and perhaps to protect the Athenian tetradrachm against devaluation. This act may be explained as a political move of the Amphictions. But it is more than probable that it was promoted by Athens and especially by the group of rich commercial families which at that time exercised power there.[9]

We see the commercial relations of Athens reflected, not only in the spread of its currency, but also in the large number of stamped amphora handles found in that city. Unfortunately these have been little studied and cannot yet be exactly dated. It is, however, significant of the direction of Athenian trade that the large majority of stamped handles found in the excavations of the Agora are Rhodian and Cnidian (of 1545 seals found there in 1931-2, 565 are Rhodian and 437 Cnidian), while Thasian stamps are comparatively rare (only 75 of these were found in the Agora in 1931-2), and Parian, Chian, and Sinopic stamps are exceptions. The proportions are similar to those which have been found in Delos. It appears that the commercial relations between Athens and Rhodes were very close in the late third and the early second centuries B.C., while less close in the later half of the second.[10]

The evidence is no doubt inadequate, but it suggests that Athens, even after the great development of Delos, continued to be an important commercial city. The geographical range of its trade was not very wide. Its currency was unable to compete with the *cistophori* in Asia Minor, with the Rhodian drachmae in the islands, or with the Macedonian, Thasian, and Maronean coins in the northern part of the Balkan peninsula. Nor did it penetrate in large quantities into the Bosporan kingdom. And yet it played an important part in Greece proper.[11] The few facts that are known, while they do not permit any firm conclusion, suggest the following explanation. It would seem that the international trading community of Delos, associated to some extent with Athenian capitalists, who became more and more dependent on their Delian partners, concentrated upon and almost monopolized the transit trade between Asia Minor, Syria, Egypt, and Italy* and left the trade between the States of Greece, which still had a certain importance, in the hands of Rhodes, Athens, Thasos, and Maronea.[12]

Besides the role which Athens played in this internal trade of Greece, there existed important direct commercial relations between Athens and Rome and Italy, in which Delos had no share. Rome and Italy were now making large purchases of all sorts of products of Athenian art and artistic industry. This we know from the frequency of works of neo-Attic art in Italy and from the abundant literary evidence, especially from Cicero. The best evidence of it, however, is afforded by the

* See Strabo x. 5. 4, p. 486.

two ships loaded to a large extent with products of Athenian artistic industry and found sunk, one off Mahdia on the Tunisian coast, the other off Anticythera. The contents of the two ships are very similar and the time when they were wrecked almost the same (86 B.C. is suggested for Mahdia, the middle of the first century B.C. for Anticythera). Besides statues and statuettes of bronze and marble, the ships carried many pieces of furniture in wood and bronze, marble decorative kraters and candelabra, bas-reliefs of marble and clay, mostly of the neo-Attic style, columns, bases, and capitals of marble; there were even early Athenian inscriptions on marble slabs in the Mahdia ship. Some of these objects were antiques, but most of them brand-new. The greater part were made at Athens. There were, moreover, among the Anticythera finds many products of Parian manufacture (especially statues), and some of the Mahdia statues were made, not at Athens, but in other centres of Greek art (for instance the statue by Boethus of Chalcedon, a contemporary of Antiochus IV). It would seem that Athens even after Sulla (and still more before Sulla) was the general clearing-house for this kind of commerce. It was Athenian merchants who carried out the orders of Italian customers and collected the objects, some of them valuable antiques, others products of contemporary artistic industry, from all parts of Greece.[13]

To these products of the industry of Athens and some other places in Greece we may safely add olive-oil, wine, certain vegetables, honey, various delicacies, &c., which were probably exported to Italy direct from Athens and never passed through the international market of Delos.[14]

Athens was no doubt the city most favoured by the Romans and was treated by the Roman administration with exceptional regard. But the treatment of the rest of Greece was free from excessive harshness. It must be remembered that the war which ended with the total destruction of Corinth and the partial destruction of Thebes and Chalcis was never looked upon by the Romans as a war against Greece in general. It was *bellum Achaicum* and nothing more.

This is not the place to consider the constitutional situation of Greece after 146 B.C., a subject that has been repeatedly

1. One of the four well-preserved marble kraters found at the bottom of the sea near Mahdia (between Susa and Sfax in Tunisia). Fragments of several others of similar shape and decoration were found in the same place. The krater represented here (the lower part of it is omitted in order to show the upper part better) is adorned with carved figures of young Dionysus and Ariadne and their thiasos. This and another almost identical one, comparatively well-preserved, from Mahdia are almost exact replicas of the famous Borghese krater now in the Louvre, while the other two better preserved specimens from Mahdia (equally Dionysiac in their decoration) stand in the same relation to the well-known krater of the Campo Santo at Pisa. The kraters from Mahdia were made of Pentelic marble and were brand-new when shipped from Athens to Italy.

2. One of the two well-preserved marble candelabra found at Mahdia. Fragments of several others were found in the same place. Made of Pentelic marble and new when shipped. Similar candelabra of a decorative character have been found in Italy and elsewhere and are preserved in various Museums.

For a detailed description of the kraters and candelabra of Mahdia see A. Merlin and L. Poinssot, *Cratères et candélabres de marbre, trouvés en mer près de Mahdia*, 1930. Here reproduced from photographs supplied by M. L. Poinssot, Director of Antiquities and Arts in Tunisia.

I have dealt with the submarine finds of late Hellenistic times in this chapter, pp. 744 ff. and n. 13. Add to the bibliography given in n. 13 the substantial article by A. Merlin, 'Submarine discoveries in the Mediterranean', *Antiquity*, iv (1930), pp. 405 ff. The miscellaneous cargo of the ship sunk off Mahdia consisted of more than 60 large marble columns, 24 m. long, and several other architectural pieces, and also of bronze and marble statues, statuettes and reliefs, bronze vessels, pieces of furniture adorned with bronze sculptures, ornamental marble kraters and candelabra. The majority of these objects were brand-new when shipped from Athens (with the exception of inscriptions on marble slabs which were taken aboard either as ballast or as curiosities). The miscellaneous character of the cargo and the fact that, though the majority of the objects were made at Athens, several pieces were products of other workshops and were brought to Athens to be dispatched, lead me to think that the ship was carrying to Italy, not the spoils acquired by Sulla, his generals, officers, and soldiers at Athens in 86 B.C., but various merchandise which one or more merchants hoped to dispose of in Italy at a good price. The Mahdia shipwreck cannot be exactly dated, but there are several reasons for assigning it to a date slightly earlier than 86 B.C. The find is a splendid testimony to the commercial, industrial, and artistic activity of Athens in the late second and early first centuries. It appears very probable in the light of this discovery that similar products of Greek industry and art found in large quantities in Italy and signed sometimes by artists who call themselves Athenians, Parians, Rhodians, etc., were made mostly in Greece for export, and not in Italy by artists of foreign origin.

PLATE LXXXIII

2. Decorative marble candelabrum

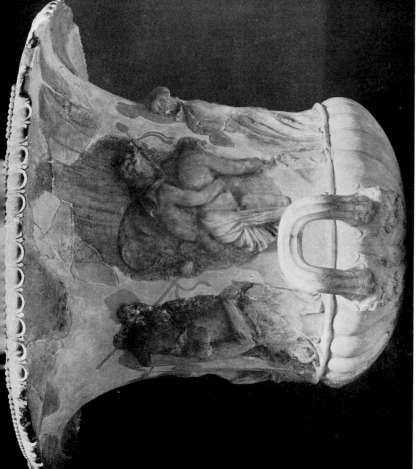

1. Decorative marble krater

ROME AND ATHENS. FIND OF MAHDIA

Tunis, Bardo Museum

PLATE LXXXIV

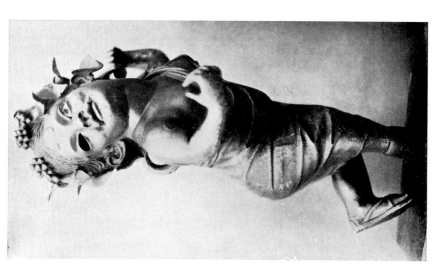

ARTISTIC BRONZE INDUSTRY OF LATE HELLENISTIC TIMES. DANCING DWARFS

Tunis, Bardo Museum

PLATE LXXXIV

Two of the three statuettes of dancing dwarfs found in the sea at Mahdia (see description of Pl. LXXXIII). Two of them represent women, one a man. All three were probably intended to be suspended from strings or chains, like the terracotta statuette of a slave being flogged found at Priene (see Pl. XXXIV, 1). The dwarfs with their distorted bodies, their disproportionately large heads, the sensual expression of their faces, and their wild movements to the accompaniment of crotala are irresistibly comic, especially if we imagine them suspended, i.e. in constant movement. It is well known that dwarfs or pygmies were very popular in Pharaonic and Ptolemaic Egypt. They are frequently represented in the art of these periods (see for example the heavy and costly sarcophagus of the dwarf Taho in the Cairo Museum, G. Maspéro, 'Sarcophages des époques persane et ptolémaïque', *Catal. gén.*, pls. xxii ff.; the description of this sarcophagus reserved for vol. ii of the Catalogue never appeared). Cf. I. Noshy, *The Arts in Ptolemaic Egypt*, 1937, p. 98, n. 2. These dwarfs often entertained their masters with wild music and dances. Professional castanet dancers (κροταλίστριαι) who moved from place to place and made a profession of their dancing are well known in Ptolemaic and Roman Egypt, and were very popular with the inhabitants of that country (see below, Ch. VIII, n. 43). They certainly appeared on the stage also and not exclusively in Egypt. The statuettes from Mahdia therefore were not necessarily made in Egypt. They are best reproduced and fully discussed by A. Merlin, 'Statuettes de bronze, trouvées en mer près de Mahdia', *Mon. et Mém. Piot*, xviii (1910), pp. 9 ff, and pls. ii, iii and iv; cf. the memoir of A. Merlin and L. Poinssot quoted above in the description of Pl. LXXXIII. Photographs supplied by M. L. Poinssot.

discussed. What interests us in this connexion is the well-ascertained fact that Greece as a whole was not organized as a Roman province after 146 B.C. The cities of Greece and the federations (first abolished but very soon restored) were to some extent under the control of the governor of Macedonia, but were not cities and κοινά under his direct administration.[15]

The whole of Greece, it need hardly be said, was not treated by the Romans in exactly the same way. Those parts which had taken an active share in the Achaean war were placed under a régime which was very similar to that of a regular province. Thus the territory of Corinth, that of Thebes and probably the whole of Boeotia, and the territory of Chalcis and probably the rest of Euboea, were declared *ager vectigalis*, and their πρόσοδοι (*vectigalia*), that is to say, the rent or land-tax which the tillers of the soil paid to Rome and the other revenues, were farmed to Roman *societates publicanorum*. This fact is attested both by literary and by documentary evidence.[16]

The *agri vectigales* were regarded by the Roman government as the property of the Roman people. The revenues from them, as stated above, were farmed out to Roman tax-collectors. It was the practice of the Senate and of the holders of *imperium* in the East to dispose of these lands freely and unhesitatingly. We hear, for example, that the larger part of the *ager Corinthius* was given to Sicyon (Strabo, viii. 6. 23, p. 381) and that Sulla gave half the territory of Thebes to the temples of Delphi, Olympia, and Epidaurus as a kind of compensation for the treasures of these temples which he had confiscated.[17] We know also from the famous *Senatus Consultum* concerning Oropus that the territory of the Oropians, including the harbours (λιμένες), was given by Sulla to the temple of Amphiaraus, the income (πρόσοδοι) to be used by the temple for religious purposes (*agones* and sacrifices), a measure which aroused the protest of the *publicani*. These tried to invalidate the clause in the *lex censoria* which treated these lands as *agri excepti* because they had been dedicated to immortal gods, by pointing out that such heroes as Trophonius and Amphiaraus were not 'immortal' gods. Finally, Sulla assigned 10,000 *plethra* of Euboean land to Archelaus, the general of Mithridates; and the famous *Senatus Consultum* of 78 B.C., by which three navarchs of Clazomenae, Carystos, and

Miletus who had rendered valuable services to Rome during the social war were made *amici populi Romani*, states explicitly that their property was to be exempt from any demands by the respective *societates publicanorum*.* The same exceptional treatment was granted by Sulla (Oropian *S.C.*) to Hermodorus, a priest of Amphiaraus, who had remained faithful to the Romans, and by a Roman magistrate to the Dionysiac artistes of Thebes.[18]

It was probably the exceptional status of the Isthmus, Boeotia, and Euboea that attracted to these regions an unusually large number of Italian *negotiatores*, some of whom were connected with the *societates publicanorum*, while others invested their money in land, industry, and banking under the direct protection of the Roman administration.[19]

It is unfortunate that we do not know what exactly were the revenues (πρόσοδοι) of these regions which the *publicani* and the sanctuaries mentioned above had the right of collecting (καρπίζεσθαι, *frui*). The use of the λιμένες refers to customs and harbour dues; the use of the land, to certain payments by the landholders, either a *pars quota* or a *pars quanta*.

We have no information about the status of the other cities which had taken part in the Achaean war. But it is probable that their territories never became *agri vectigales*, and that it was these cities, as Jebelev suggests, that paid the tribute which, according to Pausanias (vii. 16. 6), was imposed on some of the Greek cities while the majority of them paid none. The point is controversial and cannot be discussed here.

Though treated harshly from a fiscal standpoint, the Greek cities that took part in the Achaean war were not deprived of their autonomy and liberty. The Romans, it is true, favoured certain constitutional changes in these and the other cities of Greece. They preferred to see government in the hands of the propertied classes; but it is improbable that they did more to give effect to their views than patronize these richer elements and help them to reform the constitutions of their respective cities.

* l. 6: [*magistrat*]*us nostri queiquomque Asiam Euboeam locabunt vectigalve Asiae* [*Euboeae imponent curent ne quid ei dare debeant*] and in Greek l. 23: ἄρχοντες ἡμέτεροι οἵτινες ἄν ποτε 'Ασίαν Εὔβοιαν μισθῶσι ἢ προσόδους 'Ασίαι Εὐβοίαι ἐπιτιθῶσιν, φυλάξωνται μή τι οὗτοι δοῦναι ὀφείλωσι.

The rest of the cities of Greece, those which had taken no part in the Achaean war, remained what they had been: free and self-governing bodies politic, with their own revenues and taxes, paying no regular contributions to the Roman State. This does not mean that in emergencies all the cities of Greece were not liable to extraordinary contributions in kind and money ($\epsilon i\sigma\phi o\rho a i$), to requisitions, to military levies, and to the mobilization of their naval forces for the service of the Romans. I shall return to this topic in the next chapter.

The main result of the Persean and Achaean wars was a pacification of Greece which lasted for more than 50 years. We have seen how the Roman peace affected the economic life of Athens, and Athens was in all probability no exception. Many regions of Greece shared in her prosperity, and more especially the Peloponnese. Let me recall the statement of Polybius regarding the prosperity of this region (ii. 62), the sharp distinction which he draws between the Peloponnese of the end of the third century (and the conditions were not better in the early second) and the Peloponnese of his own times: 'in which all agree in thinking that it enjoys the greatest prosperity'.*

It is natural that the first Greek communities to recover after the distress of the late third and early second centuries should have been those which, lying in the more fertile agricultural regions of Greece, were self-supporting as regards foodstuffs and even able to export some of the products of their agriculture, grazing, gardening, &c. This *a priori* conclusion is borne out by a group of valuable documents which shed a vivid and unexpected light on the economic and social conditions of one of these more favoured regions, viz. Messenia. I refer to the documents concerning the $\delta\kappa\tau\dot{\omega}\beta o\lambda os$ $\epsilon i\sigma\phi o\rho\dot{a}$ of the city of Messene—an emergency tax on property assessed at eight obols in the mina—and the well-known inscription containing the $\nu\dot{o}\mu o\iota$ $i\epsilon\rho o i$ of Andania. [20] †

The extraordinary tax of eight obols, i.e. about 2 per cent. of the census or estimated property ($\tau i\mu\eta\mu a$ or $\tau\iota\mu a\sigma i a$) of each

* $\dot{\epsilon}\nu$ $o\dot{\iota}s$ $\pi\dot{a}\nu\tau\epsilon s$ $\dot{\epsilon}\nu$ $\kappa a\dot{\iota}$ $\tau a\dot{\upsilon}\tau\dot{o}$ $\lambda\dot{\epsilon}\gamma o\nu\tau\epsilon s$ $\mu\epsilon\gamma i\sigma\tau\eta\nu$ $\kappa a\rho\pi o\dot{\upsilon}\sigma\theta a\iota$ $\delta o\kappa o\dot{\upsilon}\sigma\iota\nu$ $\epsilon\dot{\upsilon}\delta a\iota\mu o\nu i a\nu$.

† This group of documents has been interpreted in a masterly manner in the light of related and contemporary evidence by A. Wilhelm.

taxpayer, was certainly very oppressive. It was levied, not because of any internal financial difficulties in Messene, but to pay a compulsory contribution to the Romans. It should be noticed that, besides this contribution, the community supplied soldiers (ii. 36) and slave-sailors (ii. 39), and that the assessment and collection of the tax were carried out under the watchful eyes of Roman magistrates (inscr. I). The occasion on which the contribution was imposed by the Romans is unknown. Palaeography and other considerations have led Wilhelm to assign the inscriptions to the end of the second or beginning of the first century B.C., but not to the time after Sulla. He has enumerated the events from the revolt of Aristonicus to the death of Sulla which might have led to the imposition of a heavy εἰσφορά and to levies of soldiers and ships. Among them the most likely are the early expeditions undertaken against the pirates (103–100 B.C.), the social war in Italy, and the first Mithridatic war, especially as it coincided with civil war in Italy, when Sulla was in urgent need of men and money, and had recourse to contributions and requisitions especially in the East (App. *B.C.* i. 102). However this may be, the tax was levied at the end of the period of prosperity and peace of which I am speaking.

The inscriptions referring to the ὀκτώβολος εἰσφορά furnish us with economic data of great importance under three heads: (1) we learn from inscr. II the general value of the property of the inhabitants of Messene as estimated by the census commission, 1256 talents of Achaean currency; (2) inscr. III, which is probably of an earlier date, gives a list of estimates of the fortunes owned by certain private individuals; and (3) inscr. II gives the sums due by taxpayers, the sums collected, and the arrears. The general estimate of the taxable property of inhabitants is probably the estimate of all the property they owned: land, houses, cattle, movable property (ἔπιπλα). It may be compared with a similar estimate of the property of Athenian citizens (5,725 talents), which is reported by Polybius (ii. 62) and refers to 378 B.C. I cannot here enter into the controversy regarding the interpretation of the passage of Polybius. In my opinion the sum that he names may be accepted, and represents the estimated value of the whole of the taxable property of the population of Athens. But a comparison with the figure for Messene is not easy. We do not know exactly the extent of the territory of Messene or the size of its population. Wilhelm's suggestion—990 square kilometres and 6,000 men—is conjectural, and I doubt therefore whether the estimate that the average fortune of an inhabitant of the city was one-fifth of a talent can be regarded as more than a possible guess. The same applies to the estimate that the average fortune of the Athenians was a quarter of a talent. Besides, more than two and a half centuries separate the two estimates. The distribution of property among the taxpayers is unknown. The comparative cost of living is a further source of difficulty. We cannot therefore press the parallel, but the comparison shows that the figure for Messene points to a comparatively high standard of general prosperity.

We may derive a little more information from another statement of Polybius (loc. cit.) relating to the whole of the Peloponnese in his own time. He says that this would hardly produce more than 6,000 talents if all the ἔπιπλα of its inhabitants were sold. He adds in the same passage that in 223 B.C. the rich and powerful Mantinea when captured yielded to the victor, by the sale of all the ἔπιπλα in the city and of the free and slave population, no more than 300 talents. Here again no close comparison is possible. But it is evident that Messene in 100 B.C. with its census of 1256 talents was probably richer than Mantinea in 223 B.C. The ἔπιπλα alone of the Messenians were hardly worth less than 300 talents.

Finally, the ease with which the inhabitants of Messene paid the contribution of 2 per cent of the value of their property— note the small percentage of arrears—shows that their general economic situation, their capacity of payment, which naturally depended on their income and savings, was not bad. We are not told that the collectors had recourse to confiscations and the compulsory sale of property, as would have happened if many of the taxpayers had been insolvent, or that the city had recourse to a loan in order to make good a deficit. The decree in honour of Aristocles states explicitly 'that there was neither borrowing nor deficit in connexion with these contributions'.*

* i. l. 4 f. καὶ] μὴ γενέσθαι μήτε δανεισμόν, μ[ήτε ἔλ]λειμμα περὶ ταύτας τὰς εἰσφοράς.

It is more difficult to discover who were the payers of the bulk of the εἰσφορά, whether the rich and well-to-do or the small farmers and artisans. An inscription found at Messene, perhaps of a slightly earlier date and in all probability not referring to the ὀκτώβολος εἰσφορά but to another tax, gives a list of twenty-three payers of this tax. At the head of the list stands Mnasistratus, whom Wilhelm identifies with the man of the same name who figures so prominently in the inscription relating to the Mysteries of Andania.* His property, whatever his payments may have been, amounted certainly to a considerable sum (if we assume the same or approximately the same rate of tax as that of the ὀκτώβολος εἰσφορά, the value of his property was about 10 talents). The rest pay less, but the sums are large enough to suggest a property of about one talent in each case. Much the same impression is conveyed by the inscription of Andania quoted above (ll. 45 ff.), according to which candidates for the commission of five who administered the revenues of the Mysteries are required to have a minimum property qualification of one talent. And, lastly, the existence of large estates at Messene is attested by the mention in the second Messenian inscription (ll. 24 ff.) of two estates (named Ἱππικά and Καλλίστα) estimated at more than eight talents, and one (named Αὐτομεία) estimated at more than two.

It seems certain from all this evidence that wealth was concentrated in the hands of a few very rich men (Aristocles, Mnasistratus, and the owners of the estates mentioned above) and of a considerable group of well-to-do people, while small landowners and artisans with a low census had a small share in the total—a concentration which appears to have begun in the preceding period (if not earlier) and is also found in other parts of the Hellenistic world in the period we are discussing. It is equally characteristic of the conditions of the time that at Messene a few very rich citizens tower high above the rest and play a leading part in the political and religious life of the country.

Among these rich citizens Italian settlers play a certain part. Νεμέριος, the owner of the large estate called Αὐτομεία, which he had acquired from a noble Messenian, Damion, was

* *S.I.G.*³ 736.

probably* the father of the two brothers Νεμέριος καὶ Μάαρκος Κλοάτιοι Νεμερίου, the well-known bankers of Gythium, of whom more will be said below. It is interesting to find that the Italian landowners enjoyed no privileges in respect of taxation and extraordinary contributions.

Of the economic situation of the lower classes in Messenia we have little information. In Messenia slave labour was of considerable importance. In the second Messenian inscription (1. 38 f.) we find mention of slaves serving as rowers, and of certain χειροτέχναι λειτουργοῦντες, who may also have been slaves; and in the Andania inscription there is a special chapter on the φύγιμον (*asylia* for runaway slaves, δραπέται).† But slave labour did not predominate. In the second Messenian inscription (ll. 11 and 17) there is reference to a special class of τεχνῖται who were not members of the φυλαί and were taxed separately. Whether free agricultural labour was also included in this class is uncertain.

The Messenian inscriptions testify beyond doubt to the existence of some measure of prosperity in the country in the late second century B.C. The same impression is derived from the study of an inscription of the same period from Thuria in Messenia. This little agricultural community was not suffering from scarcity of grain, like so many other cities of the Hellenistic world at that time. There appears to have been grain in abundance, and the only question was how to dispose of it most profitably for the community.[21]

The inscriptions of Messene are a rare exception. No similar evidence exists for the rest of Greece. There is, however, no reason to think that the conditions at Messene were exceptional. There was probably therefore a similar recovery in the other parts of Greece. It is well known that at Athens the return of prosperity led to a splendid revival of religious life. The evidence concerning this has been repeatedly collected. Parallels from other parts of Greece are not numerous. The case of Thessaly has been adduced, and I may mention also the fine Heroon of Calydon which has recently been excavated and which in all probability was restored and embellished about the end of the second century.

* Wilhelm, loc. cit., p. 63. † *S.I.G.*³ 736, ll. 80 ff.

Of no less importance than the material recovery was the psychological recovery that accompanied it. Self-confidence and pride in the glorious past are among the principal traits in the mentality of the time, especially at Athens. It is no accident that in an Amphictionic decree of 125 B.C. Athens is praised as 'established leader of all things deemed good by men'* and held up to general admiration as 'having converted men from a savage to a more civilized life',† and as the founder of social relations.‡ The whole of the decree deserves careful reading.²²

It is worthy of note that the ideas expressed by the Amphictions were shared by the Romans and became a commonplace among the leaders of the Roman educated classes. I may quote the famous utterance of Cicero: 'here are the Athenians, in whose country, we think, were born culture (*humanitas*), learning, religion, fruits of the earth (*fruges*), law and statutes (*iura, leges*), to spread from here over the world'.§

Returning to the material conditions in Greece, I may recall the fact, already mentioned, that the coinage of the Achaean League remained abundant during this period down to the fateful year 146 B.C. This coinage, like the contemporary coinage of Athens, is an excellent reflection of the status of Greece. Without any artistic value, elegant but lacking in individuality, it jealously adheres to old designs and to the venerable cults of the past.

But the picture of prosperity that I have drawn is not without its darker side. The primeval conflict between rich and poor became more accentuated than ever. Property was increasingly concentrated in the hands of the few richer families, while the poor lost all hope of an improvement in their lot and became entirely dependent on the favour of their employers. Freed from the spectre of social revolution by the intervention of the Romans, emboldened by the terrible chastisement which these had inflicted on the proletariat in the last Achaean war, the richer classes were less ready to compromise than ever. They felt themselves masters of the situation and acted

---

* ἁ[πάντων τῶν ἐν ἀνθρ]ώποις ἀγαθῶν ἀρχη[γὸς κατασταθε]ίς.
† ἐγ μὲν τοῦ θηριώδους βίου μετήγαγεν τοὺς ἀνθρώπους εἰς ἡμερότη[τα.
‡ τ[ῆ]ς πρὸς ἀλλήλ[ους κοινωνί]ας.
§ Cic. *pro Flacco*, 26 (62), cf. *De leg.* ii. 14. 36 and *Verr.* v. 187.

accordingly. The proletariat no longer counted as a political force and could be disregarded by the masters of the hour.

We know, for example, how strong the oligarchs were at Athens and how power was practically concentrated there in the hands of a few families, a situation which led to disturbances in the city and was made, as we shall see later, the pretext for Roman intervention. It also explains the readiness of the democratic party to side with Mithridates. No less characteristic of the conditions in Greece, and illustrative of the kind of régime that the Romans patronized, was the deplorable occurrence at Delphi in 125 B.C. (recorded in several inscriptions), which led to the intervention of the Roman Senate, of the governor of Macedonia, and of the Amphictiony. It is a story of maladministration and dishonesty on the part of the citizens who were in charge of the funds and revenues of the Delphian temple. The quarrel that arose on the subject was a domestic affair between two groups of local political leaders and was probably ended by a compromise. In itself the incident is of little importance, but it lifts a corner of the veil from the picture of life in Greece and reveals it in a sorry aspect. It is no hazardous conjecture that instances of similar malpractices by the ruling oligarchies occurred in other cities and sanctuaries in this period.[23]

The situation of the lower classes was made worse by the abundance of cheap slave labour, a phenomenon connected with the new growth of piracy and the active traffic in slaves in the island of Delos (of which I shall speak in greater detail presently). The main stream of slaves, it is true, went to Italy. The Italian capitalists were much richer than the few well-to-do *bourgeois* who survived in Greece. But some of the slaves from the East and elsewhere sold at Delos certainly came to Greece. Witness the two revolts of slaves in Attica (of 134/3 B.C. and between 104 and 100 B.C.), contemporary with those in Sicily, Italy, Delos, and Macedonia. The number involved in the first revolt in Attica (1,000 men) was not large, but it must be remembered that it was the slaves of Laurion alone who took an active part in it. The revolt of 104–100 B.C. was more serious and dangerous. These outbreaks, in my opinion, must be ascribed not to a kind of mental epidemic affecting the masses of slaves both in the West and in the East, but to the growing discontent of the lower classes in general. It was the slaves rather than the free proletariat who broke out in Attica, because it was easier for them than for the rest of the discontented elements to arrive at a common understanding. It should be noted that the free tenants and small landowners in Sicily were in sympathy with the slaves, and that at about the same time the risings of Andriscus in Macedonia, Aristonicus in Pergamon, and perhaps Saumacus in the Bosporus, were supported not only by slaves but in all probability by all sections of the lower classes—slaves, bondmen, and probably the city proletariat also. Each was a combined nationalist and social movement, and so was the general upheaval stirred up by Mithridates in Greece and Asia Minor.[24]

It is not surprising therefore to hear of the occurrence from time to time in certain Greek cities of outbursts of popular discontent and of attempts at political and social revolution on old-fashioned lines. We know very little about them, but they were probably more frequent than the meagre evidence would lead us to believe. One of them is revealed by an inscription found at Dyme, a letter to the city from Q. Fabius Maximus (Eburnus), consul in 116 B.C.* The populace rose against the propertied classes with elemental force. Under the leadership of three ringleaders the mob started a riot ($\tau a \rho a \chi \acute{\eta}$). The record offices with the documents kept in them were burnt in fierce rage. The cry was certainly for cancellation of debts ($\chi \rho \epsilon o \kappa o \pi \acute{\iota} a$) and of contracts ($\grave{a} \sigma u \nu a \lambda \lambda a \xi \acute{\iota} a$), a slightly modified version of the ancient slogan of Greek social revolutions, $\gamma \hat{\eta} s$ $\grave{a} \nu a \delta a \sigma \mu \acute{o} s$ and $\chi \rho \epsilon \hat{\omega} \nu \grave{a} \pi o \kappa o \pi \acute{\eta}$. New laws were drafted and no doubt adopted by the new 'democratic' government. But the rising was of course abortive. The Romans intervened and two of the ringleaders were executed, while the third was summoned to Rome. The governor of Macedonia took the revolution very seriously, investigated it thoroughly, and had recourse to stern repressive measures.[25]

While Greece was slowly recovering from the havoc brought by the wars of liberation and enslavement, MACEDONIA entered on a new period of its life. It suffered heavily during the war.

* *S.I.G.*³ 684.

Many men—and these the best—perished in the battles, and the country was devastated and exhausted by all sorts of requisitions.

After Pydna Macedonia in its turn received liberty from the Romans. But it was a peculiar liberty dictated by the desire to make the country as weak as possible. The Romans still felt an irrational dread of their old enemy. To prevent political recovery and consequent revenge various measures were adopted by the Senate and carried out by its representatives in Macedonia, some of them with slight modifications. The country was divided into four independent and theoretically 'free' regions, deprived of *ius commercii* with each other (so far as concerned land and houses), as well as of *ius conubii*. Some curious provisions were devised regarding the import of salt, which are difficult to interpret. Moreover, the Macedonians and the Roman *publicani* were forbidden to exploit the country's chief wealth, its still unexhausted mines of gold and silver and its famous forests. It was similarly forbidden to lease the former royal domains to rich Roman or Macedonian *conductores* for capitalistic development.* The *praedia rustica*† remained apparently in the hands of the small tenants.

Measures of this kind were of course futile, as the Roman Senate soon discovered. In 158 the working of the gold and silver mines was resumed. The revolt of Andriscus and of his two minor successors, who received valuable help from the Thracians, was certainly not merely the wild adventure of a pretender, but also the economic (and political) protest of a part of the Macedonian people against Roman domination. It was crushed within a year (149/148 B.C.) but certainly laid much of the country in ruins.[26]

The gradual organization of the Roman provincial government in Macedonia brought a certain measure of relief. But its northern neighbours, the Scordisci, the Dardanians, and the Thracians, were restless. We shall see later the active part taken in the second half of the second century B.C. by the Balkan Thracians in the political life of Asia Minor, first as bitter enemies of the last Attalids and later as supporters of Aristonicus. We have seen that Thracians were responsible for the partial and temporary success of Andriscus and of those

* Liv. xlv. 17–18; 29. 4–14; 32. 1–2 and 7.   † Ibid. 18. 4.

who succeeded him. Thereafter their raids and inroads were incessant. We know of one attack in 135 B.C., which was repulsed by M. Cosconius, and of several later. Destroying and pillaging, the 'barbarians' penetrated as far as the southern part of Macedonia. An inscription found at Lete describes one of these raids which occurred in 120/19 or 119/8 B.C.; Sex. Pompeius, the governor of Macedonia, was killed in it, and it was repulsed by his quaestor M. Annius. The Lete inscription gives a vivid picture of such a raid. Local militia were mobilized, the cities paying their ὀψώνια. In 107 B.C. a long struggle was brought to an end by a battle probably fought near Europus in Hemathia (or rather in Bottiaia), the Roman commander being M. Minucius. Further incursions are recorded in 101/100 B.C. and in 92 B.C., when the Maedi and Dardani penetrated as far as Epirus. We may imagine the effect of such raids upon the fields, gardens, and villages of the people. In such conditions it is impossible to suppose that the agricultural population of Macedonia enjoyed any prosperity in the late second and the early first century B.C.[27]

Conditions were better in the large coastal cities of Macedonia. THESSALONICE, now the capital of the Roman province, became a large and wealthy city. Strabo (vii. 7. 4, p. 323) says that 'it exceeds the other cities in population'.* In spite of the disturbed state of the Macedonian hinterland and of Thrace, it developed an active trade with Thrace and Illyria. This trade was partly in the hands of some rich and influential Italians, who settled at this time in the city and soon acquired wealth and a reputation that extended beyond their place of residence. We have some valuable information about one of these families, that of the Apustii. Two decrees of the city of Abdera reveal the activity of C. Apustius M. f. and his son P. Apustius, praising them highly for having in the course of their business (as ἐργάται) assured peace to the city and conferred other great benefits upon it.† The date of the two decrees is

---

* ἣ νῦν μάλιστα τῶν ἄλλων εὐανδρεῖ.

† Decree iii, ll. 36 ff.—in honour of the father—παραίτιον γενόμενον τῆς ἐλευ-θερίας τῆι πόλει ἡμῶ[ν καὶ ἄλλων μεγίστων δωρεῶν δο]θεισῶν ἡμῖν; cf. decree iv—in honour of the son—ll. 8 ff.: ἔδωκέν τε πολλὰ σ[ημεῖα ἐν καιροῖς ἀναγ-]|καίοις τῆς πρὸς τὸν δῆμο[ν εὐνοίας καὶ διετήρησεν]|ἡμᾶς ἐν εἰρήνηι.

PLATE LXXXV

1. The krater of Salpion here reproduced belongs to the group of the so-called Neo-Attic kraters which I have mentioned above in the description of Pl. LXXXIII. It is adorned with bas-reliefs of the same style and character as the craters from Mahdia. The scene represented is Dionysiac: the baby Dionysus is handed over to Nysa by Hermes. It is signed by Salpion, an Athenian artist of the first century B.C.: Σαλπίων | 'Αθηναῖος | ἐποίησε. The krater has been several times published and discussed; see the bibliographical references in A. Merlin and L. Poinssot, Cratères et candélabres, etc., p. 139, n. 2, and Lippold, P.W.K. i A. 2011. Photograph supplied by Alinari.

2. The well-known bronze herm here illustrated was found in the 'Villa dei papiri' near Herculaneum among other products of early and late Hellenistic art. It is a good copy of the head of the Doryphorus of Polyclitus. It is signed by Apollonius, son of Archias, the Athenian: 'Απολλώνιος 'Αρχίου 'Αθηναῖος ἐποίησε. On this artist see C. Robert, P.W.K. ii. 162, no. 123. His contemporary was Apollonius, son of Nestor, who made the torso of Belvedere and the bronze boxer of the Museo delle Terme Diocleziane; see bibliography in Schoenebeck's article quoted in note 13 to this chapter, p. 62, n. 1 of the article. The head has been several times published and discussed; see the short bibliography in Mostra Augustea di Romanità, Catalogo ii, p. 394, no. 33 m.

Photograph supplied by R. Soprintendenza delle Antichità, Naples.

I may emphasize again in this connexion how many were the products of Eastern, not only Athenian, artistic industry imported into Italy. I have mentioned the kraters and candelabra. A group of typical representatives of this class found chiefly in Italy, together with some of their metal counterparts, has been discussed recently by L. Curtius, Röm. Mitt. xlix (1934), pp. 268 ff. To the kraters and candelabra may be added copies of famous statues and bas-reliefs in bronze and marble, of which no. 2 of this plate is a good specimen, and copies of celebrated pictures (see next plate). I regret that lack of space prevents me from reproducing some specimens of silver plate of the late Hellenistic period. Many of them have been found in Italy and in the West in general, as constituent parts of certain treasures (for instance those of Boscoreale, the House of Menander in Pompeii, and Hildesheim), and as stray pieces. Some of them may have been made in Italy (for example at Tarentum), but many were certainly imported from the East. Such, in my opinion, was the origin of the treasure of the Casa di Menandro; see for a careful analysis of this treasure A. Maiuri, La Casa del Menandro e il suo tesoro di argenteria, 1933, and L. Curtius, loc. cit., pp. 282 ff.

PLATE LXXXV

2. Bronze copy of the head of the Doryphorus of Polyclitus.
Naples Museum

1. Marble krater of Salpion. Naples Museum

GREEK ARTISTS IN THE SERVICE OF ROME

PLATE LXXXVI

GREEK ARTISTS IN THE SERVICE OF ROME. PAINTED MARBLE PLATE
Naples Museum

PLATE LXXXVI

The marble plate with monochrome or oligochrome design reproduced in this plate was found in Herculaneum. In the same place were found four other plates of the same character. A sixth painted marble plate with the figure of Niobe was discovered in Pompeii. In the painting here shown five mythological figures are playing knuckle-bones (ἀστράγαλοι). The names of the girls are recorded by the artist: Hileaira, Aglaia, Niobe, Leto, Phoebe. To the left in the upper corner is the signature of the artist who made this rather free copy of an original of the fifth century B.C.: 'Ἀλέξανδρος 'Ἀθηναῖος ἔγραψε. I cannot here discuss this and similar copies of earlier paintings made by artists of the first century ʀ.c. The subject has already been frequently treated. The pictures belong to the same group as the so-called Neo-Attic bas-reliefs. In the first century B.c. and later these sculptural and pictorial copies were commonly used to decorate the rooms of houses owned by rich Romans. Quite recently a group of Neo-Attic bas-reliefs was found in a sumptuous house at Herculaneum *in situ*. For a more detailed description and bibliographical references see O. Elia, *Pitture murali e mosaici nel Museo Nazionale di Napoli*, 1932, pp. 32 ff. To her bibliography may be added the detailed analysis of the 'knucklebone players' by M. H. Swindler, *Ancient Painting*, 1929, pp. 323 ff., fig. 271. Photograph supplied by Alinari.

disputed. I see no reason for assigning them with Wilhelm to the time of the first Mithridatic war. It is more probable that they belong to the period when Abdera was slowly recovering from the harsh treatment that it had experienced during the Persean war at the hands of the Romans and was in danger of losing part of its territory to its rival, king Cotys. It is not unlikely that in these critical times the city suffered from internal troubles. However that may be, the Apustii were powerful enough to help the city in its difficulties, probably by material assistance and through their political influence. There is not the slightest doubt that they had had dealings with the city before, either of a commercial or of a banking character. The same Apustii had similar relations with Perinthus. One of their clan or one of their freedmen and agents died there.[28]

The Apustii of Thessalonice, their business activity, the active part which they took in the affairs of the Greek cities in which they settled or with which they stood in business relations, were no exception. Families of Italian origin appear in Greece in the second century in ever increasing numbers. It was a new phenomenon in the economic life of Greece, and merits attention. Its origin and its evolution are easy to understand.

The rapid development of prosperity in Italy during and after the Macedonian and Syrian wars, and the ever growing political influence of Rome in Greece and in the East revived the immemorial commercial and business relations between Italy and Greece, which had become less active in the fourth century B.C. and which had been almost completely interrupted at the time of the Punic wars. Large groups of Greeks and Italians from southern Italy took part in this intercourse. Many Italian *negotiatores* went to Greece in the train of the Roman armies, and became familiar with that country and the East and with the economic opportunities that they presented. Some of them, instead of returning to Italy, preferred to remain in Greece, to settle in Greek cities, to occupy themselves with Greek affairs, and gradually to become prominent and privileged members of some of the Greek communities. With the extension of Roman action in Greece, especially after the Persean war, and the subsequent Roman annexation of Macedonia, with which Epirus, Illyria, and Achaea were closely connected without becoming parts of the province of Macedonia, the number of these Italian emigrants rapidly grew, and their role in the economic life of Greece became increasingly important. In Greece they were called Romans ('Ρωμαῖοι), but a study of their names and connexions shows that most of them were South Italians. They came to Greece at a time when that country lay economically prostrate and exhausted, and when the Greek *bourgeoisie* (with few exceptions) was utterly ruined. It is not surprising that these immigrants, rich and thrifty as they were, found in Greece good opportunities to acquire land, to revive Greek banking, and to pick up the threads of Greek trade which had been disorganized as a result of war, revolution, and other calamities. These Italians, so far from being exploiters and oppressors (with the exception of a few *publicani* and their agents) were the men who helped Greece to her feet again, especially after the Persean war, and who were to a certain extent responsible for her economic revival in the second century B.C.

The Italian *negotiatores* took an energetic part not only in Greek business, but also in the political, religious, and social life of the various Greek cities of the mainland and of the islands. Being half-Greek, they easily adapted themselves to Greek life and Greek mentality and gradually became great local patriots. Some of them were more and some less prosperous; a few became very rich and influential, leaders of the social, religious, and municipal activities of their cities, though legally they remained 'Romans'. Our information about them comes to a large extent from inscriptions in their honour, praising them highly for various services rendered to divers communities, in which they resided or with which they had business connexions.

We possess only a few texts relating to the early period of Italian expansion in Greece. 'Roman' families appeared first in Illyria and later in Greece proper: Epirus, Thessaly, Boeotia. Many members of these are recorded in the Delphian proxeny lists. Somewhat later the first Italians appeared in the Cyclades and especially in Delos (on the rapid development of the Italian colony in the island and its causes, see *infra*). The spread of the Italians in Asia Minor will be dealt with later in this chapter. With the Apustii of Thessalonice may be compared the Vallii of Abdera, the Cloatii of Gythium in Laconia, who appear to have been already ancient residents there at the time when they are first brought to our notice, and the Aufidii Bassi, who are heard of both at Athens and in Tenos (later as residents in Delos).

It is worthy of note that the Italians who took part in this early expansion were probably occupied both with agriculture and with commerce (in the broad sense of this word, including banking). This is shown by the presence of Italians chiefly in the more fertile parts of Greece: Thessaly, where we have information of large groups of them settled in Larissa and Gonnus, Boeotia, and certainly also Messenia. In the Messenian inscriptions relating to the ὀκτώβολος εἰσφορά 'Roman' land-owners figure largely. They are mentioned in a manner which makes it improbable that they were new-comers. They were certainly established in Messenia for a considerable time.[29]

Not less flourishing than Thessalonice were the two important cities of MARONEA and THASOS, which were in effect cities of the new province of Macedonia closely connected with Amphipolis. Coins issued by the first Region of Macedonia and by Maronea and Thasos flooded the Balkan peninsula and became the main currency (n. 11 to this chapter). The frequency of these coins in the North testifies to an important trade between Macedonia and Thrace, mostly but not exclusively a trade in wine.[30]

Farther to the north, THRACE was in a state of unrest during the period we are considering. This is not the place to enter into the complicated and very little known history of what remained of the Scythian kingdom and of the various smaller and larger Thracian kingdoms. It will suffice for the present purpose to note that the second century was a time of misery and distress for all the Greek cities of the western and northern coasts of the Black Sea: Apollonia, Mesembria, Odessus, Callatis, Tomi, Istrus, Tyras, and Olbia.[31]

A set of inscriptions—unfortunately not exactly dated— gives a vivid picture of the sorry plight of these cities. Two long and detailed inscriptions found at ISTRUS, both of about the same time (end of the second century B.C.), one in honour of Aristagoras, son of Apaturius,* the other (still unpublished, perhaps somewhat earlier) in honour of Agathocles, son of Antiphilus, furnish information about the situation in this city. The first inscription (and the second depicts similar conditions) shows the city surrounded by enemies, suffering from shortage of food, its territory devastated, its citizens captured by the barbarians. The shortage of food made it necessary to import foodstuffs from outside, and we are not surprised to find such imports mentioned in an inscription recently discovered at Istrus. It is more surprising to gather from the same inscription that grain was imported into Istrus by a Carthaginian merchant.† Istrus was no exception. We find the same situation at TOMI vividly described in a decree in honour of certain citizens who had volunteered to act as guardians of the city, and in honour of their commanders.‡ I see no reason for assigning the inscription to the time of Byrebistas, since the name of Byrebistas does not appear in the document. These are the terms in which the city describes its situation: 'Whereas the people, perplexed and hard pressed in consequence of the circumstances of the time, were reduced to extreme despair and were above all anxious on account of the walls of the city, some having abandoned the city because of their discouragement, while the rest were unable to defend their fatherland owing to the pestilence and sickness that had developed . . . .'§ One sees the city threatened (probably besieged) by enemies, suffering from famine and epidemics, deserted by most of its citizens, unable to defend itself.

In the well-known decree in honour of Stratonax‖ and his

* *S.I.G.*³ 708.

† S. Lambrino, *Dacia*, iii–iv (1927–32), pp. 400 ff.

‡ *S.I.G.*³ 731; A. Wilhelm, *Wien. S.B.* ccxiv (1932), 4, p. 19 f.

§ i. 1 ff.: ἐπειδὴ διὰ τὰς τῶν καιρῶν περι[σ]τάσεις β[αρέως | ἀπ]ορῶν καὶ θλιβόμενος ὁ δῆμος ἐν τῆι μεγίστ[ηι καθέ|στ]η[κ]εν δυσελπιστίαι καὶ μάλιστα πάντων ἠγω[νία]κε | ὑπὲρ τοῦ περιβόλου τῆς πόλεως, τῶν μὲν διὰ τὴν ἀπ[ο]ρίαν ἐκλελοιπότων τὴν πόλιν, τῶν δὲ διὰ τὴν γενομένη[ν λοι]μικὴν περίστασιν καὶ τὰς ἀρρωστίας μὴ δυναμένων | [φυλ]άσσειν τὴν πατρίδα.

‖ E. Kalinka, *Denkm. aus Bulgarien*, 1906, p. 94; W. Crönert, *Jahreshefte*, xi (1908), Beibl., p. 105.

own city Apollonia, we have a description of similar conditions
at CALLATIS (before 100 B.C.) : a king besieges the city, Stratonax
mediates, and finally succeeds in helping the city, 'matters
being restored to their original position'.*

Nor were the citizens better off at OLBIA. In the decree in
honour of Niceratus, son of Papias,† the city is seen hard
pressed by its enemies and relying entirely on its courageous
and influential leader, who unfortunately was treacherously
killed by the enemy. The date of the inscription (before Mithridates took possession of the Crimea) may be inferred from the
mention of the settlement of affairs at Chersonesus by Niceratus, an event which could not possibly have occurred while
Mithridates controlled the place or soon after. It is not impossible that the inscription *S.I.G.*³ 707, which shows one of
the Pontic cities involved in a dangerous war ('Ολατικὸς πόλεμος),
comes from Olbia (end of the second century B.C.).³²

The situation of some other cities on the southern coast of
Thrace and on the Thracian Chersonese was not very different.
Some of them suffered heavily during the Persean war: ABDERA,
for example, was captured and pillaged by the Romans and its
population was sold into slavery.‡ A little later the city was
pleading before the Roman Senate for its territory, which (or
part of which) was claimed by the Thracian king Cotys.§
About 145 B.C. a certain Diegylis and his son Zibelmius, chiefs
of the Thracian tribe of the Kainoi, petty kings who had an
established reputation for cruelty even among their own
subjects, destroyed LYSIMACHEIA (cf. below, p. 801),‖. and
Attalus II had great difficulty in putting an end to their
exploits.¶³³

As a rule it was some very wealthy and prominent citizen
who came to the rescue of his city in an emergency. It
appears that in most of the Greek cities of Thrace wealth and

* I. 22: ἀ[ποκα|τ]ασταθέντων αὐτῶι τῶν πραγμά[των | ε]ἰς τὰν ἐξ ἀρχᾶς
διάθεσιν, cf. *S.I.G.*³ 1108, ll. 6 ff., and *A.-E. Mitt.* vi (1882), p. 10, n. 16.

† *S.I.G.*³ 730; *I.O.S.P.E.* i². 34.

‡ See above, p. 739 and n. 1, cf. p. 758 and n. 27.

§ *S.I.G.*³ 656. The date of the inscription is uncertain; a king Cotys was
active in Thrace not only during the Persean war but much later, about
100 B.C.

‖ App., *Mithr.* 6.   ¶ Diod. xxxiii. 14, 15; Pomp. Trog., *prol.* xxxvi.

political influence were concentrated in the hands of a few men, who took the lead in municipal affairs and were in relations both with other cities and with the barbarian chiefs, who were at once overlords and enemies. Some of these uncrowned leaders of the cities were foreigners (for instance the Apustii of Thessalonice); most of them were natives of the cities. They were sometimes rich and powerful enough to have their own private army and their own navy. In addition to those mentioned above I may recall the case of Python, the rich citizen of Abdera ('of eminent reputation', says Diodorus) who during the siege of his city by the Romans and Eumenes II (170 B.C.), which ended in its capture and shameful ill treatment by Hortensius, defended the most important part of the fortifications 'with two hundred of his own slaves and freedmen' (διὰ δούλων ἰδίων καὶ ἀπελευθέρων διακοσίων) and then betrayed the city.* Equally remarkable was the position of the Olbian Posideus, the commercial agent of Scilurus, the Scythian king of the Crimea and suzerain of Olbia, in the late second century B.C., mentioned above (Ch. V, p. 675). Inscriptions from Olbia† and three from Neapolis, the capital of Scilurus in the Crimea,‡ testify to his power and wealth. In one of these § he appears as the conqueror of the Satarchaioi, the dangerous native pirates of the Crimea. I may refer in this connexion to an inscription from Callatis, a decree by a *thiasos* in honour of a man who built a war-ship from his own resources, kept the city's harbour and coast free from attack, and finally presented the ship to the city.||

The energy of their own leaders, however, did not suffice to protect the Pontic cities, and these had no choice but to appeal first to Mithridates and later to the Roman governors of Macedonia and Illyria in order to save themselves from imminent capture by their dreaded neighbours. It is interesting to note in this connexion the recently published fragments of a treaty of alliance between Rome and Callatis.¶ Freed by Lucullus

---

* Diod. xxx. 6; Liv. xliii. 4.
‡ Ibid. 670–2, cf. 673.
|| *A.-E. Mitt.* vi (1882), p. 10, no. 16.
¶ M. S. Lambrino, *C. R. Acad. Inscr.* 1933, pp. 278 ff.; A. Passerini, *Athen.* xiii (1935), pp. 57 ff.

† *I.O.S.P.E.* i². 77 and 168.
§ Ibid. 672, cf. *S.E.G.* iii. 606.

from the domination of Mithridates in 72/1 B.C.,* all the cities of the western coast of the Euxine became allies of Rome, in the hope of procuring some measure of security. But between the end of the Macedonian proctectorate and the time of Mithridates the Pontic cities had experienced great hardships and misery. They were, however, able to hold out and they still had among their citizens men of great wealth who were able to help them. If it is asked whence this wealth was derived, the answer is undoubtedly that its source was trade, which was still active enough to sustain the cities. I may refer again to Posideus of Olbia. His wealth was certainly founded on the trade that he carried on in close association with Scilurus and his Crimean kingdom and the Rhodians. It must be borne in mind that behind the line of the Greek cities, the powerful and independent native kingdoms were developing their production and were eager to export it and purchase foreign wares. No doubt Scilurus in the Crimea, and his Scythian, Celtic, and Thracian contemporaries in the Balkan peninsula, would have preferred to gain the complete mastery over the Greek cities of the western and northern coasts, in the same way as the Pontic kings became masters of the cities of the southern coast. And this they attempted to do, especially in the Crimea (see below) ; but they were not strong enough to achieve it. Meanwhile they were satisfied with keeping the Greek cities in constant terror, holding them to ransom and devastating their territories. At the same time, for the export of their own wares and the purchase of Greek wine and products of Greek industry they had recourse to the services of some wealthy merchants in the Greek cities. Witness the spread of Macedonian, Maronean, and Thasian coins and local imitations of them in the late second and early first centuries all over the Balkan peninsula and far into the petty Celtic, Thracian, and Scythian kingdoms of Pannonia, Moesia, and Thrace. This eastern current of Greek trade, which was in the hands of the Macedonian and Pontic cities (including Abdera and the cities of the Thracian Chersonese), met in the Danube region two other

---

* Eutr. vi. 10 ; Ruf. 3 ; Appian, *Ill.* 30, cf. the inscription of Apollonia, Chr. M. Danoff, *Jahreshefte*, xxx (1936), Beibl., pp. 87 ff. and *Bull. Inst. Arch. Bulg.* xii (1939), pp. 237 ff.

currents of trade, which became ever stronger as time passed: that from Apollonia and Dyrrhachium (characterized by their local coins minted according to the Roman standard), and that from Italy through Aquileia (*aes signatum* and the Roman silver coins).[34]

The situation of the BOSPORAN KINGDOM and its cities and of Chersonesus and its dependencies in the Crimea was the same *mutatis mutandis* as that of the cities of the 'left' or western coast of the Euxine. The Bosporan kingdom was hard pressed both by the Scythians of the Crimea and by the Sarmatians of the Kuban and Don prairies, the Scythians being the nearer and the more dangerous enemies. The power of the Crimean Scythians constantly increased under the rule of Scilurus and of his son Palacus. The same is true of the Taurians, the vassals of Scilurus. Their combined pressure made the situation of Chersonesus almost desperate. In their distress the Chersonesites appealed to Mithridates, who saved them from the Scythians, only to make them practically his own subjects. The fate of the Bosporan kingdom was similar, but before it became a Mithridatic province it experienced a couple of years of Scythian domination. We may infer from the scanty evidence that the last Spartocid Paerisades had at his court a young Scythian, Saumacus by name, probably not his slave but a youth of noble family educated in his house, perhaps as a hostage. This Saumacus took advantage of the troubled times of the struggle between Mithridates and Palacus to foment a revolt in Bosporus. It is not easy to determine what kind of revolt it was. Risings were common in the Hellenistic world at this time both against foreign domination and against the oppression of the poor by the rich; those of Andriscus in Macedonia, of Aristonicus in Pergamon, the native revolts in Egypt, the nationalist movements in the kingdom of the Seleucids, may suggest that the rising of Saumacus was of the same type.

It must be remembered that the cities of the Bosporan kingdom were no longer what they had been. They were gradually losing their Greek character and becoming increasingly Iranized. We have evidence of this both in a few literary texts (especially in Lucian's *Toxaris*, derived from Hellenistic sources, and in other fragments of Hellenistic works, both history and fiction) and in the archaeological material. It is clear that while fresh immigrants from Greece were few, there were at that time a considerable number of Iranians—Scythians and Sarmatians—who were prepared to settle as citizens in the Bosporan cities. These immigrants no doubt became hellenized. But they nevertheless effected a considerable change in the Hellenism of the Bosporan cities, giving it an increasingly Iranian aspect. With the richer and nobler settlers there came in all probability large groups of workmen of all kinds who mixed with the older proletariat of the cities and modified its character substantially.

On the other hand, documents of the later period, and the analogy of Pontus, Cappadocia, Armenia, and Parthia, make it certain that the economic and social structure of the Bosporan kingdom was based on an aristocracy of large landowners, of whom the richest was the king (above, p. 595 f.). Next to the king came the temples. The large estates of these landowners were tilled and their flocks tended by the older inhabitants of the Crimea and the Taman peninsula whom the Greek settlers found here and whom they conquered. These native tribes performed the same functions for the neighbours of the Bosporan kingdom, the Sarmatians of the Kuban valley and the Scythians of the Crimea. They were not slaves of their overlords; they certainly belonged to the class of *laoi* or bondsmen who were a characteristic feature of the Oriental world. We know little about them, but it may be supposed that their Hellenization was slight and that their mentality was nearer to that of their Iranian than of their Greek masters. Like their fellow bondsmen in the other Hellenistic monarchies, they resented their oppression by foreigners and were ready to revolt if they found an efficient and popular leader.

We may therefore conjecture that Saumacus, who may have enjoyed the support of the Crimean Scythians, became leader of the Iranized elements of the Bosporan kingdom, especially of the bondsmen of the country, and intended to replace the Spartocids by a Scythian dynasty. The situation was the same *mutatis mutandis* as we have observed in the Balkan peninsula. The difference was that in the Bosporus the change came from within, not from without. While it was the Romans who suppressed the similar revolt of Andriscus, it was Mithridates who terminated the short-lived domination of Saumacus at Panticapaeum.[35]

II. RHODES, DELOS, AND THE OTHER ISLANDS

The end of the Persean war was the beginning of a new phase in the history of the Aegean. In the period before that war RHODES had been predominant there both commercially and politically (above, pp. 676 ff.). It had controlled the most important Aegean islands, and with their help and the resources derived from its Carian and Lycian dominions and from its transit trade it had maintained a large and efficient navy. By means of this it had curbed piracy in the Aegean, not allowing the chief pirates—the Cretans—to disturb the peace to an extent that would injure the commercial activities of the Greek world.[36]

The economic and political sanctions imposed on Rhodes directly and indirectly by the Romans—the creation of a free port at Delos and the destruction of the Rhodian Empire in Anatolia—made it difficult for the island to carry on to the full its policy of preserving peace in the Aegean. It lost its revenue from its Carian and Lycian possessions (120 talents from Caunus and Stratonicea alone) and perhaps, to some extent, from its Aegean allies, while the revenue from its transit trade fell catastrophically.* Some modern historians are sceptical about the figures quoted by the Rhodian ambassadors at Rome —a fall in customs or harbour duties from one million Rhodian drachmas to 150,000; they regard them as grossly exaggerated by the envoys for the purpose of their plea or believe that the text is corrupt. I cannot share in this scepticism. I cannot imagine that the Rhodians would produce before the Senate figures not based on, and not supported by, documents. Nor is there any necessity to believe the text to be corrupt. The Rhodians would not have insisted so strongly on this point if the consequences of the Roman sanctions had not been detrimental to the prosperity of the island.

The impoverishment of the Rhodian State and its loss of active Roman support rendered necessary a considerable change

* Polyb. xxx. 31.

in its foreign policy and a certain readjustment of its finances (we know practically nothing about the latter, but such a readjustment was inevitable and was certainly carried out). Nevertheless, impoverished as it was, Rhodes, now connected with Rome (after 164 B.C.) by a formal alliance, never completely lost its control of the Aegean Sea and of Aegean commerce. Rhodes and Pergamon, with which State Rhodes was in friendly relations, were the only powers able to maintain a comparatively strong navy and to carry out, in the measure of their capacity, the policing of the sea. Athens, though an important commercial city, had no navy. Next to Pergamon and Rhodes came the free cities of Cyzicus and Byzantium and some of the Pontic cities. Rome never kept a fleet permanently in Aegean waters and relied 'upon the Greek navies in case of urgent necessity. We are therefore not surprised to learn that it was Rhodes and Attalus II who made a combined effort to put an end to Cretan piracy, which had probably revived after the Persean war. The struggle lasted for a certain time (155–153 B.C.) and was marked by devastating Cretan raids on some of the islands of the Aegean. The situation was sufficiently serious to make the Rhodians solicit help from the Achaeans, but this was refused. It is possible that the war was ended by Roman diplomatic intervention. Whether it resulted in a diminution of Cretan piracy we do not know.[37]

We are less well informed regarding the naval side of the war between Attalus II and Prusias II of Bithynia* which broke out about the same time as the Cretan war and may have been in some way connected with it. We know that it was waged both by land and sea. It must be remembered that Bithynia, after the time of Nicomedes I and Prusias I, had some fairly good harbours and a strong navy (it was rich in forests).† We know little of the naval operations of Prusias, except that once a fleet of his was destroyed by a storm in the Sea of Marmora.‡ It was probably engaged in a raid on the Pergamene coast. In retaliation a joint naval expedition of the three leading maritime powers of the Aegean, Pergamon, Cyzicus, and Rhodes, proceeded to the Hellespont and attacked some of the maritime

* Diod. xxxi. 35; Polyb. xxxiii. 12 and 13. Cf. below, p. 800 f.
† See above, pp. 566 ff..   ‡ Diod. xxxi. 35.

cities of Prusias; five of the Rhodian ships which were fighting against the Cretans were detached for this purpose. This may suggest that Prusias, perhaps in alliance with the Cretans, was interfering, as Byzantium had done before him, with the freedom of trade in the Straits and the Propontis. It should be noticed

FIG. 7.   A man-of-war in the Aegean in late Hellenistic times. One of the three ships scratched on a wall of an *exedra* of the house of Dionysus at Delos (*Délos*, viii. 1, pp. 203 ff., figs. 86 and 87). The ship is certainly a war-ship. Men-of-war were frequent visitors to the harbour of Delos.

that Prusias was in cordial relations with some of the Cretan cities. One of them—Aptera on the north coast—paid high honours to him and to his ambassadors, citizens of the maritime cities of Bithynia, some of them hellenized Thracians.* Alliances with pirates, it may be remarked, were not uncommon.[38]

Rhodes had likewise ground for concern in the growth of Cilician piracy (see below). Strabo† states explicitly that for political reasons she took no measures against it in the early period of its development. This statement implies that Rhodes was still regarded as the chief guardian of the safety of the seas.

* *O.G.I.* 341.   † xiv. 5. 2, p. 669.

When the Cilician pirates became a great danger both to the Greeks and to Rome, it was probably on the initiative of the Rhodians, or at least with their active support (Rhodian ambassadors were in Rome when the law was voted), that Rome endeavoured to bring about a kind of common action by all the Eastern Mediterranean States—both cities and monarchies—in favour of the safety of the Eastern seas. Rome of course had chiefly in view the interests of the Romans, Latins, and Italians who at that time were occupied in business in the East. We still possess the second half (?) of a law voted at Rome for the purpose of this joint action, assigning an active part therein to the Rhodians. Rhodian ambassadors were to deliver messages concerning the law and probably the text of the law itself to the kings of Cyprus, Cyrenaica, Egypt, and Syria, and it was provided in particular that the ambassadors of Rhodes in Rome should receive a special hearing in the Roman Senate whenever they had to report on matters dealt with in the law. Here again Rhodes appears as the most active of the Eastern powers interested in the suppression of piracy; she was completely free from the suspicion, of which there is mention in the law as regards the Eastern kings, of helping the pirates by giving them the use of harbours.[39] It was probably in the interests of order in the Aegean that the Rhodians kept on good terms with Mithridates in his early years, and that later, as faithful allies of Rome, they vigorously and successfully resisted the fierce onslaught made by Mithridates in co-operation with the pirates.[40]

We shall see later that at least until the time of Cassius Rhodes was in possession of a well-organized navy and was regarded as one of the chief naval powers of the dying Hellenistic world. In consequence it retained its contact with Caria, once its own province, and its prestige in that country. The Rhodian rule in Caria had been harsh and had made heavy demands on the Carian cities. These had had to pay a heavy price for the military protection they received. Yet some of these cities after the recovery of their liberty regretted the time of Rhodian domination. The weaker cities, deprived of the support of Rhodes, were bound either to fall an easy prey to the warlike tribes of the Carian mountains (those which later supported Aristonicus), or to become practically subject cities of their stronger and richer neighbours. Such at least is the impression derived from scattered documents found in Caria. Ceramus, for example (between 167 and 133), appealed to Rhodes and begged for its alliance, and in this way secured safety (ἀσφάλεια) for the citizens and other residents in the city and the χώρα. We do not know exactly who it was that threatened the security of Ceramus. L. Robert suggests that the oppression came from the stronger city of Stratonicea, with which (probably) Ceramus had for a time been linked in a sympolity (συμπολιτεία). A similar situation existed (at about the same time) at Mylasa and Euromus, as set forth in an inscription found at Mylasa. A συμπολιτεία had been made, some time in the late second century B.C., between the two cities. Before this, Euromus had apparently been involved in some hostilities with Heraclea by Latmus, and Heraclea had taken possession of certain property belonging to the city and to some private citizens, a citizen of Euromus having been even kidnapped and abducted to Myndus. The stronger Mylasa gave protection to its new associate. Another (very fragmentary) inscription, this time of Euromus, perhaps later than the first, makes mention of troubles between Euromus and Mylasa and of appeals made by Euromus to Rome (?) and to the Rhodians. These documents show the disturbed conditions prevailing in Caria after its liberation and the regard in which the Rhodians were held as arbiters and supporters of the oppressed.[41]

We have only slight knowledge regarding the volume and the character of the Rhodian transit trade. I have discussed the evidence which refers to it above and I have mentioned the stamped jar-handles of Rhodes and Cnidus, and the problems connected with them.[42] One of the most important of these problems is that of their respective dates. A full catalogue of Rhodian stamps will certainly help us to establish their chronology. Some progress has been made in this direction. We are able to date a considerable group of stamps found at Pergamon (220 to 180). Another group of stamps found at Carthage is certainly earlier than the year of the destruction of the city. Thus we have some indications with regard to those stamps which belong to the period between 220 and 146 B.C. We are able also to recognize in a general way those stamps which are earlier than 220 or later than 146. But there is much uncertainty about the latter groups and they do not help us to estimate the comparative volume and geographical range of the trade of Rhodes before and after the time of its commercial hegemony. We require comparative statistics of the various stamps for each place where Rhodian stamps have been found in order to determine whether modern scholars are right in assuming that the Rhodian stamps of the period 220 to 146 are the most common stamps in all the centres of Rhodian commercial activity.[43]

As things stand, we must confine ourselves to some very general statements. It appears, firstly, that Rhodian commerce did not stop abruptly after 167 B.C.; Rhodian commercial relations with Carthage, for instance, were probably as active after 167 B.C. as before that date. Secondly, that Rhodian commerce endured at least until the end of the first century B.C. (probable date of the latest stamps) and very likely beyond it; it must be remembered that if no Rhodian stamped jar-handles are found of later date than the first century B.C., this must not necessarily be ascribed to the diminished volume or changed character of Rhodian trade, but in all probability to the adoption of a different method of stamping the jars or to the total discontinuance of the practice. Thirdly, that Rhodian commercial relations continued in all probability to be as wide as before, though the volume of trade may have diminished. This is shown by the discovery of Rhodian stamped jar-handles in comparatively late levels in various cities of the East, for example at Gerasa.

In any case the stamped jars indicate that Rhodes, even after 167 B.C., continued to be an important commercial centre, and their testimony is supported by some occasional literary and epigraphical evidence. I have pointed out that Rhodian influence was strongly felt in the Crimea in the second half of the second century. I referred to the activity of Posideus, an Olbian who was an intermediary between Rhodes and the Scythian kingdom of Scilurus and Palacus. His devotion to Rhodian cults, shown in his dedications in the capital of Scilurus, led older scholars to believe that he himself was a

Rhodian. There is no doubt that the trade of Rhodes with the Crimea was chiefly in grain.[44]

Similar connexions existed between Rhodes and Pergamon. Polybius[*] tells us that Eumenes II, probably not long before his death, gave Rhodes 280,000 *medimni* of grain, the proceeds of the sale of the grain to be lent out at interest, and the income to be applied to the payment of the salaries of teachers and tutors in the Rhodian gymnasia. The gift was probably not made solely with a charitable intention, but was designed to show that the period of rivalry and hostility between Rhodes and Pergamon[†] was at an end, and that Pergamon was once more prepared to make use of Rhodes as a clearing-house for the products of its flourishing agriculture and industry. I am inclined to place the same interpretation on the similar acts of Demetrius, king of Syria.[‡][45]

We may infer therefore that the creation of the free port of Delos did not oust Rhodes from its position as a clearing-house for the internal and international trade of Greece, especially in respect of the grain trade. It is highly probable that while the Roman sanctions undermined the prosperity and the political importance of the State, they did not affect to any large extent the prosperity of the Rhodian citizens. Indeed the latter, very soon after Pydna, were confirmed in their rights to private property situated in the former Rhodian dominions in Asia Minor.[§] From this it is a plausible inference that, while the State of Rhodes was considerably impoverished, the Rhodian citizens retained their former prosperity at least until the time of Cassius. They probably succeeded in adjusting their banking and commercial activities to the changed conditions.

The principal change, in my opinion, was a certain restriction of the scope of Rhodian trade. While Rhodes retained its prominence in the grain trade and in the trade between the States of Greece (a field in which its new rivals, the Italians and the Syrians, were not interested) it was probably fast losing its former predominance in the traffic between the East and the West, especially in goods brought by caravan. In addition, the important traffic in slaves had passed from its hands.

[*] xxxi. 31 (Loeb).   [†] Polyb. xxvii. 7. 5.
[‡] Diod. xxxi. 36.   [§] 163 B.C., Polyb. xxxi. 4.

This and the caravan goods trade were now almost completely monopolized by the Delian merchants—most of them Italians and Orientals. Italians, it should be observed, hardly ever figure, and Syrian and Phoenician merchants only rarely, in inscriptions relating to the foreign population of Rhodes, especially in the late second century B.C. This evidence, though negative, is conclusive. Our information about the population of Rhodes is unusually good, and the absence of Italians among the hundreds of foreigners resident there cannot be regarded as an accident.

While Rhodes made every effort to adjust itself to the changed conditions of political and economic life in the Greek world, DELOS, a creation of these new conditions, developed into a community of a peculiar character, unique in the ancient world.[46]

This exceptional development will be better understood if I recall certain notable features in the economic history of the period that followed Pydna. At first no important change was apparent. Delos passed from a position of independence to that of an Athenian cleruchy and was declared a free port; this affected the prosperity of Rhodes, but otherwise brought about no radical change in the economy of the Hellenistic world.

Certain new economic factors, however, became in time increasingly conspicuous and contributed to bring about an entirely novel situation. Of these factors the most important was the growing predominance of Italy in the economic system of the Mediterranean. I shall return to this subject later. It will be sufficient to say that Italy in the second century B.C. became the most important purchaser of Hellenistic goods, and at the same time began to compete with the Hellenistic countries in the field of production.

The social and economic reconstruction of Italy gave rise to a demand for various commodities which had to be imported from the East, such as products of Hellenistic art and industry and Oriental caravan goods, in ever increasing quantities. Moreover, a great deal of slave labour was urgently needed for the agricultural and industrial development of the country. Slave labour was plentiful at the time of Rome's eastern

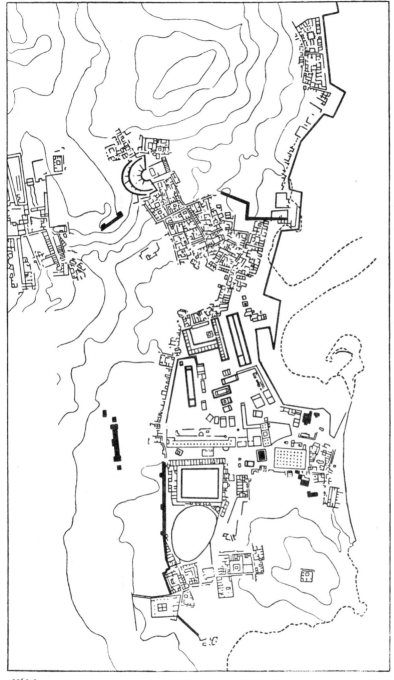

Fig. 8. Plan of the city and sanctuary of Delos (P. Roussel, *Délos, colonie athénienne*, 1916).

N

PLATE LXXXVII

1. The sacred harbour of Delos with the adjoining buildings of the sanctuary. Cf. the general plan of Delos (Fig. 8, p. 779).

2. The commercial harbour of Delos with the landing place and the adjoining storehouses.

Photographs supplied by R. Demangel, Director of the French School at Athens.

On the harbours of Delos and their history, J. Paris, 'Contributions à l'étude des ports antiques du monde grec', *B.C.H.* xxxix (1915), pp. 5 ff., and xl (1916), pp. 5 ff.; K. Lehmann-Hartleben, 'Die antiken Hafenanlagen des Mittelmeeres', *Klio*, Beih. xiv (N. F. i), 1923, pp. 152 ff. and pl. xxiv; P. Roussel, *Délos*, 1925, pp. 35 ff.: Le Port, l'Entrepôt et la Ville de Délos. Cf. below, Ch. VIII, n. 8.

PLATE LXXXVII

I

I

DELOS IN THE SECOND AND FIRST CENTURIES B.C.

wars; it became less abundant later. But the demand for it constantly increased, especially for Oriental slaves possessing some knowledge of agriculture, cattle-breeding, and industrial processes, or at least better acquainted with these than the Western slaves.[47]

A second novelty in the economic and particularly the commercial life of the Hellenistic world of the second century B.C., a phenomenon already referred to (p. 701 ff.) and of which I shall have more to say later in this chapter (p. 861 ff.), was the rapid development of Syrian trade after the time of Antiochus III. Arabian and Indian goods were now concentrated to a large extent in the hands of Syrian and Phoenician merchants. Some of these goods went to the harbours of Asia Minor overland, but the rest were in the hands of these merchants and were carried by sea. This sea route, after the Pergamene kingdom had come to an end (133 B.C.), became the main route of Syrian commerce. To the trade in these commodities the merchants of Syria and Phoenicia soon added a steadily growing trade in Oriental slaves, who were in great demand now that Cretan piracy was in its decline. The supply of slaves in Syria was abundant, for political anarchy prevailed there and dynastic, internal, and foreign wars were of constant occurrence. Moreover, in the troubled conditions of Syrian life, the kidnapping of slaves by organized robber bands became a profitable profession.

But the Italian and Sicilian demand for slaves could not be satisfied by Syria alone. As mentioned above, the supply of slaves from Cretan sources was diminishing in consequence mainly of the efforts of Rhodes. Moreover, the kidnapping and selling into slavery of free Greek citizens was arousing an ever growing indignation all over Greece. The result was that in the early period of the Roman control of the Aegean piratical raids on the shores of Greece and Asia Minor and on the islands of the Aegean became less frequent. We have no statistical data to prove this, but it is significant that inscriptions mentioning piratical raids, kidnappings, and so forth, which were common until the second Macedonian war, become scarcer after Cynoscephalae, with temporary revivals about the time of Pydna and during the second Cretan war. It must, however, be borne in mind that exactly dated inscriptions of this type are comparatively rare.[48]

A compensation for the loss of the Cretan slave-supply was furnished by the slave-dealers in Asia Minor. The revolt of Aristonicus produced large numbers of slaves. After this war the new masters of Asia Minor—the tax-farmers of the new province—appear to have taken an active part in the slave trade. Their participation is expressly stated in the well-known reply of Nicomedes III when he was asked to send troops to C. Marius during the Cimbrian war. His answer was that he had nobody to send, since the majority of his subjects had been carried off by the *publicani* and sold into slavery. It is not easy to understand how the *publicani* could carry off the subjects of an allied king, and it is highly probable that it was not the *publicani* themselves, but the warlike and hostile neighbours of the Bithynians, the professional robbers of Mysia, Phrygia, and especially of Galatia and Pontus, who did this under the benevolent eye of the Roman governor of Asia and with the co-operation of the *publicani*.

The slave trade organized by the *publicani* may have found a further source of supply in the willingness of the kings, the chief priests, and the feudal landlords of Bithynia, Pontus, Cappadocia, and Armenia to dispose of some of their bondsmen. In these countries, only slightly and superficially affected by Greek civilization and Greek ideas, the position of the *laoi* had probably changed very little in comparison with pre-Hellenistic times. While in Egypt and Syria during the reign of Philadelphus the selling of bondsmen into slavery for debts and other obligations by private people, and later even by the crown, was strictly forbidden and the legal status of the former bondsmen was essentially improved (above, pp. 341 ff.), and while we may suppose the same process to have taken place in the Pergamene kingdom, in the less advanced kingdoms of Bithynia, Pontus, and Cappadocia the status of the bondsmen was probably very similar to that which they had in Egypt and Phoenicia before the reforms of Philadelphus and of his successors. This meant that in the above-mentioned kingdoms enslavement of free *laoi* was still a traditional feature of their economic and social life. Moreover, these countries were not thoroughly pacified. One feudal lord might easily appropriate the serfs of another and sell them into slavery. It will be remembered that Bithynian and Cappadocian slaves were very numerous in Rome in the first century B.C. and in the early Imperial period.

An inscription from Delphi* affords an excellent illustration of the slave trade carried on by the Oriental kings. It is a decree in honour of king Nicomedes (apparently Nicomedes III) and Laodice, daughter of king Mithridates V, who were approached by a special embassy from Delphi with a view to obtaining slaves (σώματα) for Apollo and the city, and who acceded to this request and sent thirty slaves. It is unfortunate that we do not know their native names, which the Delphians changed into elegant Greek names. The majority of the thirty slaves given by Nicomedes were shepherds, some were artisans. The decree specifies their distribution among the various departments of the temple economy. It is more than probable that the Delphians addressed themselves to Nicomedes not only because he was a philhellene, but also because he had a large supply of slaves. He was certainly an active slave-dealer, and the slaves were in all probability, at least in part, his own serfs.[49]

A peculiar outcome of the new phenomena in the commercial life of the Hellenistic world of this time was the development of the famous Cilician piratical State or confederation. Cilician piracy is known to us in the form it took during and after the Mithridatic wars, when it replaced Cretan piracy or was associated with it in its revival, and displayed an activity very similar to that of its prototype, though more daring and better organized. Its beginnings, however, are obscure and not easy to understand. Strabo† gives a vivid though rather confused picture of it. I shall attempt to reconstruct the early days of Cilician piracy as I understand them and to explain its growth and development.

Cilicia was nominally a part of the Seleucid Empire. In fact it was almost independent, since the Seleucids, possessing a fleet of only twelve ships, were unable to control the Cilician coast and the mountains behind it. Thus Cilicia became both a base of operations and a recruiting-ground for the pretenders to the Seleucid throne, and the abode of groups of well-trained, well-

* *O.G.I.* 345.   † xiv. 5. 2, pp. 668 ff., cp. 3. 2, p. 664.

armed, and practically independent adventurers. The formation of these powerful bodies of adventurers Strabo ascribes to
Diodotus Tryphon (about 143 B.C.), who organized at Corace-
sium, a stronghold on the Cilician coast, a body of privateers
to fight Antiochus Sidetes.

These efficient groups of professional robbers, familiar with
military operations both on land and sea, soon realized how
favourable were the conditions for enriching themselves by
organized action. They began with the practice of kidnapping,
disposing of their prisoners with the help of professional slave-
traders, especially in Side. When the maritime trade of Syria
was growing by leaps and bounds, they added to their activity
on land—in Asia Minor and Commagene in close connexion
with the Isaurians and other tribes of the mountains—a rapidly
developing piracy at sea. Their instructors in this craft may
have been the Cretans, who at that time played an important
part in the dynastic wars of Syria.[50]

The Syrian waters, though frequented by a considerable and
increasing number of merchantmen, were not protected by any
organized force. It was easy for the Cilician bands to extend
their business and to combine with slave-hunting and slave-
dealing the profitable profession of piracy. No power was
willing and able to put an end to the activity of Cilician pirates
in the Syrian waters. The Seleucids were helpless. The Ptolemies of Egypt and Cyprus were glad to help the enemies of the
Syrian kings, their hereditary foes. They were willing therefore
to abet the Cilician pirates by opening their harbours to them.
The Rhodians, if we may believe the statement of Strabo, were
at this time (second half of the second century) hostile to Syria,
and would not interfere. Finally, the Romans never went
beyond diplomatic representations which were certainly never
meant seriously. They had no interest in removing what was a
thorn in the flesh to the Syrian monarchy, and was moreover
a rich source of supply to themselves of Syrian slaves. This
was exactly what they needed: cheap labour well trained in
agriculture and the care of cattle. They had not the same
compunction in employing slaves from this source as they would
have felt if the slaves had been of Greek origin. After all, these
Syrians were barbarians born for slavery. Thus Cilician piracy

developed, unchecked and unmolested, into a strong and well-organized institution.[51]

Left as they were at the mercy of the pirates, the Syrian and Phoenician merchants, and the slave-dealers in particular, soon came in all probability to an understanding with the Cilician pirates, no other course being open to them, for the conditions of the land routes were worse than by sea (see below, p. 867 f.). We may suppose that the arrangement was made through the Cilician slave-dealers, who were certainly, if not identical with the pirates, at least in close connexion with them. According to Strabo,* Side in Pamphylia became an important centre both for the pirates and for the slave-merchants of Cilicia.

The same role was played by several Cretan cities, especially by Cnossus (with its two harbours), by Cydonia and Hierapytna. I have already shown that Cretan piracy was in its decline in the early second century B.C. This decline was probably responsible for the impoverishment of the island, as reflected in the rarity of Cretan coins in this period. In the second half of the second century and in the first there was certainly a revival both of piracy and of prosperity in Crete. It is very probable that these two revivals were connected with the brisk development of Cilician piracy. The Cretans, from being teachers of the Cilician pirates, soon became their partners. This fact is mentioned by several historians of the time, and the resulting prosperity of Crete is attested by her abundant coinage, by several rich hoards found in the island, and by the aspect presented by the excavated ruins of Amnisus, one of the two harbours of Cnossus.[52]

The Cilician pirates, emboldened by their immunity from interference, gradually extended the sphere of their activity. In the atmosphere of safety in which they lived they would probably not confine themselves to the Syrian waters, but would interfere with trade in the Aegean and perhaps also in the western Mediterranean. We have very little knowledge on the subject,[53] but, unless we assume a development of this kind, which was bound to arouse the indignation of the tax-farmers of Asia and of the Italian and Roman merchants and bankers all round the Aegean, we find it difficult to understand

* xiv. 3. 2, p. 664.

why, after some fifty years of indifference, the Roman government in the last years of the second century B.C. suddenly adopted a number of serious measures against the pirates.

M. Antonius, the famous orator, was sent out in 102 B.C. to Cilicia in order to combat the pirates and was fairly successful. Cilicia, Pamphylia, Lycia, and Lycaonia were placed under Roman military control. The next step was taken about 100 B.C. A law was enacted in Rome providing *inter alia* for the organization of concerted measures by all the eastern States with a view to the isolation of the pirates. There is no mention of war in the extant fragments of the law. But the measures prescribed are of such a character that they certainly must be interpreted as preparations for an imminent war. It is probable that the law was promoted by C. Marius, who aspired to a high military command in the East. However, nothing of importance was done. Piracy throve as before and in the time of Mithridates became, as we shall see later, a real scourge and plague throughout the Mediterranean.[54]

A new commercial organization in the Aegean was demanded by the new conditions, that is to say, by the new direction and altered character of trade. This trade, being largely in eastern goods and eastern slaves and depending almost exclusively on the Italian market, was now mainly directed to the west and assumed the features of a transit trade. The chief purchasers of Eastern goods and slaves were no longer Greeks, but Italians and Sicilians, most of them rich men of various professions. A central *entrepôt* for such a trade was a great convenience to sellers and buyers, who were foreigners to each other and between whom direct communications were difficult (partly for political reasons).

There had been *entrepôts* of this kind before, such as Rhodes and Corinth. These offered better facilities than Delos, both geographically and from other points of view. Their harbours were much more commodious and much better equipped, the capital and business experience accumulated in them was much greater, and they had both been in relations with the East from time immemorial. Delos in comparison had always played a secondary part, though it was well known to foreign traders.[55]

Nevertheless, it was Delos that was chosen as their head-quarters by the Italian, Syrian, and Anatolian merchants. This momentous decision was the outcome of a combination of political, social, and psychological factors. For a time Corinth may have competed with Delos, and Carthage also may have attracted a good deal of the traffic both in Oriental goods and in slaves. But both these cities were soon eliminated from the competition. For political, not economic, reasons Corinth and Carthage, the two most flourishing international emporiums of the day, were destroyed by the Romans.

There remained the two largest commercial cities of Greece— Athens and Rhodes. Of these, Rhodes offered little attraction to the new commercial magnates. That proud and ancient city, with its political and commercial traditions, its enormous influence in banking and commerce, its contempt for foreigners, was hardly the place that upstarts in business, such as were the rich Sicilian and Italian bankers and merchants, would choose for their head-quarters. Moreover, political relations between Rome and Rhodes were strained after the Persean war, and Italians were not very popular at Rhodes.

Athens was in certain respects far better adapted. Her relations with Rome were excellent. Her commercial con-nexions with the East were of long standing, and many Orien-tals—as individual settlers or in groups—lived at Athens. At the same time Athens was the place in Greece best known to Italians. Moreover, the city was not in a position to arouse the jealousy of the Italian men of business, those new leaders in the world's affairs; her economic and commercial importance lay almost entirely in the past. All this told in favour of Athens. But her geographical position was unsuitable. She lay too far away from the main commercial route between Italy and the East.[56]

The geographical situation of Delos was much better than that of Athens, and its political status was much more accep-table to the new masters of the Aegean than that of Rhodes. I have mentioned before that Delos after the Persean war, by a brutal act of Rome which treated the free and independent city friendly to her as if it were conquered land and pro-perty of the Roman people, was given as a sort of *dorea*

(Bikerman's suggestion) to Athens and became an Athenian cleruchy. This was done, of course, not for commercial but mainly for political reasons. Athens had been a faithful supporter of Rome and was rewarded by the recovery of some of her former dependencies. This political act had, however, important commercial consequences. As an Athenian cleruchy and as a free port (another political measure taken by Rome in order to injure Rhodes), Delos met all the requirements of the Italian and Oriental merchants. Cleared of its former citizens, it became practically neutral territory. Athenian capitalists were not rich enough to compete with the wealthy and experienced traders from Italy and the East. The new Athenian government of Delos was entirely dependent in political matters on the goodwill of Rome. There was consequently no danger that it would put any obstacles in the way of the newcomers. In these circumstances it is not surprising that the foreign merchants, well aware of the advantages offered by Delos, should prefer to settle and organize their business there rather than at Rhodes. The growth of the commercial importance of Delos was a natural development, encouraged by the measures subsequently taken by Rome in respect of Corinth and Carthage. Thus it was that Delos gradually became the principal *entrepôt* for the rapidly developing trade between Italy and the East, and especially for the slave trade.

The history of Delos during the second Athenian domination has been narrated by such competent scholars as P. Roussel and F. Durrbach, and need not be repeated here in detail. For the first thirty years Delos was a regular Athenian cleruchy, with the Athenians predominant in all spheres of Delian life. About 130 B.C. or a little earlier we witness a momentous change. The Athenian cleruchic government was engulfed by the various communities of foreign traders, ship-owners, and warehousemen, corporations possessing both a national and a professional character, not mere groups of merchants but associations of men who had the same national, religious, and social interests. After 130 B.C. decrees of the Athenians, even decrees conferring honours, are no longer found, and are replaced by decrees of a composite body, including the Athenians, both inhabitants of Delos and temporary residents,

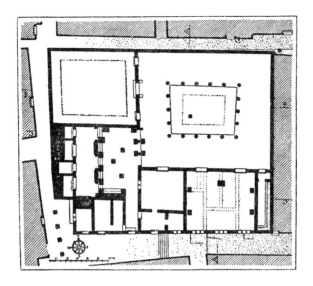

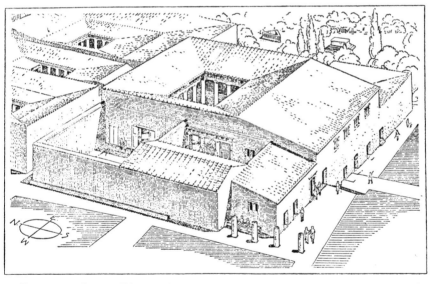

FIGS. 9 and 10. Plan and reconstruction of the 'House of the Posei-doniasts' at Delos (Ch. Picard, 'L'Établissement des Poseidoniastes de Berytos', *Délos*, vi (1921), pls. IV and X).

the 'Romans' (that is Italians), and the rest of the 'Greeks' (the hellenized Oriental merchants). The formula varies but in all its versions it is expressly mentioned that these men are merchants and ship-owners.

Delos thus ceased to be a Greek city-state and became an agglomeration of men whose connexion with the island was temporary and whose interest lay in their business, in their material prosperity. They were not citizens of Delos, and never made any effort to transform it into a city-state. Delos was their business centre, not their city; their temporary home, not a place with which they had been connected for generations. Nor was it any longer the sacred island. Whereas formerly the city of Delos had been a kind of appendix to the temple, whose religious and secular affairs overshadowed the business of the lay community, now it was the latter that predominated. The temple still existed and throve, and the merchants of the city were glad to live under the protection of its god, but it was in the harbour that the pulse of the community now beat.

A few remarks may be added regarding the economic history of the island down to the time of the Mithridatic war. The sphere of its commercial activity is illustrated by various inscriptions found there: those relating to the commercial and religious associations of Delos, those which were set up in honour of various notabilities, especially the kings of the Hellenistic monarchies and certain leaders of the Roman people, and those which mention as donors and dedicants men of foreign origin. The first are especially valuable and interesting.

The corporations which were most prominent were the several associations of Italians, some of a religious, others of a professional character. The social, religious, national, and probably business centre of the Italians was the *Italike Pastas*, their meeting-place and club-house built at the end of the second century B.C. We do not know how it was constituted, and cannot say whether all the free Italians of Delos had access to it. Besides the religious corporations, two professional associations are mentioned: the influential association of dealers in olive-oil and the less important body of wine-merchants.[57]

Alongside of the Italian associations, the richest and most

influential organized groups of foreigners were those of merchants from the two great trading cities of Phoenicia, Tyre and
Berytus ('Laodicea in Phoenicia'). The Tyrian Heracleists,
merchants and shippers, are known from one inscription only.
The Berytian association (κοινόν) of the Poseidoniasts, merchants and shipmasters and warehousemen, was probably the
oldest foreign association in Delos, and we have several inscriptions relating to it. Its head-quarters, built earlier than the
Italian *Pastas*, i.e. in the middle of the second century B.C.,
have been carefully excavated. This building was a regular
fonduq, a combination of a large colonnaded court (αὐλή?),
a sanctuary (ἱερόν), with various chapels (ναοί), a meeting-
place (οἶκος?), and some χρηστήρια. The only similar building
known to us is the recently discovered centre of the Palmyrenes in Dura-Europus on the Euphrates, again a combination
of a temple and a private house, which last contained a meeting-
room and some shops or perhaps living-rooms.[58]

I have already mentioned that the Syrian colony in Delos
was very numerous, and that in addition to it many merchants
from the various Arabian and Mesopotamian centres of the
caravan trade were probably temporary residents in the island
(Chapter V, p. 702, n. 124).

As regards merchants from Alexandria, we have no evidence
of corporations of them similar to the corporations of Italians
and Phoenicians, although large numbers of them probably
lived in the island; witness the introduction and the rapid
growth there of Greco-Egyptian cults. It seems highly probable
that trade with Alexandria was not in the hands of individual
merchants but of an Alexandrian corporation closely connected
with the Alexandrian government (the σύνοδος τῶν ἐν Ἀλεξ-
ανδρείᾳ πρεσβυτέρων ἐγδοχέων, a department of which is
known to have existed at Delos). Nevertheless it is evident that
commercial relations with Alexandria played an important
part in the business of Delos.[59]

I may mention in addition an interesting inscription in
honour of a man from Nicaea in Bithynia set up by merchants
and shipmasters who used to ply between Delos and Bithynia,
probably a heterogeneous group who had important dealings
with the latter country.[60]

PLATE LXXXXVIII

The plate and the plan reproduced here show one of the many domestic sanctuaries found in the private houses of Delos, either outside them on the street or inside. This sanctuary regularly consisted of an altar with scenes painted on the plaster which covered its core and was from time to time renewed,

and an adjoining painted panel on the wall, whose plaster coat was likewise renewed now and then. The sanctuary here reproduced was found near house C, region of the Stadium, ins. i. On the front of the altar (which had a niche above it to protect the fire) is represented a scene of sacrifice. Three men with veiled heads, dressed in white, with right hands raised in the gesture of prayer, are approaching an altar of exactly the same form as that

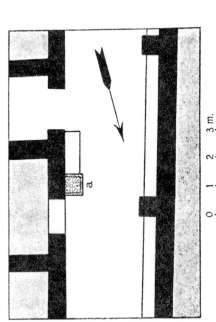

Fig. 11.

0   1   2   3 m.

on which the scene is painted. From the other side a slave or assistant is driving a pig to the altar, while behind him stands an *auletes* playing the double flute. The adjoining panel on the wall shows two wrestlers or boxers ready for the contest. Near them the prize for the victor: a piece of ham (part of the sacrificed animal) and an amphora of wine. Above, as if presiding at the game, the crowned figure of Heracles.

The meaning of this and other related, almost identical, scenes depicted in the street and house sanctuaries of Delos cannot be examined here. No completely satisfactory interpretation of them has yet been offered. It is impossible to accept entirely Bulard's suggestion that we have here a combination of the cult of the genius of the house-owner (as at Pompeii), carried out by the members of his family, with the cult of the domestic and cross-road Lares organized by the associations of slaves, and that this combination was a manifestation of the domestic cult of the Italians resident at Delos only. I am unable to detect in the pictures from Delos anything which would necessarily limit them to the Italian population of Delos to the exclusion of the Greek majority of the residents in the island: there is nothing specifically Italian in the contests represented on the altars and walls and in the scenes of sacrifice. In any case the paintings in the domestic sanctuaries of Delos introduce us to the intimate religious life of its population. See M. Bulard, 'Description des revêtements peints à sujets religieux', *Expl. arch. Délos*, ix (1926), p. 133 ff. (my plate reproduces fig. 45 and pl. xiii, 1, of this publication); cf. *La Religion domestique dans la colonie italienne de Délos*, 1926. For the parallels at Pompeii, G. K. Boyce, 'Corpus of the Lararia of Pompeii', *Mem. Am. Acad. Rome*, xiv, 1937.

PLATE LXXXVIII

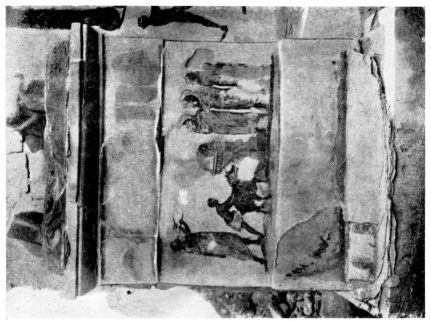

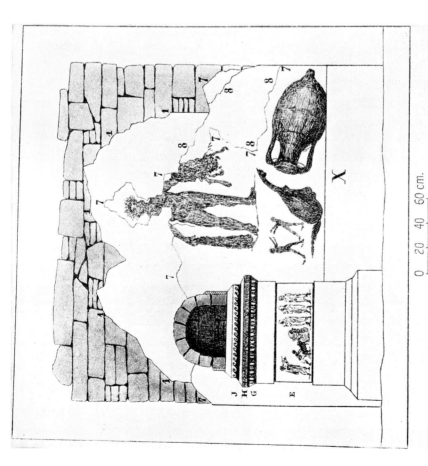

Delos. Domestic Cults and Altars

PLATE LXXXIX

SYRIAN ARTISTS AT WORK IN DELOS

Mosaic still *in situ* at Delos

The floor mosaic reproduced in this plate decorated a reception room (οἶκος) in a house in the immediate vicinity of the theatre excavated in 1930. This large and sumptuous house —one of the largest in Delos—of the usual Delian peristyle type was hastily and negligently built some time in the second century B.C., but lavishly decorated with elaborate mosaic floors. Four of them were found in four οἶκοι, built around the peristyle. Prof. J. Chamonard, who excavated the house, suggests that the cheapness and haste of its construction may be explained by its character. He thinks that the house was not a residential dwelling but was built for a corporation. The subjects of the mosaics—three of them related to the theatrical craft (tragedy, satirical drama, comedy)—may suggest, according to him, that the house of the Masks, as it was styled by the excavator, was owned by the Dionysiac technitai and was used by them as a kind of club-house and for rehearsals.

The largest and the most beautiful of the four mosaics is reproduced here. It consists of two parts: the body of the mosaic in a frame suggestive of a carpet and containing two rhomboidal medallions; and the emblema, the central square picture which was made separately in the workshop of the artist and was placed in the centre of the floor, rather negligently, either before or after the rest of the mosaic was laid. The emblema shows on a black background a Dionysiac figure in a rich theatrical dress riding in womanly fashion on a panther with an ivy crown round its neck. The Dionysiac figure wears an ivy crown and holds in its right hand a thyrsus, in its left a tympanon. The identity of the figure is doubtful: we may suppose it to be an effeminate youthful Dionysus, or more probably one of the Maenads, or even Ariadne. The emblema is of excellent workmanship, and of refined technique. Its composition is skilful and well balanced. It is full of movement

and expression, but not to excess. The polychromy is rich but harmonious. Though perhaps a copy of a famous painting, it is the work of a first-class artist. The rest of the mosaic, though probably designed by the same artist, was laid by plain craftsmen. In the rhomboidal medallions two Centaurs are facing the central emblema: one is carrying a torch-holder, the other a cantharus. In the field are strewn four crowns—two of ivy and two of laurel (won perhaps by the donor of the house or of its mosaic decoration; we know how often lavish gifts were bestowed on Dionysiac artistes), and four curiously stylized branches.

A careful stylistic analysis of the mosaics of the house of the Masks and of other mosaics in Delos, and certain other considerations (cf. Ch. Picard, Syria, xiv (1933), p. 318 f.) have led M. Chamonard to suggest that the mosaics of the house of the Masks were made under the supervision of, and in part by, Asclepiades of Aradus, the same artist who signed one of the mosaics in another rich house in Delos, styled the house of the Trident. I am inclined to accept the suggestion. We know now, after the recent excavations of Antioch, Daphne, Apamea, and Seleuceia in Pieria, how flourishing was the mosaicists' craft in Syria in Roman times. Its thriving condition was of course not a result of the Pax Romana, but a heritage of the Hellenistic period. No wonder that the rich merchants of Delos, some of whom were Syrians themselves, should commission Greek artists from Syria and Phoenicia to adorn their houses with mosaic floors (cf. description of Pl. LXXIV).

Fine coloured reproductions of the mosaics and a detailed study of them will be found in J. Chamonard, 'Les mosaïques de la maison des Masques', Explor. arch. Délos, xiv (1933). My plate is reproduced from his pl. iii. Cf. this Chapter, p. 798 and n. 68.

The impression produced by the above-mentioned inscriptions is that the principal commercial relations of Delos were with Italy on the one hand and with Syria, Egypt, and Asia Minor on the other. This is confirmed by the inscriptions set up in honour of men of political influence in the Hellenistic world. Besides many Romans, it is the Syrian Seleucids (from Antiochus IV to Seleucus VI) and the Ptolemies who are most frequently mentioned in documents of various kinds. Next come the Bithynian kings, the kings of Pontus, and those of Cappadocia.[61] The same distribution of the business relations of Delos is reflected in the foreign cults established there, as attested by temples, shrines, chapels, and scattered dedications.[62]

Our information may be incomplete, but it is certainly not misleading. Merchants from the Greek cities of Greece proper, from the islands, and from the northern part of the Balkan peninsula may have appeared at the great fair held at Delos every year now as in the past. But there is no doubt that its trade relations with Greece were of secondary importance. It was principally the merchants of Syria, Egypt, Asia Minor on the one hand and of Italy on the other who used its harbour and city for purposes of their mutual commercial relations and as their business centre.[63]

It is evident, for the fact is explicitly stated by Strabo,* that the traffic in slaves played an important, if not a predominating part in the commercial affairs of Delos. We have confirmation of this in the inscriptions quoted above. It is by no accident that the principal slave-producing countries are those which figure so prominently in the inscriptions of Delos: Syria, Bithynia, Pontus, Cappadocia. It is not to be expected, of course, that there should be inscriptions in honour of the Cilician pirates.

There are no statistics to help us to form an idea of the volume of the Delian slave trade. Strabo† in a very general way speaks of Delos as being able to receive and send out tens of thousands of slaves daily. He was not attempting to give precise figures but trying to create in the minds of his readers a general impression of the magnitude of this trade. There is

* xiv. 5. 2, p. 668.   † Ibid.

no doubt that Delos was regarded as the best place for the slave trade, at least in the opinion of the merchants themselves. The proverb quoted by Strabo is evidence enough: 'merchant, put in, unload; everything sold!'*

Next in importance was certainly a lively trade in caravan goods. The part played at Delos by the merchants from the cities of Phoenicia and Palestine, and the appearance there of Minaeans, Sabaeans, Petraeans, and Bactrians make it certain that the island was the prime clearing-house for the wares brought to Syria by caravan from Arabia, India, Bactria, and perhaps China. With these wares went the well-known special products of Oriental industry: purple, textiles, rugs, glass, &c. I am inclined to explain in the same way the renewal of the trade relations with Egypt. Delos may have been one of the *entrepôts* for the grain that Egypt sold on the Greek market. But in this respect Delos had rivals in Rhodes and Athens. Of more importance than the grain trade may have been that in the goods which Egypt received by sea from eastern Africa, Arabia, and India. I shall speak hereafter of the efforts made by the later Ptolemies to revive their trade with the East. We know that these efforts were completely successful. Since Delos was the principal clearing-house for Oriental goods, where prices were established and most of the transactions carried out, the Alexandrian exporters of African, Arabian, and Indian goods, a motley company among whom Italian merchants were conspicuous, had naturally to appear there with their merchandise in order to compete with the Syrians and Arabs. The Italians came to Delos chiefly as buyers. But thanks to the wide reputation that Italian olive-oil and wine were rapidly acquiring they had an opportunity, of which they availed themselves, of selling these commodities to the Delian population and probably to other cities of Greece, defraying with the proceeds some part at least of their heavy expenditure on slaves and luxuries. The Italians, besides being successful merchants, were the chief bankers in Delos, as they were also in Alexandria and all over Greece. This was no new pheno-menon in the history of the island. There had been many bankers there, mostly Sicilians and southern Italians, in the

* ἔμπορε, κατάπλευσον, ἐξελοῦ, πάντα πέπραται.

1. The bronze plaque reproduced in this plate has a peculiar history. It was discovered in 1908 as a stray find in the Krene Minoe at Delos. In 1921 R. Vallois observed that it fits exactly into the space reserved for an inlaid metal plaque on one of the twin stelae found years ago at Delos in the ruins of the agora bath. Vallois moreover pointed out that in the Delian inventories of the time of Athenian domination the two stelae mentioned above are described as standing in the prodomos of the temple of Ἀγαθὴ Τύχη (the best preserved description of the objects kept in this temple will be found in *Inscr. de Délos*, Actes des fonct. athén. etc., no. 1417, A ii, 26 ff.). It was thus established that the bas-relief stood from 166 B.C. in the temple of Ἀγαθὴ Τύχη. However, the fact that a decree of the Delian people of the beginning of the second century (*I.G.* xi. 1026) was engraved on one of the stelae after its dedication, showed that the temple, though never mentioned in the inventories of the time of independence, was in existence long before 166 B.C. At this time it certainly had another name. It has been suggested that in this earlier period of its history the temple may have been dedicated to Arsinoe, wife of Philadelphus, and to Ἀγαθὴ Τύχη, and in the accounts of the hieropoioi was styled Philadelpheion. The exact location of the Philadelpheion and Tycheion is unknown, but both were apparently on Mount Cynthus. It is probable that it was the anonymous Temple A recently excavated by Plassart in this region. The identification of the Tycheion with the Philadelpheion suggested by Vallois was based chiefly on his interpretation of the scene represented on the plaque. This interpretation appears to me to be not to be correct. We see the goddess Artemis with the features of Arsinoe kindling with two torches the fire on a square altar. She is assisted by two satyrs, one blowing into the flame, the other bringing an oenochoe similar to those discussed above (pl. XLI. 2) for libation, and the λίκνον, which last points to the connexion of Artemis–Arsinoe with the Dionysiac mysteries so popular in Alexandria. Behind the altar is seen a ξόανον on the summit of a slender pilaster. The bas-relief is a fine work of art of the early Hellenistic period. It has been justly described as the precursor of the so-called Hellenistic landscape bas-reliefs. Whether the bas-relief and its lost counterpart were made in Alexandria we have no means of saying. Its style is peculiar and has nothing in common, for example, with the Arsinoe and Berenice oenochoe bas-reliefs discussed above (pl. XLI. 2). The work may equally well be a product of the Delian bronze industry. It has been published and discussed several times. I give here a select bibliography only: F. Courby, *Mon. et Mém. Piot*, xviii (1910), pp. 19 ff. (with a beautiful reproduction); J. Sieveking, Brunn–Bruckmann, *Ant. Denkm.*, pl. 621; R. Vallois, *B.C.H.* xlv (1921), pp. 242 f., and *C.R. Ac. Inscr.*, 1929, pp. 32 f.; Ch. Picard, *A.J.A.* xxxviii (1934), p. 147 f., and *Mél. Maspéro*, ii (1934), p. 325 f.; cf. A. Plassart, 'Les sanctuaires et les cultes du mont Cynthus', *Expl. arch. Délos*, xi (1928), pp. 222 ff.

2. Bronze portrait head of one of the Greek or Greco-Oriental residents at Delos found in the ancient palaestra. The eyes are inlaid. Beautiful work of the first half of the second century B.C. related in style to the early Pergamene sculptures (see the head of Attalus I, Pl. v). C. Michalowski, 'Les portraits hellénistiques et romains', *Expl. arch. Délos*, xiii (1932), no. 1, pp. 1 ff., pls. i–vii, figs. I, 2.

Photographs supplied by R. Demangel, Director of the French School at Athens.

PLATE XC

2. Athens, National Museum

DELIAN METALWORK

1. Delos Museum

PLATE XCI

DELOS. PRODUCTS OF CERAMIC INDUSTRY

Delos Museum

PLATE XCI

1. One of the portable charcoal ovens found at Delos. Few intact pieces of this type are known, but fragments are very common in the ruins of Hellenistic cities. Many have been found at Athens, Thera, Priene, Delos, and scattered fragments in other cities of Greece, Italy and Sicily, Egypt and Africa (Carthage). The ovens may be divided into two classes: plain utensils without ornaments, probably used for cooking food and baking bread, and a more ambitious type, of elegant form and rich ornamentation (average height 0·54 m.), serving either for heating the rooms or for keeping food and drink warm. The ovens of the second class are of uniform shape, make, and ornamentation. They are made of a brownish-red, rather coarse clay, which assumed according to the degree of firing a red colour of different shades. The oven consists of two parts: the upper— a semi-spherical receptacle for burning charcoal, with bottom perforated (for ventilation and elimination of ashes), and with three supports within it to carry vessels placed over the charcoal; and the lower—serving for ventilation and as a receptacle for the ashes. Both parts were made on the potter's wheel and were adorned with appliqué and incised ornaments. On the above-mentioned tripod-like supports, decorated with appliqué heads, masks, figurines, etc., potters' marks are sometimes found. The ancient name of this type of utensil is unknown. We may choose one of the many names listed by Pollux, *Onom.* vi, 88; x, 10: ἐσχάρα, κρίβανος, βαῦνος, ἱπνός, πύραυνος, χυτρόπους, ἐσχαρίς, ἀνθράκιον. The portable ovens of the type described are confined to the late Hellenistic period, when Delos was flourishing. The uniformity of shape and decoration suggests that they were first produced some time in the second century B.C. in one place, perhaps by one potter (we may think of 'Εκαταῖος; ovens signed by him have been found at Athens, Delos, Rhodes, ·various places in Asia Minor, Naucratis, Tarentum, Syracuse), and that they became widely distributed. At the same time probably, in more important centres, ovens of the same type were made by local potters.

The classical paper on these objects is A. Conze, 'Griechische Kohlenbecken', *J.D.A.I.* v (1890), pp. 118 ff. The material found at Thera has been published and studied by F. Hiller von Gaertringen, *Thera*, ii, p. 82; iii, pp. 42, 127, 146, 159, 162, 178; that from Priene by R. Zahn in Th. Wiegand and H. Schrader, *Priene*, 1904, pp. 459 ff.; that from Delos (the fragments found before 1905) by F. Mayence, *B.C.H.* xxix (1905), pp. 373 ff., with a good bibliography (p. 373, n. 1). Since 1905 many new fragments have been found at Delos, among them some belonging to a third type of oven designed to burn wood, G. Bakalakis *B.C.H.* lviii (1934), pp. 201 ff. A complete collection of Delian ovens will be published by A. Deonna in *Explor. arch. Délos.*

2. One of the Pergamene red-glazed bowls with appliqué figurines (cf. pl. LXXIII) found at Delos. These figurines are not connected with each other. They represent: (1) Silenus carrying a *vannus mystica*; (2) a grotesque figure, perhaps a character in a mime; (3) a woman; (4) the Muse Thalia with a comic mask; (5) a grotesque dancing figure; (6) remains of another dancing figure, F. Courby, *B.C.H.* xxxvii (1913), p. 422, no. 716, fig. 5, facing p. 424.

3, 4. Two typical Megarian bowls of the so-called Delian factory (F. Courby, *Les vases grecs à reliefs*, 1922, pp. 378 ff. (Fabrique de Délos) ; cf., however, above, Ch. V, n. 68 and this Chapter, n. 63). On one is represented a hunting scene (Courby, loc. cit., p. 381, no. 36, fig. 79), the other is adorned with ornamental patterns (ibid., pl. xiii, no. 17).

The photographs for this plate have been supplied by R. Demangel, Director of the French School at Athens. The portable oven appears to be unpublished.

period of its independence; and the banking profession was even more prominent in the period that we are considering.

It is certainly no fortuitous occurrence that the bankers mentioned in Delian inscriptions of the period after 167 B.C. are all of them Italians: we hear of a group of 'the bankers in Delos' οἱ ἐν Δήλῳ τραπεζῖται or τραπεζιτεύοντες, of a rich banker Philostratus, native of Ascalon, but citizen of Naples; of a Maraeus Gerillanus, a Roman citizen; and finally of a Marcus Minatius, who lent money to the Poseidoniasts of Berytus and was highly honoured by them.[64]

Such was the business life of Delos. It was this which gradually made it a large city of about 20,000 to 30,000 inhabitants,[65] containing several hundreds of private houses, some of them pretentiously and gorgeously adorned with paintings, mosaics, and sculptures, scores of large *horrea*, and hundreds of shops and workshops.[66] Many of the inhabitants became very rich. It would appear that at Delos, as elsewhere, there was a group of very wealthy people who exerted great influence. I have quoted examples of such wealthy people elsewhere.[67] But, rich as it was, Delos was not an attractive place nor a centre of creative work. Products of local art and industry were poor, those of better quality being either imported or made in the island by foreign artists.[68] No Delian poet, writer, scholar, or philosopher of the period under consideration is known to us. With this may be compared the part which Rhodes, in spite of its impoverishment and humiliation, still played in the artistic and intellectual life of Greece.

While the merchants and bankers of Delos were prosperous and some of them were rich, the poorer classes probably led a very hard life. But whereas we were able to derive from the accounts of the ἱεροποιοί some idea of the standard of life then prevailing among manual or professional workers, we have no information on the subject for the period with which we are now concerned. It is probable that after the evacuation of the Delians labour was for the most part furnished by slaves. This would be natural in such a place as Delos, the principal slave-market of the ancient world, and we need feel no surprise if at a certain moment (about 130 B.C.) these slaves rose in revolt against their masters. But there were also a certain number of small shopkeepers, artisans, and so forth, who were either free-born or freedmen. Of their standard of living we are not informed, but it was probably a very low one.

We know very little of the conditions prevailing at this time in the other islands of the Aegean. There is, however, no reason to doubt that they shared in the misery or the prosperity, as the case might be, of Greece proper and the northern part of the Balkan peninsula or of Asia Minor, according to their geographical position. In one instance, however, that of the comparatively small island of PAROS, we can speak with more precision and derive from it an unexpected and much needed light on the material conditions in other parts of the Aegean world. Paros was famous for its excellent marble, which was in great demand in the archaic and classical periods of Greece. We may infer from the use still made of its marble that its prosperity was still high in the early Hellenistic period. A period of sharp decline followed in the late third and early second centuries B.C. This depression came to an end in the late second and in the first centuries B.C.; Parian marble again appeared on the market and with it Parian statues made by a group of Parian sculptors, very famous masters of the time, among them some Italians (the Cossutii). In the first century B.C. Parian statues are ubiquitous. They appear in some Greek centres: in Paros itself, in Delos, Melos, in Crete, Amorgos, Thera. But their vogue was much wider than that; many Parian statues have been found in Italy (of Cossutius, of Xenon, of Sogenes). The popularity of Parian statues and the large demand for Parian marble are shown by an analysis of the statues found in the wrecked ship of Anticythera mentioned above. Among them one is a replica of a statue by the Rhodian sculptor Antiphanes, and it is certain that all the other statues are of Parian marble.[69]

III. THE EASTERN MONARCHIES

A. *ASIA MINOR*

The political relations of Eumenes II of PERGAMON after the Persean war with the Romans were somewhat similar to those of Rhodes. Eumenes had lost his political prestige and was no longer supported by the Romans, indeed was tacitly and clandestinely opposed by them in his political designs. This became evident during the Galatian war, which broke out in 168, lasted until 166 B.C., and caused terrible havoc in Asia Minor. We know little of this war, but what we do know shows that the Romans made not the slightest effort to support Eumenes when he was hard pressed at the beginning of hostilities, and rather encouraged his enemies. It was well known in Asia Minor at this time that if the Greek cities of Asia Minor were finally saved from the danger of Galatian attacks and pillage, it was entirely due to that king's skill and courage. It is not surprising that after this war he became even more popular with the Greek cities of Asia Minor than he had been after his first Galatian war (above ch. V, p. 636, n. 45). I may mention in this connexion that in the opinion of the majority of modern scholars it was Eumenes II who at this time dedicated the famous altar to Zeus in commemoration of his great victory over the Galatians. This grand but frigid piece of decorative sculpture celebrates the victory of the Greek spirit and civilization, personified in the Greek gods, over the elemental forces of barbarism, represented by the Giants. References to the Gallic terror to be found in various literary texts and inscriptions show that the dread felt by the Greek cities at the beginning of the war and the relief after its conclusion were based on real experience, on a terrible devastation of parts of Asia Minor by the Gauls. We hear of Amlada, Sardis, and even Miletus, as being affected by the war.[70]

After the death of Eumenes II the relations between Rome and Pergamon became cordial once more and comparative quiet was restored in Asia Minor. But Pergamon was still exposed to many dangers and strenuous military efforts were required. Attalus II was twice called upon to help the Romans, at the time of the revolt of Andriscus and of the Achaean war. In Asia Minor a serious war broke out soon after the accession of Attalus II between him and Prusias II of Bithynia (156 B.C.). After its close Prusias remained hostile to Pergamon and finally, shortly before his overthrow and death, began a new war. During the first war the territory of Pergamon and of many Pergamene cities was subjected to savage devastation. Even the temples were ravaged and pillaged. It was probably at this time that the populous city of Selge in Pisidia waged war against the kingdom of Pergamon (neither the political status of the city nor the circumstances that gave rise to the war are known to us). The first conflict with Selge occurred during the reign of Eumenes II. The war broke out again under Attalus II, who sent his successor and perhaps co-ruler, the future Attalus III, against the rebels and followed soon after with the main army. Thus much we may perhaps infer from the brief references by Pompeius Trogus–Justin (prol. to book XXXIV) and from the letters of Attalus II to the city of Amlada recently published in full. Connected with the first Bithynian war was the help given by Attalus II to Ariarathes V of Cappadocia, which led to a local war against Priene (155 B.C.), a war in which the territory of that city was repeatedly devastated. The warlike half-civilized neighbours of Pergamon were troublesome. The Galatian question was far from being settled, and hostilities between the Galatians and Pergamon never ceased, as we learn from the highly interesting correspondence of Eumenes II and Attalus II with the chief priest of Pessinus.

The Thracian world was in a state of unrest. The Thracians bitterly resented foreign, especially Roman, intervention in their affairs, as they showed by supporting Andriscus. Nor were they ready to tolerate Pergamene rule in Chersonesian and Thracian territory. After the downfall of Prusias II, Diegylis, a powerful ruler of the Thracian tribe of the Kainoi and father-in-law and ally of Prusias II, launched an attack on the Pergamene cities of Thrace. Many were captured and destroyed, e.g. Lysimacheia. This led to a dangerous war which ended in the complete victory of Attalus II (cf. above, p. 766).

The political situation did not change very much after Attalus III had succeeded Attalus II. Our information is meagre, but there are occasional references to a great victory of Attalus III in a serious war, of which we have otherwise no knowledge.

In dealing with their political rivals and their warlike neighbours the last Attalids had no freedom of action. Behind them stood the Romans, and it was practically as vassals and agents of Rome that they acted, not as independent kings. The last letter (from Attalus II) in the correspondence between

PLATE XCII

1. Æ Tetradrachm of Pharnaces I, Pontus. *Obv.* Head of Pharnaces I. *Rev.* ΒΑΣΙΛΕΩΣ ΦΑΡΝΑΚΟΥ. Male figure, pantheistic deity holding cornucopiae, caduceus, and vine branch at which doe nibbles.

2. Æ Drachm of Arsaces I (?). *Obv.* Bust of Arsaces, wearing helmet. *Rev.* ΒΑΣΙΛΕΩΣ ΜΕΓΑΛΟΥ ΑΡΣΑΚΟΥ. Parthian warrior, probably the founder Arsaces, seated on omphalos.

3. Æ Tetradrachm of Mithridates I, Parthia. *Obv.* Head of Mithridates. *Rev.* ΒΑΣΙΛΕΩΣ ΜΕΓΑΛΟΥ ΑΡΣΑΚΟΥ ΦΙΛΕΛΛΗΝΟΣ. Heracles and date ΔΟΡ, 139/8 B.C.

4. Æ Tetradrachm, Magnesia (*c.* 190–133 B.C.). *Obv.* Head of Artemis. *Rev.* ΜΑΓΝΗΤΩΝ. Apollo standing on maeander patterns and magistrate's name; all in wreath.

5. Æ Tetradrachm of Alexander Balas, Tyre. *Obv.* Head of Alexander. *Rev.* ΒΑΣΙΛΕΩΣ ΑΛΕΞΑΝΔΡΟΥ. Tyrian eagle on prow; in field, club with ΤΥΡ in monogram and date ΒΞΡ, 151/0 B.C.

6. Æ Tetradrachm of Ptolemy VI, Philometor or Ptolemy VII (VIII) Euergetes II, Cyprus. *Obv.* Head of the king. *Rev.* ΒΑΣΙΛΕΩΣ ΠΤΟΛΕΜΑΙΟΥ. Eagle on fulmen; in field date ΛΑΓ, 146/5 or 135/4 B.C.

7. Æ Tetradrachm, Side (after 190 B.C.). *Obv.* Head of Athena. Both cistophoric and Seleucid countermarks. *Rev.* Nike holding wreath; in field, a pomegranate (emblema of Side) and magistrates' names.

8. Æ Tetradrachm of Nicomedes II, Bithynia, 147 B.C. *Obv.* Head of Nicomedes II. *Rev.* ΒΑΣΙΛΕΩΣ ΕΠΙΦΑΝΟΥΣ ΝΙΚΟΜΗΔΟΥ. Zeus crowning royal name; in field monogram and date ΑΝΡ.

9. Æ Tetradrachm, Thasos (after 146 B.C.). *Obv.* Head of young Dionysus. *Rev.* ΗΡΑΚΛΕΟΥΣ ΣΩΤΗΡΟΣ ΘΑΣΙΩΝ. Heracles standing.

This plate illustrates some coins mostly of the period after the battle of Pydna. Of earlier date is the first of the two specimens of Parthian coinage. The date and character of the early Parthian coinage are disputed, see the remarks of J. Wolski, *Arsaces I*, 1937 (in Polish, with French résumé). The coins of Magnesia (no. 4) and of Side (no. 7) illustrate the abundant coinage of certain Anatolian cities after the defeat of Antiochus III by the Romans, cf. our pp. 655 ff. On the coinage of Thasos after 146 B.C., this Chapter, nn. 11 and 30. On the tetradrachms of Alexander Balas, minted at Tyre, n. 126 to this Chapter.

PLATE XCII

Coins of the Second Century b.c.

Pergamon and Pessinus makes the position quite clear. This complete dependence on Rome weakened both the prestige of the Attalids and their authority within their kingdom.[71]

But this political situation did not immediately affect the prosperity of the Attalid kingdom. No economic sanctions had been imposed by Rome on Pergamon after the Persean war. No territory had been taken from Eumenes II, though an end was put to the territorial growth of the kingdom. Rome's policy in Asia Minor in the second century was chiefly to maintain the *status quo* and a balance of power. As regards the internal administration of their kingdom the Attalids remained as free as they had been, and carried on their traditional policy towards their subjects and their allies. Thus, for example, they proceeded, perhaps on a larger scale than before, with the urbanization of their territory, founding colonies in particularly fertile areas. These colonies were military strongholds as much as agricultural settlements, and centres of hellenized life, socially and economically.[72]

Nor was there any change in the character of their relations with the Greek cities outside their kingdom. Their attitude towards them remained the same. As before they sought to display their sincere philhellenism. Like the other Hellenistic kings of this period they were great benefactors both of the larger and of the smaller centres of Greek civilization, as a few examples will show. Attalus II presented a large and beautiful *stoa* to Athens; lavish gifts were made to Delphi by Eumenes II and Attalus II in the last year of the former king (160–159 B.C.); and Eumenes offered Rhodes a large gift of grain, which was accepted (above, p. 777). I have previously mentioned the favour which these kings showed to Miletus. During the Galatian war Eumenes II assigned special revenues (πρόσοδοι) to the community of the Ionians (κοινὸν τῶν Ἰώνων) to defray the cost of the celebration of his name-day (ἐπώνυμος ἡμέρα), and later Attalus II (shortly before or after the death of Eumenes II) granted the city a sum of money to enable it to buy grain for distribution among its citizens. The great honours paid at Cos to Eumenes II and perhaps to Attalus II are evidence of the important benefits conferred by these kings on the island. One is known—a contribution by

Eumenes II towards the building of the Asclepieion. There was also a gift to Calaureia (after 170/69 B.C.). I may likewise recall the loan made by Attalus I (?) to the city of Chios. This method of helping the cities was certainly adopted not only by Attalus I, but also extensively by his successors. The Hellenistic kings of this period were without doubt successful bankers, predecessors and subsequently rivals of the Roman *negotiatores* and *argentarii*. And finally, it was from motives of benevolence and business combined that Attalus II invested large sums in the improvement of the harbour of Ephesus. Ephesus was at that time the second capital of the Pergamene kingdom, a centre of its steadily growing commerce. By improving its harbour Attalus intended to render a service both to the city and to the commerce of his kingdom.[73]

There is no doubt that the Pergamene kings remained as rich after Pydna as they had been before. There is eloquent testimony to this in the history of the city of Pergamon, which became, under and after Eumenes II, one of the most brilliant capitals of the Hellenistic world, and in the lavish gifts made by that king and by Attalus II. It must be remembered moreover how meagre and fragmentary our evidence is. Certainly, too, the sources of their wealth remained unchanged. Their revenue was probably derived in the main from an intensive exploitation of the resources of the kingdom, which to a large extent were in the possession or under the control of the kings. They had also the proceeds of royal taxation and of the tribute paid by the temples, the subject cities, and the subject tribes of the kingdom.

Moreover, trade, it must be borne in mind, was an important source of wealth to the Pergamene kingdom. Though we have no direct information on the subject, we have evidence of this in certain facts. I have mentioned the great interest that the last Attalids took in Ephesus and its harbour, and their gifts to Miletus. These great centres of international trade were better places than the modest Elaea for the export of the products of Pergamene agriculture and industry. At the same time Ephesus and Miletus were in all probability the chief harbours for the export of the Arabian and Indian goods which Syrian merchants transmitted to them by the great commercial land routes across the Anatolian peninsula. Of these trade relations between Syria and the Pergamene kingdom I have already spoken (pp. 654 ff.). They are attested by several coin-hoards found in Syria consisting almost exclusively of Anatolian international silver currency (described above), as well as by stray coins of the same character. Trade became active between Pergamon and Syria in the last years of Antiochus III. The coin-hoards show that it continued and throve so long as the dynasty of the Attalids lasted. It is not by accident that Moschion, the great capitalist of Priene, was sent on embassies to Syria and to the Nabataeans (above, note 71). Although Priene was never a trading city of any importance, Moschion may have invested money in Syrian trade, of which the main centres, Ephesus and Miletus, were neighbours of Priene. He may thus have had influential friends at the court of the Seleucids and the Nabataean kings, who were trade partners of the Attalids. Lastly, we must suppose that the gifts of the later Attalids to Rhodes, Cos, and Athens were not merely political gestures intended to show the philhellenism of the donors, but that they had also an economic purpose, being designed to maintain good relations with the chief commercial cities of the Aegean.

The prosperity of the kings naturally carried with it that of even their distant relatives, and of the higher officers of the crown. While there is no direct evidence on the subject, inscriptions mention the high prestige enjoyed by such persons in the kingdom and their benefactions to various cities.[74] The city *bourgeoisie* was likewise prosperous all over Asia Minor, as we learn in connexion with the revolt of Aristonicus. Heavy demands were made by the Romans on the cities of that peninsula, and these (that is to say, their *bourgeoisie*, on whom the burden fell) were able to meet the requirements, though with complaints and under pressure. In every city of Asia Minor, as appears from the inscriptions relating to this war, there were rich citizens willing and able to help it out of the temporary difficulties in which it was involved as a result of the war. I refer to such men as Diodorus Pasparus of Pergamon, Menas of Sestus, Machaon of Cyzicus, Moschion and his brother Athenopolis of Priene, and Poseidonius of Bargylia. Craton, the famous flautist of Calchedon, later a citizen of Pergamon and *persona grata* at the court of Eumenes II and Attalus II, a benefactor of the Dionysiac artistes of Ionia, is another example of a rich and public-minded inhabitant of Asia Minor. No doubt he earned his fortune by his art, but this fact in itself shows that the cities of Asia Minor were rich enough to pay high fees to famous musicians.[75]

While the *bourgeoisie* of the Pergamene kingdom and of Asia Minor in general was prosperous and probably happy, the condition of the working classes was very different. There is reason to think that most of the estates of the kings, of the temples, of the cities, and of rich landowners were cultivated either by bondsmen and tenants (it is sometimes difficult in the East to distinguish between these) or by slaves. We have no direct information about the Pergamene kingdom in particular, but the social and economic structure of Asia Minor in general in early and late Hellenistic times was such as I have described. The city of Priene may be given as an example. Its most prominent citizens were landowners and their estates (κτήματα) were cultivated at least in part by slaves. Larichus, about 282–262 B.C., was such a landowner, and so in later times were Athenopolis and Moschion (see above). It is difficult to account otherwise for Moschion's repeated gifts and sales of grain to the city. Slaves as the principal source of rural labour are also mentioned in a fragmentary document of about 155 B.C. referring to the war over Orophernes. It must be remembered that we are dealing with a period when wars, kidnapping by land, and piracy by sea were of constant occurrence, and when the traffic in slaves was one of the most profitable branches of trade. Besides the rural slaves there were large numbers of urban slaves and perhaps of slaves working in the mines, who were owned by the kings or by private citizens.[76]

As regards the situation of the semi-independent Thracian and Anatolian tribes we have little evidence. It is certain, however, that they resented the firm rule of the Attalids, which prevented them from raiding the rich plains of the Pergamene kingdom and forced them to pay tribute. It is highly probable that punitive expeditions against them were frequent and provided more slaves for the Pergamene market.

The richer and the more civilized the cities became, the

sharper grew the conflict between the working classes and the government, which enjoyed in general the support of the *bourgeoisie*. There is ground for thinking that during the rule of Attalus III the situation may have been tense and the working classes unruly. This would account in part for the decision of Attalus III to bequeath his kingdom to Rome and for the measures taken by the city of Pergamon to conciliate the masses immediately after this decision had become known.* The rebellion of Aristonicus was the natural result of this situation: one régime broke down, another was not yet established; the interval provided a good opportunity for active protest against the social and economic conditions then prevailing. Like the risings of Andriscus and later pretenders to the Macedonian throne and of Saumacus in the Bosporan kingdom, like the revolts of the natives in Egypt, of the slaves in Sicily and Italy, in Delos and at Athens, the rebellion of Aristonicus was an outburst of the discontent prevailing among the masses of the people and in the main a protest against the existing social and economic order, rather than an expression of strong national or religious feeling.[77]

The war that resulted has been frequently related, and this is not the place to describe it in detail.[78] I may, however, insist on certain points of interest. Strabo's account shows that Aristonicus in the early days of the revolt sought to obtain recognition as the legitimate heir of Attalus III and to win the support of the cities of the kingdom, which had always been the main pillars of the Attalid rule. His first act therefore was probably to secure a part of the royal navy (perhaps stationed at Leucae) and with its help to occupy the chief maritime bases of the kingdom—Elaea and Ephesus. Most of the cities, however, refused to support him. The Ephesian fleet, which was perhaps another squadron of the royal navy, met his ships off Cyme and defeated him. The motives which led the cities to repudiate Aristonicus are unknown. He may have started subversive propaganda among the lower classes from the outset; or the cities may have been afraid of Roman intervention.[79]

In any case Aristonicus failed in his attempt to secure recognition by the cities as legitimate king. He realized that the

* *O.G.I.* 338.

bourgeoisie was against him. In fact numerous inscriptions show that most of the cities of the kingdom remained faithful to the Romans. There were apparently only three exceptions, Cyme, Phocaea and Pergamon. At Pergamon a group of men appear to have made an abortive effort to win the city for Aristonicus, an effort that was put down by the energetic measures of king Mithidrates of Pontus.[80]

The failure of Aristonicus in his naval venture and the hostility of the cities transformed a war of independence, such as this rebellion probably was at the beginning, into a war of the 'oppressed' against the oppressors, a war of the country against the cities, of slaves and serfs against their masters. This character of the war was well known to contemporaries and is emphasized in our scanty literary tradition (see note 76).

Most modern scholars believe that Aristonicus was inspired by, or adopted for purposes of propaganda, certain semiphilosophical social and political theories set forth in Utopias such as the novel of Euhemerus and the 'Sun-state' of Iambulus, which certainly had a wide currency in the Hellenistic period. This belief is based on the presence in Aristonicus' camp of Blossius of Cumae, the Stoic philosopher, adviser of Ti. Gracchus, and on the name Heliopolitai which Aristonicus gave to his supporters. The evidence is slight and inconclusive. Iambulus' Utopia is not Stoic, and Blossius cannot be held responsible for the use made of it by Aristonicus. Blossius may have joined Aristonicus in the hope of influencing him later when the victor might be disposed to organize his State on new lines. On the other hand, the name Heliopolitai may equally well be connected with the Oriental belief in the Great Sun, the Supreme God of Oriental solar henotheism, the God of Justice (Ἥλιος Δικαιοσύνης) and the protector of those who have suffered wrong. In any case, whether he was acquainted or not with the Heliopolis of Iambulus, Aristonicus certainly promised his followers all sorts of blessings and a happy life under his rule. The emphasis in his propaganda lay probably on the religious, not on the philosophical, aspect of his new State of Justice.[81]

However this may be, the war of Aristonicus lasted for three full years (132–129 B.C.) and was still proceeding after the great victories of Perperna and the capture of Aristonicus in some part of Asia Minor, probably near Stratonicea in Caria.* It was a great calamity, for it spread far and wide, though not all parts of Asia Minor were affected by it. The inscriptions of Moschion and Herodes of Priene, discursive as they are, do not mention the war as having affected the welfare of Priene. But Caria was in flames and the cities of the Thracian provinces were in great danger. There is no doubt that the Thracians took an active part in the operations, and so did some mountain tribes in their strongholds and refuges, for example the inhabitants of Mysia Abbaitis.†

We have no detailed descriptions of the war similar to those on which Diodorus drew for his account of the slave wars of Sicily. Nevertheless it is evident, given the character of the war, that it was cruel, bloody, and ruinous, a struggle for life on the part of the *bourgeoisie* of Asia Minor and a great danger to the neighbouring monarchies. Though only a few cities were captured by Aristonicus, the rural territories of many towns were devastated, farmhouses burnt down, cattle driven off, and so forth (inscription of Sestus). On the other hand the Romans, who had no army in close vicinity to the Pergamene kingdom (the small Macedonian army was busy fighting the Thracians‡), tried first to suppress the revolt by employing the military resources of the cities of Asia Minor. The military forces of the cities and of the allied kings were mobilized. When these proved unsuccessful and the Roman army appeared in Asia, the allied troops (σύμμαχοι) were retained and compulsory levies (ἀνδροληψίαι) were organized on a large scale.§ This compulsory military service was a great burden to the cities and a cause of bitter complaint.‖ It must be remembered that although the Pergamene kings recruited for their army from among the inhabitants of their cities, and for this purpose gave

---

* Inscriptions of Bargylia and Stratonicea.
† Inscriptions of Bargylia.
‡ See the inscriptions of Cyzicus and of Sestus.
§ This is frequently mentioned in the inscriptions relating to the war (Pergamon, Cyzicus, Halicarnassus, Bargylia); Halicarnassus had to man a ship. Of course, ἀνδροληψία may also mean 'taking of hostages'.
‖ Inscriptions of Pergamon and Bargylia.

a more military character than usual to the training of the ephebes and *neoi* in the gymnasia, the Pergamene army nevertheless consisted mostly of mercenaries, and the majority of the younger citizens were therefore unaccustomed to military service.

Moreover, when the Roman army appeared in Asia Minor, it lived at the expense of the cities and established its headquarters and its winter quarters in them. This involved a heavy charge upon them, ruined as they were by the rebellion. Requisitions and compulsory extraordinary contributions (εἰσφοραί) were constantly enforced (Pergamon, Methymna.)[82]

The lamentable plight of the cities of Asia Minor during the war of Aristonicus may be illustrated by a few facts taken from the above-mentioned inscriptions. At Pergamon business was disorganized by the compulsory levies of men (or taking of hostages, ἀνδροληψίαι), by the expenses connected with the maintenance of detachments of σύμμαχοι, and by the use of the city as winter quarters (παραχειμασίαι) for the troops. Diodorus Pasparus, while on an embassy in Rome, obtained some relief for the city. It was exempted from further compulsory levies and from providing winter quarters; nor were further obligatory contributions (ἐπιταγαὶ ἐκτὸς τῶν φόρων ἐπιτασσόμεναι) demanded from it. Since many citizens were completely ruined, while many others had lost their property (βίοι), and all were suffering severely from the high rate of interest on loans, contracted perhaps with Roman money-lenders and probably for the purpose of paying the forced contributions, the rate of interest on these loans was lowered (ἐλαφροτοκία). Contracts made under compulsion and of a fictitious character (κεναί) were annulled. The confiscated estates of the rebels, whether dead or alive, were handed over to the city. This list of the concessions obtained by Diodorus shows the difficult position in which well-to-do citizens of Pergamon were placed during the revolt.

At Methymna the *neoi*, the sons of the burghers, came to the rescue of the city by subscribing for its service 'irrecoverable money' (χρήματα ἀναπαίτητα) to the amount of 3,100 staters. The difficult financial situation of the city is attributed in the decree of the *neoi* to repeated bad harvests which made heavy subscriptions necessary for the purchase of grain, and

to the εἰσφορά levied to defray the 'many large expenses' connected with the Asiatic war of Rome, the friend and ally of
Methymna.

A passage may be quoted from the eloquent and illuminating
description of the situation of Sestos at this time contained in
the decree of that city in honour of Menas. It runs as follows
(ll. 53 ff.): 'Summoned [by the city] to the office of gymnasiarch
for the second time, he discharged its duties in difficult times.
We were all hard pressed for many years by the inroads of the
Thracians and by the wars which surrounded the city, wars in
which everything was carried off from the fields and most of
the land remained unsown.' The repeated bad harvests that
resulted reduced both the city as a whole and the individual
citizens to poverty, and among them Menas himself was very
hard pressed. The war was certainly a severe calamity for
Asia Minor and great was the country's relief when it was
over.

After the revolt of Aristonicus the Pergamene kingdom
became a Roman province designated by the ambitious name
of Asia. Whether the Roman domination thus established
changed the economic aspect of Asia Minor as above described
we have little means of knowing. Literary texts relating to
this period are scanty and the inscriptions few and most of
them fragmentary.

Of the contents of the last will and testament of Attalus III
very little is known except that he made Pergamon a free city
and assigned to it a territory (πολιτικὴ χώρα) and that his orders
were confirmed by the Roman Senate. In the capacity of a
free city the *demos* of Pergamon, before the testament was
accepted by the Roman government, voted certain measures
which affected various classes of the population of the city and
of its territory. Whether these measures were adopted in
conformity with the desires of Attalus III expressed in his
testament or were emergency devices dictated by the political
and social situation, we do not know. These were apparently
not cancelled by the Roman government. In any case they
referred exclusively to the city and territory of Pergamon.[83]

Not very much more is known of the organization of the new
province of Asia as settled after the annexation, and again in

129 B.C., after the revolt of Aristonicus.[84] The only positive evidence that we possess, in addition to the inscriptions quoted above which testify to the acceptance by the Romans of the organization of their new province as it was devised by the Pergamene kings, is contained in the famous speech of Antony reported by Appian.* The speech was delivered at Ephesus before the embassies of 'the Greeks (i.e. the Greek cities) and other peoples (ἔθνη) who inhabited Asia around Pergamon'. According to the introductory paragraph of this speech, the Romans after the death of Attalus III first remitted to the new province all the taxes that it had formerly paid to the Attalids. But this immunity, he says, did not last very long. Very soon some popular agitators at Rome (he means of course C. Gracchus) imposed taxes on Asia. However, Antony insists, the new taxation was very liberal. The new φόροι were levied not 'by assessments' (πρὸς τιμήματα) but as a *pars quota* of the harvest (by which is plainly meant the *decuma*). The *decuma* mentioned by Antony is well known. The new tax, according to Cicero, was collected by Roman *societates publicanorum* in conformity with regulations contained in a special law, the *lex Sempronia* of C. Gracchus. I shall discuss this tax and its history in greater detail below and in the next chapter.[85]

Antony's statement as reported by Appian presents many difficulties. Are we justified in accepting it in full? When speaking of the temporary immunity of Asia, does Antony refer to the time immediately after the death of Attalus III or to the reorganization of the province after 129? Is it a fact that the whole of the province was for a time completely free of taxes? Or, since Antony was addressing especially the Hellenes though speaking before representatives of the whole of Asia, was this immunity restricted to the Greek cities only, the rest of the province being subject to taxation? Was Antony referring only to the land tax or to other taxes also, especially the customs duties (*portoria*) and the cattle tax (*scriptura*) levied in the province later? And finally may we infer from Antony's statement and the words of Cicero quoted above that before the time of C. Gracchus no *societates publicanorum* were active in the province?

* *B.C.* v. 4 ff.

We have no means of deciding these questions. Some doubt, however, is cast on the accuracy of the statement of Appian by two contemporary inscriptions which refer to the conditions of Pergamon and its *chora* at the time during and immediately after the war of Aristonicus. The first is the famous inscription of Pasparus referred to above (n. 80 and p. 810). In it we find mention of regular *phoroi* which the city of Pergamon paid during and after the war of Aristonicus. This suggests that the city of Pergamon was free but not immune (ἀφορολόγητος) and implies that the other cities of Asia were in the same position. The second inscription is the well-known fragment of the *Senatus Consultum* and decree of the praetor and his council found at Adramyttium, recently supplemented by another fragment found at Smyrna. The Senate and the praetor were considering a dispute between Pergamon and the *publicani* which related to the *chora* of Pergamon. The precise subject of this dispute is unknown. It may have concerned the immunity of the whole of the *chora* of Pergamon or, of only one part of it, for example, the land owned by a temple. In any case the dispute makes it probable that in 129 B.C. (which is almost certainly the date of the document) taxes were imposed on the new province of Asia by the censors and collected by the *publicani*.*86

This evidence throws doubt on the statement of Appian and suggests that the province of Asia was never (even between the death of Attalus and 129 B.C.) immune from taxation, not even the cities of the province, to say nothing of the parts of the province not organized as cities, and that the appearance in the province of *publicani* was not deferred until the time of C. Gracchus.

Whatever the situation may have been before C. Gracchus, Antony's statement as reported by Appian implies that C. Gracchus carried out an important reform in the field of taxation. He appears to have considerably simplified the Attalid fiscal system. We may conjecture that most of the royal taxes and monopolies were abolished. The main tax collected by the Romans was a general land tax, the *decuma*. In addition to it, according to later evidence which will be

* l. 14 f.: [ἄρχοντες ἡμέτεροι οἳ τῇ ᾽Ασίᾳ | προσόδους ἐπιτιθῶσι ἢ τὰς] τῆς ᾽Ασίας προσόδους μι[σθῶσι].

discussed below and in the next chapter, two general taxes only were levied in Asia by the Roman State and collected, like the *decuma*, by the Roman *publicani*: the customs duties (*portoria*) and a cattle tax (*scriptura*), both of which had formerly been royal taxes.

These taxes were certainly paid after the time of C. Gracchus by the cities of the former Attalid kingdom, perhaps with some exceptions (such as possibly Pergamon). Less is known of the fiscal situation of those parts of the new province which had not the status of cities, viz. the temples, the semi-independent tribes, and, no less important, the large tracts of land studded with villages which were inhabited by thousands of peasants, *laoi* in the ancient terminology, who tilled the soil and were bound to their respective villages.

Of the temples and tribes I shall speak presently, after dealing briefly with the villages that did not belong to city and to temple territories. In Hellenistic times this part of the province was termed *chora* or *chora basilike*. What exactly is meant by these two terms is uncertain and disputed, and has already been discussed above. According to one theory, the whole of the *chora* was regarded by the kings as their property and called therefore *chora basilike*. According to another opinion, the term *chora* is not equivalent to the *chora basilike*, the former denoting the open land of the kingdom in general, the land that was not in the hands of cities, temples, and tribes, while the latter was applied only to that part of it which consisted of the private estates of the kings. In general this was more or less the same distinction as existed in the Roman provinces: *ager publicus* and *ager stipendiarius*.

Now, whichever opinion we adopt, the problem before us in this chapter is as follows. How did the Roman administration deal with the *chora* (and with the *chora basilike*, if distinct) and with the cultivators thereof? The *laoi* of the *chora*, even if we accept the view that only part of them were *laoi basilikoi*, had undoubtedly paid certain rents or dues to the kings for the right of cultivating the land. Were these payments now replaced by the *decuma* mentioned by Antony? We have no direct information on this point.

The solution of the problem stated above would be easier if

we knew the legal status in the Roman province of Asia of what had formerly been the *chora*. Was it that of *ager publicus* or of *ager stipendiarius*? Or was the status of the royal property that of *ager publicus*, and the status of the rest of the *chora* that of *ager stipendiarius*? For it may be thought that there was a substantial difference in the legal and economic status of the tillers of the land according as one or other of the Roman legal terms was applicable to that land. As cultivators of *ager publicus*, the former *laoi* may have retained their previous social and economic position, that of tenants and *adscripti vicis*; as holders of *ager stipendiarius*, they may have been treated as possessors of their parcels of land, bound to pay not a rent but a tax, perhaps the same *decuma* that was certainly paid by the landowners in the city territories.

Unfortunately we possess no trustworthy evidence on this point. In his *De lege agraria* Cicero speaks in legal terms of the disposal of the territories of cities and kingdoms of Hellenistic times. We have seen above that according to him part of the territory of Achaea became *ager vectigalis* after the Achaean war, that is to say, *ager publicus populi Romani*. The territories of some cities of Asia Minor and of Mytilene were treated in the same way. When speaking in this connexion of Bithynia (see below, Ch. VII, n. 65), he states positively that the whole of that kingdom became public property of the Roman people, and says a little later that the *agri regii* of Bithynia were rented to *publicani*. He also mentions that the *regii agri* of Pontus, Paphlagonia, and Cappadocia, the *agri Attalici* in the Chersonese, and the land of king Apion in the Cyrenaica, likewise became *ager publicus populi Romani*.[87]

In an earlier work I expressed the opinion, founded on the passages adduced above, that, since in early Hellenistic terminology *chora basilike* appeared to me to be equivalent to *chora*, this *chora basilike* of the former Pergamene kingdom became in Roman times *ager publicus*, as such land did in other Roman provinces at an earlier and a later date. From this I concluded that the situation of the *laoi* in the Roman provinces of Asia Minor remained unchanged. Other scholars are inclined to assume that the *chora* of Hellenistic times, except for the private estates of the kings, was treated by the Romans as *ager stipendiarius*, and that consequently most of the former tenants and *adscripti vicis* of the Asiatic provinces of Rome became *possessores* of their parcels of land, liable to the payment of the *decuma*, and so ceased to be *adscripti vicis*. The former estates of the Pergamene kings in their opinion became *ager publicus*, which, however, disappeared very soon as if by magic.

The problem of the treatment of the *chora* of the Attalids in Roman times cannot be solved with certainty. The contemporary evidence is too scanty, while the later texts are open to various interpretations. For myself, I still regard my interpretation of the facts as no less probable than that suggested by my opponents.[88]

Besides the cities and their territories and the *chora* with its villages, there were in Asia Minor many temples of various types. Some were connected with cities, other were treated by the Seleucids, and later by the Pergamene kings, as distinct territories similar to those of the cities and villages. The land which the temples owned was sometimes very large. We know very little of the history of these temples in early Roman times. Some of the temples in city territories enjoyed an immunity granted to them by former rulers of Asia and in most cases recognized by the Roman government. The *publicani*, we hear, repeatedly endeavoured to encroach on this immunity under one pretext or another. In some instances the efforts of the cities to save the temple land of their territories from the *publicani* were supported by the Roman government.[89]

Of the temple-states of the former Attalid kingdom in Roman times very little is known. In Pontus, in Cappadocia, and in Cilicia their status was in most cases left unchanged, and we may assume (though it is a pure hypothesis) that in their province of Asia the Romans followed the same policy.[90]

Whether, besides the owners of land in the city territories—who, being staunch supporters of the Romans, were certainly not molested by the Roman government—there still existed in Asia Minor owners or holders of estates which included one or many villages and did not belong to city territories, there is no evidence to show. Attalus III was harsh to his relatives and to the richer members of the Pergamene aristocracy: we hear of his murders and confiscations. It is quite possible that these landowners practically disappeared under the Roman régime.[91]

Of the status of the semi-independent tribes under the Roman Republic we know practically nothing.

We similarly lack information regarding the disposal of the various other sources of revenue of the Attalids specified above. The mines, quarries, forests, and lakes became in all probability the property of the Roman people. We hear incidentally that under the Romans the salt-pans (*salinae*) were in the hands of the *publicani*,* which may suggest that the other similar possessions of the kings were dealt with in the same way. We know nothing of the royal herds and studs; nor do we know the fate of the various royal factories. The *vestes Attalicae* and the famous *aulaea* retained their former reputation, and so did the parchment. This is all that is known on the subject, and we cannot tell whether the royal factories passed into the possession of the city of Pergamon or whether the work done formerly by royal slaves was carried on by private artisans.[92]

The *publicani* were a new element in the economic life of the former Pergamene kingdom. They played an important part in the administration of the province. They underwrote contracts with the Roman censors for the collection of the State taxes—the *decuma* of which I have spoken, the *scriptura*, a general tax on live stock, perhaps for the use of the pasture land which belonged to the Roman people, and the *portorium*, the customs duties on land frontiers and at the ports. In addition, as I have mentioned, they may have collected the rents from the cultivators who tilled the *ager publicus*, and they may have managed the other State property in the province.

Of their operations before the time of Sulla we hear very little. All our information, even in regard to the taxes that they farmed, is of later date. We have no precise knowledge about their relations with the various types of cities in the province or about their method of tax-collection at this time. I shall speak of the later period in the next chapter.

The 'Romans', the Italian *negotiatores*, were already not unknown to the Pergamene cities. We hear of a group of them at Pergamon and of others in other cities. With the

* Cic. *De imp. Pomp.* 6. 16; the reading *salinis* has been corrected to *saltibus*.

establishment of the Roman province their numbers certainly increased rapidly. To them were added the *publicani* and their numerous subordinates.[93]

If we had only the epigraphical evidence, we should be unable to form even a conjecture of the number of the 'Romans,' *publicani* and *negotiatores*, in Asia. There are very few references to either class in the evidence relating to the time before Sulla. We are therefore somewhat surprised to learn that at the bidding of Mithridates 80,000 Romans were massacred all over Asia, and that many others escaped. The figures are trustworthy and are derived in one way or another from official sources, though these may for some reason have exaggerated the greatness of the catastrophe.

The very character of the business of the *publicani*, their efforts to extend the range of their operations by encroaching on territories which were immune from the *decuma*, their natural desire to invest their money in the exploitation of the natural resources of the country in competition with the natives, and finally the support which they received from the governors and subordinate administrators of the province when their interests conflicted with those of the native population, could not fail to arouse indignation and jealousy among all classes of the population. This indignation was justified. The *publicani* certainly were ruthless tax-collectors, and dangerous and unscrupulous rivals in business. They were often dishonest and probably always cruel. All this was known in Rome, and led to acute conflicts between the *equites* and the ruling aristocracy. It is sufficient to recall the affair of Rutilius Rufus, whose residence in Asia Minor was far from uneventful and who knew by experience the mood of its population.[94] We may suppose that the *negotiatores* were no better, for they were in all probability connected with the *publicani* and enjoyed certain privileges which made it difficult for native merchants and landowners to compete with them.[95]

It would, however, be unfair to say that the *publicani* of the period before Sulla ruined the country, especially the *bourgeoisie*. Such evidence as we have does not support this view. There were in the late second century and the early first plenty of rich men in Asia Minor who were ready and willing to make generous donations to their respective cities. I have already quoted some instances of this. Further typical examples are set forth on the 'walls of honour' (the west and east short walls) of the portico of Orophernes or 'sacred' portico at Priene. A long series of complimentary decrees covered the two walls. They start about the year 130 B.C. and come to an end about 50 B.C. Members of various rich and public-spirited families of Priene appear before us: men who were active during the revolt of Aristonicus and before it, men who afterwards defended the privileges of the city against the *publicani*, and men who had lived through the horrors of the Mithridatic war. All these, however difficult the situation, showed their readiness to help the city. It is significant that the series ends not in the days of Mithridates and Sulla, but in those of Caesar, that is, in the last phase of the civil wars of Rome. It is possible, however, that this is an accident, and that another public building was then chosen on which to record the decrees in honour of later benefactors, just as the portico of Orophernes succeeded the great temple of Athena.[96]

Now, Priene was a very small and not a very wealthy city. Other larger and wealthier cities of Asia Minor certainly had similar groups of rich and influential families. These families had not yet completely lost their confidence in the Roman government. We have seen how doggedly they struggled to defend the interests of their cities against the *publicani*, and we know how fervently they praised and honoured the Roman magistrates who supported them in their struggle or gave them other assistance. I need only refer to the games celebrated throughout Asia Minor in honour of Mucius Scaevola, and the high honour in which the cities of that country and of the islands held Rutilius Rufus, the victim of the *publicani*. I may also mention the cult of P. Servilius Isauricus, the proconsul of Asia in the days of Caesar (46 to 44 B.C.) and the lifelong enemy of the *publicani*, a cult of which there is evidence in many inscriptions.[97]

An idea of the wealth and influence of some of the members of the *bourgeoisie* of Asia Minor may be derived from the well-known inscription found at Nysa in Caria.* It is a decree of the

* *S.I.G.*³ 741.

PLATE XCIII

1. The market place of Priene, a southward extension, as it were, of the main street, surrounded on three sides by porticos, was the chief social, political, religious, and business centre of the city. The south wing of the portico here reproduced in reconstruction was not treated like the other wings, that is to say as a hall fronting a series of shops. By elimination of the shops its central part was transformed into a spacious hall divided into two parts by a row of columns and protected against sun and rain by a roof. Further protection (against the north wind) was given by a low wall in front. The hall was certainly intended to be a meeting place for various purposes, among them the transaction of business. The reconstruction of this hall, made by Prof. F. Krischen, is reproduced here with the permission of the author and of the authorities of the German Archaeological Institute. On the city of Priene in the second century B.C. in general and on the further embellishment at this time of the market place (by the addition on the north side of the main street of the 'sacred hall' of Orophernes or Ariarathes VI) *c.* 130 B.C. see pp. 819, 824.

2. The Artemision of Magnesia on the Maeander with its monumental altar. I have mentioned (p. 824 and n. 100) that this temple of Artemis Leukophryene was built about 130 B.C. by Hermogenes, the greatest architect of the time, and was regarded as the classical example of the later Ionian style. The temple was described in a special work by its builder, and this monograph was extensively used by Vitruvius. I cannot here describe this building, which has been excavated by the German Archaeological Institute (a description will be found in the works quoted in n. 100). I need only emphasize once more that the construction of such a temple in the second half of the second century B.C. testifies to the still unexhausted creative genius of Greek artists and to the material wealth of their employers. The reconstruction (by Prof. F. Krischen) is here reproduced with the permission of the author and of the authorities of the Staatlichen Museen of Berlin.

PLATE XCIII

1

2

THE CITIES OF ASIA MINOR IN THE SECOND CENTURY B.C.

city in honour of one of its richest citizens, CHAEREMON, son of
Pythodorus, whose wealth was probably acquired from the
exploitation of the large estates which he possessed in the
territory of Nysa and probably of Tralles (to which city his son
Pythodorus migrated later). The descendants of this Chaere-
mon played a very important part in the history of the Roman
Empire in the first century B.C. and later.* He himself was a
bitter enemy of Mithridates and a staunch supporter of the
Romans. The dossier of his services begins with a letter from
C. Cassius, to whom in 88 B.C. he offered a gift for the army of
60,000 *modii* of wheaten flour ([ἀλ]εύρων μοδίους ἑξακισμυρί[ους]).
There follow two letters from Mithridates directed against
Chaeremon and his sons and their pro-Roman activity. The
estate of Chaeremon's son PYTHODORUS, inherited by him from
his father, is estimated by Strabo as worth more than 2,000
talents. It was confiscated by Caesar (Pythodorus was a friend
of Pompey), but bought back by Pythodorus and left intact to
his children. Pythodorus married a daughter of Antony. The
offspring of this marriage was the famous Pythodoris, queen of
Pontus.

Other families as wealthy and powerful as the family of
Chaeremon and Pythodorus of Nysa, so far from being uncommon, are even characteristic of Asia Minor and of some of the
richer islands. They are known to us from documents and
literary evidence (particularly Strabo) of the first century
B.C. and especially of Caesar's time, but they were certainly
flourishing in their respective cities long before his day.
A few instances may be quoted.

An interesting figure is MITHRIDATES OF PERGAMON, son of
Menodotus, a citizen of Pergamon, and of the Galatian princess
Adobogiona, daughter of the Galatian tetrarch Deiotarus. He
regarded himself as son of the great Mithridates and received
his military training in the king's camp. As a citizen of Pergamon he rendered great service to his city. We hear from Cicero
that in 62 B.C. he went to Rome, as bearer of a psephism of
Pergamon, to appear in the law-suit against Cicero's client
Valerius Flaccus, the former governor of Asia. Cicero speaks
of a lavish banquet given by him to the citizens of Pergamon

* Strabo xiv. 1. 42, p. 649, tells us the story of this family.

before the psephism was voted, and of his great political influence in the city. In Rome he was the most dangerous enemy of Valerius Flaccus and the most important witness against him. He thought his life in danger and walked about Rome wearing a cuirass. He was acting probably not only on his own account, but also in the interests of his influential Roman friends, enemies of Valerius Flaccus and his clique. In Asia Minor he had a brilliant career. His embassy to Rome was not the last. He repeatedly intervened there in favour of his city. Especially great was his influence in Rome during the rule of Julius Caesar, whose staunch supporter he always was. It is well known that he came at the head of an army to the rescue of Caesar when he was besieged in Alexandria and that he was rewarded for his assistance by the eminent dictator. For his great services to his native city he was highly honoured by it. We still possess many inscriptions which speak of his services and of honours bestowed on him by Pergamon. In one of these inscriptions he is praised as νέος κτίστης of the city after Pergamus and Philetaerus. There is no doubt that he was a very rich man. Adobogiona would not have married his father Menodotus if he had not been both rich and politically prominent. The army which he raised to help Caesar was without doubt paid, at least in part, out of his own resources.

Laodicea in Phrygia was the abode of the family of the famous rhetoricians, orators, and politicians, ZENON and his son POLEMON. Zenon rendered great services to Rome during the invasion of Asia Minor by the Parthians under Pacorus and Labienus (40 B.C.). His son Polemon became a friend of Antony and later of Augustus, and was appointed by the latter king of Pontus and Bosporus. The family of Zenon had been prominent at Laodicea long before Antony's time. In connexion with Laodicea Strabo mentions another millionaire of this city, HIERON, who bequeathed to it more than 2,000 talents and adorned the city with many beautiful gifts. It should be noted that Laodicea was famous for the exceptional quality of its wool. Mylasa in Caria in the first century B.C. was ruled by two distinguished rhetoricians, who were at the same time prominent politicians and practically tyrants of the city—EUTHY-DEMUS and his successor HYBREAS. Strabo gives a vivid account of them. Euthydemus belonged to a very rich family, while Hybreas was a self-made man. I shall have occasion to speak of him in the next chapter. Cnidus in Caria was the home of two prominent families, that of CALLISTUS, son of Epigenes, and that of THEOPOMPUS, son of Artemidorus, the friend of Caesar, many times mentioned in literary texts, perhaps the same who met Q. Cicero in Asia. Even more distinguished were the two Lesbians of Mytilene, THEOPHANES, the friend and historiographer of Pompey, and the well-known POTAMON, son of Lesbonax, whose monumental *heroon* has yielded a remarkable series of highly important inscriptions. And finally, at Cos we have the curious figure of CURTIUS NICIAS, Epicurean philosopher, poet, and man of letters generally, friend of prominent Romans (Memmius, Pompey, Cicero, Atticus, Dolabella, and Brutus), who at the end of his life became tyrant of Cos for about eight years (from 41/40 B.C.).[98]

To this short list many names might be added by readers of Cicero's orations and letters. He mentions repeatedly, especially in his speech *pro Flacco* and in his letters to Quintus, wealthy and outstanding members of the *bourgeoisie* of Asia Minor. They were well known at Rome and had many friends in the great city, among both the senatorial and the equestrian classes. Many of them were intimate friends of Cicero. In this connexion the *pro Flacco*, Cicero's very interesting 'Anatolian' speech, deserves perusal. It brings before us a great variety of members of the Anatolian middle class: of some of them Cicero has hard words to say, which does not mean necessarily that they deserved them; some others he praises highly (if we had the speech of Laelius, we might find praise and blame reversed). They all belong to highly honoured families of the cities of Asia Minor, and had probably all of them inherited their fortunes from their ancestors. Of one of them, Mithridates of Pergamon, I have already spoken.

To the rich *bourgeoisie* was due the splendid architectural development of many, perhaps of all, the cities of Asia in the late second century B.C. The archaeological exploration of Asia Minor, the careful study of the ruins of various cities and temples, has shown the remarkable abundance of fine buildings that this region produced in the second century B.C., not excluding the latter half of it. Priene may be taken as an example. Archaeologists note with astonishment that its citizens had at that time the means of executing an ambitious building programme: the completion of the beautiful temple of Athena with its altar and cult statue, the rebuilding of the theatre, the erection of a gymnasium and of three splendid porticoes, one near the temple of Athena, another in the market-place, and the third in the stadium. Some scholars are inclined to connect the whole scheme with the money of Orophernes. But we have no information that any part of the money deposited by Orophernes was given to Priene. Nor is there any suggestion that other royal benefactors were interested in that city. It is simpler to attribute this outburst of building activity to the steady growth of the city's prosperity before and after Aristonicus.[99]

Nor was Priene an exception. A study of the Artemision of Magnesia on the Maeander has shown that this temple, built, according to Vitruvius, by the famous architect Hermogenes, must be dated not earlier than 130 B.C. In addition to the Artemision, Hermogenes, according to the same author, built the temple of Dionysus at Teos. The little that remains of this temple shows the same plan and the same style of architecture and sculpture as we find at Magnesia. To these must be added the temple of Apollo at Alabanda, which, Vitruvius says, was constructed on the same plan as the two temples of Hermogenes. Here again the style of the remains is very similar to that of the temples of Magnesia and of Teos. Further, the plan, the style of the architecture and sculpture, and the data furnished by an inscription engraved on one of its walls, lead us to ascribe the elegant temple of Hekate at Lagina near Stratonicea with great probability to the period following the war of Aristonicus. We have seen the part played by Stratonicea in this war and we know the favour shown to the city by the Romans.[100]

Finally, it should be noticed that the Didymeion of Miletus was not in decay in the second half of the second century B.C. Gifts from kings (such as Antiochus VII and his queen Cleopatra), from cities, and from private persons are recorded in the inventories, and building operations were not interrupted.

A special significance attaches to the gifts from some of the cities of Asia Minor. They show that the comparative prosperity of Miletus was shared by many other cities. The gift of Myrina, for instance, may be noticed, and we know, moreover, from the systematic excavation of the necropolis of this city, that the graves therein attributed to the second and the early first centuries B.C. were exceptionally rich. The participation of rich Milesian citizens in the celebration of the Didymeia is no less significant.[101] We may conclude with certainty from all this evidence that the second century B.C. and the early years of the first were not a period of economic decay for Asia Minor. The ruin of the country did not begin until the Mithridatic war.

The wealthy magnates of the first century B.C. to whom I have referred may be regarded as exceptions. They were clever enough to emerge unharmed out of the miseries of the late second century and of the first century B.C. They were, however, true children of the *bourgeoisie* of Asia Minor, and the foundations of their wealth were laid before the great catastrophes of Mithridates, Sulla, and the Roman civil wars. How many such families there were in Asia Minor we do not know. It is probable that the majority of the middle class fared less well and were ultimately ruined more or less completely. But the ruin of the entire class took some time.

My impression is that the economic situation of the Roman province of Asia deteriorated during the first fifty years of its existence, but the decay was far from desperate or catastrophic. It was reserved for Mithridates and for Sulla and still more for his successors to make the ruin of the Hellenistic world almost complete.

I am inclined to believe in the accuracy of the preamble to the famous speech which Sulla delivered after the close of the first Mithridatic war to the representatives of the cities of Asia Minor at Ephesus.* He begins his speech with a short history of the relations between Rome and Asia Minor. He mentions Antiochus III, Eumenes, and the Rhodians, and their relations with the Anatolian cities, and proceeds: 'That, then, is the way in which we have behaved toward you; but you on your part, when Attalus Philometor left his kingdom to us by will, fought

* App. *Mithr.* 62 ff.

on the side of Aristonicus against us for four years, until
Aristonicus was captured and until most of you were reduced
to helplessness and terror. And although you fared thus, nevertheless, when in twenty-four years you had progressed to a
high level of wealth and splendour in private and public possessions, peace and luxury caused you to break out into wanton-
ness once more, and after waiting until we were busied with
Italy, some of you brought Mithridates and others made
compacts with him when he came' (translated by A. M.
Harmon).

The sources of the wealth of the Anatolian *bourgeoisie* are
evident. Asia Minor, it need hardly be said, was a very fertile
country. Its rich *bourgeois* were in all probability most of
them landowners. Industry, as I have said, continued to
flourish in many cities. There were rich and unexhausted mines
of silver and copper, and large forests. All these sources of
wealth were still at the disposal of the native population.

Nor was the trade of Asia Minor declining. I shall show later
in this chapter how the active commercial relations between
Asia Minor and Syria (above, pp. 655 ff.) came to an end after
the disappearance of the Attalids, and shall try to explain this
phenomenon (below, p. 867 f.). The loss, however, was compensated by the lively trade between Asia Minor and Italy, a trade
chiefly in slaves, as already described. I may refer in this
connexion to a hoard of coins found in Picenum (later than 77
B.C.) which contained many *cistophori*. It should be noted that
cistophori were still minted in the Roman province of Asia
apparently in large quantities and of good quality.[102]

Some changes took place in the period we are considering in
the state of the independent kingdoms of the north and east
of Asia Minor.

BITHYNIA was politically in its decline. Prusias II, the successor of Prusias I, whom we have seen engaged in 'modernizing' Bithynian life (above, p. 662 f.), followed in the main the
policy of Nicomedes I, Ziaëlas, and Prusias I. But, despite
his servile attitude towards the Romans and the humiliation
of his great rival Eumenes II, by which he hoped to profit, he
was unable to achieve anything of importance. Heraclea
Pontica, supported by the Romans, retained its liberty and

the important position in the trade of the Euxine that it had inherited. An attempt to increase the territory of Bithynia at the expense of Pergamon and perhaps to establish control over the Straits and the Propontis—a matter of vital consequence not only to Pergamon but also to the two greatest commercial cities on the Greek seas, Rhodes and Cyzicus—failed in spite of some military successes. The failure was due not to any mistakes or lack of ability on the part of Prusias (who was stronger than Attalus II both on land and sea) but to the vigorous intervention of Rome. Prusias misunderstood the policy of the Roman Senate. He hoped that Rome would be willing to let his kingdom grow in order to weaken Pergamon, but he was mistaken. Bithynia under Prusias I had become too strong and too self-confident. The early successes of Prusias II alarmed Rome. Thus the war ended without bringing gains to any of the combatants.[103]

Prusias II was succeeded by his son and murderer Nicomedes II Epiphanes (149–128/7 B.C.). Next came Nicomedes III (128/7– c. 95/94 B.C.), and finally Nicomedes IV, who bequeathed his kingdom to Rome in 74 B.C.[104] The first two successors of Prusias II kept strictly to the policy of the great kings of Bithynia. Faithful and obedient to Rome, they endeavoured to increase their territory and their wealth in rivalry with Pontus and Pergamon, and to display themselves in the Greek world as strong supporters of Hellenism. Epiphanes was highly honoured by the Ionian κοινόν (a dedication by Epiphanes of a temple to his mother Apame, found at the Piraeus, may have been brought there from Bithynia in modern or ancient times). He was a familiar figure in Delos and kept up friendly relations with other crowned vassals of Rome, such as Massinissa of Numidia. Nor was his son Nicomedes III less popular in the Greek world. His relations with Delos were very close. His philhellenism was well known at Delphi, where he was a figure of no less importance than Eumenes II and Attalus II before him. He had relations with Epidaurus and friends in that place, and was the benefactor of the *technitai* of Argos, who erected a statue of him. This is not the place to deal with the foreign policy of Nicomedes II and Nicomedes III. I need only say that all their efforts to add to their territory, whether

3261.2   Q

by courting Rome (as Nicomedes II did), or by diplomacy, intrigues, and wars (the methods used by Nicomedes III), met with failure. Rome was opposed to their endeavours, being anxious that none of her vassal allies should become too strong.[105]

Political failure did not entail decline in prosperity for Bithynia. There is evidence here and there that the kings remained as rich as before. It was not without good reason that the Ionian κοινόν had established the cult of Nicomedes II and granted him high honours. Granius Licinianus states that Nicomedes III had the reputation of being the great benefactor of all who were in need, meaning probably the Greek cities in particular. He adds that Nicomedes gave 500 talents to his concubine, Hagne of Cyzicus, when he sent her with their son Socrates to Cyzicus for safety.[106] The kings naturally derived their wealth from the same sources as in the past. The country was well cultivated. The forests provided timber, pitch, and tar, of which there was abundance for the kings to export. There was, moreover, the active traffic in slaves of which I have already spoken. The pointed remark of Nicomedes III to the Senate that the *publicani* of the province of Asia had carried off his subjects betrays his annoyance at their efficient competition in the slave trade. His keen interest in trade is attested by the dedication to him of a still extant *Periegesis* attributed to Scymnus, which pays great attention to the contemporary conditions of the Pontic regions. In his dedication the author of this work shows great enthusiasm for Nicomedes III and for the Bithynian kings in general. He was in all probability a native of one of the Greek cities of Asia Minor, though not a subject of Nicomedes.[107]

Finally, it seems highly probable that the Bithynian kings competed with the Romans in the field of banking also. Pliny, referring to the endeavour of Nicomedes, probably Nicomedes III, to obtain the famous Aphrodite of Cnidus, twice repeats the same version of the story:* Cnidus was heavily indebted to the king ('grave aes alienum'; 'aes alienum quod erat ingens'), and Nicomedes was prepared to cancel the debt if Cnidus gave him the great Aphrodite. I suspect that it was some measure

* Plin. *N.H.* vii. 12, and xxxvi. 21.

connected with the activity of Nicomedes II as money-lender that so endeared him to the Ionian κοινόν. The steady development of Bithynian trade and the concomitant growth of Bithynia's own harbours, founded by the Bithynian kings, could not but impair to some extent the prosperity of Heraclea and Cyzicus, the two chief commercial cities of the southern coast of the Euxine and of the Propontis, the nearest neighbours of Bithynia and for a long time its commercial agents.

HERACLEA was certainly in its decline. I have already said that it lost the greater part of its fertile territory to the Bithynian kings and suffered heavily not only from their attacks but also from the Galatians. The political history of the city in the second century B.C. was uneventful. Memnon, its enthusiastic historiographer, has nothing to record between the siege of the city by Prusias I and the Mithridatic War except its dispatch to Rome, its ancient ally, during the Social War, of a small squadron of two ships—a very small contribution indeed for a city that had in the past equipped much larger squadrons for the support of its friends and allies.

Yet its commerce was still flourishing, and the accumulated wealth of the city and of its individual citizens was very large. The former conclusion may be drawn from the fact already stated that a large number of Heracleans resided at·Athens in the second and first centuries B.C.; of the latter we have proof in the fact that, when the city, a reluctant ally of Mithridates, was captured during the third Mithridatic War by Cotta and Triarius after a siege which lasted for two years, it yielded to the ruthless victors an enormous booty in gold, silver, objects of art, and the like. After the war it recovered rapidly and regained its former prosperity.[108]

CYZICUS, the Rhodes of the Propontis, fared better. The city adhered to its traditional policy—preservation of the freedom of the seas in alliance with Rhodes, cordial relations with its powerful neighbours the Pergamene kings and the kings of Bithynia, and of no less importance, a continuous and unwavering support of Rome. It was prepared to resist, arms in hand, every encroachment on the freedom of the seas. We have seen the city active in the war against Pharnaces and in that against

Prusias II. On the other hand, its faithfulness to Rome brought great tribulation upon it in the time of Fimbria, and again when it was besieged by Mithridates, a siege not less famous and dramatic than the great siege of Rhodes by Demetrius Poliorcetes.

The prosperity and reputation of Cyzicus did not decline in the period with which we are dealing. Its alliances with Pergamon and Rome were probably more profitable to the city than its former relations with the early Seleucids. It retained the large and fertile territory which rendered its population self-supporting in normal times. Its trade continued to flourish. Strabo's description of the city* holds good both for the early and for the late Hellenistic period. Relying on personal acquaintance with the city, as well as on literary sources, he praises Cyzicus in terms similar to those which he and other ancient writers applied to Rhodes—a large and beautiful city, famous for its good organization both for peace and war (εὐνομία πρός τε εἰρήνην καὶ πόλεμον), well equipped with ships, arms, engines of war, and food for all eventualities. Its large storehouses, in particular, struck Strabo's imagination.

The coins of Cyzicus were no longer what they had been in the past, the prime currency of the Pontic regions and highly esteemed in the rest of Greece. But they were still a respected currency. As an ally of Rhodes, Cyzicus had at first adopted the Rhodian standard, but about 200 B.C. substituted the Attic. We have seen that in the second century this was the predominant standard of international trade.

The great sufferings that Cyzicus endured in the Mithridatic Wars did it no vital damage. In the days of Tiberius it was once more an international market, where merchants (ἔμποροι) and visitors (ξένοι) from all over the Roman world (οἰκουμένη) met to take part in its famous assembly (πανήγυρις).[109]

Pharnaces (see above, pp. 663 ff.) left PONTUS as strong and as rich as Bithynia. Its capital was now SINOPE, the principal emporium of the south-eastern coast of the Euxine. After its conquest by Pharnaces and its adoption as the capital of the Pontic kings, its commercial importance did not decline. It remained (with Amisus, the second capital of Pontus) the chief

* xii. 8. 11, p. 575.

port from which the products of Pontus itself were exported, and at the same time an important centre of transit trade, especially for metals and for the caravan goods which came from Asia to Phasis by the South Caucasian route and to Pharnacia by the Euphrates route. The wide range of the trade of Sinope is attested, as I have already remarked, by the frequent occurrence in all the important cities of the Euxine and even occasionally in such cities as Athens and Delos, of jar-handles stamped with the names of *astynomi*. A comparison of the stamps with the coins of Sinope leads us to assign a large proportion of these handles to the time when Sinope had ceased to be an independent city and had become the capital of the Pontic kingdom. With the Sinopian jars came Sinopian merchants. Sinopians were familiar figures, now as in the past, in the principal centres of Greek life, especially at Athens, though perhaps not so important as were the merchants of Heraclea, Panticapaeum, Chersonesus, and Olbia; for the products of Sinope were in less demand in Greece than the grain, fish, hides, and slaves of the other Greek cities of the Euxine. In these cities themselves, however, where the need of metals and of cheap olive-oil was urgent, the importance of Sinope was paramount.[110]

The trade relations of Sinope and its close connexion with the other cities of the Euxine coast determined to a large extent the policy of the two most prominent kings of Pontus, Pharnaces and Mithridates VI Eupator. The policy of Pharnaces, of which I have already spoken, was neglected 'for a time by his immediate successors, Mithridates Philopator Philadelphus and Mithridates Euergetes, so far as it concerned the Euxine. They were both of them faithful allies of Rome and sought to use this alliance to promote the Anatolian side of the policy of Pharnaces, the extension of the territory of Pontus in Asia Minor at the expense of its neighbours—Bithynia, Paphlagonia, Galatia, and Cappadocia. In the main they were successful. Rome for some reason believed in their loyalty and did not oppose the expansion of their kingdom, especially during the rule of Mithridates V Euergetes, her efficient supporter in the third Punic war and in the war with Aristonicus. Mithridates Euergetes was certainly the wealthiest and the most powerful king in Asia Minor in the last decades of the second century B.C.

His wealth and strength were inherited after his death by Mithridates VI Eupator. But Rome became conscious of what from her point of view were the abnormal features of the situation, and at one stroke deprived the heir of all the acquisitions of his father, thereby reminding him of his modest role as a vassal king, ruling by the grace of Rome. This act led to a change in the policy of the new king of Pontus. His two predecessors had endeavoured to enlarge their kingdom with the permission of Rome. Eupator decided to do so as he saw fit without consulting Rome. His main political conception he inherited from Pharnaces. It was that of a Pontic Empire, the fusion in a single political and economic unit of the territories round the Euxine, in spite of their peculiar structure: a belt of Greek commercial cities and a hinterland of native tribes and villages, closely connected with the Greek cities economically but quite different from them in their mode of life and mentality. As a man of Greek civilization, a sincere philhellene and the recognized king of his own Greek cities, one of which was his capital, assisted by advisers and generals who were mostly Greeks from Amisus and Sinope, Mithridates designed to become the ruler and the leader of the other Greek cities of the Black Sea. As a descendant of the great Persian kings and hereditary ruler of part of Asia Minor, he regarded himself as the natural master and leader of all the tribes that lived behind the Greek cities on the Euxine—Iranians, Anatolians, Celts, and Thracians. And certainly his dynamic figure appealed to them and they were ready to support him. Nor was he unpopular among the Greeks, hard pressed as they were all along the coast (except of course in Bithynia and in Pontus) by the greedy and cruel chiefs of native tribes, their nearest neighbours. They certainly preferred incorporation in a Hellenistic kingdom, in which they were assured of a leading part politically and economically, to the role of victims and subjects of barbarians only slightly tinged with Greek civilization.

It is not astonishing that in these circumstances Mithridates succeeded in adding to his dominions the ancient customers of

Sinope—the Greek cities of the Caucasus, of the Crimea, and of the northern and western coasts of the Euxine. The tribes of their respective hinterlands were not averse from accepting him as their ally and serving in his armies for good pay in the combined qualities of allies and mercenaries.

The great influence of Mithridates V in Asia Minor and the marvellous successes of Mithridates VI in the East contributed to their popularity in the Greek world in general; achievements of the latter were presented to the Greek public by his historiographers in the same light as the fabulous exploits of Antiochus III, 'the Great', of Syria had been glorified in the past. The steady growth of the trade of Pontus which was reflected in the cordial relations between Delos and Athens on one hand, and the kings of Pontus, especially Mithridates V and Mithridates VI, on the other, confirmed the Greeks in the idea that the Pontic Mithridatids were the richest kings of the world, and that their treasury was full of gold and silver. The abundant and spectacular coinage of Mithridates VI supported this idea.[111]

We are therefore not surprised to learn that at Delos in 102/1 B.C. a priest of the gods who protected maritime commerce (Poseidon Aisios and the Dioscuri-Cabiri), Helianax, son of Asclepiodorus, an Athenian, built in the sacred precinct of the Cabiri a little *heroon* dedicated to Poseidon and the Cabiri and to King Mithridates (identified with Dionysus), with a statue of the king in military dress which was the cult statue of the shrine. With Mithridates were associated some of his highest dignitaries, members of his military and civil staff—the well-known Dorylaus, 'classmate' of Mithridates (σύντροφος), chief of his body-guard (ἐπὶ τοῦ ἐγχειριδίου) and chief commander of his army (ἐπὶ τῶν δυνάμεων); his private confidential chancellor (ἐπὶ τοῦ ἀπορρήτου, *a secretis*); his chief doctor and chief judge and other members of his court, most of them having the court rank of τῶν πρώτων φίλων and most of them Greeks of Amisus. Beside them appear kings, friends of Mithridates, and probably personal acquaintances of Helianax—Ariarathes Philometor of Cappadocia, Antiochus VIII Grypus, and two members of the court of Mithridates II of Parthia. With this noble company was associated the father of the dedicant. Portraits of all these dignitaries were carved on shield-like medallions (ὅπλα) with the corresponding inscriptions below or above the medallions.[112]

It is evident that it was not only for political reasons that an Atheno-Delian of wealth and position dedicated a *heroon* to Mithridates. It is highly probable that Helianax played an important part in the commercial relations between Delos and Pontus, especially Amisus.[113] The same suggestion may be made as regards Dicaeus, son of Dicaeus, priest of Sarapis, who about 94/3 B.C. dedicated at Delos a chapel in the Sarapeum for the safety of Athens, Rome, King Mithridates Eupator Dionysus, and his own father and mother. Another dedication of the same Dicaeus to Isis Aphrodite again associates Mithridates and his own mother; and still another is preserved in fragments.[114]

The significance of these Delian dedications is clear. We see how the popularity of the young, ambitious, and valorous king, the saviour of the Greeks of the Euxine, the rich benefactor and business associate of Athens and Delos, spread gradually from these two places to the rest of Greece and to Asia Minor, and how he came to be looked upon, where the Roman methods of dealing with the Greek cities had provoked impatience and disgust, as the eventual saviour of Greece in general.

So long as the action of Mithridates was confined to far distant regions bordering on the Black Sea, Rome remained undisturbed. She was not interested in the fate of the Greek cities in that quarter and saw without concern the glorification of Eupator, saviour and benefactor of Greek civilization. But without the possession of the Bithynian coast and the Thracian Bosporus, the work of Mithridates remained incomplete and his Pontic kingdom insecure. His principal efforts were now directed, after the conquest of the southern and northern coasts of the Euxine and of the northern part of the western coast, to the Bithynian coast. In the long history of Bithynia and Pontus it had been repeatedly demonstrated that it was easy for a strong Bithynia to close the Bosporus and thus deprive Pontus of its main source of income, commerce with the Mediterranean world. It was no accident that the conflict between Rome and Mithridates began with an attempt by Bithynia to cut off Pontus from the Mediterranean (in 88 B.C.).

These designs of Mithridates, however, met with the determined resistance of Rome and finally resulted in a protracted war between them. Of this war I shall have to say a few words in the next chapter. Here I need only remark that in the course of the struggle the cardinal political ideas of Mithridates underwent a notable change. He realized that the Pontic kingdom which he had created could not enjoy a lasting security while the Greek world remained under the control of Rome. So his endeavour now was to restore the unity of the Hellenistic powers and to make them, under his own leadership, politically independent of Rome. His Pontic kingdom was now no longer an object in itself, but a means of realizing and sustaining his Greco-Anatolian Empire.

The kingdom of Pontus under Mithridates certainly marked a step in the development of the Hellenistic world. While the Oriental tide was rapidly submerging the hellenized parts of Syria, without any effective measures being taken to stem it, Mithridates endeavoured to check a similar process in the regions of the Euxine, by supporting Hellenism against Orientalism, or rather by establishing a *modus vivendi* between the two, in which Hellenism would keep its identity and continue to play a leading part in civilization and economics. He failed because he substituted for the sound and realizable idea of a Pontic kingdom, which might have been tolerated by Rome indefinitely, the dream of an independent Panhellenic monarchy, which of course was unacceptable to Rome. The result was to plunge the Greek world into unheard-of sufferings and to bring about a rapid and general economic decay, of which more will be said in the next chapter.[115]

We may, however, note here that the Mithridatic War was the closing phase of the great struggle between Hellenism and Romanism. The Greek world once more mobilized its resources, not so much in men as in wealth. It is amazing to see how great this accumulated wealth was, especially in Asia Minor. Army after army, fleet after fleet, were thrown into the struggle by Mithridates. Enormous issues of coined money were struck to cover the vast military expenditure, which was naturally borne in the main by Asia Minor and especially by the Greek cities. We may see in this wealth striking evidence of the success that had attended the economic policy of the Anatolian Hellenistic monarchies in the two centuries of their independence, and of the profit that the Greeks of Asia Minor had derived from it.

The conditions in GALATIA were unsettled. Under the influence of the surrounding Hellenistic States and of the Galatians who returned to their country after long service in one of the Hellenistic armies, its kings and chieftains developed a keen resentment at their isolation in their remote towns amid a semi-barren country. Like their neighbours, they wanted a freer and more civilized, that is to say, a hellenized life. It was a new phenomenon in Galatian history when a little before 190 B.C. they organized an expedition not of mere robbery but of conquest. Their aim was to seize Heraclea Pontica and thus to get an outlet to the sea (Memmon 28). Their attempt was doomed to failure since they had not learned how to besiege and capture fortified cities. We have evidence of another venture, perhaps of the same kind, in an obscure incident which took place between the flourishing city of Lampsacus and the Tolistoagian Galatians.*

The events that followed the Roman victory over Antiochus III brought these aspirations to a close. The Romans acceded to the suggestion of Eumenes II and decided to put an end to the inroads of the Galatians into Asia Minor and to their efforts to enlarge their territory. It is probable that Cn. Manlius Vulso was spurred to action by tales of the fabulous wealth of the Galatians. The result was that the country was thoroughly laid waste and that many thousands of Galatian slaves were thrown on the Greek and Italian markets. Later, after a new outburst of Galatian temper under Ortiagon, Galatia was made subject to Pergamon, in a kind of vassalage. We have seen that the Galatians reacted to this turn of events by a tremendous war of revolt (of 168 B.C.), in which Eumenes II saved Asia Minor from the horrors of a new Galatian devastation. After the war of 168/7 B.C. Galatia was ready for annexation. But Eumenes II had become too strong and too popular for Rome, and the 'liberty' of the Gauls was restored as it had existed before Vulso's conquest and Ortiagon's War.

* *S.I.G.*³ 591.49.

This political measure, however, could not arrest the gradual transformation of Galatia into one of the Hellenistic countries of Asia Minor, that is to say, the spread of Greco-Phrygian civilization to the Galatian aristocracy. The first sign of this was the appearance of Galatian chieftains in the ancient 'cities' of Phrygia, Tavium, Ancyra, Pessinus, and the active part taken by them in the administration of the Pessinuntian temple-state, of which we have a vivid reflection in the correspondence between the chief priest of Pessinus, Attis, and the kings of Pergamon, Eumenes II and Attalus II (163–156 B.C.).* We are unfortunately unable to follow the process of the subjection of Galatia to Greek and Phrygian cultural influences in the late Hellenistic times. It reached its greatest intensity after the Mithridatic wars, when all Galatia was gradually united under a succession of single rulers, kings by the grace of Rome. Of these Deiotarus is the best known. The last was Amyntas, after whose reign Galatia became a Roman province (25 B.C.). An interesting testimony to the hellenization of Deiotarus and his family is furnished by their graves, recently found at Karalar—impressive tumuli of the Anatolian and Thraco-Macedonian type, so well known from the South Russian variety of them with solid stone grave-chambers of Greek type. It is a pity that these graves had been looted before their excavation. The scanty remains that they yielded in sculpture, grave-furniture, and minor finds have a Greek aspect and were the work of Greek craftsmen. Some of the vessels had been imported either from Egypt or from Syria, for example the glass dish with gold ornaments. The only funeral inscription which was recovered is in Greek. The evidence, however, is too slight for general conclusions. The weapons, gold and silver vessels, and the horse-trappings might have presented a different aspect.[116]

In the period under review the wave of hellenization reached CAPPADOCIA.[117] I have already described the aspect of Cappadocia before its superficial hellenization, which began in the middle of the third century B.C. and was intensified in the second century and the early first. At the time of the Galatian War of Manlius Vulso the native Iranian dynasty of the

* Welles, *R.C.*, Nos. 55–61.

Ariarathai of Cappadocia entered for good into the orbit of Roman policy and became practically a dynasty of vassal kings. It was Ariarathes V Eusebes Philopator (163–130 B.C.) who was regarded as the real Hellenizer of Cappadocia. His successors followed his policy, though the turmoil of political events at the end of the second century gave them very little chance of carrying out his programme. The best testimony to their efforts, besides the dynastic marriages, are their relations with the great centres of Greek life and of Greek commerce of the time, Athens and Delos. It will suffice to recall a few facts. Ariarathes V was educated at Athens and was there a classmate of Attalus II ; both of them were made Athenian citizens and honoured their common teacher Carneades with a statue.* The letters which Carneades wrote to Ariarathes are still extant. I may also mention the Athenian decree of the Dionysiac artistes in honour of Ariarathes and the statue of his sister Stratonice, wife of Eumenes II and Attalus II, erected at Delos by the Athenian people. Once started, the cordial relations between Athens and the Cappadocian kings were never interrupted until the tragic end of the dynasty in the convulsion of the Mithridatic wars.[118]

The little we know of Cappadocia of this time (Cappadocia is the least known part of Asia Minor) does not allow us even to conjecture the extent to which Cappadocian economic and social life was hellenized by the Cappadocian philhellenic kings. For a country like Cappadocia hellenization meant urbanization. Now Strabo,† our best authority on Cappadocia, had very little knowledge of it. He speaks of two places only which may claim the honour of being called cities (πόλεις), Mazaca and Tyana, which both received from one or other of the Cappadocian kings of the second century a new Greek name, Eusebeia. But even Tyana, which he once calls πόλις, he describes another time as πόλισμα.

The epigraphic and numismatic evidence supports this sceptical attitude of Strabo as regards the urbanization of Cappadocia. His picture of the country is certainly true to the actual conditions as they were in his time or in that of his late hellenistic sources (probably anterior to the reign of the last royal

* *S.I.G.*³ 666.   † xii. 1. 4 ff., p. 537.

hellenizer of Cappadocia, Archelaus, whom Antony appointed king of Cappadocia).

'Cities' (though not in the sense of the Greek *polis*) existed in Cappadocia long before the second century B.C. In this respect it was not unlike the other parts of Asia Minor. They were either temple-cities with their priest-kings (for example Comana), or city-states with their own dynasts. Some of these were slightly hellenized, as is shown by the rare coins of the early third century B.C. of the city-kingdoms Tyana, Morima, and Anisa. Their kings appear on the coins in Persian garb, but the inscriptions on the coins are in Greek.[119]

These city-kingdoms were absorbed by the new united Cappadocia created by the efforts of Ariaramnes and his successor Ariarathes III. The latter was the first 'hellenistic' king of Cappadocia. He showed his hellenizing policy by building for himself a capital in the style of Antigoneia, Cassandreia, Lysimacheia, Demetrias, and Antioch, to which he gave his own name (Ariaratheia). This policy was further developed by his successors in the second century. It is highly probable that under their protection and under the influence of the development of the natural resources of the country many Greeks or hellenized Anatolians and Syrians, landowners, artisans, and merchants, settled in the existing city-like centres (κωμοπόλεις or πολίσματα according to Strabo) and gave them a more or less hellenized aspect. The first instance of this is to be seen in the new capital of Cappadocia, Mazaca-Eusebeia. It replaced, perhaps under Ariarathes V, the earlier capital Ariaratheia, which sank into oblivion (it is entirely unknown to Strabo). The founder of Mazaca-Eusebeia gave it a Greek constitution of an antiquarian character: Strabo* reports that it was governed by the laws of Charondas and had a special official to interpret them, a sort of constitutional jurisconsult or expert. Nyssa, if it really was another dynastic city of Ariarathes V, as has been suggested, was perhaps similarly treated.

Other cities, large and small, also adopted Greek constitutions and assumed a more or less Greek aspect. So it was with Tyana. The discovery in this city of a catalogue of gymnasiarchs of the second century B.C., dedicated to Hermes and

* xii. 2. 9, p. 539.

Heracles for the safety of Ariarathes VI Epiphanes, makes it likely that the city had a kind of Greek political organization, probably since the time of Ariarathes V.*

Lastly, we have the interesting inscription of the city of Anisa, one of those 'cities' whose name appeared on the dynastic coins of the early third century. It is a decree of the city bearing the date of the year 7 and the Macedonian month Dius (the seventh year being certainly, according to the practice followed on these coins, the regnal year of one of the last Ariarathai, not the year of the Pompeian or an unknown era); the decree is in honour of a distinguished citizen of Anisa who went to the capital Eusebeia and made good, before the supreme 'manager' (ἀρχιδιοικητής) of the kingdom and the royal governor of the city (ἐπὶ τῆς πόλεως), the claim of the city to a contested heritage of a man who had died intestate (ἀκληρονόμητος). The city appears in possession of a regular Greek constitution, has Greek festivals—Διὸς Σωτήρια and Ἡράκλεια—and has the rights of a juridical person and its own property. And yet it is called not πόλις but πολίτευμα, and depends in many respects on the royal officers. Its position was the same as that of Uruk in Babylonia, of Seleuceia on the Eulaeus, and of Dura-Europos on the Euphrates when they were cities of the Parthian kingdom. It should also be noted that the citizens of Anisa use Greek and local names indiscriminately.

The urbanization of Cappadocia, with the Greek type of economic life which it implied, was shortlived. Anisa, like Morima, faded out of sight. They are unknown to Strabo. Perhaps they will emerge some day under another name, like Mazaca, which became Caesarea. Whether their disappearance was due to the activity of the following line of kings with the dynastic name of Ariobarzanes or to the absorption of the smaller urban centres by the larger we do not know. A revival of urbanization may be noticed shortly before the Roman annexation, under Archelaus. But even under Roman rule (from 17 B.C.) Cappadocia still appears as a mainly Oriental borderland of the Roman Empire.[120]

* S.E.G. i. 466.

B. THE SELEUCID EMPIRE AND ITS NEIGHBOURS

After its days of greatness and glory under the rule of the first Seleucids and after a spectacular revival in the time of Antiochus III, which continued, despite the Roman victory over Antiochus, under his successors Seleucus IV and Antiochus IV, the Seleucid kingdom under the successors of Epiphanes was in a state of gradual political decay. Continuous dynastic strife, both ruinous and aimless, gradually undermined the military and financial strength of the late Seleucids and made Syria helpless against its foreign enemies, against disintegration from within, and against the mounting Oriental tide which threatened its very existence.

In the East the PARTHIANS advanced steadily in spite of all the efforts of the Seleucids. They gradually occupied the Iranian lands and finally under Mithridates I established their rule on the banks of the two rivers in Babylonia and Mesopotamia. Their further advance was temporarily checked, partly by the growth of ARMENIA, which reached its peak in the time of Tigranes I, and partly by events unknown to us which took place within the Parthian kingdom and on its northern, eastern, and southern frontiers.

In the South JUDAEA under the Maccabees was engaged in a long and bloody struggle with the Seleucids. Successful in the main, this struggle secured for Judaea and its new rulers first an almost complete autonomy and later full political independence. The new kingdom, under the sway of some able descendants of Judas, embarked on an imperialistic policy and became for a while one of the strongest States of the Near East.

The neighbours of Judaea, the NABATAEAN ARABS, likewise seized their opportunity. The Nabataean kings showed their ability by steadily building up their empire both in the south and east and in the north. Their principal aim was undoubtedly to obtain control over the main caravan routes of the Arabian desert, those which connected South Arabia through Petra with Gaza in Egypt on the one hand and with Damascus and the Phoenician cities on the other, and those which led from Gerrha and the northern coast of the Persian Gulf across the desert to Petra and Bostra respectively, the two most important centres of the Nabataean State. At the same time they developed the natural resources of their own country.

Between the Parthian Empire and Syria the ARABS of the Syrian desert continued to lead an almost independent life. Some of these tribes which lived in close proximity to certain important Macedonian military colonies succeeded in establishing their control over several of the Greco-Macedonian cities. The city of Edessa-Orrhoe-Antioch on the Kallirhoe was ruled by the Osrhoenian Arabs through their own dynasty— most of the kings had the name of Abgarus—from 130–127 B.C. onwards. This was probably a consequence of the troubled conditions that prevailed when Mesopotamia was occupied by the Parthians. Much nearer to the main centres of Seleucid Syria, at Hemesa near Arethusa, the tribe of the Hemesenes took possession of the city and made their sheikhs rulers of the new State. In the time of Pompey the dynasty of the Sampsicerami and Iamblichi was already firmly established. Its previous history is unknown. We have later evidence (of the time of Crassus) of the existence of similar petty native monarchies or Greek tyrannies in several other cities. Their previous history is likewise unknown. Some of these petty monarchies (e.g. Hemesa) depended nominally on Seleucid Syria, most of them (e.g. Edessa) on Parthia.

Another native state—that of the ITURAEANS—was established in Coelesyria between the Lebanon and Antilebanon. Its capital was Chalcis ὑπὸ τῷ Λιβάνῳ and its second capital Heliopolis. Stephanus Byzantius speaks of Maniko, an Arab, as the founder of a dynasty of native rulers at Chalcis. In the time of Pompey the ruler was Ptolemy, son of Mennaeus, a hellenized Ituraean who started a coinage of his own and bequeathed his rule to his descendants.

Finally, in the North, COMMAGENE asserted its independence, first for a short time between 140–130 B.C., then permanently from 96 B.C. onwards.

The gradual progress of Syria's disintegration, on which our meagre and scattered sources of information throw very little light, cannot be dealt with here in detail. Suffice it to say that, while it was slow at first, it progressed rapidly in the last decades of the second and the first decades of the first century

B.C. Attempts to restore the unity of the Seleucid kingdom
were not lacking. Many efforts were made by the Seleucids
themselves. All were thwarted by the dynastic strife fostered
by the Romans. Later the task was taken up by the strongest
rivals of the Seleucids. It is highly probable that the Parthians
had it in mind at the time of Mithridates II. Tigranes I, in the
atmosphere which led to the Mithridatic wars, succeeded for a
short time in uniting almost the whole of Syria under his rule.
The Parthian efforts failed because of the intervention of the
Romans. They would not tolerate the existence of any strong
Syrian State.[121]

The Syrian State was thus gradually reduced to a small
territory comprising the Tetrapolis, its nucleus, Phoenicia, and
what was left of Coelesyria and Cyrrhestica. However, even
within this limited territory the tendency to break up into
separate autonomous fragments spread like fire. The satraps
of the kings took up the attitude of feudal lords. Petty
dynasts established their rule, probably with the consent of
the kings, in various cities. Pompey put an end to some of them.
Others maintained themselves for a longer time. Our information, derived mostly from Josephus and Strabo, records in
the main conditions that prevailed in the time of Pompey. We
hear for example of a tyranny at Lysias near Apamea; of
Beroea with Bambyce and Heraclea repeatedly in the hands
of tyrants, first during the reign of Grypus and again in 88 B.C.;
of the rule of tyrants in several Phoenician cities, Byblos,
Tripolis, Tyre, Dora, Stratonos Pyrgos, Gaza, and in Philadelphia and Gamala in Transjordan.[122]

Moreover, almost all the important cities of the kingdom
claimed political liberty and obtained it gradually from the
kings to an ever increasing extent. The climax of the process
was the grant of 'autonomy', which in Syria meant practically
almost complete political independence. A study of the coinage
of the cities enables us to follow the steps by which this
autonomy was reached: from royal copper minted by the cities
to autonomous copper, and from autonomous copper to autonomous silver, these changes marked the steps which led from
self-government to political independence. To the minting of
autonomous silver corresponded, in international relations, the

3261.2   R

inclusion of the autonomous cities in international treaties and special announcements to foreign powers concerning the new autonomous, i.e. almost independent, status of the cities.

I cannot here deal in detail with the highly interesting history of the autonomy of Syrian cities. This has been frequently treated and with great care. I will confine myself to some general remarks which have a bearing on the subject of this book and to a few illustrations.

In most instances the grant of complete autonomy was preceded by the recognition of a given city as ἱερα and ἄσυλος (in some cases we have an advance from the title ἱερά to that of ἱερὰ καὶ ἄσυλος). Lists of cities recognized by the kings as 'holy and inviolable' have been compiled by many modern scholars and need not be repeated here. I will only observe that in none of the Hellenistic kingdoms was the grant of *asylia* to cities so common as in the late Seleucid monarchy and in none did the *asylia* present such peculiar features.

I have dealt above with *asylia* as one of the most interesting Greek international institutions and pointed out the political, social, and economic role it played in the Hellenistic world in the third and second centuries B.C. Its spread was due to the great uncertainty of life typical of the time. It was used as a means of neutralizing this uncertainty, as a kind of international insurance against it.

In Syria the possession of the right of *asylia* by certain cities, almost all of them commercial cities of the coast, may have had, as has been recently suggested, the same meaning and may have been achieved by the same means as in the rest of the Hellenistic world. The cities may have endeavoured to protect themselves in this way from attacks by certain foreign powers, including the pirates, their most dreaded enemies. By special embassies they would request their pro-spective enemies, certainly wth the permission and approval of the king, to recognize their *asylia*. Such may have been the procedure and the implication. But it must be emphasized that this assumption is highly conjectural, based on one posi-tive fact only, that all the cities in possession of *asylia*, as attested by the coins, were maritime cities. It involves some grave difficulties. Since the most dangerous enemies of the maritime cities were the pirates, it would mean that the pirates were treated by the Syrian cities and implicitly by the Syrian kings as a legally recognized body politic, a fact not attested in our evidence. It would mean also that the pirates—perhaps for a substantial fee—were inclined to accept the bargain and to bind themselves by religious sanctions, a fact otherwise unattested.

Be this as it may, recognition of their 'holiness' and 'inviolability' by the kings, even without the problematic international implication, may have brought with it substantial privileges for the cities and may have therefore effected an important improvement of their situation. In the disturbed conditions of the late Seleucid period the cities, hard pressed by the financial exactions and arbitrary jurisdiction of the kings, saw that their salvation lay in obtaining by some means complete or partial exemption from these royal exactions and jurisdiction. Royal recognition of the city as ἱερά and ἄσυλος may have met these requirements. By becoming 'holy' the city perhaps acquired certain privileges in respect of royal taxation; by being *asylos* it may have been exempted from royal jurisdiction. In addition it became a place of refuge for all those, rich and poor, who were persecuted and oppressed, politically or financially, by the king and his agents. It meant for the city an influx of capital, an increase of population (that is, of military strength), and abundance of cheap labour. The grant of *asylia* may thus have been an important economic factor in the life of Syrian cities.

It was natural that the cities should use all means at their disposal to secure recognition by the kings of 'holiness' and 'inviolability'. One method in all probability was to offer to purchase the *asylia* at a good price. The kings yielded to the demands. They were too weak to resist the cities, which were still rich and possessed in some instances considerable military strength. Moreover, the purchase money paid by the cities was undoubtedly of great assistance to the kings in their chronic financial difficulties. Thus *asylia* spread far and wide all over Syria and Phoenicia.

The next stage after *asylia* was of course recognition of a more or less complete autonomy. From 'holiness' to 'inviolability', from 'inviolability' to 'autonomy' was, as I have said, a progress characteristic of the history of many of the Syrian cities.[123] Here are, *exempli causa*, a few typical cases.

SELEUCEIA IN PIERIA was one of the strongest and richest cities of Syria. It enjoyed under the Ptolemies a certain degree of autonomy, perhaps greater than other Ptolemaic cities. When it became once more a Seleucid city the Seleucids (as we know in the case of Seleucus IV) showed high regard for it. From Demetrius II it received the title 'holy' (about 145 B.C.), and a little later that of 'holy and inviolable' probably from Tryphon (certainly before 138 B.C.) Finally, in 109 B.C. it received freedom (ἐλευθερία) from Antiochus Grypus. This was announced by letters written by Grypus to Ptolemy IX Alexander I, and to the Romans. Part of this correspondence was published at Paphos in Cyprus. From 109 B.C. Seleuceia used its own era and from 108 B.C. minted silver in large quantities.

An interesting phenomenon in the same sphere is the formation in the middle of the second century B.C. of a monetary league of the *Tetrapolis*. This league emitted coins with the inscription ἀδελφῶν δήμων.[124]

Still stronger was the tendency to separatism among the Phoenician cities. The geographical situation of ARADUS and MARATHUS, the most northern of the Phoenician cities and therefore the most dangerous rivals of Seleuceia and Laodicea in Syria, gave them a peculiar position among those cities. They were practically independent at the time when the Ptolemies and Seleucids divided between themselves the rule over the Syrian, Phoenician, and Palestinian coast. They kept this semi-independence during the Seleucid rule, Aradus having received from Seleucus Callinicus the right of *asylia*. In the period which we are considering they coined large quantities of silver. The coinage of Aradus of a special standard was particularly abundant between 137 and 45 B.C., while Marathus used the Attic standard, minting without interruption until probably 64 B.C.[125]

A little later than Aradus TYRE received the right of *asylia* from Epiphanes. From 125 B.C. onward it enjoyed complete autonomy. Its silver at that time was abundant and excellent, and it occasionally minted even gold. The coins Τυρίου κόμματος were highly appreciated all over Syria and had a wide circulation; they retained their reputation for a long time. The other Phoenician cities, Byblus, Sidon, Tripolis, Ace, and Ascalon, became autonomous a little later, most of them after 111 B.C., having previously received the right of *asylia*. In the case of Tyre we know that the city paid in money for its autonomy. Other cities, those which retained their free constitution and those which preferred another type of autonomy, the rule of tyrants (above, p. 843), not improbably did the same.[126]

Being autonomous, the cities sometimes settled their quarrels among themselves without appealing to the kings. We know how Aradus organized a treacherous plot against its neighbour Marathus. The plot failed. Strabo, however, states positively that Marathus was destroyed by Aradus and that its territory was divided among the Aradians. If this is true, Strabo got his information from some literary source of the late second century contemporary with the destruction of Marathus. The city was certainly soon restored to its former splendour, since there is no long and notable interruption in the issues of its silver coins.[127] Another city war, this time between two cities of the kernel of the Seleucid kingdom, is recorded by Posidonius. With fine humour he describes how about 142 B.C. a regular war broke out between Apamea, the military capital of the Seleucids, and its dependent neighbour Larissa. The Macedonians, says Posidonius, took up their rusty swords and spears, donned their helmets (or hats) with visors, and moved in the fashion of a Dionysiac *komos*, followed by donkeys carrying wine, food, and musical instruments.[128]

In this atmosphere of anarchy and continuous internal struggle the Seleucids further indulged in wars with their hereditary enemies, the Ptolemies.

No wonder that in such conditions robbery became endemic in the kingdom and piracy rife at sea. Even Pompey was unable to restore order. Mountains on the coast and certain maritime cities afforded refuge for pirates. In caves near the caravan roads professional robber bands lay in wait for the caravans. Other tribes preferred to rob the peasants of the fertile plains of Syria. Strabo, who notes with care the various strongholds and refuges of these brigands, mentions for example the robbers who infested the rich oasis of Damascus and those who pillaged the valleys of Coelesyria.[129]

Political disintegration and the creation of new independent States out of the fragments of the Seleucid Empire did not involve the thorough orientalization of these fragments and a radical change in their economic and social life. It must be remembered that the long domination of the Seleucids and, in some parts of the later Seleucid Empire, of the Ptolemies, that is to say of Macedonians and Greeks, had as its consequence a far-reaching hellenization of at least the upper classes of the native population. The 'Hellenes' of Syria now included many natives, especially inhabitants of the cities, natives who spoke Greek, had become Hellenic in their mode of life, and gave a Greek education to their children. We know that this was the situation in Palestine in the time of Epiphanes, and we may guess that Palestine was no exception. Greek civilization and the Greek mode of life were regarded by this class of natives as the pre-eminent civilization, as a higher form of life.[130]

When political anarchy in the Seleucid kingdom and national revival in the borderlands replaced the rule of the Seleucids by that of native dynasties, the new rulers were certainly not hostile to Greek civilization as such. Most of them belonged to the hellenized upper class of the native population. Those who did not very soon learnt to appreciate the benefits of that civilization. They never thought of uprooting it in their kingdoms and replacing it by something wholly different. In fact they were all more or less philhellenes, as their contemporaries were in Bithynia, Pontus, and Cappadocia. Their object was not to create States of a new type or to go back to conditions which had prevailed in the Near East before Alexander. In fact they knew nothing of these conditions. They had grown up and had been educated in a different atmosphere, and this atmosphere was Hellenistic.

We need not be surprised therefore if the States they set up were of the Hellenistic pattern, reproductions and imitations of the great Seleucid monarchy, and this we know many, if not all, the new States to have been.

COMMAGENE may be taken as an example. The new kings, natives of this small but wealthy country, had genealogies drawn up for them by some of their Greek assistants connecting them both with the glorious Achaemenids and the Seleucids and through the latter with Alexander. The monumental Heroon erected by one of them on the lofty summit of the Nemrud-Dagh, and the elaborate Greek inscriptions set up by him in this and other sanctuaries, are faithful illustrations of the new civilization and the new mentality, at once Greek and Oriental, of which the Pontic and Cappadocian kings offer somewhat similar examples. The bronze coinage of the kings of Commagene, a continuation as it were of the Seleucid coinage, shows the same blend of influences. It should be noted that their royal names were either Mithridates or Antiochus.

How much the dynasty of Commagene contributed to the urbanization of their own country we do not know. In the late first century (69–34 B.C.) the structure of the country was in the main feudal and rural. In the famous inscription of Nemrud-Dagh Antiochus speaks of the king, of the dynasts (feudal lords of the Iranian type), of the priests, and of the ἄρχοντες, that is to say the magistrates of the cities.* It should be observed that the ἄρχοντες come last. In the social and economic life of the country, alongside of the king and the feudal lords, an important part was played by the temples and the villages; of the latter some were assigned to the temples by the king.† The cities were treated by the king exactly in the same way as the villages.‡ The inscriptions of Nemrud-Dagh and other inscriptions of the kingdom point in their general tenor to a rural, agricultural, and pastoral life, with city life very little developed.[131]

There is no doubt that if we knew more of the Ituraean, or of the Hemesene, or even of the Osrhoenian dynasty, we should find approximately the same picture. Ptolemy, son of Mennaeus, the tetrarch and *archiereus* of CHALCIS, issued a regular Greek coinage. His coins (85–40 B.C.) bear the head of his god Zeus on the obverse and his name and title coupled with various

---

* *O.G.I.* 383; Jalabert et Mouterde, *Inscr. gr. et lat. de la Syrie*, i, no. 1, ll. 171 ff., cf. l. 228.

† Ibid., ll. 191 ff.   ‡ Ibid., ll. 94 ff.

PLATE XCIV

1. The funeral monument of Antiochus I of Commagene (69–34 B.C.) is well known to students of the ancient world. It consists of a majestic tumulus about 45 m. in height and of three terraces. Two of these were intended to be sanctuaries or heroa of the deceased king. Here the king was associated (in statues and bas-reliefs) with the ʳᵒds and with his royal ancestry. This last linked him on one side with the Achaemenids, on the other with the Seleucids. The bas-relief represented here shows one of the Persian ancestors of Antiochus I (the inscription on the back is too imperfectly preserved to permit of the identification of this ancestor). We see a Persian king or a member of the Persian royal house in the traditional Persian royal dress performing an act of worship. In the right hand he holds a patera, in the left the sacred bundle of twigs—the *baresman*. The royal garb consists of the stiff tiara (τιάρα ὀρθή) adorned with golden stars, the diadem also adorned with golden plaques, the golden torc (στρεπτός) on the neck, the kaftan (κάνδυς) richly embroidered, open in front, held together across the breast by a knotted strap fastened to two golden brooches, the shirt (covered by the kaftan), the breeches, and the shoes again richly adorned with gold embroideries and plaques. The two circular brooches fastened to the lapels of the kaftan are especially interesting. They are described by Curtius, iii. 8, as one of the insignia of the Persian king: *pallam auro distinctam aurei accipitres velut rostris inter se concurrerent adornabant* and were apparently made either in open-work or in repoussé. This bas-relief has been minutely described and illustrated by K. Humann and O. Puchstein, *Reisen in Kleinasien und Nordsyrien*, 1890, pp. 299 ff., pl. XXXVI. 1 (cf. XXXV. 3 and XXXVII. 1). Here reproduced from a cast in the Staatlichen Museen in Berlin (photograph supplied by the authorities). Cf. pp. 842 f., 849 of this chapter, and notes 121 and 131.

2. The two gold brooches reproduced here were certainly, as Prof. R. Zahn has pointed out to me, used for the same purpose as those of the bas-relief described above. They probably formed part of the treasure of Karen Pahlav found at Nihavand. The brooches consist of circular frames and figures of eagle-griffins soldered to these circular bands. The griffins are in repoussé work. They are shown frontwise with outspread wings and heads turned one to the right, the other to the left, holding in their claws an ibex. Slots on either side of the brooches are decorated with an erect half-acanthus leaf. The birds, the prey, the circular frame, and the leaves are inlaid in cloisonné technique with greenish-grey paste. The style and workmanship of these brooches are strikingly similar to those of the products of Bactro-Siberian or Neo-Iranian art discussed in the description of pl. LXII. 3. See M. Rostovtzeff, *Arethuse*, 1924, pl. xv. 5; E. Herzfeld, *Burlington Magazine*, lii (1928), p. 22, pl. fig. c; D. M. D(alton), *Brit. Mus. Quart.*, ii (1928), pp. 88 ff., and Frontispiece LIB; Ph. Akerman in A. U. Pope, *A Survey of Persian Art*, i, 1939, p. 465, pl. 138 A, B.

PLATE XCIV

2. Gold buckles. London, British Museum, and New York, Metropolitan Museum of Art

1. An ancestor of Antiochus I of Commagene. Nimrud Dagh in Commagene

THE REORIENTALIZATION OF THE FORMER CONSTITUENT PARTS OF THE SELEUCID EMPIRE

PLATE XCV

The Sheikhs of Hemesa

PLATE XCV

The monument on Mount Hermel in Syria, shown in this plate, as restored by the Service of Antiquities of Syria, is described in the text. The association of this monument, whether it be of a funerary or a commemorative character, with the rulers of Hemesa is fully established by a comparison of the pyramid of Mount Hermel with the now destroyed mausoleum of Sampsiceramus in Hemesa itself (see n. 133). The date of the monument cannot be exactly determined, but its architectural features and the peculiar style of the sculptures point to late Hellenistic rather than to early Imperial times. The bas-reliefs which adorned the monument are puzzling. The absence of the hunters is surprising, the hunting implements are peculiar. For a more detailed discussion of the monument see the paper by P. Perdrizet quoted in n. 133. I may in this connexion emphasize the more modest and more 'Hellenistic' character of the monument of Mount Hermel as compared with the funeral tumuli of the Commagene dynasty. The Hemesenes stood in closer relations with Greek civilization than the Commagenians.

Photographs supplied by H. Seyrig, Director of Antiquities of Syria.

religious and political devices on the reverse. His son Lysanias replaced the head of Zeus by his own likeness.[132]

Near Hemesa on Mount Hermel still stands a majestic monument, which has recently been thoroughly excavated and restored by the Syrian Service of Antiquities. The excavators of this monument (a pyramid on a square two-storied base adorned with interesting bas-reliefs) have discovered no grave-chamber either above or below the ground. Nevertheless it may have been a funeral monument. The building is beautiful and imposing (see Pl. xcv), displaying a mixture of Greek and Oriental elements both in architecture and in sculptural decoration (hunting-scenes of a peculiar character, in which the hunted animals and the weapons of the hunters are shown, but not the hunters themselves). It is regrettable that the bronze tablet with an inscription which once adorned the façade of the monument has disappeared, for it certainly would have told us by whom the monument was built and to what period it belongs. As it stands, we are reduced to conjecture, and the most probable is that it was erected by one of the Hemesene kings of the late Hellenistic times, an excellent parallel to the funeral *temenos* of Antiochus of Commagene.

Strikingly similar to the pyramid of Mount Hermel is the sepulchral monument, a real mausoleum built for himself by the last Sampsiceramus at Hemesa itself before A.D. 78/9. Unfortunately, the monument, which was still intact in the nineteenth century, has been utterly destroyed in our 'civilized' times. Its remains show once more a mixture of Greek and Oriental elements in architecture and decoration. An instance of this is the incrustation style of the wall decoration now known to be a feature of Babylonian art, as is shown, for example, by the remains of the wall decoration in the palace of the kings of Mari (Tell Harir).[133]

The history of the Maccabees and the Hasmonaeans in JUDAEA is interesting. I have already (pp. 703 ff.) referred to the policy of Epiphanes in regard to Judaea. This policy led to a fierce revolt against the Syrian rule and against Hellenism, finally resulting in the creation of an independent Jewish State. This State, however, was far from being a restoration of the ancient Jewish State. In the hands of the later Hasmonaeans it became an adaptation of the Seleucid State to the life and religion of the Jews. Of this we may see an illustration in the Hasmonaean coins, which begin with John Hyrcanus (135–106 B.C.). The types of these coins imitate those of the Seleucid kingdom. No less characteristic are the graves of the late Hasmonaean period at Jerusalem and elsewhere in Palestine— thoroughly hellenized imitations of older forms of burial, with Hellenistic entrances and sometimes with Hellenistic mausoleums. The earliest and the most famous example is the mausoleum built for Jonathan at Modeïn and described by Josephus.* The successors of the Hasmonaeans, the Idumaeans, developed much greater activity and have left us more monuments of it. But they were not the first to hellenize their kingdom politically and socially.[134]

Beyond Palestine the NABATAEANS developed their own kingdom (from 169 B.C. onwards) on the same lines. Shrewd traders, they remained at the same time skilled shepherds and cultivated as much of their territory as they could. They may have also taken over from their predecessors the exploitation of the copper and iron mines of Edom (below, Ch. VIII). The hellenized kings of the Nabataean dynasty in the late second and early first centuries B.C. developed their growing kingdom on Hellenistic lines, with perhaps a slight admixture of Parthian elements. The administration of their foreign dominions was Hellenistic. Partly Hellenistic also was their dynastic coinage, which began under Aretas III the Philhellene (87–62 B.C.); for this they adopted the Ptolemaic standard. The Greek inscriptions and the types of their coins are not different from those of the other Hellenistic dynasts of the former Seleucid kingdom.

The early rock stronghold of Petra, the city of rock dwellings and rock sanctuaries, was transformed by the kings of the Nabataean dynasty into a typical Hellenistic city with a beautiful main street and several religious and public buildings. The temple known under the name of Kasr Firaun (its exact date is disputed), for example, is Hellenistic, and likewise the pretty Heroon or Tychaeon of El Khazne (the dates assigned

* Note the purely Hellenistic character of the painted decoration of the graves at Marissa of the second and first centuries B.C., Pl. LVIII.

PLATE XCVI

1. The beautiful bronze head found in South Arabia has been mentioned in this chapter, p. 855 (cf. n. 136 for bibliography). I cannot here describe it in detail, but the reader will find an excellent account of it in the paper by R. P. Hinks quoted in n. 136. I may, however, draw attention to the peculiar dressing of the hair. 'The hair hangs', says Mr. Hinks, 'in loose curls behind the nape of the neck; in front, over the forehead, it is combed forward into corkscrew locks arranged with a right- or left-hand twist on either side of the central parting, so that the ears are completely covered.' This arrangement of the hair appears, as Mr. Hinks has pointed out, on the coins of the Himyarite kings of the early Roman Empire. It is evident, however, that the Himyarites did not invent this fashion but borrowed it from elsewhere. We may recall the late Hellenistic Nabataean kings who dressed their hair similarly (see below, nos. 2 and 3) under the influence probably of the late Ptolemies (I. Noshy, *The arts in Ptolemaic Egypt*, 1937, p. 125). One of these—the famous Cleopatra Thea—imported this Libyan coiffure into Syria (see her coins and the famous bronze bust with cork-screw locks from the Villa dei Papiri, Herculaneum, now in the Museum of Naples, ingeniously recognized as a portrait of Cleopatra Thea by E. Pfuhl, *J.D.A.I.*, xlv (1930), pp. 43 ff., and figs. 26 and 27). The style of the head, its similarity to the coins of Malichus and Obodas reproduced below, proves, to my mind, that the head must be assigned not to Roman but to late Hellenistic times and was probably imported into South Arabia from Egypt or the Seleucid kingdom. We know how keen was the traffic in bronze statues about this time in the Parthian Empire (see below, pl. xcviii). The same was probably the case with the Nabataeans and the South Arabians, who received their supply of bronze objects from Egypt or the Seleucid kingdom, or both, and used them as patterns for their own bronze industry. We must not forget that the flourishing state of the caravan trade in the second century B.C. is attested by the prosperity of the Nabataean kingdom and of the trading cities of Phoenicia on the one hand, and by the revival of Egyptian trade relations with Arabia and India on the other. Add to the bibliography concerning the bronze head given in n. 136 R. Dussaud, *Syria*, xix (1938), p. 98. Photograph supplied by the authorities of the British Museum.

2. Æ Didrachm of Malichus I (*c.* 60–30 B.C.), king of the Nabataeans. Obv. Head right, beardless, moustached (?), with hair in long curls, diademed. Rev. Eagle with closed wings standing left; Nabataean inscription, in addition ΙΚϹ, perhaps a date. London, British Museum, *B.M.C.*, Arabia etc., p. 3, pl. 1, 5. Enlarged.

3. Æ Drachm of Obodas III (*c.* 30–9 B.C.). Obv. Busts jugate of Obodas with long hair, draped and diademed, and of Queen, draped, wearing stephane and necklace. Rev. Eagle standing left; Nabataean inscription. London, British Museum, *B.M.C.*, Arabia etc., p. 4, pl. 1, 6. Enlarged.

PLATE XCVI

1. Bronze head. London, British Museum

2, 3. Nabataean coins. London, British Museum

ARABIA AND HELLENISM

to which vary considerably). Minor finds in the city of Petra are scarce. The most notable are specimens of a peculiar type of pottery, a continuation of earlier local pottery under the strong influence of the contemporary Syrian *terra sigillata* and with elements borrowed from the Hellenistic painted pottery of Egypt and Asia Minor (for example the Hadra vases and the *lagynoi*).[135]

Being themselves hellenized, the Nabataeans contributed to the rapid hellenization of their customers and business partners, the south Arabian SABAEANS and HIMYARITES. We have evidence of this hellenization, for example, in an interesting find made in 1933 in the interior of South Arabia, south-east of the capital Senaa in the province Chaulan, and now in the possession of Imam Yahya, king of Yemen. A beautiful bronze head forming part of this find was recently given by him to King George and is now in the British Museum (see Pl. XCVI). Some of the bronze objects included in the find bear Sabaean and Himyaritic inscriptions and were certainly made in South Arabia; but the bronze head shows such a similarity to Nabataean coins of the first century B.C. that we are justified in regarding it as imported from the Nabataean kingdom. All the objects, including the architectural fragments, show strong Hellenistic influence.[136]

The most striking example of the prestige of the Seleucid Empire is the PARTHIAN KINGDOM. Iranian in its origin, in the character of its central government, and in the social organization of the ruling people, it inherited a large part of the Seleucid Empire and therewith its subdivisions, its administration, its financial organization, its social and economic structure, and its coinage. Heirs of the Seleucids, the Arsacids made no change in the organization of the provinces which they inherited, but left it intact. For the benefit of these provinces they continued the coinage of the Seleucids, using the same types with slight modifications, similar legends in Greek, the same standard, the same system of dating. The only change was the appearance on the coins of their own portraits and names, and perhaps on some coins the substitution of the Arsacid for the Seleucid era.[137]

What has been said of Parthia applies equally to the

ARMENIAN KINGDOM, also formerly a Seleucid satrapy. The Armenian dynasty emitted coins (from the 2nd cent. B.C. on) similar to those of Cappadocia, with Greek legends and portraits of the kings. The most enterprising of the Armenian kings, Tigranes I (97–56 B.C.), during his shortlived rule over Syria approached his Seleucid predecessors very closely in the form of his coinage. His philhellenism is well known. His capital— Tigranocerta—was designed to be a second Antioch and a semi-Greek city. It was formed on the ancient Hellenistic plan of a *synoikismos*.[138]

The disintegration of Syria involved therefore no radical change in the social and economic conditions that had pre-vailed in the new kingdoms before they became independent. The Greek cities remained the foundation of the wealth and prosperity of the new rulers. The Macedonians and Greeks of the cities no longer formed, to the exclusion of other races, the ruling class of the population, but they certainly were a privi-leged class. The cities retained their old political system, that is to say, a certain degree of autonomy. They remained in possession of their large and fertile territories, and no change was apparently carried out in their social and economic struc-ture. They were not molested as regards their cults and their intellectual training. We know this with certainty as regards two of the Macedonian cities which became parts of the Par-thian kingdom: Dura-Europus on the Euphrates and Seleuceia on the Eulaeus (Susa).

DURA-EUROPUS, as known from its numerous inscriptions and parchments of the late years of the first century B.C. and of the first and second centuries A.D. presents the appearance of a typical Macedonian colony. Its chief magistrate during the Parthian domination was the *strategos* (originally probably elected), who at the same time was an *epistates* (royal governor or representative, probably appointed by the king). This office at Dura in Parthian times appears to have been practically hereditary in one and the same aristocratic Macedonian family. The origin of this combined office is obscure. It may have been an innovation of the Parthian régime, or it may have been inherited by the Parthians from the late Seleucid period, when similar hereditary offices, styled tyrannies, had been established in several Greek cities, probably with a view to more efficient protection against the attacks of neighbours. Whether Europus in the late Seleucid and Parthian times had a *boule* and a popular assembly we are unable to say. The chief magistrate of the city was subordinate to the Parthian governor of the province, an official inherited by the Parthians from the Seleucids. The military representative of the provincial governor in the city may have been the commander of a Parthian garrison, a *phrourarch* in Seleucid terminology. But it is not certain that a Parthian garrison was permanently stationed in Europus and in the other Greek cities of the Parthian Empire. In normal times the city was probably protected by the local militia under the command of the *strategos-epistates*. There were other royal officers in the city. Royal judges (βασιλικοὶ δικασταί, cf. above, Ch. IV, p. 271) presided over courts organized on Greek lines, certainly another heritage from Seleucid times. They were appointed by the king and belonged to local Macedonian families. Some minor royal officials may have watched over the interests of the crown in the field of taxation (for example the *chreophylakes*). Other minor functionaries may have belonged not to the royal but to the municipal administration, being subordinate to the *strategos*. Eponymous priests of municipal Greek cults (among them Seleucid dynastic cults), who were members of the Macedonian families, were in charge of official religious observances.

We have no reason to suppose that the Parthians deprived the city of its large territory with its many native villages. Many documents of the Parthian period, found at Europus and kept apparently in the archives of that city, relate not to the affairs of the citizens of this city, but to those of inhabitants of various villages. One of these villages was Paliga, an important settlement and fortress far away from Dura at the mouth of the Khabur. It is evident therefore that Parthian Europus remained the centre of a large agricultural district. It is, moreover, certain that the Parthians did not encroach on the property rights of the citizens of Europus. It may be added that there was no change in the forms of business life or, probably, in the civil laws. They remained in Parthian Europus the same as in Seleucid times.

Important changes in the economic and social life of Parthian Europos were not due to any action on the part of the Parthian government. They were the result of the changed economic aspect of the Syro-Mesopotamian regions, of which I shall speak presently. These changes affected Europus because in Parthian times it was not only the centre of a flourishing agricultural district and of local industry, but became also a minor centre of the caravan trade, one of its frontier stations controlled by the new and rapidly growing caravan city of Palmyra. This change in the role of Europus accounts for its increasing prosperity, reflected in the size and splendour of its civil and religious buildings, and for its gradual but steady orientalization. It must be remembered that the caravan trade at this time was in the hands, not of the Macedonians of the city, but mainly of Oriental merchants. The Macedonians still formed the upper stratum of the population of Europus, but they shared their social position with many rich families of Semitic nationality.[139]

Still nearer to the Greek pattern of the past were the constitution and life of SELEUCEIA ON THE EULAEUS as known from several documents of the second and first centuries B.C. and the first century A.D. The city constitution of the first century A.D. was probably exactly the same as it had been in Seleucid times. Two archons, a treasurer, and probably other magistrates, were elected by the *demos*. The existence of a *boule* is probable. The youth of the city was trained in the Greek way. In the first century B.C. a certain Nicolaus, a Macedonian (?) and a distinguished citizen of Seleuceia, himself a victor in Greek *agones*, was gymnasiarch of the city and built a stadium for it. Similarly we have evidence of the existence of a gymnasium and of city games at Babylon in the year III B.C. Business life had not changed. Manumission documents were published in the same way as before and the form of manumissions remained the same. Finally, two metrical honorary inscriptions of the first century A.D. attest the fact that the descendants of the old settlers of Seleuceia were still in possession of their ancestral κλῆροι.[140]

The same persistence of Hellenistic traditions is illustrated by the interesting finds made recently at Shami, a little village near Malamir, about 100 kilometres east of Susa. Careful exploration of a temple of Hellenistic and Parthian times by Sir Aurel Stein showed that it was a sanctuary adorned with bronze statues of Hellenistic rulers (above, Ch. IV, n. 237) and of high Parthian dignitaries. An almost intact statue of one of the last (now in the Museum of Teheran, see Pl. xcviii) admirably illustrates the metrical inscription from Susa* engraved on the base of a 'bronze-image' of Zamaspes, *stratiarches* and satrap of Susa. It is interesting to find that the head of the statue from Shami was imported and was probably made at Susa, while the body is of local manufacture.[141]

Life at Europus, at Babylon, and at Seleuceia had, therefore, not changed much in Parthian times. The only difference was that the cities had now to obey the orders not of a Seleucid but of an Arsacid, and not of Greek but of Iranian governors— satraps and *strategoi*. There was, however, nothing to prevent the citizens from being honoured by the Parthian king with court titles of the Seleucid type and from becoming members of the royal administrative staff.

What is true of Parthia was certainly true of the other semi-Hellenistic monarchies of the time which happened to have Greek cities within their boundaries. It is regrettable that we know so little of the Greek cities that were incorporated in the Hasmonaean kingdom of Judaea. Some of them were destroyed by John Hyrcanus and Alexander Jannaeus. But we hear of no attempts by the Hasmonaeans to suppress Greek city life in Palestine altogether, and, that being so, there is no reason to suppose that they interfered with their constitution and their social and economic organization. The Nabataeans and the Armenians certainly did not.

Our scanty information does not allow us to form a confident opinion regarding the effect of the political conditions of the time upon the prosperity of the country. We have seen that this prosperity was based mainly on four pillars: agriculture (including viticulture, culture of olive-trees, and gardening), extensive grazing, industry (particularly in the Phoenician cities), and trade (including local trade, but especially caravan and maritime trade).

* *S.E.G.* vii. 13.

I have quoted above the passage of Posidonius which depicts in brilliant colours the fertility and the wealth of Syria in the time of Antiochus Sidetes.* The same impression of wealth is produced by the account given by the same writer of the war between Apamea and Larissa already referred to. The general tone of Strabo's description of Syria does not conflict with the picture drawn by Posidonius. Strabo of course makes frequent mention of brigandage, robberies, raids, and the like, and we must not underestimate the detrimental effect of such disorder upon the economic life of Syria. He often insists, however, upon the fertility and the agricultural prosperity of certain regions of Syria, and never speaks of any decline in this respect. It is therefore probable that these fertile territories had not been devastated as a result of the anarchy of the time. The wars were apparently not very destructive, the belligerents being careful not to arouse the indignation of the farmer-soldiers, their former and future subjects, on whose support they ultimately depended. The new dynasts were probably even more considerate as regards both their own subjects and their neighbours. Their taxation was probably not very oppressive.[142]

Nor were the last kings of the Seleucid line needy and impoverished. I have referred to a number of passages, which of course are mere stories and amusing anecdotes, with the object principally of illustrating the τρυφή of the kings and their demoralization; at the same time these passages show how great was the wealth at their disposal and how lavishly they used it, especially for the purpose of bribing their soldiers. I again draw attention to the army that Antiochus VII Sidetes led to Parthia, with its enormous train, and all the comforts that the supply service provided for the officers and men of the army.[143]

There was no lack of rich men in Syria either. At the most critical moment in the life of Babylonia, perhaps in 129/8 or 124/3 B.C., Posidonius tells of a rich Babylonian giving a banquet to Himerus, tyrant of both Babylon and Seleuceia, and to his three hundred companions. Each guest received from the host a silver drinking-cup worth four minas.[144] Or

* Fr. 10, *F. Gr. Hist.* 87.

I may cite again the banquet that was given by one of the chief assistants of Antiochus VIII Grypus, Heracleon of Beroea, to the soldiers, a copious feast served on tables that accommodated one thousand soldiers each.[145]

The situation of the Greek cities that came under the sway of the Parthian kings was a difficult one. At the moment of the Parthian conquest they had without doubt suffered heavily. The end of the second century and the first half of the first century are the darkest and most miserable period in the history of Dura. No extant buildings can be assigned to it and hardly any objects belonging to it have been found. The same may be said of Seleuceia on the Eulaeus. The two metrical inscriptions of the time of Phraates IV quoted above are in praise of governors of the district and their assistants for having restored the irrigation system and therewith the fertility of the κλῆροι of the Macedonian colonists of that city. The transitional period between Seleucid and Parthian rule was disastrous likewise for the two principal cities of Babylonia, Babylon and Seleuceia. Their sufferings were especially severe during the rule of the tyrant Himerus.

However, while on the whole the wealth of the Seleucid kings, though still considerable, was diminishing, and certain cities, formerly rich, were in a condition of temporary decline, many cities of the kingdom were as wealthy and perhaps wealthier than before. Strabo praises the purple industry of Tyre and the striking industrial activity of Sidon, especially as regards glass. And Tyre and Sidon were no exceptions. The same impression is left by the little we know of Aradus and Marathus, of Antioch and Seleuceia in Pieria, and of Berytus. Wherever the momentous invention of blown glass may have been made, it is certain that one of the chief centres of its production and export was Sidon, a vigorous rival of Egypt. I may add that this invention must have been made some time in the first century B.C. and that the export of large quantities of blown glass followed on the heels of the invention.[146]

Nor have we any reason to suppose that the volume of trade of the Syrian and Phoenician cities was declining. I have already referred to the important and influential position that the Phoenicians and Syrians held in the commercial and social

PLATE XCVII

1, 2. Two sections of the famous painting dedicated by Conon, a prominent inhabitant of Dura, in the middle of the first century A.D. to the great god Bel in his temple situated in the north-western corner of the city of Dura-Europus. The painting represents a sacrifice offered by Conon (fig. 1 to the left) and his family (not reproduced in my plate) and performed by two priests (to the right of Conon in fig. 1 ; bust of one of them fig. 2). The picture of Conon's sacrifice is an admirable illustration of the gradual orientalization of the Hellenistic Macedonian settlers in Dura-Europus. Conon, as we know from several records found there, belonged to one of the oldest and most prominent Macedonian families of the city. However, as our painting shows, while keeping his Macedonian name and transmitting it to his male posterity, he was married to a Semitic woman (Bithnanaia) and his daughters had Semitic names. He and his family wear a mixed Greco-Syrian dress (perhaps with some Iranian elements) and they worship a Semitic god, the great Bel of Palmyra and Babylon. The priests who are officiating for him are pure-blooded Semites, their priestly garb is Semitic, and the rite which they are performing is neither Greek nor Macedonian. And finally, the architects who built the temple and the painters who made the picture (though perhaps semi-Greek, like Conon and his family) were deeply influenced by traditions of Oriental art and were creating, together with other artists of the same type all over Mesopotamia, a new Mesopotamian style in architecture, painting, and sculpture. On the temple of Bel and its pictorial decoration see J. H. Breasted, *Oriental Forerunners of Byzantine Painting* &c., 1924; F. Cumont, *Fouilles de Doura-Europos*, 1926, pp. 41 ff., pls. XXV–XL: and the later contributions listed in my *Dura-Europos and its Art*, 1938, p. 146, n. 42; on the architecture of the temple cf. the works quoted ibid., p. 142, n. 26.

3. Cult bas-relief of a shrine found in the sacred precinct which stood in the south-western corner of the city of Dura-Europus. It represents a bearded god with curly hair standing frontwise on a double base of stone, each base being adorned with the protome of a winged griffin. The god wears a polos and a diadem; on the neck an Iranian torc (στρεπτός). He is dressed in a semi-Iranian fashion: tunic with long sleeves, trousers, and high shoes. Over the tunic he wears a Hellenistic cuirass with a leather belt. Four stars are engraved on the cuirass and similar stars adorn the shoes. In his right hand a sceptre, in his left something like a stilus. Before the god stands a priest, or the dedicant in priestly dress. He wears a conical cap and a long tunic. His legs are bare, his face beardless. He is offering a libation and a sacrifice of incense. A long Greek inscription states that the shrine was built for the god Aphlad, patron of the village Anath (on the Euphrates, about 100 kil. south of Dura, modern Anah) by Adadiabus, son of Zabdibol, grandson of Silloi. The same name appears in an inscription found in the same place which records the names of the members of a religious association of worshippers of the same god, all (with one exception) Semites (A.D. 54). The cult bas-relief is again an excellent illustration of the mixture of Semitic, Greek, and Iranian elements in the life, religion, and art, this time of the Semitic part of the population of Dura in the early Roman period, a mixture without doubt inherited from the late Hellenistic time. For details see my *Dura and the problem of Parthian Art*, 1935, pp. 226 ff., and figs. 36 and 38, cf. *Dura-Europos and its Art*, 1938, pp. 142, n. 26, and 145, n. 39.

PLATE XCVII

1   2

The Conon paintings. Damascus, National Museum

3. The god Aphlad. New Haven,
Yale Gallery of Fine Arts

DURA-EUROPUS IN PARTHIAN TIMES

PLATE XCVIII

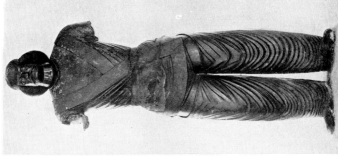

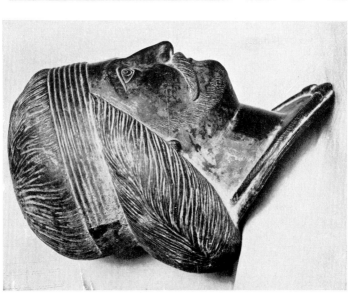

A local ruler. Teheran, National Museum

HELLENISM IN PARTHIA

PLATE XCVIII

Bronze statue found at Shami near Malamir in Susiane. The statue is a little more than life size (1·94 m.). Head and body were made separately, as is shown by the metal used and by the style of workmanship. In all probability the head was brought from elsewhere (from Susa?) and the body made on the spot. The man represented in the statue wears an Iranian dress, two Iranian daggers, and an Iranian torc on his neck. The head with a long moustache (no beard) is bound by a peculiar broad diadem, not of the royal pattern, since its ends do not float behind the head as is usual in royal and divine diadems. The statue therefore represents not a god nor a Persian king, but a local dynast or a Parthian satrap. It shows striking similarity in style to the sculptures of Dura and Palmyra, and was certainly made by Oriental sculptors: the head by one subject to some degree of Greek influence, the body by a local artisan who followed the traditions of Oriental art. It is difficult to assign the statue to a definite period. However, comparison with certain statues and bas-reliefs from Dura points to late Hellenistic or early Roman times, not later than the first century A.D.

The style of the statue is important also from an economic standpoint. It reveals commercial relations between Mesopotamia and the East, on the one hand, and Mesopotamia and the north-western part of the Syrian desert, on the other. The close stylistic connexion between the early Palmyrene sculptures and the statue from Shami, and between this last and the Gandhara statues and bas-reliefs representing Boddisatvas, seems to suggest that Luristan and the adjacent regions, rich in metals, especially in copper, supplied the leading cities of Babylonia and Susiane, and of other parts of the Parthian kingdom also, ancient centres of splendid metal-work, with abundance of metals, and that these were used for the production (among other things) of bronze statues in the Parthian style, which were exported to the East, to the North, and to the West. One of the chief places where the new 'Parthian' style in sculpture was created may have been Seleuceia on the Tigris. I may remind the reader that the famous 'tariff' of Palmyra (*C. I. Semitic.* ii. 3913, ll. 128 ff.) expressly mentions bronze statues as imported into Palmyra, certainly not from the West (the style of the stone reproductions of these bronze statues found at Palmyra has nothing in common with Greco-Syrian sculpture, and we must not forget that Syria was not very rich in metals). The carriers of this commerce in metal products and probably in metal ingots were the Palmyrene caravans of which I have spoken in the text. See this chapter, p. 858 f., and n. 141; add to the bibliography the excellent article by H. Seyrig, *Syria*, xx (1939), pp. 176 ff.

life of both Athens and Delos. In the business, social, and religious activities of Delos the Poseidoniasts of Berytus were second only to the Italians. This seems strange, seeing that Strabo states that Berytus was destroyed by Tryphon and was not restored until this was done by the Romans. The destruction of Berytus is well attested and so is its restoration to its former prosperity by the Romans in Strabo's time. The first fact Strabo probably learnt from his Hellenistic source, the second from his contemporaries. He found, however, no information in his sources regarding the intervening period and conjectured that Berytus had lain desolate during the whole of it. His supposition is contradicted by the coins and is probably wrong. The city after its devastation by Tryphon may have recovered very soon. Then came gradual decay caused probably by the decline of Delos, with which Berytus was so closely connected. Tyre transferred its business relations in time to Puteoli, Berytus apparently did not. And so the Romans found it a minor and insignificant city.[147]

Berytus therefore was an exception. The coinage of Seleuceia in Pieria and of the Phoenician cities, especially of Aradus and Tyre, of which some account has been given above, shows that there was no interruption in the commercial prosperity of the cities of the Syrian coast, at least until the time of the Roman civil wars. Purple dyed stuffs of Tyre, the various manufactures of Sidon, certain products of Syrian agriculture, were still popular on the foreign markets.[148]

In the first place there was a growing demand for and a corresponding supply of Arabian, Indian, and Chinese luxuries, which were carried by the caravans to the Syrian and Phoenician ports. I have repeatedly referred to this trade. The establishment of the Parthians in some of the Iranian satrapies of the Seleucids and the occupation by Mithridates II of Babylonia and Mesopotamia hardly diminished its volume. On the contrary, it was in the time of Mithridates II that direct diplomatic relations (the two embassies of Chang-K'ien of 128 and 115 B.C.) were first established between China and countries as far west as Parthia. This without doubt led to a better organization of the trade routes (the so-called 'silk route') between China and Parthia and to intensified and regularized commercial relations between these two countries. For Syria this brought about a considerable increase in imported goods.[149]

Nor was the demand for the caravan goods declining in the Mediterranean world. We must bear in mind that for Italy the period that followed the establishment of the Roman protectorate and partial domination over the East and even that of the civil wars were times of great prosperity. Italy was rich and its consumption of all sorts of foreign products was not declining; on the contrary, it was constantly growing. There were a large number of wealthy or well-to-do men both in Rome and in the rest of Italy. We must also take into consideration the kingdoms of Numidia and Mauretània in Africa, Gaul and perhaps Spain in Western Europe. Nor must we overlook the demand for Oriental goods in the monarchies of Asia Minor, to which I have already alluded.[150]

No doubt the caravan trade suffered heavily from the anarchy of the time. The Euphrates route was unsafe, especially in its northern section. The petty dynasts of Upper Mesopotamia and the Arab sheikhs of the Syrian and Mesopotamian deserts levied heavy tolls on the passing caravans. The route from Petra to Damascus was likewise insecure. The Ituraeans had the well-earned reputation of being professional robbers.

Yet the resourcefulness of the caravan leaders (later called συνοδιάρχαι at Palmyra) devised methods by which trade relations gained some measure of security. Strabo describes one of these. His description is certainly drawn from earlier sources (unfortunately of uncertain date) and contains a good deal that is puzzling. It may be in the main reconstructed as follows. In order to avoid the organized robberies of the Arabian chieftains (φύλαρχοι) on the right and left banks of the Middle Euphrates (these chieftains were very poor, says Strabo, and therefore exceedingly greedy; they were apparently not under the control either of the Seleucids or of the Parthians), a change was made in the route of the caravans which travelled from the ports of Syria to the East. It started as before on the Syrian coast, crossed the Euphrates at Anthemusia (i.e. in all probability at Zeugma-Apamea), and then, instead of descending the Euphrates, it struck off to Edessa. This part of the route was safe: it passed through Syrian territory and then through the principality of Edessa. From Edessa, in order to avoid the blackmail of the φύλαρχοι, the caravans proceeded across the desert to a new city called Σκηναί, a capital of nomadic Arabs (Strabo calls them σκηνῖται and καμηλῖται, 'tent' and 'camel' Arabs), who guaranteed to the caravans water, peace, and moderate tolls while they travelled through the desert to Skenai and thence to Babylonia. This means that in the Mesopotamian desert, probably by agreement with the merchants of Babylonia and Syria and perhaps with the Osrhoenes also, a new Arab State was formed with a caravan-city as its centre, exactly similar to the Nabataean State with Petra as its capital, or later Palmyra with its territory. This State was strong enough to protect the caravans against the petty robber-sheikhs of the banks of the Euphrates. The city of Skenai has not been located. It cannot be Hatra.[151]

A similar device was apparently adopted by the caravans which started from Aradus or Tyre. The roads from Tyre to Damascus and from Aradus to Hemesa or Hamath were not quite safe, but could be sufficiently protected by the cities themselves. From Damascus, Hemesa, and Hamath two alternative ways of reaching the Euphrates were open to merchants: either to take the route to Beroea and thence to Thapsacus on the Euphrates, or to cross the desert and so reach either the Middle or the Lower Euphrates. The first route was apparently in use as long as orderly conditions prevailed in the Syrian State and the Euphrates route was well protected. It was less arduous and safer. In the troubled period of the late second and early first century the route across the desert became more convenient, provided there was a power which would guarantee its safety and water supply. Such a power was constituted by one or several tribes of the Syrian desert in the oasis of Palmyra (Tadmor), and Palmyra became the Skenai of the Syrian desert. Though unknown to the Hellenistic source used by Strabo, Palmyra was nevertheless a rich settlement and an important centre of caravan trade in the late Seleucid times. We know that it aroused the greed of Antony during his Parthian expedition and that before the time of Augustus the settlement possessed at least one temple of the Hellenistic type. This growth of Palmyra cannot be accounted for unless we assume a change in the caravan routes such as is described above. Its development into a real Hellenistic city, whose ruins are so well known to all lovers of antiquity, occurred later, shortly before and under Augustus, as the result of a political and commercial understanding between Parthia and Rome.[152]

Similar methods were certainly resorted to by the Nabataeans in order to safeguard the caravan routes that connected them with Babylonia. Here also settlements of native Arabs reinforced by Nabataean colonies protected the caravans and secured their water supply. There is evidence of this in Nabataean inscriptions found between Dumatha and Forat (the latter a Parthian caravan-city of Babylonia, known from some Palmyrene inscriptions). Dumatha or Thaima or both may have played in the Arabian desert the role of Palmyra and Skenai. Efforts no less successful were certainly made by the Nabataeans to safeguard their northern route from the robberies of the Ituraeans, as is indicated by the Nabataean domination over Gerasa, Bostra, and Damascus.[153]

The above measures, taken by the parties interested in the Syrian and Phoenician caravan trade, certainly saved it from utter disorganization. But the situation was difficult and the trade in all probability was not so well organized as it had been in the third and early second centuries B.C. It was reserved for the Romans to restore it to all its former regularity. Meanwhile Egypt benefited by the situation and certainly made good use of its opportunity. A considerable part of the Nabataean trade was probably attracted to Alexandria, and Egypt got a fair chance of reviving the maritime route from its harbours in the Red Sea to South Arabia and India. I shall speak of this in greater detail presently.

But the most important new phenomenon in regard to the trade of Syria was the almost complete change in its orientation. For more than a century Seleucid trade had been directed towards Asia Minor and Greece and had used mainly the land routes across the Anatolian peninsula leading to the great ports of Ephesus and Miletus, the main outlets of this trade, while the Seleucid Syrian ports of Laodicea and Seleuceia in Pieria played a secondary part so long as the Ptolemies were masters of the sea. This was the position when Asia Minor was a part of the Seleucid kingdom and so it remained after Magnesia and Apamea, when Asia Minor was lost to the Seleucids and was governed by the Attalids. I have observed above that an *entente cordiale* was reached between thc Seleucids and the Attalids and that the land routes of Asia Minor and the ports of Ephesus and Miletus were as extensively used by the Seleucids of the early second century B.C. as they had been by their predecessors. This situation began to change in the second half of the second century B.C., especially after the disappearance of the Pergamene dynasty. Syrian trade abandoned the Anatolian routes, as is shown by the Syrian coin-hoards of the time. Coins struck in Asia Minor which had prevailed in such hoards in the early second century vanish almost completely from them at the end of the second and in the first century. The hoards of this period consist of Seleucid coins, of Syrian municipal issues, and occasionally of Athenian 'owls'. At the same time Syrian trade became more and more concentrated in the Phoenician ports, especially Tyre and Berytus. This coincides with the change in the orientation of the caravan roads, as described above. The Phoenician cities, now masters of the Syrian trade, gave it a new direction. Their business relations with Delos and Italy have already been dealt with. Another similar phenomenon is the closer commercial connexion between the Phoenician cities and Alexandria. This found its most striking expression in the adoption of the Phoenician, that is to say, the Ptolemaic standard by the Syrian kings (among others, of course) from Alexander Balas onwards and by some of the minting cities of the Seleucid kingdom, especially Tyre. This innovation was certainly not exclusively a political measure. Political and commercial interests here went hand in hand.

This change in the orientation of Syrian trade is not difficult to explain, and the explanation is that already given. I have pointed out the growing importance of the Western market for Eastern commerce and the steady fall in the purchasing power of the Greek world, especially of Asia Minor, as compared with what it had been in the third and the early second centuries

B.C., and this in spite of a certain improvement in the economic situation of Asia Minor and Greece in the late second century and the early first. But the change is not to be attributed solely to the diminished purchasing capacity of the Aegean and Pontic world. It is more than probable that it was caused to a large extent by the political conditions which impaired the security of the Anatolian land routes. The Attalids disappeared and with them the efficient protection of the caravans. Rome had no military or police forces in its province of Asia. Thus the principal route across Asia Minor, the southern, was no longer as safe as it had been under the Attalids. This state of things explains Rome's endeavour to establish the new province of Cilicia and the efforts of Servilius Vatia to combat and to crush the Isaurians.

It is not surprising that the great merchants of Phoenicia, forced to choose between two evils, found it more profitable, cheaper, and safer to arrive at a tolerable *modus vivendi* with the Cilician pirates and to use the cheaper sea route, the route to Delos, than to take the risk of sending caravans by the long and expensive land routes to Ephesus and Miletus.[154]

We may notice at this point a feature of the economic and social life of Syria in the period we are considering, which certain scholars have connected with the commercial decay of that country. While 'Roman' *negotiatores* were common in Asia Minor at this time, actively transacting business not only in the Roman province of Asia but also in the still independent kingdoms, especially Bithynia, we have hardly any evidence of the presence of either *negotiatores* or other Romans in Syria and Phoenicia except in the capacity of political envoys or occasional visitors. J. Dobiaš has attributed this fact to the insecurity of traffic in Syrian waters, to which insecurity even Pompey's annexation of Syria did not put an end. The Roman merchants waited for quieter times before appearing in force in the Syrian and Phoenician ports. I doubt this interpretation of a 'fact' which is itself established only by negative evidence. We know that there were large numbers of Italians in Asia Minor, but they are very seldom mentioned in our literary and epigraphical evidence. The absence of such evidence as regards Syria is therefore not conclusive. Better archaeological exploration of the principal cities of Syria and Phoenicia may yield such evidence. But, assuming the absence of Italians from the Syrian ports, this absence is much better explained by the existence of Delos. Why should the 'Romans' go to distant Syria when they had Delos with its Syrian merchants at their disposal? So long as Delos throve, there was no reason why the 'Roman' *negotiatores* should go to Syria. As soon as it sank into neglect these merchants found their way thither. After the time of Pompey there was certainly no lack of 'Romans' in the province of Syria, and their numbers constantly grew with its gradual pacification.[155]

I will conclude with a brief observation on the reasons which led Pompey to annex Syria. He certainly did not do so in order to open that country to Roman business men by putting an end to piracy and to the unsettled conditions that prevailed there. This consideration may have played a secondary part in Pompey's decision, but in the main he was guided by political considerations. The episodes of Mithridates VI and Tigranes I showed how easy it was for a man of ability backed by large material and military resources to re-establish the unity of the hellenized East. A new Tigranes might appear at any time. And it was very probable, though at the moment Parthia was not particularly strong and enterprising, that the role of Tigranes and Armenia might in the immediate future be taken up by Parthia and one of its kings. There was no Parthian danger at the moment, but Pompey knew Parthia too well to underestimate its capabilities and its ambitions. War against Parthia in the very near future seemed inevitable (Crassus' expedition was already in contemplation) and it was strategically important to have a pacified and well-organized province and not a chaos of petty kings and robber-dynasts as the starting-point and base of a major military expedition. Pompey's ambitions were great and Alexander's fame was still alive in the East.[156]

C. *EGYPT*

After the death of Philometor, who fell on the field of battle in Syria during one of the interventions of the Ptolemies in the affairs of the Seleucids (145 B.C.), Ptolemy νεώτερος returned from Cyrene to Alexandria, reached an understanding with Cleopatra II, widow of Philometor, made her his wife, and was recognized as ruler of Egypt. His cult name was Euergetes.

With his reign begins a new period in the life of Egypt, a period full of dynastic strife, accompanied by skilful propaganda and internal troubles, by ghastly crimes and bloody executions. In politics the heavy hand of Rome, which was first extended over Egypt at the memorable meeting of Antiochus IV and Popilius Laenas at Eleusis, was felt more and more strongly. The period ends with the annexation of Egypt by Rome.

I cannot deal in detail with the political history of this period which, though it has been carefully studied, is very imperfectly known. It will be sufficient to mention a few cardinal facts to enable the reader better to understand its social and economic features.

Its best known personalities are the king Euergetes II himself and his two wives—Cleopatra II, styled his sister in official documents, and her daughter, the niece of Euergetes, Cleopatra III, called officially his wife. Euergetes made a great and very unfavourable impression on his contemporaries. We still hear their voice in the excellent description of his character by the author whom Diodorus used as his source.* We must, however, remember that his situation was very difficult. He inherited a kingdom grievously shaken by foreign and civil wars, deprived of its foreign dominions, faced by the greatest financial and economic dangers. The population was far from tranquil. Unrest was rife both in the 'country' and in Alexandria. Even the army was unruly. Opposition to the king was vigorous and his throne was insecure. He was forced by circumstances and perhaps by the pressure of Rome to marry and associate with himself on the throne Cleopatra II, an ambitious and unscrupulous woman, though very popular in Alexandria, whom he hated no less than she hated him. As a counterpoise to her Euergetes married her daughter Cleopatra III, who was as ambitious and cruel as her mother. The two women cordially detested each other and struggled unceasingly for power. It is therefore not surprising that the long reign of Euergetes was

* xxxiii. 6.

PLATE XCIX

1. Fragmentary, badly damaged basalt head of a statue wearing the *nemes* head-cloth with the uraeus on the front (h. 0·27 m.). The eyes were inlaid. The head was certainly intended to be a portrait of one of the Ptolemies, perhaps Philopator. It shows an inorganic mixture, or rather juxtaposition, of Greek (see the hair and some traits in the modelling of the face) and Egyptian elements.

2. Fragment of a granite statue representing one of the Ptolemaic queens with the features and symbols and the dress of Isis (h. 0·485 m.). Though the conception is Egyptian, some traits in the face and body reveal Greek influence. Late second century B.C. Statues of Ptolemaic queens represented as Isis have been frequently found in Egypt.

Unpublished. Place of origin unknown. Photographs supplied by the Yale Gallery of Fine Arts.

I have reproduced the two sculptures (of rather poor workmanship), which belong to a well-known and frequently illustrated class of sculptures of the Ptolemaic period found in Egypt, because they show the Egyptian aspect of the policy of both the earlier and especially the later Ptolemies. For a more detailed stylistic analysis of works of this kind I may refer to the summaries of I. Noshy, *The arts in Ptolemaic Egypt*, 1937, pp. 138 ff., cf. p. 126; A. Scharff in W. Otto *Handb. d. Arch.* ii, 1938, pp. 612 ff., and to the more special works quoted in these summaries. Cf. A. Adriani, *Bull. Soc. Arch. Alex.* xxxii (N. S. 10, 1), pp. 103 ff. and figs. 12–14. The Ptolemaic sculptures of the Yale Gallery have been studied by Miss W. Needler, Toronto, in a paper soon to be published.

PLATE XCIX

2. Statue of a queen

1. Head of a king

New Haven, Yale Gallery of Fine Arts

EGYPT IN THE SECOND CENTURY B.C.

an agitated and feverish period in the history of Egypt and that the king himself and his throne were constantly exposed to serious danger. The fact that he succeeded in maintaining his power for about thirty years and the methods by which he did this show that he was a clever politician, resourceful, courageous, and energetic, though utterly devoid of scruple and moral sense, and unusually cruel and cynical.

At the beginning of his reign (in 145/4 B.C.) Euergetes, following in this the example of his predecessors, published at least two 'peace proclamations' or 'amnesty decrees', one in Egypt, another in Cyprus. The second was directed mainly to the soldiers of his Cyprian army, which had faithfully supported him during his struggle for power. Then, in 144, followed the understanding with Cleopatra II. Peace was established between them and their long and dramatic joint rule began. With this joint rule Cleopatra III was associated in 142. We may see in the association of Cleopatra III and in the feelings which it aroused in Cleopatra II some connexion with the dangerous revolt of one of the grandees of the kingdom, Galaistes, son of Amynandrus, king of the Athamanians. Galaistes appears in our literary texts as leader of the exiles, the political opponents of Euergetes. He and his followers were supported by a small part of the royal army (140/39 B.C.). This revolt, of which we know very little, may have led the king to bestow about that time certain privileges on the priests, who had perhaps upheld his cause in the struggle.

The most conspicuous event in the life of Euergetes II, an event which had grave political, social, and economic consequences, was the political crisis which began in 132/1 B.C. and lasted until 127 B.C. Cleopatra II and the other enemies of Euergetes forced him in 132/1 to leave Alexandria (with Cleopatra III) and to take refuge in Cyprus. From Cyprus Euergetes began an obstinate struggle with Cleopatra II for the recovery of Egypt. That country was in a chaotic condition. The population was divided into two camps (ἀμιξία): Alexandria, at least part of the 'Greeks', the Jews and part of the army, supported Cleopatra II; many (probably the majority) of the natives, under the leadership of the priests, and the rest of the army, sided with Euergetes. In fact the war was a combination of a dynastic war and a 'native' revolution, and consequently took chaotic forms. In this turmoil, however, Euergetes managed his affairs cleverly. In a few months he became master of almost the whole of the open country. Alexandria resisted. The city was not taken by Euergetes until 127 B.C., after Cleopatra II had fled to Syria (129/8 B.C.). Its rebellion was visited with cruel punishment. But Cleopatra II remained powerful even in exile, and Euergetes was forced finally to acknowledge this by a reconciliation with her (in 124 B.C.) and the re-establishment of their joint rule.

The close of the dynastic strife did not bring with it the end of the native revolution. Outbreaks in one place or another continue to be mentioned in our documentary evidence, meagre as it is. In 123 Hermonthis in Thebais was conducting a regular war against its neighbour Crocodilopolis.* It should be noted that on this occasion the Hermonthites mobilized their λαοί or πλήθη. In 122/1 B.C. disturbances broke out in the Thinite nome.† They are described as an ἀμιξία.‡ Later it was Panopolis which caused trouble. The affair was so serious that the Panopolites were not included in the general 'amnesty' of 118 B.C.§ Finally, as late as 118 B.C. local *laoi* of the Thinite nome attacked a royal embankment.‖ The impression produced by the *amixia* in the minds of the people is reflected in many documents. There is a characteristic example in the expressions used in a complaint lodged by a *paraschistes* ¶ to describe the outrageous conduct of his adversary. He is acting, the plaintiff says, in the manner of a rebel (ἀποστατικῷ τρόπῳ) and as if there were no king in the country (ὡσανεί τις ἀβασιλευσίᾳ περιεχόμενος). Euergetes and his co-rulers tried to stop this avalanche of risings, revolts, and disturbances by a new decree, or rather set of decrees, of 'amnesty' published in 118 B.C. (below, pp. 878 ff).

Euergetes II died soon after his attempt to pacify the country (in 116 B.C.). But the situation remained as complicated after his death as during his lifetime. He himself pre-

* Wilcken, *Chr.* 11.   † *P.S.I.* 171.

‡ l. 34: ἐν τῇ γενηθείσῃ ἐν τῷ ⸤τόπῳ ἀμειξίᾳ.

§ *Teb.* 5. 134 ff. and 147 ff.   ‖ *P.S.I.* 168.

¶ *U.P.Z.* 196. col. ii. 65 ff. and 82 ff.

pared the ground for further disturbances by his testament. Disregarding established traditions, he dealt with Egypt as if it were his private property. According to Justin* he left the kingdom to his younger wife Cleopatra III with full powers to choose as her co-ruler one of their two sons: the elder, Ptolemy Philometor Soter II, or the younger, Ptolemy Alexander. Moreover, Euergetes separated Cyrenaica from the kingdom and gave it to his bastard son Apion. He may have acted in the same way as regards Cyprus, which he perhaps intended to make a separate kingdom under the rule of the legitimate son who should not be chosen as co-ruler with queen Cleopatra III. This will and testament of Euergetes remained for a time a dead letter. The people of Alexandria refused to accept it and forced Cleopatra III to take as co-ruler not Alexander, the son she preferred, but Soter II, whom she hated. Whether this was done at the instigation of Cleopatra II and with the approval of Rome, we do not know. Nor do we know whether Cyrenaica was taken over by Apion in accordance with the will of Euergetes or remained under the control of Cleopatra and Soter. An inscription recently found at Cyrene, if correctly dated 109/8 B.C., may be regarded as evidence that Cyrenaica either remained part of the kingdom despite the testament of Euergetes or was temporarily annexed by Soter after a brief period of rule by Apion.

The real ruler of Egypt after the death of Euergetes II and Cleopatra II (who certainly was no longer alive after 116 B.C.) was Cleopatra III. Her limitless ambition and unrestrained violence involved Egypt in continuous dynastic strife, in which the Seleucids of Syria took an active part. The joint reign of Cleopatra III and Soter II was not a time of tranquillity for Egypt. Certain documents suggest that breaches between the two rulers occurred twice before Cleopatra finally succeeded in driving Soter out of Egypt. In 107 a revolution broke out against Soter, and Cleopatra proclaimed as her colleague her younger son Alexander, at that time governor of Cyprus. Soter found refuge and support in Cyprus. About the same time or a little later Apion occupied Cyrene. He was certainly king there before 100 B.C. Egypt was thus split into three

* xxxix. 3. 1; 5. 2.

independent kingdoms hostile to each other. Nor was the situation in the country itself satisfactory. Cleopatra would not tolerate any initiative on the part of her new colleague. Hostility and hatred therefore reigned in Alexandria. Finally, after a violent struggle, Cleopatra died in 101 B.C., murdered, as some scholars suppose, by her son.

After Cleopatra's death Alexander remained sole ruler of Egypt until 89 B.C., when he was driven out by the Alexandrians and perished in a naval engagement while trying to reach Cyprus from Lycia. Soter reunited Egypt with Cyprus and ruled over his kingdom until his death (80 B.C.). A little earlier, in 96, Cyrene and the Cyrenaica became by the last will of Apion a Roman possession.

After the death of Soter the dynastic strife began afresh. The royal house was exterminated at the very outset and there appeared on the throne, a tool in the hands of certain Roman politicians, the well-known Ptolemy Auletes, a bastard son of Soter II, who ruled until 51 B.C., exploited by his Roman friends and supporters, surrounded by intrigues and plots, hated and ridiculed by the Alexandrians. These in the end succeeded in expelling him from the country, but he returned with the help of Gabinius in 55 B.C., this time supported by a Roman armed force.

His death ends the period of the gradual decay of Egypt. With its last queen Cleopatra the country rises again to great political importance, destined after this short phase of glory to be annexed by Rome in 30 B.C. The events of this period are too well known to be related here.

The sombre internal conditions that had prevailed under Euergetes II continued under his successors. Rebellions and revolutions were still of frequent occurrence. An *amixia*, for example, is mentioned in a petition of 111 B.C. (from Thebais) as having taken place not long before the date of the document.* This *amixia* seems not to be identical with that of 132/1 B.C. As usual, it led to confusion in rights of property: an abandoned vineyard of one Greek settler was appropriated by another, just as, for example, the house of the famous Hermias at Thebes and many other houses and parcels of land in

* *P. Lond.* ii. 401. 20.

the Thebaid and elsewhere had been taken from their rightful owners in the time of Epiphanes. One of the rebellions of the first century B.C. is better known than the others. It is the στάσις of the year 88 B.C., during the second reign of Soter II. Some chance documents which refer to it show that it did not differ from the other revolts, but was a rebellion of the lower classes against the government, with some admixture of nationalistic aspirations and religious fanaticism. Like the other rebellions, its focus was in the Thebaid, that part of Egypt which was nearest to Nubia and Meroe. It was terminated by the capture and ruthless destruction of Thebes, an act which made a certain impression on contemporaries and is mentioned in our literary texts.*

We have less information about the troubles, apparently of the same character, of the reign of Auletes and probably of the first years of Cleopatra. Inscriptions from Hermupolis and papyri from the Heracleopolite nome show how disturbed the situation was in 79/8 and 64/3 B.C. To maintain some degree of order strong detachments of soldiers were stationed in various villages and cities, and squadrons of the royal navy, under the direction of the *dioecetes*, ensured the safety of traffic on the Nile. In 58 B.C., when dynastic strife prevailed in Alexandria, we hear of a kind of formal civil war around Heracleopolis, in which a certain Hermaiscus played an important part.† The doings of Hermaiscus exasperated the population to such an extent that the government was threatened with a general strike. Whether Hermaiscus was, like Dionysius Petosarapis, an officer of the crown who became leader of a rebellion or a chief of organized robbers we do not know. Organized robbers we meet again in *B.G.U.* 1858 (date lost). The woman who writes this petition speaks of the conditions as ὡς ἐν πραγμάτων ἀναρχίᾳ. She complains of open robbery. We have the same theme of robbery in *B.G.U.* 1780 (51/50 B.C.): a ὑποστράτηγος (vice-governor) had been attacked by a certain Diocles who had summoned to his aid his own brother ἄνωθεν ἐπὶ λῃστῄαις γεγονότα (whether this means engaged in robbery in the North or engaged in resisting the robbers is not clear).[157]

The series of civil wars which began under Philopator and

* Paus. i. 9. 3.   † *B.G.U.* 1762, cf. 1763 and 1764.

878 The Roman Protectorate and the CHAP.

became endemic in the country until the end of the Ptolemaic régime shows that the conditions of life there were far from satisfactory. I drew attention in the last chapter to certain features in the economic and social system of the time of Philopator, Epiphanes, and Philometor which were in one way or another connected with the civil strife, and to the remedies adopted by the government. I showed how unruly and discontented was the mood of the people. Similar conditions continued to prevail in the period we are now considering, for which we have much better and fuller evidence than for the preceding reigns. We may therefore pause and ask once more what were the reasons for the continuous civil and dynastic wars and for the public discontent that lay behind them. It will be convenient, however, first to set out the few known facts which may help us to explain the unrest that was prevalent in Egypt and contributed to the gradual decline of the financial and economic power of the country.

Most illuminating is 'the proclamation of peace', or the 'amnesty' decree, or, to use the ancient term, the φιλάνθρωπα of Euergetes II of 118 B.C. The copy of the document which we possess is fragmentary. There are many lacunae, and many paragraphs are hard to decipher completely. Moreover, the scribe who wrote the copy made many mistakes, some of them difficult to correct. And finally, even if we had the full and correct text of the copy, we could not be sure that it may be regarded as a complete copy of the original. I am inclined to think that the document as we have it is an abbreviation of the original proclamation. The historical section, which we found a constituent part of the proclamations of Philopator and Epiphanes and which contained a report of victories and concomitant gifts to the army and to temples, is here completely omitted. The φιλάνθρωπα alone, preceded by the announcement of amnesty, have been copied, and of these only a selection, many paragraphs being omitted. Some of those which have been copied have probably been abbreviated. Thus the document is incomplete. Nevertheless, it gives a very instructive picture of the conditions of life that prevailed in Egypt in the late second century B.C.[158]

The 'proclamation of peace' or φιλάνθρωπα of Euergetes II

was not the first document of this kind published in Egypt. Philopator may have published one, and others were certainly issued by Epiphanes and Philometor (above, pp. 713 ff.). Euergetes himself had previously published one or two decrees similar to that of 118 B.C., in 145/4 B.C. (above, n. 157) and perhaps in 140/39 B.C. (above, n. 157). We have later quotations from the φιλάνθρωπα of 118 B.C. or from an amendment to them.* The later Ptolemies probably made similar proclamations; we know that Auletes did so.† Chance has preserved for us a substantial part of the decree of 118 B.C. and only fragments and quotations of the earlier ones. But it is highly probable that all the φιλάνθρωπα had the same general form. This form may have been initiated by Philopator or Epiphanes. But I am disposed to think that the idea of such a proclamation and its general form may have been traditional in Egypt. I have no direct proof of this, but my suggestion receives some support from the Ptolemaic ἐντολαί or *mandata*. Egypt was a country of traditions, and conditions similar to those of the reigns of Philopator, Epiphanes, Philometor, Euergetes II, and Auletes, that is to say, of pacification following periods of anarchy, were no novelty in the history of Egypt. In their φιλάνθρωπα the Ptolemies were addressing themselves mainly to the natives, and it is possible that for this purpose they chose a form familiar to them.[159]

The φιλάνθρωπα were first and foremost proclamations of peace or grants of amnesty.‡ They all begin with the same formula: the kings give general pardon (ἀφιᾶσι) to all their subjects for 'errors, crimes, accusations, condemnations, and charges of all kinds' up to a certain date. Peace was thus offered to every one involved in the rebellion. More specifically all those who had left their homes (ἀνακεχωρηκότες) and were in hiding were invited to return to their dwellings (ἴδιαι) to resume their former peaceful occupations, and to reoccupy so much of their property as had not yet been disposed of by the government, in other words, had not been sold (ἄπρατα) as

---

* In *U.P.Z.* 162, col. 7, 13 ff., cf. *Teb.* 124. 22 ff. (about 118 B.C.) and 73 (113–111 B.C.).

† *B.G.U.* 1185 (59 B.C.).

‡ συγγνώμη, *O.G.I.* 116.

ownerless (ἀδέσποτα). Then followed a general concession to all the population: a remission of taxes until a certain date.

This solemn general proclamation to all (πάντες) was followed by special orders (προστάγματα) mingled with ἀφέσεις (amnesty orders). These relate either to the whole population or to particular classes—those which formed the main pillars of the economic and social life of the country: the Greeks on the one hand—merchants of Alexandria, soldiers, landowners—and the natives on the other—the working class. Between the two stood the privileged natives—the native soldiers and more especially the priests.

This portion of the document deals first with the privileged classes, both native and Greek, such persons as were not engaged in manual work: merchants of Alexandria, soldiers, priests, and landowners. It deals secondly with the labouring classes: the royal peasants (βασιλικοὶ γεωργοί) and all who were occupied in other economic fields, or, to use the expression of the Ptolemies, those who were connected in one capacity or another with the revenues of the king (the ὑποτελεῖς and the ἐπι- or ἐμπεπλεγμένοι ταῖς προσόδοις). These two sections of the document have a different character.

The paragraphs dealing with the higher privileged classes are most of them of a confirmatory character and probably emergency measures intended to restore order after the chaos caused by the civil war. Two governments had been in existence. Each had granted certain favours to the privileged classes in order to secure their support, and given its sanction to arrangements, frequently of an irregular character. The compromise between the two governments was based on mutual concessions. It involved substantially the confirmation, with certain restrictions, of the measures taken and grants made by the other side.

However, though chiefly concerned with the settlement of the troubles of the time of *amixia*, the first series of προστάγματα reflect at the same time the grievances and the claims of the privileged classes. They are based without doubt on divers petitions submitted by the representatives of these classes to the king and his higher officials. The προστάγματα φιλάνθρωπα are thus an answer to these claims and contain a number of concessions to the requirements of the several bodies.

From these προστάγματα we may gather what were the more dissatisfied groups among the privileged classes. Whereas the merchants of Alexandria are granted some trifling privileges as regards various customs duties, and only two paragraphs are devoted to the soldiers (one relating to the κληροῦχοι, another to the μάχιμοι), the bulk of the first part of the document deals with the priests and with the private landowners. It would appear that it was these two groups which were the cause of the greatest concern to the government, while the soldiers and the Alexandrians gave comparatively little ground for uneasiness (unless perhaps they were dealt with in special proclamations).

Still longer and still more diversified is the second section, which deals almost exclusively with the labouring classes. Here it is no longer a matter of confirmation of rights or re-adjustment of conditions after the civil war. The government had, no doubt, been overwhelmed with the petitions, complaints, and recriminations of the labouring classes, and the king and his ministers recognized the justice of their claims and endeavoured to give them satisfaction. Most of these grievances arose from the unlawful acts of the officials of the crown in the various departments of the administration. The picture is a gloomy one, reflecting the atmosphere of oppression, arbitrary acts, violence, bribery, and corrupt practices amid which the labouring classes were living. I shall return presently to this formidable list of the misdeeds of the administration.

The picture drawn by the φιλάνθρωπα is completed and extended by many contemporary and later documents. Among them two groups are of special significance. One consists of the documents and private letters of the archives of a certain Menches, a village scribe of Cerceosiris, and dates from the late years of Euergetes II and the early years of Soter II.* For the late Ptolemaic period this group of official documents and private letters has almost the same importance as the Zenon papyri for the reign of Philadelphus and the early years of Euergetes I. It reflects in many important aspects the life of a village in the Fayûm, while behind it we see the activity of the

* It has been published by Grenfell and Hunt in *P. Teb.* i. and has been the subject of several commentaries.

government, beginning with the king, his chief officials (among them the *dioecetes* Irenaeus, one of the best successors of the famous Apollonius), and ending with the impressive array of the higher and lower functionaries of the nome. On them depended the life and welfare of Menches. But on Menches in turn depended the life and prosperity of many of his subordinates and colleagues: minor officials, agents of the government rendering compulsory service (the various φυλακῖται), collectors of taxes, contractors in the government monopolies and in other concerns controlled by the government. Finally in the background stand the mass of the βασιλικοὶ γεωργοί and of all those who laboured for the government.¹⁶⁰

The second group of documents comes from the government offices of the Heracleopolite nome and dates from the time of Auletes and of the last Cleopatra, that is to say, from the last years of Egypt's independence.* It contributes to our understanding of the internal situation of Egypt at this momentous stage of its history. Various other documents help to complete the picture and make it more illuminating.¹⁶¹

Egyptian life as depicted in the φιλάνθρωπα of Euergetes II and the contemporary and later documents shows no essential change when compared with that of earlier times (see above, Chs. IV and V). Nothing fundamental had been altered in the system established by Philadelphus. If we consider, for example, the question of the relations between the two main elements in the population of Egypt, the 'Greeks' and the natives, we certainly find that there was now greater interpenetration of the two groups than in the past. Many Egyptians became thoroughly hellenized, received Greek education, spoke and wrote fluent Greek. Some of them acquired comparatively large fortunes and rose to high office in the service of the late Ptolemies. Others, less rich, occupied important posts in the middle and lower administration. The higher priests of Egyptian temples belonged in part to the first group and were held in great regard both by the government and by the Greeks of Egypt. The policy of 'association' initiated in the time of Philopator had taken its natural development.¹⁶²

* It has been recently published by W. Schubart and D. Schäfer in *B.G.U.* viii.

On the other hand, many Greeks became thoroughly acclimatized in Egypt, learned the Egyptian language, took an active interest in Egyptian affairs, and accepted with a real devotion the slightly hellenized Egyptian gods. Many Greco-Egyptian families were formed, families in which Greek and Egyptian names are equally frequent. Such, for example, was the well-known Theban family of Hermias and Apollonius. Some Demotic documents of this family were buried or kept in the late second century B.C. in one of the Theban graves. The family stood in business relations and lived on friendly terms with the χοαχύται of Thebes; it may at the same time have been related to the family of the brave Greek officer of Omboi, the famous 'colonel' Hermias, the bitter enemy of the χοαχύται, whom he accused of having occupied his ancestral house during the troubles of the civil war in the reign of Epiphanes.[163] Some, perhaps most, of the Egyptianized Greeks (we have no precise information), retained their wealth and their social prominence. But there were many who were much poorer than the hellenized, and even than some of the non-hellenized, Egyptians. From the social and economic standpoint the dividing line between the upper and the lower class was no longer between the Greeks forming the upper, and the Egyptians forming the lower, but between the rich and poor in general, many Egyptians being among the first, many Greeks among the second. Many documents might be adduced in support of this statement; one may be taken as an example. It is the letter* of a mother to her son, both Greeks. The mother congratulates the son on having learnt the Egyptian language and having obtained employment as tutor in the family of an Egyptian ἰατροκλύστης (doctor for internal diseases).

Although the ruling class became in course of time more numerous, having absorbed many natives and semi-natives, and although the general character of its mentality was rapidly changing, Egyptian influences making themselves more and more strongly felt, the old division into a privileged class of 'Greeks' (which comprised now many hellenized Egyptians) and a subordinate class of natives remained as it had been. We hear of a governor on his inspection tour. He travels in

* *U.P.Z.* 148.

a ship. At the landing-place he is met by the inhabitants of
a κατοικία. The first to greet him are the high priests—the
προφήτης and other priests (ἄλλοι ἱερεῖς). Then come the military Greek settlers, probably those actually serving in the
army—the πεζοὶ καὶ ἱππεῖς. After them an obscure group of
people connected in some way with an οἰκία, perhaps clients
of the governor (see below). Next to them stand σύμπαν τῆς κατ-
οικίας πλῆθος—families of the soldiers serving in the forces,
κάτοικοι who were not actually serving and their families. And
finally ξένοι (people not resident in the κατοικία), and far in the
background the λαοί (the natives). It is a pity that this interesting document is in such a bad state of preservation. The
priests of course are highly honoured, for this is a tribute to the
gods of the country. But the natives are a negligible element,
a mere *plebs*.[164]

The high position occupied by the priests in this document
is typical of Egypt in the second and first century B.C. The
priests and temples were the object of much solicitude to the
government, which listened attentively to their grievances and
endeavoured to remedy them. The relative sections of the
φιλάνθρωπα of Euergetes II afford eloquent testimony of this.
The grievances alleged were not new. They were probably
the same as had been presented from time to time to the
early Ptolemies. They reappear in the time of Epiphanes* and
again in the early years of Euergetes II before the φιλάνθρωπα
of 118 B.C. I may also refer once more to the interesting decree
of Euergetes II of 140–139 B.C.† The grievances are all of the
same character, most of them complaints connected with the
economy and finances of the temples‡: encroachments on the γῆ
ἱερά, orders concerning the well-known wine and garden tax
(ἀπόμοιρα), subsidies paid to the temples by the government
(συντάξεις), violent and unlawful acts connected with the gifts,
especially of land, made to the temples (ἀνιερωμένα), exaction
of arrears, contributions and deliveries of textiles due by the
temples, harsh treatment of the minor sanctuaries in similar
matters, difficulties arising out of the government's liability for
the expenses of the burial of sacred animals, encroachments on

---

* Rosetta Stone, *O.G.I.* 90.   † *Teb.* 6; Wilcken, *Chr.* 332.
‡ *Teb.* 5. 50 ff.

the rights of the temples as regards the priesthoods and other sacred offices 'bought' by the temples from the crown, and violations of the right of ἀσυλία.

I have said that similar complaints were probably submitted by the priests and temples to the early Ptolemies. But they are not mentioned in the early official utterances of the priests —in the decrees of their meetings at Canopus in the time of Euergetes I and at Memphis in that of Philopator. They appear first in the decree of Rosetta, which quotes extensively from the φιλάνθρωπα granted to the temples by Epiphanes, in part identical with those granted by Euergetes II. These complaints and concessions may be taken as a phenomenon typical of the period. The kings were increasingly anxious to satisfy the temples, while the priests and the temples, ever more molested by the royal officials in spite of the orders of the king, show a grim and pugnacious mood in defending their ancient privileges and demanding new ones.

It is interesting to observe the importance attached by the temples to their right of receiving and of managing without interference the gifts made to them by the kings and by private persons. There is no reference to such gifts in the Rosetta Stone. But the subject is prominent in the φιλάνθρωπα of Euergetes II (ll. 57–61). It led to many acute conflicts between the temples and the administration. The agents of the government had recourse to violence (βία) and even to torture (πειθανάγκη). The priests protested and complained, and the question was settled by Euergetes II in favour of the temples. The point was certainly an important one: the unrestricted right of the temples to receive gifts and to own and manage them meant, in a country so deeply religious as Egypt, a rapid increase of their wealth and prestige.

The same is true as regards the *asylia*, which is not mentioned in the Rosetta Stone. I shall return to this subject presently.

In the case of the temples two points deserve special notice. We see the kings in conflict with their own agents, who were apparently more royalist than the kings themselves. The φιλάνθρωπα here, as in other departments of Ptolemaic administration, were directed chiefly against the officials of the crown and were intended to place a powerful weapon in the hands

PLATE C

1. Limestone statuette of a priest dressed in the Egyptian fashion and carved in the Egyptian style. Two inscriptions are incised on the statuette: one on the front of the girdle, the other on the back support under a figure of Osiris seated beneath the winged disk. I am indebted to Mr. I. E. S. Edwards for a tentative translation of these two inscriptions: (1) 'The priest, beloved of the lord of happiness Ḥer, nicknamed . . .' (illegible); (2) 'The priest, beloved of the lord of happiness [follows a list of Ptolemaic titles, many of which are obscure] Ḥer, true of voice, son of a [priest of similar titles] Nes-Min, son of Uaḥ-àb-Rā, true of voice, born of the 'Mistress of the House' [? ?] Áḥat-Rā.' H. R. Hall, *Br. Mus. Quart.*, iii (1928–9), p. 13, pl. VI a. Photograph supplied by the authorities of the British Museum.

2. Fragmentary basalt statue of a standing man in the Egyptian garb typical in statues of the Hellenistic and Roman periods: a short sleeved shirt and a long and narrow cloak wound several times around the body. A short inscription on the back of the support gives the name of the man: 'Hor, son of Hor, the justified'. Another much longer inscription enumerates his deeds. It is probable but not certain that Hor was a priest. The statue is a fine work of art. The portrait represents an intellectual, hellenized Egyptian or an egyptianized Greek in the style of Isidorus, the author of the hymns of Mādinet Māḍī. It has been assigned to early Imperial times. But it is probable that F. Poulsen's date (early first century B.C.) is more correct. See P. Graindor, *Bustes et statues-portraits d'Égypte romaine*, s. d. (1937), pp. 138 ff., no. 74, pls. LXV–LXVI; F. Poulsen, 'Gab es eine alexandrinische Kunst?' *Coll. Ny Carlsberg Glyptothek*, ii (1938), p. 31 f., fig. 31; G. A. S. Snijder, 'Hellenistisch-römische Porträts aus Ägypten', *Mnemos.*, 3rd ser., vii (1939), pp. 268 f., cf. 278 ff. (in these three papers a complete bibliography will be found). Photograph lent by Prof. F. Poulsen.

3. Votive statuette of black basalt found at Dimeh (Fayûm). Dressed in the same fashion as no. 2. Greek inscription of two lines engraved on two parallel folds of the chiton (*S.B.* 3454): Εἰρηναῖος νεώ(τερος) Πισόιτος προσ|τάτης Σοκνοπαίωι Θεοῦ (sic) μϵ(γίστωι). The man represented in the statuette was therefore a hellenized Egyptian 'president' (προστάτης), probably of the temple of Soknopaios at Soknopaiu Nesos. On the office of προστάτης, W. Otto, *Priester und Tempel* &c., i, p. 362; ii, p. 75 and Index, s.v. προστάτης; F. Preisigke, *Wört.* iii, sect. 20, s. v. προστάτης; cf. *Teb.* 781 (164 B.C.), and above, p. 282. The date of the statuette is disputed. Milne and Graindor for example assign it to the time of Augustus, while Breccia and Poulsen suggest an earlier date (*c.* 70–60 B.C.). I am inclined to accept the latter date. Slightly later is the related statuette of Pa-du-asar, a late Ptolemaic dignitary (P. Graindor, loc. cit., p. 129, no. 66, pl. LIX). See P. Graindor, loc. cit., pp. 127 ff., no. 65, pl. LVIII; F. Poulsen, *Rev. É. A.*, xxxix (1937), p. 390; G. A. S. Snijder, loc. cit., pp. 268 ff. and 278 ff. Photograph supplied by the authorities of Alexandria Museum.

It is very instructive to compare the three statuettes reproduced in this plate with each other; they well reflect the various aspects of the mentality of the priestly class in the late Ptolemaic period: 'traditionalism' dominates in the statuette of Ḥer, intellectual refinement and far-reaching hellenization are the leading traits in that of Hor, and brutal materialism in the statuettes of Irenaeus and Pa-du-asar. Some considerations of the same kind regarding the mentality of the priests, as reflected in their portraits (though going too far), will be found in the memoir by G. A. S. Snijder quoted above, where the reader will also find an up-to-date bibliography of works dealing with the many problems connected with the dating and stylistic analysis of the Ptolemaic and Roman portraits made in Egypt.

PLATE C

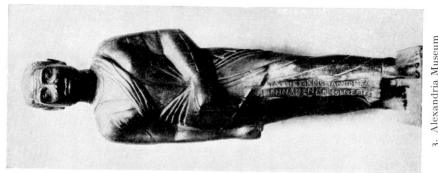

3. Alexandria Museum

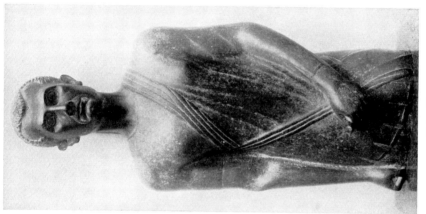

2. Cairo Museum

1. London, British Museum

EGYPTIAN PRIESTS AND OFFICIALS OF THE LATE PTOLEMAIC PERIOD

of the priests against the royal administration. On the other hand we may notice that the orders of the kings deal with matters of detail rather than of principle. The relations between the king and the priests remained unchanged. The φιλάνθρωπα are no more than partial concessions to the clergy: they involve no surrender on the part of the crown, no victory of the priesthood over the king. In general the clergy show a loyal attitude and the king an increasing regard for the priests and a deep devotion to the gods of Egypt. It is therefore, to my mind, a gross exaggeration to speak of the revolts of the natives as organized and fostered by the priests, and of the temples in general as focuses of the native opposition to the Ptolemaic régime. I have pointed out that many temples remained loyal at the times of the invasion of Antiochus IV and of the revolt of Dionysius Petosarapis. And when I come, later in this section, to the *asylia* I shall show that the priests, or at least some of them, were less afraid of the royal administration than of the revolutionary mood of the masses.[165]

No less important than the priesthood, probably even more important for the security of the dynasty, were the Greek and other foreign settlers in Egypt, the political and military backbone of the country and the chief supporters of the kings. Among them the most prominent position was occupied by the territorial army, the settled soldiers, the κάτοικοι and κληροῦχοι. It is interesting to note that in the φιλάνθρωπα the settled soldiers as such are mentioned in one paragraph only after the μάχιμοι. And yet while there is no further reference to the μάχιμοι, the κληροῦχοι receive much attention, not in that capacity nor as a separate group, but as part of a much larger group, that of the landowners of the country.

I have already spoken of this class (pp. 732 ff.). We should like to know more of the evolution of this country *bourgeoisie*, which was closely connected with the *bourgeoisie* of Alexandria. Most of its members who lived in the country were landowners. I have shown that they acquired their holdings in various ways: as settled soldiers, by buying land from the State, by planting waste land (ἐμφύτευσις, καταφύτευσις), by renting land εἰς πατρικά, that is, as hereditary tenants, and by converting land into vineyards and gardens.

It is in their capacity as landowners that these men chiefly figure in the φιλάνθρωπα of Euergetes. The long section dealing with them is only partially preserved, for a large lacuna inter-rupts the series of orders relating to them (ll. 104–134). Yet it is evident that most of the orders of this section deal with their interests as landholders: these are referred to first in the order addressed to the κληροῦχοι relating to the royal land which has been illegally occupied by them and by other landowners (ll. 36 ff.), and again later in a series of dispositions all concerned with land: the failure of landowners to plant land acquired from the crown (ll. 93 ff.), the purchase by them from the crown of houses, vineyards, gardens, ships (ll. 99 ff.), the re-building after the revolution of houses held by them on various titles (ll. 134 ff.), the billeting of soldiers in their houses (ll. 100 ff.), the falsification of weights and measures used by agents of the government in collecting from them taxes and other payments in kind (ll. 85 ff.). Of the paragraphs which stood in the place of the lacuna most dealt with land questions, two perhaps with government contracts and similar matters.

It is clear that this class remained what it had previously been, the class, to apply modern terms, of the middle and small *bourgeoisie*. It is unfortunate that we are unable to say what proportion of it was Greek. It played apparently an increas-ingly important role in the economic and financial life of the country. Now as before, and perhaps more than before, it was from this class that the officials of the crown were recruited: the contractors who collected the royal revenues from taxes and from the various industrial and commercial concerns owned or controlled by the government, the minor function-aries serving under the system of liturgies, viz. the numerous tax-collectors and especially the various types of φυλακῖται and φύλακες—the economic police force of the state. Other members of the same class, if not actually in government service, stood behind those so employed as their sureties (ἔγγυοι), that is to say, as responsible for them in case of deficiency.*

It is regrettable that we know so little of the gradual evolu-tion of this class. The foundations of their prosperity were laid at the time of Egypt's great economic development (see above,

* An interesting case is *Teb.* 853 of 173 B.C.

Ch. IV). Many of them made their money in the military or civil service of the crown. They invested it in houses or in parcels of land of various kinds. I may instance, for the period which we are considering, the family of Hermias, the ἡγεμὼν ἐπ' ἀνδρῶν of Omboi in the late second century B.C. His 'ancestors' had, before the great revolution, owned many houses at Thebes and probably several plots of land in the surrounding χώρα.* Many other members of the same class were residents in Alexandria who had invested in the χώρα the money they had made in that city. Lastly, the same class included members of Greco-Egyptian families and a large group of hellenized natives. An excellent example of the latter is Menches, the village scribe of Cerceosiris, and many other Egyptians of the same type.[166]

How this class fared in the late second and early first century we are unable to say. It seems, however, that the government, conscious of their growing economic strength, became more and more desirous of obtaining a share in their prosperity. It employed for this purpose with increasing vigour its right of requiring from them various services (λειτουργίαι). When members of the class showed a diminished readiness to offer themselves as contractors, as collectors (πράκτορες), and as guards, these functions having become less profitable, and when their patriotism, in emergencies, no longer stimulated by the hope of profit, became less ardent, the government probably had recourse to compulsion, constantly extended the sphere of liturgical service, and included within its range undertakings that had previously been simple matters of business (the various government contracts). Our evidence, however, is too scanty to enable us to trace this process in its gradual development. It was no doubt slow, and the measures of the government were probably spasmodic, not systematic. It appears, however, that the tendency to resort to liturgies grew in intensity and began gradually, in conjunction with the general impoverishment of the country, to undermine the prosperity of the class in question. I may cite in this connexion the ἐντολαί of Herodes and the documents illustrating the situation of the tax-contractors referred to above.[167]

In the period we are considering, the general situation of this

* *U.P.Z.* 161 and 162.

class appears to have been difficult but not critical. They had some grievances and complaints, such as high taxation and liturgies (see below, p. 891), and the kings wished to give them satisfaction; but these grievances, as we have seen, were not very important and the complaints probably not very acrimonious. In general the majority of these persons belonged to the privileged class of the population.

A constituent part of the body of landowners were the settled soldiers, the κληροῦχοι and κάτοικοι. We should like to know more of their social and economic conditions. We learn from certain documents that by the second century B.C. their κλῆροι had become definitely hereditary in their families. From soldiers remunerated for their military service by the income of a plot of land in place of money, they had passed into real soldier-farmers, κληροῦχοι not κάτοικοι, and thus were now members of the large class of landowners, sharing the interests and the mentality of the landholding *bourgeoisie*.[168]

Of their life and the degree of their prosperity we know little. I have mentioned the low rate of pay of soldiers while actually serving. The case of Apollonius, brother of Ptolemy the Recluse, is probably typical. There are good reasons for thinking that the government was not averse to cheating the troops by an unfair *adaeratio* (valuation) of the payments they received in kind. But what the soldier-farmers especially resented was the burden of taxation and of compulsory civil service (liturgy). We know from *Teb.* 27 that in the period with which we are concerned the onerous liturgy of the γενηματο-φύλακες was largely imposed on the στρατευόμενοι Ἕλληνες. No mention, however, is made of this or the burden of taxation in the extant text of the φιλάνθρωπα of Euergetes II.

Whether this omission was an oversight on the part of the king, or whether, when publishing his general φιλάνθρωπα he intended to deal with the soldiers in a separate decree, cannot be said. In any case soon after the publication of the φιλάνθρωπα the king issued a special edict, a sort of supplement or amendment of his φιλάνθρωπα. This is still extant in a mutilated and probably incomplete or abbreviated copy difficult to interpret and to restore.* It is, however, a highly interesting document.

* *Teb.* 124.

Its first paragraph corresponds to the first chapter of *Teb.* 5, and contains a general amnesty. Then follows an order confirming the *status quo* as regards the holders of κλῆροι, including all the changes that had occurred in the time of *amixia*. Next comes a most important disposition, by which, apparently for the first time in the history of the cleruchs, the crown confirmed changes in the ownership of the holdings effected under the pressure of poverty by the cleruchs themselves. Such changes had taken the form of cessions of holdings or of parts of them in discharge of debts to other cleruchs or perhaps to ἰδιοκτήμονες or men of other status, or of exchanges of holdings between one cleruch and another. This was a momentous novelty. Hitherto the κλῆρος though hereditary could not be ceded, even with the permission of the king. Now it entered, of course with many important restrictions, into the category of privately owned land.

The following paragraph is of no less importance. It shows that, in spite of all the hardships to which the cleruchs had been subjected and the resulting poverty and indebtedness, their position was better than that of an ἰδιοκτήμων, especially as regards the liturgies connected with it. For this order confirms the acts of royal officials by which certain ἰδιοκτήμονες· had been granted the status of κάτοικοι and prescribes explicitly that the new κάτοικοι shall be subjected only to λειτουργίαι κατοικικαί.* We may infer from the last disposition that the λειτουργίαι of the non-military members of the landowner class were much heavier than those of the κάτοικοι.

The emergency measure of Euergetes permitting the cession of a κλῆρος became a precedent. Conditions of life did not change in Egypt, or changed only for the worse in the first century B.C. There was no abatement of the oppressive taxation or of the liturgies. It is not surprising that such soldier-farmers as were not very capable agriculturists or good men of business (and this applies more especially to their widows and children under age) should find the burden intolerable and should ask

* It is not clear whether this change of status was the consequence of the purchase of a *kleros* or whether the persons concerned remained in possession of the same parcels of land as before, their own status and that of their holdings being alone transformed.

permission to cede their holdings or parts of them to stronger
and more efficient farmer-soldiers in payment of debts incurred
for the payment of taxes. Such petitions became very common
and a special type of transaction was evolved, a precursor of
the later παραχωρήσεις of Roman times. A considerable series
of such documents formed part of the archives of the Heracleopolite nome.*[169]
    We may now turn to the situation of the lower working-
classes. It was from these and the native soldiers (μάχιμοι) that
the rebels were mainly recruited. It was natural that some of
the rebels, even after an amnesty, should not return home, but
should prefer the life of robbers to that which they had
previously led. This was the reason of the gradual decrease in
the number of working men, and in the supply of labour. It is
to be regretted that we have so little information about the
exposure of children (see the bibliography above, pp. 623 ff.).
One would not be surprised, however, in view of the conditions
in which the natives lived, to find the practice of exposing
children gradually extending from the Greeks to the natives
in general and to the working classes in particular.[170]
    The policy of the government towards the working class
remained on the whole unchanged. The chief function of the
βασιλικοὶ γεωργοί and of the ὑποτελεῖς and ἐπιπεπλεγμένοι ταῖς
προσόδοις continued to be to provide revenue for the king
and to serve as tools in the hands of the government, enjoying
very little economic freedom. The government tried in a
variety of ways to convince the labouring classes that they
existed primarily for the purpose of increasing the royal
revenues by their toil. It was natural that the millions of
fellahin, though officially pretending—in their petitions—to
share the opinion of the government, should go about their
work without much enthusiasm,[171] and should try to cheat the
government as best they could. Careless cultivation of the
land, slovenly work on dikes and canals and in shops and
factories, abstraction of grain from the threshing floors, of
vegetable oils from the oil-presses, and so forth, were of common occurrence. The *laoi* showed lack of initiative, reluctance
to cultivate land that required any exceptional degree of care

* *B.G.U.* 1731–40, cf. *P. Oxy.* 1635; the earliest document is of 99 B.C.

and attention, and indifference to the increase of production in agriculture or industry. These two factors, the decrease of the working population and their apathy, had their natural consequences in the field of agriculture: deterioration of dikes and canals, a rapid increase of waste land, and an accumulation of arrears of taxes. Similar phenomena may be observed in the field of industry.

The government as usual blamed the officials and insisted on the adoption of energetic measures. The officials, responsible to the government in property and person (there was no *habeas corpus* for them any more than for others), exerted pressure on their subordinates, the minor functionaries, and these in turn on the workers. To increase the efficiency of the administrative machinery the government gave a fairly free hand to its officials, and a large amount of jurisdiction in fiscal affairs was transferred to them.[172] The result was what might be expected.

We see it illustrated in the formidable array of measures adopted by the government against the arbitrary rule of its own agents. We possess a series of such measures in the φιλάν-θρωπα of Euergetes II, which are certainly based on an enumeration of the grievances and complaints of the *laoi*. It is an impressive and melancholy list, more impressive because more detailed than that derived from the Rosetta Stone. The more important parts of it are as follows (ll. 155 ff.). Orders were issued by Euergetes to repress the following misdeeds of his agents:

(1) The governors of the nomes, the police officers, the financial agents and their subordinates, made a practice of collecting payments from the *laoi* for their own private benefit, a kind of organized blackmail.

(2) The same officials would select for the cultivation which they were themselves required to undertake, not unproductive land of inferior quality (ὑπόλογος), but the best plots, thus defrauding both the government and the royal tenants.

(3) The labouring classes suffered a terrible scourge in the σταθμοί or billeting of soldiers in their dwellings, a burden from which they were exempt by law.

(4) Royal officials were in the habit of impressing the inhabit-

ants for private services. For the same purpose they requisitioned cattle, draught animals, and ships. They caused men and animals to work for them without payment. They forced the royal peasants and workmen to feed (without remuneration?) sacrificial animals (pigs and calves) for public sacrifices. They demanded from them geese, fowls, and grain at an (arbitrary?) price or as gifts on the occasion of the renewal of their offices. These exactions were probably connected with regular payments by officials to the crown—a kind of organized sale of offices.

(5) A paragraph forbids collectors of debts to apply, without the decision of a court of law, coercive measures (especially arrest and imprisonment) to the person of a debtor, instead of proceeding against his property. The paragraph notes that the selling into slavery of debtors of the crown has been abolished by the king's predecessors. It was probably of common occurrence in the time of Philadelphus (above, pp. 341 ff., on the conditions prevailing in Syria).

(6) Royal officials would force textile workers to work for them personally without payment or at reduced prices.

(7) Collectors of rents, arrears, &c., would confiscate the dwellings, cattle, and tools of the *laoi*, though these were exempt from seizure by law.

(8) Officials would arrest persons and keep them imprisoned in their houses, for the purpose of extorting the payment of private debts, or as vengeance in private quarrels.[173]

It is evident from the φιλάνθρωπα that the principal evil from which Egypt was suffering—at least in the eyes of the government and of the *laoi*—lay in the insubordination, dishonesty, violence, and arbitrary acts of government agents of divers kinds. The central government desired to improve in all possible ways the economic and legal status of the various classes of the population, especially that of the workers. Many new and important fundamental rights were, for example, granted by law to the *laoi*, rights which would enormously improve their legal and economic situation provided that they were strictly observed by the agents of the government. I may cite for example the order prohibiting the sale of the *laoi* into slavery and even their imprisonment for debt to the fisc, and that protecting their private property. The trouble was that the government was unable to enforce its own laws and orders. It was not master of its own subordinates, who refused to co-operate with it. The measures taken by the government against its own agents and the publicity given to these measures proved unavailing. We may infer this from several documents which demonstrate that the situation of the working classes in Egypt was not improving in the late second and in the first century B.C., and that the arbitrary and lawless acts of the administration were as frequent as before. I shall, without aiming at completeness, adduce some of these documents in the following pages.

We may first consider the various royal officials, their mentality, and their functions.

Appointments as government officials (other than appointments of a liturgical character, which were dreaded by the richer classes of the population)*, especially those connected with the financial and economic administration, were much sought after. They gave the holders power and good opportunities of enrichment. No doubt they were also attended by many dangers, of financial ruin, disgrace, even imprisonment. However, the various grades were so closely interconnected by common interests and probably by a highly developed system of corruption and bribery that the dishonest agents of the government felt fairly secure. Menches appears in his official correspondence as a highly honourable member of the village community, and as an efficient executive agent of the government; yet there is good ground for suspecting him both of bribing his superiors and of receiving bribes from his subordinates.[174]

The government was well aware of the popularity of these offices, and of the reasons for it. Apparently incapable of sweeping away the whole system and setting its house in order, it acquiesced in the *status quo* and made the distribution of offices one of its sources of revenue. The offices, like the priesthoods, were practically sold to the highest bidders. We have an instance of this in the case of Menches, which was certainly

---

* See *Teb.* 27; Wilcken, *Chr.* 331, 113 B.C., cf. *P.S.I.* 168, 118 B.C. on the conditions of service in these.

not exceptional but typical.[175] The same desire of the government to allow its servants to derive profit from their offices, of
course at the expense of the population, may be seen in the
ever growing practice of granting to favourites of the king, as
a kind of a *dorea*, the right of collecting certain minor taxes.[176]

No wonder that under such conditions the government itself
had a very low opinion of its own agents. I have mentioned
above (p. 721) what Herodes thought of his subordinates. The
estimate formed by the *dioecetes* Irenaeus of his village scribes
was not much better. Two officials were sent by him (?) on a
tour of inspection to examine the books of the village scribes.
Their report to him and to Ptolemy the *strategos* is acrimonious*. The village scribes had placed all sorts of hindrances in
their way and had behaved with insolence. They could not
have done this unless they had been confident of support in
higher quarters. Still more acrimonious are the remarks of an
unknown officer† on the ἀρχιφυλακῖται (?). One passage of his
report is worth quoting: 'the majority of them have been
appointed with the cognizance of the *dioecetes*, and some
have wormed themselves into positions of *oeconomus*, toparch,
sitologus, comarch, and other offices inconsistent with their own
work, others have transferred their duties to their sons, who are
quite young men, and sometimes to other persons altogether,
others are engaged in the duties of *topogrammateus* and control
at least two *comogrammateis* in each division, and have handed
over the posts of *epistatae* into which they have crept to . . . or
some of their brothers contrary to decrees . . .' (translation of
the editors). A student of the history of bureaucratic government will find nothing new in this picture. Cumulation of
offices, nepotism, control by various means of many offices, are
well-known phenomena in any decaying bureaucratic régime.

It is no exaggeration to say that in the late second century
B.C. and in the first Egypt was governed not by the king and
some of his honest and well-meaning ministers but by a clique
of selfish, greedy, and lawless officials who formed a new,
wealthy, and influential aristocracy of the kingdom. The
wretched conditions in Alexandria itself, the rule of favourites
like Eulaeus and Lenaeus, may partly account for such con-

* *Teb.* 28 (114 B.C.).   † *Teb.* 24 (117 B.C.).

litions. The main cause, however, lay deeper. I shall speak of
t presently.[177]

We are not surprised to learn that such an administration
ιcted in the way described in the φιλάνθρωπα and illustrated by
nany documents. Some of these may be taken at random.
Ͻases of most outrageous violence were of common occurrence.
Ɪn 141 B.C. a 'royal tenant', in a petition extant in fragmentary
:orm complains of torture.* In a petition of 51/50 B.C. some
persons appeal from prison for justice. They state that, though
ınnocent (καθαροί), they have been subjected to torture (βασα-
νισθέντες).† In both these cases the petitioners may have been
guilty, but the fact remains that torture was a recognized
procedure in the administrative practice of the time. In 112
B.C.‡ a certain Senpoeris had planted a piece of land with palm
trees, over an area two cubits in excess of what was her right.
Ѕhe was sentenced to a fine. This fine was extorted from her
πειθανάγκης προσαχθείσης. Acts of violence by the crown officials
are described in many other documents, none so graphic as the
petition addressed to the chief of police of Cerceosiris by
the comarch of the village and its 'royal tenants'§. 'Marres the
topogrammateus is in the habit of coming to the village with
numerous others all armed with swords, and with the utmost
insolence making continual attempts at extortion upon wives
of some of us and of others' (translation of the editors).

Violence, arbitrary exercise of authority, and peculation
prevailed in so important a department of public administration as the management of waste lands. The growth of these
lands was rapid and fraught with danger. I have in the preceding
chapter described the policy adopted by the government in the
early second century B.C. in the matter of waste lands, and I
shall return to the subject later in this section. I need only
state here that the method principally resorted to by the
authorities was force and compulsion.[178]

Nor was the situation better in respect of industry and retail
trade. The régime of monopolies had always been unpopular
and the public had always sided with the smugglers and illicit

* *Teb.* 789.   † *B.G.U.* 1847.
‡ *P. Amh.* 31 ; Hunt–Edgar, *Sel. Pap.* ii. 367.
§ *Teb.* 41, of 119 B.C., one year before the φιλάνθρωπα.

dealers, and against the agents of the government and the contractors. It was so under the early Ptolemies and still more in the period we are considering. Two petitions* give us a vivid picture of the struggle successfully conducted by an illicit dealer, aided by almost the whole of a village, with the agents of the oil monopoly.

It was natural that the population, deprived of legal means of combating the oppression to which it was subjected, sought for some method of escape from it. Open rebellion was tried from time to time, but all the revolts failed, for the rebels though numerous were disorganized and ill equipped. They had against them not only the wealth and prestige of the king, but the regular army which, though not well trained or very contented, was yet ready to fight for the king and for its own privileged position. The people on the other hand were not a united body, for the richer natives regarded the poorer with suspicion and sided with the government. Finally, the movement had no inspired leaders, for the priests in this struggle played an equivocal part. This explains why all the revolts proved unsuccessful, and ultimately led, in spite of the φιλάν-θρωπα, to even greater misrule and impoverishment.

In times of peace the *laoi*, when exasperated by their sufferings, would resort to the immemorial Egyptian device—the silent and passive revolution, the 'strike' (ἀναχώρησις or ἐκχώρη-σις, *secessio*). Groups of men or individuals in a resentful mood (ὑπόπτως σχόντες) would abandon their work, leave their place of residence, and either retire to a temple or go to another village. In the temple they would be under the protection of the god, in the village they would live in hiding with the connivance of their fellow-sufferers. If a striker, through some act of his, were in danger of his life and in utter despair, he would flee to the swamps or to the desert and live the life of a robber. 'Secessions' were always common in Egypt. I have referred to them in connexion with the time of Philadelphus and later. They were tolerated by the government, though certainly never regarded by it as legal. It is, however, appalling to see how frequent they become in the period under consideration.

* *Teb.* 39; Hunt–Edgar, *Sel. Pap.* ii. 276 (114 B.C.), and *Teb.* 38; Wilcken, *Chr.* 303 (113 B.C.).

Fragmentary and inadequate as our evidence is, we hear of them repeatedly. They were especially frequent among the royal peasants and others connected with agriculture.* They were less frequent among men engaged in State manufactures† and State retail trade.‡ They were certainly a great calamity, for they deprived the king and the country of the most important element in their economy—labour, which was never very abundant or very efficient in Egypt.[179]

Under the early Ptolemies a few sanctuaries of high reputation possessed the right of *asylia*, sometimes combined with the rights of immunity from liturgies and freedom from taxes (ἀτέλεια); but this right of *asylia*, though recognized by the government, was gradually restricted by several royal edicts.§ The greater the influence acquired over the king by the priests and the more helpless the king in his conflicts with his own officials, the more insistent became the priests—not without the tacit support of the government—in demanding that the right of *asylia* enjoyed by their respective temples should be respected and confirmed by the government. We have seen how Euergetes II included in his φιλάνθρωπα a special provision confirming the right of *asylia* of those temples which possessed it. In the first century B.C., especially under Alexander I and Auletes, the right of *asylia* was extended to many temples both old and new, large and comparatively small, sometimes to several in the same place. There is evidence of this in many inscriptions found in the villages of the Fayûm and elsewhere, which proudly inform the visitor that the place is ἄσυλον and give the text of the petition by which the temple obtained from the king the right of *asylia*. The petition has sometimes been submitted to the king by the priests, sometimes by powerful protectors of the temple—as a rule military or civil officers of high standing. It is highly probable that

* Without attempting to present the evidence in full, I may quote: *Teb.* 895 (175 B.C.); 1008 (second century); 787 (138 B.C.); 41, l. 40 (119 B.C.); 61 *b*, 357; 72, 352; 707 (118 B.C.); 24, l. 34 (117 B.C.); 26 (114 B.C.); *B.G.U.* 1815, 18 (61/60 B.C.); 1835 (51/50 B.C.); 1843 (50/49 B.C.).

† *Teb.* 790, second century B.C.

‡ *Teb.* 724 (175 or 164 B.C.), οἰνοκάπηλοι.

§ See the fragmentary φιλάνθρωπα of Philopator, which refers to an earlier edict of Euergetes I, *B.G.U.* 1212 *c*.

PLATE CI

1. Stele (h. 0·35 m.) of Greek type with pediment adorned with acroteria. The pediment is supported by two Egyptian pilasters surmounted by Caryatids (Egyptian naked goddesses seen frontwise). On the surface of the stele, below, a painted scene: the Apis bull facing an altar, and above, a Greek, apparently metrical inscription: ἐνύπνια κρίνω | τοῦ θεοῦ πρόσταγμα ἔχων. τύχ᾽ ἀγαθᾶι. Κρής ἐστιν ὁ | κρίνων τάδε. ('I interpret dreams having this commission from the god. Good Fortune! A Cretan is the interpreter'). The stele—an advertising poster—was found in the Serapeum of Memphis. Dream interpretation by licensed interpreters was apparently a profession carried on in various sanctuaries, especially in the Serapea, by men of various nationalities. An ἐνυπνιοκρίτης is mentioned in one of the papyri of the Serapeum, U. P. Z. 84. iii. 79, cf. U. Wilcken, ad loc. and p. 69. O. Rubensohn, 'Das Aushängeschild eines Traumdeuters', Festschrift J. Vahlen, 1900, pp. 3 ff.; S.B. 685; G. Raskin, 'Handelsreclame en soortgelijke praktijken bij Grieken en Romeinen', Phil. St., Kath. Univ. te Leuven, 1936, p. 39 f. and pl. 1.

2. Terracotta figurine (h. 0·19 m.) representing a negro or negroid, perhaps a Nubian warrior with full military equipment: an axe, a peculiar shield, and a heavy cloak with fringes. Date uncertain. However, even if of Roman times and representing an actor in a mime, the figurine gives a good idea of the southern enemies of Ptolemaic and Roman Egypt. Allard Pierson Museum. Algemeene Gids, 1937, p. 50, no. 465 and pl. xxv.

3. A fine bronze figurine of a naked fettered negro slave or prisoner with hands chained behind his back (h. 0·132 m.) found in the Fayûm. He is looking at somebody with a smile of defiance. Hellenistic. A. de Ridder, Les bronzes antiques du Louvre, i, 1913, p. 57, no. 361, pl. 30.

On the Nubians and negroes in Alexandrian art, I. Noshy, The arts in Ptolemaic Egypt, 1937, p. 98 (with bibliography).

PLATE CI

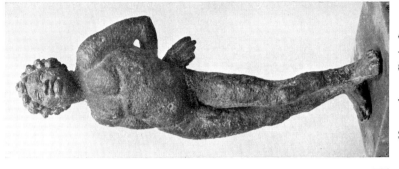

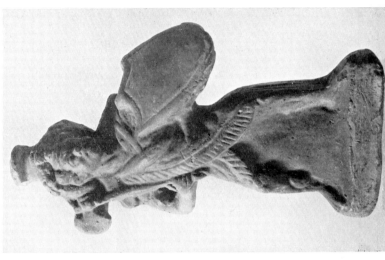

1. Interpreter of dreams. Cairo Museum

2. Nubian warrior. Amsterdam, Allard Pierson Museum

3. Negro slave. Paris, Louvre

EGYPT OF THE LATE PTOLEMAIC PERIOD

temples, like individuals, had their special patrons among the magnates of the day, under whose σκέπη (protection or patronge) they lived. These petitions afford most valuable information ⸱n the economic and social importance of the right of *asylia*.

The most important feature of the right of *asylia* was undoubtedly the privilege of the temple to admit into its precincts only those whom the priests regarded as desirable and to exclude those who were not. Having received such authority, they posted proudly in the most conspicuous places the notice: ὧι μὴ πρᾶγμα, μὴ εἰσιέναι—'no admission for those who have no business in the temple'. This right of admission was particularly mentioned in the petitions. The priests insisted that no one should have the right to force himself into the sacred precincts (εἰσβιάζεσθαι) in order to molest either the priests themselves or those who had taken refuge in the temple (τοὺς αὐτόθι καταφεύγοντας). Such intruders were further to be prohibited from removing out of the precincts (ἐκβιάζεσθαι or ἐκσπᾶν) either the priests themselves or the refugees, the suppliants (ἱκέται) of the god.

Who were the intruders against whom the temples sought to protect themselves? No doubt all such as had some private or public claim on the permanent or temporary residents in the temple: private creditors who desired to have their debtors imprisoned with the help of the government, agents of the government who wished to collect taxes or arrears by coercive measures, or to press the residents into some form of compulsory service (liturgy), and so forth. The priests, of course, were prepared to submit to existing laws and regulations. They frequently repeat in their petitions that the right of *asylia* involves no detriment to the State (ἀβλαβής or ἀβαρής). It was not against the laws, but against violence, against the arbitrary or unlawful acts of the officials of the crown, that they protested.

However, it was not only government agents whom the priests regarded as undesirable visitors. There was another class no less obnoxious, viz. groups of ἱκέται who tried to force themselves into the temples in a disorderly and violent manner, without the permission of the priests. In a petition of the second century B.C.* addressed to the *strategos*, the priest-

* *Teb.* 790.

guardians of the temple of Arsinoe of Oxyryncha (a village in the Fayûm) complain bitterly of some ὑποτελεῖς, workmen of the monopolies or other State concerns, belonging to the village, who have forced their way into the temple, imposed some burden upon it, and are making exactions, having improperly taken refuge in the temple and that 'with insolence and injury' The priests demand help from the government and a πρόσταγμα which may be engraved upon the outer gate of the precinct below the existing tablet (dedication?), in order to protect the temple against undesirable intruders (apparently a tablet with the formula ὧι μὴ πρᾶγμα, μὴ εἰσιέναι). The document shows the unruly temper and violent proceedings of the lower classes of the population. These regarded refuge in the temple as their sacred right. When rebuked by the priests and refused admission, they forcibly introduced themselves into the temple. Once within the sacred precincts they demanded food and quarters. The law-abiding priests appealed to the government. Their conduct explains why Dionysius Petosarapis and his predecessors and followers destroyed Egyptian temples.

The *asylia* decrees show that the institution in itself caused little inconvenience to the State. The latter in all probability protected itself against it and the concomitant grants of immunity from taxes and liturgies by many laws, orders, and regulations. By conferring the right of *asylia* on the temples, the kings sought to flatter the priests and to secure their loyalty, perhaps also to increase the prestige of the temples and to promote to a certain extent their material welfare (for they could employ the refugees in their workshops, collect donations from them, and sell them food). At the same time the *asylia* was regarded by the government as a means of protecting the priests and temples themselves and those who took refuge in the sacred precincts from the lawless acts of its own officials, whom it was unable to control. We have here further evidence of the impotence of the government to maintain discipline among its own agents and at the same time of its reluctance to introduce radical changes. Like the other φιλάν-θρωπα, the *asylia* was a *testimonium paupertatis*, a futile attempt to improve the conditions of life in Egypt.

And yet, limited as it was in its scope, the *asylia* was an important factor in the social and economic system of the country. The number of refugees was certainly large; they included many workers, who sat idle in the temples, while the government was in urgent need of their labour. The restrictions imposed by laws and regulations on the temples were often ineffective, for the government hesitated to enforce them. Restricted as it was, the *asylia* nevertheless served the oppressed classes of the population as a kind of substitute for civic rights.[180]

The same helplessness of the individual in his relations with the State and its agents gave rise to certain other institutions. In many cases the gods appeared less powerful than the government and its officials. The priests themselves were not secure in their sacred and 'inviolable' (ἄσυλος) precincts. Those who were in need of protection were aware of this and knew that there was another power in the State which was perhaps greater than that of the temples. This power was the aristocracy composed of bureaucrats—officers of the crown—of royal favourites, and of the magnates. I have already referred to the bureaucracy in the service of the crown. Of the magnates who surrounded the kings and who sometimes were the real rulers of the State we know less. But they were certainly very rich, sometimes enormously so. Part of their wealth consisted of royal gifts (δωρεαί) of which I have already spoken but besides such revocable gifts they certainly possessed land in the *chora* and invested their money in banking operations (loans) and probably in commerce also. The size of the fortunes of these magnates may be inferred from the statement of Diodorus* that a certain Hierax, otherwise unknown, one of the best generals of Euergetes II, paid the army of Euergetes which was fighting against the rebel Galaistes, another 'nabob' and member of the Alexandrian aristocracy, out of his own funds—by way of a loan advanced to the king. If a man could attach himself to a member of this group by ties of some kind or by common material interests (for instance by obtaining a loan from him), he would be dependent on him, but would be protected against every one else, even the courts. Protection (σκέπη), like the *asylia*, was of immemorial antiquity in Egypt. We find some examples of it in the earlier Ptolemaic period in

* xxxiii. 20. 22.

the circle of Apollonius (above, p. 325). We meet it again in full vigour—and it had probably never ceased to exist—at the time of the decay of the royal power and of the growth of the power and influence of certain individuals.* It developed rapidly in the period we are now considering. In the late second century Egypt increasingly resembled Rome in the Republican period or the late Empire, in that it comprised a number of οἶκοι, of great houses. Many inhabitants belonged to some οἶκος, and were under the σκέπη of some person of importance. I may cite a few examples. In *Teb.* 40 (117 B.C.) two contractors for the beer and nitron tax in Cerceosiris have learnt that the whole village is under the special protection of Amenneus, the royal scribe. In their petition they ask that the same privilege may be granted to them 'because it devolves upon you (or upon us?) before all others to watch over the interests of the crown', and that the administration of the village may be notified of the grant. *Teb.* 34 (about 100 B.C.) is the letter of a certain Philoxenus, who has interceded for a man who was arrested for debt but happened to be ὑπὸ σκέπην καὶ γεωργός of Demetrius, probably a very important personage. In *Teb.* 41, 35 (about 119 B.C.) it is Lysanias, the *strategos*, who is the protector of some royal peasants, and in *B.G.U.* 1833 (51/50 B.C.) a woman appeals to Seleucus, the *strategos*, as being τῶν ἐκ σῆς οἰκίας (certain debts are in question). I have mentioned that certain temples, in the same way as villages, were under the protection of influential persons. Thus σκέπη interfered in all sorts of economic processes and relations: royal agriculture, royal manufactures, private debts and obligations.[181]

While the 'oppressed' strove to find some form of protection against their oppressors, these in their turn tried to safeguard their interests by more or less ingenious devices. The government had at its disposal all the machinery of laws, decrees, and orders. But in many cases this machinery was useless. It was so where the interests of two departments of the State clashed or where the civil law was in conflict with the public law, or even where the right of *asylia* removed a man from his ordinary work in order to protect him against claims

* *Teb.* 750. 19 (187/6 B.C.) and 758, 30 (early second century), above, Ch. V, n. 137.

of a private or public character. I refer, for example, to conflicts between tax-collectors, who arrested and imprisoned a man working for a department of the State, and that department, which had urgent need of his labour. Or it happened that a private debtor was imprisoned for failing to repay a loan, and was consequently unable to sow or to reap for the State; or again a 'royal tenant' might take refuge in a temple to escape some impending calamity. The State in these cases, being unable to avert the conflict of interests, resorted to measures which would secure for itself the man's labour at least temporarily. It gave him a πίστις, a safe-conduct for a certain time, in order to enable him to carry out his work for the government. Such πίστεις were issued, sometimes promiscuously, by the king himself and by various royal officials. Their validity was confirmed by special προστάγματα.* Influential persons protected themselves in the same way, but more efficiently and enduringly. *U.P.Z.* 119 (99 B.C.) is the petition of a priest, by which he procures from the king an order declaring his house 'inviolable' (ἄσυλος), conferring on it, that is to say, more or less the rights of a temple.[182]

The same desire of the government to protect itself against individuals may be seen in its tendency to bind them by oaths; by which is meant not a general oath of allegiance, but oaths to the king in routine documents of an economic or financial character, such as the χειρογραφίαι ὅρκου βασιλικοῦ, obtained from royal peasants who received loans of seed grain from the government. The government believed that the increased responsibility of the man, when bound by an oath to the king, would prevent him from breaking in some manner his contract with the government.[183]

While the government thus protected its interests against institutions for which it was responsible, private individuals tried to do the same for themselves. Conflicts between civil law and public law were frequent. The royal φιλάνθρωπα, decrees concerning public work, πίστεις granted by the government, right of sanctuary, the σκέπη of government officials, interfered with private credit and made any kind of business hazardous. In order to protect themselves, creditors would

* *B.G.U.* 1812 (49/8 B.C.)

grant no loans, nor would business men make contracts, without being guaranteed by a special clause in the contract that the other party would not avail himself of any of the protections extended to him by the State. This meant of course full liberty to the collectors to disregard any protection of this kind.[184]

The various developments set forth in the preceding pages disorganized the economic life of the country. Both state and private interests suffered. Not only did the authority of the king, undermined by these factors, decline rapidly, but his wealth diminished concurrently. His principal sources of revenue—the rent of the royal land and the revenue from the 'monopolies' and taxes, constantly decreased. The estates of the temples, the 'private' land, including that of the settled soldiers, and the gift-estates, grew mainly at the expense of the royal domain, and their growth, despite the heavy taxation of private land, contributed to the decline of the royal revenue. Even more detrimental were the rapid decrease in the area of the cultivated land—royal and other—and the increased difficulty of renting it, which have been described above, and the concomitant depopulation of the villages, of which something will be said presently. Finally, the growing dishonesty of the royal officials and their neglect of royal interests conduced in a marked degree to the impoverishment of the king.

All the efforts of the government to arrest this decline in its revenue proved in most cases unsuccessful. All sorts of devices were adopted in respect of royal tenants, royal workmen, taxpayers, contractors and officials of the crown: mutual understanding, exhortation, and in the last resort forcible measures. I have already described how these methods were applied in order to stop the increase of waste land and to reclaim areas which had gone out of cultivation. Similar processes were adopted in regard to state-controlled industry and to taxation. If the milder measures failed, the final resource was the confiscation of the property of the persons responsible for the cultivation of the land, for the management of the industry or trade, or for tax-collection. This responsibility, whether of the persons bound to the State by some form of contract (tenants, industrial workers, retail traders, contractors of various kinds), or of the agents of the State for the full collection of the revenues, was a tradition derived from the ancient, pre-Ptolemaic financial administration. But never had it been enforced so frequently and so systematically as under the Ptolemies, especially in the second and first centuries B.C. It was at this time, for instance, that a momentous innovation in this respect was introduced. Alongside of individual responsibility, an experiment was tried in collective responsibility. This collective responsibility was applied first, not to the government agents, but to those who paid rent and taxes to the crown, to the villages of royal tenants. We have evidence of this in several documents of the second and first centuries, while similar documents for the preceding period are unknown.[185]

Another peculiar feature of the royal economy of the time, closely connected with the developments described above and especially with those affecting royal and private land, was the rapid growth of 'ownerless' property (ἀδέσποτα), especially of ownerless land. It is unfortunate that we have so little information on this subject, and in general about the private property which for one reason or another was claimed by the State.* Ownerless property and that claimed by the State were closely connected with one another. The most typical ἀδέσποτα were the property of private persons who died intestate and without heirs. Much more important, however, were *res derelictae*, abandoned property. These *res derelictae* were especially common in troubled times, when the owners fled from their place of residence and left their property behind them. To the same class, substantially, belonged the confiscated property of insolvent debtors of the State: defaulters in payment of rent and taxes, officials and State contractors (including their sureties) responsible for the collection of revenue and for the management of 'monopolies'. Such defaulters in troubled times became very numerous. No wonder that there is frequent reference to ownerless, abandoned, and confiscated property in our sources of the late second and the first century B.C., especially in what are known as the amnesty decrees published in Egypt, in Cyprus, and in the Cyrenaica. This type of State property had of course always existed.

* In Roman times it was styled τὰ εἰς τὸν Καίσαρα πίπτειν ὀφείλοντα, in the Ptolemaic probably τὰ εἰς τὸν βασιλέα πίπτειν ὀφείλοντα.

The government naturally tried to dispose of it, that is to say, to sell it. And there were certainly special officials who were in charge of it. But it is worthy of note, as I have mentioned above, that a special department called ἴδιος λόγος and a special official of the same name, first appear in documents of the second century B.C. It is evident that it was in this turbulent period that the problem of ownerless and confiscated land became acúte. Its solution was not easy, and the government tried various methods. But it is apparent that at a time of labour scarcity, of economic stress, and of general impoverishment, ownerless land, so far from being a valuable source of steady revenue to the crown, was merely a cause of additional worry and preoccupation.[186]

Detrimental as was this state of things to the interests of the king, it was no less detrimental to those of the general public, especially the working classes. I have already referred to their situation, but some further features of it may be mentioned here. A striking illustration of the miserable economic and social conditions in which they lived is the depopulation of the villages. In some cases it was temporary and was due to secessions. In others, however, it was enduring. The depopulation of particular villages is often alluded to in the documents of the second and first century B.C. *Teb.* 803 (late second century B.C.) is a petition addressed by the tenants of the village of Oxyrhyncha to the *epistates* of the village, and states that, whereas they had formerly numbered 140, they are now, in consequence of various acts of injustice, only 40. In *B.G.U.* 1815 (61/60 B.C.) it is the ἐπιβολή that has ruined the village of Machor and has led the inhabitants to go on strike. *B.G.U.* 1835 (51/50 B.C.) is a report of the priests of a temple at Hiera Nesos, expressing anxiety about the treasures of the temple, for all the inhabitants of the village have departed, δι' ἀσθένειαν καὶ ὀλι⟨γ⟩ανδρίαν, and left the priests quite alone (μονωτάτους). In 50/49 B.C. similar conditions were produced in the village of Tinteris by drought, all the strangers (ξένοι) temporarily resident there having left for their homes.*

Archaeology supports the evidence of these documents. The systematic excavations of Karanis in the Fayûm carried out

* *B.G.U.* 1843.

by the University of Michigan have shown that the area of the village became smaller in late Hellenistic times than it had been under the early Ptolemies. The discovery of the Zenon papyri in the basement of a private house at Philadelphia shows that the house of Zenon was in all probability a ruin in the late Ptolemaic period. Another house was built on this ψιλὸς τόπος, but not before Roman times.[187]

Such being the conditions in the villages, we shall not be surprised to learn the disastrous effect on Egypt in the first century B.C. of so ordinary a phenomenon as a low Nile, and the impotence and perturbation of the government when confronted with it. In 50/49 B.C. a royal order was issued at Alexandria* by which it was forbidden under penalty of death to export grain from Middle Egypt either to Lower or to Upper Egypt, and it was ordered that all grain should be sent to Alexandria. The interpretation of the document is far from certain, but in my opinion is probably as follows. The harvest of the year of 50/49 B.C. was probably deficient.† Both Lower and Upper Egypt had need of imported grain, and there was danger of famine in Alexandria. Middle Egypt may have had some surplus, which the owners of the grain would naturally have sent to the places where the price was highest. The government, fearing the temper of the Alexandrians, intervened and ordered all surplus grain to be directed to Alexandria. The case was therefore exceptional. A low Nile did not depend on bad or good government. Nevertheless the depopulation of the villages probably aggravated the situation. The hysterical tone of the πρόσταγμα betrays the alarm of the government, and the measure adopted shows that its first thought was to secure its own safety, to the detriment of the country as a whole, by methods of compulsion and oppression.[188]

Poverty therefore was the sign under which Egypt lived in the late second and the first century B.C., poverty for the State and for the majority of the people. An unmistakable symptom of this may be seen in the prices, which rose spasmodically and feverishly. This derangement of prices was promoted by the state of the currency. A new outburst of inflation may be observed in the period of *amixia* under Euergetes II, and it is

---

* *B.G.U.* 1730.   † Cf. *B.G.U.* 1843.

well known how adulteration impaired the quality of the silver coins of the late second and first centuries.[189]

But the evil must not be overstated. The country was not utterly ruined. The Ptolemies still had the reputation of being the richest kings in the world, and their credit remained good. They certainly did not squander the private treasure gradually accumulated by the dynasty. This is evident from the large resources wherewith Auletes was able to bribe his Roman supporters, and the last Cleopatra to finance Antony's Actium expedition. Even after this expedition Augustus derived enormous booty from the royal treasure. The wealth of Cleopatra was not due to any notable improvement in the economic conditions of Egypt under her rule. The few papyri of her time and her coinage show that conditions during her reign were not much better than during that of Auletes. She may have been more popular than her predecessors with the natives. I much doubt, however, whether this was due to any improvement in the administration and general state of the country.[190]

Such were the social and economic conditions that prevailed in Egypt in the late second and in the first centuries B.C. To explain them is one of the crucial problems of the history of Ptolemaic Egypt. The easiest solution is to make the individual rulers responsible for the country's decay. Ptolemy Soter, Philadelphus, perhaps Euergetes I, it may be said, were good and efficient kings, and Egypt was prosperous and flourishing under them. The later Ptolemies were degenerate descendants of noble ancestors and gradually effected the utter ruin of the country. The same solution has been suggested for the similar problem relating to the Roman Empire. Some of the later Ptolemies may have had good intentions. But they were in the hands of wicked advisers and favourites. Others died too young to improve the wretched conditions. Bad rulers form one side of the picture. On the other we have the nationalistic tendencies of the masses of the population and their religious fanaticism. And finally there was the sinister influence of Rome, which deprived Egypt of her foreign possessions and sucked her blood in the first century B.C.

In my opinion, the responsibility for the decay of Egypt cannot be placed on its rulers alone. The system of government, as I have described it, underwent no radical change from the time when it was first established by the common efforts of Soter and Philadelphus. Why should it, if it was impeccable, work smoothly in the third century, less well in the early second, and disastrously in the late second and in the first century B.C.? The documents show that all the Ptolemies were constantly repeating, in accordance with the immemorial tradition of Oriental kingship in general, that they wished every one to be happy in their kingdom; nor have we any reason to disbelieve them. They did not like oppression for its own sake, and they endeavoured to repress the misdeeds of their agents by all means in their power and to protect so far as they could the oppressed classes. Why should the same sentiment be sincere in the mouth of Philadelphus and a mere empty formula when expressed by his later successors? Why should the same methods of government be beneficent under the former and pernicious under the latter? It may be objected that the same instrument may be creative or destructive according as it is employed, and that is no doubt true. But the difficulty here is that the machinery created by Philadelphus was managed in the same way, with the same aims, and by the same methods, and mostly by well-meaning men. Yet the results were good in the early period and evil in the late.

Nor can I attribute the decline in late Ptolemaic times to the nationalistic aspirations of the Egyptian masses, which caused the revolutionary upheavals of the second and first centuries. No doubt, it was the masses who were ultimately responsible for the decay. They refused actively or passively to respond to the call of the kings. But it is evident—and the point was understood fully by the kings themselves—that they did so not because they resented the rule of foreigners as such and felt it an offence to their national and religious pride. This may have been a secondary, but not the principal motive of their insubordination. The Ptolemies strove to appear to their Egyptian subjects as much like Pharaohs as possible, and never offended their religious feelings. They showed the highest reverence for the Egyptian gods and the Egyptian temples, and most of the latter were their supporters. There is, moreover, no reason to believe that the kings of the second and first century had any pro-Hellenic policy, that is to say, that they favoured the foreign element in the population as such. The policy of association started by Philopator was never abandoned. The higher classes of the hellenized natives had *de iure* the same opportunities as the gradually Egyptianized foreigners. In the late Ptolemaic period, as I have repeatedly emphasized, the privileged classes belonged to a mixed race, though a prerequisite of success was no doubt a certain degree of Greek culture, which was accessible to the richer sections of the population alone. The mass of the poorer people had no share in it.

What the non-hellenized natives, the *laoi*, who constituted a large majority of the population resented, was not the presence of foreigners in their country. To this they gradually became accustomed and they took it for granted. It was the system of government as applied by the privileged classes: economic oppression, heavy taxation, compulsory work, services of all kinds, requisitions, and above all the unfair and unjust management of the various branches of administration. The mass of the population of Egypt was opposed not to the 'Greeks' in that capacity, but to every one who formed part of the administrative machine and of the ruling class. Their resentment was naturally intensified by the fact that the oppressors spoke a different language, lived a different life, and regarded themselves as far superior beings. In a sense the members of the upper classes were foreigners to the natives, though in many cases as good Egyptians racially as the latter. The same conditions prevailed in many European countries in the eighteenth and early nineteenth centuries and they are not unfamiliar to those who know modern Egypt.

Nor can I regard Rome as bearing a large share of responsibility for the gradual decay of Egypt. Her heavy hand was certainly felt by the Egyptian kings. But in comparison with what Rome did for the ruin of Macedonia, of the monarchies of Asia Minor, and of Syria, her contribution to the ruin of Egypt was slight. Rome did not restore the Ptolemaic Empire after the first war with Macedonia; but neither did the Ptolemies themselves do much to further the restoration. On the other hand it was Rome that saved the independence of Egypt

in the time of Antiochus IV, and without seeking for remuneration. Her subsequent intervention was very slight. The
situation became different in the time of Auletes, but Egypt
then was already in full decay.

It may be conceded that all the factors discussed above had
their share in the decline of Egypt, but in my opinion they
were secondary, not primary, causes. To my mind it was the
mood of the population that was decisive, especially the mood
of the lower classes. And this mood was created gradually and
slowly by certain features of Egyptian life which I have already
discussed.

These may be recapitulated as follows: the economic oppression of the working classes; the division of the population of
Egypt into two groups, one socially and economically privileged and consisting to a large extent of foreigners, and the
other treated by the government mainly as a source of revenue,
as labour necessary for the production of goods; the antinomy
between the economic, social, and 'political' structure of life
of the two classes, which found its expression in the division
of Egypt into πόλις and χώρα, into γῆ βασιλική and γῆ ἐν ἀφέσει,
into λαοί and Ἕλληνες; and the coexistence of two types of economic life, one reserved for the Ἕλληνες another for the λαοί, one
based on a certain amount of freedom and initiative, another
regulated from above and subject to a far-reaching state-control.
Now these predominant features, which could not remain
unnoticed and unresented by the natives and which affected
their private life and their prosperity, were all of them creations
of the early Ptolemies and were inherited from them by their
successors. Add to this that the private law of the natives,
which was individualistic and opposed to state-control, but in
spite of this was never altered by the Ptolemies, accentuated
the antinomy inherent in the Ptolemaic organization. It is not
exact to say that the people began to resent this state of things
late in the history of Ptolemaic Egypt. It did so from the outset, at first tacitly through strikes, later openly by revolts.

But it took some time for the natives to feel the oppression
of the new system, more to realize that they could not hope to
better their situation by petitions and complaints, and still
more to become conscious of their strength and to organize

open resistance. On the other hand the system, so long as it was new and not yet rigid, worked comparatively smoothly. It took time again for the government to become an inhuman machine, and for the bureaucracy to learn how the population might be oppressed without too much danger to the oppressors. The bureaucratic system became indurated and developed an inflexible routine just at the time when the political conditions became complicated and threatening and the series of native revolts began.[191] The result was the situation that I have described above.*

We know very little of the conditions that prevailed in the second century B.C. in the two foreign dominions held by Egypt at that time—CYPRUS and CYRENE, the last remains of the once great Ptolemaic Empire. I have already set out (pp. 333, 339) the scanty evidence that we possess concerning the social and economic aspect of these two countries in the third century B.C. As regards the second century B.C. the evidence is more abundant.

For Cyprus it consists of several inscriptions. Most of these, like those of the third century B.C., relate to affairs of members of the Ptolemaic army of occupation. Others furnish some information on the Ptolemaic administration of the country and on the conditions prevailing in some of the cities[192].

More important light is thrown on the social and economic evolution of the island by a text recently discovered there. It is the fragment of a proclamation containing a series of φιλάν-θρωπα granted to Cyprus by Euergetes II, accompanied by a letter from the king to the army of occupation. The little we possess of the text of the φιλάνθρωπα shows extensive coincidences with *Teb.* 5, the proclamation dealt with above, though the Cyprus document is much earlier (145/4 B.C.) than the other, and suggests that the situation of Cyprus during the reign of Euergetes II was not very different from that of

---

* The above interpretation of the course of Ptolemaic history, more than once put forward by me in the past (in my *Staatspacht* (1902), my *Kolonat* (1910), and in many articles), has been criticized by eminent scholars as biased and founded on an erroneous analogy with certain events in the history of the modern world. But my view was expressed before the events in question were dreamt of, is based solely on consideration of the evidence, and remains substantially unaltered.

Egypt.*   The letter addresssed to the 'land and sea forces' (πεζικαὶ καὶ ναυτικαὶ δυνάμεις) is even more interesting. It shows the king's dependence on the support of the army in 145/4 B.C. and of course later, a support which he was prepared to secure by flattery and by various benefactions. Among these favours none is more remarkable than his promise to grant pensions for life to the soldiers and sailors.† These pensions were necessarily an extremely heavy burden on the resources of the impoverished kingdom of Euergetes II.[193]

As regards Cyrene our information is less copious but more substantial. I have mentioned (Ch. IV, n. 128) the inscription from Cyrene containing the last will and testament of Euergetes II made at the time when he was ruler of Cyrene. Of a little later date is a fragmentary inscription recently found at Cyrene. It contains copies of at least four separate documents and is dated in the ninth year of Ptolemy Soter and his co-ruler and wife Cleopatra, probably Soter II and Cleopatra Selene (109/8 B.C.). The date, however, is disputed, and the inscription may belong to an earlier time, to the reign of Philometor.[194] Be that as it may, the dossier engraved on the Cyrenean *stele* is of great interest. The first document is a decree of the city of Cyrene prescribing in full detail a religious celebration in honour of the rulers, their family and their ancestors. It recalls the famous inscription of Gythium of the time of Tiberius. The celebration prescribed in the decree is intended as a mark of the city's gratitude for the φιλάνθρωπα conferred on it by the rulers (ll. 13 ff.). Next comes the fragmentary conclusion of a second document, either a decree of the city or a *diatagma* of the rulers concerning a group of prominent citizens of Cyrene, some of whom were lying under grave accusations. The document directs that as regards these people the royal orders and laws shall take their course but with this qualification, that their property shall not be confiscated but shall pass to their heirs. Then follow two well-preserved documents: (1) a letter from the rulers to the Cyreneans forwarding letters addressed to their own officials in Cyrenaica (τοῖς ἐπὶ

---

* See especially the paragraph on the ἀνακεχωρηκότες.

† 27 ff.: διὰ βίου τε τὰς σιταρχίας ἅπασιν ἐτάξαμ[εν, ὃ οὐδεὶς] | [τῶ]ν προγόνων μνημονεύεται πεποιηκώς.

τῶν πόλεων τεταγμένοις) and an order of the rulers (πρόσταγμα), and (2) the beginning of the *prostagma* referred to in the covering letter. This *prostagma* deals (as probably also did the letters to the royal governors of the cities, which are lost) with land which either has been declared ownerless (ἀδέσποτα) and has thus passed into the hands of the crown or was in an inter-mediate state: its owners are under accusation and it is in danger of being confiscated (or declared ownerless) by the crown (such land was known technically as κατῃτιαμένα). It appears that parcels of land of these two classes were still, at least to some extent, in the hands of their former owners. The kings prescribe that such land shall not be sequestrated ('placed under seal') nor the owners and their slaves arrested by administrative action, but that the legal procedure shall first be carried out.

I cannot here enter into a detailed discussion of all the problems to which the Cyrenean inscription gives rise. They are numerous and of different kinds: political, constitutional, administrative, &c. I shall confine myself to the social and economic aspects of the new document.

It is evident that the whole dossier records a set of φιλάνθρωπα. It is no less evident that behind the measures taken by the kings may be detected conditions that are far from normal. The country is in a state of unrest. Many prominent persons in the cities are under accusation and await trial. Certain other persons in the *chora*, not in the city—have forfeited, apparently because of breaches of the law, their right of property in their land, and their holdings have become ownerless (*adespota*). Another group, probably of the same class, have not lost their property yet, but they are under accusation and are liable to do so at any time. These two groups have been treated harshly by the royal officials. They appear to be not native cultivators but in all probability military settlers. It may be noted that the same terms as regards land, confiscated and semi-confiscated, are used in the land surveys of Tebtunis of about the same time in connexion with γῆ κατοικική, and in the φιλάνθρωπα of Cyprus discussed above.[195]

The inscription, to whatever part of the second century it

may belong, reflects unsettled conditions in the country and implies unrest and probably civil war. The history of Cyrenaica is too little known to permit us confidently to connect the document with particular events, but in any case the rulers who appear in the documents had emerged victorious from a struggle, probably dynastic or civil; and seem to be endeavouring to restore peace and order, without, however, proclaiming a full amnesty. They intend to punish their enemies but to do so without violence, through the regular courts of law. Similar situations were frequent in Egypt during the second century in the reigns of Philometor, Euergetes II, and Soter II, and Cyrenaica was certainly involved in the troubles of Egypt.

Like the document from Cyprus, the Cyrenean dossier reveals the wretched and unsettled state to which a rich and thrifty country had been reduced, as a consequence in the main of civil war and maladministration.

The grievous conditions that reigned in Egypt in the late second and first centuries undermined its production and prosperity. They impoverished the labouring classes and reduced the revenue that the government derived from internal sources. But they had no direct influence upon the development of the commercial relations of the Ptolemies.

I have already pointed out that these commercial relations were profoundly shaken first by the state of the Western market during the Punic and the first Oriental wars, and then through the loss by Egypt of its maritime hegemony in the Aegean. Finally, the commerce of Egypt suffered a severe blow in the occupation of Syria by Antiochus III, and the concentration of the caravan trade of Arabia in the hands of the Seleucids.

It did not, however, take the Ptolemies long to readjust their commercial relations and adapt them to the changed conditions. Their loss of their hold on the Aegean did not of course involve their exclusion from the Aegean trade, which, moreover, was losing its importance with the economic decay of Greece. Furthermore, the rapid economic development in the second century B.C., especially as regards agriculture, of the Pergamene kingdom, of Bithynia, and of Pontus, and the partial revival of the Bosporan kingdom, made it difficult for

Egypt to retain the role it had played in the third century of chief distributor of grain in the Aegean area. In addition to this, the agricultural production of Egypt, as we have seen, was declining, and it is probable that the quantities of grain for export and of oil for consumption were gradually decreasing. But Egypt undoubtedly still exported some grain and certain other products (e.g. papyrus, linen, glass, &c.) to the Aegean cities. There can be no question, therefore, of anything resembling a complete ruin of Egypt's Aegean commerce in the second and first centuries B.C.[196]

But it was no longer the Aegean market that played the leading part in the trade of those centuries. The largest consumers of Hellenistic goods were now Italy and the West. I have already referred to this change when discussing the development of Syrian commerce. What Italy needed was not so much Egyptian grain as the products of Egyptian manufactures and the luxuries imported to Egypt from the Somali country, Arabia, and India. It is unfortunate that we have so little information regarding the various branches of Alexandrian manufacture, especially as concerns the history and development of Egyptian textiles, both wool and linen. Egypt at this time was naturally not the only purveyor of textiles on the world market. Pergamon and several other cities of Asia Minor were offering their stuffs; Cos was still active, and so were Phoenicia and Syria. We should like to know how much each of these centres of production exported to Italy. Though no original fabrics of the period have survived and there is very little hope of finding any of them even in Egypt, we have a source of information which may prove helpful, at least as regards one kind of textiles. I refer to the wall paintings of Rome and Pompeii of the early Second Style, which frequently reproduce hangings, rugs, and the like. No doubt most of these wall paintings of the Second Style belong to the Sullan and Augustan times, but some of them are earlier, and I much doubt whether there was in this respect any notable difference between the first century B.C. and the early first century A.D. An analysis of the ornaments of these painted rugs and hangings may reveal their place of origin.[197]

Nor are we better informed about glass. We know nothing

of the types of glass which were used in late Hellenistic times, before the invention of blown glass. The burials of the period we are concerned with are few and very difficult to date. Not very many of them are richly furnished. Careful excavations of burial grounds of the late Hellenistic period carried out with exact observations are exceptional both in Italy and in the East, including Egypt. In fact I know of only one instance— that of Myrina, a small provincial town of Asia Minor. This means that as regards the last period in the development of moulded glass there is a gap in our knowledge.[198]

The situation in respect of toreutics is similar. I have already pointed out how difficult it is to distinguish between the various local types of silver and bronze plate of the Hellenistic period: the Pergamene, the Egyptian, the Syrian, the Tarentine, the Campanian. It is even more difficult to discriminate between the third century B.C. and the later Hellenistic times. The evidence is abundant but it has never been collected. A *Corpus* of silver and bronze plate with careful registration of the circumstances in which the several pieces were found might prove of great assistance to the historian of ancient economic life. So it is also with jewels, which again have never been collected, distributed according to their place of origin and their types, and carefully dated. This applies especially to Egypt, Syria, Asia Minor, and Italy, and to the period we are studying.[199]

Lastly, as regards pottery, we know practically nothing of the ware used and made in Egypt and especially in Alexandria in the second and first centuries B.C. No comprehensive study of the pottery of this period has ever been made. We are able to some extent to distinguish between Hellenistic and Roman ware, but we are completely incapable of discriminating between the early and the late Hellenistic period. We are similarly ignorant in respect of Italy. Apart from the local brands of pottery, Calenian, Italo-Megarian and early Arretine, we know very little about the types that were used in Italy in the late Hellenistic period. Attention such as has been paid to the subject in the excavation of cities and burial grounds in Greece and the East, for example at Corinth, Athens, Priene, Pergamon, Miletus, Olbia, and in some other minor places, has been very rare in Italy. If even in respect of these careful excavations, where the finds have been studied with painstaking accuracy,* it is difficult to distinguish between early and late Hellenistic ceramics and to separate local from imported ware,† how much more difficult is it to apply the same principles of classification to pottery found in Italy!

Such being the conditions, we have no means of ascertaining or even of conjecturing the volume of the export of manufactured goods from Alexandria to Italy and of comparing this volume with that of the exports from Asia Minor and Syria. And yet there is not the slightest doubt that Alexandria was, in fact, sending products of her manufacture to Italy and probably in large quantities. We may infer this from the development in southern Italy in the late Hellenistic times of those branches of industry which flourished at Alexandria: the textile industry, toreutics, jewellery, scented oils and perfumes. The activity of these branches of industry at Pompeii in the first century A.D., reflected in Pompeian paintings of that time which reproduce scenes of industrial life, makes it probable that this emancipation of southern Italy from Alexandria was preceded by a period when importation from Alexandria was an ordinary feature of its business life. A careful investigation of the various objects found at Pompeii, especially jewels and silver plate, may support or refute my suggestion. I fully realize that all the branches of industry which I have mentioned were flourishing in Italy before the Hellenistic period, and that their activity in the first century A.D. at Pompeii may have been a local revival and not the result of a transfer of those industries from Alexandria to Italy.[200]

The existence of an active trade between Alexandria and Italy may likewise be inferred from another fact. There was an ever increasing number of Italians in Alexandria in the second century B.C., who were probably both temporary visitors and permanent residents. There is a group of inscriptions from Delos which point to lively commercial relations between the Italian merchants of Delos and Alexandria. I refer in the first

* It must be noted, however, that the minor finds of Miletus have not yet been published.
† Note the case of Megarian pottery discussed above.

place to the dedication at Delos by a group of Italian merchants of a statue of Lochus, son of Callimedes, in recognition
of 'benefactions conferred on them when Alexandria was
captured by king Ptolemy Theos Euergetes'.*
This short and apparently simple text presents many difficulties of interpretation, which I cannot here discuss in detail.
It is certain that the Roman merchants were helped by Lochus
(and also by Euergetes?)† in 127 B.C. when Alexandria was
taken by Euergetes after the *amixia*. Lochus is known from
many other documents. He was a high dignitary in the service
of Euergetes, *strategos* of the Thebais in the same year 127/6
B.C., and probably took an active part in the capture of Alexandria. In what way the Roman merchants received benefactions
from him (and Euergetes?) is beyond our knowledge. They
may themselves have been in Alexandria in 127 B.C., or they
may have had agents, ships, and goods in the Alexandrian
harbour which were saved by Lochus. I see, however, not the
slightest reason to think that the benefactions were bestowed
on them by Euergetes as recompense for services rendered by
them to the king, for they would certainly not have failed to
mention these in their dedication. To the same class of Italian
negotiatores belonged the two Pedii, permanent residents at
Delos, who honoured there another dignitary in the service of
Euergetes, Polemarchus.‡ We have a similar dedication at
Delos to C. Marius by *Alexandreae Italicei quei fuere.*§ As there
were Italians of Delos at Alexandria, so there were Alexandrians at Delos. I may remind readers of the well-known dedication of the σύνοδος τῶν ἐν Ἀλεξανδρείαι πρεσβυτέρων ἐγδοχέων
at Delos in honour of Crocus, governor of Cyprus under Euergetes II.‖ Close business relations between Alexandria and
Delos in the reign of Euergetes II were preceded by similar

* Ῥωμαίων οἱ εὐεργετηθέντες ναύκληροι | καὶ ἔμποροι ἐν τῆι γενομένηι
καταλή|ψει Ἀλεξανδρείας ὑπὸ βασιλέως | Πτολεμαίου Θεοῦ Εὐεργέτου | Λόχον
Καλλιμήδου . . . ἀρετῆς ἕνεκεν καὶ | εὐεργεσίας τῆς εἰς ἑαυτούς, κτλ., O.G.I. 135;
Durrbach, *Choix*, 105; *Inscr. de Délos* 1526.

† Are we to connect the name of the king with εὐεργετηθέντες or with κατα-
λήψει?

‡ O.G.I. 133; Durrbach, *Choix*, 106; *Inscr. de Délos* 1527.

§ Durrbach, *Choix*, 107; *Inscr. de Délos* 1699.

‖ O.G.I. 140; Durrbach, *Choix*, 108; *Inscr. de Délos* 1528, cf. 1529.

relations in the time of Philometor, as is attested by the dedication by Areus, an Athenian, of a statue of Chrysermus, a
prominent man at the court of Philometor,* and perhaps by
the choice of Delos by the Cretan mercenaries of Philometor
as the place of publication of their decree in his honour.† They
were followed by similar relations between Soter II and Delos,
as is attested by many documents: his well-known dedication
at Delos‡; two dedications in his honour, one by a priest of
Ammon§, the other by an Alexandrian ‖; and in addition two
dedications, one in honour of Stolus the Athenian, a magnate
of Alexandria, by Simalus, a rich man, member of a Cyprian
family, resident at Delos, the other by Stolus in honour of
Simalus.¶ Finally, we may note the rapid growth of Alexandrian
cults at Delos and the presence there of many Alexandrians.²⁰¹

Evidence pointing in the same direction is to be found in the
famous papyrus recently published by U. Wilcken, the contract of a loan on bottomry, probably of the early second
century, granted to a group of importers of goods from Somaliland by a certain Archippus, son of Eudemus. The five trade
partners, all bearing Greek names, have different *ethnica*: the
ethnica of three of them are unknown; of the other two one is
a Lacedaemonian, another a Massaliote. The loan was arranged
through a certain Gnaeus, no doubt an Italian, probably a
banker (of Alexandria?) or a broker; three officers of the army
and two merchants, one from Massalia, another from Carthage,
figured as sureties. It is certain that all these men were permanently or temporarily resident at Alexandria and were engaged
there in business of different kinds. The large proportion of
Westerners among them may be noticed and the complete
absence of men from Syria and Asia Minor. The Western
members of the group had certainly not lost contact with their
native cities. Similar companies probably exported Alexandrian goods to the West: to Italy, Carthage, and Gaul.²⁰²

* *O.G.I.* 104; Durrbach, *Choix*, 90; *Inscr. de Délos* 1525.
† *O.G.I.* 116; *Inscr. de Délos* 1518, cf. Durrbach, *Choix*, 92; *Inscr. de Délos* 1517.
‡ Durrbach, *Choix*, 124; *Inscr. de Délos* 1531, cf. 1530 and 1537.
§ *O.G.I.* 170; Durrbach, *Choix*, 125; *Inscr. de Délos* 2037.
‖ *O.G.I.* 171; Durrbach, *Choix*, 126; *Inscr. de Délos* 1532, cf. 1535 and 1536.
¶ Durrbach, *Choix*, 127 and 128; *Inscr. de Délos* 1533, 1534.

It is improbable that the merchandise exported by the rading companies at Alexandria whose members used to visit Delos, or by the Italian merchants of Delos who visited Alexandria, consisted mainly of goods of Alexandrian manuacture. There was no reason why articles of Alexandrian and Egyptian manufacture should take the circuitous route by Delos in order to reach Italy. It was otherwise with the goods which came to Alexandria from Arabia and India and were in part merchandise in transit. Since similar commodities were exported in large quantities to Delos by Syrian, Anatolian, and perhaps Bosporan merchants, and since Delos probably fixed he prices, distributed the stock, financed the enterprises, &c., in a word acted as a clearing-house for this trade, it was natural hat Alexandrian merchants should not export their 'Oriental' wares straight to Italy but should send them first to Delos. I may point out that it was two governors of southern Egypt who protected the Italian merchants at Alexandria in the time of troubles. It was necessary that importers of 'Oriental' goods should maintain good relations with the viceroys of southern Egypt, the centre of the 'Oriental' trade of Egypt. It may have been otherwise as regards the imports from Somaliland, of which Alexandria had complete control.

If the above explanation is correct the relations between Alexandria and Delos are evidence of a revival of the trade of Egypt with the South-East and East, which for a while had been disorganized by the Seleucid annexation of Palestine and Phoenicia. The Ptolemies undoubtedly succeeded, soon after the battle of Panium, in reorganizing their Oriental trade. We find hem active at Delos under Philometor, and they kept up their business relations with the island State until its untimely end after the Mithridatic war.

Scanty and disconnected as it is, our evidence nevertheless allows us to reconstruct the main lines on which the Ptolemies revived and reorganized their commercial relations with the East. Philometor may have begun the process by intensifying the trade with Somaliland and by renewing the connexion between his merchants and Delos. But it was probably Euergetes II who was the chief restorer of Alexandria's foreign trade. The reputation which, as we have seen, he and his chief assistants acquired at Delos, was no doubt due to his success in securing command over Oriental and African merchandise in constantly increasing quantities, far greater than his predecessor had controlled. This he did by resuming the task of the first Ptolemies, Philadelphus and Euergetes I, that is to say, of establishing a safe and well-organized maritime route between South Arabia and Egypt. For these early kings the Red Sea route, thanks to their control of Phoenicia and Palestine, was of only secondary importance so far as Arabian commerce was concerned, while direct relations with India were of no great consequence. Their attention towards the South was chiefly directed to the organization of the systematic capture, taming, and transportation of war elephants. The efforts of Euergetes II, on the other hand, were devoted principally to the development of his maritime trade relations with Arabia and Africa; these he rendered easier and safer by various improvements affecting the Red Sea route, its harbours, and the roads connecting the harbours with the Nile. The capture of elephants came to a natural end. I may cite two texts as illustrating the interest taken by Euergetes II in the navigation of the Red Sea. The well-known inscription *O.G.I.* 132 of 130 B.C. mentions an officer who was in charge of a flotilla of ships in the Red Sea (probably guard-ships protecting the merchants trading in that sea and the boats collecting precious stones on its islands), and of the desert road by which incense and other foreign goods were transported from the Red Sea to Coptos. A chance remark of Posidonius* shows that the eastern shore of the Arabian gulf was likewise well guarded, no doubt against Nabataean pirates, who certainly did not look with favour on the revival of Ptolemaic south Arabian trade and were ready to rob the Egyptian ships, exactly as they had done earlier in the days of Philadelphus. Whether or not Euergetes II engaged in a regular war against the Nabataeans is a controversial point. Nor do we know anything positive about his connexion with the important harbour on the Nabataean coast—Leuce Come. There is no reliable evidence of his being the founder of the city.[203]

* Strabo, ii. 3. 4, p. 98.

I may quote in this connexion the name of Agatharchides of Cnidus, the well-known grammarian, philosopher, and geographer of Alexandria. His ἀκμή fell in the time of Philometor and Euergetes II. In his capacity as a member of Cineas' household (above, pp. 715, 731) and as secretary to Heracleides the Lembos, the two well-known political advisers of Philometor, he was certainly not unknown to the rulers of his time. No wonder therefore if in writing in his advanced age his famous treatise on the Red Sea, which is still extant in substantial fragments, saved for us by Diodorus and Photius, he was not only able to use literary sources but had access also to official documents, to the ὑπομνήματα βασιλικά kept in Alexandria, and to the reports of αὐτόπται, probably explorers and merchants who apparently carried out their voyages of exploration and business not without the knowledge of official circles.

It is interesting to note that the ὑπομνήματα βασιλικά contained so much material on Agatharchides' subject, material which came to the cognizance of the king either directly from the travellers or was incorporated in reports of certain officials of the crown. Still more interesting is the fact that Agatharchides lays the blame for the unfinished character of his work on the interruption in the flow of official reports due, as he says, to τὰς κατ' Αἴγυπτον ἀποστάσεις, caused by the *amixia* of the time of Euergetes II.

All the facts adduced above show the great interest of Euergetes II in the Red Sea, in its further exploration, and in the possibilities of development of the Red Sea trade which would result from this exploration. Of course the chief aim of Agatharchides, the famous and brilliant writer, was in all probability not to supply the merchants with a reliable guide to the Red Sea but to awaken general interest in it by reminding possible future merchants and explorers of the efforts to promote its exploration already made by Philadelphus and Euergetes I and of the importance Euergetes II attached to that region.[204]

Thus the intense interest of Euergetes II in the Arabian and African trade of Egypt is beyond doubt. But his eyes were open to even wider possibilities. Of this we have good evidence in the well-known story of Eudoxus of Cyzicus.* It tells how an Indian, stranded in the Arabian gulf, was brought to Alexandria and, after having learnt Greek, furnished information to the court about the commercial route to India. An expedition was sent out, among the members of which was Eudoxus, who happened to be in Alexandria as sacred envoy and herald to proclaim the truce for the festival of Persephone at Cyzicus (θεωρὸς καὶ σπονδοφόρος τοῦ τῶν Κορείων ἀγῶνος). The expedition reached India, and Eudoxus' ship came back laden with valuable goods (ἀρώματα and precious stones). Whether all the members of the expedition, supposing that it included a number of other ships, came back as successfully as Eudoxus we do not know; in all probability they did. On the return of the expedition the merchandise brought by Eudoxus from India was taken over by the crown, to his great disappointment, which it is difficult to understand. He certainly cannot have been ignorant of the Ptolemaic regulations regarding the import of goods subject to monopoly. He may have thought that what he, a foreigner, imported, perhaps in his own ship, would be exempted from these regulations.

The first expedition of Eudoxus was despatched probably in the last years of the reign of Euergetes. It appears that the success of this venture made the king desirous that another expedition should be sent, and that the same Eudoxus should take part in it. This second expedition, however, took place, not under Euergetes, but soon after his death. A careful analysis of our sources by W. Otto and H. Bengtson suggests that it started during the short rule of Cleopatra II in 116 B.C. From this second expedition Eudoxus came back not without adventures. His ship on its return voyage was driven on the Somali coast. When the expedition reached home Cleopatra II was no longer alive, and Soter II was king. The cargo brought back by Eudoxus was again, to his great vexation, taken over by the crown. We may suppose that this time he had received formal promises to the contrary before sailing.

The success of the two expeditions probably led to an active development of Egyptian trade with India. We may assume

* The story was told by Posidonius and borrowed from him by Strabo, ii. 3. 4 ff., pp. 98 ff.

that the example of Eudoxus was followed by other merchants, already engaged in the trade in Somali, Arabian, and Indian goods. This may explain the position held by Soter in Delos, that great mercantile clearing-house. It was probably Soter, the man of business, the great merchant, the holder of large stocks of Indian goods and thus a serious rival to the Syrian merchants, not Soter the king, who was so popular in the island.

It is more than probable that the Egyptian trade with India owed its development to some new factor previously unknown. This may have been the discovery of the monsoons, which allowed the Egyptian merchants to establish direct relations between Egypt and India. Eudoxus may have received information on the subject from the stranded Indian merchant, and may have carried out his first expedition with his help.

But our literary texts associate the discovery of the monsoons, not with Eudoxus, but with a sailor, a captain (κυβερνήτης), Hippalus by name. The later *Periplus of the Red Sea* is positive on the matter. Its author states explicitly that it was Hippalus who first carried out a direct voyage to India with the help of the south-west monsoon, after having first explored the *emporia* and the character of the sea. It was under his name that the south-west monsoon was known to the Greeks* and it was he who gave his name to an important promontory and to a sea†.

The date of Hippalus and of his discovery is disputed. Many eminent scholars are inclined to assign him and his discovery to the time of the early Roman Empire, since his name first occurs in that period and is unknown to the Hellenistic authors (for example to Juba). I find it difficult to accept this conclusion. It is based on negative evidence exclusively, and *argumenta ex silentio* are very hazardous. If Juba really never heard of Hippalus, it may have been due to his own negligence. Several weighty considerations on the other hand support an earlier date for Hippalus. I have pointed out above that the expeditions of Eudoxus and the subsequent development of trade relations between Egypt and Delos can be easily explained by assuming the discovery of the monsoons by

---

* *Per. Mar. Eryth.* 57; Plin. *N.H.* vi. 100 and 104.
† Ibid. vi. 172; Ptol. iv. 7. 12.

Eudoxus and the common use thereafter of this knowledge. Otherwise these events are puzzling. It must be remembered that the sea route from Egypt to India in general, the traditional coastal voyage, was well known to the Ptolemies from the beginning of their rule in Egypt. If it was not made use of, this was due to its dangerous character, to its length, and to the expense that it involved. What reason had Euergetes II for engaging in so risky an enterprise, containing no element of novelty, and that at a time when conditions were not very favourable?[205]

Moreover we possess some positive evidence besides the story of Eudoxus and the Delian material dealt with above. In the late second and the early first centuries B.C. we come upon an unexpected innovation in the administration of Egypt, connected apparently with a new situation in the Red and Indian Seas. It is about this time that we first find mention of a special officer in the Ptolemaic service charged with the care of Egyptian interests in those two seas and styled ἐπὶ τῆς Ἐρυθρᾶς καὶ Ἰνδικῆς θαλάσσης. This new post was at first perhaps combined with the office of *strategos* of the nome of Coptos, later certainly with that of *epistrategos* and of *strategos* of the Thebaid.[206]

This innovation cannot be explained unless we assume that the Red and Indian Seas, which had hitherto been of little or no interest to the Ptolemies, began at that time to play an important part in their policy. Some change had taken place in this respect, and this change was certainly not political but economic. It was undoubtedly the growing importance of the Indian trade, connected with the discovery of the monsoons and with the ever-increasing demand for Indian goods in the ancient world. This developing trade needed protection and organization. Protection on the desert routes from the Nile to the Red Sea had already been arranged. How and to what extent it was provided in the Red and Indian Seas we do not know. It is possible that a squadron of Ptolemaic ships cruised in the Red Sea permanently or at least during the trading season. Moreover the trade had to be carefully watched from the fiscal point of view, the goods imported being subject to monopoly. It was therefore imperative to concentrate the control of this trade in the hands of a single official, and the governor-general of the Thebaid, who was at the same time the commander of the Red and Indian Seas, was indicated or the purpose.

It therefore seems to me highly probable that the monsoons were discovered about the time of Eudoxus, probably by Eudoxus himself. Hippalus was apparently his contemporary, perhaps the naval chief of his expeditions, or one of those who succeeded him in the systematic exploration and exploitation of the new route, and who first supplied copious and trustworthy information about it, oral or literary. We know nothing about the volume of this Indian trade. Strabo tells us that in the time of the Ptolemies not more than 20 ships sailed yearly from the harbours of the Red Sea, while in his own days there were each year fleets of about 120 ships. This statement must be taken *cum grano salis*. We do not know the source of Strabo's information regarding the Ptolemaic trade, nor the date of this source. The statement may relate to early Ptolemaic times or to the last years of the Ptolemies, when political events may have affected the development of trade. Unfortunately Delos, after the time of Sulla, furnishes very little evidence. However this may be, it is certain that the reigns of Euergetes II and Soter II were a period of substantial expansion of the commercial relations of Egypt both with the West, where Alexandria profited by the destruction of Carthage, and with the South-East, where political conditions in Syria made it comparatively easy for those kings to restore and expand their trade relations with Arabia and India. In conclusion, I may remind the reader of the well-known intention of Cleopatra VII, after Actium, to sail to India and establish there a kingdom for herself and Antony. Cleopatra would not have thought of such a venture had there not been in her time regular relations between Egypt and India, which were under the control of the Egyptian government and supplied the rulers of Egypt with full information about the conditions in the latter country.[207]

VII

ROMAN DOMINATION

SOURCES OF INFORMATION

THIS chapter may be regarded as an epilogue to the history of the economic and social development of the Hellenistic world. It contains a brief review of the conditions prevailing there at the time of the Mithridatic and civil wars down to the battle of Actium. This period, I need hardly observe, is at once an epilogue and a prologue: an epilogue to the development of Hellenistic economy as created by Alexander and developed by his successors, a prologue inasmuch as it heralds the new phase in the economic life of the ancient world brought about by the stabilization and reorganization of the Roman Empire by Augustus. It is evident that a new economic system was not substituted at this juncture for the old. Such breaks in evolution do not occur in history. Economic life in the East developed after Augustus on much the same lines as before. Hellenistic economy and social order were too firmly rooted in the life of the East to be abruptly changed by any act of Augustus or of his immediate successors. Nevertheless, the firm establishment of the *Pax Romana* in the united civilized world and the stable and uniform organization of the Roman Empire of which the foundations were laid by Augustus set in motion new and powerful forces which deeply affected the ancient world in general. I have dealt with this period of economic history in another work, where I have indicated the links that connected the Roman Empire with the Hellenistic countries.

The period in question is that in which Roman domination, firmly established in certain parts of the East, was challenged by the elemental uprising of part of the Hellenistic world, on the initiative and under the leadership of the hellenized king of Pontus, Mithridates VI Eupator, and then re-established and extended to almost the whole of that world amid the stormy atmosphere of the Roman civil wars.

We are not here concerned with the history of the Mithridatic and civil wars, which has been repeatedly studied. My purpose is to investigate the effect of these wars, and of the subsequent reorganization by Rome of the administration of the old and new provinces of the Hellenistic East, upon the economic and social life of those regions. It is important to know the form that the Senate's Hellenistic provinces had assumed when it handed them over to Augustus. With Egypt, which became a Roman province after Actium, I have dealt in the previous chapter. The social and economic evolution of this country in the first century B.C. was not directly affected by the Mithridatic and civil wars, except the war of Actium. These wars were not the cause of the crisis previously described, from which, by this time, Egypt was suffering, though they may have made it more acute. In this chapter I shall confine myself to Greece, including Macedonia and Thrace, the old Roman provinces of Asia and Cilicia, and the new provinces of Bithynia, Pontus, and Syria after their annexation to the Roman Empire.

No general survey of the economic and social aspect of these regions in the first century B.C. will be found in modern histories either of the Hellenistic period or of Rome. Most of the former end their narrative at an earlier date, while the latter are naturally much more concerned with the political, military, administrative, and social and economic development of the Roman State in general than with the agony of the Hellenistic world, a moribund survival which plays a secondary part in these general surveys. The only exception, as regards a portion of the period in question, is the brilliant picture of the whole of the Hellenistic world (Egypt excepted) given by Th. Reinach in his masterly book on Mithridates Eupator. Among other valuable contributions may be mentioned the surveys of Greece at this time by Finlay and Hertzberg in their excellent histories of Greece under Roman domination and recently by J. A. O. Larsen, and similar surveys of the history of the Roman province of Asia by Chapot, of Asia Minor in general by T. R. S. Broughton, and of the province of Syria by Dobiaš. The reader may also consult certain monographs on the Roman Senate's methods of provincial administration in the late first century B.C.[1]

PLATE CII

1. Head of Pompey, made in modern times into a bust. The best-known and the best preserved plastic portrait of Pompey (even the nose is intact). It shows all Pompey's principal features as we know them from coins minted in Spain and Sicily soon after his death, and from the many references in contemporary and later literary sources. Note the massive almost square head, the low forehead with three deep wrinkles, the luxuriant hair of the type called by the Romans *crispus*, the small eyes, the short nose, the full cheeks, the double chin, and the short massive neck. The most individual feature in the appearance of Pompey, which was often noticed and described by his contemporaries, lay in the rebellious curls of the hair over the forehead, the famous ἀναστολή. Note also a tendency to introduce into his portrait certain traits borrowed from the portraits of Alexander. The Ny Carlsberg head was held by some scholars to be a contemporary portrait of Pompey, a product of late Hellenistic art. Other students, however, regard it as a work of a much later time, a portrait study by a Hadrianic sculptor based on the earlier portraits and on literary sources. The similar *mutatis mutandis* to the biography of Plutarch. The bust has often been discussed. I may refer to the admirable paper by F. Poulsen, 'Les portraits de Pompeius Magnus', *Rev. Arch.* 6 sér, vii (1936), pp. 16 ff., where the reader will find references to the earlier studies. Photograph supplied by Vilhelm Tryde.

2. Head of a statue of Caesar. The dictator and founder of the Roman Empire is represented standing in full military dress. The statue was made by a sculptor of the time of Trajan, but is based on a careful study of the many portraits of the dictator then existing. It is well known that none of the extant plastic portraits of Caesar goes back to his own time or is an exact copy of one of the statues set up to him in his lifetime. The only contemporary portraits of Caesar will be found on his coins (see for instance pl. cv, no. 8). The busts and statues in stone or other material are all later, and reflect the conceptions of Caesar's character and role prevailing at one or another period of the Roman Empire. The majority of the many fine and impressive portraits of the time of Augustus show him, not as he really was, but as an ideal 'princeps', the true 'father' of Augustus and of the Roman State. In the time of Domitian Caesar appears as the ruthless autocrat, inaccessible and divine. For the time of Trajan and for Trajan himself Caesar was the great predecessor of the *optimus princeps*, the good, clement, and serene ruler of what was to become the prosperous and happy world-state ruled by Trajan. On the iconography of Caesar see the recent studies by L. Curtius, *Röm. Mitt.* xlvii (1932), pp. 212 ff.; E. Boehringer, *Der Cäsar von Acireale*, 1933, and the remarks of F. Poulsen, loc. cit., p. 50 f. Curtius has devoted several pages to an excellent discussion of the statue in the Palazzo dei Conservatori (pp. 235 ff. and pls. 56 and 57). Photograph supplied by Anderson.

PLATE CII

THE FOUNDERS OF THE NEW WORLD

Our information is better for the period we are considering than for any other in the history of the Hellenistic world, which does not mean that it is completely satisfactory. Appian in his *Mithridatica* and in his history of the civil wars, Plutarch in many of his biographies, fragments of Cassius Dio for the years 133 to 69 B.C. and his continuous narrative of events from 68 to 44 B.C. (books XXXVI, preserved in part, to XLIV), and the *periochae* of Livy, contain a wealth of information regarding the social and economic life of the East. Still more evidence will be found in the works of Cicero, especially in his orations and letters, some of which* give a vivid though not an unbiased picture of the conditions in Asia Minor, Syria, and Greece, with a wealth of details. The same, to a lesser extent, is true of the *corpus Caesarianum*. All these literary works and some later historical compilations, it must be admitted, represent, in the main, the Roman point of view, and the same remark applies to the work of the great Posidonius, so far as we are able to form an idea of it, and still more to such Greek writers, panegyrists of Rome, as Nicolaus of Damascus and Theophanes of Mytilene, the friend and protégé of Pompey.

We must regret that the voice of those Greeks who were hostile to Rome, or rather, who were not prejudiced in her favour, giving their interpretation of the course of events and their reaction to it, is not heard, or only reaches us very faintly through the literary texts. The work of Pompeius Trogus survives only in the very meagre abbreviation of Justin, and contains nothing that relates to the social and economic life of the Hellenistic world. Josephus and still more the books of the Maccabees represent the Jewish point of view, and give some idea of the atmosphere surrounding one of the most peculiar sections of that world. Memnon's history of Heraclea Pontica is invaluable as presenting the events from the standpoint of one of the strongest Greek cities of the period. And finally the great historian and geographer Strabo gives us here and there in an historical excursus a substantial and unbiased

---

* e.g. the *Verrines, De imperio Cn. Pompei, Pro Flacco, Pro Sestio, De provinciis consularibus, In Pisonem, Pro rege Deiotaro,* and several letters in his correspondence with his brother Quintus and with Atticus.

picture of the conditions prevailing at this time in various cities of Asia Minor. Especially interesting are his descriptions of his native Pontus and of Cappadocia and his digressions concerning the history of those parts of Asia Minor, Mithridates and his successors, and the history of the Bosporan kingdom. It is probable that these passages are derived from a local historian of Pontus, Hypsicrates, a native of Amisus.[2]

However, none of these last-named authors represents at all adequately the point of view of the unprejudiced Greeks. We should therefore pay the more attention to those reflections of the real life of the Hellenistic world which we may detect in many inscriptions found in various parts of it, chiefly in Greece and Asia Minor. Most of these, no doubt, are either official Roman documents or of a pro-Roman character—inscriptions set up in honour of the masters of the day and of their partisans. Nevertheless, such as they are, they contain valuable documentary information regarding the life, sufferings, and hopes of the population of the Hellenistic countries. The coins and the archaeological material are of a more restricted scope.

I do not pretend to have exhausted this rich material. I am offering here a mere sketch, a short epilogue. I have quoted in the course of it some (not all) of the literary texts and inscriptions, a selection exhibiting mainly the dark side of the picture and not always strictly related to its social and economic aspect. This course is rendered inevitable by the character of our sources of information. A more detailed treatment would involve difficult and complicated discussions, such as would require a volume to themselves, regarding the general character of Roman dominion before Augustus, its principles of government, its administration, its economic and fiscal policy, and so forth. This fascinating subject calls for fuller and more adequate examination by some younger scholar, not so much as an epilogue, but as the prologue to a new chapter in the history of the Ancient World.

I. MITHRIDATES

I shall not be expected to relate the history of the first Mithridatic war.[3] But certain important aspects of it, to which allusion has already been made, may be pointed out, in view of their great and enduring influence on the social and economic life of the Aegean world.

After his conquest of Pontus Mithridates naturally directed his efforts to the consolidation and organization of his kingdom. This was not yet complete, for part of the Pontic territory remained in the hands of the Bithynian kings. Moreover, to be master in his dominions, Mithridates required to exercise full control over the Straits. At these two points the interests of Mithridates were irreconcilable with those of Rome, and the issue accordingly could not be settled without war.

No war could be conducted against Rome with any hope of success so long as she had the control and enjoyed the support of Greece and Asia Minor. The stability and prosperity of the Pontic kingdom of Mithridates depended to a large extent upon their assistance, and this could be assured only if there were sympathy and co-operation between him and them. Sincere Philhellene or not, Mithridates realized that without the active help of Greece, without the accumulated resources of Greek wealth and Greek intelligence, any endeavour to create a strong State in the East and to assert its independence against the Romans was doomed to failure. It was of vital importance to him to get the Greek purse and Greek brains on his side.

In particular, no efficient army or navy could be organized without extensive Greek help. Mithridates' own Pontic soldiers and Thracian and Iranian mercenaries were good war material, but not a match for Roman legionaries. To face these on equal terms, the troops of Mithridates had first to be transformed into a real modern army, and this could not be done without the active help of Greeks, who in military science were still regarded as second only to the Romans. And the same was true of the navy. In the ancient world, especially after the downfall of Carthage and the decay of the Ptolemaic and Seleucid navies, there were no experts in naval matters other than the Greeks of Greece proper, of the islands, and of Asia Minor.

Thus it was an indispensable condition of success that Mithridates should gain the sympathy, support, and co-operation of the Greek world, especially of the Greek *bourgeoisie*. In this, especially after his first victories, he was fairly successful.

PLATE CIII

1. Æ Tetradrachm of Heliocles, the last Greek king of Bactria (c. 140 B.C.). *Obv.* ΒΑΣΙΛΕΩΣ ΔΙΚΑΙΟΥ ΗΛΙΟΚΛΕΟΥΣ. Bust of Heliocles. *Rev.* Kharosthi inscription of king's name, Zeus radiate holding fulmen.

2. Æ Tetradrachm of Mithridates VI, Pontus. *Obv.* Head of Mithridates VI. *Rev.* ΒΑΣΙΛΕΩΣ ΜΙΘΡΑΔΑΤΟΥ ΕΥΠΑΤΟΡΟΣ. Pegasos drinking. Date ΗΣ (90–89 B.C.). All in a crown of flowers.

3. Æ Tetradrachm of Antiochus VIII Grypus (125–95 B.C.) Antioch. *Obv.* Head of Antiochus VIII. *Rev.* ΒΑΣΙΛΕΩΣ ΑΝΤΙΟΧΟΥ ΕΠΙΦΑΝΟΥΣ. Zeus Ouranios, crowned with crescent and holding star. To the l. two monograms. All in a laurel crown.

4. N Stater of Mithridates, Athens (struck for use in his war with Rome). *Obv.* Head of Athena. *Rev.* ΑΘΕ ΒΑΣΙΛΕ ΜΙΘΡΑΔΑΤΗΣ ΑΡΙΣΤΙΩΝ. Owl on amphora; in field Mithridatic symbol, star between crescents.

5. Æ Drachm of Ariobarzanes I, Cappadocia, 75 B.C. *Obv.* Head of Ariobarzanes I. *Rev.* ΒΑΣΙΛΕΩΣ ΑΡΙΟΒΑΡΖΑΝΟΥ ΦΙΛΟΡΩΜΑΙΟΥ. Athena holding Nike; in exergue regal year ΚΑ (75 B.C.).

6. Æ Tetradrachm of Athens, c. 91–89 B.C. *Obv.* Head of Athena. *Rev.* ΑΘΕ ΞΕΝΟΚΛΗΣ ΑΡΜΟΞΕΝΟΣ. Owl on amphora, and symbol, seated Metellus. All in a laurel crown.

7. Æ Tetradrachm of Tigranes, king of Armenia (97–56 B.C.), Antioch. *Obv.* Bust of Tigranes wearing Armenian tiara. *Rev.* ΒΑΣΙΛΕΩΣ ΤΙΓΡΑΝΟΥ. Seated Tyche of Antioch. All in a laurel crown.

8. Æ Nicias, tyrant of Cos. *Obv.* ΝΙΚΙΑΣ. Head of Nicias. *Rev.* To the r. ΚΩΙΩΝ, to the l. ΕΥΚΑΡΠΟΣ. Bust of Asclepios.

9. Æ Tetradrachm of Ascalon with portrait head of Cleopatra. *Obv.* Head of Cleopatra. *Rev.* ΑΣΚΑΛ[ΩΝΙΤΩΝ ΙΕ]ΡΑΣ ΑΣΥΛΟΥ. Date ΝΕ˙of the local era (49 B.C.). Eagle.

10. Æ Tetradrachm of Cleopatra and Antony, Antioch. *Obv.* ΒΑΣΙΛΙΣΣΑ ΚΛΕΟΠΑΤΡΑ ΘΕΑ ΝΕΩΤΕΡΑ. Bust of Cleopatra. *Rev.* ΑΝΤΩΝΙΟΣ ΑΥΤΟΚΡΑΤΩΡ ΤΡΙΤΟΝ ΤΡΙΩΝ ΑΝΔΡΩΝ. Head of Antony.

The coins in this plate (with the exception of that of Heliocles of Bactria, which is reproduced here because the reign of Heliocles was the turning-point in the destinies of Bactrian and Indian Hellenism) reflect in part the conditions prevailing in the East in the time of Mithridates the Great and in part (Nicias and Cleopatra) those of the civil wars. On Nicias see pp. 1007 f. and n. 120. The tetradrachm no. 9 (Brit. Mus.) belongs to the set of Ptolemaic coins of Ascalon which have been frequently discussed, most recently in the articles of Mrs. Brett and Ph. Lederer cited above, Ch. VI, n. 190. It is highly probable that the coins are dated by the Ascalonian era, which began in 103 B.C., and testify to the strength of Ptolemaic influence in the free city of Ascalon. It is, however, puzzling that the portrait of Cleopatra is that of a woman of somewhat advanced age and not that of a young girl.

PLATE CIII

COINS OF THE LATE SECOND AND FIRST CENTURIES B.C.

Asia Minor and Greece lent him their support spontaneously and with a certain enthusiasm. But this support was not unanimous and not altogether enthusiastic.

The majority of the population of Greece and Asia Minor was certainly impressed by the spectacular display of Mithridates' armed forces and by his early military successes in the Pontic regions and later in Asia Minor and Greece. The effect of these was increased by the strong resentment against the Roman rule felt by all classes of the population of these countries. But hatred of the Romans and the exaltation of Mithridates must not be over-emphasized The taxation, war contributions, compulsory levies, and requisitions imposed by Rome though affecting to a certain extent the *bourgeoisie* weighed mostly on the lower classes. It must be borne in mind that the Roman resistance to Mithridates before the arrival of Sulla rested exclusively on an army levied in Asia Minor and consisting mainly of artisans and peasants.* These classes were of course eager for *res novae* from whatever source they came. Mithridates offered them the prospect of *res novae* and they sided with him and were prepared to exterminate their oppressors, at least such of them as were foreigners.

On the other hand, the well-to-do classes, especially the urban *bourgeoisie*, though resenting the activity of the *publicani*, the war burdens, and the competition of the *negotiatores* in business, could not possibly have had very strong feelings against the 'Romans'. The scores of thousands of Italians who settled in Asia Minor were not all of them foreign oppressors. Many were quiet and honest business men and landowners, who had lived in Greece and Asia for several generations, in close contact, both social and economic, with the native *bourgeoisie* of the cities. It must be remembered that most of the so-called Romans were south Italians, some of them of Greek origin, and that all of them were more or less hellenized.

It is not surprising therefore that the support given to Mithridates by the cities and their middle class was far from unanimous. I may first review the situation in Asia Minor. Some cities resisted Mithridates, among them Magnesia on the Sipylus, Tabae, Stratonicea, and perhaps other cities in Caria,

* App. *Mithr.* 17.

and some cities in Lycia, Pamphylia, and Pisidia. It was not without hesitation that Ephesus and Chios threw in their lot with Mithridates. Rhodes and its dependency Cos showed the same attitude as the cities of Caria, Lycia, and Pamphylia. It is evident that many members of the ruling classes in the cities of Asia Minor were diffident and suspicious. The action of Chaeremon of Nysa mentioned above (p. 821) is characteristic, and affords a good illustration of the attitude of these classes.

It is therefore certain that the Greek middle classes cannot be regarded as the sole perpetrators of the great 'pogrom' organized by Mithridates in Asia. Nor do I believe that the whole population of the cities took an active part in it. Like most such acts, both in ancient and modern times, the Asiatic massacre was carried out by the rabble of the cities. These murderers and pillagers would certainly have much liked to include others than Italians among their victims. Slaves certainly took an active part, both as actual murderers and as informers ($\mu\eta\nu\nu\tau\alpha\iota$), and were rewarded by Mithridates for their share in the work by the grant of freedom. I am convinced that the massacre evoked a sentiment of terror rather than delight among the higher classes. This, however, did not prevent them from taking their share of the plunder. We hear that the cities were able to pay their debts from the profits of the 'pogrom'.

After the massacre Mithridates needed the support of the Greek *bourgeoisie* more than ever. For a time he was well provided with money, having appropriated an ample share of the booty. He therefore made a gesture of liberality, and remitted the taxes of the people of Asia for five years. This was supplemented by some acts of generosity to the Greek cities: he gave a subsidy to Apamea which had suffered from an earthquake, supported the celebration of games (at Smyrna), bestowed gifts on temples, confirmed and extended the *asylum* of Ephesus, and so on. His acts were similar to those of Aristonicus in the first months of the latter's power. Certain of his measures caused some alarm to the *bourgeoisie*. Such were, for example, the grant of privileges to slave-informers ($\mu\eta\nu\nu\tau\alpha\iota$), and the confiscation of Jewish money in the island of Cos. However, the *bourgeoisie* would certainly not actively oppose Mithridates or betray him to the Romans, so long as he was successful on the field of battle.

The situation in Greece was similar. There the chief moral and strategic victory of Mithridates was the defection of Athens from Rome. Under the leadership first of Athenion and then of Aristion, or, much less probably of Aristion whom Posidonius calls Athenion by mistake or on purpose,[4] the Athenians declared themselves allies of Mithridates. This act has been explained in various ways. The ancient relations of friendship between the Mithridatids and Athens, the bitter feeling against Rome, the elemental and romantic craving for liberty, have been put forward. In my opinion it was in the main an act of the same kind as many others in the history of Athens. It was a victory of 'democracy' over the oligarchical régime established and supported by the Romans. The upper classes remained true to their philo-Roman policy. It was the mass of the population that was responsible for the change in the direction of Athenian policy. They were lured into the adventure by ambitious demagogues, who promised them the usual economic and social reforms, and they were blinded by exaggerated reports of the successes, strength, and wealth of Mithridates. And the same happened all over Greece.

For this Greece paid a heavy price. All the calamities of the war of liberation and of the war of enslavement were renewed on a larger scale. The 'pentecontaetia' of the recovery and prosperity of the middle class in Greece under the protection of the Romans came to an abrupt end. This is not the place to repeat the sad story of the Sullan war in Greece. The sufferings of the country began as soon as Sulla appeared with his army on its soil. The Mithridatic occupation of Greece was a short prelude; it was immediately followed by the conflict between Mithridates and Sulla.

The army of Sulla was not very large. But cut off as it was both from Italy and the East, having no fleet to support it, it relied entirely on the resources of Greece. Food for the soldiers, fodder for the horses, means of transportation, quarters for the army, material and labour for the construction of military engines, supplies of clothes, shoes, armour, and weapons for the re-equipment of the soldiers, had all to be furnished by the

people of Greece. Nor was Sulla well supplied with money.
Moreover his small army, which experienced heavy losses
during the campaign, had to be reinforced by compulsory
levies from the more warlike elements of the Greek population.
Finally, havoc was wrought by the continuous sieges and
captures of cities, by the raids of the Thracian Maedi and the
Bastarni (one of which, carried out by the former, reached
Delphi and resulted in the capture and pillage of the city and
temple) and by the attacks of pirates on the helpless cities and
temples (for example, the sack of Epidaurus in 88 B.C.).[5]

I may illustrate what I have said by a few examples. The
best-known episode, in fact the central episode of the war, was
the siege and capture of Athens and the Piraeus by Sulla.
Appian and Plutarch give a vivid picture of the siege. Its
success depended entirely on the perfection of the siege engines.
Sulla had none, and had them built on the spot. Skilled labour,
material, and especially iron were furnished by Thebes, wood
was cut in Attica—it is well known how the famous plane-trees
of the Academy fell victims to this operation; ten thousand
pairs of mules were occupied transporting the material and
operating the siege engines; the mules and the drivers were of
course requisitioned in the country.[6]

The result of the siege is well known and need not be recalled
in detail: the sack of the city, the massacre of the population,
the execution of the leaders, the confiscation of property. It is
significant of the standard of wealth in the city that all that
Aristion, after a thorough campaign of confiscations and
robbery, was able to store in the Acropolis amounted only to
40 pounds of gold and 600 pounds of silver.* Sulla, in his
urgent need of money, did not hesitate to confiscate or to
borrow gold and silver from the richest and most famous
sanctuaries of Greece: Olympia, Delphi, and Epidaurus, and probably also from others. There is good ground for thinking that
we must regard the gifts of Sulla to the sanctuary of Amphiaraus at Oropus in the same light as the concession of half of
the territory of Thebes to Olympia and Delphi, that is to say
as compensation for the confiscation of its accumulated capital.[7]

The abuses resulting from the billeting of soldiers on the

* App. *Mithr.* 39.

cities of Greece are clearly suggested by two inscriptions. One is a decree of the city of Chaeronea (of 87–86 B.C.) in honour of Sadalas, commander of a detachment of soldiers sent to Sulla by the Thracian king Amatocus. Sadalas is highly praised by Chaeronea for having kept discipline among his soldiers stationed in the city.[8]

The other is an inscription from Daulis. It affords a good illustration of the evil plight of some of the minor cities and of the dangers that threatened them amid the turmoil of war. It should be observed that Daulis was situated in a region which suffered severely from the hostilities. Archelaus had sacked the neighbours of Daulis, Panopeus (Phanotea) and Lebadea, and Daulis itself naturally feared for its existence (Sulla was very lenient to his soldiers).* Surrounded as it was by terrors and dangers,† it had recourse (successfully) to the good offices of Hermias, a man of Stratonicea of Caria (a city which staunchly supported the Romans) and probably a person of influence with Sulla. The city asked him to intervene in its favour ἐπὶ τῶν ἀγειμένων.[9]

Even more eloquent are two inscriptions from Delphi, one mentioning a Phocian of Drymus whom the city asked for his help, another in honour of Caphisias of Orchomenus who succoured the city in difficult times by a gift of grain. It is to be observed that the Pythia of 86 B.C. were never celebrated.[10]

The facts are well known and I cannot cite them all. It should be noted that the Pontic troops behaved during the struggle in exactly the same way as the Romans. Sulla in his interview with Archelaus‡ was not exaggerating when he said that the men of Pontus after having invaded Greece killed a large number of the inhabitants and appropriated 'both the public and the sacred property of the cities and the private property of the slain'.§ I may remind the reader of Archelaus' expedition against Delos. After the capture of the city many Italians and other residents of the city (some of them Athenians who took the side of the Romans) were killed (the figure

---

* Sall. *Cat.* 11.
† l. 1 f.: περιστά[ντων] τὰ[ν] | [πόλιν φόβων πολλ]ῶν καὶ κινδύνων μεγάλων.
‡ App. *Mithr.* 54.
§ τά τε κοινὰ καὶ ἱερὰ τῶν πόλεων καὶ τὰ ἴδια τῶν ἀνῃρημένων.

given is 20,000), their wives and children were sold into slavery, and their property was confiscated and divided between Athens and Mithridates.[11]

A picture of Greece as a whole at that time, based on literary sources,* may be found in Hertzberg (Fr. transl., p. 359): 'Macedonia suffered severely and Thessaly experienced great hardships. To the south of Thermopylae even regions which were not the theatre of war were grievously harassed by war-contributions, requisitions, and levies . . . and the fields of Boeotia and Attica in particular were practically devastated by the armies of the belligerents.' In many places recovery was impossible. There is evidence that certain cities never revived. Such were Panopeus of Phocis and Alalcomenae of Boeotia, whose sanctuary was pillaged. Thebes in the time of Strabo was no more than a miserable village.

Meanwhile in Asia Minor[12] the news of the great victories of Sulla effected a considerable change in the mood of the population. The burden of war was heavily felt by it. We do not know how many free men levied in Greece and Asia Minor were serving in the armies of Mithridates, but an incidental mention of the enrolment of slaves is suggestive. At the battle of Chaeronea† the first ranks of the Pontic phalanx included 15,000 slaves whom the royal general had freed by edicts and enlisted among the hoplites. These slaves came probably from Greece, but the same was certainly done in Asia Minor also. How many free men in addition served in the army of Mithridates? There is, moreover, no doubt that the navy of Mithridates, like the navy which was collected by Lucullus for Sulla, consisted almost exclusively of ships which with their crews and rowers were supplied by the cities of Asia Minor and of the islands. Finally it must be remembered that the part of Mithridates' army which was with him in Asia Minor certainly lived at the expense of the country.

The heavy charges, exactions, and arbitrary confiscations of property, the expectation of still heavier burdens, the terror spread by the invincible Romans, the wholesale liberation of slaves by Mithridates, increased the feeling of aversion to the

* It is supported by the epigraphical evidence, unknown to Hertzberg which I have cited in part above. † Plut. *Sulla*, 18, 5.

latter among the leading men in the cities and in the country.
There was general unrest throughout Asia Minor. Mithridates
knew this through his spies and acted accordingly. Tyrannies
were established in several cities (Tralles, Adramyttium, Colophon), a military governor was appointed at Ephesus. Nevertheless, the hostility to the king grew ever stronger, and
provoked him to reprisals. Certain Galatian tetrarchs who
were accused of having organized a plot against him were
ambushed and killed. Chios, which was suspected of Roman
sympathies, was subjected to ignominious treatment: the whole
of its population was transported to Colchis under the guard of
their own slaves, and Pontic settlers replaced them in Chios.[13]
Ephesus was threatened with the same fate and rose in revolt.
The demagogic measures of Mithridates had made an impression, and the leaders of the city were distrustful of the loyalty
of the lower classes. A still extant decree or law of the city
shows how it endeavoured, by the grant of various economic,
social, and political privileges to the population of the city
and especially to the lower classes, to gain their support. The
example of Ephesus was followed by Tralles, Hypaepa, Metropolis (?), and a little later by Smyrna, Sardis, Colophon, and
perhaps Miletus. There is reason to think that these cities
tried to secure the loyalty of the lower classes by measures
similar to those adopted by Ephesus. Finally Galatia rose in
revolt.[14]

The counterstroke of Mithridates was terrible. Several cities
were besieged, captured, and sacked.* Executions were of
constant occurrence. The province was systematically robbed
and pillaged.† But the king's most radical measure was a social
and economic revolution imposed from above in the manner of
Aristonicus. Sulla in his Ephesian speech, after having spoken
of the great massacre organized by Mithridates and carried out
by the cities, notes with a certain satisfaction: 'For all this,
punishment has been inflicted upon you by Mithridates himself, who proved faithless to you, and gave you your fill of
bloodshed and confiscations, caused lands to be redistributed,
debts to be cancelled, slaves to be freed, tyrants to be set over
some of you, and robberies to be committed in great number

* Liv. lxxxii.   † App. *Mithr.* 54.

both on land and sea, so that you learnt at once by trial and comparison what sort of protectors you had before, and what sort you chose instead'.* In his historical narrative, Appian† thus describes Mithridates' measures: 'Afraid of a defection of the other cities he gave freedom to the Greek cities, proclaimed a cancellation of debts, gave citizenship to the metics in every city and liberated the slaves'. We are not surprised to learn that a number of leading men in the cities organized a conspiracy against Mithridates, which was betrayed and resulted in a wholesale slaughter of the conspirators. About 1600 of them perished. After the battle of Orchomenus the situation became even worse.‡ ¹⁵

I have recalled these well-known facts because they show the atmosphere of ruin, oppression, and mutual suspicion that pervaded Asia Minor during the decisive duel between Mithridates and Sulla in Greece. The situation was further aggravated when the centre of hostilities was transferred to Asia Minor, where Fimbria was active for a while, committing acts of barbarism and cruelty in competition with Mithridates. His plunder of Nicomedia, his devastation of the territory of Cyzicus and of the Troad, and especially the cruel treatment of Ilium, are mentioned in the records.

With the appearance of Sulla in Asia Minor and the surrender of Fimbria's army the day of reckoning came for the province of Asia. At the meeting at Ephesus to which I have referred Sulla first declared his attitude towards the policy of Mithridates and his measures: 'far be it from the Romans, he says, even to entertain the thought of impious massacres, senseless confiscations, revolts of slaves or all the barbaric rest of it' (transl. by A. M. Harmon).

Nevertheless, his own measures were not less radical and thorough, though tending in the opposite direction. The social and economic conditions which had prevailed before the social revolution of Mithridates were re-established. This was a difficult operation, for some cities refused to obey. Punitive expeditions against them resulted in massacres of slaves and free men, pillaging, and devastation. Mytilene was besieged and offered a staunch resistance. Several cities were plund-

* App. *Mithr.* 62.　　　　† Ibid. 48.　　　　‡ Ibid. 92.

red by pirates, after having been spared by Sulla (Iasus, Clazomenae, Samos, Samothrace). The province as a whole had to pay a heavy penalty for its conduct. It had profited, by the munificence of Mithridates, from the remission of the regular taxes. Now the whole amount of these taxes for five years was required by Sulla in one year. Moreover the province was ordered to pay the cost of the war and of its reorganization. This amounted to 20,000 talents. And, lastly, the army of Sulla, after all the hardships of the two campaigns, was given an agreeable holiday at the expense of the provincials. The soldiers were billeted on private houses during the winter of 84 and perhaps also that of 83. Each soldier received from his host 16 drachmas a day and free meals for himself and his guests, whatever their number. The centurions ($\tau\alpha\xi\iota\alpha\rho\chi o\iota$) received 50 drachmas a day. Clothes, too, had to be supplied, one suit for use in the house, another for out of doors.

A heavy financial burden was thus imposed on the cities of Asia, which had suffered so severely at the hands of Mithridates, Fimbria, and Sulla. It was made to appear even heavier by contrast with the privileges granted to those cities which had remained faithful to Rome: Ilium, Chios, Magnesia on Sipylus, Laodicea on the Lycus, Stratonicea and Tabae in Caria, Rhodes, probably Cos, some cities in Lycia, perhaps also Ephesus and Apollonis; also by the favours bestowed on private persons and corporations (the Dionysiac _technitai_). It is not surprising that the cities were unable to meet their financial obligations from their accumulated resources, and were forced to borrow money and to pledge their public buildings, their municipal customs duties, and other revenues.[16]

It was not so much the amount demanded that caused difficulty as the necessity of paying it at once and the extraordinary and brutal method of exacting it. For the payment both of the $\phi\acute{o}\rho o\varsigma$ and of the fine the cities were made jointly responsible. The _publicani_ were eliminated for a time. The cities were required to deliver the sums collected from the taxpayers to the agents of Sulla direct. To make the collection effective Sulla divided Asia in forty-four regions and appointed one of his legates, with an armed force at his disposal, to each region.

The withdrawal of the *publicani* was of course not permanent. They certainly returned on the heels of Sulla's army. Plutarch and Appian speak of them as oppressing the cities alongside of the money-lenders. They may have continued to collect the yearly taxes, including the *decuma*, and to manage the public estates of the Roman People, but the point is disputed. A passage in Cicero suggests that after Sulla's time they had nothing to do with the *decuma*, which was collected, like the *phoros* and the fine, directly by the cities. But they may have secured the contracts for the collection of the *scriptura* and the *portoria* and for the management of the public estates. In any case they did not disappear from the province. Being present and in possession of money (the crisis produced on the Roman money market by the massacre of 88 B.C. was severe but of short duration), they probably took part in the money-lending operations of the professional bankers.[17]

As might be expected, it proved impossible, despite all the efforts of the legates of Sulla, to collect in one year the full sum imposed by him on Asia. After his departure his quaestor Lucullus was commissioned to carry on the collection. Lucullus did the best he could during the four years that he held the office (84–80 B.C.). His work was highly praised by contemporaries, e.g. by Cicero. According to Plutarch* he endeavoured to moderate and humanize the methods of the money-lenders and tax-collectors and to overcome the fierce resistance of the cities, which persisted in spite of the punitive expeditions of Sulla. He succeeded in pacifying the cities, but even he was not able to collect in full the sums due from them. Ten years later there were still enormous arrears, with which Lucullus had to deal at the time of the third Mithridatic war.[18]

The first Mithridatic war came like a violent storm, and left Greece and Asia Minor in ruins. But recovery was not impossible. A few years of peace and benevolent administration would have gradually helped the stricken inhabitants to their feet again. Unfortunately peace and rest were not accorded.

When Sulla left Greece (83 B.C.) he was faced in Italy with a dangerous civil war. His army was not large and his financial resources were insufficient for the conduct of prolonged

* *Luc.* 4. 1.

hostilities. It was natural that he should reinforce his army in Greece and Macedonia by compulsory levies* and demand a heavy contribution from the countries that provided his financial resources—Greece, Macedonia, and Asia Minor. Appian† says expressly that during the civil war in Italy 'all the provinces and the allied kings and the cities, not only tributary cities, but those also which had surrendered on special conditions under special oath or were as allies, or for some service, autonomous and immune, all of them were now ordered to pay contributions and to serve. Some of them lost part of their territory or the revenue from their harbours given to them by treaty.'

Some traces may be found of these εἰσφοραί in Greece. I have mentioned the ὀκτώβολος εἰσφορά of Messene, which may be assigned to these years. Similar contributions were paid, perhaps at the same time, by Sparta.‡ The city was over-burdened with imposts (ἐπιτάγματα), some of which were in arrear. It had recourse to a voluntary contribution (ἐπίδοσις) from well-to-do citizens, and obtained a loan from a certain Diotimus, probably a banker.

Appian's allusion to the confiscation of the harbour revenues of allied cities may perhaps find an illustration in the well-known *lex Gabinia-Calpurnia* of 58 B.C. relating to Delos. The island had at one time been *sacra lib[era et immunis]*, but probably at some moment in its late history was subjected to *vectigalia*.§ The law in question restores the immunity of Delos. May we not connect the suspension of its immunity with the measures of Sulla described by Appian? Delos, it will be noticed, had no navy and was unable to supply ships like other maritime cities.[19]

Finally, I may suggest that the renewal in 72 B.C., by a special tribunician law, of the privileges of the city of Termessus in Pisidia—privileges granted, some of them as early as 91 B.C., others after the first Mithridatic war—may have been connected with subsequent encroachments on these privileges by the Roman administration. Of these encroachments the earliest

---

* Peloponnesians and Macedonians, App. *B.C.* i. 79.
† Ibid. i. 102.   ‡ *I.G.* v. 1. 11.
§ Special mention is made of the duty [*pro* ?] *custodia publica fe* . . (or *fr* . .).

may have been the εἰσφοραί of Sulla, and his confiscation or seizure of the customs duties of the city.*[20]

It was apparently C. Antonius Hybrida, left perhaps in Greece by Sulla in command of a small force, who carried on the enforcement of Sulla's orders as regards the contributions. His work was continued by C. Cornelius Dolabella, governor of Macedonia (81–78 B.C.), whose legate was the notorious Verres. It is unnecessary to remind the reader of all the misdeeds committed by Verres during his residence in Greece and Asia Minor.[21] I have already mentioned that it was Lucullus who was in charge of the collection of funds in Asia.

The first Mithridatic war left behind it a grievous legacy in the Aegean Sea, in the form of piracy. It is well known that the pirates were allies of Mithridates and took an active part in the war. In his day Cilician pirates throve as never before, and the Cretans resumed their old profession. Sulla and his quaestor Lucullus were unable to restrain their depredations effectively. After the end of the war their ranks were joined by large numbers of those who had sided with Mithridates and who had profited by his social revolution, especially slaves liberated by him. Piracy became an intolerable nuisance.

The first expedition against the pirates after the departure of Sulla was organized in 82 B.C. by A. Terentius Varro, legate of L. Licinius Murena governor of Asia, and was connected with the so-called second Mithridatic war, the war of Murena against Mithridates. This expedition has left several traces in our literary texts and in inscriptions. It was probably conducted on a large scale and with success. Varro's fleet consisted exclusively of ships supplied by various Greek cities. Cicero† mentions ten Milesian ships. An inscription in the temple of Zeus Urius was dedicated by Coan marines who served in Varro's fleet.‡ And finally three dedicatory inscriptions (two were recently found at Cos and the third may have

---

* Note that the immunity of the city from ἐπισταθμία and εἰσφοραί and the right of the city to collect customs duties according to its own νόμος ὠνῆς (except from the *publicani*) are dealt with in detail (*Lex de Termess.*, col. ii. 1. 7 ff. and 1. 33 ff.).

† *Verr.* II. i. 34, 87.   ‡ *I.G.* xii. 8. 260.

come from the same place) were set up respectively by a detachment of the Rhodian navy, by the Milesian crew of an ἄφρακτος, and by Halicarnassians who served on a quadrireme.[22]

Cicero describes how the strong fleet of Varro was got together:* 'decem enim naves iussu L. Murenae populus Milesius ex pecunia vectigali populo Romano fecerat, sicut pro sua quaeque parte Asiae ceterae civitates.' Does this mean that the sum required for ship-building was deducted from the yearly payments (*phoros*) due by the cities to the Roman State under Sulla's dispositions? Or are we to suppose that the *pecunia vectigalis* was an addition to the regular tribute? The second appears to have been the usual arrangement, that of Sulla before Varro and of Pompey and Valerius Flaccus after him.† In any case the contribution was paid in one way or another by all the cities of the province either in kind or in money.[23]

We know that Varro was tried later on a charge of *repetundae* in Rome and was acquitted as the result of shameless bribery. It is certain that his conduct in the collection of the naval contributions from the *socii*, like that of Flaccus later, was dishonest and arbitrary.[24]

Varro was succeeded by P. Servilius Vatia (78 B.C.), whose Isaurian expedition was supported by naval action against the Cilician strongholds of the pirates. It is certain that his fleet consisted of ships supplied by the Greek cities of Asia Minor. It is tempting to connect an Athenian inscription in honour of a navarch with this expedition. The stone is decorated with crowns within which are named crews of his τριημιολίαι, the κοινόν of the Lycians, the cities of Phaselis, Myra, Side, Celenderis, Cythnos, and Athens.‡ It is unnecessary to assume that the person honoured commanded a detachment of ships supplied by Athens; he may have been a Rhodian. The date of the inscription, however, is uncertain; it can equally well be assigned to the time of Pompey's great operations against the pirates. I may also mention that three inscriptions from Xanthus in Lycia § tell us of the victories and services of a

---

* *Verr.* II. i. 35. 89.   † Cic. *Pro Flacco*, 14. 33.
‡ *I.G.* ii.² 3218.
§ *O.G.I.* 552, 553, 554; *T.A.M.* ii. 1. 264, 265, 319.

PLATE CIV

Circular support or base of a trophy. Base and trophy were probably dedicated to Mars by a victorious Roman general. Italic marble. H. 1·04 m. The slightly damaged bas-relief which covers the surface of the base (except the rear, which is adorned with a bucranium) shows a scene of sacrifice. A bearded man wearing a winged helmet and a belted cuirass, and holding a spear, is pouring a libation over a square altar, on which a fire is burning and fruit is piled, before a triad of gods: Mars, wearing a crested helmet and cuirass and holding a trophy and a spear, Venus Genetrix with sceptre and mirror, and Vulcan in his usual dress and with his usual attributes. As he pours the libation, the armed man is being crowned by a Victory. The central figure of the bas-relief may be an anonymous victorious general of the time of the civil wars who adopted the Greek fashion of wearing a beard (his beard is very similar to those of Philip V and Perseus of Macedonia, see pl. VII, 5), or a half-mythical figure—Aeneas or Romulus—identified with or personifying one of the victorious leaders of the period that followed Caesar's death. The base is not dated, but we may safely assign it to the years after 46 B.C. (the figure of Venus Genetrix was first created for the temple dedicated to her by Julius Caesar in 46 B.C.), but before the establishment of the principate when the sculptors were working in quite a different style. The sculptures of the base have been carefully studied by R. Herbig, *Röm. Mitt.* xlii (1927), pp. 129 ff., and pls. XV–XIX, cf. F. W. Goethert, *Zur Kunst der römischen Republik*, 1931, p. 20, and Mrs. E. Strong, *C.A.H.* ix, p. 829 f. and vol. of pls. IV, p. 90. Here reproduced from a photograph of the cast of the base exhibited in the Mostra Augustea. The photograph was made at my request by the authorities of the Mostra.

PLATE CIV

THE CONQUERORS OF THE HELLENISTIC EAST

Cività Castellana, Cathedral

certain Aechmon, commander of the Lycian army and navy, who fought the pirates. He may have done this in the service of the Lycians and not at the bidding of the Romans, or he may have been one of the local generals under the command of Servilius Isauricus.[25] The cities of Asia Minor, while they were robbed and pillaged by the pirates, had in addition to bear the burden of the war, known as the second Mithridatic war, initiated by Murena, a sort of prelude to the third Mithridatic war. Greece of course suffered from the pirates no less than Asia Minor. Moreover her northern neighbours were more restless than before, for they were supported and instigated by Mithridates.[26]

Then came the third Mithridatic war. Greece was not affected by it directly, but it was a very unhappy period in her history. The pirates greatly hampered the operations of Lucullus against Mithridates. A vigorous effort was made to curb their activity. A special command was created, the precursor of that held by Pompey. M. Antonius, father of the great Antony, was appointed commander-in-chief with *infinitum imperium* (74 B.C.). He achieved nothing, but was a great burden on the Greek cities. So Cicero states expressly,* and several inscriptions support his statement. It is perhaps an accident that all the inscriptions connected with this war come from the Peloponnese, but it may be suggested that Gythium and Epidaurus, where the inscriptions were found, were the naval bases of Antonius. In fact, these two cities were good starting-points for his expedition against Crete, which ended in complete disaster.

The inscriptions from Gythium and Epidaurus speak of contributions, compulsory levies, billeting of soldiers, and the existence of famine and financial distress in the two cities. A few remarks regarding these inscriptions will make it easier to understand the situation of Greece at this time, and to realize the implications for the Greek cities of so apparently harmless an operation as an expedition against pirates. The first inscription is a decree of Epidaurus in honour of Euanthes.†　Antonius placed a strong garrison in the city, thereby creating difficulties in the matter of food-supply and causing a shortage

---

* *Verr.* II. iii. 91. 213.   † *I.G.* iv.² 66.

of grain (σπάνις σίτου). Euanthes, as *agoranomos*, was nevertheless able to procure a sufficiency of the latter and sold it at
about half the current price. In addition, he helped the city to
celebrate a festival and on this occasion paid for a sacrifice and
for a banquet and made a general distribution of grain at the
rate of half a medimnus a head. Though he himself enjoyed
immunity (ἀτέλεια), he acted as *agonothetes* during the Dionysia,
and finally, when a levy of soldiers was ordered, he was able to
obtain exemption from it for the city. It is tempting to refer
to the same time another inscription from Epidaurus, a decree
in honour of Aristobulus,* a benefactor of the city, who sold it
grain at a moment of difficulty.

Still more explicit are two inscriptions from Gythium. One
is the famous decree of the city in honour of its rich bankers,
the two brothers Cloatii.† The city contracted several loans
with them and received help from them on several occasions in
connexion with various burdens imposed on the city. First
came a compulsory levy and various requisitions. The Cloatii
intervened with P. Autronius and L. Marcilius (whom they
entertained in their own house, thus relieving the city from
this heavy obligation) and secured the city's liberation from
these burdens. A little later the *legati* of Antonius, C. Julius,
P. Autronius, and Fulvius, appeared in the city and once more
the Cloatii intervened in its favour. Then C. Gallius demanded
from the city a contribution of grain, and Q. Ancharius a supply
of clothing, contributions which had been spread over the
cities of Greece (in accordance with Sulla's procedure). Again
the Cloatii intervened and with success. Finally Antonius
himself arrived, and imposed a heavy εἰσφορά on the city. It
had no funds and no one would lend it money. The Cloatii
agreed to lend it 4200 drachmas at 48 per cent., but reduced
the rate of interest the following year to 24 per cent.

We have a fine picture of nobility of character in the second
inscription from Gythium, a decree in honour of a physician,
Damiadas, a Lacedaemonian.‡ He served the city for two
years as its doctor and showed himself 'worthy of his profession'.§ He never discriminated between rich and poor, slave

* *I.G.* iv.² 65.   † *S.I.G.*³ 748.   ‡ *I.G.* v. 1. 1145.
§ l. 22 f., ἄξιος γινό[μενος τᾶς] τέχνας ἇς μεταχειρίζεται.

and free. After holding his office for two years, in the year of Biadas (73/2 B.C.), he saw the city 'overburdened and exhausted by contributions' (ἐξαντλου]μέναν ἐν ταῖς εἰσφοραῖς) and offered it his professional services for nothing.[27]

Thus the period from the end of the first Mithridatic war to the end of the third afforded Greece no breathing-space in which to recover from its sufferings. The same is true of Asia Minor. The province of Asia itself was not affected by the third war directly, for the hostilities were confined to Bithynia and Pontus, and these were utterly devastated. The Greek commercial cities that alone had escaped the miseries of the last fifteen years—Cyzicus, Heraclea, Sinope, and Amisus—now experienced the horrors of a siege, the last three even of capture and pillage.

Though not affected directly by the war, Asia had to bear certain burdens similar to those which were imposed on Greece. Lucullus' fleet was recruited exclusively in his own province. When the Senate offered him 3,000 talents for the construction of a fleet he proudly declined the grant, saying that he would overcome Mithridates at sea with the help of the *socii* alone.* In addition the province certainly supplied the army of Lucullus with food and other requisites, and its cities furnished it with winter quarters. Meanwhile the province was still suffering under the pressure of Sulla's contributions, which were not yet discharged in full. Arrears were accumulating, debts were growing, and hardships becoming more severe. The loans contracted with the *negotiatores* and *publicani*, though twice discharged by the cities *de facto*, had constantly increased *de jure*, and now (in 71–70 B.C.), if we are to believe the correctness of the statement and of the text of Plutarch,† amounted to the fabulous sum of 120,000 talents. Plutarch gives a terrible picture of the consequences of this monstrous situation. Some of the debtors were forced to sell their sons and daughters, and were themselves reduced to slavery. Cities sold their votive offerings, pictures, and sacred statues. Torture was freely resorted to. Plutarch may have exaggerated the amount of the debt and the sufferings of the population, and probably did so in order to glorify his hero Lucullus. But

* Plut. *Luc.* 13. 4; see note 29.   † Ibid. 20. 4.

the fact cannot be denied that cruel misdeeds were perpetrated and that dishonesty reigned at this time in the province.

Lucullus after his decisive successes—the capture of Heraclea and Amisus—returned to Asia (71–70 B.C.) and devoted himself to setting his province in order. His measures appear in two groups, recorded, the one by Appian,* and the other by Plutarch.† Plutarch speaks of the liquidation of loans contracted by the cities. Three measures were adopted to enable debtors to satisfy their creditors: the rate of interest was reduced to the normal 12 per cent. *per annum*, all (arrears of) interest which exceeded the principal were struck off, and finally the amount payable annually to the creditor was restricted to the fourth part of the debtor's income. Moreover, any creditor who added interest to the principal (charged compound interest) forfeited the whole of his claim.

Appian on the other hand records certain measures taken by Lucullus to facilitate the payment of the arrears of Sulla's contribution. He says that Lucullus imposed new taxation, probably of a temporary character. Landowners were required to pay a tax of 25 per cent. of the harvest, and a tax on slaves and on houses was introduced. These taxes were probably collected by the cities themselves, since the system of tax-collection instituted by Sulla—by which the *publicani* were eliminated—was still in force in 71 B.C.[28]

The measures of Lucullus, if we may believe Plutarch, had an almost immediate effect: in less than four years (that is, before Pompey took charge of the province) 'the debts were all paid and the properties restored to their owners unencumbered'.

But Lucullus, successful as he was in his war with Mithridates, was helpless against the pirates. His fleet—mostly recruited from the Greek cities—was not strong enough even to prevent the capture and sack of Delos (in 69 B.C.) by a daring pirate Athenodorus. C. Valerius Triarius, the commander of the Roman fleet, arrived too late to save the city. It had already been sacked before he reached the island. Nevertheless, he was highly praised by the Delians for having fortified the city

* *Mithr.* 83.   † *Luc.* 20. 23.
‡ Phleg. Trall. 12, in *F.H.G.* iii. p. 606.

after Athenodorus' raid. The fate of Delos was no exception.
The pirates had never been so daring as they were during the
first phase of the third Mithridatic war. For a detailed account
of their activities, I must refer the reader to the vivid narra-
tives of Appian* and Plutarch.† [29]

Nor is this the place to discuss the great naval expedition of
Pompey against the pirates (67 B.C.), preceded by the occupation of Crete by Metellus. Suffice it to say that Pompey
succeeded in a few months in clearing the sea of most of these
pests. Of course the cities of Greece had again to pay contributions and to supply ships. Sulla's system of distributing
the burden among the cities was again put into force (above,
p. 948 f.). But the result compensated for the sacrifices. The
sea was almost free of pirates.

When Pompey in 66 B.C. succeeded Lucullus as commander-
in-chief in the East, his administrative policy was as fair and
just as that of Lucullus. The *publicani*, who had probably
succeeded in 70 B.C. in resuming their function of collectors of
the *decuma*, and in addition had been enriched by collecting the provincial taxes in Bithynia, kept quiet and behaved
with moderation for a time.

2. FROM THE TIME OF MITHRIDATES TO THE CIVIL WARS

The period that followed the pacification of Asia Minor by
Lucullus (70 B.C.) and Pompey's war with the pirates (67 B.C.)
was one of peace in the Hellenistic world, interrupted only by
invasions of the Thracians, Celts, and Illyrians in the Balkan
peninsula and of Arabs and Parthians in the new province of
Syria. It lasted continuously for about twenty years until the
outbreak of the civil war between the Senate and Caesar. We
should expect this period to be not only one of peace but also
of recovery. The economic development of the constituent
parts of the Hellenistic world may accordingly be considered
from this point of view.

A certain recovery is noticeable in the province of Asia, and
particularly in the cities to which Sulla had granted valuable
privileges, known to us with certainty through official documents: the law regarding the privileges of Termessus and the

* *Mithr.* 91–6.   † *Pomp.* 24.

Senatus consulta regarding Stratonicea and Tabae.[30] Exempted from federal taxes, from extraordinary contributions from requisitions, and from the burden of billeting (ἐπισταθμία) in undisputed possession of the revenues from their land, their public buildings, and their harbours, enjoying in addition in some cases the privilege of *asylia* for themselves and for the temples in their respective territories, these cities were able to devote part of their resources to 'luxuries'. We hear that certain cities, Tralles and Miletus and probably some others restored their municipal games, which had been suspended since the first Mithridatic war.[31] Building activity was resumed in some of the most important cities, such as Samos and Halicarnassus, 'which'—with some other cities—'had fallen into ruin and almost into desolation'.* Cicero† ascribes the revival of these places to the blessings of his brother's government, but we must take this *cum grano salis*. It is certain that building work started afresh in several cities because the *bourgeoisie* began to recover from their wounds. And this is not surprising, for the province of Asia was a very rich country and retained a reputation for wealth even at the time we are considering. I may quote the well-known passage of Cicero:‡ 'Asia'—as contrasted with the other provinces—'is so rich and fertile, that in the productiveness of its land, the variety of its crops, the range of its grazing, and the quantity of commodities that are exported, it is superior to all other countries'. The recovery of Tralles, for example, certainly must be ascribed to the fertility of its territory—exceptional even in Asia Minor—and to its advantageous situation as regards commerce. Strabo describes the city as one of the richest and most populous of the province.[32]

The recovery of which I am speaking is manifested not only in the few random facts that I have cited. More important is the general tone of the literary texts and especially of Cicero's references to Asia Minor in the days of Lucullus and Pompey. Behind the complaints and bitter censures of Roman administration that are found in all the literature of the time, especially in Cicero's letters and speeches, we are conscious of a background of quiet undisturbed work which the people are

* Cic. *Ad Q. Fr.* i. 1. 25.   † Loc. cit.   ‡ *De imp. Pomp.* 6. 14.

pursuing in every economic sphere: agriculture, industry, and commerce. We get glimpses of a life of ease and comparative comfort in most of the Anatolian cities. In Cicero's speeches and in his letters we meet many representatives of the Anatolian *bourgeoisie*. The majority of them are quiet, well-to-do, respectable citizens, well-known and highly respected in Rome, and maintaining friendly relations with the leading Roman families.

It would seem therefore as if the times of the Attalids and of the early Roman domination had returned, at least in a measure, and as if, after the great hardships of the days of Mithridates and Sulla, the *bourgeoisie* of Asia (of the rural population we know nothing and very little of the city proletariat) had been able to resume its habitual pursuits and the accumulation of wealth. Such is the general impression that one derives from a careful and unbiased reading of our sources of information. This impression is confirmed by the later history of the country. Unless we assume at least a partial economic recovery, we shall not be able to understand how Asia Minor, in the general turmoil of the civil wars, hard pressed as it was by the rulers of the day, could withstand this pressure and supply the revolutionary leaders with the material means of conducting their disastrous wars.

The recovery to which I refer was due to many factors. The most important were the great resources of Asia Minor and its highly developed economic life, firmly established in most of the Anatolian cities. Next comes the liberal attitude of the Roman government towards taxation. The regular taxation imposed by Rome, as described above (cf. below, pp. 965 ff.), was not heavy, less heavy, we may conjecture, than that of the period of the Seleucids and Attalids. It is evident that the principal tax—the tithe of the crops—cannot be regarded as high or oppressive. The cattle tax—*scriptura*—was familiar to Asia and was probably administered on the same lines as under the Attalids. And finally the *portoria*, the customs duties, were probably not higher than in the past or later under the Roman Empire, presumably $2\frac{1}{2}$ per cent. on exports and imports. The other provincial taxes, which corresponded to the former royal taxes, were not permanent as in the past, but, as we have seen and as we shall see later, local and temporary emergency taxes.

It is not easy to estimate the total amount of the revenues that the Roman State derived from the province of Asia and from the other Anatolian provinces. Careful, though necessarily hypothetical, calculations lead to the conclusion that the total in the period with which we are dealing did not exceed 15 million *denarii* a year, a sum which even from a contemporary standpoint, with due attention paid to the rather low intensity of economic life in the ancient world in general, cannot be regarded as very high.[33]

Another important factor in the economic life of the time must not be overlooked: the influx of foreign capital to Asia Minor after the Mithridatic wars and the investment of a large proportion thereof in Anatolian enterprises. This capital was brought to the country by the 'Roman' *negotiatores* who now returned, after having been temporarily driven from Greece, Asia Minor, and the islands by the Mithridatic wars. It is significant that the best and the most copious information about them that we possess, derived both from literary sources and from numerous inscriptions, relates to the period between Sulla and Augustus.[34] The evidence as collected and analysed by Hatzfeld allows us to form a general idea of some aspects of their business in Asia Minor in the middle of the first century B.C. This was not very different from that which they had developed before the time of Sulla (above, pp. 762 ff.). They came back in order to resume their former activities. As in the past, they invested their money chiefly in agriculture, vine- and olive-growing, gardening and grazing. Asia Minor and the islands remained, of course, as before, mainly agricultural countries. In managing their estates, mostly acquired in some way from native landowners, the *negotiatores* inherited the methods which had been evolved under the Attalids and in the early times of Roman domination by the local landowners, that is to say, progressive methods based on experience carefully collected and examined by individual agriculturists and formulated in scores of treatises on agriculture in book form. It is unfortunate that we know hardly anything of these treatises beyond the names of the authors (below, Ch. VIII). We may form some idea of their contents and general character from a study of the versions of them published in Italy (especially Varro's book). But it must be remembered that the Italian manuals of agriculture were not mere translations of Greek and Punic originals, but productions based as much on careful consideration of the economic and physical conditions of Italy and on the accumulated experience of Italian peasants and land-owners as on treatises of foreign origin.[35]

Besides occupying themselves with agriculture, the *negotiatores* certainly participated with the local merchants in the internal and external trade of Asia Minor. Delos, as we have seen, gradually died a natural death. It still existed, but its leading role was played out. Direct commercial relations were established between Asia Minor and Italy, especially with the growing harbour of Puteoli. We are not surprised to find some of the great trading families of Delos established in Asia Minor. Ephesus was probably the chief centre of the Asiatic trade, heir, at least in part, of Delos. It is evident that no important changes in the methods of trade or in the character of the goods exchanged took place in the Greek world at this time, except that for some time after the extermination of the pirates the slave trade temporarily declined.[36]

Much of the activity of the *negotiatores* was devoted as before to banking operations, especially to loans of different kinds. There had been a heavy drain on the accumulated capital of Asia and the islands in the time of Mithridates and Sulla, and the market was therefore scantily supplied with ready money. On the other hand, money was urgently needed for the revival of agriculture, industry, and trade, and to satisfy the demands of the Roman government (see below). It was to be expected that both the *negotiatores*, whether new-comers or old residents in the East, and the rich capitalists of Italy, who had plenty of funds to invest, would be ready and eager, in competition with the few surviving local capitalists (for example the former bankers and merchants of Delos), to put their money out at interest.

There are many contemporary references to the credit operations of that time. Public attention was naturally attracted to those of an unusual kind, transactions which often led to cruel and ruthless exactions. We must not forget that among the creditors were many men prominent in Roman political life (for example Pompey, Brutus, Atticus, and others). But alongside of these abnormal operations, frequent as they were, a good deal of ordinary quiet business was proceeding. It appears that this ordinary business was not very different from what it had been in the past. The normal rate of interest seems to have been 12 per cent. yearly. Such at least was the opinion of Lucullus and Cicero.[37]

Economic conditions in Asia in the time of Cicero are well reflected in its coinage. The *cistophori*, the popular Anatolian coins of the previous period, were still minted in many cities, and were still a stable and reliable currency. We have no means of estimating the volume of silver coined in the country at this time. It is highly probable that the number of mints was reduced and that the minting was concentrated in a few of the richer and stronger cities such as Ephesus. But we know from Cicero that the *cistophori* were still at this time the predominant currency of Asia, supplemented in times of emergency by temporary issues made by the Roman magistrates. Of these issues the only examples known to us belong to the time of Sulla and to that of the civil war.[38]

I have indicated above the symptoms that point to a gradual economic recovery in Asia Minor during the period that preceded the civil wars. But the extent of this recovery must not be overstated: it was partial and local. Its limited character was due exclusively to the misgovernment of the Asiatic provinces, which reached its culminating point during the confusion that prevailed between Pompey's return to Italy and the beginning of the civil war between him and Caesar. The vices of the administrative and financial system adopted by Rome in the provinces are seen at their worst in this period of political anarchy and distress.

Her general policy in the provinces remained, no doubt, unaltered, and need not be discussed here. The system of administration may be regarded as in itself efficient and well adapted to the conditions of the time and to the aims and ends of the Roman government. But it was unquestionably in its main features a 'colonial' system of government, based on the dea of the predominance of the conquerors over the conquered, f one people or race over the other, of the *Romani rerum omini* over the provincials. Such a government may be ometimes just and efficient, but it is always arrogant, arbirary, selfish, and often ruthless and cruel.

In the Greek territories this system of government was omewhat modified and mitigated by the respect that the Romans felt for Greek civilization, for the Greek past, for the Greek genius. But this admiration for the Greek past never prevented the Romans from regarding most contemporary Greeks with deep contempt, while recognizing their cleverness and their intellectual gifts. They viewed with peculiar disdain he Greeks of mixed descent, the Levantines, such as the Mysians', 'Lydians', 'Phrygians', who in fact at this period were as good Greeks as the Greeks of the mainland.[39]

Amid the turbulent conditions of the Mithridatic wars Roman philhellenism became little more than an empty formula and hardly affected the conduct of the masters of the East. There was no lack, even at this time, of just and honest men among the Roman senators. The Senate and the courts of law stood in principle for a fair and just treatment of the provinces. But the provincial administration rapidly degenerated and became more and more 'colonial' in the corrupt atmosphere of the Roman political life of this time. Men like Lucullus, Pompey, the two Ciceros, and Servilius Isauricus the younger became rare exceptions; they knew that they were exceptions and emphasized the fact repeatedly in their actions and in their public and private utterances.[40]

At the moment with which we are dealing, when one civil war had come to an end and another was in prospect, the despotic, self-seeking, almost anarchical character of the provincial government reached its climax. No doubt, it is not easy to assign their proper weight to Cicero's praise of Valerius Flaccus or his denunciations of Gabinius and Piso. We must be careful to take with a grain of salt his panegyric of the administration of Asia by his brother Quintus and the contrast he draws between his own administration of Cilicia and that of Appius. But after making all allowances one must still admit that in respect of administrative methods the short period of peace which I am considering was no better, but perhaps worse, than that of the Mithridatic wars which preceded it.

It is unnecessary to collect once more, chiefly from the works of Cicero, the material relating to the proceedings of the officials and of the tax-contractors in the Eastern provinces at this time, for this has been done repeatedly. It will be sufficient to indicate the principal features of the situation and some outstanding facts. The burden which pressed most severely on the taxpayers was not the regular taxes, which were not heavy. Far more exasperating, as I have pointed out, were the irregular payments imposed by the administration, and all sorts of requisitions. The demands of this kind, the distribution of the charges, and the methods of collection (carried out as a rule by special agents of the government) were of an arbitrary character. We should have expected these irregular and despotic measures to disappear from the surface after the end of the Mithridatic wars. But it was not so. The governors availed themselves of their power of imposing them, on the flimsiest pretext, not so much for the benefit of the State as for their own profit.

I have already mentioned the introduction of new temporary taxes by Lucullus as an emergency measure and as the most effective and least oppressive way of liquidating the arrears of the ill-fated fine exacted by Sulla. The same extraordinary measure was resorted to, probably on the pretext of the Parthian threat and with very little justification, by Appius Claudius in his province of Cilicia. An extraordinary *tributum*, a head-tax (ἐπικεφάλαιον, *exactio capitum*) and a house-tax (*exactio ostiorum*), were imposed by him and levied ruthlessly and cruelly. When Cicero was on his way to his province he was overwhelmed with the complaints of the cities: ' we heard ' he says in his letter to Atticus, ' nothing in the cities, but that they could not pay the ἐπικεφάλαια that have been imposed; that their ὠναί (leases of the taxes) were all sold; groans and lamentations everywhere '. He certainly means that a sum had been imposed on each of the cities of his province calculated *pro capite* of its population, and its immediate payment required. The cities were not able to pay the sums imposed on them, for all the taxes had been let to and paid for by the contractors and the money had been spent. Cicero himself was indignant and in full sympathy with the oppressed cities. He describes the proceedings of Appius as 'acts of savagery worthy of some wild beast, rather than of a man'.[41]

I have repeatedly referred to the heavy burden involved in the obligation of the *socii* to contribute to the conduct of wars by supplying the Roman State with an efficient navy. It might be expected that such levies would disappear after the pacification of the Aegean by Pompey and the end of the Mithridatic war, and that emergency levies would be replaced by some more satisfactory and better organized system. But, once established and legalized by the Roman government, levies of ships became a routine, and the right of mobilizing Greek ships for the use of the government or of raising a special naval contribution was freely exercised by the successors of Pompey on the pretext that the Aegean was not completely free of pirates (which of course was true) and that the existence of a strong fleet in Aegean waters was the best way of preventing their recrudescence. The general idea was sound and a permanent fleet was necessary for the policing of the sea. But to deal with the problem by means of repeated emergency measures was outrageous and vexatious, though in conformity with the special laws voted by the people and confirmed by the Senate. The distribution of the burden and the collection of ships, men, and money were entirely in the hands of the governor. The procedure was that adopted by Sulla for the collection of his fine and probably for the formation of his navy, and the practice had been followed later by all those who assembled a fleet for the Roman people in Aegean waters (see above), including Pompey himself. Special agents were employed, assisted by soldiers, and their way of dealing with the matter was arbitrary and ruthless. It was certainly the worst possible method of organizing an effective defence of the long coast-line of Asia Minor, the islands, and Greece. The complaints put forward by the province of Asia against Valerius Flaccus in this respect were certainly fully justified, and Cicero found it difficult to defend his client against them. It is not surprising that more honest governors, like Q. Cicero, preferred to dispense with a permanent fleet in order to prevent abuses and to remove the well-founded grievances of the *socii*.[42]

The Mithridatic wars were over, but the emergency war measures were not. Like the levy of ships, they became a recurrent charge, which pressed severely on the provincials. The army stationed in the Anatolian provinces was not large. Nevertheless, the burden imposed on the cities of providing winter quarters for detachments of troops remained heavy. The requisitions of various kinds for the needs of the army were no less onerous. Even more burdensome were the constant demands, connected with movements from place to place of the provincial administration, for means of transport, food, and quarters; and that not only for the regular staff, but also for officials travelling on tours of inspection and for holders of *legationes liberae*. These persons were arrogant in behaviour and exacting in their requirements. Never before had the complaints of these evils been so bitter and so frequent. We hear frequently, for example, of the *frumentum aestimatum* and *cellae nomine* for the governor and his staff.* Cicero is never weary of insisting that he and his staff never have recourse to such measures, though in themselves they were not illegal but in full accordance with the traditions of Roman administration.†[43]

No doubt none of these demands made by the authorities on the population were new to the inhabitants of Asia Minor and other parts of the Hellenistic world. I have more than once referred to them in earlier chapters and shown that they formed part of the fiscal system of all the Hellenistic kingdoms, especially of Egypt. Such were, for example, the ἐπισταθμία— the quartering of troops—and the ἀγγαρεῖαι and παρουσίαι— the obligation imposed on the population of transporting, housing, and feeding the ruler, his officials, and his military forces when they moved from place to place. The Hellenistic kings also resorted freely to requisitions of various kinds, especially in time of war, but mostly in enemy countries.[44]

It was not, therefore, any novelty in these exactions that exasperated the population. It was the fact that they were prescribed by foreigners, and enforced with arrogance, and often in a manner contrary to the Roman law (*Lex Porcia* and later *Lex Iulia*) and to Hellenistic tradition.

* Cic. *Verr.* II. 3. 83. 192, cf. 191 ; 90. 209 f. ; *Pro Flacco*, 45.
† *Ad Att.* v. 10. 2 ; 16. 3 ; 21. 5.

One of the principal grievances of the population was the Roman system of tax-collection. Even Cicero, a political friend of the *publicani* and partner in many *societates vectigalium*, recognizes explicitly the irreconcilable conflict between their interests and those of the provincials; he admits likewise the selfish and ruthless conduct of the former. I may recall the well-known passage in his letter to Quintus concerning the *publicani*:* 'However, to your good will and careful policy the great obstacle lies in the *publicani*: for if we oppose them, we alienate from ourselves and the State an order which has deserved exceedingly well of us and which has been linked to the State by our efforts; if on the other hand we comply with them in every case, we shall allow the complete ruin of those for whose welfare and interests we are bound to have regard.' Similar utterances occur frequently in his letters and orations and in other writings of the time. 'The publican is a nuisance' was a commonplace in the first century B.C.; another, that it was the duty of every honest administrator to combat them. What was the reason of the disfavour with which they were regarded? I have touched upon the Roman system of taxation and tax-collection in the eastern provinces in the section of this book which deals with pre-Sullan times. Our information in respect of that period is very poor; for that which we are now considering it is somewhat better. I will therefore resume the topic and endeavour to reconstruct, in its main outlines, the Roman fiscal system in the East.[45]

The evidence available relates, in the main, to the province of Asia. Some additional information concerns the later Roman provinces: Cilicia, Bithynia, Pontus, Syria, Cyprus. Very little is known of Macedonia and Greece.

In the province of Asia, and probably in the other eastern provinces likewise, there existed before Sulla's time, during his time, and also later, two groups of regular taxes. One was that of the Roman provincial taxes collected by agents of the Roman government for its treasury. The other was that of the local municipal taxes. I will first deal briefly with the former.

I have already mentioned the three regular provincial taxes—the *decuma*, the *scriptura*, and the *portoria*—and the

* Cic. *Ad Q. Fr.* i. 1. 11, 32.

various emergency taxes. The three regular taxes were farmed out before Sulla's day and again in the period we are studying to associations of contractors, the *societates vectigalium publicorum*, that is to say, to the *publicani*. In addition, the *publicani* managed (*frui*, καρπίζειν: see above, p. 748 f.) the estates of the Roman people in Asia. I have already (pp. 814 ff.) dealt with the question of the arable *ager publicus* in the province of Asia. Besides this we hear of the salt-pans, and we may add the mines, quarries, forests, fisheries, &c.

The other group of taxes comprised the municipal taxes inherited from the past, and already mentioned by me. These were collected according to ancient tradition by municipal tax-collectors, *telonai*, on behalf of the particular city. The Roman *publicani* had nothing to do with them. Contractors were also engaged to manage the public estates of the cities. Some cities were exempt from Roman provincial taxation.[46]

We have no information regarding the mode of collection of the provincial taxes by the *publicani* before Sulla's time. Sulla, as we have seen, probably eliminated the *societates vectigalium publicorum* from the collection of the *decuma*, but may have left them in charge of the collection of the other provincial revenues. After Sulla, the *decuma* appears to have been administered by the cities themselves, its proceeds being paid to the provincial quaestor. We may assume that the *decuma* was collected by the cities from the taxpayers through the agency of municipal *telonai* (see note 17). The Roman *decuma*, therefore, was at that time a kind of modified Hellenistic φόρος.

When the *publicani*, probably in 70 B.C., succeeded in regaining their hold on the *decuma*, the basis of Sulla's system, that is, the collection of the *decuma* by the cities, was retained. The *publicani* were superimposed on the cities as underwriters and guarantors to the Senate and people of Rome of the full payment of the *vectigalia*.[47] A special *lex censoria* specified the sums to be paid by the *publicani* and the mode of payment, and defined the extent of their rights and duties. Additional regulations were published in the yearly edicts of the provincial governors.[48]

The approximate amount of the payment which every city

was required to make was of course known to the censors in Rome and to the governors of the provinces. The cities had their archives and their accounts were carefully kept.⁴⁹ But the exact amount necessarily varied from year to year, especially in such a country as Asia Minor, where the harvest depends largely on the rainfall.

This is the reason for the existence of yearly contracts or agreements (*pactiones, συγγραφαί*), which were made by the cities with the *publicani*. We know of these *pactiones* and their importance to the cities and to the contractors in Cilicia and Syria, and it is highly probable that they were likewise the basis of tax-collection in Asia and in Bithynia-Pontus. As regards Greece and Macedonia we have no information.⁵⁰

The *pactiones* were settled probably (no information on this point is available) after careful estimates and repeated inspection of the fields and crops by the city authorities and the agents of the *publicani*. The procedure was probably very similar to that followed in Egypt and Sicily. Before and during the harvest representatives of the city and members of the *familia publicanorum* carefully watched the crops and especially the gathering of them and the payment of the *decuma* by the cultivators. Such operations required the employment of a large staff by the *publicani*, not only in the cities but also in the country (*in agris*).⁵¹

We do not know exactly when the *pactiones* were drawn up. Cicero in two of his letters to Atticus* written on his journey to his province at the end of July 51 B.C. (i.e. in June according to the Julian calendar) refers to them as having already been completed. This may suggest that the *pactiones* were settled at the time of the harvest as in Sicily and Egypt.

The contents of the *pactiones* are unknown. But it is certain that they included the amount to be paid, the mode of payment, and the treatment of arrears. In one of his letters to Atticus† Cicero mentions that the contracts made in his province contained provision for exorbitant rates of interest on arrears, provisions confirmed by the edict of Servilius Vatia. But Cicero changed the practice. He allowed a reasonable time for payment with a rate of interest of only 12 per cent. If the

* Quoted in note 49.   † vi. 1. 16.

payment was not made within that period, interest was there‑
after payable at the rate stipulated in the contract. In another
letter* he speaks of all the arrears having been paid to the
publicani by his province during his year of governorship.

The account that I have given of the fiscal system includes
no doubt, many hypothetical elements, for we possess no
detailed information relating to the East. But there are good
grounds for thinking that the system of assessment and
collection there was not very different from that which was in
force in Sicily and which was regulated ultimately by the *Lex
Hieronica*, a modified version of the νόμοι τελωνικοί of the early
Ptolemies. The system was not in itself a bad one. It proved
very efficient in Egypt and in normal times in Sicily. In the
East, however, it had disastrous results. Bidding for the
collection of taxes in the East was essentially a hazardous
enterprise, for success depended on many incalculable factors.
Poor crops, war, raids by pirates, or (as happened in Syria under
Gabinius and in Macedonia under Piso) the stubborn hostility
of governors, might upset the most careful calculations.[52] Still
in most cases, the powerful *societates publicanorum* knew the
situation well and played a safe game; and in case of mis‑
calculation they were able to get reductions from the Senate.[5]

The situation of the cities and of the taxpayers was quite
different. These were adequately protected by the law and the
regulations. Provided that the governors fulfilled their duty
towards the State and its subjects, the taxpayers were safe.
The governors certainly knew the terms of the *pactiones* and
could modify or annul them if necessary.† The trouble lay in
the great power of the *societates publicanorum*, their wealth
and their enormous political influence. They ruined Rutilius
Rufus and Lucullus, and Cicero's speeches show that they
knew how to get the assistance of capable lawyers in under‑
mining the reputation of their enemies Gabinius and Piso.

Another prejudicial factor was the dishonesty of the Greek
magistrates themselves. In the turbulent conditions of the time
they often acted in concert with the *publicani* and peculated
on their own account. Cicero‡ tells how, by gentle pressure

* *Ad Att.* vi. 2. 5.   † Cic. *De prov. cons.* 5, 10 ff.
‡ *Ad Att.* vi. 2. 5.

and after careful investigation, he forced the magistrates of his province to confess their guilt and restore what they had misappropriated.

Accordingly it is not surprising that the main preoccupation of so honest and well-meaning a governor as Cicero, who was at the same time the champion of the *concordia ordinum* and politically dependent on the support of the *equites*, was to find a way of safeguarding the interests of the *publicani* while treating the cities of his province fairly. That is what (in 60 B.C.) he advised his brother Quintus to do* and what he himself did ten years later. The principal stumbling-block lay in the *pactiones*. When these were completed and duly signed, he felt happy.[54]

In many cases, however, the cities were forced to sign unfair and oppressive *pactiones*, which led to arrears and obliged them to borrow at exorbitant interest from the same *publicani* and from other money-lenders in the province and in Rome. The same method was used to meet the payment of the supplementary imposts to which I have referred. Nor were the money-lenders very tender to their clients. It is hardly necessary to recall, for example, the famous case of Brutus and the Salaminians of Cyprus† which caused Cicero so much trouble, but was not regarded by him as anything exceptional. I may remind the reader that the well-disposed benefactors of the city of Gythium—the Cloatii—at first fixed the rate of interest on their loan to the city at 48 per cent., and that the reduction of this rate to 24 per cent. (the legal rate fixed by Cicero in his province was 12 per cent.) was regarded by the city as a great favour (above, pp. 951 ff.).[55]

It is interesting to note that while Cicero and our other authorities supply us with so much information about the relations between the Roman government and the *publicani* on the one hand and the cities of the provinces on the other, they never mention the territories, arable or other, which were not in the control of the cities. Yet such territories existed and yielded revenue to the Roman government (below, note 85). Was the reason that the cities were outspoken and contentious and a source of real danger to the governors and the *publicani*,

* *Ad Q. Fr.* i. 1. 11–12.   † Cic. *Ad Att.* v. 21 ; vi. 1–3.

while the country with its villages was long-suffering and silent? It is hardly possible to suppose that the villages with the land assigned to them were all attributed to one city or another and that their taxes were collected by the city magistrates and the city *telonai*.

It is evident and it was a commonplace in the literature of the time that the *publicani* secured for themselves (including their partners and shareholders) a fair, sometimes an excessive return on the money invested in tax-farming. What the volume of the capital so invested was is unknown and cannot be calculated even approximately. Still less can we form an approximate idea of the net profits of the *societates*, even if we assume that legally they were entitled to no more than 10 per cent. of the amount of each *pactio* as compensation for their risk and trouble. Dealing with large amounts of grain and handling substantial sums of money, the *publicani* certainly did not confine themselves to the business of tax-contractors. They were at the same time important corn-merchants and money-dealers, who engaged in all sorts of banking operations. In these capacities they were dangerous rivals of the local business men.[56]

In the conditions described above, we cannot suppose that life in the province of Asia was altogether tranquil and happy. Nor was it. The policy of the Romans was to establish in the cities of their eastern provinces an aristocratic, or rather an oligarchic régime, the rule of the well-to-do class. The wealthy *bourgeoisie* of the Hellenistic past had always been supported by the Roman government and was now thriving. The facts relating to certain very rich and prominent families of Asia Minor in the second and first centuries B.C. have been set out in the two preceding chapters. A careful study of Cicero, as I have already remarked, would add to this list the names of a number of other men of position, wealth, and culture, members of good Anatolian families, who formed the ruling aristocracy of the cities. The *bourgeoisie* were, no doubt, often cheated and maltreated— to serve private interests—by the provincial government. I have mentioned examples of this, and many others might be added; the speech of Cicero in defence of Flaccus is sufficiently illustrative of this point.

However, these rich Anatolian aristocrats had many friends in Rome and were capable of defending themselves.

Their position in the cities was solidly established. They were the masters there and knew how to make use of their opportunities. Rome granted many of them the privilege of immunity from taxation including exemption from extraordinary imposts, both Roman and municipal. Cases of such grants were frequent from Sulla's time to that of Pompey and became still more frequent in the days of the civil war; Pompey and Caesar, Brutus and Cassius, Antony and Octavian, were lavish in this respect. Some of their supporters even received the grant of Roman franchise in addition to the grant of immunity, as a reward for their services. Evidence on the subject is scanty, but I may recall Euanthes of Epidaurus, who became *agonothetes* while enjoying immunity, and the Cloatii of Gythium who entertained Roman officers in their house although without doubt they had the privilege of ἀνεπιστάθμία (above, pp. 951 ff.). I have mentioned above the *Senatus consultum* of 78 B.C.* conferring immunity on three Greek naval officers. A similar grant was made by Octavian to Seleucus, a navarch of Rhosus in Syria, during the civil war. And there is no doubt that many others succeeded, in one way or another, in obtaining the privileges involved in the grant of immunity.[57] For the cities these grants to individuals were a source of trouble. We know how acutely such favours to Greeks, Italians, and Romans were resented by their fellow-citizens. Those who should have been the first to bear the burden of Roman and municipal taxation and of Roman and municipal liturgies, the richest members of the community, were exempted from them, and the burden was borne entirely by the middle class and the poorer citizens and residents. If the rich chose to assume their share of the burden, this was regarded by themselves and those around them as a benefaction, not as a duty.

No wonder that the Mytileneans complained bitterly of this state of things and insisted that everyone should bear his share of the τέλη, a request which was forwarded to Caesar and settled by him in favour of the city.† Similar conditions

* C.I.L. I². 588.
† I.G. xii. 2. 35, col. b, ll. 26 ff.; I.G.R. iv. 33.

PLATE CV

1. *N* Aureus probably struck in Greece, *c.* 83–82 B.C. *Obv.* L. SVLLA. Head of Venus right, in field, Cupid holding palm branch. *Rev.* IMPER ITERVM. Jug and lituus between two trophies. The obverse honours Venus under whose protection Sulla believed he was granted victory in battle. The jug and lituus of the reverse refer to Sulla's election to the college of Augurs, and the trophies, probably to the battles of Chaeronea (86 B.C.) and Orchomenus (85 B.C.).

2. Æ Tetradrachm of Athens, time of Sulla. *Obv.* Head of Athena. *Rev.* Owl on amphora between two trophies having the same import as those on the coin above (on these coins see n. 7 to this chapter).

3. *N* Stater, Ephesus, 88–84 B.C. *Obv.* Bust of Artemis. *Rev.* ΕΦ. Cultus image of Ephesian Artemis.

4. *N* Stater, Smyrna, 88–84 B.C. *Obv.* Head of Kybele. *Rev.* ΙΜΥΡΝΑΙΩΝ ΠΡΥΤΑΝΕΙΣ. Aphrodite Stratonikis holding Nike.

5. Æ Proconsular cistophorus, Ephesus, 57 B.C. *Obv.* Cista mystica and serpent in ivy wreath. *Rev.* Tripod flanked by serpents; above it, Apollo. The inscriptions give: the name of the mint (ΕΦΕ(ΣΟΣ)), the mint official (ΕΡΜΙΑΣ ΚΑΙΥΣΤΡ), the governor of Asia (T. AMPI. T. F. (T. Ampius Balbus) PROCO(N-) S(VLE)), and the date ΟΖ, year 77 of the Province.

6. Æ Tetradrachm of Gortyn, Crete, *c.* 69 B.C. *Obv.* ΡΩΜΑΣ. Head of Roma in winged helmet adorned with elephant's head; in front, monogram ΚΑ. *Rev.* ΓΟΡΤΥΝ. Ephesian Artemis; in field, bee and elephant's head. The elephant's head, emblem of the Caecilii Metelli, associates this coin with the occupation of Crete by Q. Caecilius Metellus.

7. Æ Tetradrachm of Amyntas of Galatia (36–25 B.C.), struck at Side. *Obv.* Head of Athena. *Rev.* ΒΑΣΙΛΕΩΣ ΑΜΥΝΤΟΥ. Winged Nike holding torch.

8. Æ Julius Caesar, Corinth, *c.* 46–44 B.C. *Obv.* LAVS IVLI CORN. Head of Julius Caesar. *Rev.* Bellerophon mounted on Pegasus, and the names of the duoviri L. CERTO AEFICIO and C. IVLIO.

9. Æ Denarius, struck in the East by L. Plaetorius Cestianus *c.* 43–42 B.C. *Obv.* L. PLAET CEST BRVT IMP. Head of Brutus. *Rev.* EID. MAR. Cap of liberty between two daggers. The reverse commemorates the liberty of the country achieved through the daggers of Cassius and Brutus on the fateful date, the Ides of March.

10. *N* Aureus, *c.* 40 B.C. *Obv.* ANT IMP III VIR R.P.C. (triumvir reipublicae constituendae). Head of Antony. *Rev.* CN DOMIT. AHENOBARBUS IMP. Prow with star above. These coins celebrate the reconciliation of Antony and Ahenobarbus when their fleets met in the Adriatic.

11. *N* Aureus. Probably issued at Sardis, *c.* 43–42 B.C., and coined from booty to be distributed to the soldiers. *Obv.* LEIBERTAS C. CASSI. IMP. Veiled head of Liberty. *Rev.* LENTVLVS SPINT Sacrificial implements. P. Cornelius Lentulus Spinther, member of the college of Augurs, quaestor of Syria, joined Cassius and Brutus in the East.

I may remark that the gold staters of Ephesus and Smyrna of 88–84 reproduced in this plate (and the similar staters of Miletus) were coined by these cities in connexion with their vicissitudes during the first Mithridatic war. The issues were not very abundant. The coins are rare.

PLATE CV

COINS OF THE TIME OF SULLA AND THE CIVIL WARS

prevailed in Cyrene in the time of Augustus, a legacy of the past.[58]

These wealthy members of the upper class were not only free of the burdens that marred the lives of their fellow-citizens, but used their influence and their exclusive right of admission to the magistracy and *Boule* for their personal advantage. I have cited the case of the Phrygian notables who confessed their crime before Cicero. Their case was certainly not exceptional.

It was natural that Asia should be restless. Riots, accompanied by murders, were frequent in the cities. Robber-bands infested the highways, and burglars and thieves made urban life insecure, while denunciations of private enemies poisoned the atmosphere.

These were the conditions when Lucullus was proquaestor and such they remained in the first years of his governorship, and even after his benevolent rule and that of Pompey. Cicero, in his famous letter to his brother Quintus, in trying to glorify his brother's administration, draws a lamentable picture of the state of Asia in 60 and 59 B.C. A passage from this letter may be quoted:* 'It is the duty not only of those who govern allies and citizens but even of those who are in charge of slaves and dumb animals to serve the interests and advantage of those under them. In this respect I see that everybody agrees that you do your utmost: no new *debt* is being contracted by the cities, while many have been freed by you from large and heavy old ones. *New life* has been given by you to many cities that had become dilapidated and almost deserted; among them are one of the most celebrated cities of Ionia and another of Caria—Samos and Halicarnassus. There are no *riots* in the cities, no civil strife. You take care that the cities should be administered by the *best class* (*consiliis optimatium*). *Brigandage* in Mysia has been stamped out. *Murder* (*caedes*—is common murder meant or political assassination?) has been suppressed in many places. *Peace* has been established throughout the province. Not only *robberies* on the highways and in the country have been completely stopped but also the more numerous and more serious thefts

* *Ad Q. Fr.* i. 1. 8. 24 f.

and robberies in the towns and the temples.* *Calumny* (does he mean 'insidious accusations' or 'vexatious prosecutions' or perhaps the activity of *delatores*?), that cruel instrument of the greed of governors, has ceased to undermine the reputation, the fortunes, and the tranquillity of the rich. The *expenses* of the cities and the *taxes* imposed on them are now borne equally by everyone who lives in their territories (Cicero refers of course to the unfair distribution of the burden of taxation and of liturgies and to the privileges granted to the richer and more influential citizens, of which I have spoken above). *Access* to you is as easy as possible, and your ears are open to the complaints of all. No men, however poor and isolated (i.e. unsupported by friends) they may be, are excluded from access to you, not only in public and on the tribunal, but even in your house and private apartment.'

This is a grievous revelation of what Cicero believed to be the 'normal' conditions of life in the province of Asia. Many other passages in his orations and letters confirm the inferences that may be drawn from the above extract.†

The system of government applied by the Romans to their province of Asia was extended to their other Asiatic dominions: the province of Cilicia, first organized about 101 B.C., consolidated by Servilius Vatia, and reorganized by Pompey after 67 B.C.; that of Bithynia, annexed in 74 B.C.; that of Pontus added to Bithynia after the third Mithridatic war; and finally the most recent of the Asiatic provinces, that of Syria annexed by Pompey after his Mithridatic war. I cannot here enter into the history of these countries under Roman rule, especially their organization as Roman provinces, for which in the main Pompey was responsible, for this would far exceed the scope of the present book. I may, however, mention certain facts connected directly or indirectly with the economic changes that took place in these countries in the first years of Roman administration.

---

* The meaning of *furta* and *latrocinia* in this passage is not quite clear: does Cicero mean attacks of robber-bands on the cities and temples or thefts and robberies within them?

† Those passages should be collected and thoroughly examined in the light of contemporary documents. This cannot be done here, but I strongly recommend this subject to the attention of younger fellow-students.

I need not repeat what I had to say of CILICIA when dealing with the province of Asia. It is well known that the name Cilicia' given to the new Roman province was in fact a misnomer. The province in its early days consisted of certain parts of Phrygia, Pisidia, and Pamphylia, of the Milyas, and nominally of Lycia. Cilicia proper was added to this administrative unit by Pompey after he had crushed the Cilician pirates. Cyprus also formed for a time part of the province. For the Romans the province at the outset was chiefly a base of military operations first against the Cilician pirates and afterwards against the mountain tribes that threatened the military roads connecting Asia Minor with Syria.[59]

The coastal part of the province was very rich in natural resources. The soil was exceedingly fertile. The vineyards of Cilicia had been famous from time immemorial. The chief god of the region of Tarsus—Sandon—was a god of fertility and protector of viticulture. His cult flourished at Tarsus in the late Seleucid period and in Roman times. Hellenistic and Roman coins and late Hellenistic terracottas represent him in his temple or in some other cult edifice. No less flourishing than viticulture were the cultivation of flax and the linen industry connected with it. Tarsus was from a very early date and until the late Roman Empire one of the chief centres of linen-weaving, as also were Anazarbus and Corycus. Even more prosperous were the coastal cities of Pamphylia. I have mentioned the important part played by their issues of silver in the commercial life of Syria in the middle of the second century B.C. Nor were the resources of some of the inland cities of this large province less abundant.[60]

The province was consequently the source of a steady and substantial revenue to the Roman treasury and a favourable field for the *publicani*. However, the early days of Roman domination were not a time of prosperity for most of its cities and tribes. Several of the former profited by the development of piracy, especially in its early stage, but most of them suffered heavily from the slave-hunting and the occasional raids of the pirates, especially during the Mithridatic wars. Moreover, the resources of the cities were freely used by Roman governors for the purpose of their operations against the pirates and the predatory tribes of the interior. An excellent picture of the economic life of the province and of the hardships it endured may be found in the letters written by Cicero during the short period of his governorship of Cilicia. I have already utilized this material when speaking of the province of Asia, and the conditions it reveals are the same as those which prevailed in Asia. The chief preoccupations of the cities were their relations with the *publicani* and the military burdens imposed on them by the governors: levies of men, various requisitions, and especially the billeting of soldiers. Cyprus was paying 200 Attic talents a year to secure exemption from furnishing winter quarters for Roman troops, and the free cities of the province (e.g. Termessus) were striving to obtain immunity in this and other respects.[61]

Better times came when Pompey, after his war with the pirates, reorganized the province, especially Cilicia proper. He found some of its cities in utter decay and extreme poverty. We learn from Appian that Pompey repopulated Adana, Epiphania, and Mallus with captured pirates; he probably did the same for Zephyrium, Mopsuestia, and Alexandria, which all adopted the Pompeian era of 67 B.C.[62]

Roman rule in Cilicia did not extend very far inland. The warlike tribes of the interior and the few half-Greek cities were left in the hands of local dynasts, as vassals of Rome. One of them was Tarcondimotus (64–31 B.C.), known from Cicero's mention of him and from the historians of the time, as well as from some inscriptions. His capital was Castabala Hieropolis and his tetrarchy or kingdom was of considerable size. One of the inscriptions gives us a glimpse of the organization of his capital. It was set up by the *demos* of the city in honour of a certain Isidorus, who was chief magistrate (*demiurgos*) and at the same time holder of a court title and military governor (στρατηγός and φυλακάρχης) of the city. He held in addition the office of war minister to the king (ἀρχυπηρέτης τῶν κατὰ τὴν β[α]σιλείαν δυνάμεων). It is interesting to observe the strength of Seleucid influence on the structure of the petty kingdoms of Asia Minor and the similarity of the organization of the cities to that of Cappadocia, Commagene, and especially the urbanized parts of Parthia.[63]

More ancient than the kingdom of Tarcondimotus was that of the Teucrids, the hereditary priest-kings of Olba whom I mentioned above (Ch. IV, n. 230). Their dynasty was dying out, though the kingdom still existed at this time. The rest of the mountainous regions of Cilicia, Pisidia, and Isauria was nominally in the hands of the neighbouring vassal kings of Galatia, Cappadocia, and Commagene, but was in fact independent and a great danger to the more civilized parts of the province.

The northern part of Asia Minor—BITHYNIA, PAPHLAGONIA, and PONTUS—and the great and prosperous Hanse of the north—comprising Cyzicus, Byzantium, Calchedon, Heraclea Pontica, Sinope, and Amisus—were not, with the exception of Cyzicus and Byzantium, directly involved in the first Mithridatic war.[64] A period of misery and distress began for them with the third Mithridatic war. Bithynia, after the death of its last king, became a Roman province in 74 B.C. by the last will and testament of Nicomedes IV. A revolt of the population against the new Roman rule, similar to that of Aristonicus, was quickly followed by the occupation of Bithynia by Mithridates. Immediately after the occupation of the province by the Romans its revenues were farmed out to a *societas publicanorum*. The inclusion of Heraclea, a free city and an ancient and faithful ally of Rome, in the sphere of operations of the *publicani*, in other words its treatment not as an allied but as a subject city (under the pretext that it had furnished supplies to Mithridates, and that two rich citizens had put at his disposal five triremes), aroused the indignation of the people and led to the massacre of the *publicani* and their *familiae.** The Roman treatment of the city probably made it easier for Mithridates to gain possession of it a little later.†

A full narrative of the third Mithridatic war cannot be given here. It will be sufficient to say that it was concentrated at first in Bithynia and later in Pontus. The story of the siege of Cyzicus and of the operations that ensued reveals the severity of the city's sufferings and the thoroughness of the devastation of Bithynia. Then came the turn of Pontus. The principal cities of the Pontic coast—Heraclea, Amisus, Sinope—were

* Memnon 38. † Ibid. 42.

captured by the Romans and suffered heavily. Panticapaeum, the last refuge of Mithridates, was never captured, but its resources and those of the Bosporan kingdom were exhausted by the indomitable king, who before his assassination was preparing a final expedition against Rome.

Of the organization of the province of Bithynia by Lucullus we know nothing, nor do we know much of the *Lex Pompeia*, which reorganized Bithynia and Pontus. It is highly probable that in Bithynia there was no change of system so far as city life, administration, and taxation were concerned. The place of the king was taken by the governor, that of the royal tax-collectors, whether contractors or officials, by the *publicani* and their agents. How much of the χώρα or χώρα βασιλική was assigned to the cities we do not know. Cicero* states positively that the *regnum Bithynicum*—with its *agri, urbes, stagna, portus*—was *publicum populi Romani*; and also that the *agri Bithyniae regii* were in the hands of the *publicani*.† [65]

In Pontus the situation was different. Here Pompey effected a radical reorganization—an urbanization of the country on Greek lines and on a large scale. However, it is doubtful how far the rule of Pompey's eleven cities—some of them the great ancient Greek cities (Amisus, Sinope, Abonuteichus, and Amastris), others the more thoroughly hellenized royal cities (Amasia, Cabira and Zela, Eupatoria (Magnopolis)), others again new foundations by Pompey (Pompeiopolis, Neapolis, Megalopolis)—extended over the territory of Pontus. The temple of Comana retained its ancestral organization and its territory. We may assume the same as regards some of the other temples. The large estates of the nobility may have been confiscated in part or *in toto*. Since they legally formed part of the χώρα βασιλική, it is not improbable that they and the portions of the χώρα βασιλική not assigned to the eleven Pontic cities are referred to by Cicero‡ when he speaks of the *regii agri Mithridatis qui in Paphlagonia qui in Ponto qui in Cappadocia fuerunt*, which became *ager publicus p. R.* by Pompey's conquest and were offered for sale by Rullus. Whether or not the revenues of Pontus and its *ager publicus* after the settlement of the province were leased to a special *societas vecti-*

* *De leg. agr.* ii. 40.   † Ibid. 50.   ‡ Ibid. 51.

galium we do not know. There is no mention of a *societas
Pontica* alongside of the *societas Bithynica* in our sources of
information, though we know from Caesar that there were
publicani in Pontus at the time of Pharnaces.[66]

The mountainous region of Paphlagonia south of the
Olgassys range, which lies between Bithynia and Pontus, had
its own chequered history and its own dynasty in the second
century B.C. In the first century it was a bone of contention
between Bithynia and Pontus. The Senate declared it free,
and it split up into many small *dynasteiai*. Pompey reunited
it and restored Attalus, a scion of the ancient dynasty of
Morzaeus and Pylaemenes, to the throne. About its social and
economic structure, which resembled that of Pontus and
Commagene, we have little information either in the second
century or in the first. We do not know exactly where the
agri regii of Mithridates, to which I referred above, were
situated. The country remains no better explored than
Bithynia and Pontus. A more careful study of it may reveal
some interesting features.[67]

Pompey's reorganization of Bithynia survived him, and his
lex was still the foundation of its administrative, social, and
economic life in the time of Pliny the Younger. The radical
changes introduced by him in the political system of Pontus
were on the contrary of short duration. Its feudal structure
was soon revived, and even the Pontic monarchy, after the
abortive attempt of Pharnaces to restore the great Pontic
kingdom of his father, was reconstituted by Antony, the
Pontic throne being given to Darius, the son of Pharnaces and
grandson of Mithridates.

A large part of Asia Minor, even after Pompey's reorganization of the East and his attempt at modernizing, that is to say,
urbanizing, the backward regions, remained in the hands of
native kings, who became CLIENT or VASSAL KINGS of Rome;
such were the rulers of Cappadocia, of Galatia, of Commagene,
and others whom I have mentioned. Their legal status does
not concern us here. Their economic situation was certainly
not better than that of the provinces. Extraordinary contributions formed their heaviest burden. Detachments of cavalry
and infantry, money and all sorts of supplies were repeatedly

demanded from them. Heavy bribes had to be paid by the kings to their patrons and their enemies in Rome to secure the retention of their thrones. Their miserable situation is illustrated by Cicero's description of Ariobarzanes, his poverty, his scanty revenues, his debts to Pompey and Brutus. The arbitrary character of Roman policy towards the vassal kings is shown by many facts, for example, by the treatment of Galatia, and especially of the temple of Pessinus. Cicero* mentions that by a special *lex tribunicia* of 59 B.C. the chief priest of Magna Mater of Pessinus was deprived of his office, which was sold for hard cash to the well-known Galatian Brogitarus, a scoundrel of the worst type, if we may believe Cicero. Whether he was a scoundrel or not, the transaction, on the part of Rome, was arbitrary and somewhat brutal.[68]

A few words may be said in conclusion about SYRIA.[69]

The former kingdom of the Seleucids was annexed to Rome by Pompey and became the Roman province of Syria. Practically this province consisted of the territories of the cities, which had been formerly, at least in name, parts of the Seleucid State. To these were added many cities which had hitherto been in the hands of the Jewish rulers. Some of the cities comprised in the province had in Seleucid times been free and autonomous, others had been in the hands of tyrants, others again had been tributary. So they remained, subject to certain changes (such as the abolition of some of the tyrannies), after the annexation.

This nucleus was surrounded by a set of petty vassal kingdoms, most of them ruled by native dynasties of Arab sheikhs. Behind these vassal States, in the north, east, and south, lay the larger independent and semi-independent Oriental monarchies: the great enemies of the Seleucids and Rome—Armenia and Parthia, and the lesser kingdoms of the Nabataeans, the Jews, the Ituraeans, Commagene, and Cappadocia, all more or less politically dependent on Rome.

The province of Syria was organized on approximately the same model as the other Roman provinces in the East. The king was replaced by the governor, his court and administration by the governor's staff. With the governors came the *publicani.*

* *Pro Sest.* 26. 56.

Despite the political anarchy of the decades that preceded the annexation, the country was still rich and offered Roman business men a good field of activity. Cicero* speaks of the *pacatissimae et opulentissimae gazae* of Syria, of the large quantities of gold they contained, of the *veteres inlibataeque divitiae*. The picture must be true, at least in some degree. The fertility of Syria had not diminished, and we have seen that the caravan trade, although its normal development had been hindered by the third Mithridatic war, was still a source of wealth to the cities of Syria, Phoenicia, and Palestine, especially during the few years of Tigranes' domination and later in the period immediately after the annexation of Syria. Pirates and robbers had not been completely exterminated by Pompey, but the conditions were much better than before.

Soon after the annexation Roman *negotiatores*, of whom there had hitherto been very few in Syria, became more numerous there and took an active part in the business of the country.[70]

We know very little of the economic situation of Syria after its annexation, or of the influence thereon of the annexation, of Roman methods of government, and of the *publicani*. Certain statements made by Cicero illuminate, for one brief moment, the conditions that prevailed there. These statements relate to the time between 57 and 55 B.C., when the famous A. Gabinius was governor of the province. He was a bitter enemy both of Cicero and of the *publicani*. Cicero, in his denunciations of Gabinius and his contemporary Piso (see below, pp. 986 ff.), gives us from time to time, amid rhetorical outbursts of indignation, glimpses of the governor's activity in Syria which are certainly based on first-hand information.[71]

This fragmentary evidence shows us many Syrian cities in complete decay. Their prosperity had for years been undermined by anarchy, brigandage, and piratical raids. Gabinius understood this and tried to help the cities at the expense of the *publicani* and not without profit to himself. Many of the cities had received from the later Seleucids liberty, autonomy, and fiscal immunity (above, pp. 843 ff.). Gabinius in several instances confirmed these privileges and perhaps extended

* *Pro. Sest.* 43. 93.

them; Tyre was a famous example, and it was no exception. It may be that Gabinius (for a substantial fee) liberated certain cities from their dependence on the *publicani*, without granting them full immunity, by allowing them to pay their taxes directly into the treasury of the province. In other cases he may have partially remitted the amount which, under the terms of their *pactiones*, they were required to pay to the *publicani*.[72]

The operations of the *publicani* certainly did not extend to those cities which were ruled by tyrants. These had once been numerous in Syria, but Pompey had put an end to several of the tyrannies. Many, however, remained, and it is possible that Gabinius increased their number in consideration of fees paid to him personally. The tyrants collected the taxes of their cities and their territories directly, without participation of the *publicani*. Their tribute was paid by them to the governor, and their *pactiones* were made with him, not with the *publicani*. The position of the many native dynasts, some of them Arab chieftains, appears to have been similar.[73]

The remainder of the province was in the hands of the *publicani*. They collected the *stipendium* and the *vectigal*. The difference between the two taxes as imposed in Syria escapes us. Whether the *stipendium* was a fixed φόρος based on the *decuma*, and *vectigal* the revenue from the *ager publicus*, or whether *stipendium* was the tribute of the cities and *vectigal* that of the *chora* and its villages, we cannot say. In any case we learn from Cicero that the *publicani*, for the purpose of collecting these revenues, made *pactiones* with the cities, *pactiones* which Gabinius would occasionally cancel though they were contracted *sine ulla iniuria*. Are we to suppose that in the case of such cancellation the governor would make his own *pactiones* with the cities?

The *portorium*, or customs duty, was also collected by the *publicani*. Cicero says that Gabinius removed their *custodiae*, that is, the guards who watched over the harbours and the land frontiers; which suggests that he may have intended ultimately to replace the *publicani* by his own agents, in other words, to introduce direct collection of the *portoria*.

As in other eastern provinces, lawsuits between the *publicani* and the taxpayers were brought before the court of the governor. We learn that Gabinius refused to act as a judge in such cases. The motive underlying this attitude remains obscure. If not he, who was to act as judge in these suits? Nevertheless, we hear that Gabinius never missed an opportunity of thwarting the *publicani* and of subjecting them to heavy payments, infamy, and even death. They were numerous and ubiquitous in Syria, as in other provinces. We are told that Gabinius would not tolerate their presence or the presence of their agents in any city in which he himself happened to be residing.[74]

Many of Cicero's statements referred to above are short and therefore obscure. His audience understood him, but we are in a different position. It would appear, however, that Gabinius had a definite policy as regards tax-collection in his province. He had no power to eliminate the *publicani* altogether, but he did his best to narrow the scope of their activity by collecting taxes directly, thus perhaps taking the first step—after Sulla— towards the system which gradually replaced that of tax-collection through contractors.

The bitter war that Gabinius waged against the *publicani* does not imply that they behaved worse in Syria than in other provinces. The measures taken by him were not dictated by any exceptional misconduct on their part. On the one hand, these measures were of a political character, directed against a system from which the *equites* drew their political influence; on the other, they may have been suggested to Gabinius by the conviction that the *publicani* were not needed for the collection of the taxes, since this could easily be organized without them, to the benefit of both the taxpayers and the State. It is not quite correct to say that the measures of Gabinius were detrimental to the treasury. The *publicani* no doubt obtained a reduction of their payments to the State. But in all probability this reduction was amply covered by the sums collected by Gabinius from the taxpayers directly.[75]

Syria, like the other provinces, had to bear, besides taxes, the heavy burden of contributions, requisitions, billeting of soldiers, &c. It is incidentally mentioned that, even before the annexation, Philip, one of the rival kings of Syria, had to pay to Q. Marcius Rex, governor of Cilicia in 67 B.C., a heavy contribution, probably on the pretext of helping Pompey in his operations against the pirates, but in fact as a fee to secure, for a brief period, Roman recognition.[76] We may be sure that after the annexation the new rulers would not give up the practice of conducting their wars in the province at the expense of the province itself. In 49 B.C. Q. Caecilius Metellus did not hesitate to impose heavy contributions on Syria for the purpose of helping Pompey in his struggle with Caesar. Among other things he forced the *publicani* to hand over to him the money which they owed to the State, in other words, he laid hands on the funds deposited in their provincial treasury.[77] Similar acts, though not on the same scale, were probably of common occurrence between 64 and 49 B.C.

In fact this short period was not one of peace for Syria. I cannot enter into details, but will confine myself to recalling some outstanding facts.[78] Soon after the annexation a war with the Nabataeans was begun by Scaurus, the agent of Pompey. The two governors of Syria who succeeded him were occupied in resisting repeated raids by Arab tribes. Nor was the rule of Gabinius peaceful. Cicero speaks of his great losses and we know a good many details regarding his war with the Jews and the Nabataeans and his intervention in the affairs of Parthia. We hear incidentally that during his governorship of Syria the pirates were very active along the Syrian coast and that after his departure in 55 their raids became so frequent and so devastating that the *publicani* were unable to collect in full the sums due to them.[79]

As soon as Gabinius left, his successor Crassus, after careful financial preparation, began his ill-fated expedition against Parthia. After his death, his quaestor C. Cassius had to deal with a revolt of the Jews and a dangerous raid of the Parthians (52 B.C.). Before Cassius left Syria and was succeeded by M. Calpurnius Bibulus, the Parthians, led by Pacorus, the son of King Vorodes, invaded the whole of Syria in force. The raid was short but ruinous, and ended with the partial victory of Cassius. But it was renewed under Bibulus at the end of 51 B.C. and the whole of Syria except Antioch was again for several months in the hands of the Parthians.

All the expeditions of their Roman masters and all the raids of their hereditary enemies were obviously paid for by the cities and dynasts of Syria. Of even more importance was the fact that the conflicts with the Nabataeans and the Jews, the war of Crassus, and the Parthian counterstroke utterly disorganized the caravan trade and the foreign commerce of the Syrian cities. Syria's loss was Egypt's gain. The Nabataeans preferred to deal with the Ptolemies rather than with the Roman *publicani*, and the sea route from Egypt to India, when once discovered (above, p. 927 f.), remained in favour with Egyptian and international merchants.

The scanty information that we possess about MACEDONIA and GREECE in the period we are considering shows that the conditions there were much the same as in Asia Minor. The principal disturbers of the peace were the northern and western neighbours of Macedonia. Many Illyrians (especially the Dardanians), Thracians, Celts (Scordisci and Bastarnae), and Germans (Sciri), were allies of Mithridates and helped him in many ways, especially by raids on the territory and cities of Macedonia. From the time of Sulla's operations in Greece all the successive governors of Macedonia were engaged in hostilities with the northern enemies. All had victories to report and triumphs to claim and to receive. Cicero, endeavouring to show by contrast the ignoble spirit and inefficiency of Piso, gives a list of them: Cn. Dolabella (80–78), C. Curio (*bellum Dardanicum*, 75–73), M. Lucullus (see below), and quite recently, he says, L. Torquatus (64–63).* He omits Appius Claudius Pulcher (78–76) and C. Antonius Hybrida, the latter probably because he was not as successful as his predecessors and contemporaries, and had a bad reputation as an administrator.

Some of these expeditions were real successes. Such were those of Curio and of M. Terentius Varro Lucullus (72–70 B.C.). These generals succeeded in breaking the resistance of the Dardanians and Thracians and in reaching the Danube. Lucullus gained possession of the Greek cities of the western Euxine which had hitherto been in the hands of Mithridates and were defended by his garrisons. We know from Eutropius†

* *In Pis.* 19. 44. † vi. 10.

and other sources that he occupied Apollonia, Callatis, Parthenopolis, Mesembria, Dionysopolis, Tomi, Istrus, Bizone.* The result was the extension of Roman domination to the Danube and to the western coast of the Euxine. The relations between Rome and the Greek cities of the latter region took the form of alliances. We still have a fragment of a treaty of alliance between Rome and Callatis, which is not dated, but probably belongs to the time of Lucullus or a little later.

All the gains of Curio and Lucullus were lost in 62–60 B.C. A revolt having broken out among the Dardanians, an expedition conducted against them by C. Antonius Hybrida ended in a crushing defeat of the Roman forces (62 B.C.). Another against the Thracians and especially the Greek cities which had broken away from the Roman alliance, probably in consequence of arbitrary exactions, likewise miscarried. The Greek cities received help from the Bastarnae with whom they had entertained friendly relations since the time of Mithridates, and these Bastarnae inflicted a serious defeat on Antonius under the walls of Istrus.† The disastrous governorship and unlawful proceedings of Antonius led to his trial in 59 B.C., in which Cicero defended him.[80]

Under the impression of these calamities—for the governors who followed, and among them C. Octavius, the father of Augustus (59 B.C.), were unable to do much to retrieve them—the Senate decided to take more efficient measures. L. Calpurnius Piso Caesoninus, the consul of the famous year 58 B.C., father-in-law of Caesar and bitter enemy of Cicero, was sent to Macedonia with extraordinary powers (58–55 B.C.). In contravention of the *Lex Iulia* the whole of Greece, including Achaea, Thessaly, and Athens, was added to his province, that is, full power was given him to treat Greece as part thereof. This means that he received a free hand to draw on the resources of Greece, since Macedonia was unable to bear alone the burden of the great war. He conscribed a strong army in Italy and received ample financial support from the treasury.[81]

We know a good many details of the expedition and of the

* Cf. Ruf. Fest. 9. 2–4; App. *Ill.* 30.
† Cass. Dio, xxxviii. 10. 2–3; Liv. ciii; Jul. Obs. 61a (122), cf. *S.I.G.* 762, winter quarters taken up by C. Antonius near Dionysopolis.

proceedings of Piso in Greece from his enemy Cicero, who speaks of him in many speeches delivered at this time (*Pro Sestio, De domo sua,* and especially *De prov. cons.* and *In Pisonem*). The picture drawn by Cicero is of course unfair and infused with bitter hatred. However, with the help of our knowledge of the usual practice of governors during important wars, we may try to disengage from the passionate rhetoric of Cicero the lamentable facts of Piso's campaign.

The details of his military operations cannot be given here. It appears from the statements of Cicero that Piso tried to arm a part of the Thracians against the rest. He advanced subsidies to King Cotys (of the dynasty Cotys-Sadalas),[82] and delivered to him the envoys of the Bessi. At the same time he engaged in operations against the Dardanians and waged war on the immediate neighbours of Macedonia, the Dentheletae, who had been Rome's faithful friends in the past. The result was a crushing defeat of his army and a tremendous invasion and devastation of Macedonia by the Dardanians, Bessi, and Dentheletae. The Romans lost control of the via Egnatia, and Thessalonice was threatened. Finally Piso dismissed his army and left the province defenceless. Two of his legates, L. Valerius Flaccus and Q. Marcius, restored order to a certain extent in central Macedonia.[83]

To finance his expedition and either to supplement the funds received from the Senate *vasarii nomine,* or, if we are to believe Cicero,* to save the Senate's money for himself, Piso resorted to the same expedients that had been adopted by all his predecessors, for example by Antonius Hybrida and Antonius Creticus, and by so many governors in Asia Minor.

(1) Yearly contributions (εἰσφοραί) were imposed on the cities of Achaea and probably on other cities of Greece and Macedonia. These εἰσφοραί were in all probability not identical with the *aurum coronarium* in respect of which the Achaeans were supposed to pay 100 talents.[84]

(2) A new provincial tax was introduced (after the manner of Lucullus and Appius Claudius): a tax on sales (ἐπώνιον). The collectors were not the *publicani,* but Piso's slaves, who acted as his agents; this mode of collection was probably one

* *In Pis.* 35. 86.

of the grievances of the *publicani* against Piso. The fact in itself is interesting. I have pointed out that Gabinius probably acted in the same way in Syria. This mode of collection was the precursor of the later collection of taxes by the imperial slaves and freedmen.[85]

(3) At Dyrrachium Piso sequestrated the *vectigal* and *portorium* of the city, that is to say, he set aside the *publicani* and collected these taxes himself. This act was probably detrimental not so much to the city as to the *publicani*, since the *vectigal* and *portorium* were probably not municipal ὠναί but provincial taxes.[86]

(4) Requisitions were carried out on a very large scale. We hear of *frumentum imperatum, aestimatum, honorarium*. Cicero refers with special bitterness to the *frumentum honorarium*, a counterpart to the *aurum coronarium*. The contribution was extorted *vi et metu*; the greatest sufferers were the Bottiaeans, the Byzantines (a free city), Chersonesus, and Thessalonice. In this way Piso concentrated in his own hands the whole grain supply of his province.*[87] He dealt in the same way with hides. All the cattle of the province (or at least part of it) were requisitioned to provide equipment for the army (armour, shields, horse-trappings).[88]

(5) Ships, probably transports, were demanded from the cities.[89]

(6) Troops were billeted on cities regardless of their status. The soldiers behaved as usual. Especially cruel was the treatment of Byzantium, a free city which had just passed through a dangerous internal crisis. An εἰσφορά was probably imposed upon it. As it was unable or unwilling to pay, Piso assigned it as winter quarters for several cohorts and himself took up his residence there. In this free city he acted as judge (in virtue of his extraordinary powers, see above, p. 986), issued death warrants, and was the cause of the suicide of an innocent girl. In default of the εἰσφορά he confiscated some statues. Other Greek cities were similarly treated.[90]

(7) Finally, in order to restore the cities of his province to solvency, he interfered with the transactions of the numerous

* We know the nature of the above-mentioned contributions from the practice of Verres.

Italian *negotiatores* of Macedonia and Greece in favour of the debtors.[91]

The reader of the preceding pages will see that there was nothing unusual in the conduct of Piso. He acted within the limits of the extraordinary powers conferred on him in legal form, and to some extent in the interests of the Greek cities (direct collection of some taxes, protection of the provincials against the money-lenders). In this respect he did what Gabinius had done. This does not mean, however, that his proceedings were not selfish, ruthless, and cruel, and disastrous for his province. Cicero, it may be noted, was well acquainted with the public opinion of the province, since he himself stayed in Macedonia (at Thessalonice and Dyrrachium) in 58 and 57 B.C.

Comparative order was restored in Macedonia by the successors of Piso. But the country remained surrounded by enemies, and the projected extension of the province to the Danube and to the Black Sea was abandoned. Complete freedom was given to the capable Dacian king Byrebista to build up his great if ephemeral Thracian, Illyrian, and Celtic kingdom, which comprised, besides numerous tribes, almost all the Greek cities of the western Pontus, including Olbia (those which resisted being captured and destroyed). It was a rich and powerful kingdom, although it never succeeded in absorbing all the Thracian tribes and kingdoms and all the Greek cities in question. Byrebista's strength was recognized both by Pompey, who tried to win his support, and by Caesar, who intended to conquer his kingdom as a prelude to his Parthian expedition. But internal revolution brought his empire to an end before the stage was reached of armed conflict between him and Rome.[92]

3. THE CIVIL WARS

Less than twenty years had elapsed since Pompey had established comparative peace on land and sea when wars on a great scale once more rent the Hellenistic world, as it was very slowly recovering from its depression. In 49 B.C. began the armed conflict between Pompey and Caesar, which (with its sequels—the Alexandrian war and the war against Pharnaces) lasted in the East for more than two years. Close upon it followed a fresh civil war, the bitter struggle between the Senate and the heirs of Caesar's ideas and of his power, Antony and C. Caesar (Octavianus) (42 B.C.). This again was fought out in the East. It was short, but it deeply affected the whole of the Hellenistic world, which, after a short lull of about ten years (interrupted by the violent raid of the Parthians into Syria and Asia Minor (41–38 B.C.)), was once more overwhelmed by an even more formidable war—the mortal duel between Antony and C. Caesar.

The people of Greece and the Hellenistic East had no sympathy with either of the contending parties. The war was foreign to them. The cities and rulers of the East sided with one or other of the combatants because he was nearer and imposed an iron will by armed force upon unwilling allies. Yet it was the Hellenistic countries that bore the major part of the burden of the Roman civil wars.

If in the past the East had been forced to pay for such Roman wars as were waged on its soil, there had been at least this semblance of justification, that the Romans claimed to be fighting on Greek territory in order to protect Greeks from oppression by a barbarian king (Mithridates) or by foreign enemies (the pirates, the northern tribes of the Balkan peninsula the Armenians, or the Parthians). If the Greek cities had had to pay heavy taxes and exhausting contributions during these wars and in the intervals between them, well-meaning Romans such as Cicero would tell them that they were thus purchasing for themselves peace, internal and external, and security. The sacrifice was heavy, but it was compensated by some hope of a quiet future.

But even this faint hope the civil wars showed to have been illusory. Brute force and compulsion reigned supreme. The rivals were fighting for their lives, and in such a struggle all means were good. There was no difference in this respect between Pompey, Caesar, Brutus, Cassius, Antony, and C Caesar. None of them ever pretended that the war would benefit in any way the Hellenistic countries. Greeks and other Orientals were expected to support one or other of the combatants, not as free men exercising their choice, but as subjects almost as slaves.

The demands made on Greece and on hellenized Asia by their Roman masters were exactly the same as during and after the Mithridatic war. Besides the regular taxes various contributions were required: man-power (soldiers, rowers, and labour), warships, money, means of transport, quarters, food, clothes, and arms for the troops. And the methods of collection remained the same. The contributions were a sheer loss to those who made them, without prospect of any compensating benefit. Refusal of compliance on first demand brought cruel punitive expeditions upon the recalcitrant city or vassal dynast, while enormous fines were the penalty for siding with the enemy, as if a Hellenistic government had even the semblance of free choice. In my opinion there is no ground for supposing that the Greeks were in sympathy with any of the combatants. In the depth of their hearts they hated them all. The expressions of gratitude and the honours heaped by them on the rulers of the day were mostly flattery and adulation, sometimes emotional thanks for unexpected favours and prayers for their renewal.

A narrative of the civil wars, even from the point of view of Greece and Hellenistic Asia, would here be out of place. We hardly hear the voice of the Greeks in this terrible period of their history. Inscriptions are few and mostly of a depressing banality. Without aiming at completeness I will confine myself to a short selection of such facts as relate to economic conditions in Greece and the rest of the Hellenistic world.

It is well known that Pompey, in his struggle with Caesar, relied to a large extent on Greece and the East for his supply of funds and provisions, and for the recruiting of his navy and to a certain extent his army, especially certain special troops (archers and slingers and cavalry). We possess some detailed information on the last point. Pompey began by mobilizing the few Roman veterans in Macedonia and in Crete and probably also the Roman citizens in Greece, in the islands, and in Asia Minor. There were many of these, for the number of Italian settlers in the East had been rapidly increasing since the first Mithridatic war, and Italians now formed a substantial part of the *bourgeoisie* of many a Hellenistic city. The land-owners and business men (*negotiatores*), the *publicani* and their

PLATE CVI

An impressive tomb relief representing one of the soldiers of the revolutionary armies and his family, said to have been found near Rome. Marble block about seven feet long and over two feet high. The heads are nearly life-size. Three busts are presented. The central one is that of *P. Gessius P. f. Rom(ilia)*, to the left of him *Gessia P. l. Fausta*, to the right *P. Gessius P. l. Primus*. The tomb was built: *ex testam(ento) P. Gessi P. l. Primi*, the executor being his mother Fausta: *arbit[ratu] Gessia[e P.l.] Fausta[e]* ('under the supervision of Gessia Fausta'). It is evident from the above inscriptions that P. Gessius P. f. Rom., a veteran or soldier, as indicated by his military dress (tunic, leather cuirass, sword belt, and cloak; his left hand grasping a broken object, perhaps a sword-hilt), lived in concubinage with his slave Fausta and had by her a son Primus. He manumitted both of these. After him died his son, and the monument was built by the surviving Fausta. The monument is not dated, but the style, the dressing of the hair of Fausta and Primus, and the form of the letters of the inscriptions suggest a date before Augustus, about the middle of the first century B.C. The relief is an astonishing product of Roman portrait art. I may quote the words of L. D. Caskey: 'The sculptor has concentrated his chief effort on the heads, reproducing faithfully not only their underlying structure, but all their superficial peculiarities—creases and wrinkles in the skin, veins on the temples of the old man, even a large mole on the left cheek of the woman. But the bodies and the drapery, though they are less carefully executed, contribute to the effect of the whole. The three people, seen as if at a window, holding themselves stiffly upright and directing their solemn gaze towards the spectator, have an astonishing air of reality.' It is highly interesting to compare the massive, heavy, almost square heads of the Gessii, so brutally realistic, a true product of Roman art, with the tall, slender, elegant figures of the base from Città Castellana (pl. CIV), which, though probably the work of a Roman artist and showing some peculiarities of Roman art, are nevertheless very Hellenistic in their proportions, conception, and style. L. D. C(askey), *Bull. Mus. Fine Arts, Boston*, xxxv (1937), pp. 20 ff.; id., *A.J.A.* xli (1937), pp. 527 ff., figs. 8–12; F. Poulsen, *Probleme der römischen Ikonographie*, 1937, p. 23, no. 7, figs. 52–3, cf. his article, 'A Roman of Republican days', Δράγμα, *M. P. Nilsson ... dedicatum*, 1939, pp. 409 ff. Photograph supplied by the authorities of the Museum of Fine Arts, Boston.

PLATE CVI

A Soldier of the Roman Army of the Times of the Civil War and his Family

Boston, Museum of Fine Arts

staff of freedmen and free men, were probably not first-class war material, but they were numerous.

The defence of the western coast of Greece was entrusted to Aetolian, Epirotic, and Thracian militiamen in addition to the Italians. The legions were completed by levies in Macedonia, Thessaly, Epirus, Boeotia, Achaea, Athens, and the Peloponnese. Laconia, Crete, Pontus, Syria, and other places supplied the army with archers and slingers, and Macedonia, Thessaly, Thrace, Galatia, Cappadocia, and Commagene with horsemen, some of them mounted archers.

The large fleet at the disposal of Pompey (500 to 600 ships) was almost entirely Greek and Oriental: it was composed of Egyptian, Rhodian, Syrian, Phoenician, Cilician, Pontic, and Bithynian ships, together with ships of Chios, Lesbos, Cos, Smyrna, Miletus, the Cyclades, Athens, Achaea, Byzantium, and Corcyra. It was divided into four squadrons according to the origin of the ships: Egyptian, Asiatic, Syrian, and Achaean and Liburnian. It is certain that none of the maritime cities of Greece or the East was exempt from the naval burden, that is to say, from the obligation actually to build and man ships. The rest—the inland cities—were required to pay a heavy naval contribution in money.

We have no exact information about the size of the rival armies. But on the most moderate estimate, we must reckon that the number of armed men who lived for more than a year on the resources of Greece and the Hellenistic countries was not less than 100,000; to which must be added the navy and the trains of the two armies, especially that of Pompey with his itinerant Senate. Each senator was no doubt accompanied by as many members of his family as possible and certainly by many slaves.

In addition to the provision of men and ships, heavy contributions were required from Syria, Asia, the vassal kings and dynasts, and from Achaea. Moreover, requisitions of food, of war material, of clothing were of everyday occurrence throughout Pompey's sphere of influence, including Egypt and the Cyrenaica.

Caesar in his *Civil War** gives a vivid picture of what

* iii. 31–3.

happened in this respect in Syria and Asia Minor, where Scipio was acting on behalf of Pompey. Scipio began operations in Syria, imposing heavy contributions on cities and tyrants, and appropriating from the *publicani* the money due by them to the State under their contract for the last two years, and in addition, by way of an advance, for the ensuing year.

Then he moved with his army to Asia. His first act was to distribute his troops in winter quarters among the rich cities of Asia (including Pergamon), allowing the soldiers to pillage at their pleasure. Next came exactions of money. Contributions were extorted, and extraordinary taxes, after the manner of those instituted by Lucullus, Appius Claudius, and Piso, were imposed on the population: a poll-tax (ἐπικεφάλαιον) on free men and slaves, and a house-tax under various names (*columnaria, ostiaria*). Levies and requisitions were organized on a large scale: soldiers and rowers on the one hand, armour and weapons, engines of war, and means of transport on the other. These were demanded not only from the cities but also from villages and fortified villas (*vici* and *castella*—an interesting proof, incidentally, of the existence in the province of villages and farms not included in the territories of the cities).

The mode of collection was that used by Sulla and his successors in Asia: special agents were employed with extraordinary military power (*imperium* with *lictores*), and certainly with detachments of soldiers at their disposal. Caesar calls them *praefecti* and *exactores*. They certainly did not omit, while exacting money for Pompey, to fill their own pockets.

The usual result followed. Money was borrowed from moneylenders and the indebtedness of the province increased rapidly. In two years it doubled.

The Roman *negotiatores* and *publicani* suffered no less than the provincials. They were dealt with both individually and as organized communities, which Caesar calls *conventus*, and also as groups of foreigners residing in particular cities; these two latter categories appear not to have been identical. It was probably under colour of compulsory loans that the money was exacted from them. The *publicani*, for example, were required to advance to the treasury their payment for the following year. On the other hand, money deposited by private persons with the *publicani* was appropriated by the agents of Pompey; such confiscations were probably regarded as compulsory loans by individual capitalists. It was thus that Cicero lost at this time the savings that he had deposited with the *publicani* at Ephesus. Pompey intended to deal in the same way with the money deposited in the temple of Ephesus; it was twice saved by accident.*[93]

While the problem of financing his expedition and of forming and keeping up his army and navy was solved by Pompey as above described, Caesar's situation was different. We are not here concerned with his mobilization of the West. Once in the East, Caesar relied for his supplies almost exclusively on the resources of Greece proper. We know that his forces gradually occupied the whole of central and north-western Greece. This was done, no doubt, mainly for strategical reasons, but the question of supplies played a certain part in this occupation.

A couple of texts engraved on the Cnidian treasure-house at Delphi reflects the conditions now prevailing in central Greece. They show that Caesar was accompanied in Greece by two Cnidian notables, the famous Theopompus and another influential man, Callistus. They played, on his staff, the same role of advisers and experts in Greek affairs as Theophanes of Mytilene on that of Pompey. At Delphi they helped with their advice Fufius Calenus, who was charged with various tasks in central Greece certainly in some way connected with the military operations. An obscure sentence in one of the inscriptions suggests that he was responsible for the safety of the Corinthian Gulf and the harbour of Delphi—Cirrha. He may have had to deal with local pirates and his duty may have been to protect the transport of food-supplies. It may be recalled that some pirates captured by Pompey in the course of his operations had been settled at Dyme, and took advantage of the turmoil of the civil wars to resume their old vocation.[94]

We may imagine how disastrously this war affected Greece, and especially Thessaly. I may cite the fate of Gomphi and the sieges of Athens and Megara, that of the latter ending in the

* Caes. *B.C.* iii. 33 and 105.

capture of the city, the massacre of the population, and the enslavement of the survivors.[95] We are not surprised that Servius Sulpicius, in his letter of 45 B.C. to Cicero, should describe the condition of Greece as worse than it had been after Sulla's campaign there: 'behind me was Aegina, before me Megara, to the right the Piraeus, to the left Corinth, cities which had been flourishing in the past and now lay before my eyes in ruin and decay'.[96]

The end of the war did not mean the end of exactions and contributions. Caesar needed money and did not hesitate to collect it in one way or another. Exactions began as soon as the war was over, witness the large sums demanded from the vassal kings who had sided with Pompey. Deiotarus of Galatia, for example, held three auctions in order to satisfy the victor.* [97] Cassius Dio† gives an illuminating survey of Caesar's activity after his victory over Pharnaces (who, by the way, contributed a good deal during his invasion of Pontus to the ruin and desolation of that country, Cappadocia, and Armenia Minor). Caesar went first to Bithynia and thence to Greece on his way to Italy, 'collecting much money and upon every pretext from everybody, just as he had done before (i.e. during and immediately after the war). In the first place he exacted all the money that any one had previously promised to Pompey, and made still further demands under colour of various accusations. He appropriated all the votive offerings to Heracles of Tyre, because the Tyrians had shown hospitality to Pompey's wife and son. He also obtained many golden crowns from potentates and kings in honour of his victories.' Moreover, for the purposes of his Alexandrian expedition and afterwards of his war with Pharnaces, he assembled land and sea forces, especially in Syria and Asia Minor. Thus the East, which was slowly recovering from the blows dealt it by Sulla and Mithridates, was again most ruthlessly despoiled, first by Pompey, then by Caesar.[98]

Caesar, however, during the short period of his rule, did something to compensate the East for his depredations. In

---

* We should much like to know what was sold at these auctions: land, cattle, gold and silver plate?

† xlii. 49, cf. 6.

Greece he granted certain privileges to Thessaly,* restored Corinth, and presented gifts to Athens. The reparation he made to Asia was more substantial. The most important of his measures were his remission of one-third of the sums paid to the *publicani* by the cities of the province of Asia, and his restoration of the Sullan system of direct tax-collection by the cities themselves, without the intervention of the tax-farmers. We have little evidence about the latter reform, but it seems clear that Caesar returned to the system originally instituted by Sulla, which the Senate had subsequently modified by introducing the *publicani* as intermediaries between the cities and the government, to act as underwriters and guarantors. Caesar set aside the *publicani* and established or re-established direct relations between the cities and the provincial government. Each city remained liable for the payment of a lump sum, but this sum it paid, not as before to the *publicani*, but to the quaestor of the province. Whether this tribute or φόρος was a sum fixed once for all and was calculated on a basis representing in the main the *decuma* of a normal harvest, or was determined yearly and arranged by an annual *pactio* between the city and the governor (the system of Gabinius, a modification of that which had prevailed in the time of the *publicani*), we do not know. In any case the owners or cultivators of the land continued to pay a *decuma* as before. Antony, when referring in his speech to Caesar's reform, makes no allusion to any change in this respect.[99]

We find occasional mention of other measures advantageous to the cities of Greece and Asia Minor. I referred above (p. 971 f.) to the complaint of the Mytileneans regarding the number of privileged persons residing in their city but bearing no share of its burdens; to this complaint Caesar gave redress. But he was himself lavish in granting privileges and exemptions to individuals. The Roman franchise and other favours were frequently bestowed by him on those who supported and assisted him in the war.† He was no less lavish in granting privileges to cities. Such grants were made in 48 B.C. to Cnidus, the home of

---

* App. *B.C.* ii. 88 and Plut. *Caes.* 48 speak of liberation, which may have included temporary remission of taxes.

† I have collected the evidence on this point elsewhere.[100]

the friends of Caesar mentioned above, and to Ilium, and later to Amisus and Mytilene. Cyzicus, Miletus, Pergamon, Athens, Megara, Thespiae received from him privileges of one kind or another. Even distant Chersonesus in the Crimea benefited by his favour. An inscription there mentions an ambassador sent by the city to Caesar and the Roman Senate in 47 or 46 B.C. The question at issue was the liberty of the city. Chersonesus had in the past been politically dependent on Mithridates and on his successor Pharnaces, and after the latter's death on Asander, the ruler of Bosporus. It is very probable that Caesar granted the city the liberty it requested.[101]

Some of his benefactions were dictated by considerations of sentiment and propaganda (Ilium, Athens, perhaps Thespiae and Megara), others by the desire to satisfy influential friends in the East (such were the cases of Cnidus and certain other cities supported by Caesar's Cnidian friends; also probably of Mytilene and certainly of Pergamon). But the main reasons for his liberal policy in the East were of a political character. During the civil war the force of circumstances had driven him to treat Greece and Asia with harshness and to subject them to spoliation. When his great struggle was over and he had become the sole and supreme ruler of the Roman Empire he had imperative need of the support, both moral and material, of the East. He was planning his great expeditions against Byrebista and the Parthians. To ensure the success of these campaigns he must have in his rear a pacified, quiet, happy, and prosperous people, and his measures were directed to this end.

Corinth was restored as one of his principal bases in Greece, an excellent connecting link between Italy and the East. The people he sent to reside there were expert in business and profoundly devoted to him. He was not interested in Delos, which received its *coup de grâce* in the restoration of Corinth.

Peace and prosperity were needed in Macedonia and Greece in order that these countries should support his expedition against Byrebista, who had grown too strong for him and could threaten his communications with Italy.

Full control of the Straits, of the Propontis, of Pontus, and of supplies from the Crimea was a vital condition of the success of his Parthian expedition. This was why he crushed Pharnaces and conferred favours on Cyzicus, Heraclea, Sinope, and Amisus. It should be noted that in the last two, and also in Apamea, Myrlea, and Lampsacus (or Parium?), he planted Roman military colonies.[102] And this explains likewise his policy in the Crimea: the emancipation of Chersonesus and the humiliation of Asander short of a breach with him.

The evidence regarding the political measures of Caesar in Greece and in the East is of course very meagre and incomplete. It is certain, however, that the settlement of this quarter of the world was one of his main preoccupations in the last years of his life. We know that in 46 and 45 B.C. he was continuously occupied with Oriental affairs. Scores of ambassadors came from the East to Rome at that time, and many *Senatus consulta* regulating the affairs of the East were submitted to the vote. Very illuminating in this respect is a letter from Cicero to Paetus in the second half of 46 B.C.* in which Cicero speaks of being the sponsor, without knowing it, of several *Senatus consulta* and receiving letters of thanks from potentates in the East of whom he had never heard before.

In the light of the reforms of Caesar in Asia Minor, which in the main were modelled on the rearrangement of taxation by Sulla (and the system of Sulla seems to have been at least a partial return to the Hellenistic traditions), we may perhaps better understand the little we know of Caesar's fiscal policy in Syria. Though we have no direct information about this, we may form some idea of its character from a study of his two edicts of 47 and 44 B.C. concerning Judaea, which are reproduced, certainly in abbreviated form, by Josephus.†

After the annexation of Syria by Pompey and the conquest of Judaea, the latter became practically part of the Roman province of Syria. I have described the Hellenistic system of taxation in force in Judaea as we know it from the books of the Maccabees and from Josephus. Under Jonathan in 152 B.C. the country paid a tribute and a very high land-tax (one-third

---

* *Ad fam.* ix. 15. 4.

† *A.J.* xiv. 10. 5 and 6 (200 ff.). I dealt with this topic thirty-five years ago in my *Staatspacht* and see no reason to modify the interpretation of the edicts that I then put forward.

of the harvest and half the crop of the fruit-trees), besides a number of royal taxes and a tax on the revenue of the priests.

The history of the high land-tax, which does not appear among the taxes of Judaea in the time of Antiochus III, is obscure (above, pp. 467 ff.). We shall see that it reappears in Judaea in the days of Caesar and probably was the basis of the taxation there throughout the period between the end of the Seleucid rule and Caesar's conquest of the country. It may have been the fundamental tax of Judaea from time immemorial, a tax which formed the basis of the tribute, and may have been temporarily collected by the Seleucid government as a separate impost additional to the tribute, that is to say as a punitive emergency tax, corresponding to similar taxes imposed by Lucullus, Appius Claudius, and Ariobarzanes. Under the Hasmonaeans it became once more the chief tax of Judaea, and as such was inherited by the Romans.[103]

This of course is merely a surmise. We know little of the system of taxation established by the Hasmonaeans, but it is very probable that they did not change that which they inherited from the Seleucids, and that Pompey took the same system over from them. Pompey, however, adopted the same course in Judaea as the Romans had followed in the East generally. He simplified the relations between Rome and Judaea by ordering it to pay to the Roman government a *stipendium*,* a certain quantity of grain and money calculated probably on the normal yield of the Hellenistic and Hasmonaean land-tax and other taxes. The collection of the *stipendium* in the time of Gabinius was farmed out to the *publicani* of Syria, a procedure which was certainly not initiated by him. He divided Judaea for fiscal purposes into five districts, each with its own metropolis. With these district capitals the *publicani* made their *pactiones*, which were sometimes cancelled by Gabinius, who thereupon probably made his own *pactiones* with the cities. I have already referred to this system of direct *pactiones* practised by Gabinius in emergency cases.

This procedure—its reconstruction is of course conjectural—remained in vigour until the time of Caesar, who introduced some changes. He may have temporarily maintained the

* Fl. Jos. *A.J.* xiv. 4. 4 (74); *B.J.* i. 7. 6 (154).

Pompeian system with slight modifications in favour of Judaea: the tribute was calculated on the basis of one-fourth (not one-third) of the harvest in the second year of the *lustrum*, while complete exemption was granted in every seventh (i.e. sabbatical) year. The payments in kind had to be delivered at Sidon, probably to the central granaries of the province of Syria. Such may be the meaning of the edict of 47 B.C., though its interpretation is very difficult and doubtful. Joppa, restored to Judaea, formed a separate fiscal district.

In 44 B.C. a more radical change appears to have been introduced. For the new *lustrum* the *stipendium* of Judaea ceased to be farmed out to the *publicani*, and the system of taxation was modified. But the privilege relating to the second year of each *lustrum* and probably to the sabbatical year was maintained. There is reason to think that it was the ethnarch—Hyrcanus II—who was made responsible for the payment of the *stipendium*.

It is more than probable therefore that in Judaea, as in Asia, Caesar put an end to the activity of the *publicani*, to the great satisfaction of the Jews, who moreover were exempted from military service and from the ἐπισταθμία. By these measures Caesar kept the Jews in good humour, secured for himself their support in his projected Parthian war, and filled his military granaries at Sidon.

May we go farther and suggest that Caesar acted more or less in the same way in Syria also? We know that he bestowed many favours on some of the dynasts of Syria and on several Syrian cities, especially Antioch. It is significant that he founded the first military colony in Syria, that of Berytus. It is perhaps permissible to think that, as he freed Asia Minor and Judaea, so he freed Syria for ever from the *publicani* and entered into direct relations with the cities, in this following the lead of Gabinius.[104]

The Hellenistic world hardly had time to recover from the previous depredations in the brief period of Caesar's benevolent rule. In 44 B.C. Caesar was killed, and in 43 began the activity of Brutus and Cassius in Greece, Asia Minor, and Syria. They arrived in the East without money or men, their intention being to create from its resources an army and a fleet, and to secure enough money to pay their forces and finance the war in general. The time of Pompey's and Caesar's exactions returned, with only this difference, that Brutus and Cassius showed a more ruthless energy than either Pompey or Caesar. They had to obtain men, ships, money, and equipment with all possible speed and they did not hesitate, for this purpose, to resort to the most violent measures.

Brutus and Cassius found the East distracted and chaotic. In Syria civil war had begun before the death of Caesar, Caecilius Bassus, a Pompeian in alliance with Parthia, offering staunch resistance to Caesar's generals. On the top of this came Cassius, who succeeded in getting the upper hand over both Bassus and his Caesarian opponents, and in winning the allegiance of their legions. There was no less confusion in Asia Minor, where Trebonius, the legitimate governor of Asia, refused to yield to Dolabella, who was on his way to Syria. Dolabella brutally murdered him, but was himself overtaken by Cassius, besieged in Laodicea, and driven to commit suicide. In Greece the situation was less complicated. Here the success of Brutus was rapid and complete. But Greece was now exhausted, and Brutus, to obtain the means of maintaining and increasing his forces, soon set out for Asia Minor.[105]

All the temporary rulers of Syria lived with their armies at the expense of the province. We have some information about their methods in the case of Cassius. His measures in Syria were designed to force the cities and vassal kings into unconditional submission and to extract from them all the money and military help that he needed. Those who opposed him had to pay a heavy penalty. Josephus* tells us how Cassius went from one city of Syria to another collecting arms and soldiers and imposing heavy contributions, and treating the vassal rulers in the same way. Antipater and Hyrcanus in Judaea† had great difficulty in collecting the contribution of 700 talents imposed on them. Some cities which were unable or unwilling to pay saw their population sold into slavery.

We have more detailed information regarding the fate of the two cities that had given their support to Dolabella—Laodicea and Tarsus. Laodicea was captured by Cassius. Its public and

* *A.J.* xiv. 11. 2 (272).   † Fl. Jos., loc. cit.

sacred treasuries were robbed, the city was partly destroyed, and a heavy fine was exacted from it. Even more cruel was the treatment of Tarsus. According to Cassius Dio, Cassius here used the method later applied by him and Brutus to Rhodes and Lycia: he confiscated all the public money and ordered the private citizens to surrender all their gold and silver. Elaborate measures were taken to procure the success of this operation, among which spying and denunciations proved very effective. Appian gives a slightly different account: he speaks of a contribution of 1,500 talents. For the payment of this sum, he says, the city used up all its resources, both public and sacred, and finally, being unable to meet the demand in full, sold into slavery a large part of its own population.[106]

In addition to these measures, Cassius, in order to fill his war-chest, had recourse to a device which earlier rulers of Syria had frequently adopted. He sold the government of various cities to wealthy applicants, in other words, established tyrannies in them.[107]

Similar methods were followed by Dolabella, Cassius, and Brutus in Asia Minor and Greece. Dolabella during his short stay in Asia Minor acted with promptitude and cruelty. Lentulus, the proquaestor, reporting to Rome in the summer of 43 B.C.*, speaks of the province of Asia being devastated by Dolabella, who seized the *vectigalia* and showed especial severity to Roman citizens. Appian† mentions in addition the contributions which he imposed on the cities, while as regards the navy he preferred to hire ships from the Rhodians, Lycians, Pamphylians, and Cilicians. Nor did Dolabella fail to reinforce his army by compulsory levies. Like Metellus, he exempted from these levies the Jewish population of Asia Minor.[108]

The proceedings of Cassius and Brutus are well known and need not detain us, but a few outstanding facts may be mentioned. Rhodes offered resistance to the former, and the city was captured after a difficult siege. It was not pillaged by Cassius' troops, but paid heavily for its resistance. Its ships were confiscated, as also was the money found in its temples and public treasury. In addition, an order was given that private citizens should deliver, under penalty of death, all the

---

* Cic. *Ad fam.* xii. 15. 1.   † *B.C.* iv. 60. 58.

gold and silver that they possessed. This order, enforced in the same way as at Tarsus, produced more than 8,000 talents. And, lastly, if we may believe Plutarch (who, however, does not mention the confiscation of the public and sacred funds) a fine of 500 talents was imposed on the city.[109]

In Asia Minor the Lycians and Ariobarzanes III of Cappadocia suffered the same fate as the Rhodians. Brutus and Cassius led military expeditions, the first-named into Lycia, the second into Cappadocia. In Lycia the cities had refused to pay the contributions and to furnish recruits, and Brutus retaliated with his expedition. Xanthus, which offered resistance, was besieged and finally captured, whereupon its inhabitants destroyed themselves and their city. Its tragic fate made a profound impression on contemporaries. Patara surrendered and according to Appian suffered at the hands of Brutus the same treatment that Cassius had applied with success at Rhodes. All the gold and silver in the possession of private citizens was seized, and in addition, according to Plutarch, the cities of Lycia paid a joint contribution of 150 talents.[11] Cappadocia was invaded and the treasury and war material of Ariobarzanes were confiscated.[111]

No resistance was offered by the province of Asia. Under strong pressure its cities did their best (by selling their plate and jewels) to satisfy Brutus and Cassius, who imposed on them (as on the other provinces of Asia Minor) a contribution equivalent to the amount of their *phoros* for ten years. For the collection of this enormous sum the tyrannicides no doubt adopted the system of Sulla and Pompey.[112]

I may note in passing that in Asia Minor, as in Syria, the rulers of the day preferred to deal, not with free cities, but with cities governed by tyrants. Several tyrannies are mentioned by Strabo as institutions characteristic of his time, and we may derive information about some of the tyrants from coins and inscriptions. I have already referred to the most typical representatives of this class, and I shall return to the subject later in this chapter. Some of these potentates were fully constituted tyrants; others, though not tyrants in the true sense of the word, were practically masters of their own cities. Their influence and power were based on their relations with he rulers of the day, and the support which they received from these was certainly not given for nothing. If they did not pay regular tribute out of their own pockets, they certainly helped their protectors to obtain contributions from their fellow citizens.[113]

Besides contributions, the East as usual supplied the Roman leaders with men for their army, and ships, together with their crews and rowers, for their fleet. Two legions were formed of Macedonians in 43 B.C. Almost the whole of the cavalry of Brutus and Cassius (17,000, if we may believe Appian) consisted of Thessalians, Thracians, Illyrians, and Orientals (Arabs, Medes, Parthians, Galatians).[114]

And last but not least, during two years Asia Minor and Greece had to support the large and constantly growing army of Brutus and Cassius (at Philippi it numbered according to Appian 100,000 men), and their fleet, and later the army of C. Caesar (Octavianus) and Antony.[115]

The end of the war at Philippi brought no relief to Asia and to Greece. The triumvirs were in urgent need of money for the pay and discharge of their soldiers. Of the legionaries alone 170,000 had to be provided for.* At the same time, Antony had no intention of remaining idle, but was preparing his Parthian expedition.

His proceedings in the East, as might be expected, were exactly the same as those of Sulla, Pompey, Caesar, and Brutus and Cassius. We possess substantial accounts of them in the reports of Appian, Plutarch, and Cassius Dio, all of course hostile to him.

Like Caesar, Antony conferred privileges on the cities, dynasts, and private persons that were loyal to him and had suffered heavily before and during the war of Philippi. Lycia became *immunis*, Xanthus was rebuilt, Rhodes received an increase of territory, as also did Athens. Laodicea and Tarsus were treated in the same way as the Lycians, and by a special edict ($\delta\iota\acute{a}\tau\alpha\gamma\mu\alpha$) the Tarsians who had been sold into slavery were restored to freedom. In all probability the Caesarian system of collecting the taxes was maintained.[116]

At the same time privileges were freely granted to groups

* Ephesian speech of Antony, App. *B.C.* v. 5.

and to individuals who had no special political claims. We stil possess Antony's letter to the *koinon* of Greeks in Asia (τὸ κοινὸ τῶν ἀπὸ τῆς Ἀσίας Ἑλλήνων), strikingly similar to the letter o Sulla previously quoted, in which is mentioned his grant o various immunities and favours,* at the request of his frienc Artemidorus, a famous athlete, to the world-wide associatior of victors in the festival games (σύνοδος τῶν ἀπὸ τῆς οἰκουμένη ἱερονικῶν καὶ στεφανειτῶν). This document may be dated ir 42/41 B.C. or in 33 B.C., during Antony's great mobilization of the East. We may also recall the large number of provincials, botl soldiers who had served in his army and civilians of variou: standing, who received from him the Roman franchise.[117]

On the other hand, the measures taken by Antony to obtair money from the Asiatic provinces were vigorous and unsparing In his famous speech at Ephesus in 41 B.C. he ordered the citie: of the province of Asia to pay him within one year the sam: sum as they had paid to Brutus and Cassius, both as a punish ment for their support of Caesar's murderers and as their shar: in the liquidation of the civil war. After some bargaining i was decided that Asia should pay a nine-years' *phoros* in two years. Such is the report of Appian, and Plutarch adds som: interesting details. Describing what was probably the sam: meeting at Ephesus, he records that Hybreas of Mylasa, the famous rhetorician with whom Strabo has made us familia (above, p. 822 f.), remarked sarcastically in his speech: 'If yo can take a contribution twice in one year, you can likewis: give us summer twice and harvest twice.' The same speec of Hybreas contained a caustic comment on the methods o Antony's fiscal agents. The sum exacted from Asia amounted according to him, to 200,000 talents, which is of course : gross exaggeration, either by Hybreas himself or by Plutarc and the author on whom he drew.[118] This sum was collecte by the same means as had been adopted by Sulla. Specia agents were appointed for groups of cities and these levied th contributions with the help of soldiers.†

---

* ἀστρατευσία, ἀλειτουργησία, ἀνεπισταθμία, ἐκεχειρία περὶ τὴν πανήγυρι ἀσυλία, and πορφύρα.

† One of these collectors was Anaxenor, a musician, who was appointe φορολόγος for four cities (Strabo, xiv. 1. 41, p. 648).

It is highly probable that Roman citizens in the Greek East suffered as much as the native population. It is certain, for instance, that Antony confiscated the landed estates and other property of the proscribed, and may have appropriated tracts of what was actually or had been formerly *ager publicus*, part of which may have been at that time in possession of Romans of high standing. It is an interesting fact that we hear of many Antonii with foreign *cognomina** in the first century A.D. in the rural districts of Asia. This can be most easily explained by assuming the existence in these regions of estates belonging to Antony. The Antonii would then be the descendants of native members of Antony's domanial staff or of his freedmen. An alternative but less probable explanation would be to connect them with veterans of Antony's army.[119]

Antony, it must be said, survived in the memory of the people of Asia Minor as a reckless and hard-hearted robber. Augustus in his *Res Gestae*† thought fit to refer to the plunder of the temples of Asia that Antony had appropriated: 'in templis *omnium* civitatium provinciae Asiae victor ornamenta reposui quae *spoliatis templis* is cum quo bellum gesseram privatim possederat'.

It may be added in this connexion that Antony, like his predecessors Dolabella, Brutus, and Cassius, protected the tyrants and imposed new tyrannies on certain cities hitherto free. I have already alluded to Hybreas of Mylasa, noted for his resistance to Q. Labienus, and a *persona grata* with Antony. We have, in Strabo's account of Tarsus, a vivid picture of the conditions then prevailing in some of the cities of Asia Minor. Antony installed there as tyrant Boethus, 'a bad poet', says Strabo, 'and a bad citizen', and during his reign, until he was deposed by Augustus, he played havoc with the affairs of the city. Of the same type was Straton, tyrant of Amisus by Antony's favour. But the most picturesque figure was Curtius Nicias, whom I have already mentioned. R. Herzog has drawn a capital portrait of this man, a personage highly characteristic of his time. He was an eminent scholar and philosopher, and

---

* We must take into consideration that our information for the first century B.C. and the first century A.D. is very scanty.

† *Mon. Anc.* iv. 49–51.

probably a poet, a man who as the friend of Memmius, Pompey
Cicero, Atticus, Dolabella, and Brutus, played an important
part in the social and political life of Rome. To judge by his
style of living in Rome, he was very rich. He returned to his
native city of Cos during the disorders that followed the death
of Caesar. Once in Cos, he took a leading part in the affairs of
the city and, by his friendships and connexions and his
political tact, saved it from the fate of its patron and ally
Rhodes. At the time of Antony's predominance he became
a regular tyrant of the city and during eight years coined, in
the name of the city, his own money with his own portrait
(Pl. CIII, 8). He died a natural death, and though his remains
after the fall of Antony, were thrown out of his mausoleum, he
remained famous as a benefactor of the city and its great hero
Fourteen inscriptions have been found in various parts of the
island of Cos—dedications to the *patrōoi theoi* for the safety of
Nicias, the son of the city, the patriot, the hero, the bene
factor of the State.[120]

Antony's procedure was the same in the rest of Asia Minor
and Syria, which he visited on his tour of inspection in 41 B.C
Everywhere he imposed heavy contributions, which sometimes
gave rise to acute conflicts. Thus Aradus, severely pressed for
money by Antony's troops, rose in revolt and killed (Hierony
mus says burned alive) four cohorts of Roman soldiers. The
motives of Antony's policy in Syria were partly financial
partly political. He wished to raise money, but he also wished
to safeguard his rear during his projected Parthian expedition
He therefore deposed several city tyrants, mostly pro-Parthian
who fled to Parthia and incited it to attack Rome. From the
cities and the rest of the population (including probably the
vassal dynasts of the borderlands) he demanded large sub
ventions. Especially famous was his abortive raid on the
Palmyrenes, who were reputed to have become very rich as
intermediaries between Rome and Parthia, by reason of
their control of the new caravan road across the Syrian desert
He complained of their maintaining strict neutrality between
Parthia and Rome.[121]

The exactions of Antony undoubtedly aroused a wave of
indignation both in Syria and in Asia and provided favourable

conditions for the Parthian invasion of Syria and Asia Minor under the leadership of Q. Labienus and Pacorus, which began late in 41 or early in 40 B.C.

It is unnecessary to repeat here the little we know of this invasion. It will be sufficient to recall that Labienus remained master of a large part of Asia Minor for about a year and a half, and that the war in Syria was not brought to an end until 38 B.C. The sufferings of Asia Minor were severe. Cities which, like Mylasa and Alabanda, resisted Labienus were taken and sacked. But most of them willingly surrendered, and so did many of the dynasts.[122]

We have some documentary evidence regarding the hardships suffered by Asia Minor in the times of Dolabella, of Brutus and Cassius, and of Antony and Labienus. A fragmentary honorary inscription from Tabae, which has recently been published, concerns a notable of that city who had been a member of the *consilium* of Dolabella. The enumeration of his services, dry and incomplete as it is, is very illuminating. He went on embassies to the 'chief among the rulers' (ὕπατοι τῶν ἡγουμένων) and to the 'dynasts who came to Asia Minor'. By the word ὕπατοι is probably meant, not the consuls nor even the governors of the province of Asia, but perhaps the changing masters of the day, whatever their title may have been, who one after another appeared on the soil of Asia. The term 'dynasts' probably signifies vassal rulers of Asia on their way to the camps of the Roman rulers. At a time of crisis this notable mobilized the cavalry of the city, whether by order of one of the rulers or for the purpose of defending the city against the Parthians does not appear. It is regrettable that the text of the inscription is so imperfect.[123]

Even more eloquent are the inscriptions relating to the Parthian invasion. This produced a great impression on the people of Asia Minor. The time of the Galatian raids seemed to have returned and with it came stories of divine help granted to various cities by their gods and protectors. A long text engraved on the walls of the temple of the Great Zeus of Panamara (near Stratonicea) gives a vivid account of the epiphanies of the god and of the succour lent by him to his sanctuary when the Parthians, marching against Stratonicea,

PLATE CVII

1. Cup (scyphus) with two handles said to have been found at Homs (Syria) ; imitation of metal ware. Coloured with a thick layer of deep-green glaze which blurs the modelling beneath it. Adorned with appliqué figures representing two pairs of fighters. The first group consists of a Greek on horseback fighting with a barbarian, perhaps a Scythian of Mongolian type. The Scythian holds a round shield in his left hand, the gorytus (bow and arrows case) hangs down his right leg. His horse has collapsed, but he is still on its back. For the motif G. M. A. Richter, *Metrop. Mus.St.* iv. 1 (1932), p. 124 and figs. 16, 17, cf. the gorytus of Solokha, my *Iranians and Greeks*, p. 104, pl. XXI. The second group comprises a horseman in Parthian dress riding full gallop to the right and shooting an arrow back at his mounted Greek enemy, who is pursuing him. H. 0·06, diam. 0·085 m. Unpublished. Short mention in *Augustan Art. An Exhibition* &c., 1939, p. 21. I am indebted to Mrs. William H. Moore for permission to reproduce here, though inadequately, her highly interesting cup, which deserves fuller treatment.

2. Cup (scyphus) said to have been found in Syria. Green glaze. Adorned in chequer pattern with lozenges in relief on which palmettes are engraved, alternating with rosettes. H. 0·08 m. *Bull. Metr. Mus.* 1916, p. 65, fig. 6.

3. Askos covered with greenish-yellow glaze. On one side is a bull in relief; on the other (shown on our reproduction) a cow. The handle is in the form of a panther or lioness springing forward, the front paws on the edge of the mouth. H. 0·115 m. H. B. Walters, *B.M.C. Roman Pottery*, 1908, p. 6, K 34.

I have mentioned the type of faience ware illustrated in this plate on p. 1024 and in note 130. It was not produced in large quantities but had a wide distribution. Specimens of it have been found all over the Greco-Italian world from South Russia, on the one hand, to Italy, Gaul, and Germany, on the other. The imported ware was soon replaced, at least in South Russia and Italy, by one made locally. The cup in the possession of Mrs. Moore may perhaps contribute to a clearer insight into the problem of the location of the early factories of this so-called lead-glaze faience. The group of the Parthian fighting with a Greek is most peculiar. It has no parallel in the art of the late Hellenistic period. The 'Parthian shot' as shown on the cup is a common motif of Iranian and Nomadic, but not of Greek or Roman art (see my 'Dura and the problem of Parthian Art', pp. 270 ff., figs. 67, 69, 70). Since a borrowing from Central Asiatic art is most improbable, it may be suggested that the motif was introduced into Greek art as the result of actual observation of the methods of the Parthian archers. There was occasion for this in the first century B.C. at the time of Crassus' expedition and of the later Parthian invasions of Syria and Asia Minor, when the Greeks of Syria and Asia Minor had frequent opportunities of seeing the Parthians as unwelcome and terrifying guests in their own country. I venture therefore to suggest that the new type of faience very probably originated in the first century B.C., and probably in Syria, where many specimens of it have been found. Note that many fragments of this type of pottery have been found in the ruins of Tarsus (many are in the Louvre, several in the Metropolitan Museum).

PLATE CVII

1. New York, Coll. Mrs. William H. Moore

2. New York, Metropolitan Museum of Art

3. London, British Museum

SYRIAN OR ANATOLIAN FAIENCE OF THE FIRST CENTURY B.C.

PLATE CVIII

1. Paris, Louvre

2. New York, Metropolitan Museum

3. Munich, Museum of smaller antiquities (Kleinkunst)

SYRIAN OR ANATOLIAN FAIENCE OF THE FIRST CENTURY B.C.

(1011)

PLATE CVIII

1. Askos reproducing a metal original (see the double handle) covered with green and brown glaze. On the body a vine branch with grapes beautifully modelled in very low relief in imitation again of metal work. H. 0·13, l. 0·17 m. O. Rayet and M. Collignon, *Hist. de la Céramique grecque*, 1888, pl. xiv, 3; F. Courby, *Les vases grecs à reliefs*, p. 514.

2. Cup (scyphus) said to have been found near Homs, Syria. Bequest of Mrs. H. O. Havemeyer. Green glaze. Decorated in low relief with plane-tree twigs bearing leaves and fruit. These are tied with fillets at the stem ends (under the handles) and are separated by two eight-pointed flowerets at the tips (centre of each side of the cup). Description kindly supplied by Miss Chr. Alexander. H. 0·075 m. *Catalogue of the Havemeyer Collection*, 1930, no. 1946; *Bull. Metr. Mus.*, 1930, p. 75. Photograph supplied by the authorities of the Metropolitan Museum of Art, New York.

3. Cup (scyphus) covered with brown (?) glaze. On the body in low relief various objects probably related to the agones or to the Bacchic cult, such as a large lebes, a crater, a hydria on a columnar support, a sacrificial or agonistic table, a large dish, a torch, a wreath, &c. Photograph supplied by the authorities of the Munich Museum.

Two of the specimens reproduced in this plate are decorated with fine vegetal ornaments. Similar ornaments, typical both of the scyphi and the askoi, and very different from those familiar to us in the products of Augustan art, such as the *Ara Pacis*, recur on several metal vases of the late Hellenistic period and on Neo-Attic decorative marble vessels. This treatment of twigs, leaves, and flowers on the Syro-Anatolian faience makes it certain that the finest and earliest specimens of this type of pottery are pre-Augustan. See H. Kusel, *J.D.A.I.*, xxxii (1917), Anz., p. 55, fig. 1; L. Curtius, *Röm. Mitt.*, xlix (1934), p. 274.

The Syro-Anatolian faience ware in imitation of contemporary metal ware is a peculiar phenomenon in the history of Hellenistic pottery, and has been very inadequately studied. It was, to my mind, an attempt by Hellenistic potters, using and improving the technical devices of Egypt and Mesopotamia for the production of fine faience, to create on this basis a purely Greek, Pan-hellenistic type of pottery which would appeal to the whole of the Hellenistic world. I have shown above that neither the hellenized Mesopotamian faience (pl. lxxx) nor the earlier Egyptian faience of the Hellenistic period (pls. xxxvi, xli, 2, and xlii, 1 and 2), though very popular in Mesopotamia and Egypt respectively, ever had a wide circulation in the rest of the Hellenistic world. Quite different was the history of the faience ware discussed here. Though late in origin, it soon became one of the most popular, though expensive, types of Hellenistic pottery, similar in many respects to the earlier Megarian bowls and other kinds of relief pottery used (like the Syro-Anatolian faience) as sub-stitutes for expensive metal ware; similar also to the painted *lagynoi* and the related wares. See below, Ch. VIII. However, any kind of generalization in this respect is premature so long as the material is not fully collected and classified, and the whole group studied on the basis of careful technical analyses of clay and glaze and with the help of a minute stylistic investigation.

endeavoured to storm it. Less fortunate was another temple of the κοινόν, that of Lagina.[124]

In general Labienus showed no consideration for the cities of Asia Minor. He, like the other Roman plunderers of the province, was in need of money, which he exacted ruthlessly from the cities, besides sacking many temples.* The ambassadors of Mylasa who appeared before C. Caesar (Octavianus) at Samos in 31 B.C. draw a gloomy picture of the state of their city after its siege and capture by Labienus:† many citizens had been killed, many others captured, the temples inside and outside the city had been pillaged, the countryside devastated, the farms burnt down, and calamities of every kind had descended upon the city.

It is tempting to connect with the same events the fragmentary decree of Aphrodisias in honour of a man who helped the city at a moment of famine, was magistrate in war-time, and perhaps took an active part in one of the battles.[125]

The devastations of Labienus did not induce Antony to relax his own efforts to raise funds. He was in urgent need of money for his Parthian expedition and afterwards for the great struggle with C. Caesar. He had determined from the outset to acquire a large and powerful fleet. This he collected and organized at the expense of his Asiatic and European provinces. He lent a number of his ships in 36 B.C. to C. Caesar for the purposes of his struggle with Sextus Pompeius, and some of these or of the more efficient members of their crews were probably retained by C. Caesar in his service. We still possess the dossier of the brave captain of one of the larger war-ships, who was a native of Rhosus in Syria, distinguished himself in the war against Sextus Pompeius, and after the war took up service with C. Caesar, and remained in his navy probably without interruption until the battle of Actium. The triumvirs honoured him with the franchise and immunity, and later, after the battle of Actium, Caesar at his request granted pardon and certain privileges to his native city, and recommended him to the attention of his fellow citizens.[126]

Nor was Greece, any more than Asia, left unmolested after all its previous hardships. It is certain that at least

* Cass. Dio, xlviii. 26.   † *S.I.G.*³ 768.

Achaea had to pay heavy contributions to Antony, which he rigorously exacted from the cities before handing over the country to Sextus Pompeius in accordance with the treaty of Misenum.[127]

The epilogue to this long story of pillage and oppression was the final duel between Antony and C. Caesar, in which the East was once more forced to participate and of course by the usual methods. The facts of this last struggle are well known and add nothing to the picture that I have drawn. It must, however, be borne in mind that the armies and navies mobilized in this war were the largest ever seen. The army of Antony comprised at least 75,000 foot and 12,000 horse, while his fleet of 500 large war-ships and hundreds of transports carried crews which must be estimated at between 125,000 and 150,000 men. In addition he had reserves of 11 legions and many auxiliaries. The army and fleet of C. Caesar were of about the same size. To feed, pay, and clothe forces of this magnitude and to provide rowers for the fleet, Antony was naturally forced to call upon all the resources of Greece and of the East. Egypt supplied part of his requirements, but the bulk of them were met by Syria, Asia Minor, and Greece.[128]

It may be appropriate to end this survey by referring to the well-known passage of Plutarch* in which he describes the hopeless misery and the unexampled humiliation of the population of Greece on the eve of Actium. After the battle C. Caesar sailed to Athens, came to terms with the Greeks, and distributed the grain that remained at the end of the campaign among the cities, for these were in a sorry plight, having been stripped of money, slaves, and beasts of burden. The corn which Caesar distributed was no doubt that which he had previously requisitioned from the Greeks. Plutarch concludes his statement on a personal note: 'My great-grandfather Nicarchus', he says, 'used to tell how all his fellow-citizens (he was a Chaeronean) were pressed into the service of carrying wheat on their shoulders down to the sea at Anticyra, their pace being quickened with the whip; they had carried one load in this way and a second had been assigned to them, but just as they were about to start word was brought that Antony had

* *Ant.* 68. 6–8

been defeated, and this was the salvation of the city; for immediately the agents and soldiers of Antony fled and the citizens divided the corn among themselves'.[129]

4. EPILOGUE

I have now surveyed the extension of Roman rule over part of the Hellenistic world at the end of the second and in the first century B.C., and have endeavoured to show the effect of its successive phases upon the social and economic development of the conquered territory. I may here pause and draw some general conclusions from the material I have set out.

Rome intervened in the East on the pretext of restoring liberty to the Greek world. According to Roman official theory the protectorate that she established over the Greek cities as a result of this intervention was a real boon to her allies (*socii*), as her associates in the East, both cities and monarchs, were officially called. As regards the cities it was said to guarantee them freedom and self-government, to put an end to royal oppression and royal encroachments on their liberty, and to bring them safety from foreign enemies and internal peace, that is to say, a cessation of petty wars among themselves and of civil strife and social and political disturbances. For the monarchies it was supposed to mean the establishment of a solid political equilibrium, undisturbed by wars or by the ambitions of individual rulers.

During the short period from the intervention of Rome to the Mithridatic wars, her benevolent protectorate proved more or less harmless to her city-allies. Some of the blessings described above were, at least in a certain measure, realized. But it brought no real progress comparable to that which the Greek cities had achieved under the royal protectorate and domination.

As regards their constitutional standing, no fundamental change was introduced by Rome. Roman theory regarded them as independent bodies politic in alliance with her. But in practice they had no more political independence than had the city-allies or subjects of the Hellenistic monarchies. Rome never hesitated to impose her will on the cities when necessary, exactly as the Hellenistic rulers had done.

Nor did Roman protection against foreign enemies surpass or even equal in efficiency that which the Greek cities had received from former protectors and masters, especially the Antigonids and the Seleucids, and the successors of the latter, the Attalids. Finally, civil strife within the cities was never eliminated so long as they retained a semblance of their political independence.

As regards Rome's relations with the Hellenistic monarchies, the boasted balance and equilibrium never existed. The stronger monarchies were smashed by her mailed fist, but the result was not political freedom for the weaker. In fact all the Hellenistic monarchies lost their independence almost entirely, and became practically vassals of the Roman State.

Even so, the period of Roman protectorate and partial domination contributed in Greece to a certain economic recovery from the havoc caused by the first great wars of liberation and enslavement. In Asia Minor it was a time of brilliant progress, which was not greatly impaired even by the transformation of the Pergamene kingdom into the Roman province of Asia. The most important factor in the economic life of the Hellenistic world at this time was not so much the dubious peace established by Rome as the closer economic contact between the East and the West, and the increasing demand for Hellenistic goods on the western market. Moreover, the new capital and the new energy which the many immigrants from Italy, the *negotiatores*, brought into Greece and Asia Minor helped those countries further to develop their economic resources.

With the Mithridatic wars begins a new phase in the relations between the Hellenistic East and its Roman rulers. In theory the situation of the former remained the same, but in fact it had changed completely. During and after these wars it became evident to every one in those regions that the blessings of Roman protection were a mere fiction. The political liberty both of the cities and of such kings as remained independent was seen to be an empty formula. The military defence of Hellenistic territory against foreign enemies proved to be badly organized and seriously defective. The

successive wars in the northern region of the Balkan peninsula,
the Mithridatic wars, the repeated expeditions against the
pirates, the unsuccessful attempts to hold in check not only the
great Parthian Empire but even such minor Powers as Armenia
and the Nabataeans, strikingly displayed the inefficiency and
inadequacy of Roman military organization. The partial
victories were gained at the cost of the utmost effort and of
enormous expense, the burden of which fell upon the allies of
Rome.

The final stage of this evolution was reached with the civil
wars. Whereas the Romans had some plausible ground for
arguing that their wars in the East and the struggle with the
pirates were after all enterprises in which Rome and the allies
had a joint interest and that their successful issue was perhaps
of more importance to the latter than to the former, the Roman
civil wars, as I have remarked, had manifestly nothing to do
with the safety, prosperity, and liberty of the allies. Yet it was
on the allies that the burden of them fell most heavily. When
Sulla punished Greece and Asia Minor for having supported
Mithridates and for having taken part in the massacre of
the 'Romans', when his successors applied to them for help
against the allies of Mithridates, the tribes of the northern
Balkans and the pirates, the *socii* accepted the heavy fines and
the arbitrary requisitions as a great calamity but may have
understood their justification. But when Pompey and Caesar,
who both claimed to be the legitimate rulers of Rome, demanded
allegiance and material support from the 'allies', when the
same was done by Brutus and Cassius on one side and by
C. Caesar and Antony on the other, and again by Antony and
by C. Caesar, and when each party punished with the utmost
severity those who sought to remain neutral, the 'allies' were
reduced to utter bewilderment and despair.

Thus, so far as the provision of security was concerned, the
Roman régime proved a gross and cruel imposture. Never
before had the Hellenistic countries suffered so terribly from
wars with the causes and objects of which they had as a rule
no concern whatever, if they even understood them.

Nor was the political control established by the Romans in
the East successful in its methods. After a period during which

a protectorate was exercised from Rome by means of legations, commissions, and embassies, a more direct system of control, known as the provincial régime, was gradually set up in some of the former Hellenistic monarchies. In theory the aim of this régime was the same as that of the protectorate: to secure for the provincials, usually referred to as 'allies' (*socii*) of Rome, peace, justice, fair administration, and equitable taxation, and concomitant happiness and prosperity. The difference was one of method: in lieu of sending temporary missions to the East, the Roman Senate and People now had permanent representation there, in the persons of governors of the provinces armed with full civil and military powers and holding office for a year. This change in the system of control proved a complete failure. The new yearly governors practically carried on in their provinces the system of administration and taxation of the Hellenistic kings. No essential factor was changed, except one—the spirit in which this system was applied. In place of the personal, paternal, benevolent rule of hereditary kings whose interests were identical with those of the country, a rule regarded as at least tolerable by the people, there was substituted a truly 'colonial' régime, arrogant, selfish, corrupt, cruel, ruthless, and inefficient. Some of the governors were men of high principles, enlightened, well-meaning, and benevolent. But all of them, the good and the bad alike (and the latter rather than the former were typical of the class), ruled over the provinces as over 'estates' of the Roman People (*praedia populi Romani*), mere annexes, not constituent parts, of the Roman State, inhabited by an inferior race. This unfortunate attitude was aggravated by the employment of tax-farmers, the *publicani*, Romans, not local people, imbued with the same spirit as the governors and their staffs. The institution in itself was not bad, but it assumed grotesque and oppressive forms in the atmosphere of 'colonial' exploitation that prevailed in the provinces and of political corruption at Rome. The Roman provincial administration was a real 'pasha' rule of the kind with which we have been made familiar by the practice of Turkish Sultans and Persian Shahs of the past. It was certainly far inferior to the rule of the Antigonids, Seleucids, and Attalids.

Such conditions were unfavourable to the economic development of the countries subjected to them. The provincials were
inevitably conscious that they were mere tools in the hands of
foreigners, without rights or liberty even in the economic field.
They laboured and suffered not for their own advantage, nor
even for that of their own country, but for strangers, for
foreign rulers who absorbed all their gains, in normal times by
an elaborate system of fiscal oppression, and in emergencies by
violent and arbitrary exactions.

The provincials could not indeed suspend work and production, but they carried these on from necessity and in an
atmosphere of utter demoralization. The enormous majority
sought nothing more than to keep themselves and their
families alive and to escape imprisonment and death.

No doubt all the provincials were not treated alike. There
was an *élite*, the rich and influential magnates of the cities, who
by servility and bribes, and a judicious choice of friends and
protectors, succeeded in retaining and increasing their fortunes
and in securing an exceptional and privileged position among
their fellow citizens, as *immunes* among the masses of oppressed
provincials. I have mentioned several such magnates, and the
civil wars produced conditions favourable to the growth of
their number. To these must be added the Italian immigrants,
the *negotiatores*, who formed another privileged group amid the
multitude of those who had many duties but no rights. As
owners of land or shops, as merchants and ship-owners, or
as money-lenders, they fared much better than the natives
similarly engaged.

Thus the burden of Roman rule lay with especial weight
upon the working and middle classes of the towns and of the
country.

And yet the conditions above described formed no more than
a superstructure on the economic life of the East, of which the
core remained sound and full of promise. As I have said, the
period of the domination of the Roman Senate and People was
not merely the sad conclusion of a long process of development,
a time of destruction both systematic and spasmodic. It was
also the preparation for a renascence. Wars and oppression
were an important factor in the economic evolution of the East,

though of an exclusively negative character. But alongside of this negative and restrictive factor there was another, of a positive kind, for which the Romans were responsible. I refer to the new opportunities for economic expansion which the gradual establishment of the Roman world State offered to the East. New impulse was given to its economic efforts in the second century B.C. by throwing open Italy as a market for its products and by the rapid increase in the buying capacity of its Italian customers. During the period of civil strife, this new western market, though severely shaken by wars at home and abroad, continued to expand, to become more united and consolidated, and to demand Eastern commodities of all kinds in ever increasing quantities. The economic unity of the ancient world, which had been partly achieved in the East by Alexander, was now gradually restored there and extended to the West. From the standpoint of economic history the close contact between East and West that resulted from Roman rule was as important as had been Alexander's opening of the East to western trade. New material resources in the West were added to the world's stock, new economic possibilities were opened by its gradual urbanization and pacification. No new land, of course, was discovered. Here again the comparison with Columbus and America is misleading. Western Europe had been in commercial and economic contact with eastern Europe and the Near East from time immemorial. The new phenomenon was not any discovery of entirely new markets and of completely unknown resources. It was the incorporation of the West in the fabric of the East, an extension of the eastern economy and of the eastern mode of life, with all its requirements, to large areas hitherto little affected by them. The East and the West were not only politically united. They were knitted together into one economic unit by the establishment of lasting and uninterrupted social and economic relations between the united West and the equally united East.

This process began early, but was slow and hardly perceptible in its beginnings. In the turmoil of the civil wars, in the stormy atmosphere of the first century B.C., solid foundations were laid for the new unity of the world. In this period the West underwent a momentous evolution such as, in the East,

had begun long before. We have seen how there, slowly
and gradually, before and especially after Alexander, a new
'oecumenical' Greek nation, with one and the same language
one and the same civilization, one and the same mentality, and
the same forms of economic and social life, was created and
consolidated. And so it was, with certain differences in the
West. An Italian nation came into being, in spite of the
diversity of the ethnographic units composing it. The evolu
tion began with the latinization or romanization of Italy
which made astonishing progress in the time of the civil wars
Out of a chaos of languages and civilizations arose a new and
compact Italian nation with a single language and a single
civilization. This new nation streamed to the North and to the
West on the heels of the Roman legions. It first superimposed
itself upon, and then gradually penetrated deeply into, the
areas of Berber, Celtic, Iberian, Illyrian and to some extent of
Thracian civilization, where it brought about the gradual and
successful development of a new type of men and a new people

The romanization or latinization of the West was a compli
cated phenomenon not easy to understand. The new Latin
civilization, from its very origin, was connected by thousands
of ties with the Greek city-civilization of the East. In the field
of cultural and intellectual life and to a large extent in economic
and social structure, it was, in fact, a new western edition of
Greek and especially of Hellenistic civilization. Its rise and
consolidation contributed decisively to the unification, on lines
mainly devised by Greece, of the ancient civilized world in
general. And it was in the time of the civil wars that this uni
fication was effectively realized, not only in its political aspect

No endeavour was made by the West to latinize the East and
still less was there any attempt by the East to hellenize the
West. But by independent internal evolution each of these two
sections of the civilized world reached a point at which union
between them became possible and natural. Their conception
of life, their mentality, their social and economic organization
though different in many respects, were of one and the same
type. The 'Romans' of the West and the 'Hellenes' of the
East understood each other very well, and had more or less
the same requirements and the same desires and ideals. In

economic respects the result of unification was that the West was prepared to absorb a greatly increased quantity of eastern goods, in fact as large a quantity as the East was able to produce; and that the East was disposed to open its markets to western commodities provided that these were as good as, or better than, its own products.

Wars and oppression never completely undermined the economic foundations of the East. Greece no doubt had seen her territory laid waste, her population drained by race suicide and emigration, demoralized by the Roman methods of government, and reduced to general poverty. Her economic leadership was at an end and she never regained her former prosperity. She had always been poor in natural resources and in this respect she became even poorer in late Hellenistic times by progressive deforestation, exhaustion and erosion of the soil, the exhaustion of certain mines, and so forth. Her ancient wealth and splendour had been due, not to the bounties of nature, but to her unique creative genius, which had secured her supremacy in the intellectual and artistic sphere, and to her economic pre-eminence. But these times were gone, and in the economic life of the united world Greece was bound to play a very modest part. Greek products, except antiquities and education—and prosperity could not be based on the export of these—were not in demand in the rest of the civilized world.

The situation of Asia Minor, Syria, and Egypt was different. The fertility of their soil had not diminished. The demand for their special products had been maintained and was rapidly increasing. They retained their position as countries of transit, and their role as carriers, for the trade with Iran, India, and China. Neither the calamities of war nor the hardships of oppression could kill the active and enterprising economic spirit of the Near East. It is evident that Asia Minor and Syria could not have paid the enormous sums that were demanded from them had they not possessed perennial sources of wealth such as war and oppression could not utterly destroy. These sources were their agriculture, their pasturage, their industry and commerce.

It is curious to notice that one of the greatest inventions in the field of ancient industry, that of blown glass, an invention which revolutionized the market for pottery, was made either

PLATE CIX

1. One-handled glass jug. Brown. Inscription Ἐννίον | ἐποίει (on a *tabella ansata*). Neck decorated with flutes; ovoid body with three friezes: (1) palmettes, (2) the inscription bound by a honeycomb pattern of lozenges, and (3) vertical flutes. The jug, said to have been found in Italy, was blown in the same mould as the intact jug in the Metropolitan Museum (D. B. Harden, *J.R.S*, xxxv (1935), p. 168, pl. XXIII, *c*). The knob at the bottom is probably wrongly restored. H. with the knob o·228 m. For a fuller description D. B. Harden, loc. cit., cf. *Augustan Art. An Exhibition &c.*, 1939, p. 22. Photograph supplied by Mr. R. W. Smith.

2. A large bronze crater found at Antium. Fluted. Handles and foot modern. On the shoulder a chased frieze of lotus flowers inlaid with silver. On the rim inscription in letters consisting of dots: Βασιλεὺς Μιθραδάτης Εὐπάτωρ τοῖς ἀπὸ τοῦ γυμνασίου Εὐπατορισταῖς, and in cursive a little farther, on Σύρα διάσωζε. H. without the foot o·70 m., diam. (at lip) o·43 m. Th. Reinach, *Mithridates Eupator*, p. 460, no. 10 and pl. facing p. 284; H. Stuart Jones, *A Catalogue of Ancient Sculptures preserved in the Municipal collections of Rome: the Sculptures of the Palazzo dei Conservatori*, 1926, p. 175, no. 10, pl. LXII (with bibliography). The crater came to Antium probably as part of the war booty of Sulla, Lucullus, or Pompey. It is to be regretted that we do not know from what city it came. It may have stood in Delos, or Athens, or one of the Greek cities of the Euxine, or any city of Asia Minor and the islands. In any case the existence of an association of Eupatoristai would testify to the enthusiasm with which some of the Greek cities began by greeting the rule of the philhellenic king. The crater is a beautiful specimen of late Hellenistic bronze work. Photograph supplied by Alinari.

PLATE CIX

2. Bronze krater. Rome, Palazzo dei Conservatori

1. Ennion's glass jug. Coll. of R. W. Smith (on exhibition, New York, Metropolitan Museum of Art)

GLASSWORK AND METALWORK OF THE LATE HELLENISTIC PERIOD

PLATE CX

1. New York, Metropolitan Museum of Art

2. *a–e* and *g*. Alexandria Museum. *f*. New York, Metropolitan Museum of Art

LATE HELLENISTIC GLASS

PLATE CX

1. Six-sided glass amphorisk with two handles found in Potamia near Golgoi, Cyprus. Blue. Inscription 'Εννίων | ἐπώησεν. Short cylindrical neck, plain. Convex shoulders divided by palmettes into six panels each containing a rosette within a semicircle. Sides taper downwards. Each side forms a panel variously decorated: (a) double flute hanging from a palmette; (b) jug hanging from an ivy spray; (c) pipes hanging from a palmette; (d) inscription; (e) bunch of grapes hanging from a palmette; (f) cantharus hanging from an ivy spray. Base flat. Blown in a (?) tripartite mould. H. 0·143 m. I have repeated in abbreviated form the description of the amphorisk by D. B. Harden, *J.R.S.* xxv (1935), p. 168, no. 6, who gives a complete bibliography, cf. *Augustan Art. An Exhibition* &c., 1939, p. 22, fig. 49. I may remind the reader that similar decoration is typical of the painted lagynoi.

2 *f*. Two-handled cup. Greenish yellow. Inscriptions: 'Εννίων | ἐποίη|σεν in a tabella ansata and μνη⟨σ⟩θῇ | ὁ ἀγορά|ζνω (*sic*) (μνησθῇ ὁ ἀγοράζων) likewise. On the body two friezes: one containing the inscriptions and between them ivy sprays and vine sprays, and the other adorned with vertical flutes. Sloping bottom with honeycomb pattern of lozenges. Flat base. Blown in tripartite mould. H. 0·062 m. Description borrowed from D. B. Harden, loc. cit., p. 166, no. 2, *d*, who lists three other cups of the same mould and gives the bibliography, cf. *Augustan Age. An Exhibition* &c., p. 22. On the invention of blown glass Ch. VI, n. 146.

2 *a–e* and *g*. Decorative glass plaques. See Ch. IV, n. 167.

in Syria or in Egypt probably in the second half of the first century B.C. (Pls. CIX and CX). Less important, but still symptomatic, was the production of a new type of glazed pottery, the elegant pottery of yellow, brown, and green colour covered with what is known as 'Bleiglazur'. It was invented probably in the second half of the first century B.C., perhaps somewhere in Asia Minor, and was exported far and wide to the East and West, but especially to Italy (Pls. CVII and CVIII).

The date of these inventions is admittedly controversial. We may ascribe them to the time of the Augustan peace, and compare their conquest of the market with the notable achievement of the Arretine potters. But it is evident that such improvements and discoveries were in the air and that the way had been prepared for them by a long series of experiments.[130]

Another significant feature is the keenness of the merchants of the time to devise new methods of trade and to try new trade-routes. Witness the discovery of the monsoons and the use made of it by the Greek merchants of Egypt.* [131] Similarly in the Mediterranean the channels of trade were radically altered in the late first century B.C., to accord with the new situation, and we notice a change of orientation similar to that which followed the Persean war and the destruction of Corinth. Delos had lost its position as the great Italian emporium in the Aegean and was slowly dying. Peculiar political and commercial factors had made it a great clearing-house for the trade between the Hellenistic world and Italy. These factors ceased to exist in the time of the civil wars. Syria was now a Roman province, the pirates had vanished, Corinth was about to be restored to life. It was natural that the Syrian merchants should prefer to establish their *fonduqs* in southern Italy and that Anatolian and Pontic traders should do the same or make use of Corinth rather than Delos for their commercial relations with Italy. It was not Mithridates and the pirates who destroyed Delos. It died a natural death. Trade gradually abandoned it and it became once more what it had been before Antigonus Gonatas—a famous sacred island and an occasional port of call for merchants.

* It is interesting to observe that at the same time the great 'silk route across Asia was being organized by China.

Rhodes was better situated, but it never recovered the position that it had held before Delos entered on the brilliant phase of its history. It remained a convenient port of call for Syrian and Egyptian merchants trading with the Aegean and the Euxine. But those merchants, when trading with Italy, had no real need to make use of impoverished Rhodes as a commercial centre. Nevertheless, Rhodes remained an excellent and well-organized port and was never completely forsaken by international trade.

The great commercial cities of the new age were the Syrian and Phoenician ports, Alexandria, the ports of Asia Minor, Corinth, and the ports of the south-eastern and south-western coasts of Italy. We observe no change in the orientation of the Pontic trade, nor was any possible.

We have no means of estimating the volume of the trade of the ancient world in the late first century B.C. No statistical data are available. The archaeological material is dispersed and has never been made an object of careful study from the economic standpoint. It is evident, however, that the ground was well prepared for the brilliant economic revival of the age of Augustus. All that was required for this was peace and good government. Of these both East and West had urgent need and were prepared to make good use, and they presently attained them, thanks to the unity of the ancient world established by Rome. However, the crucial problem remains: was this unity an unmixed blessing? did it not bring with itself germs of stagnation and decay? This question cannot be discussed here. I have dealt with it in another book and have shown what were the ultimate results of that unity.

VIII

SUMMARY AND EPILOGUE

NEW FEATURES IN THE SOCIAL AND ECONOMIC LIFE OF THE HELLENISTIC WORLD

INTRODUCTORY: PHASES OF EVOLUTION

I HAVE traced in the preceding chapters the economic and social development of the Hellenistic world during the three centuries that followed Alexander's death. I may now, for the convenience of the reader, briefly summarize what I have written. The conquest of the Near East by Alexander relieved the Greek city-states of continental Greece and of the islands from an acute political, economic, and social crisis which had found its expression in the economic and social sphere in a growing overpopulation of Greece, in the reduction of the masses to indigence and the concentration of wealth in the hands of a small class; while a diminishing demand for the products of Greek industry on both the home and foreign markets brought about a gradual decrease in industrial production and a corresponding decline of commercial activity.

Alexander's Eastern conquests provided the Greeks with new markets for their wares and offered them excellent opportunities for emigration and the recovery of economic status. They helped to set Greece on her feet again and led to a period of great commercial activity and prosperity. But this revival was of short duration. It was impeded from the outset not only by the incessant wars of Alexander's successors, which especially affected Greece, but also by the buoyant economic development of the Near East on Greek lines, which slowly but continuously reduced the demand for Greek products in the Asiatic and African parts of the former empire of Alexander.

The years that followed, known as the period of the political balance of power, witnessed a certain stabilization of economic and social conditions in the Hellenistic world. The three leading monarchies that emerged from the turmoil of the time of the Successors were actively occupied in consolidating their position and remodelling their economic and social life. In the East this was done with the help of an ever-increasing host of Macedonian and Greek immigrants distributed throughout the former Oriental monarchies in larger and smaller groups. The same process was begun in certain minor monarchical States and in some of the leading Greek city-states which had succeeded in retaining their political independence.

The leading role, both politically and in other respects, was played by the two largest and wealthiest regions of the Hellenistic world—Egypt under the Ptolemies and Syria under the Seleucids. Both the Ptolemies and the Seleucids had a great task before them in the organization of their States on new administrative, financial, social, and economic lines, with a view to their strength, wealth, and contentment, and in their political consolidation. The main problem before them was to establish a reasonable *modus vivendi* between the two constituent parts of the population of their kingdoms, the two foundations on which their dominion rested—on the one hand the new settlers, for the most part associates of the king and instruments in his hands, chiefly Macedonians and Greeks; on the other the natives, the economic backbone of the two countries. These two groups had at first very little in common: their mentality was utterly different and so was the structure of their relations, social, commercial, and industrial. A new economic organization that would produce the harmonious co-operation of the two parts was indispensable in each kingdom, but to achieve it was a matter of extreme difficulty. Without this co-operation the Ptolemies and the Seleucids could not attain their principal objects, the fusion of their kingdoms into solid political units and their strengthening and enrichment by the development and more rational exploitation of their natural resources.

The efforts of the first Ptolemies, of whom we know much, and of the early Seleucids, of whom we know much less, appear to have met with fair success. Egypt and the Asiatic empire of the Seleucids became, if not solid and enduring political, economic, and social units (for the problem of the amalgamation of the Greeks and the natives was not satisfactorily solved either by the first Ptolemies or by the Seleucids), at least strong and wealthy States; these enabled their rulers to play in the Hellenistic world the part not only of political but also of economic leaders, at the expense of, but without crushing detriment to, the other constituent parts of it, especially the Greek cities of the mainland and the islands. The result of this hegemony was a certain stabilization and political and economic balance of power, which seemed likely to endure.

But the stabilization and balance of power thus established were never firmly founded and never remained undisturbed for long. They were undermined from the very start by certain elements in the situation: by the political rivalry between the three leading monarchies, entailing recurrent wars in which the minor States took an active part; by the fierce struggle of the Greek cities for political independence and their conflicts among themselves, aggravated and complicated by internal discords and social revolutions in some of the leading cities; by the gradual but steady disintegration of the Seleucid monarchy under the pressure of foreign wars, of the Galatian invasion of Asia Minor, and of the revival of national spirit in India and Iran. The consequences of the instability of the balance of power were most acutely felt in Greece, the weakest and least consolidated part of the Hellenistic world. A gradual impoverishment, connected with the steadily growing economic emancipation of the East from the Greek motherland, became the leading feature of its life, and this impoverishment was responsible for the revival of acute social and economic unrest.

A strong effort to give greater political and economic stability to the Hellenistic world, on the basis of the political hegemony of the leading Powers, was made at the end of the third century B.C. by Antiochus III of Syria and Philip V of Macedonia, to the detriment of Egypt, which had hitherto been the strongest Hellenistic State and the pivot of Hellenistic equilibrium. Under the combined military pressure of Macedonia and Syria Egypt lost its control of the Aegean and its leading position in the commercial life of the Hellenistic world. These it was unable to recover, for it was involved in a difficult internal struggle, due to the inability of the Ptolemies to find a satisfactory solution of the main problem that confronted them—how to develop friendly relations between the Greeks and the natives and secure their harmonious co-operation in the economic life of the country, which they were organizing on the basis of a strict State control. The result was a gradual decline in the prosperity of Egypt and its growing isolation.

Meanwhile the efforts of Antiochus and Philip, successful at the outset, were disconcerted by a new development. The minor States, whose very existence was threatened by these endeavours to unite the Hellenistic world, called into the political arena a new force, which proved unexpectedly decisive. They appealed to Rome, the new predominant Power of the West.

The intervention of Rome had two important consequences. The protagonists in the attempt at stabilization—Macedonia and Syria—were eliminated by Rome in a series of effective strokes. Rome herself assumed the task of pacifying and stabilizing the Hellenistic world under her benevolent hegemony, and carried it out successfully for a time. After a period during which the Greek city-states, in particular, of the mainland, the islands, and Asia Minor, experienced great sufferings and suffered severe losses as a result of the wars of liberation and enslavement, the Hellenistic territories were at last granted a breathing-space. For about fifty years they lived in a condition of peace and unity enforced upon them by the heavy hand of Rome and only temporarily interrupted by short periods of local wars. This enforced peace had its beneficial results. Greece and Asia Minor enjoyed a phase of prosperity, more conspicuous in the latter, less so in Greece. But this prosperity was not shared by Egypt and Syria; for Egypt was still helplessly struggling with its internal problems and was rapidly decaying, while Syria, in its Oriental seclusion, was prevented from quietly enjoying its natural wealth and its economic opportunities by the forces of disintegration, supported and intensified by the political action of Rome.

Still more important than the partial and compulsory peace was another factor in the economic development of the Hellenistic States, which also was a consequence of Roman intervention and protectorate. I allude to the closer political, social, and economic connexion of the two parts of the civilized world of that time: the Western, centred around Italy and Rome, and the Eastern, more or less reunited under the pressure of the Roman protectorate. For the Eastern region the increasingly intimate interpenetration of the two worlds meant not only a new market for its goods, a market continuously increasing in size and purchasing capacity, and perhaps a new field for emigration (mostly through slavery), but also an influx of new capital and new energies from the West. These made their way into the East with the steady flow of enterprising and well-to-do new settlers, the 'Roman' *negotiatores*. What the *negotiatores* brought with them was not only a brisk business spirit but also capital ready for investment. This was no doubt capital that had formerly been accumulated by the East and had been transferred to the West in the form of loot, booty, and indemnities. Nevertheless, it was some compensation to the East that at least in part it was not invested in the West, but returned to its original home to revivify and reorganize the anaemic and disorganized economy of the East.

The recovery of the Hellenistic world brought about by the Roman protectorate was, however, partial and local. It did not affect the richest parts of it—Syria and Egypt—and therefore never restored in full the prosperity that had prevailed under the Successors and under the creators of the Hellenistic balance of power. This blessed age never returned. Moreover, the recovery was short-lived. It was interrupted and shaken to its very foundations by the revolt, led by Mithridates, of Asia Minor and Greece against Roman domination; and was completely reversed during the civil wars that followed, when the East was ruthlessly exploited and utterly humiliated by its masters, who were fighting their own fierce battles for power on Greek soil and with the help of the resources of the East. Even in the short intervals between the successive stages of the Roman civil war the East had no rest. Roman domination and the Roman system of provincial administration weighed heavily and unremittingly upon it.

Such in brief were the successive phases of the economic and social development of the Hellenistic world. It had failed to find solutions for its principal problems: the establishment of political unity or at least of a more or less peaceful political co-operation, that is to say, of a durable balance of power. This was made impossible by the ceaseless struggles for political hegemony, which had a disastrous effect not only in the political but also in the economic and social spheres. No doubt these struggles stimulated the energies of the rivals, compelling them to efforts whereby the productivity and trade of their respective territories might be increased. But, on the other hand, the wars absorbed or destroyed an enormous volume of human energy which otherwise would have been active in the economic field, and large quantities of actual or prospective goods; they encouraged and developed the destructive spirit of individuals and groups (for example, piracy); and they created in the masses of the population an ever-increasing sense of uncertainty, which gradually and inevitably induced depression and apathy.

Within the great monarchical States (other than Macedonia) the rulers never succeeded in attaining stabilization and consolidation. They never found a way of escape from the great antinomy in the political, social, and economic life of their dominions, to which the conquest of Alexander had given rise: the conflict between the two leading forms of civilized life, the Eastern and the Western, between Greek city-states and Oriental monarchies—between Greek 'politai' and Oriental subjects; between the Greek economic system, based on freedom and private initiative, and the State economy of the East, supervised, guided, and controlled. And finally they were faced with the great eternal problem of human society, as acute in the ancient world as it is in the modern: the antinomy between the rulers and the ruled, the 'haves' and the 'have-nots', the *bourgeoisie* and the working classes, the city and the country.

It was in the main the inability of the Hellenistic world to find, if not the solution of these problems, at least an acceptable compromise, which was responsible for its easy defeat by Rome and its incorporation in the fabric of the Roman Empire. The destinies of the old Hellenistic States as parts of the Roman Empire have been dealt with by me in another work and do not concern us here. I may, however, observe that although the problem of political unity was solved by the Romans, at least for a certain time, the other problems were not; and it was this inability to solve them that was the underlying cause of the political dissolution of the Roman Empire.

In the three centuries of the existence of the Hellenistic world many new social and economic features came into existence in the course of its evolution, features which were unknown to the Oriental empires and to classical Greece. I have drawn attention to these and done my best to elucidate them in the preceding chapters, both in their essence and their gradual development. The attentive reader of my book could, without my help, arrange them in systematic order and form an idea of their character and importance. But in order to make this process easier, I may—at the risk of repeating myself—offer a brief systematic survey of the more prominent of these new features as our meagre evidence reveals them, in the form rather of problems than of ascertained facts. In doing so I shall deal more explicitly with certain features to which I have devoted less attention in my historical narrative. It is not my purpose to treat systematically in this chapter all the new features of economic and social life, for this would probably require an entire volume. I shall confine myself to a small selection, to those which I regard as of the greatest interest to students of the ancient world. In the first part of my survey I shall address myself to the social aspect of the period, and proceed to the economic aspect in the second.

I. SOME FEATURES OF SOCIAL LIFE

1. UNITY OF THE HELLENISTIC WORLD

ALEXANDER'S conquest of the Persian Empire made a considerable change in the aspect of the Eastern section of the ancient world. It added to the Greek share of it the former constituent parts of the Persian Empire, its various satrapies. The whole extent of these satrapies was familiar to the administration and to many of the inhabitants of the Persian State. They were intersected by roads, which were well organized and carefully kept in repair, and these roads, military and commercial, formed a well-balanced system. Though direct evidence on this subject is lacking, there is no doubt that the

Persian administration was in possession of itineraries, that is to say, descriptions of these roads with a record of distances between the stopping-places; such itineraries were later known to the Greeks as ὁδοιπορίαι or σταθμοί, and to the Romans as *itineraria*. For purposes of taxation and preparedness for war the Persian kings and satraps certainly had in their hands lists of the inhabited centres of each satrapy, and at least an approximate idea of the territories belonging to these inhabited centres, their population, and their material resources. Of course all the satrapies of the huge Persian Empire were not equally familiar to its rulers. Such parts of the empire as Egypt, Asia Minor, Phoenicia, Palestine, Mesopotamia, Babylonia, centres of high civilization and thoroughly developed administrative and economic organization, were known in all their details, and this knowledge was certainly registered in written form. With their Iranian satrapies and their Arabian dependencies, as well as with certain parts of Asia Minor, Armenia, and the Caucasus, the Persian rulers were less thoroughly acquainted. But even in respect of these regions we may credit the Persian civil and military administrators with some degree of information.[1]

Well known as they were to their own rulers and to the merchants resident in the Persian Empire, the Persian satrapies were not unfamiliar to the Greeks. I have mentioned in the second chapter how active were the trade relations of the Greeks with certain portions of the Persian Empire, especially Egypt, and the Syrian, Phoenician, and Palestinian coastal cities. I may add that these trade connexions are well illustrated by the data contained in the well-known Periplus of pseudo-Scylax, belonging to the middle of the fourth century B.C. It is unfortunate that the section of this Periplus dealing with the Syrian and Phoenician coast is very poorly preserved, but its general character is sufficiently well known. Moreover, diplomatic relations between the leading States of Greece and Persia, a constant exchange of embassies, were an established practice of the fourth century B.C. Finally, large bodies of Greek mercenaries were in the service of the Persian kings and of the rulers of Egypt. Nevertheless, the acquaintance of the Greeks with Persia was partial and far from exact. A glance at the descriptions of the Persian Empire by Herodotus and of the march of the Ten Thousand by Xenophon enables us to realize how vague and imperfect was the information that the Greeks possessed regarding Egypt and the Asiatic territories of the Persian Empire.

With Alexander and under his successors the situation changed completely. Most of the former satrapies of the Persian Empire became constituent parts of the Hellenistic world. Alexander and the rulers of the Hellenistic monarchies inherited from their predecessors their knowledge of their own dominions. Of the extent to which Alexander and his successors made use of the information accumulated in the central archives of the Persian kingdom and in the archives of the satrapies there is no evidence. But we know with certainty that the administrative machinery of Alexander and of his successors was practically a continuation of that of the Persian kings, and it is equally certain that no such continuation would have been possible without the help of the documents and information assembled in the Persian archives. The new settlers of Macedonian, Greek, and in general foreign origin—soldiers, colonists, merchants—supplemented their personally acquired knowledge of the country by information regarding other parts of it obtained in the same or a similar way. They soon became thoroughly familiar with the new additions to the Greek world and they certainly did not keep their information to themselves. This new acquaintance with certain portions of the Persian Empire would inevitably become before long the common property of the Greeks in general.

And so it was in fact. The extent and character of the newly acquired territories were duly recorded and described in contemporary literature, in works of divers kinds—poetical, dramatic, historical, geographical.

I cannot analyse in detail the attitude of the Hellenistic writers towards this new accession to the Greek world, for this would far exceed the scope of the present book. But I may offer some remarks on certain special points which may help the reader to a better understanding of the Hellenistic world in its general aspect, as it appeared at least to the leading Greeks of the day.

I have mentioned above (Ch. IV) that most of the few extant literary works of the Hellenistic period view with enthusiasm the new world opened to them by the conquests of Alexander. This enthusiasm is especially marked in regard to Egypt and the activities of the Ptolemies. I pointed out that in general the judgements of contemporary writers on this subject, especially in the third century, were a mixture of flattery and propaganda. But there were exceptions. We possess expressions of opinion of a different character; some of them are censorious, others impartial. If we had more literary texts of this kind regarding the Seleucid kingdom we should probably find the same diversity. All these judgements, flattering, censorious, or impartial, take one cardinal point for granted. The new world which they describe or mention was in their eyes an extension, a continuation of the Greek world. The new kings are Greek kings and pursue a Greek policy; they rule over Greeks and are surrounded by Greeks, and they are prepared to offer excellent opportunities to other Greeks who may be willing and ready to emigrate to the new world.

In this respect the geographical works of the period are especially valuable. Their main purpose was practical and scientific: to register and describe, not to praise or blame. It will be appropriate, therefore, to deal at greater length with the picture that the Hellenistic geographers gave of the new world.

Geographical works were a form of literature familiar to Greeks of the classical period. With the more general aspect of this well-known fact I cannot here deal; a few words will suffice to bring out certain salient points bearing directly on the subject of the present book.[2] Various types of geographical treatises of a semi-literary or literary character were current in the Greek world of the fourth century: περίπλοι, σταθμοί, ὁδοιπορίαι on the one hand, and γεωγραφίαι, περίοδοι, and περιηγήσεις on the other, were the titles most commonly given to them. All of them were either practical or scientific in their character and tone.

The earliest works were the περίπλοι. They were based on personal experience of travellers and merchants (ἐμπειρία), sometimes embodied in written accounts of exploration of hitherto unknown regions. The aim of the earliest περίπλοι wa practical. They were intended as aids to seamen and mer chants, to supplement the knowledge they had personall acquired. They contained an enumeration of stopping-places especially harbours, in geographical sequence, with hints a regards orientation and with records of distances betweer them. They covered either the whole of the Mediterranean o certain parts of it. We have, for example, *periploi* dealin exclusively with the Pontic regions, the Euxine. The dat contained in these guides were not always reliable and wer never precise. Those on orientation, for example, were rathe vague (the compass is a modern invention), and the reckonin of distances was always approximate, the methods of measure ment used by the Greeks being somewhat primitive.

Some of these *periploi* were intended for the use of seamer exclusively, containing data mostly of a nautical characte (σταδιασμοί), others were guides for merchants. But most o them were of a mixed character, guides for travellers i general. In these there was soon added to the dry enumeratior of stopping-places and distances information of various kind concerning the nature of the regions, their physical aspect their population, their history, and their peculiarities. Mos of the early *periploi* are lost, except for some fragments anc one complete manual of nautical directions, that of pseudo Scylax (about 350 B.C.) mentioned above. But it is certair that several later *periploi* of Roman and Byzantine time derive from earlier works and well illustrate their genera character. Invaluable, for example, are the nautical guide *Stadiasmus Maris Magni*, of the late Roman Empire and th merchants' guide, *Periplus Maris Erythraei*, of the first century A.D. I should add in this connexion that in early times itiner aries for land voyages were of minor importance and therefor left hardly any traces in pre-Hellenistic literary tradition.

On the *periploi* and *hodoiporiai*, combined with speculation on the general form of the inhabited world, were based th early attempts at a general description of the Earth (γεωγραφίαι or γῆς περίοδοι and περιηγήσεις), with all sorts of data concerning especially human geography. The intention of these treatises was to give a comprehensive picture of the whole of the in habited world, including regions that were little known or practically unknown. But naturally the bulk of these descriptions concerned that portion of it which was known, the Mediterranean area, including the Pontic regions, with special attention to the best-known part of it—the Aegean and the countries bordering on it.

In the Hellenistic period geography underwent a spectacular development. No new literary forms were invented, and geographical works retained the same character as before. They appeared in Hellenistic times under the same titles as in earlier days and treated the material at their disposal by the same methods. But their contents were no longer the same. I am not concerned here with the fundamental progress in the field of mathematical geography connected with the names of Eratosthenes and Hipparchus, nor can I deal with the many valuable additions to the knowledge of the past in the field of physical geography. I can only mention in passing the extension of the geographical horizon of the Greeks, due in part to the absorption by Greek geographers of the new knowledge of the East and in part to the efforts of the Seleucids and the Ptolemies to explore the borderlands of their respective kingdoms, efforts which I have recorded above. I must confine myself to certain aspects of the development of human geography which have a direct bearing on the subject of this book.

In the first place I may draw attention to one cardinal feature of the geographical treatises of the period. The attentive reader of what remains of these will perceive that for their authors the territories of the greater and lesser Hellenistic monarchies of the East were no longer remote outlandish countries on the periphery of the civilized world, little known and superficially described, as they appear in earlier geographical works, but constituent parts of it, a section of the Greek nucleus of the οἰκουμένη. These Oriental regions were now as well known as those encircling the Mediterranean and are described in the same spirit, with the same interest and accuracy, and by the same methods, as the latter.

This was undoubtedly due, especially as regards the territories of the Eastern monarchies, to the fact that the Hellenistic geographers had access to fresh sources of information, which enabled them to collect an abundance of new and trustworthy material, to incorporate it in their treatises, and thus to give a new picture of the Greek world. This new material, let me repeat and emphasize, was ultimately derived from the official records of the Hellenistic monarchies and in particular from their military and administrative itineraries, which were based as I have stated, on similar Persian itineraries. These last— called by the Greeks σταθμοί—were certainly checked, improved, and hellenized, first by the well-known *bematistae* of Alexander, and later by those in the service of the Seleucids the Ptolemies, and the rulers of the Anatolian monarchies.

These itineraries may have been accompanied by maps in which the stations (σταθμοί), enumerated in their sequence in the itineraries, were indicated and located. Maps such as the military map of *stathmoi* painted on a Roman soldier's shield found at Dura may go back to earlier Hellenistic maps. It may be mentioned that the only extant itinerary, derived without doubt almost directly from the itineraries of Alexander and his successors, was compiled under the early Roman Empire by Isidorus of Charax and was certainly based on the Parthian official itineraries, successors of those of the Hellenistic kings. The Seleucid itineraries, though based on the Persian, were unquestionably more complete and more accurate than the latter, and were compiled in a new Greek style since they were intended for the use of Greek administrators and military officers.[3]

The basis on which they were compiled was the new, more diversified, and better-planned system of roads. We know very little of the system of roads established by the Seleucids, the Attalids, and the Ptolemies. But the little we know shows that to the great highways and the local roads of Persian times the Hellenistic kings added many new ones, both main roads of a strategical and commercial character, which connected their new capitals with the existing system of ancient highways, and local roads. These last certainly joined the new Macedonian and Greek settlements to each other and to the main roads new and old. We know little of this system of communications except for the great roads which ran from Antioch to Mesopotamia and Iran on the one hand and to Asia Minor on the ther. But it is obvious that without a well-planned network of main and local roads no mobilization of the military forces of the Hellenistic kingdoms could be carried out smoothly and without undue delay. It is regrettable that we know so little of the efforts of the Hellenistic monarchs in respect of road-building. But it is fair to suggest that the Romans, though they improved and enlarged the road system of their Eastern provinces, inherited in the main that of their predecessors, together with some of their technical devices in road construction.[4]

Geographical writers were certainly eager to profit by the activity of the administration and to register all the progress made in regard to the building and description of roads. They were certainly encouraged by the rulers of the day, since it was in the interest of the latter that their subjects should have at their disposal trustworthy guides for their frequent travels in their respective kingdoms; moreover, such descriptions were a powerful means of propaganda. Official interest in geographical treatises is attested by such works as the *Periplus of the Red Sea* by Agatharchides.

The results of the diligence of the Hellenistic geographers in the field of descriptive or human geography are still perceptible in the few fragments that survive of their principal productions. I refer to such famous works as those of Eratosthenes, to the geographical sections of the history of Polybius, to the comprehensive geographical treatises of Agatharchides of Cnidus written in the time of Philometor and Euergetes II) and of Artemidorus of Ephesus (composed at the end of the second century B.C.), and to the contributions to descriptive geography made by Posidonius. It is to be regretted that these works are extant in fragments only, but we are to a certain extent compensated for their loss by the great compilation of Strabo, preserved almost in its entirety. Strabo, of course, belongs to the new world of the Roman Empire. In his descriptive geography, so far as it concerns the East, he added to the old stock of geographical information his own personal contributions, the results of his own observations, and some material collected in the East by the Roman conquerors, especially by Pompey and his geographical staff. But the core of his work, as far as the East is concerned, is Hellenistic, and almost reproduces the description of the East that had been given by Eratosthenes, Polybius, Agatharchides, Artemidorus, and Posidonius.

It is unfortunate that we cannot compare the picture of the East given by Strabo with those of the last geographers of the days before Alexander, whose accounts were so vividly reflected in the geographical parts of the historical works of Ephorus and Theopompus. The *Periplus* of pseudo-Scylax is but a poor substitute for their lost writings. But it is almost certain that in them the East was still presented in the same light in which Herodotus displayed it to his contemporaries. The changes were partial and the improvement slight. Quite different is the picture given by Strabo, and even more different, in all probability, was that supplied by his Hellenistic sources. In Strabo's description the East, that is to say, the Oriental provinces of Rome, appears as a part of the civilized world, exactly known, comparatively safe for travellers, full of interest, rich, and highly organized. It is taken for granted that cities mentioned by Strabo are Greek cities, if not otherwise specified. Strabo's period and that of his immediate sources, Artemidorus and Posidonius, was one of grave disturbance, and his picture reflects these conditions. How much more attractive and civilized, we may believe, must Egypt, Syria, and Asia Minor have appeared in the descriptions of Eratosthenes and Agatharchides and their sources. The student will do well to glance through Strabo's sixteenth and seventeenth books.

The geographical treatises were thus a demonstration, accessible to everyone, of a well-established fact—the unity and homogeneity of the Hellenistic world from the point of view of civilization and mode of life. The reader could at once learn from them where the civilized world ended and the half-civilized and only partially known world began. They gave attractive and well-balanced descriptions of the territories newly added to the domain of Greek civilization, and conveyed the idea that a visit to them was after all attended with no very serious risk, hardly more difficult and dangerous than a voyage round the Aegean. It might further be gathered from the *periploi* and itineraries that life in these new regions of the Greek world was not very different from what it was in

he motherland, but was probably more attractive and offered
better prospects.[5]

The impression thus given was not misleading. A traveller
from the Aegean setting out for the Hellenistic monarchies of
the East, were he a business man, a merchant, a soldier, or a
prospective colonist, could easily plan his voyage and choose
his route by consulting the best and most recent *periploi* and
periodoi.[6] By personal inquiry he could learn how numerous
and varied were the opportunities of sailing from his home to
the harbours of Egypt, Syria, Phoenicia, and Palestine. Many
ships of various classes were, in fact, plying frequently between
the ports of the Aegean and those of Egypt and Syria. He knew
of course from his experience of the Aegean that travel in
general by sea was neither fast nor comfortable and safe. But
to this he was accustomed. He knew also that in spite of the
rapidly increasing sea traffic of Hellenistic times the conditions
of navigation had not much improved. Even in these times
progress in Greek maritime methods was slow and partial.
No basic innovations in nautical science were introduced. The
merchant-ships, which carried also passengers—there being no
special passenger traffic—were more numerous and of more
varied types than before; ships were frequently of increased
size, and they were in general a little more comfortable. The
voyage may have been a little faster and perhaps a little safer
(from the nautical point of view), thanks to some new instruments (for example, the sextant) and to improvements in the
form and management of rudders and anchors. But in the
main the conditions of navigation remained the same as in the
past. Nor did they improve later in Roman, Byzantine, and
even modern times until the invention of steel ships and steam
propulsion. The principal handicaps from which sea traffic
suffered remained unaltered—the difficulty of orientation (before the compass was invented), helplessness in the face of
heavy storms, and lack of security from attack (the reader
will recall what was said in previous chapters regarding the
development of piracy); these disadvantages could not be
overcome by the means at the disposal of sailors.[7]

On their way travellers would call at various ports. The
voyage was slow, for ships hugged the coast, and frequent stops

were imperative for repairs and to renew supplies of water and provisions. There was no lack of good harbours in the Mediter- ranean and the protection offered by most of them was in- creased by moles and jetties, cleverly and efficiently con- structed. Well-designed *emporia* were built along the shores of these harbours and there were market-places connected with them. So it had been in classical Greece and so it remained in Hellenistic times, except that the harbours, protected by piers and jetties, became more numerous and the old ones larger and better organized, though constructed or rebuilt on the same lines as before. In this respect, also, no radical in- novations were introduced. But some of the harbours, old and new, though developed on the old lines, were models of really clever and efficient planning and artistic creations of a high order, beautifully laid out and adorned with imposing buildings and decorative sculptures. Such was, first and fore- most, the most famous harbour of the ancient world, that of Alexandria or rather of the whole of Egypt, devised by Alexander and constructed by the Ptolemies. This is not the place to describe it in detail. I need only remind the reader of its two main divisions (the Great Harbour and the Eunostus) separated by the famous heptastadion, a wide dam which con- nected the mainland with the island of Pharos; of the wide and monumental entrance into the Great Harbour marked at one end by the impressive mass of the lofty Pharos tower, which may or may not at this time have been a lighthouse; and of the splendid basin within it reserved for the king and con- nected with the royal palace. This basin, small in dimensions but cleverly planned, was in fact a pocket of the great harbour near Cape Lochias, protected against waves and storms by two special jetties. On one side of it towered Cape Lochias with its decorative buildings and perhaps its royal park, while on the other lay the elegant little island of Antirrhodos, possessing its own small harbour and perhaps studded with villa-like royal buildings. We may conjecture that a fine mosaic of the second century A.D. found in Leptis Magna represents this little harbour and the entrance to the royal villa (Pl. XL, 2). The Hellenistic original of this mosaic was probably intended to glorify the achievements of Ptolemaic commerce under the protection of the powerful Ptolemaic navy, a combination emphasized by the planning of the Great Harbour, where the 'neorion' was in close proximity to the 'emporion'. It was off the southern shore of the Great Harbour, opposite the Pharos tower, that Antony later built his famous Timonion. The dam which connected it with the mainland isolated the royal basin from the commercial and military ports, with their 'emporion' and 'neorion', and from the harbour market which served as a connecting link between the Great Harbour, the gate of the Mediterranean world, and the Eunostus harbour, the distributing centre for the goods that were floated down the Nile to Alexandria.

Alexandria had rivals in the reorganized harbours of Miletus (Pl. LXXV and Fig. 5) and in the splendidly remodelled harbour of Carthage, the latter almost as famous in the Hellenistic world as that of Alexandria. Nor were the harbours of Rhodes (Pl. LXXVI, 1; cf. Pl. CXII, 1—harbour of Cnidus) less impressive, though the Rhodian counterpart to the Ptolemaic Pharos tower, the Colossus of Rhodes, was soon after its erection destroyed by the famous earthquake. It may further be suggested with great probability that Seleucus, when planning and constructing the harbours for his new Syrian ports of Seleuceia and Laodicea, did not neglect the new devices adopted by Alexander and Soter at Alexandria and later by the Greek architects in the service of Carthage.

Other harbours were developed on different lines. Such were those of Corinth (the Lechaion) and especially of Delos (Pl. LXXXVII and Fig. 8), which last, like the city itself, was growing by natural process out of its modest beginnings with the rapid development of Delos as the chief commercial port and clearing-house for Mediterranean trade.[8]

Behind the harbours lay the seaport towns, in which travellers often spent several days. The atmosphere of these cities was familiar to them. They were all of them, even in the new Greek lands, either Greek (as were Alexandria, Seleuceia, and Laodicea), or thoroughly hellenized (as were the Cilician and Phoenician cities and those of the Palestinian coast). They had a certain exotic character, but there was nothing new in this for the Greek.

If the traveller decided to proceed inland from the seaports of Anatolia, Egypt, or Syria, he found no difficulty in doing so. Traffic both by river and by land was well organized in Egypt, likewise in Asia Minor, Syria, and Mesopotamia. As regards the last, I have already referred to the system of royal roads developed by the Seleucids and the Attalids. There was certainly a similar development in the minor Anatolian monarchies. The roads were well provided with stopping-places and rest-houses, and these were probably at the disposal of other travellers besides agents of the government.[9]

We have hardly any information about the conditions of land travel in Hellenistic times in the Asiatic kingdoms. They certainly varied from time to time and from place to place. It is certain that travel by land as by sea was never safe. Brigandage on land was as well-established an institution of the ancient world as was piracy on the sea. In the mountains and in the desert raids of professional robbers or of local half-savage tribes were probably of frequent occurrence, especially during war. But in normal times the main roads and the rivers were well protected. We know that this was so in Egypt. An elaborate and numerous police force was organized by the Ptolemies, especially for the desert and for the river.[10] I see no reason to suppose that conditions were different in the Seleucid monarchy and in the Anatolian kingdoms. Here, as in Egypt, in normal times the main and the local roads and the few navigable rivers were certainly well guarded by a special police force, the main roads perhaps also by military detachments. We have good evidence for Roman times regarding the organization of municipal police, especially in Asia Minor, the chief police officer being a παραφύλαξ or an εἰρηνάρχης. The παραφύλαξ was mounted, his subordinates (known under various names) were not. It is certain (see above, p. 451 and n. 250) that this institution was inherited by the Romans from their Hellenistic predecessors. Whether all the παραφύλακες and policemen of Hellenistic times were municipal officers, or whether some of them, like certain financial agents of the Crown (for example the χρεοφύλακες), were in the service of the central government, we have no means of deciding. I am inclined to believe that there existed in the Seleucid kingdom as in Ptolemaic Egypt, not only a municipal but also a State police force, though we know practically nothing of the organization of this department of administration. I cannot help thinking that the system of guarding the desert roads by mounted gendarmes, mostly mercenaries, of which there is evidence at Palmyra in Roman times, was not a new scheme devised by the Palmyrenes or prescribed to them by Rome, but a heritage of Seleucid times, an imitation of a similar institution of the Seleucid government.[11]

Besides being somewhat unsafe, journeys by land were very slow. The royal couriers, riding on swift horses or on camels, travelled fast. But ordinary persons, who mostly used donkeys and mules, and generally for safety's sake travelled in groups, forming larger or smaller caravans, probably made very slow progress. Riding on horseback or in horse-driven carriages was certainly restricted to the wealthy.[12] But travel by land in the Eastern monarchies did not, in respect of its slowness and insecurity, differ from travel in Greece and in the city-territories of Asia Minor. I may remind the reader of the description given in Chapter IV of brigandage in Greece in the third century B.C., and the conditions in this regard that prevailed later in Asia Minor, as we know them from occasional documents (above, Ch. VI).

In the new countries, as in the motherland, the roads led travellers through villages and hamlets from one city to another. These cities, in the Hellenistic monarchies of the East, were all of them either Greek or, if Oriental, included considerable groups of Greeks among their inhabitants. The Greek traveller, if he halted in one of them, found himself in a congenial atmosphere. He did not need to know the Oriental languages. Greek in its new form—the κοινή—became to an ever-increasing extent the lingua franca of the Near East in competition with Aramaic. We have seen that it was the language of the government and the army, and that it gradually became the language of business. It is not surprising, therefore, that the Orientals were eager to learn it for practical reasons, while it is doubtful whether the Greeks took very kindly to the Oriental languages. The κοινή was a flexible and not very complicated instrument. It could be easily learnt by foreigners and presented no difficulty to such Greeks as still spoke the various Greek dialects.[13]

Everything else in the new section of the Hellenic world was as familiar to the Greek new-comers and travellers as was the language. Notwithstanding the political disintegration of Alexander's monarchy, its parts continued to be governed in much the same way. In the form of the central government, in the system of administration, in the organization of the law courts, in taxation, there was very little difference between Seleucid Syria and the Anatolian monarchies, or between the Asiatic monarchies and Egypt. And what differences there were the new-comers were readily able to grasp.

The same was true of business life. All the Hellenistic monarchies were rapidly adopting the use of money as a medium of exchange in place of barter in both official and private transactions. All the Hellenistic kings minted an abundant and trustworthy currency for their own use and for that of their subjects. This currency was a continuation of that of Alexander, that is to say, it was Greek. It was uniform, with slight variations from monarchy to monarchy. Most of the monarchies retained the Attic standard which Alexander had adopted for his currency. Such coins as were not minted on the Attic standard could easily be reduced to it. In all the cities both of the motherland and of the Hellenistic monarchies of the East there were Greek bankers—royal, municipal, and private—who were prepared to exchange foreign money for the local currency and to transact business for their clients in the Greek fashion. The prices of commodities naturally varied from place to place, but these variations were not considerable. All parts of the Hellenistic world were connected with each other by active and almost uninterrupted trade relations, and it was this international trade which ultimately determined the prices of the most important commodities, especially corn (see below).[14]

We should like to know more of the current forms of business transactions. But a comparative *Urkundenlehre* such as U. Wilcken demanded still remains a *pium desiderium*. It appears, however, that business was transacted in Greek circles almost in the same forms all over the Hellenistic world. An instructive comparison may be made between the few business documents found at Dura-Europus and those found in larger numbers in Egypt. Very few differences, if any, are noticeable. The contracts found in Avroman in Media show greater differences, but are still of the Greek type.[15] The problem of the basis of the various business transactions, the civil law in force in the various parts of the Hellenistic world, is one of greater difficulty. I shall return to the subject in the next section. Our material is very scanty. We are well informed on this question in regard to Egypt, we possess some information in respect of Asia Minor; and finally we have the documents of Dura, mostly of later times. It is natural that the subject should give rise to lively debate among modern scholars. My impression is that here also we have a kind of common foundation with local variations, a legal Hellenistic κοινή in course of development.

Perhaps more important than the uniformity in government and business was the uniformity of the mode of life adopted by the Greeks in their new eastern homes. A visitor to one of these Oriental Greek cities found himself in an environment thoroughly familiar to him. Everywhere he met the same forms of 'political' life based on constitutions borrowed from those of the cities of Greece or Asia Minor, the same *boule* and *demos*, the same magistrates, the same organization of city finances, the same municipal taxation, and so forth. Nor was it otherwise in the sphere of religion. Greek gods with the addition of the new gods—Alexander and the ruling dynasty— were worshipped in Greek temples, with the assistance of Greek priests who performed the same rites as in the mother country.

Boys were educated in Greek schools. There is good evidence that there were Greek private elementary schools in all the Greek settlements in Egypt, and they were certainly as numerous in the Seleucid monarchy. Greek gymnasia were as much a fundamental institution of Greek life everywhere in the Eastern monarchies as they were in Greece and Asia Minor. I shall have more to say on this subject in the next section.

An important feature of the civilization and life of the Greeks was their mode of spending their hours of leisure—their amusements and recreation; but on this point also it is unnecessary to dwell at length. Dramatic performances and music on the one hand and sports on the other were as essential in Greek life as was gymnasial education. They were, in fact, a part and a continuation of this education. It need hardly be said that the Greeks did not change their habits in this respect when they emigrated to the East, nor is any evidence on this point necessary.

I may, however, offer one important illustration. I refer to the relations of the Hellenistic kings with so typical a creation of their times as the professional and religious associations of what were known as the Dionysiac *technitai*, members of the dramatic and musical crafts grouped around Dionysus, their patron.[16] It was not until early in the third century that any professional organization came into being in Greece and it is characteristic of the Greek mentality that it was in the field of artistic and religious activity that the first association was constituted. The Athenian organization was the oldest, and it was soon followed, in continental Greece, by the Isthmian and Nemean. The existence of these associations made easier the celebration of the great religious festivals, and they were therefore patronized by the Amphictions of Delphi and by the chief cities of Greece. The latter conferred upon them and their members many important privileges (above, Ch. VI, n. 18) of vital consequence to them in the troubled political atmosphere of Hellenistic times.

It is interesting to find that very soon after the creation of the Athenian association a corresponding association was formed in Egypt, probably on the initiative of Philadelphus and in close connexion with the dynastic cult.* The activity of this association was not limited to Alexandria (the *technitai* for example, took an important part in the great *pompe* of Philadelphus) but was extended to Ptolemais† and perhaps to other centres of Greek life in Egypt. A similar organization—a local branch of that of Alexandria—was soon formed in the island of Cyprus to satisfy the needs of its Greek population and we may conjecture, though we have no evidence, that

---

* *O.G.I.* 50 and 51, middle of the third century B.C.
† See the above-quoted inscriptions.

provision was made in some way by the Ptolemies to meet the like requirements of the Greeks in Syria and Phoenicia.

The policy of the Pergamene kings in this respect was not dissimilar to that of the Ptolemies. They entered very soon into close relations with the association of the Ionian and Hellespontine *technitai*, which was founded in Asia Minor perhaps in the middle of the third century if not earlier, with its seat in the small city of Teos. To this they affiliated their own creation—the association of *technitai* attached to the cult of Dionysus Kathegemon in Pergamon. These two associations were closely connected with the dynastic cult of the Attalids, and were under the strict control of the Pergamene kings.

It is unfortunate that we have no information about the policy of the Seleucids in regard to the Dionysiac *technitai*. Their relations with the Ionian and Hellespontine association in the third century B.C. are unknown. Nor do we know whether they followed the policy of the Ptolemies and had their own association of Dionysiac *technitai* for the purposes of their own religious celebrations in Antioch and elsewhere. Such an association was certainly greatly needed. How large and widespread was the demand is shown by the striking but not surprising discovery by Koldewey of the ruins of a Greek theatre in Babylon, in that part of the city (Homerah) which was probably the centre of the Greek population of Babylon. The theatre was built of bricks, and was rebuilt at least once. Its date has not been fixed with certainty. But the forms of the letters of the inscription recording its construction point to a time not later than 150 B.C. (the date suggested by C. B. Welles), and experts in the history of ancient theatres have assigned to it the same date. The theatre must therefore no doubt be connected with the efforts of Antiochus IV and of his immediate successors to reinforce and organize the Greek and hellenized population of their Oriental cities, and it must be regarded as a testimony to the deep attachment of the Babylonian Greeks to their ancestral habits. If the Seleucids had their own association of Dionysiac *technitai*, its members certainly travelled far and wide all over the Seleucid kingdom.[17]

Lastly, I may recall what I have already said regarding the relations of Ariarathes V of Cappadocia with the *technitai* of

Athens, and of Nicomedes III of Bithynia with those of Argos. The intimate character of these relations and the great honours conferred by the *technitai* on the kings point to the enthusiasm of the latter for drama and music, and reflect their phil-hellenism in general. But it is not improbable that the two kings availed themselves of their close relations with the *technitai* to invite companies of actors and bands of musicians, or individual actors and musicians, belonging to these associations to give performances from time to time in the capitals and other Greek cities of their kingdoms. It must be remembered that the Ionian and Hellespontine association, which was nearest to them, was completely dependent on the Attalids, who were not always in friendly relations with the Cappadocian and Bithynian kings.

Together with the peculiarities of their political, religious, and intellectual life the Greeks carried to their new homes the leading features of their family and social organization. Much might be said on this subject, but I must confine myself to a few remarks. It is interesting to observe that the Greek marriage contracts of Egypt in the Hellenistic period were substantially reproductions of the Athenian marriage contracts of the fourth century B.C. They remained essentially Greek until the end of the rule of the Ptolemies, and underwent only slight modifications of a purely formal character. These were intended to make more definite and explicit certain basic features of Greek family life; they are not borrowed from the Egyptian law of marriage, which differed in many respects from the Greek, and show no signs of an interpenetration of the two laws, despite the existence of intermarriage between Greeks and natives. The same seems to be true of the Seleucid State. In Dura-Europus, in Parthian or Roman times, the purely Greek law of intestate heritage was still valid, with slight modifications resulting from the peculiar relations between the settlers of Europus and the king, but showing no local influences. Greek family tradition was as persistent in the East as was Greek civilization.[18]

I may finally remark that the Greeks of the Hellenistic *diaspora* continued in their new homes to display their fondness for associations and clubs of various types and characters religious, social, sometimes professional. We have abundant evidence of this in Egypt. Here the Greek associations show in their organization hardly any difference from those of Greece and Asia Minor. As regards the Seleucid kingdom we have no evidence. But certainly the conditions in this respect were not different from those prevailing in Egypt. I shall return to the subject later in this chapter.

There remains to be mentioned in this brief sketch one aspect of the Hellenistic world which emphasizes its unity as strongly as the other features of Greek life to which I have referred, and that is the uniform character of Greek settlements in the various parts of the Greek East in regard to town-planning and the types and forms of buildings, both public and private. The evidence available is limited. Of the cities of Egypt and the Seleucid kingdom that were founded or rebuilt by the Hellenistic kings very few have been excavated, and these have revealed to us their later aspect, as a rule that of Roman times. I may name for example the ruins of Dura-Europus in Mesopotamia and of the village of Karanis in Egypt, which have both been carefully excavated. I need not repeat what I have said in an earlier chapter with regard to the impressive ruins to be seen in Syria and the Transjordan. They are all of them either Roman or Byzantine.

However, even the scanty material at our disposal shows, as I have said, that those cities of Syria and Mesopotamia which were built or thoroughly rebuilt by Hellenistic rulers were laid out according to one and the same design, which in all cases that have been closely examined has proved to be the Greek Hippodamian plan. This was probably adopted in Antioch and Apamea, certainly in Laodicea, Damascus, and Dura-Europus. In Egypt, Alexandria and Ptolemais were very probably built on this plan, and it may be found to have been followed in the new Greek village-like settlements, especially in the Fayûm. It may be noted that the adoption of the Hippodamian plan for the new cities of the Greek East did not conflict with the Oriental tradition of town-planning. The late Babylonian cities and some of the Pharaonic cities of Egypt present an aspect not dissimilar to that of the Greek Hippodamian cities.[19]

A discussion of the designs and architectural forms of public and private buildings in the new cities of the Greek East presents greater difficulty. We possess very little evidence. The little that remains of the Hellenistic temples in Dura-Europus shows Greek plans and Greek architectural forms. But apart from Dura we possess very few data, even in Egypt. The vogue of Greek architecture in the former Seleucid kingdom and to some extent in Egypt in Roman times may be the continuation of an old tradition, but may, on the other hand, be due in large part to a Greek renaissance only slightly connected with the past.

Even vaguer is our information as regards private houses, and we have little material to go upon. In Egypt we have many descriptions of private houses in the Ptolemaic papyri. They convey a general idea of the type of the house, but nothing more. A few tombs in Alexandria appear to represent houses, but they are not reproductions. Moreover very few ruins of Ptolemaic houses have been excavated. It is therefore extremely difficult to say whether the Greeks in Egypt built houses of their own type; or whether they soon learnt to appreciate the comfortable character of the Egyptian houses, which were suited to the climate and cheap to build, and either remodelled their own peristyle house (not very different from the Egyptian) in the Egyptian fashion, or built houses of a purely Egyptian type for themselves and their families.

Our information is still more disappointing as regards the Seleucid dominions. The types of Greek house used in Hellenistic times in the Greek cities of the mainland and of the islands, and in the ancient cities of Asia Minor, are clearly revealed by the ruins of houses, especially those of Olynthus, Olbia, Priene, and Delos, and by the treatise of Vitruvius. But we are ignorant whether in the new cities of Syria, Phoenicia, Palestine, Mesopotamia, the Iranian countries, &c., the emigrants built themselves Greek houses or houses of the local types, which last varied according to place, climate, and tradition. Many private houses have been excavated in Dura-Europus. Naturally all these are known to us in the shape they assumed in Parthian and Roman times. Houses built of un-baked bricks soon decay. The houses of the Parthian and

Roman periods at Dura are certainly Oriental in plan and construction, with some Greek secondary elements (the use of the Greek column, Greek cornices, &c.). Their prototypes are local Mesopotamian houses, which are similar to the Babylonian, but show many local peculiarities. Of the earlier Hellenistic houses we have very few remains, and we are therefore unable to say which type they represent.[20]

The short sketch which I have given, based as it is on few facts, shows that the Hellenistic world possessed such a thing as unity, in spite of its political differentiation and rapid disintegration. By the efforts of Alexander and of his successors the Greek world was undoubtedly extended far into the East. Large areas were added to it in Asia Minor, in Syria and Mesopotamia, and in Egypt.

But the further the traveller advanced to the south and east in the Seleucid kingdom and to the south, east, and west in Egypt, the less did the regions through which he passed present a Greek appearance to his eyes. There were no Greek bases in Arabia, except in so far as Petra was one; very few were created by Alexander and his successors in the Iranian territories, except in Bactria; and the upper course of the Nile retained its pre-Ptolemaic social structure and cultural features. These regions, however, were never, or only for short periods, constituent parts of the Hellenistic monarchies.

2. THE GREEKS AND THE NATIVES IN THE ORIENTAL MONARCHIES AND THE GREEKS OF THE MOTHER COUNTRY

The unity of the Hellenistic world of which I have given a rapid sketch in the preceding pages was a peculiar phenomenon, unique of its kind in the evolution of mankind. It was a unity which comprised the whole of the Greeks (including those of the mother country), but not the whole population of the Eastern monarchies, where it was restricted to its Greek superstructure. The natives, forming the vast majority of the population, were not (with few exceptions) absorbed into this unity. The native population remained as diversified in its national, social, religious, economic, and cultural life as it had previously been, and retained all the principal characteristics of this life until the end of the Hellenistic period.

I have frequently referred in the preceding chapters to thi important feature in the structure of the Hellenistic world and have traced its evolution. Having regard to its funda mental importance for the proper understanding of that world I may now sum up in a systematic survey the facts adduce above and develop the short exposition of them contained i the preceding pages. I shall begin with the upper stratum the Hellenes in the Eastern monarchies, and point out thei peculiar organization and the most salient features of thei social life. I shall then say a few words of the natives, an end with a sketch of the new social elements in the life of th Greeks of old Greece.

A. THE GREEKS OF THE DIASPORA

(a) Greek Emigration to the East.

During and after the conquest of Alexander thousands c immigrants poured into the various parts of his empire, whic subsequently became independent Hellenistic kingdoms. The were mostly men of Greek civilization, Macedonians, citizen of various Greek cities, groups of more or less hellenize country folk from the northern Balkan Peninsula and, in th case of Egypt and the Iranian countries, from Asia Mino Palestine, Phoenicia, and Syria. Many of these probably ha originally no intention of settling permanently in the ne world, but most of them finally did so in one way or anothe The emigrants to the East and to Egypt were men of var ous nationalities, occupations, and social status. The uppe stratum, the aristocracy of the emigrants, was formed b various groups of men of Macedonian and Greek nationalit and of Greek civilization: political refugees (members of roy families, statesmen, political leaders of Greek cities, an others), talented generals and officers of the army and nav men of political training and experience or distinguished i intellectual and artistic spheres, eminent specialists in variou fields. These mostly settled in the new capitals of the Heller istic world around the royal courts. We know the names c many of them, and in some cases we can follow their destini in their new homes. But these were a small minority. Th bulk of the emigrants consisted of thousands of soldiers of the royal armies and thousands of civilians of various occupations, various classes, and many nationalities: men of liberal professions (teachers of different kinds, doctors, lawyers, artists connected with the theatre, architects and engineers, painters, sculptors, most of them Greeks), merchants and other business men prepared to invest their money in profitable business, private or official, various craftsmen of ability, and finally enterprising individuals without employment or prospect of obtaining it in their old homes and ready to engage in any occupation that might present itself.

I have already observed that we have no statistical data regarding the number of the immigrants, but it is certain that in all the Hellenistic monarchies, especially in the East and in Egypt, they formed an important element in the population superimposed on the natives.

Some of them came to their new homes at the invitation of the rulers and were settled there in accordance with a well-devised plan. In the Seleucid kingdom compact groups of them of larger or smaller size—soldiers and civilians—were organized either as city-states of the Greek type or as military village-like settlements enjoying a certain measure of self-government. In Egypt the immigrants were dealt with somewhat differently. Two cities only were built for them: Alexandria, the capital, and Ptolemais, the southern stronghold of Hellenism. The rest were distributed throughout the country, as individuals and groups, either in pre-existing native towns and villages or in new centres of the same type created by the Ptolemies.

Besides these organized groups invited by the rulers, thousands of immigrants came to Asia and Egypt on their own initiative and at their own risk. We know little of them. But it is natural to suppose that they settled in various cities, towns, and villages, Greek and Oriental, as groups or individuals, in a haphazard way according to the economic opportunities that presented themselves.

The emigrants to the East belonged, as I have pointed out, to various nations. Macedonians and Greeks formed the core, the most civilized and active part. The Macedonians soon assumed the aspect of Greeks and certainly did not, in the third century B.C., differ from them in language and civiliza tion. The process of amalgamation in these respects, in othe words the hellenization of the Macedonians, began early. In the time of Philip and Alexander there was little differenc between educated Greeks and Macedonians of the upper class Under Alexander, and still more under his successors, helleniza tion was extended to the middle and lower classes of the Macedonians of the *diaspora*. The great hellenizing influenc on the Macedonians at this time was the army. There is no doubt that, at least in the third century, the official languag of all the Hellenistic armies and their general structure wer Greek. And the same must be assumed as regards the militar settlements of the Macedonians. Into this process of helleniza tion were drawn the non-Greek and non-Macedonian element of the Hellenistic armies.

This hellenization of the Macedonians and of the non-Greel elements among the emigrants penetrated even more deepl as the colonization was consolidated and extended. The nev settlements—military and civil—were all of them organize on Greek lines. The bulk of the settlers were either Greek o already in great measure hellenized. It is not surprising tha the hellenization of the remainder proceeded rapidly in thes settlements and was thorough and complete. Colonizatio was therefore, in fact, an extension of the Greek nation an of Greek civilization to the East. At the outset a medley o nations, the stratum of the emigrants soon became Greek i its mode of life and civilization.

Nevertheless the Greeks of this Oriental dispersion, it mus be noted, never, except during the short rule of Alexande formed part of a single State. Alexander's empire disintegrate soon after his death, and with this disintegration the Gree network of settlements was split into smaller and larger grouq under the rule of his successors, the various Hellenisti dynasties. More than that, even within the several Hellenisti monarchies the groups of Greeks that composed the uppe stratum of their population were never treated as 'politica units, they never formed a single corporate body. They live in smaller or larger bodies within the monarchies, and thes bodies were never connected with each other. The only 'political' connecting link between them was the fact that their members were all individually subjects of one and the same king.

And yet in reality they formed a unit and were conscious of it. Their unity was not political, as it never had been in the long history of the Greeks, nor was it racial. It was, as I have indicated in the preceding section, a unity of civilization, the bond between the members of this unit being identity of language, of education, of mentality, of group organization, of mode of life, and of religious conceptions. This bond united settlers living in small and scattered groups, surrounded by multitudes of men of a quite different type and some of them highly civilized. How in the absence of any political organization did it prove possible not only to maintain and consolidate this unity, but even gradually to extend it by absorbing into it certain native elements? We have here one of the principal, most fundamental problems of Hellenistic history, and further consideration of it will not be out of place.

I shall therefore in the following pages give a more detailed, though still imperfect, picture of the conditions in which the settlers lived in their new homes, since it is these conditions that explain in a large measure the persistence of Greek civilization in the East and the role it played in the life of the Hellenistic Oriental world.

(b) *Status civitatis* **of the 'Hellenes'. Education. Forms of Corporative Life.**

I have emphasized the fact that the Greeks in the several Hellenistic monarchies never formed one 'political' body. From the constitutional standpoint the foreigners were not a distinct element in the State. Their political standing was exactly the same as that of the rest of the population. They were all of them subjects of the king.

But—and this is a very important fact—the kings never wished this group of their subjects to become absorbed by and amalgamated with the remainder, the natives. They desired that the Greeks should keep their national and cultural identity, and they took measures to ensure this.

In Egypt the kings required that their foreign subjects should indicate, when naming themselves in official documents, the city or country of their origin, that is to say, their national and to a certain extent their political status. In this way the foreigners were sharply distinguished from the natives and from each other. This rule, this distinction, was maintained by stringent royal orders to the above effect, which moreover forbade under penalty of death any arbitrary shifting from one group of the population to another, any change in the national or political status of an individual. For such a change the special permission of the king was necessary. There is good evidence of the existence of this regulation in both the third and second centuries B.C. The same practice existed in all probability in one form or another in the Seleucid kingdom also.[21]

Furthermore, although individually subjects of the king, the foreigners were presumed to live not as isolated individuals but in organized groups. Some of them became citizens of Greek *poleis*, created for them by the will and decision of the king. These *poleis* were not independent political bodies, but they all possessed the self-government inherent in the notion of the Greek *polis*. Other groups, not organized as cities of Greek type, were not prevented from forming, were even probably encouraged to form, associations, κοινά or *politeumata*, framed on the lines of Greek *poleis* and possessing a certain degree of self-government.[22]

Within these 'political' groups the national and cultural cohesion of the Greeks was based on the education of the young on the Greek model. This education was organized around the Greek gymnasium. The gymnasia, as is well known to all students of the Greek world, had been the foundation and support of Greek life and mentality in all Greek cities since very ancient times. They were carried to the East with the emigrant Greeks and became as fundamental an institution where these settled as they had been in the mother country. In the Hellenistic monarchies they were never established and conducted by the kings as an instrument of their policy. They were and remained private or municipal institutions, but they certainly were patronized and sometimes materially supported by the kings.

Gymnasia spread far and wide over the Hellenistic countries, that is to say, such parts of them as were first opened to Greek settlement by Alexander and his successors. The most abundant, though still somewhat meagre, information comes from Egypt. Here we have proof of the existence of gymnasia not only in the few Greek cities but also among the smaller groups of immigrants, who lived in towns and villages of the native type, both old and new. In them the young generations of foreigners received the old-fashioned Greek intellectual and physical training. About this training we know very little, but what we know indicates that it was exactly the same as that of which we have evidence in many documents of Hellenistic times found in the ancient Greek cities of Greece and especially of Asia Minor.

But the role of the gymnasia in the foreign communities of Egypt was not confined to the education of the young. The gymnasia were as important in the life of the adult Greeks as in that of their children. They were the rallying-point of all those who themselves had received Greek education, οἱ ἐκ τοῦ γυμνασίου. These formed compact groups organized as corporative units and recognized as such by the government. Their main purpose was to support the gymnasia by their contributions, donations, and foundations, and to regulate and supervise them. In this capacity, the gymnasial associations received from the kings important privileges, for instance that of owning property: money, buildings, furniture, land. At their head stood an elected gymnasiarch. The educational work was in the hands of a *cosmetes* and of larger or smaller staffs of teachers.

For οἱ ἐκ τοῦ γυμνασίου the gymnasia were not only schools. They were also the centre of their own intellectual and recreative activities, which were essentially Greek. The gymnasium played in their lives the part of a permanent club-house: it was their main social centre. Within the larger group of οἱ ἐκ τοῦ γυμνασίου there existed various subsidiary associations of different types, for example those of the *alumni* of particular years, the so-called αἱρέσεις.

Since the chief supporters of the gymnasia were on the one hand the cities and on the other the army, especially the settled soldiers, the associations of οἱ ἐκ τοῦ γυμνασίου were closely connected with the cities and with the various communities, mostly ethnical, the *politeumata*, which were certainly as much 'political' as military institutions. Our defective information unfortunately does not allow us to be more precise on this point.

Admission to the gymnasia and to the group of οἱ ἐκ τοῦ γυμνασίου was regulated by the laws of the several corporations and by the decrees of their 'popular assemblies', probably also by laws and ψηφίσματα of the cities. Unfortunately no details on this point are known to us. Whether there also existed special royal laws and regulations of a general character we are unable to say. It is certain, however, that οἱ ἐκ τοῦ γυμνασίου consisted exclusively of men of Greek education, though not exclusively of Greek nationality.[23]

The existence of the gymnasia and the important position that they held in the life of Egypt partly accounts for the efforts made by the higher classes of the population to give their children an adequate primary education on Greek lines. Scores of text-books and school exercises found all over Egypt, especially in the villages of the *chora* (the earliest dating from early Ptolemaic times), fragments of manuscripts of Greek classical writers, some of them remnants of school or private libraries, and a few texts which refer to schoolmasters and pupils, are an eloquent testimony to the efforts of the 'Greeks' of Egypt to teach their children the Greek language and the elements of Greek primary education, in order to make them eligible for the gymnasia. It must be noted that primary education was not as a rule promoted by organized groups of Greek settlers, but was left to the private initiative of individual families. The system of primary education, as revealed by the documents that I have indicated, shows an amazing degree of stability and uniformity. The text-book of the early third century B.C. mentioned above, which has been recently discovered and published, is almost exactly the same as another text-book of Christian times found in Egypt.[2]

What we know about the education of the young Greeks in Egypt is in all probability true, *mutatis mutandis*, of the Seleucid kingdom and of the minor Asiatic monarchies. We have only scanty and haphazard information, but we know positively that gymnasia, and *agones* connected with them, were leading features of the life of the new cities created by the Seleucids, not only the capital Antioch and the larger cities of the Seleucid monarchy, but also such far distant places as Babylon and Seleuceia on the Eulaeus.* I may remind the reader in this connexion of the part played by gymnasial education in the hellenization of Jerusalem in the time of Antiochus III and Antiochus IV, and of the probability that there was a *palaestra* in Dura-Europus.

As regards Greek primary education and the acquaintance of the Greeks of the Seleucid kingdom with Greek literature, especially Homer, I may point to the fact that the Greeks of Dura-Europus and of Seleuceia in Hellenistic and Parthian times spoke and wrote good Greek, and were able without assistance to compose poems that were metrically correct and good in point of style, and contained classical allusions. A group of such poems of late Hellenistic and early Roman times was found at Seleuceia on the Eulaeus,† and I may mention that quite recently many scraps of literary papyri, fragments of various books in Greek, have been found at Dura.‡ A batch of these was identified by Professor L. A. Post as belonging to a fine manuscript of Herodotus of about the second century A.D. (the fragment contains Bk. V, 113–14). These fragments will shortly be discussed by him and Professor C. B. Welles. They may have belonged either to a school or to a private library.

Less important than the cities, the organized 'political' groups, and the gymnasia, were other cells of corporative life of the Greek type that were distributed far and wide over the Hellenistic world, namely, the various private Greek associations of a religious and social character, of which we have much information so far as Egypt is concerned, but very little as regards the Seleucid kingdom and Asia Minor. In Egypt they existed among the foreigners before the time of the Ptolemies, but it was under the latter that they became

---

* *S.E.G.* vii. no. 39 (111/10 B.C.)—Babylon; and ibid., no. 3 (about 100–50 B.C.)—Susa.

† Ibid., nos. 11–14.   ‡ *Rep.* vi, p. 417, pl. xxxvi. 2.

prominent and important. In speaking of these associations in Egypt we must, according to my interpretation of the evidence —of which by far the greater part belongs to the Ptolemaic and Roman periods—be careful to discriminate between associations of foreigners and those of natives.* The same may be true of the Seleucid kingdom and of the monarchies of Asia Minor. We should remember that even our vague and meagre information regarding the Saite and Persian periods and earlier times establishes, in my opinion with full certainty, the existence in Egypt of at least three types of native associations: private associations, those pertaining to the religious and economic life of the temples, and those connected with the State and the royal economy.

Of the purely private native associations we have very inadequate knowledge. They were in all probability closely related to the religious life of the country, to the gods and goddesses, and their temples and shrines. They were apparently not unlike the Greek *thiasoi* and the similar native associations of Syria and Mesopotamia (of which we have particularly good evidence at Palmyra and Dura in the later times), and perhaps of Babylonia. We must not confuse them with the various groups of priests, especially minor priests, and of 'sacred slaves' of the temples, which may also have been organized into corporative bodies of a kind (for example the *choachytai*, the *taricheutai*, &c.), according to the part they played in the business of the temples. Different again (and no less imperfectly known than the first two types) were the apparently corporative professional fellowships closely connected with the affairs of the State and perhaps organized by it: local communities of royal tenants, of men working for the State in the fields of industry, transport, mining, building, hunting, &c. Some of them may have been loose groups of a temporary character, but others were certainly intended by their organizers as permanent institutions.

All these types of native associations continued under the Ptolemies, and their existence in this period is attested by many documents. Some of them, at least, gradually assumed certain Greek features and are therefore not easily recognized

* Cf. Ch. IV, n. 105.

as originally native institutions. This is the case with the private religious and social associations, which were not very different in purpose and organization from the Greek associations of the same type. With the interpenetration of Greeks and natives in Egypt and with the growth of the importance of Egyptian cults in the religious life of the Greeks of Egypt, the members of both types of association may have been recruited from Greeks and natives alike, and the organization of the associations themselves may have been affected by mutual influences.

The same is true of the second and the third types of association, the temple associations and the professional State associations. We know little of the first except as regards the organization of the *choachytai* preserved for us in the well-known Theban documents, which have been admirably re-edited and interpreted by· U. Wilcken in his *Urkunden der Ptolemäerzeit*. The professional State associations probably remained in Ptolemaic times what they had previously been: local groups of men of one and the same profession, organized and closely supervised by the economic and financial administration of the king. These also may have been gradually hellenized, that is to say, they may have assumed some features of Greek collegiate life. But it must be borne in mind that, apart from Egypt, we have hardly any evidence regarding professional organizations in other parts of the Hellenistic world. In Roman times, with the general change in the economic management of Egypt, the Ptolemaic guilds of artisans continued to exist, assuming the form of private professional associations, and their organization may have been influenced by that of the Roman *collegia* of the same kind.

Greek private associations of various types and names superimposed themselves, in late pre-Ptolemaic and in early Ptolemaic times, on the pre-existing native associations which I have described. Many of them were probably founded in early Ptolemaic times. Our information, however, refers almost exclusively to late Ptolemaic times, when they had already been exposed to local influences. In organization they did not differ very much from those of the Greek cities of the motherland. Their popularity in Egypt may be connected with the general tendency of the Greeks of the Hellenistic period to support and develop collegiate institutions. Of this tendency I shall speak in greater detail later in this section. I may here mention that, in Greek city-states, it was most noticeable among those inhabitants who did not belong to the body of citizens of the particular city (this is well known in the case of Athens and Rhodes). For these 'foreigners' the associations were a kind of substitute for city life. The same, *mutatis mutandis*, may have been the ultimate reason for the growth of private associations in Egypt. It must be remembered that in Alexandria a minority only of the Greek residents were citizens of the *polis*, the majority having the status of *Alexandreis*, which was not dissimilar to that of metics in other Greek cities. In the *chora* the Greeks lived, not in cities, but scattered over native towns and villages. It was natural, in these circumstances, that they should create for themselves various substitutes for city life, among which were the private religious and social associations.

The government looked favourably on this spontaneous growth of corporative life, so long as the associations were not the cause of political trouble, as from time to time they were at Alexandria.* They gave them a legal status and granted them some important privileges such as the right of owning property.[25]

We are much less well informed about Greek private associations in the other Hellenistic monarchies. In respect of the Syrian, Mesopotamian, and Palestinian sections of the Seleucid kingdom we have direct evidence only concerning the gymnasial associations. We may assume therefore that Greek private associations were not so numerous in these territories as they were in Egypt. In Syria, Mesopotamia, and Palestine most of the Greeks lived in cities with full rights of citizenship.

On the other hand, native collegiate institutions were not unknown in the Syrian, Mesopotamian, Phoenician, and Palestinian sections of the Seleucid Empire before Alexander. Religious associations certainly flourished throughout the Semitic world long before his day. They were the progenitors

---

* See above, Ch. VI, on the measures taken against them and the gymnasia by Euergetes II.

of the later *thiasoi* of Palmyra and Dura of which we have evidence in some inscriptions and *tesserae* of the Roman period. As regards professional associations, it is probable that the κοινὸν τῶν μαχαιροποιῶν mentioned in an inscription from Sidon of 47 B.C. (metal-working was from very ancient times a special industry at Sidon) was, as Clermont-Ganneau suggested, a native guild slightly hellenized. In these conditions, the Greeks of Syria, Phoenicia, Mesopotamia, and Palestine, who certainly had a great reverence for the native gods and had close economic ties with the natives, may have desired to join the ancient Semitic 'mazzah' and 'gev' of the cities in which they had settled, and thereby gave these institutions an externally Hellenic character. It must be remembered that the native members of these associations, which grew up mostly in the large cities, were themselves gradually hellenized, that they formed a part of the same well-to-do *bourgeoisie* to which the Greeks also belonged, and that they had many religious and economic interests in common with the Greeks. It was natural that they should willingly admit the Greeks into their religious and professional associations. But this process was slow. In Dura a ἑταιρεία formed for the worship of Aphlad, the patron god of Dura's neighbour, Anath, though it recorded its dedications (of A.D. 54) in Greek, yet consisted exclusively of Semites (with only one exception: probably a Semite who had assumed a Greek name). The position was similar at Palmyra.[26]

We are no better acquainted with collegiate institutions in the Anatolian satrapies of the Seleucids and in the minor Anatolian monarchies. The old Greek cities of Asia Minor had certainly developed corporative life on the same lines as the other Greek *poleis*. On this point we possess some information in respect, for example, of Miletus. The development continued in the Hellenistic period. I have already mentioned the Ionian and Hellespontine Dionysiac *technitai*, whose seat was at Teos, and their peculiar relations with the Pergamene kings. I may add that Teos was in general a great centre of collegiate activities in the Hellenistic period. We are aware also of the prosperity and striking development of the gymnasia, and of the associations connected therewith, in all the

Greek cities of Asia Minor. In the Anatolian kingdoms the were certainly patronized and controlled by the kings (se above, Ch. V, as regards Pergamon).

The history of professional associations in Asia Minor is distinct question, but I cannot deal with it here at length. I is well known that in Roman imperial times there existed i Asia Minor, alike in the larger and smaller cities, scores if no hundreds of such associations, especially of artisans, manua workers, and merchants, variously named and of various type more numerous perhaps than in Egypt. This phenomenon— exceptional in the Greek world of this period—has been com monly explained as the result of the brilliant economic pro gress of Asia Minor during the first three centuries A.D. Th professional associations grew spontaneously on the patterns and under the influence, of the collegiate groups which wer so prominent a feature of the social and economic evolution o the western part of the Roman Empire. In brief, accordin, to this view, it was a new development, of foreign origin without precedent in the past. But another interpretation o this phenomenon has been suggested. Professor Radet an the late Sir William Ramsay have briefly indicated the possi bility that these associations were the continuation of the pre Hellenistic guilds which existed for example at Sardis and ma have been, as in Egypt, an important feature in the organiza tion of the Oriental temples of Asia Minor before the days o Alexander. As in Egypt, these guilds may have survived i Hellenistic times, as free corporations in the hellenized cities an as temple institutions. In the Roman age, under the influenc of peace and prosperity, their development was remarkabl the temple associations being freed from the control of th priests. Gradually they spread all over Asia Minor. I accepte this second interpretation in my *Social and Economic History c the Roman Empire* and I still regard it as probable. It must b borne in mind, however, that we possess no direct evidenc and that conclusions *ex silentio* are always dangerous.[27]

(c) Civil Law.

The same tendency on the part of the Hellenistic kings of th East to help the Greeks to maintain their national and cultura

dentity may be seen in the little we know of their policy in
egard to the civil law valid in their respective dominions.
Vhat I shall have to say on this subject is mostly based on
he evidence supplied by Egypt. It is, however, highly pro-
)able that in this respect the policy of the Seleucid monarchy
ollowed a similar course.

The Ptolemies, the Seleucids, and the monarchs of the
\natolian States found in their respective territories a well-
stablished civil law which regulated the social and economic
ife of the population. It is not surprising that they accepted
t in its entirety, introducing through their own laws, orders,
ιnd regulations only such very slight changes as were required
)y the reorganization of their kingdoms. We know that this
vas so in Egypt and Babylonia. The foreign immigrants
)resented a more difficult problem. The Greeks came from
heir homes accustomed to the civil law of their respective
)oleis. Other foreign settlers, especially the Jews, were in a
imilar case. The Hellenistic kings were therefore faced with
ι very serious difficulty. How they overcame it is but im-
)erfectly known. The newly founded Greek cities naturally
eceived from their founders their constitutions and codes of
aws. Of the character of these we know little. In the case of
\lexandria the code of laws was apparently modelled on that
)f Athens. In other cases other models may have been adopted,
vith alterations and adjustments suited to the conditions of
ife of the new settlers. The position was more complicated
vhere the Greek immigrants were not connected with some
)articular city. The royal judges who, in the name of the king,
,dministered justice among these* may have taken into con-
ideration the laws of their various communities, the national
)oliteumata. The same course may have been followed in
espect of certain foreign groups other than the Greeks,
:specially the Jews. These, in Egypt, may have been allowed
he use of their own code *in toto*, under the jurisdiction of
heir own representatives.

This variety of juridical systems was dominated by the
oyal legislation and jurisdiction. It is evident that a royal

* We have evidence of their existence in the cities also, for example in
)ura-Europus, above, Ch. IV, p. 440, and n. 241.

law, order, or regulation, if it conflicted with other laws, was always regarded as overriding them, and that the royal verdict in lawsuits was final. The same may be true of the decisions of certain royal officials, who often rendered justice in the name of the king concurrently with the regular courts. It is clear that the royal authority was actively exerted in the sphere of civil law. This was inevitable, having regard to the various legal problems that would constantly be submitted to that authority as a natural consequence of the reorganization of the Hellenistic States and of the business and social relations that necessarily developed where natives and foreigners lived in close contact.

In these circumstances it is certain that there was no uniformity in the legal aspect of life in the Hellenistic monarchies. Nevertheless, certain facts point to some degree of approach to unity in this respect, especially as regards the Greek civil law. The codes given by the kings to the various cities founded by them, though different in details, were certainly based on certain general legal principles characteristic of Greek civil law as a whole. And it is probable that the adjustment of these laws through the exercise of the king's legislative and judicial authority tended towards unification and not differentiation. We may assume that there was a similar tendency as regards the civil law which gradually emerged from the exercise of this authority where those Greeks were concerned who did not belong to any particular city and were gradually losing their former 'national' status. Thus it was that slowly and by degrees there was probably developing in the Hellenistic monarchies of the East a new law, which was based on Greek principles but took into account the conditions peculiar to the various parts of those regions, a kind of legal κοινή, similar to the linguistic κοινή which gradually emerged from the chaos of Greek dialects.

About this legal κοινή our information is miserably inadequate. It relates almost exclusively to Egypt (with a little additional evidence regarding Syria and Mesopotamia), and it is derived from the study of business documents in which the law is reflected but very rarely textually quoted, and which are accordingly subject to different interpretations. Yet it

ppears that contemporaries were aware of the existence of
such a Greek κοινή, remodelled and adapted by the royal laws
and orders (διαγράμματα and προστάγματα). To distinguish this
common Greek law from the native law (ἐγχώριος νόμος), they
called it the law of the πολῖται, πολιτικοὶ νόμοι; it was supplemented by decrees (ψηφίσματα) of the various Greek political
communities in Egypt. By the term πολιτικοὶ νόμοι were
probably understood both the law of Alexandria and the other
Greek cities, and that of the various πολιτεύματα, including the
legal innovations and changes introduced by royal authority.
In the Roman period the terminology appears slightly modified.
At that time the 'Greek' *bourgeoisie* residing in the χώρα
was still sharply opposed both to the Alexandrians and to
the natives. On the other hand, the various earlier national
groups also residing in the χώρα had all become merged into
one class, distributed among the towns and villages and
following one and the same mode of life. It is not surprising
then that documents of this period should speak of the
χώρια νόμιμα, by which they mean the legal Greek κοινή
valid for the χώρα, distinguishing it from the law of the natives,
the law of Alexandria (ἀστικοί νόμοι), and the Roman law.

The legal κοινή created in Hellenistic times was essentially
Greek in character, as I have said. But it is natural that in the
process of its formation some features of the native Egyptian
law should have penetrated into it. We must bear in mind
that the social and economic life of the 'Greeks' in Egypt was
connected by thousands of ties with that of the natives. And
correspondingly, the kings in their legislative and judicial
capacity must inevitably have remodelled the native law to
some extent and so created here again a certain compromise,
kind of κοινή. In this respect we may therefore follow some
modern students in speaking of the adoption of Greek law in
Egypt, though the main feature of the legal evolution of
Hellenistic Egypt was not the acceptance of a fully developed
system of law by populations which previously had quite
different civil laws of their own, but the adaptation of various
forms of Greek law to the social and economic traditions of
Egypt. And the same may also be true of the other eastern
Hellenistic monarchies. What little we know about Dura

points to a similar though not identical development in th Seleucid monarchy.

The new Greek law of the eastern Hellenistic monarchie was in course of formation when their political decline begai We need not therefore be surprised if we see no signs of an endeavour on the part of the Hellenistic kings to codify th law valid in their respective monarchies, and to establish single legal system for all the constituent parts of their king doms. Moreover, such an idea was probably, in a general way foreign to them, and was not in conformity with the mai principles of their internal policy or with the political and soci: conditions of their dominions.[28]

(d) Social Role of the Hellenes in the Life of the Easter Monarchies.

The political, educational, social, religious, and legal featur described above exerted a powerful influence on the destinie of the foreigners in the Hellenistic monarchies. They helpe the Greeks to maintain their national life and to resist wit success the natural process of orientalization. Even mo effective in this regard was the part assigned to foreigners b the kings in the political, military, and economic affairs of th country. In these departments no legal discrimination wa ever made between foreigners and natives. It rested wit the king to employ members of either group as his associat and assistants, and to confer on them individual or grou privileges. *De facto*, however, it was the consistent policy of th kings throughout the Hellenistic world, for the reasons pr viously set forth, to treat the Greeks as a privileged class, fa superior in social standing to the mass of natives. I hav dealt with this subject repeatedly in the preceding chapte and I may therefore here very briefly summarize my concl sions. It was from the foreigners that the kings recruited the army, both officers and men. Foreigners assisted the kings the administration of their realms. The natives were of cour not excluded legally either from the army or from the admi istration. But, in fact, they played a minor and subordina role in both these fields. It is even more noteworthy th foreigners had an important, perhaps the leading, part in th

:onomic life of the Hellenistic monarchies of the East. The
1ajority, or at least a substantial proportion, of them were
1ccessful in their economic ventures and became prosperous.
.s well-to-do men they became the upper class of the population
f Egypt, the upper stratum of what we may call the *bour-
eoisie* of this country. And the same thing occurred in the
ther monarchies. This was the result not of any definite
rivileges bestowed on them by the kings, but of their *de facto*
rominent position in the business of the country in general.
.s officers and soldiers of the army, as higher civil officials,
1ey had exceptional opportunities of earning and saving
1oney and of investing it profitably, often as partners and
gents of the kings in the management of their estates and
1eir revenues from the royal land, from monopolies, from
1xes, from the management of the royal money; or as holders
f gift estates, as tax and monopoly farmers, as concessionaires
1 the field of trade, as bankers, and so forth.

This privileged position of the foreigners made their status,
hat of a 'Hellene' as described above, very attractive to the
atives, especially to the higher class among them. Since
minence in the administrative and to a certain extent in the
:onomic world depended in practice not so much on legal
rivileges as on the aspirant's degree of hellenization, Greek
ducation and the Greek mode of life were adopted by many
rominent native families. It was a natural process, and it
ecame increasingly common as time went on. I have quoted
everal instances of it both in Egypt and in the Seleucid king-
om. I have mentioned for example several distinguished
'hoenicians of Sidon who assumed Greek names and Greek
1anners and in consequence played an important part not
nly in the affairs of their own city but also in those of the
'tolemaic kingdom in general. I may add here two instances
elating to Phoenicians of Cyprus. One of these is Zenon, son
f Mnaseas (or Demeas), a native of Citium in Cyprus, the
horoughly hellenized founder of the Stoic school in Athens.*
'he other is the hero of one of the stories told in Book II of
he *Leontium* of Hermesianax of Colophon, a contemporary of
'hiletas of Cos. The heroine presented by Hermesianax is

* Diog. Laert. vii. 1; on Citium see Oberhummer, *P.W.K.* xi. 535.

Arsinoe, the daughter of Nicocreon, king of Salamis (probabl, the ally of Ptolemy in his struggle against Antigonus). Th lover of Arsinoe is Acreophon, a rich Phoenician like Zeno and his father. Nicocreon opposes the marriage, 'because of th shame of his descent, his ancestors being Phoenicians'.* Th reverse process was of course also in operation. In the new surroundings, owing to frequent intermarriages with natives the 'Greeks' of the Hellenistic monarchies became somewha orientalized. But this natural orientalization was less prom inent, at least it is less easy for the modern student t detect, than the process of hellenization among the uppe classes of the natives.

The rulers were not opposed to the tendency toward hellenization. Association with natives, not domination ove them, became, for many political and military reasons pre viously indicated, the leading feature of their internal polic from the time of Philopator in Egypt and at least from tha of Antiochus IV in the Seleucid kingdom. The kings wer more and more inclined to increase the numbers of the rulin class, not by bringing more immigrants into Egypt and Syri, but by employing natives in the higher administration. I must be noted, moreover, that for many reasons the suppl of immigrants of Greek civilization became gradually scarce and most of the new mercenaries were supplied by Thrace, th Anatolian regions, and (especially as regards Egypt) the Syria countries (above, Chs. V and VI).

But association had its limits. The kings were not prepared by carrying the policy of association too far, on the one han to transform their dominions into Oriental States, and on th other to undermine their economic system, which depende on the steady work of natives under their minute contro They required therefore that the new members of the rulin class should be hellenized, Greek in language, in education, an in mode of life. These hellenized natives they were willing t treat as the equals of the ruling *bourgeoisie* of the old stock And they naturally would not tolerate the effacement of th

---

* Νικοκρέων δ' οὐκ ὑποδέχεται τὸν γάμον κατ' αἰσχύνην γένους τοῦ Ἀκρεοφῶντς ὅτι αὐτῷ πατέρες ἦσαν Φοίνικες, Antoninus Liberalis, *Met.* 39; cf. E. Rohd Der gr. *Roman*, 2nd ed., pp. 84 ff.

sharp dividing line between the ruling hellenized *bourgeoisie* and the working classes, the first being the 'Hellenes', the second the natives.

As a result of the process of amalgamation described above and of the policy of the kings, the upper class in Egypt, in the Seleucid kingdom, and probably in the Anatolian kingdoms also, remained Greek in the second century B.C., though many of its members were hellenized natives.[29]

e) Mentality of the Hellenes.

In the preceding pages I have endeavoured to describe the *status civitatis* of the 'Hellenes' in their new homes in the East, as well as some peculiar features of their social life which were partly of their own creation and partly the outcome of the policy of their rulers. I may now say a few words of their mental outlook, of the ends and aims which they pursued, and of the means by which they achieved them. Here again our material is scanty. Besides the works of the Hellenistic poets, and of the scholars and other authors, mostly Alexandrian, of this period, who very seldom speak of themselves and only rarely give us glimpses of the real world about them as they saw it, we have the Egyptian papyri, in which various aspects of the actual life of the Greeks in Egypt are reflected. The petitions and lawsuits of these people are especially instructive, but above all their private letters. In some cases, as I have stated (Ch. IV, p. 256), substantial fragments of domestic archives have been preserved. Most of these belonged to men of the class of the 'Hellenes'. Such are the archives of Zenon, those of the architects Cleon and Theodorus, and, coming to a later period, those of Ptolemy the recluse and of a typical hellenized native, Menches the village scribe of Cerceosiris.

We do not know (except in a very few cases) what had been the conditions of life and the social standing of the Greek emigrants to the East in their former countries. It has been suggested that most of them—in this resembling the mercenary soldiers of the fourth century—were metics or κατοικοῦντες in their old homes, that is to say, in one of the Greek cities of continental Greece, the islands, or Asia Minor, and that they naturally carried with them in their migration the 'political' or rather 'non-political' outlook of this class with its buoyant creative spirit and its concomitant experience in the various fields of economic and social activity. It is well known that for instance at Athens, and in other large and important centres of economic life in the fourth century such as Rhodes commercial and other kinds of business and to some extent the liberal professions were in the hands of foreign residents, and not of members of the exclusive group of *politai*. In fact we shall see presently that the spirit of the new settlers in the Hellenistic monarchies of the East closely resembled the spirit of the metics in old Greece. But this does not necessarily mean that the majority of them had had the standing of metics in their cities of origin. Our knowledge on the point is of course defective, but it is interesting to note that in one of the rare cases where we possess trustworthy information, the evidence does not support the above sweeping general statement. I am not speaking of the political and intellectual aristocracy, but of the mass of the immigrants. Zenon, the famous assistant of Apollonius, for example, belonged to a family of respectable citizens of the Carian city of Caunus, and the other Caunians who played so important a part in the *dorea* of Apollonius probably belonged to the same social class.

The new settlers in the Hellenistic East, who had been metics or citizens in their former countries, brought with them and developed in their new homes a very peculiar attitude of mind, differing greatly from that of the fourth century though ultimately derived from it. I may briefly point out some of its features, those best known to us and having the most important bearing on the subject of the present book; but, for a thorough understanding of the matter, students should supplement this sketch by reading the relative passages in books and articles which deal with the topic at greater length.[30]

Of the political spirit of the new settlers, their attitude as *homines politici*, we know very little. In the early period the Macedonians of the armies of the Hellenistic monarchies still regarded themselves as the traditional body-politic of their motherland, closely connected with the kings. But these political aspirations of the Macedonian armies evaporated very rapidly. If the armies (which in fact ceased to be Mace

ionian) played a certain role in the political affairs of the great
Hellenistic kingdoms (especially in questions of dynastic succession), they did it mostly, not as a regularly organized body
with political rights, but as a constituent part of the population of the great Hellenistic capitals, which in troubled times
exerted a certain political influence.[31]

As regards the Greeks other than soldiers and residents in
the great capitals, I may observe that, in my opinion, one of
the reasons for the Seleucid colonization of the East was the
desire of the kings to create in their monarchies nuclei of
Greek political spirit, possessing a natural, inborn devotion to
their *poleis*, and a readiness to defend them against attacks
from without. Coupled with attachment to the dynasty, this
devotion would constitute a guarantee of the stability of those
monarchies. So it was, *mutatis mutandis*, in the Ptolemaic
Empire. In fact, though our information on this point is very
meagre, the Greeks of the eastern *diaspora* showed in their
new abodes the same devotion to their *poleis* that had characterized them in their original homes. In this respect the
mental outlook of these Greeks cannot be described as non-
political or cosmopolitan. They were proud, not only of being
'Hellenes', but also of being members of a Greek political
community, whether this was a *polis* or some substitute therefor. This was their spirit in Egypt and under the Seleucid
rule, and it survived even after their incorporation in the
Parthian and the Roman Empires. I refer the reader to what
I said on this subject when dealing with Dura-Europus and
Seleuceia on the Eulaeus, not to speak of larger cities such as
Seleuceia in Pieria. But no doubt this spirit should perhaps
be styled not so much 'political' as 'municipal'.

We may see this attitude illustrated in the history of the
Greek, Macedonian, and hellenized native cities of the Seleucid
kingdom. I have shown (Ch. VI, pp. 843 ff.) how anxious they
were, as soon as political conditions became favourable to
their aspirations, to secure for themselves, by any means, a
liberty and autonomy which would ultimately lead to political
independence. Their reasons were in part economic, but the
underlying motive of their efforts was the innate love of the
Greeks for independent political life. It is irrelevant that, as

a rule, they did not win their liberty by action, but received it as a gift and a concession from the hands of their overlords.

While traces of the *homo politicus* are not easy to detect in our evidence, the *homo domesticus* and in particular the *homo oeconomicus* and *technicus* are amply manifested. Less perceptible are the intellectual and artistic interests of the Eastern Greeks, by whom I do not mean the Greeks of the large capitals, least of all Alexandria. Here, in the small circle of those highly educated people to whom the great poets and writers of the capitals principally addressed themselves, literary and artistic interests were very keen and highly refined. The Greeks I have in mind are those of the *chora*. It may be an accident that in the documents which illustrate their life (I refer principally to the papyri of Egypt) domestic, economic, and technical interests prevail over those connected with literature and art. One would hardly expect business documents and private letters to be concerned with other matters than economic, professional, and domestic affairs. We may adduce as evidence of the existence of literary interests among these Greeks the frequent discoveries in the *chora* of fragments of literary papyri. Most of the books of which they are the sorry remnants were probably used in the schools, but some belonged to private, domestic libraries.

Nevertheless I am inclined to regard the correspondence of Zenon and fragments of the correspondence of other Greeks of early Ptolemaic times (and the same is true of the late Ptolemaic period) as true reflections of the prevailing mental outlook of the persons who appear in them. Their real concern was with material life, with their economic and mercantile affairs. Even family cares, not to speak of intellectual interests, are of secondary importance to them. We must remember that it was not exclusively business documents that Zenon filed. He probably did not discriminate between his letters but kept them all in his domestic archives. In fact, among them we occasionally find highly interesting family letters (especially his correspondence with his home folk in Caria) and letters which reflect his social relations and his sporting and intellectual tastes, and even fragments of books which show that he was not indifferent to literature and music. But these are exceptions. Their small number is an eloquent testimony to the predominance in his mind of interests and preoccupations of an economic and technical character.[32]

It is therefore evident that the Greeks in their new Eastern homes were mainly concerned to secure for themselves and their families a life of material prosperity and if possible social prominence. To attain this they worked diligently and with enthusiasm. A study of the means by which they attained their object, fuller than I have given in the previous chapters, will be of interest.

(f) Professionalism.

Most of the emigrants to the East, whether to Egypt or to the Asiatic parts of the Hellenistic world, are presented to us as professionals, trained specialists in some craft (τέχνη). They were originally, or became in their new homes, *technitai* in the broad sense of this word. For such men there was a demand in the Eastern monarchies, since it was on their work that the prosperity and political role of all these kingdoms to a large extent depended. In all the Hellenistic monarchies the governing principle of life was technical efficiency: vocations became highly specialized. I may dwell shortly on this topic, for it bears directly on the subject of the present book.[33]

The Kings. To begin with the kings: their office was not a sinecure nor their task an easy one. It required not only personal ability but also a high degree of special training. This was fully understood by all the Hellenistic dynasties. Their founders were self-made men who had acquired their proficiency by arduous work and earnest thinking, and had developed an admirable adaptability to the conditions with which they had to deal. Having made their own way, they endeavoured to transmit to their heirs the knowledge they had won by experience, their ἐμπειρία. They gave them, to begin with, an excellent general education designed to make them respected and admired in the Greek world. Even more important was the professional training that the royal princes received from the king himself and those who shared with him in the administration of the country. This was achieved not by theoretical instruction, but by initiating them, and in particular the heir apparent, early in life, into the affairs of the kingdom, so as to prepare him or another prince to become, at first co-ruler with the king, and later his successor. This was the practice of the early Ptolemies and Seleucids, and it was followed in the house of the Attalids. The royal princesses had their share in this practical training, and some of them became excellent rulers, not inferior to their brothers and husbands. I need hardly remind the reader of such examples as Arsinoe, sister and wife of Philadelphus, of the several Cleopatras of the Ptolemaic dynasty, culminating in Cleopatra VII, the wife of Antony. The technical training of the future kings was, as has been said, not theoretical but practical, training by action. There were no written manuals intended for the education of future rulers. The many treatises περὶ βασιλείας offered them the philosophy and the moral background of kingship, not professional training in the craft of ruling men. This was natural, for philosophers were not interested in practical life, while the kings had no real need of written manuals for themselves and their successors. What everyone in the Hellenistic world—philosophers, kings, the reading public, each one in his own way—required was to understand kingship from the philosophical standpoint, to grasp its essential character and to become convinced of the necessity and beneficence of this new form of Greek government, so different from the city-state. This is exactly what the philosophical schools, vying with each other, offered to their readers. Since most of the treatises, so far as we can judge from our exiguous information, in accordance with the general philosophic ideas of their authors, accepted kingship with some restrictions and under certain conditions, and gave it a kind of philosophical legitimation, they were welcome both to the kings and to their Greek subjects. In return for such a philosophical legitimation the kings were prepared to recognize and adopt the moral principles of conduct dictated to them by the philosophers. On the other hand, their subjects were glad to be given reasons for accepting, without scruple or regret, subjection and obedience in place of the old liberty of the *polis*.[34]

Bureaucracy. The duties of a king could not be discharged

without the help of a trained body of professional assistants, a well-organized bureaucracy. The speedy and successful creation of this army of officials, this Greek bureaucratic machinery, was one of the greatest achievements of the Hellenistic kings. We are beginning gradually to reconstruct it from scattered documents, to grasp its organization, its hierarchy, its sphere and mode of action. It is a difficult and laborious task. It is even more difficult to understand how the kings were able to create such a machinery in a foreign country, in new and somewhat bewildering conditions, out of elements entirely devoid of suitable qualifications. It must be remembered that the higher members of this personnel, the directors of various departments and their subdivisions, were almost exclusively Greeks whose antecedents had in no way prepared them for the complicated task assigned to them.

No doubt the bureaucratic machinery of the Ptolemies, and probably that of the Seleucids and Attalids also, was in part inherited from the past. To a certain extent, but to a certain extent only, it was a continuation and hellenization of Oriental bureaucracy. Of the latter we know very little, but if we compare it as it was in Egypt, where the information about it is fullest, with the bureaucratic machinery of the Ptolemies, we see how much more refined, more logical and coherent the latter was, and how many new Greek features it contained. This new Greek element was not confined to the Greek names of the offices, to the elaborate Greek administrative and financial terminology, vague at the outset, but becoming ever more precise as time went on; nor to the use of the Greek language in administration and taxation; nor to the Greek accounting system; it consisted above all in the general design of the administration and the spirit that permeated it.

The task required of the civil officials was also new. In the early days the kings were not satisfied with routine work such as had mostly been inherited from the past by their subordinates. They had their own ends, which were far different from those of their predecessors. To suit these ends they endeavoured to reorganize the old administrative, financial, and economic systems that they found in existence in the countries over which they ruled. They required therefore creative, not routine work from their staff. I may recall what I said in Chapter IV about the economic system of the early Ptolemies (about their monopolies for example), and draw attention to the high degree of skill needed on the part of the royal officials to draw up such a document as the so-called Revenue Laws of Ptolemy Philadelphus, an elaborate, logical, and precise regulation of certain branches of the new Ptolemaic financial and economic organization. It is more than probable that similar work of reorganization and adaptation was done in the other Hellenistic monarchies of the East.

The reconstruction and transformation of the bureaucratic system of the East, according to a general plan and with a definite purpose, must be recognized as one of the most astonishing achievements of the Greek genius, and as evidence of its flexibility and adaptability.

The feat accomplished by the early Hellenistic kings was the more remarkable because they and their assistants brought with them, as I have said, no special knowledge or professional training for the task. Their private concerns had been conducted in their own countries in a rather primitive fashion. The management of their municipal affairs, of which some of the emigrants may have had a certain experience, was more developed, but still quite elementary as compared with the Ptolemaic system. The remainder, that is to say, the greater part of this system, had to be evolved by their own quick and fertile brains, which at once grasped the main lines of the Oriental organization and were able to remodel them to suit the royal policy. The general scheme was certainly formulated by the kings themselves and their chief assistants and personal advisers. But the machinery had to be built up by the efforts of minor officials, and it was these who had the task of transforming written rules into actual practice.

This task the Ptolemaic bureaucracy carried out efficiently and successfully in all departments of administration. The machinery, though not perfect (no perfect bureaucracies ever existed), proved quite adequate to the purposes of the kings. Certainly it was not free from defects: inconsistencies and irregularities, conflict of authorities, lax terminology, somewhat vague conceptions of responsibility, and so on; but on the whole the result, as we dimly perceive it and as I have described it in Chapter IV in respect of Egypt and Syria, was marvellous in its logic and clearness of conception, in its co-ordination with the past, and in the flexibility that made changes of detail easy.

It is notorious that in the later stages of its history the Ptolemaic bureaucracy (the only one of which we know the evolution) degenerated, and became an intolerable and dishonest instrument of oppression. This was due, however, not to the design of the machinery, but to the general conditions, previously discussed, under which it operated, and to the character of the purposes for which it was set up.

At the outset the kings selected their officials more or less at haphazard, taking the best that were at their disposal. These men, like the king himself, accumulated a stock of professional knowledge, partly borrowed from the past, but partly elaborated by themselves through hard work and practical experience. They had no one to guide them in their efforts. Like the kings, they bequeathed their accumulated experience to their successors and established a tradition. Their offices were probably from the very first at once departments of the government and training schools for the younger 'scribes'—young clerks and copyists as we should call them. Officials could not, any more than the kings, learn their craft from books. The general principles of conduct they may have found explained to them in some special philosophical treatises similar to those περὶ βασιλείας, especially the many συναγωγαί compiled by Aristotle and his pupils; and these could certainly be gathered from the general instructions issued by the kings, the so-called ἐντολαί or ὑπομνήματα, later the Roman *mandata*, which in their general admonitions showed the influence of contemporary philosophy. But the practice of administration they learned from their chiefs. When the Romans came to the East, they found ready to their hand a well-established administrative system and an army of specialists in this craft. It depended on them whether they would employ it, and if so, how.[35]

Army and Navy. The army and the navy constituted two other large and important groups of trained craftsmen in each of the Hellenistic monarchies. I shall not be expected to deal here again at length with this fundamental subject. The one point in the organization of these armies and navies which I wish to emphasize in this place is their purely professional character. The kings themselves were, first and foremost, leaders of their armies and navies, experienced *technitai*. And so were their generals, admirals, subordinate officers, and most of the men. War, whether on land or sea, was a highly specialized occupation, in which untrained men were of no use. On the contrary, thoroughly trained men were needed and sought for. How the rank and file of the army received this training we do not know. The soldiers settled on the land may have learned the first rudiments of their craft in their gymnasia. Games of a military character were taught in the gymnasia of the ancient world (see Ch. VI, n. 82). Professional mercenaries were drilled by the officers who recruited and commanded them. 'Barbarian' mercenaries, such as Galatians and Thracians, were educated at home in their hamlets and villages; war was their traditional occupation, and training for war the substance of their education. But the final training was given to the men in the camps and on the ships, especially when one of the frequent wars was threatening or had broken out. The same applies to the officers. We have no evidence of the existence of military schools. The strategists and tacticians of the ancient world became professionals and specialists by actual experience in military service.[36] No doubt they had some books to help them. There were general books on tactics and strategy and interesting collections of so-called stratagems. But they were mostly of a purely theoretical character and probably played a secondary part in the military training of commanders and subordinate officers. Some of the Hellenistic officers may also have studied the reports on the campaigns of Alexander compiled by specialists in military affairs (for example, Ptolemy Soter) and those on the wars of the Successors in the historical works written by competent contemporaries. The same may probably also be said of the naval officers.[37]

Technical staff of army and navy. The task of those who formed the technical staff of the army and the navy was far ess simple. Here purely empirical training was insufficient. Engineers in building and operating the increasingly complicated siege engines and pieces of ancient artillery, architects in constructing the imposing fortifications of which some examples still survive, had to keep abreast of the new inventions which followed one another in rapid succession. It was the same in respect of naval engineering. Distinguished scholars, acquainted with the achievements of pure science, applied themselves to this department of military technique and sometimes made spectacular discoveries. It will be sufficient to recall such well-known names as Ctesibius, Philon, Biton, and perhaps Heron and Athenaeus, and the most eminent and famous of them all, Archimedes. Except Archimedes, all these scientists recorded their inventions in special treatises (πολιορ-ητικά, βελοποιϊκά and the like), and we are justified in supposing that these books were extensively used by the technical staffs of the Hellenistic armies and navies. I cannot dwell here at length on the complicated problems connected with the evolution of war technique in general and in Hellenistic times in particular. I need only say that, according to the most noted modern specialists in this field, Hellenistic scientists and engineers exhausted the possibilities that the mechanical knowledge of the day placed at their disposal in the rapid improvement of siege engines, the artillery of the age, and of methods of fortification. In respect of artillery they were limited, for propellents, to torsion and compressed air (which last they did not in fact use), since explosives were unknown to them. These two forces they studied thoroughly and with great success. Their discoveries formed the basis of military technique for many centuries to come. The Romans added very little.

What I have said about military operations on land applies also to naval warfare. I have mentioned the competition among the Hellenistic kings in the construction of men-of-war of ever greater size and in their equipment with all the latest inventions. I emphasized (in Ch. V), the point that in the Rhodian navy the technical staff played as important a part as the naval personnel and the marines. It is unfortunate that our information on this topic is vague and general. But the fact is very well established.

It is therefore evident that no Hellenistic king who was ben on making his own State as powerful as possible could neglec the great technical achievements of the time. For this purpos all these rulers needed large and efficient staffs of professiona specialists.[38]

Liberal Professions. Professionalism was not confined to thos who were in the service of the State, whether in the civi administration, the army, or the navy. It developed rapidl at this time in all spheres of life. Later in the present chapte I shall return to this phenomenon as an economic factor o importance in agriculture, industry, and commerce. Here may speak of the rapid growth of professionalism in what ar known as the liberal professions.

Museum of Alexandria. The prominent part played by the famous Museum of Alexandria in the development of litera ture, learning, and science is highly significant. The most dis tinguished scientists and men of letters of the day lived in thi institution, housed and fed by the kings, enjoying immunit from taxation and other burdens, and entirely devoted t their work of research or literary creation. Some of them carried out special tasks entrusted to them by the king, such as the organization of the library and the cataloguing of it contents, with which the name of Callimachus is associated and perhaps a rational organization of the medical service;[*] but the majority were simply engaged, year after year, on their own studies, without preoccupations of a material o political order. Their material needs were looked after by their ἐπιστάται and ἀντεπιστάται,[†] appointed by the king, while for political activity there was no opportunity in Alexandria. The members of the Museum became therefore professiona poets, writers, philosophers, scholars in the true sense of the word. A somewhat similar situation was to be found in the other Hellenistic monarchies. No institution exactly like the Museum of Alexandria is known to have existed at Antioch and Pergamon. But the Library of Pergamon vied with that

---

* See below, p. 1091.

† Note the title of the latter: 'in charge of supplies to the tax-free men who are fed in the Museum'—καὶ ἐπὶ τῆς εὐθηνίας τῶν ἐν τῶι Μουσείωι σιτουμένων ἀτελῶν—S.E.G. viii. 652, first century B.C.

of Alexandria and was the rallying point of the literary men, philosophers, scholars, and artists patronized by the Attalids; and it is difficult to suppose that the Seleucids made no efforts in the same direction, though with less vigour and success than the Ptolemies and the Attalids. In support of this contention I may mention that Syria in the Hellenistic times produced a numerous group of writers, philosophers, and scholars, some of whom followed their vocations at home and others in certain more ancient centres of Greek civilized life, such as Athens or Rhodes. Their names are well known and have frequently been collected.* The Hellenistic literary foundation was so strong in Syria that in Roman times that country was as prolific in eminent writers and scholars as the other provinces of the Roman Empire.† [39]

Dionysiac technitai. The Dionysiac *technitai* of whom I spoke above offer another example of the same tendency. The professional character of these corporative bodies is evident. Only those were eligible for membership in these associations who were craftsmen connected in some way with the theatre, such as artists, stage managers, actors, musicians, dancers, and other professionals occupied in staging and producing plays or in organizing musical performances, that is to say, those who made Dionysiac work their permanent profession. The rest were either honorary members (πρόξενοι) or φιλοτεχνῖται and συναγωνισταί, which may mean 'friends of the art' and 'aspirants' respectively. While in Greece the *technitai* were organized as free self-governing corporations, in the Eastern monarchies, as I have mentioned, while retaining their peculiar corporative organization and a large measure of self-government, they became more or less dependent on the rulers. The situation of the *technitai* in the Ptolemaic kingdom recalls, *mutatis mutandis*, that of the members of the Museum, and may be regarded perhaps as the first attempt in the Greek world to give a completely official character to one branch of artistic life. [40]

* I may refer, for instance, to the impressive pages on this subject in W. W. Tarn, *The Greeks in Bactria and India*, 39 ff.

† See the list in F. M. Heichelheim, 'Roman Syria' in T. Frank, *Econ. Survey*, iv, pp. 167 ff.

Thus organized as religious and professional associations, the members of the Museum, and certainly also those of the Dionysiac associations, became by force of circumstances teachers as well. The great specialists of the Museum, like the heads of the philosophical schools of Athens and prominent individual philosophers elsewhere, attracted young men who were eager to learn, and the *technitai* certainly needed pupils and younger associates and apprentices to assist them in their crafts. It is well known that in Europe the theatres used to be, and still are, efficient schools of all that pertains to the dramatic art.

Poets, &c. Many poets, lecturers on various subjects, musicians, and so forth, did not belong to the Dionysiac associations or any other professional organizations, but pursued their callings in independence. Nevertheless, they were as much professionals, *technitai*, as those who formed part of organized groups. In the Hellenistic period they very frequently earned their living by travelling far and wide about the Hellenistic world, delivering recitations or lectures, or giving muscial performances to the public for payment. Many traces of their activity and success are recorded in our evidence, which refers, I must admit, mostly to the mainland of Greece.[41]

Mimes. Another class of professionals vied with them in ubiquity and popularity, viz. those actors, dancers, and musicians who cultivated not the old-fashioned kinds of dramatic and musical, more or less classical, performances, but the more modern and lighter *genre* of what in ancient times was called the mime or pantomime, with its several subdivisions. The popularity of this new type of drama, a combination of light comedy or farce with ballet, which is but rarely mentioned in literary texts and inscriptions, is attested by several clay statuettes, found in graves and private houses, which in all probability reproduce the most famous and popular characters in the mimes (see Pls. XXXI and XXXIII). They are perhaps of more frequent occurrence than the popular statuettes of comic and tragic actors (Pl. XXII), though less easily recognizable. I may mention, moreover, that scenes from mimes were sometimes used to decorate what are known as 'Megarian bowls' and early specimens of Italian *terra sigillata* (Pl. XXV).[42]

On a lower plane we find the never-failing entertainers of the populace, in streets, squares, fairs, and private houses, in cities and in villages. We know little of them, but they were certainly as numerous and as popular in the Hellenistic world as they had been before and remain to-day: itinerant musicians and singers, acrobats of various kinds, such as rope-dancers (σκανδαλισταί) and fancy dancers (for example, castanet dancers —κροταλίστριαι or κροταλιστρίδες—in Egypt and elsewhere), snake-charmers, exhibitors of monkeys, bears, and other trained animals, conjurers and wonder-workers (θαυματοποιοί), &c. These cannot be omitted from my survey, for they belonged to the large family of professionals of which I am speaking, though they stood somewhat lower in the social scale.[43]

Athletes. Finally I may mention a fact well known to all students of the ancient world: the increasing professionalism of sports, the growth of a class of professional athletes who were as famous and as popular as the most successful actors and singers. Among these, the fashion of the day assigned the highest place to the wrestlers and the boxers. The famous bronze statue of the boxer in the Museo delle Terme at Rome shows the great vogue and honour that these men enjoyed in late Hellenistic times.[44]

Schools. From the theatre and other amusements we may pass to the schools. I have pointed out the importance of these in the life of the Hellenes of the Eastern monarchies. The teachers, both private and public, were not specialists in their craft. There were no special establishments for training them in the Greek world, even in the Hellenistic period. In Greek cities public teachers were elected like other city officers. Many of them may have been schoolmasters only temporarily. We hear of no special qualifications being required other than a high moral standard of general conduct. But, in practice, the majority of the teachers were professionals. Our information about them relates almost exclusively to Athens and to some of the ancient cities of Asia Minor. But we may safely deduce from it a general idea of the life of a schoolmaster in the Eastern monarchies also. The employment was not highly remunerated, and indeed has never been so in the history of mankind. We know that, at the end of the third century B.C.,

teachers in the public school of Miletus received one drachma
or a little more a day,* the salary of a skilled workman, and
at Teos somewhat later a little more.† Nevertheless, then as
now, many made teaching their life profession and were highly
esteemed and honoured by their pupils. I may remind my
readers of the sepulchral bas-relief of Hieronymus of Rhodes
set up by his devoted and grateful pupils. How popular the
teacher was both in life and as a character of drama is shown
by the numerous clay statuettes which permit us to follow the
education of a child (boy or girl) from its first school years: we
see him or her in the hands (or on the shoulders) of a domestic
pedagogue (generally a slave), then learning the elements of
knowledge from the schoolmaster (see Pls. XXX and L, I).

Physicians. No less important a figure in the life of an
educated Greek was the doctor. His profession was well
established in Greece in the fifth and fourth centuries B.C.
References to doctors and discussion of their craft abound in
the literary works of this period. The sick would go to the
great temples of healing gods (especially Asclepius) and would
look for healing to their miraculous intervention (incubation).
But at the same time scientific medicine, that of Hippocrates
and of his Coan school, became increasingly popular as it progressed. In Hellenistic times physicians (and veterinaries also)
were ubiquitous. There was no self-respecting city in the old
Greek world—on the mainland, the islands, and in Asia Minor
—that had not had at least one public doctor and some private
practitioners. In emergencies—epidemics, wars, and on the
occasion of great festivals and fairs when the large crowds
assembled lived in utterly insanitary conditions—the cities
would borrow famous physicians from other cities, especially
from Cos, or invite distinguished private practitioners from
other places, and would acknowledge their gratitude to them
by public honours recorded in honorary decrees. Honour
would be done in the same way to doctors resident in a city
in recognition of extraordinary ability and outstanding service.
Many of these decrees are still extant, and they form the bulk
of the evidence relating to the social role of physicians in the
life of the Greek cities.[45]

* *S.I.G.*³ 577. I. 51 ff.   † Ibid. 578. I. 10 ff.

From the Greek point of view, physicians were craftsmen (τεχνῖται), and their art a τέχνη. Like other trained craftsmen they were highly nomadic. They travelled far and wide, and in most of the cities where they resided for some time they were not citizens, but foreigners or metics. In their art they depended not only on their own theoretical and practical training but also on certain products of other crafts. From very early times surgical and other instruments were in common use. They were much improved in delicacy of construction with the progress of mechanical skill in Hellenistic times. We still possess detailed descriptions of various surgical instruments of the early and late period, and many fine specimens have been found·in ancient graves and in the ruins of ancient cities. The specimens preserved in our museums belong mostly to Roman times, but there is no doubt that the bulk of them derive from Hellenistic originals. As elaborate and finely made as the surgical instruments were the various forms of bandages. These are known to us exclusively from descriptions in medical treatises. The preparation and application of the bandages required special skill. Finally, I must mention the hundreds of different drugs, prepared and sold by the physicians themselves and their apprentices. Here they met with competition from professional druggists (φαρμακοπῶλαι) who had a very bad reputation in the ancient world, acting as doctors though they had no professional training, selling all sorts of drugs of their own preparation (among them poisons), and impressing the public by various tricks, which led to their being classed among the θαυματοποιοί. Nevertheless, they were very popular with the common people, as their successors continue to be in modern times.[46]

Such was the situation of the medical profession in ancient Greece. Somewhat different conditions prevailed in the Eastern monarchies. Medical craft here was as highly specialized as in Greece, and doctors were as much in demand, but their relations with the State assumed a different form. We have much less information regarding the medical profession in the Hellenistic monarchies than in the Greek city-states. As regards the Seleucid kingdom evidence hardly exists; as regards Egypt it is a little more abundant. And yet, such as it is, it shows clearly that the Hellenistic kings did not neglect a department of such interest to the public, and that doctors played as important a part in the life of the Eastern monarchies as they did in that of the old Greek *poleis*.

It need hardly be said that the kings employed the best physicians they could obtain to attend to themselves, their families, and the members of their large οἶκος. We know, for example, that Diphilus of Siphnos was physician to Lysimachus,* that Menander the Pergamene looked after the health of Eumenes II,† that Antigonus Gonatas employed several famous doctors, and that the Seleucids also had many practitioners of high reputation to attend to them. I may mention among the last the famous physician Metrodorus, a native of Amphipolis, who healed the wound in the neck received by Antiochus I in a battle in Asia Minor about 270 B.C.‡

Certain inscriptions attest the existence of a high court title ἀρχίατρος in the Seleucid kingdom and in the kingdoms organized on the same model. The fact that 'chief doctor' was a court title suggests that those who bore it were in all probability specially charged with the court medical service, though not necessarily themselves physicians. Partly to secure the best medical assistance for themselves, and partly, it may be, with a view to the efficient organization of the medical service in their respective kingdoms, all the Hellenistic monarchs vied with each other in obtaining the services of the best physicians of the day and in establishing in their capitals medical schools, conducted as a rule by doctors of Coan Hippocratic training. There is good evidence of such medical schools at Alexandria; we have less information regarding Macedonia, Pergamon, and Antioch.[47]

More importance attaches to the fact that all the Hellenistic monarchies appear to have endeavoured to organize special medical services both for the capitals and the armies, and for the civil population at large. Though our information on the point is very poor, it is sufficient to make the existence of such a service in Egypt highly probable. Its origin must be sought

* M. Wellmann, *P.W.K.* v. 1155.
† *I.G.* ii.² 946—166/5 B.C. (?); cf. Suidas, s.v. Λεσχίδης.
‡ *O.G.I.* 220; cf. Welles, *R.C.*, p. 64.

partly in local traditions: a sort of royal medical service probably existed in Egypt before the Ptolemies. On the other hand, the Greeks were accustomed in their own country to the services of public city doctors (δημόσιοι ἰατροί),* and they expected to find a similar service organized for them in their new homes, either by the new cities or by the central government. The Ptolemies, in their cityless kingdom, appear to have combined local traditions with those of the Greek city-state and to have created what was the first State sanitary service and 'socialized' system of medical assistance of which we have evidence in the history of civilized mankind. It will therefore not be out of place to review the meagre evidence on this subject.

The existence of a public medical service in Alexandria may be conjectured from an interesting Delian inscription of the second century B.C. set up in honour of a noble Alexandrian, Chrysermus, son of Heracleitus, holder of some high royal offices in Alexandria.† The offices were: *exegetes* of Alexandria, ἐπὶ τῶν ἰατρῶν (chief of the doctors), and *epistates* (president) of the Museum. The offices may have been held concurrently or successively. They are all restricted to Alexandria. It is therefore difficult to share the unanimous opinion of modern scholars that Chrysermus was the chief of the royal medical service both in Alexandria and in the country (*chora*). But it is evident that he occupied a high position in the medical service. Since his medical office led to, or was connected with, the presidency of the Museum, it is safe to assume that he was head of the medical section of the Museum, which very likely consisted of members who were at the same time court physicians. We may perhaps go further and regard him as responsible for the royal medical service in the city of Alexandria, including the garrison. But I hesitate to extend his sphere of action beyond this, because of the Alexandrian character of his office and the existence of other evidence pointing to a somewhat different organization of the medical service in the *chora*.

---

* See above, p. 1088.

† *O.G.I.* 104; F. Durrbach, *Choix*, 90; *Inscr. de Délos*, 1525, time of Philometor.

This evidence appears to show that there was a centralized medical service for the whole of the Egyptian *chora* with head-quarters at Alexandria. Diodorus (i. 82), probably repro-ducing Hecataeus of Abdera, a contemporary of Soter, who was his main source, says that the soldiers of the *chora* while on active military service or otherwise on duty were treated by the local doctors without payment: the doctors were sup-ported ἐκ τοῦ κοινοῦ, that is to say, were in public or royal service. This institution appears to have been inherited by the Ptolemies from the past. The medical profession was highly specialized and widely diffused in pre-Ptolemaic Egypt (Herod. ii. 84). In Ptolemaic Egypt medical assistance was a well-organized branch of the public service. We know that a special head-tax (ἰατρικόν) was levied at this time from all the inhabitants of the *chora*, including the settled soldiers. In the Roman period this tax was apparently abolished. The tax has the same name as that levied in the Greek cities to finance the public medical service, and it could hardly have had another meaning in Egypt. It may be mentioned that in one case the individual contribution of a taxpayer went direct from him to the doctor (*Hib.* 102).

Other texts supply additional evidence regarding the charac-ter and organization of this medical service. In a private letter of the first century B.C.* a Greek, Athenagoras, styled ἀρχίατρος, gives an order to the mummy-dressers (στολισταί) and their priests of the Labyrinth in the Fayûm to release the body of his assistant who had happened to die there. To transport the body as far as Ptolemais Athenagoras sent two of his agents, Nicias and Crocus, and he mentions in his letter that the mummy-dressers of Alexandria have written to their colleagues in the Labyrinth in the same sense. This suggests that Athena-goras resided at Alexandria, that he was an official of high rank, and that his office was connected with the functions of the large and important body of priests, minor priests, and attendants who were charged with the highly complicated business of preparing for burial and burying the bodies of Egyptians who died in Alexandria and in the *chora*. This was

* Hunt–Edgar, *Sel. Pap.* 104; cf. C. C. Edgar, *Arch. Pap.* xiii (1938), p. 76.

a charge of extreme importance from the sanitary point of view, for burials required great care and medical supervision if epidemics of many kinds were to be avoided. It must be remembered that Egypt in our own day is a land where many highly infectious diseases are endemic.

Another person apparently connected with the same business of sanitary supervision was Tatas, an Egyptian (?), who is styled βασιλικὸς ἰατρός (see Ch. VI, n. 162). He figures in the lawsuit of Hermias,* where he is mentioned as having sent a report to the *strategos* regarding the residential restrictions imposed on the ταριχευταί of Thebes, referring in the course of it to a special order about this matter issued by the king.

We appear, therefore, to be justified in suggesting that there was a royal sanitary and medical service operating over the *chora* in general. At the head of it was a chief doctor, residing at Alexandria and assisted by a large staff of Greek officials. His subordinates in the *chora* were 'royal doctors', some of them perhaps Egyptians. It was his duty to supervise from a sanitary point of view the functions of the priests in connexion with burials. The same service and the same royal doctors, in addition to their sanitary duties, probably attended to the health of the inhabitants of Egypt. A separate service may have been organized for Alexandria under the ἐπὶ τῶν ἰατρῶν.[48]

In addition to the public medical service, private practitioners probably existed in Egypt as elsewhere. We may regard as belonging to this class a Greek doctor (?), a certain Demas, who is praised in his epitaph of the second century B.C. as 'helper of many men by means of his knowledge (or wisdom)',† and an Egyptian one (mentioned in Ch. VI, p. 883), who was styled in a private letter ἰατροκλύστης.‡

We have less information about the organization of the medical service in the Seleucid and Pergamene dominions. We may suppose that the ἀρχίατρος of the Seleucids and of Mithridates mentioned above (n. 47), like the ἐπὶ τῶν ἰατρῶν of the Ptolemies,

---

* *U.P.Z.* 162, col. ii, l. 25 f.
† πολλῶν ἀνθρώπων βοιθὸς ἐὼν συν[έσει] or σο[φίαι] (*S.E.G.* viii. 483).
‡ Wilcken, *Chr.*, 136; *U.P.Z.*, 148.

was in charge not only of the court doctors but also of the medical service of the capitals and of the armies. The cities of the Asiatic kingdoms probably organized their own medical services on the model furnished by the cities of old Greece. As regards the *laoi* I am afraid that it was left to the gods and the priests to help them to die in peace.

Lawyers. In the complicated legal life of the eastern Hellenistic kingdoms, where several codes of law were in force side by side, and the courts had often to deal with conflicts among these laws and between them and royal edicts and regulations, the parties in the lawsuits and even the judges themselves (who were nòt professionally trained, especially those who acted as judges in their capacity of administrative officials) had urgent need of trained lawyers to advise them. Such lawyers (συνήγοροι and ῥήτορες on the one hand and νομικοί on the other) are abundantly proved to have existed in Roman times. Our evidence respecting the Ptolemaic period is much scantier, but sufficient to show that professional lawyers were an ordinary element in the Egyptian social system of this period. The government gave them its recognition, but endeavoured to restrict their activity so that they should not interfere with the collection of taxes. By an order of the king (mentioned in *Amh.* 33 of 157 B.C.) lawyers (συνήγοροι) were not permitted to appear in criminal cases connected with taxation. Otherwise they were familiar figures in the courts. We know that a special lawyer-tax (συνηγορικόν) was levied by the government.* The nature of this tax and the mode of its assessment are unknown. It may have been a tax levied on those who wished to be assisted in their suits by lawyers, or a tax levied on a larger group of payers for the remuneration of lawyers in general, who in that case would be specialists controlled by the government.

Finally, we may form some idea of the methods and ability of the lawyers from the documents of the lawsuit of Hermias. In these there figure two lawyers, both of them Greeks, one representing the interests of Hermias, the other those of the *choachytai*.† It is evident that lawyers (whose competence and cleverness in handling the lawsuit of Hermias evoke our ad-

---

* *U.P.Z.* 172 of 126/5 B.C.　　　† *U.P.Z.* 161, 34–5, and 162, iv, 35.

miration) were not trained in special law schools, for we hear nothing of such schools. They acquired their knowledge by practice, by ἐμπειρία, and transmitted it to their assistants and apprentices.[49]

The men who followed liberal professions formed a large part of the 'Greek' population of the Hellenistic monarchies of the East. To them we must add another important group, perhaps equally large, but less known: men who only occasionally participated actively in the economic business of the State and mostly worked on their own account. They were probably more numerous in the Seleucid kingdom and in Asia Minor than in Egypt, where no sharp dividing line can be drawn between private business and that of the State, whether as regards the lower or the upper class of the population. I shall speak of this second group presently when I review the economic innovations that first appeared in the Hellenistic period.

(g) Temper of the Hellenes.

A few words may be said on the spirit animating the foreigners in the Hellenistic monarchies. The subject is a difficult and delicate one. Our evidence is poor and is open to various interpretations. I can therefore only give my own impressions, which cannot be strictly proved but are supported by the general tone and character of the information available. I shall confine myself in these remarks to the Hellenistic East. Of Greece and the old Hellenic world I shall say a few words presently.

My impression is that the prevailing mood of the Eastern Greeks of early Hellenistic times was not one of depression and pessimism, of mourning for lost political liberty. On the contrary, a buoyant optimism prevailed. There was confidence, a faith, supported by the teachings of the leading philosophical schools, in the unlimited capabilities of man and his reason; there was an aggressiveness, a striving for life and happiness. Such a spirit one finds in all the great leaders of the time in the political, intellectual, and economic spheres. I may recall the great generals of Alexander, the founders of the new world; their successors, the daring builders of the new States; the great poets and scholars, engineers and architects, sculptors and painters, actors and musicians. They were all engaged not in routine, but in creative work. They were all bringing new values into existence. With due respect for the past they were endeavouring to say their own, sometimes revolutionary word, to recast and reshape the old life. There is no need of evidence in support of this statement. To prove it would mean repeating the political history of the time together with that of the literature, art, and civilization in general of the early Hellenistic period.

This spirit was shared by the minor personages of the day. We know little of them. But I may remind the reader of what I said above of Apollonius, the financial and economic manager employed by Philadelphus, of his assistant Zenon, and of the group of men about them. The dominant note in the letters and other documents of the archives of Zenon is relentless work, feverish activity for the benefit of the State, of one's superior, and of oneself. In this atmosphere no pessimism could survive and none would have been tolerated. I am inclined to extend the picture presented by Zenon's correspondence and the other surviving letters of this period to the majority of the Greeks both in Egypt and in the rest of the eastern Hellenistic world.

Of course the eager activity that we find in the pioneer days could not be maintained indefinitely. The Eastern monarchies became by degrees firmly established and were systematically organized for a long time to come. The phase of experiments and construction gave place to daily routine. Moreover, the political evolution of the second and first centuries undermined the foundations of the Hellenistic monarchies of the East, leading to political enfeeblement, to impoverishment, to misgovernment, and to the demoralization of the ruling class. It is no wonder that in these conditions creative spirit and throbbing optimism were gradually replaced by resignation, and the European rhythm and purposeful alacrity of work by the slow tempo of the East; that part of the Hellenistic world was gradually relapsing into Oriental passivity, and so a strong Oriental flavour characterizes the productions of this time. Interests other than intellectual, economic, and pro-

fessional appeared in the forefront, especially religious preoccupations. I cannot deal with this subject in the present
work. I need only say that chance has bequeathéd to us
documents relating to this period which make us acquainted
with men of a quite different type from those of the past, such
as the afore-mentioned Apollonius, Zenon, Cleon, Theodorus,
and their entourage. I have mentioned above certain representatives of this later time whom I am inclined to regard as
typical: Hermias, the garrison officer in the south of Egypt,
Menches, the village scribe of Cerceosiris, a representative of
the class of hellenized members of the late Ptolemaic bureaucracy, and above all Ptolemy the recluse in the Serapeum of
Memphis, and his young brother Apollonius. It is regrettable
that no similar evidence exists in respect of the Asiatic East.
But I may recall what I said in Chapter VII of the *Graeculi*,
according to the Roman definition of the day. I must, however, emphasize that the change was very slow and gradual,
and the process only in its initial stage when the eastern
Hellenistic monarchies ceased to exist as independent political
bodies.[50]

(h) Stability of Hellenism in the East.

The evolution sketched above in its general outlines, and
dealt with in more detail in the preceding chapters, accounts
for the remarkable stability of Hellenism in the Eastern
monarchies, notwithstanding political tribulations, rapid disintegration, internal troubles, growing economic decay. It is
a fact that the islands of Greek culture in the East never lost
their Greek character. They were never obliterated to any
great extent by their Oriental surroundings. They showed in
this respect an amazing tenacity and persistence. Without it
all the efforts of the kings to maintain the Greek identity of
their kingdoms would have been vain. Not only the Greek
city-states of Asia and Egypt but also the minor corporative
organizations showed remarkable success in withstanding the
pressure of their Oriental environment. The Hellenistic
monarchies, while they survived, continued to absorb and
hellenize their Oriental elements without suffering themselves
to be disintegrated by these and finally surrendering to them.

Their concessions to Orientalism were slight in Egypt and in Syria, where the Hellenistic rule endured until their incorporation in the Roman Empire. Even the outposts of Hellenism in the Parthian kingdom, and in Bactria and India, though they lost the support of the government, kept intact some prominent features of their Hellenism—their language and their ancestral institutions—though they succumbed to Orientalism in their religious and domestic life. More than this: the Oriental kings who succeeded the Hellenistic rulers in some parts of Asia Minor and Syria never, in their early history, discarded the Hellenistic traditions. They carried on in essence the political organization of the Hellenistic monarchies and never sought forcibly to destroy the nuclei of Greek life within their States.

We may therefore speak of a unity of the Hellenistic world from the social and even the political point of view. It was maintained by the network of Greek settlers on which rested the political structure of all the States which constituted that world. The fundamental institutions of civilized life inherited by the Romans in its Western portion, and by the Parthians in its Eastern, owed their Greek character ultimately to the existence of this same network.

B. THE NATIVES IN THE EASTERN HELLENISTIC MONARCHIES

The unity of which I have been speaking was, however, as previously stated, partial and limited. It never penetrated very deep. The Hellenistic kings never succeeded in converting their dominions into national States possessing one and the same language, social and economic structure, and mode of thought. The antinomy between the West and the East which faced Alexander after his conquest of the Persian Empire was attenuated but not eliminated by the efforts of his successors. It assumed a somewhat different aspect but remained, in substance, as acute as it had been in the time of Alexander.

This situation, as it developed in the various Hellenistic monarchies, has been discussed in the preceding chapters; I would now emphasize briefly the partial character of the unity of the Hellenistic world, supplementing my description of the destinies of the 'Greeks' in those regions by a few words about the natives.

I shall begin with Egypt. I have pointed out that the modern term 'natives', as applied by modern scholars to Ptolemaic Egypt, has somewhat different meanings in the early and the late Ptolemaic times. In the third century it is still applicable in its original national connotation, as opposed to the term 'foreigners', most of the latter being Greeks who had become the rulers of the country. It is much less appropriate if applied in the conditions that prevailed in Egypt during the second and first centuries B.C., after the policy of association had long been in force and a *bourgeoisie* of mixed nationality had been formed. Natives were now to be found in large numbers in the group of 'Greeks' and Greeks in the group of 'natives'. The real meaning of the Greek term *laoi* in Egypt during this period is not 'natives' as opposed to foreigners, but the labouring class as opposed to the bureaucracy, the clergy, the army and navy, and the *bourgeoisie*. The mass of the *laoi* practically consisted of those who earned their living by manual work: of royal peasants, of tenants of richer landowners, of hired agricultural labourers on the one hand and on the other of all the artisans of different types possessing more or less economic freedom; the slaves formed a group by themselves, and, except as household slaves, played a minor part in the economic life of the *chora*, especially in the second and first centuries B.C. It is no doubt true that the majority of the labouring class were Egyptian in language, religion, life, and outlook, while the upper class were Greek in this respect. This was inevitable, since Greek education was expensive and the Greek schools somewhat exclusive. For the millions of *laoi*, to merge with the Greeks, to become hellenized, was impossible, even if efforts had been made in this direction. Officially no attempts to hellenize the *laoi* were ever made. The notion of 'hellenizing' was completely foreign to the Ptolemies. This difference in language, religion, and outlook added a good deal to the contrast between the two classes and to an ever-growing antagonism between them.

The division into two social and economic groups as sketched above was not new in Egypt, it was not a creation of Ptolemaic

PLATE CXI

1. Bronze statuette of the former Fouquet collection found at Hermonthis in the Thebaid. A priest, with face and head clean shaven and wearing a linen dress (which deserves careful study) and sandals, is represented standing with his head slightly raised and inclined to the left and his eyes gazing into space. The hands of the priest are covered by his upper garment. In them he probably held a jug containing sacred water of the Nile. It is well known how prominent a role Nile water played in the religious ceremonies connected with the cult of Isis (on this cult F. Cumont, *Rel. Orient.*, 4th ed., ch. IV, and especially notes 76 ff.). The religious ecstasy which holds the priest is strongly expressed in his head and eyes. It is a mild and somewhat romantic and mystic ecstasy and well illustrates what we learn from our sources, both pagan and Christian, about the chastity, purity, and deep religious sentiment of the priests of the Egyptian cults. The statuette—late Hellenistic or early Roman—is a fine product of an art which had a conception of religious sentiment quite different from that expressed in Greek classical art. The nearest parallel to the statuette in this respect will be found in some of the monuments of Dura, especially in the figures of the priests illustrated above (pl. xcvii, 2). Note, however, the difference: the stern fanaticism of the Dura priests contrasts sharply with the romantic and mystic rapture of the Egyptian priest of this statuette. One may fancy one sees in the sharp contrast between the two figures a foreshadowing of the same contrast between the religious sentiment of the East and West in Christian times. H. 0·133 m. The statuette has been published, minutely described, and excellently illustrated by P. Perdrizet, *Bronzes grecs d'Égypte de la Collection Fouquet*, 1911, pp. 48 ff., no. 82, pl. xxii. Cf. a similar statuette found at Hermonthis, O. Rubensohn, *J.D.A.I.* xxi (1906), Anz., p. 139, fig. 10.

2. Terracotta group found in Alexandria in a tomb of the late Ptolemaic and early Roman necropolis in the gardens of the royal palace of Ras-el-Tin. Near a base adorned with a garland on which rests a statue of a couchant sphinx (the head turned to the spectator is missing) is seated a man, apparently a priest, with his head clean shaven except for a long curl of hair which hangs down on the right side of the head, typical of Harpocrates. His dress is peculiar and should be carefully studied. It appears to consist of a sleeved chiton and an ample cloak with fringes, which is wound round the figure. From his left arm is suspended a cloth bag. He is seated in a somewhat cramped position, the head inclined to the left playing a flute with rapture. Near him stands a low, massive, apparently bronze tripod piled with fruit, the centre being occupied by a large cedar- or pine-cone. The base supporting the sphinx reminds me of similar bases typical of the dromoi and the entrance doors of Egyptian temples of Greco-Roman times (see for example the temple of Pnepheros at Theadelphia, E. Breccia, *Mon. de l'Ég. gr.-rom.* i. 2, 1926, pl. li—two sphinxes before the entrance into the second court). The scene takes place apparently in one of the temples of Egypt. Similar scenes are seen daily in the Brahmanic temples of India. Music certainly played as large a part in the religious life of the temples of Egypt and Syria as it now plays in India (no references are needed for Egypt; for Syria, see pl. lix, 4). Late Hellenistic or early Roman. H. 0·13, l. 0·195 m. E. Breccia, *Le Musée gréco-romain*, 1922–3, p. 20, pl. xvi. 1, and *Mon. de l'Ég. gr.-rom.* ii: *Terrecotte figurate greche e greco-egizie del Museo di Alessandria*, part i, 1930, no. 163, pl. xvii. 2. Photograph supplied by the authorities of Alexandria Museum.

PLATE CXI

2. Priest playing a flute. Alexandria Museum

EGYPT. LIFE IN THE TEMPLES

1. Priest. Paris, Louvre

mes. The same conditions had existed in pre-Ptolemaic
gypt. The *laoi* had always formed there the foundation of
ιe State, and the ruling class had always been a superstructure
pon this foundation. Labour, as is well known, was always
ιore or less bound to the State by numerous obligations.
he relations between the working classes and their overlords
ι pre-Ptolemaic times were probably based, not on specific
ιws and regulations, but on custom and tradition. In this
:spect the Ptolemaic régime, which in general was a con-
nuation of the past, represents almost a complete break with
. The Ptolemies, in planning their national economy, were
ot satisfied with custom and tradition. They required more
recision, more regularity, more logic, and sought therefore
ι transform the old-fashioned traditional relations into re-
ιtions based on laws, regulations, orders, instructions, &c.,
nd to a large extent on individual contractual obligations.
y this array of more or less precise rules the situation of the
ιoi became legally fixed in all essential respects. The royal
ιrmers became *de jure* free peasants, tenants of the king;
ιe artisans were set to work for the king on a contractual
ιsis. There were, of course, important limitations of their
ersonal freedom, a necessary part of a planned economy, and
:rtain accessory obligations were imposed on the labouring
ιasses which were not exactly regulated nor based on con-
ιacts. But in the main the relations between the king and
ιbour were organized on a legal basis and very little room was
:ft for arbitrary action on the part of the administration.
gainst unlawful acts by officials or private persons the *laoi*
ιere protected by another set of royal laws and orders.
ι eedless to say, contractual mutual obligations, protected
y law, regulated the economic relations between labour and
ιe richer classes and among themselves.

It must be recognized that the Ptolemies never pursued a
ιass policy favourable to the *bourgeoisie* and bearing oppres-
ιvely on the labouring classes. They were impartial and
ιst, and were inclined rather to protect the weak and the poor
ιgainst the officials and the *bourgeoisie* than to give a free hand
ι the latter.

While thus the social and economic status of the *laoi* was

regulated and, it may be, improved (from a European poin of view), and their personal freedom and the king's interest i their welfare remained undiminished, their general conditio did not in practice show any marked amelioration. On th contrary, their obligations to the king, now legalized an systematized, weighed probably much more heavily upon ther than before, in consequence especially of the minute contr that the royal officials exercised over their work, of the heav rents and the ever-increasing variety of taxes, and of com pulsory labour of both a regular and an emergency characte From all these obligations, strictly regulated and rigoroush exacted by a host of officials, there was no escape. The onl means of protest against the burdens imposed upon them an against the natural development of dishonesty and harshnes on the part of the officials lay in secession, flight, or ope revolt. When such conditions prevailed, in sharp contrast wit the legal rights and the personal freedom of the labourin classes, while the situation of the upper class, foreigners in th eyes of the Egyptians, was (at least from the latter's point c view) infinitely better, it is not surprising that disconten increased, and that, at certain moments, when the controllin power was weak, organized resistance broke out in the form c revolts. This was the natural consequence of the country' general evolution under the system of planned economy buil up by the Ptolemies.

Against these revolts the Ptolemies endeavoured to protec themselves by mobilizing and enlarging the upper class, whicl in the main but with some exceptions, remained loyal to then and by granting to the *laoi* some further partial concession without making any fundamental change in the general econc mic and fiscal system as established. The first measure wa successful on the whole. It enabled the Ptolemies to remai rulers of Egypt until the battle of Actium and the occupatio of Alexandria by Octavian. The second measure—conces sions to the *laoi*—not being accompanied by radical an decisive reforms and strict measures against their oppressor proved ineffective. In fact, it aggravated the situation.

In the other section of the eastern Hellenistic world, tha is to say, in the territories of the Seleucids and in parts of Asi

Minor, the situation of the lower working classes and their relations to the king and the upper class were different. There he *laoi* in pre-Hellenistic Persian times were probably not ss numerous proportionately than in Egypt. Some of them depended directly on the Persian king and lived on royal land n their hamlets and villages, others were 'sacred slaves' of the temples, others again resided in the commercial and industrial owns. Our information regarding their status before the time f the Seleucids is hopelessly inadequate. It is, however, more han probable that in Asia as in Egypt the relations between ing, temples, feudal lords, and holders of parcels of royal and, in the period before Alexander, were based on religion, ustoms, and tradition, not on royal laws and orders. The Seleucids introduced some radical changes in these relations. Their colonizing activity necessarily led to a far-reaching dismemberment of the royal and probably of the temple land. Large tracts of it were assigned to the new cities, and to Macedonian and other military settlements. Many villages with their territories were sold or given to the pre-Hellenistic Greek cities of Asia Minor. Many others were assigned as revocable gift-estates to the members of the royal family and to officers and officials of high rank. What happened to the villages of the *laoi* which were sold or assigned to cities new and old we do not exactly know. Since the villages of the city territories of the Seleucid kingdom, both in pre-Hellenistic and in Roman times, were inhabited by men called κάτοικοι or πάροικοι, we may suppose that the same terms were applied to those who had been *laoi basilikoi* of the Seleucids, but whose villages had become parts of city territories. It is regrettable that we know so little of the status of these κάτοικοι or πάροικοι in Hellenistic times and about their obligations to their new masters. But we must take into consideration that bondsmen (*laoi*), as the foundation of rural economic life, were a familiar feature in many large and independent cities of the northern part of Asia Minor (Cyzicus, Zelea, Byzantium, Heraclea Pontica, see Ch. IV, pp. 587 ff.) and that we hear very little of any radical change in the relations between the *laoi* and these cities in the Hellenistic period.

More is known about the situation of those *laoi* who became

dependent on the temporary holders of gift-estates. It i
certain that they retained the status which they had held whe
they worked for the king directly. As in Egypt, they were no
slaves. They were free men who were not strictly bound t
their village and parcel of land. They had a certain amoun
of freedom of movement (probably under the control and witl
the permission of the overlords). Their obligations to thei
masters consisted of the payment of a rent and probably o
concomitant royal taxes, and a certain amount of compulsor
work for their landlord and for the State. Whether their enjoy
ment of a limited personal freedom was an innovation due t
the Seleucids is unknown. Nor can we say whether, as in Egypt
their obligations to their masters were determined by laws
orders, instructions, and regulations. We are equally ignoran
of the extent of self-government which they were allowe
within their villages (in Roman times there is evidence of th
existence of a kind of village self-government) and whethe
this corporative organization (if there was one in the Seleuci
period, as is probable) remained purely traditional or wa
regulated and legalized by their rulers.

On the whole it appears not improbable that some kind o
legalization of the status of the *laoi* was effected by th
Seleucids as regards both those who became πάροικοι of
Greek city and those who lived in villages on the royal land
One of these innovations may, as in Ptolemaic Egypt and th
Ptolemaic dominions, have taken the form of certain restric
tions on the eventual right of the overlords to transform th
bondage of their *laoi* into regular slavery. It is less probabl
though not impossible, that certain changes were made b
the kings in the relations between temples and their 'sacre
slaves', in the direction of giving more personal freedom to th
laoi, fixing their obligations to their masters, and developin
their corporative organizations on the lines of a limited sel
government.

Very little is known about the history of that part of th
working class which was connected with the industries of th
country, in the temples on the one hand, and in the industri
cities of the East on the other. I have referred to this whe
discussing the evolution of professional associations. No direc

evidence is available, and we must await further information before we can form a judgement on the social status of industrial labour in pre-Hellenistic and Hellenistic times.

The measures taken by the Seleucids for the benefit of the lower classes did not bring tranquillity. The *laoi* in the Seleucid kingdom were unhappy and dissatisfied with their lot. It is unfortunate that we know nothing of their grievances, but the fact of their dissatisfaction is certain. In the Seleucid kingdom this discontent developed on somewhat different lines from those which we have observed in Egypt. In the urbanized kingdom of the Seleucids, with its hundreds of cities old and new, where the Greek and hellenized *bourgeoisie* resided, there grew up an antagonism, unknown in Egypt, between town and country, between cities and villages, between the 'Greeks' of the cities and the villagers, among whom Greek manners and culture had very little penetrated. In Mesopotamia and Syria it was probably the city *bourgeoisie* rather than the officials of the Crown who were regarded by the *laoi* as the oppressors and innovators. Since religion was an enormously important factor in their lives, their resentment took the form of a struggle on behalf of the ancestral gods against the new gods worshipped in the cities.

This movement resulted in revolts and secessions, in the establishment of the independent State of Palestine, of several semi-independent Arab States in various parts of the Seleucid Empire, and of tyrannies in certain Greek cities of Syria and Mesopotamia. It probably also contributed to the success of the Parthians and Armenians in their attacks on the Seleucid Empire. It may be that the movement towards the practical independence of the Syrian cities was not merely the result of a revival of the Greek political (i.e. separatist) spirit of the cities, but should be regarded as in part a manifestation of the *bourgeoisie*'s resistance to the rising tide of Orientalism, which was supported by the natives and the villages and not resisted with sufficient vigour by the kings.

In Asia Minor the course of development appears to have been somewhat different. We know too little of the structure of the Pergamene kingdom and of the policy of the Attalids to indulge in sweeping generalizations. The Attalids inherited their kingdom from the Seleucids. They did not continue on the same scale as their predecessors the policy of urbanization and of breaking up the royal and temple lands. But they certainly, even after Magnesia, founded some new cities and established some new κατοικίαι. We hear nothing of any action taken in respect of the *laoi* whom they inherited from the Seleucids. We know, however, that the antagonism between the villages and the cities was as acute in their kingdom as it was in the Seleucid Empire. So long as the Attalids were strong, this antagonism remained quiescent. But as soon as the rule of the Attalids collapsed, the rural districts showed their mood by supporting Aristonicus and by fighting on his side against the Romans supported by the *bourgeoisie* of the cities. The same happened again in the time of Mithridates. The active participation of the slaves in the movement and their co-operation with the rural population aggravated the situation. It is certain, as I have already pointed out, that slavery played a far more important part in the economy of the Pergamene kingdom and probably of the Greek and hellenized cities of Asia Minor than of Egypt and perhaps of Syria also. It is impossible to understand the life of Asia Minor in Hellenistic times without assuming that the Attalids employed large numbers of slaves and that there were many in the larger and smaller Greek cities, used in agriculture and industry as well as in domestic service. The importance of the slaves is illustrated not only by the proceedings of Aristonicus and Mithridates, but also by the concessions made to them by various Greek cities of Asia Minor, such as the grant of legal holidays (the same as those of schoolboys) and perhaps facilities for obtaining a good education.[51]

All the facts and considerations adduced above show that complete unity was never achieved in the Oriental monarchies of the Hellenistic world. The mass of natives was never absorbed by Greek civilization and never became hellenized. They retained their traditional way of life, in its religious, social, economic, legal, and cultural aspects. They never felt themselves to be part of a larger unit of which the upper stratum was formed by the Greek and hellenized *bourgeoisie*. To what extent they regarded the Hellenistic dynasties of the lay as their own kings, not as chiefs of the Greeks, as foreign masters, not legitimate rulers, the evidence available does not enable us to say. But it is certain that the eternal social and economic antagonism between labour and the *bourgeoisie* was aggravated and complicated in the eastern monarchies by national and religious contrasts, which were hardly less acute in the late than in the early Hellenistic period. Externally the Hellenistic world was a unit, internally it was split into two unequal parts, one Greek, the other native, one centred in the cities and city-like settlements, the other spread over the country, in its villages, hamlets, and temples.

C. THE GREEKS OF OLD GREECE

While in the East the Greeks were building up for themselves a new life by adapting to the new conditions and surroundings the traditional forms of Greek culture which they had brought with them in their migration, Old Greece, in its hundreds of cities, remained outwardly unaltered. The general aspect of most of the cities remained the same. No extensive rebuilding was carried out in any of them in Hellenistic times. Nor did the daily routine change in the cities. Political and religious duties were regularly discharged by the body of citizens, lively discussions took place in the popular assemblies and at the meetings of the *boule*, speeches were delivered there and in the courts, war interrupted from time to time the peaceful flow of events and citizens were mobilized for military service, internal conflicts arose within the cities and led in some cases to revolutions, civil war, and changes in the form of government. The young frequented the schools and received there their mental, artistic, religious, and physical training. Business and social pursuits followed their normal course: the agora was full of shops, artisans, retail traders, and pedlars, workshops were active in streets and public squares, ships sailed in and out of the harbours bringing and exporting various goods, banks transacted their daily affairs, clubs and associations met on given days for banquets and other celebrations, and current events were discussed in streets, squares, around the temples, in barbers' and smiths' shops, and on the harbour quays. Resident foreigners continued to take as active a part as the citizens in the economic and social movement, and slave were occupied in public service, in domestic work, in shops and at the harbours. It is unnecessary to describe in detail th daily life of the Greek cities in Hellenistic times. It would show much the same aspect as in the fifth and fourth centuries B.C.

Nevertheless, there were some momentous changes. Thes were closely connected with the political events and th economic developments of the time. Of the political events have already spoken, and I shall deal with the new economi phase in the second part of this chapter. Here I may briefly review the principal new features in the social conditions and in the mental outlook of the period we are considering, sum marizing what I have said on these subjects in the preceding chapters.

These new features, as I understand them, were on the one hand the growing consciousness, among the Greeks of the motherland, of their national and cultural unity, of thei cohesion, and of the common interests and dangers that formed the background of their existence, and on the other the growth and consolidation of a city *bourgeoisie*, more or less sharply divided from the working classes and gradually evolving a peculiar mental attitude of its own. These two developments were common to the Greeks of the motherland and of the *diaspora*, but show some fundamental differences in their character and progress in the two parts of the Hellenistic world.

Unity of the Greeks.

The unity of the Greeks of which I am speaking was never political. Politically Greece remained divided into hundreds of independent States. All the efforts to unite the country politically, as I have described them, met with failure. Centri fugal remained stronger than centripetal forces. Yet the consciousness of national unity was rapidly growing, in spite of political rivalry and conflicts among the city-states including the Leagues. This consciousness found expression in certain new phenomena both in the political sphere and in the general trend of social life in the Greek cities. The phenomena in question have been more than once assembled and discussed by modern scholars, pre-eminently by W. W. Tarn.[52] It is therefore unnecessary to deal with them in detail in this short summary. It will be sufficient to mention some of the most prominent.

In the political sphere I may cite as instances of national consciousness the development of certain ancient institutions which had never played an important part in the past, and the creation of some new ones. I refer not only to such outstanding events as the growth and consolidation of the Aetolian and Achaean Leagues, but also to some minor factors: for example, the rapid development of arbitration for the settlement of minor political conflicts between cities; the more frequent conclusion of treaties of *isopoliteia* between individual States; the protection of certain cities and sanctuaries against reprisals, privateering, and piratical raids through the recognition by particular States of the 'holiness' and 'inviolability' of these places; some measure of agreement between States regarding the enslavement of their respective citizens who might become prisoners of war or might be captured by pirates; the lavish grants of honorary citizenship and proxeny to citizens of other cities; the frequent recourse to foreign judges for the decision of lawsuits within a city; regular compacts between States regarding the settlement of private disputes between their citizens; and the loan by one city to another of experienced specialists (other than the judges above mentioned) in emergencies, as for example of capable physicians to attend the sick in epidemics or the wounded in war or in an earthquake. I have discussed all these political innovations in preceding chapters, especially in Chapter V, and have endeavoured to show that most of these measures were intended to protect the cities against the growing insecurity of life. But even so these protective measures, which all of them meant the substitution of co-operation for antagonism, testify by their frequency to the growth among the Greeks of the motherland of a consciousness of their unity and solidarity, of the existence of vital common interests among them. Greek 'political' exclusiveness was gradually giving way to a broader conception, of a kind of brotherhood among all who were entitled to call themselves 'Hellenes'.

This broader conception did not lead to political acts alone. It manifested itself also in the private daily life of the Hellenes of Old Greece. I have frequently referred to such manifestations of brotherhood, and may recall some of them. Greek public opinion in the third and second centuries B.C. vehemently resented the brutal treatment of Greeks in the frequent wars between Greek States: the wholesale massacre and enslavement of the population of captured cities, the violation of sanctuaries, the savage and purposeless devastation of the country by belligerents. It never accepted but took strong exception to the enslavement of individual Greeks by pirates. I have mentioned cases of help privately given to persons thus enslaved, of kindness and charity shown to them, notwithstanding the fact that they were complete strangers and that those who succoured them could derive no immediate benefit from what was, in fact, an act of pure benevolence. Nor did cities and individuals remain indifferent to hardships suffered by their compatriots in consequence of some calamity. Of this there are many examples, for instance, the help afforded by Cyrene to Greek cities during the great famine of the end of the fourth century, the gifts and loans of private merchants and bankers to various cities in similar circumstances, and the outburst of sympathy among the Greeks when Rhodes was destroyed by the famous earthquake.

Parallel with the development of the notion 'Hellene', which found expression in acts of various kinds, went another still broader conception, that of the brotherhood of man, of human beings in general. The idea was in the air. It was formulated and advocated in logical discussions by several philosophical schools of the time, especially the Cynics and Stoics, who endeavoured to show, with restrictions varying in different schools, how artificial, conventional, and irrelevant from a philosophical standpoint were the distinctions between man and woman, barbarian and Greek, slave and free. The new idea appealed to many in the Greek world, especially in Old Greece. No doubt it was never generally adopted nor became socially operative on a large scale, but it influenced the behaviour of some, and may be dimly perceived in the proceedings of certain cities.

It never led, for example, to a far-reaching emancipation of women. But it made it possible for some of these to co-operate with men on the same level in various fields of activity. I need hardly remind the reader of the spirited and talented princesses, some of whom played an important part in the political life of their day. There were also well-known women among the philosophers and poets. These, it must be admitted, were exceptions, and the vast majority of women remained as before confined to the *gynaeceum*. But they are nevertheless characteristic of the period.

Nor can it be said that the new idea of brotherhood brought any radical and essential change in the situation of the slaves. In general the law of slavery remained what it had been. But that the idea exerted a certain influence may be inferred from a few innovations in the treatment of slaves by individual owners and by some of the cities. I may remind the reader of some facts which I have previously mentioned. Certain cities granted the slaves legal holidays, the same as those allowed to schoolboys. Educational opportunities may have been given to slaves in some cities. Private donors sometimes refused to discriminate between slaves and free men in the distribution of food organized by them on certain occasions. Certain private founders of religious associations also declined to make this distinction and admitted slaves to membership, as in the case of the famous association of Philadelphia in Asia Minor.* Many similar instances will be found also in the history of Rhodes. Slaves in several places, for example at Athens and Rhodes, especially the highest class of them—the public slaves —were not precluded from forming associations of their own for religious and social purposes. Greater economic freedom may have been granted to slaves, enabling them to accumulate savings and ultimately to purchase their freedom. This would account for the frequency of manumissions in Hellenistic times, as attested by several documents. The rights of freed men were probably better protected than before, being guaranteed both by the cities and by the sanctuaries.

In most cases the more liberal treatment of slaves was not dictated solely by humanitarian considerations. Economic and

* *S.I.G.*³ 985, first century B.C.

social motives may be detected behind these, and may have been decisive. But no one can fail to see the influence of the new ideas in the changed relations between slaves and masters that developed in Hellenistic times. This altered conception of their relations is excellently illustrated, for example, by the praise which the city of Gythium bestowed on Damiadas of Sparta, an eminent physician, who was for a time in its service (above, Ch. VII, p. 952). In the decree in his honour the city lays stress on the fact that in the exercise of his profession 'he made no difference between rich and poor, free and slaves'. It is not only a testimony to the noble character of the physician, but also an expression of the current idea of what constituted fitting conduct towards one's fellow-men. The same spirit may be seen in the well-known epigram of Theocritus on the banker Caicus which I have previously cited (Ch. V, p. 689). Theocritus, describing the banker's activity, lays the emphasis not so much on his efficiency as on the social service he renders, by day and night, to all his clients whoever they may be (cf. below, on the philosophy then current).

The solidarity and unity of Greeks in their motherland was not the result of having 'barbarians' for neighbours; it was not a huddling together, so to speak, for mutual protection, as it was to a large extent in the new Hellas of the East. It was an organic development of Greek life and thought in the atmosphere of the Hellenistic period. One of the factors that contributed most powerfully to produce it was the mobility of the Greeks, an outcome of the extension of the Greek world. The Greeks never felt themselves bound to one place. They liked change and movement and were never afraid to emigrate and to build up a new life for themselves in new conditions, whether in one of the Greek cities as metics, or in foreign countries as settlers and colonizers. In Hellenistic times mobility became a salient characteristic of the Greeks, perhaps more so in Old Greece than in the East. I do not mean that travel then became easier and safer than it had been. But, as I have explained, it became a part of the routine of life, not only within the Aegean world but far beyond it. New economic possibilities, the hope of escaping misery and starvation by moving from place to place or by definite emigration from the homeland, were potent factors in the evolution of Hellenistic Greece, and tended greatly to widen the hitherto narrow horizon of the *polites* of a Greek city.

I may remind the reader in this connexion of some eloquent facts which afford an excellent illustration of the mobility of the Greeks of this period, the constant intercourse that prevailed among the Greeks of Old Greece, and between them and their compatriots in the East. With the professional travellers —the merchants—I shall deal in the second part of this chapter. But I may mention here that thousands of Greeks were constantly travelling from one place to another, selling and buying. Another force that kept hundreds of men moving was political activity. Embassies were frequently sent by various cities, large and small, to wait upon the Hellenistic kings, to discuss matters of more or less importance with the government of some other city, as representatives at the great festivals organized by kings or cities, as arbitrators and judges, or for other similar purposes. Among professional travellers other than merchants there were many specialists, experts in some craft, τεχνῖται according to ancient terminology. Especially nomadic were the members of liberal professions, in particular physicians and artists. I have already referred to them and need only add a few words. Physicians and artists rarely regarded themselves as bound to one place, but were constantly moving—*ubi bene ibi patria*. And this they did not merely from material considerations. Some physicians, for example, were genuine idealists. They wished to be active and useful, and were ready to go wherever they were needed.

This mobility of Greek life was a potent factor, to which, in some measure, the ancient world owed certain important innovations. Foremost among these was the development of a common language, which alone made political and social intercourse possible among the cities of Old Greece and between Old and New Greece. I have already referred to the Greek κοινή. It was not an artificial creation superimposed on the variety of Greek dialects. It was a natural outgrowth of the new conditions of Greek life.

But all the political and social changes described above

involved no radical transformation of the old-fashioned traditional life of the Greek cities. These changes were all partial
the outcome of special circumstances, palliatives to counteract the dominant characteristic of Greek institutions, the city
particularism. We need not therefore be surprised that no
attempt was made to introduce uniformity—by agreement
apart from pressure from above—into some of the most vital
features of Greek usage. The list of diversities that were never
reconciled is long, and I need only mention some of them. No
uniform system of chronology was ever attempted; each city
had its traditional method of dating the events of its history
and its traditional calendar, and there was no one to impose
unity in this respect upon them, as was done to a certain extent
by the Hellenistic kings in their respective dominions. If there
was a certain approach to monetary unity among the Greek
cities, it was not because the cities desired it. So long as they
could they retained their traditional city currency. No one
ever suggested to them the advantage of an efficient improvement of the roads and of a well-designed system of highways
for the whole of Greece. In spite of all the inconvenience
arising, in the altered state of business relations, from the
diversity in the laws of the various cities, no effort was ever
made to reorganize civil law on general principles common to
all the cities of Greece, or to appoint for this purpose a pan-
Hellenic law-giver after the fashion of the city law-givers of
the past. The only exception was the so-called Rhodian
maritime law. But, as I have pointed out, this law was perhaps
never codified and was probably no more than a set of regulations of a practical character whose utility was tacitly recognized by the navigators of Greek waters. The practice of the
courts, especially that of the foreign judges, may have led to
some unification of civil law, but this is a mere conjecture
unsupported by any facts. In such a state of legal confusion
one would expect to find in the Greek cities many legal experts
trained lawyers prepared to assist the parties and to advise the
judges. We have seen some of these at work in Hellenistic
Egypt, and there are several references to their existence elsewhere even in our scanty evidence. I may quote as examples
the lawsuit between the city of Calymna and certain Coans

rbitrated by the Cnidians,* and the dispute between the city
f Thestia in Aetolia and the tax-farmers of the enigmatic τὰ
ιάλαυρα, in which each side had a lawyer.† But it is inter-
sting to note that the famous brothel-keeper Battarus of the
econd mime of Herondas pleads his own cause (eloquently
nd efficiently it must be said) before the Coan judges. No
awyer assists him, nor does he mention one assisting his rival,
he foreigner Thales. Perhaps they were too poor to employ
dvocates.

The Bourgeoisie.

So much for the unity of Greece. To the extent to which
t existed, it was in fact the creation not of the whole people
 out of part of it only, that is to say, of the upper and *de facto*
uling class of the population, the *bourgeoisie* of the Greek
ities. A *bourgeois* class was not a social novelty in Greece of
he Hellenistic period. I have pointed out that Athens in the
ate fourth century B.C. was a city of *bourgeois*, if we may
rust the picture of it presented by contemporary authors
uch as Menander and other dramatists of the New Comedy
nd Theophrastus in his *Characters*; so also were other
ities as we see them in the mimes of Herondas, Theocritus,
nd elsewhere. Little attention has been paid by students
o the part played by this class in Greek history in pre-
Hellenistic and especially in Hellenistic times. I have made
requent references to it, and need only supplement these
ere by a few words.

The *bourgeois* class in the Greek cities was both a social and
conomic, and a political phenomenon. It was an important
nd often a decisive element in Greek politics during the
icissitudes of the Hellenistic period. It is not, however, the
olitical but the social aspect of the *bourgeoisie* that I wish to
mphasize, and the part that it played in the formation of a
ew Greek mode of thought.

I may begin by stating what I mean precisely by the
omewhat ill-defined modern term *bourgeoisie*. I understand

* *S.I.G.*³ 953, ll. 18 f. and 88 ff., second century B.C.; cf. below, Add. to
h. VIII, n. 49.
† G. Klaffenbach, *Berl. S.B.*, 1936, pp. 380 ff., second century B.C.

by it—in the Hellenistic period and especially in respect o the Greek cities of that time—a class of men who had achieve by their efforts or inherited from their parents a certain degre of prosperity, and lived not on the income derived from thei manual labour but from the investment of their accumulate capital in some branch of economic activity. In the field o agriculture the *bourgeois* of the Greek cities were landowner whose land was tilled by tenants, hired hands, and slaves, or wh were themselves tenants employing labour of the latter classes In the field of industry they were owners of workshops, super vising and directing their employees, slaves or free men. I the field of commerce they were owners or tenants of shops i the retail trade, or of ships and storehouses for trade betwee cities or States. Many of them were money-lenders of on kind or another, who lent their accumulated capital mostl on mortgage to those who needed it. Some may have bee professional *trapezitai* (bankers), though this vocation, wa classed as a τέχνη and the bankers as *technitai* (see below) Many were slave-owners and derived their income from thei slaves, hiring them out to owners of mines, shops, or ships, o permitting them to conduct a business of their own on conditio of paying a regular fee. In many cases their investments wer diversified and they were interested in a variety of enterprises

The main and most characteristic feature of the *bourgeoisi* from an economic standpoint was, however, not their manne of investing their capital, but the fact that they were not pro fessionals, craftsmen of one kind or another, salaried employees or the like, but investors of accumulated capital and employer of labour.

It was this class which formed the respectable society o the Greek cities and which is prominent in the literary an epigraphical evidence relating to the life of those cities in th Hellenistic period. As a rule its members were citizens of thei respective cities. But some of them may have been metics The sharp dividing line between these two groups, typical i the pre-Hellenistic period, was gradually vanishing in Hellen istic times. The *bourgeois* were not necessarily aristocrats o descendants of aristocratic families of the past, though som may have claimed such a standing. In fact they were in th mass the middle class, probably of mixed origin, though the majority of them belonged to the old stock of citizens of their city. Nor can we say that they were a kind of plutocracy, a small group of very rich men. Most of them were well-to-do, judged by the ancient standard, which does not mean that they were wealthy. There were some rich persons among them, but these were exceptions. The exceedingly rich man who towers high above his class and exerts an overwhelming influence on city life was not a typical figure in the third or even in the second century. Such men became common in the times of general misery and ruin, that is to say, in the late second and the first centuries B.C.

From the modern point of view we should be inclined to class with the above the members of the so-called liberal professions, specialists in some branch or other of the technical, intellectual, or artistic crafts. This group of men became more and more numerous and played an increasingly important part in the cities of the Hellenistic period. The growth of professionalism was not confined to the eastern Hellenistic monarchies. By such specialists (*technitai*) I mean officials in the service of the cities, some of them public slaves (δημόσιοι), mercenary soldiers and officers, teachers, either salaried employees in public schools or independent tutors receiving fees from their pupils, doctors either in the city service or free practitioners, engineers and architects, sculptors and painters, artists of various kinds, and lawyers. But I must emphasize the fact that from the Greek point of view, i.e. the point of view of the Greek cities, which was not entirely adopted by the Greeks of the Hellenistic monarchies, these were *technitai*, not differing in kind from the various artisans. Most of them lived, like other artisans, on wages paid them by their employers or on fees which they received from their clients. Their salaries—including those of the mercenaries—were very modest, a little more than the wages of hired hands in the various professions, and their fees—with rare exceptions—were not very high. Most of them were foreign residents in the Greek cities and some of them even slaves. They were of no interest to the dramatists of the New Comedy, and they were not members of the respectable city society.[53]

The leading traits of the *bourgeoisie* of the Hellenistic cities, their moral tone and the characteristic features of their political, social, and economic activities are comparatively well known to us from various sources. As regards Athens in the late fourth century, I have referred to the extant comedies and the many fragments of the lost comedies of Menander, and the similar comedies of the 'new' style by other authors (in Greek and in the Latin versions). I have also cited the *Characters* of Theophrastus in the same connexion. And I have pointed out the importance of the mimes of Herondas and Theocritus as throwing light on the conditions that prevailed in Cos in the early third century B.C.

The materials relating to this subject to be drawn from the works of these professional painters of human life are rich, varied, and highly instructive. But they have their limitations. Their evidence is confined to two places and to two comparatively short periods. Moreover, the pictures drawn by these authors, detailed and fascinating as they are, are not, and were not intended by them to be, complete representations of the life of the *bourgeois* class as a whole, or even of individual members of it. Menander, Theophrastus, Herondas, and Theocritus had in view quite other ends, chiefly of a literary character. They were creators of new *genres* of literature, and they endeavoured to produce the best possible specimens of these.

To achieve their literary aims, which are well known and cannot be discussed here, they naturally chose as subjects of their observation and analysis the people whom they knew best, with whom they lived, whom they met every day——typical representatives, that is to say, of the city *bourgeoisie* and its dependants. In dealing with these, in producing them on the stage, they naturally confined themselves to such traits in their characters as best revealed them, and in analysing these traits they were careful that their public, their judges, men and women of the class which was the object of their psychological study, should not be too deeply offended. Their object was to stimulate their audiences by amusing and delighting them, not by lashing them with bitter sarcasm. This accounts for the elimination from their pictures of many salient features of the life of the time, which are of much interest to us, but were irrelevant to them. Instead, they present the predominance of purely personal motives, such as love, jealousy, and avarice. And even in these fields the pictures are not realistic and individualized; they are typical, and represent typical situations and typical actions. If in forming our estimate of the city *bourgeoisie* in its social aspect and role we were restricted to the authors indicated above, our information would be hopelessly incomplete and misleading.[54]

Fortunately we are able to supplement these by knowledge derived from other sources of a documentary or literary character. I allude to those occasional passages in other texts which illuminate one side or another of *bourgeois* life, especially some highly instructive pages in the work of Polybius, and to the hundreds of inscriptions scattered all over the Hellenistic world and belonging to all periods of its history. It is on these sources mainly that I have drawn when referring to the city *bourgeoisie* in the preceding chapters, and on them are based the rapid outlines here presented.[55]

It is impossible to estimate the numbers of this class in the various cities of the Hellenistic period and at various times. As regards most of the cities, we have not the slightest idea of the proportion that it bore to the working classes (including the *technitai*) and the slaves. There are no statistics at our disposal, apart from some figures relating to Athens, which are susceptible of more than one interpretation.[56]

The *bourgeoisie*, however, whatever its numerical strength, formed the backbone of the Hellenistic cities. The cumulative evidence that we possess is decisive on this point, and cannot be interpreted otherwise. The most salient trait of their behaviour and mental attitude is their fervent devotion to their respective cities, to the traditional features of urban life, political, religious, and social.

Some modern scholars are wont to speak of the political death of the Greek cities after the days of Philip and Alexander, and to regard the Greek *homo politicus*, the main support of these, as consequently dead also, or confined to a very modest role in contemporary affairs. This conception of the political condition of the Hellenistic world is not, I think, supported by the facts, which, as set forth above, rather point to the contrary. No Hellenistic monarch would have admitted it, still less the Greek cities themselves. Every Hellenistic king looked upon the Greek cities as a factor in politics not less powerful than his rivals, the other Hellenistic monarchs. Such was also the opinion of the Romans when they first appeared on the political horizon of Hellenism. Every reader of the preceding chapters will realize, I hope, the importance of the part played by almost all the Greek cities, whether politically independent or not, in the political evolution of the Hellenistic world and of each of the Hellenistic monarchies. If the city-state was still an important factor in Hellenistic history, it was certainly because the Greek was still pre-eminently a *homo politicus* especially in the mother country.

That the heroes of Menander and of his fellow-dramatists, the characters of Theophrastus, the personages of Herondas and Theocritus hardly ever mention politics and show apparently no great interest in them, is not to be interpreted as suggesting their complete indifference to the subject. Nor does it indicate such indifference on the part of Menander and Theophrastus, or even of Herondas and Theocritus. It merely signifies that the reactions of their characters to political events and problems were, from an artistic standpoint, of no interest to any of them, and that their public preferred not to be reminded of this grave and melancholy topic when they sought recreation, aesthetic impressions, and amusement.

Nor does it appear possible to invoke the philosophers of this period in aid of the thesis that the city-state and the *homo politicus* had died a premature death in Hellenistic Greece. No doubt all the philosophies in question had their interest centred in the individual. They all were dogmatic philosophies of conduct, semi-religious doctrines intended to guide the individual in his life, in his relations with God, the Universe, the State, the family and himself, all this in accordance with the general structure of the world as the various schools of thought conceived it. This trend in philosophical thought may be explained in part by the political and social conditions of the time, by the growing demand of the intellectual citizen for guidance and help in his doubts and difficulties, but it must

be remembered on the other hand that the general development of philosophy had been in this direction since the time
of the Sophists, and that the new Hellenistic schools were not
in this respect innovators or revolutionaries. This is not the
place for a full discussion of the subject, but I may point out
that none of the Hellenistic philosophies ignored the existence
of the State, of the *polis*, and its importance in the life of the
individual. Each school treated the problem of the relation
of the individual to the State differently, but none neglected
it or regarded it as irrelevant. The Epicureans and the Cynics
repudiated any such relation and recommended complete retirement from political life. The most influential of the new
schools, the Stoa, at the outset ignored the State as it existed
and substituted its own ideal, the universal State, in which
the unity of the world found expression; but it very soon
changed its attitude. In view of the important part which the
actual State played in the lives of its pupils, of whom many
were statesmen in Rome and Greece, the Middle Stoa made
strenuous efforts to reconcile its individualism and 'cosmopoli-
tism' with the State as it existed, which to them again was the
city-state. They did not pay so much attention now to βασιλεία
(see note 34), but concentrated their efforts on the guidance of
statesmen and citizens of the city-state. In this direction the
activity of Panaetius was decisive, and in framing his 'political'
philosophy he had in mind not his influential Roman friends
alone.[57]

It may perhaps be suggested that the upper, intellectual
class in general lost its interest in politics, which survived only
among a few politicians and in the mob. This I regard again
as unsupported by the facts. If the *homo politicus* was dead
and politics a matter of complete indifference to so large and
influential a group of the urban population as the *bourgeoisie*,
including the intellectuals, how can we account for the political
struggle of the Greek cities, which never abated until the last
days of the Hellenistic period? It was not under the compulsion of a few politicians and of the proletariat alone that
the middle class built ships and organized armies to defend the
political liberty of their cities, or to extend their territories and
their sphere of influence. They preferred to employ mercenaries

to wage their wars. Was this exclusively because they were cowardly and unwilling to risk their lives, or was it partly because the military and technical superiority of mercenaries over citizens was universally recognized in the Hellenistic world? In my opinion it was the city *bourgeoisie* that was chiefly responsible for the great struggle for liberty carried on by the cities, an often disappointing and, as it proved, a hopeless struggle.

Devoted to his city as a body politic, the *bourgeois* was no less devoted to its traditional gods and ancestral religion. It was members of his class who built new temples and repaired old ones, who adorned them with statues and pictures by the best artists, and filled them with votive offerings, sometimes of a costly character. It was the *bourgeoisie* again that maintained the old festivals and inaugurated new ones, where professionals and the young men of the cities competed in games and contests,* and that organized the gorgeous processions, so typical of the religious life of the period. It was members of the same class who made pilgrimages to the great Panhellenic shrines (all of them highly prosperous at this time), who sent sacred embassies (θεωροί) to represent their cities at important celebrations in these and other notable sanctuaries, and who filled their treasuries with gifts and instituted foundations for the support of certain religious ceremonies in them. The hundreds of inscriptions at Delphi, Delos, Olympia, Epidaurus, which record honours conferred on foreigners, and the lists of *proxenoi* of these sanctuaries, are eloquent of the religious zeal of the *bourgeois*.

It is customary with modern historians of Greek religion to attribute these practices to the vainglory of the *bourgeoisie*, not to their real religious feelings. The city-states, they say, were dying, and with them the devotion to the great Olympians and to the gods of the city; the splendour of their cults was an empty mummery. Most of the educated Greeks of the Hellenistic period, they assert, were sceptics or agnostics, some of

---

* I may remind the reader of Magnesia on the Maeander and of the propaganda conducted by it in favour of the new festival of its city goddess Artemis Leucophryene; I may also mention the Asclepieum of Cos among many other examples.

them atheists; if some were religious, their devotion was to
new gods and new religious conceptions. It is no doubt true
that Greek religion was not static in Hellenistic times: religious
conceptions were certainly changing; new cults were being
organized, new forms of religious thought were growing, new
gods and among them many foreign gods were being worshipped. But this does not mean that the old religion was
dead. We have no means of penetrating into the souls of those
who worshipped their ancestral gods in the manner above
described and we are not warranted in decrying their religious
practices as demonstrations of mere traditionalism and ostentatious vanity. Such outbursts of religious feeling as that which
swept over the Hellenistic world when the Gauls almost captured Delphi were certainly genuine. Later phenomena of the
same kind in Asia Minor connected with catastrophic events,
the belief in the epiphany of the ancestral gods in critical
moments of the city's life, the registration of such manifestations in special historical works (of which there is evidence in
Lindus, in Chersonesus in the Crimea, and elsewhere), were
likewise unmistakable displays of religious feeling. This was
understood by the philosophy of the day. Epicurus, in spite
of his materialistic conception of life, never discarded the gods
completely. The Stoics made the greatest efforts to reconcile
their philosophical conceptions with the traditional piety.
Without discussing the subject in detail, I may say that,
everything considered, I regard the devotion of the Greek
bourgeoisie to the Panhellenic and city gods as a genuine
reflection of their religious sentiment, not less genuine than
the worship of the Τύχη, of the great men of the time, and of
certain foreign gods.[58]

Besides supporting the traditional religion, the *bourgeois* of
the cities did their best to make these beautiful and comfortable. As in modern America, they liked, in the measure
of their means, to present to them beautiful new buildings of
various kinds. If they were not sufficiently wealthy to do this
individually, they contributed what they could to the subscriptions organized by the cities for these and similar purposes.

They showed great enthusiasm in maintaining and extending the traditional education of the young, such as they had

themselves received in their youth. Several donations and foundations of this kind are known. The office of the gymnasiarch was one of the most important in the city. They endeavoured to secure the most meritorious and trustworthy teachers for their schools, laying stress on their moral, as distinguished from their technical, qualifications. Being themselves well educated, they took a lively interest in philosophy, literature, and art. They demanded the best companies of actors for their theatres regardless of cost; they were ready to pay high fees to travelling lecturers, reciters of their own poems, and musicians; they spent lavishly on the adornment of their temples and public buildings with the finest statues, bas-reliefs, and paintings; they liked to ornament their own houses in the same way, and they buried with their dead exquisite products of the minor arts. They were not indifferent to public health, witness the spread of public medical attendance, of which I have spoken. And they strove hard to avert the spectre of famine from their cities, a vital problem for them all, which I have already discussed. The offices of *agoranomoi* (market managers) and σιτῶναι and ἐλαιῶναι (buyers of corn and of olive-oil) had an importance in the life of the cities equal to that of the gymnasiarch.

It is true that in many cases the *bourgeoisie*, as I have explained (Ch. V, p. 622), was acting wholly or to some extent under compulsion in these matters. The attention that they paid to supplies and to displays, their frequent distributions of foodstuffs and oil, must be attributed in part to their desire to keep the proletariat quiet, to preserve concord (ὁμόνοια) between the classes, to avoid social and political revolutions. Again, it might often happen that a liturgy was undertaken by some member of the *bourgeoisie* under pressure from the government. But this does not mean that all such things were done under compulsion, and that other, and especially patriotic, motives were not the most potent factors in evoking the zeal of the *bourgeoisie* on behalf of their native or adoptive cities.[59]

To sum up this brief sketch of the urban *bourgeoisie*, which might be made much longer and more impressive and convincing, I may say that it was owing chiefly to their conservatism and patriotism, to their sincere devotion to their civic institutions and traditions, that the Greek cities experienced no radical changes in their political, social, economic, and cultural structure, such as might have been imposed either by pressure from above, from the autocratic rulers of the Hellenistic States, or from below, from the proletariat. It is idle to speculate what course of action the kings would have followed had they not met with such staunch fidelity to the traditional features of their mode of life on the part of the population of the cities, and especially of their leaders, the *bourgeoisie*. The kings no doubt showed great respect for the Greek city-state and of course the *bourgeoisie* was often prepared to make far-reaching concessions to the kings, especially when faced with social revolution from within. But the kings apparently knew very well that extreme measures would lead to endless conflicts, and on the other hand they understood that Greek civilization, which was their own civilization, would die out if the foundations of the traditional Greek city-state were undermined. This is the main reason why they accepted the Greek city as such, never tried to make any fundamental change in its constitution, and preferred endless negotiations and sometimes great political inconvenience to any radical reform.[60] What would have happened to the city-state if the proletariat had been successful in its attempts to modify profoundly its social and economic structure, it is difficult to say. Social revolution was always in the air in the Greek cities of the Hellenistic period. But it never met with any enduring success, at least on a large scale. The joint efforts of the *bourgeoisie* and of the kings, and later of the Romans, always averted this danger, sometimes at the last moment.

Some of my readers may feel that the description that I have given of the urban *bourgeoisie* is too glowing and too flattering, and does not accord with the rather sombre picture to be found in most of our literary sources. The Athenian *bourgeois* depicted by Menander or Theophrastus and the respectable citizens of Cos as drawn by Herondas are not very attractive figures. The *Graeculi* of the Romans were in many respects their lineal descendants and reveal to a large extent the same character. They certainly were selfish, their conception of life was materialistic, their ideals somewhat distasteful, and their morality low. What they wanted was a quiet and easy life of pleasure, with the minimum of work and worry. They showed very little interest in the State or in religion. Their main endeavour was to increase their material possessions and to bequeath them to their posterity. Love plays an important part in their lives, but it was not the basis of marriage: the latter was simply a business transaction. They showed some tenderness for their infant children, but were ready, in case of necessity, to expose those that were not wanted, especially the girls.

This picture is certainly a true one, though a little exaggerated. But its fundamental elements apply, to a certain extent, to the *bourgeoisie* of all times and of all countries. It does not contradict and is not irreconcilable with that which I have drawn above. No human beings are perfect, and the *bourgeoisie* of Hellenistic times was no exception to the rule. Moreover, as time went on, it deteriorated even further in respect of its failings. And yet what I have said of its ultimate role in the destinies of Greece is exact. It was in the main the Hellenistic *bourgeoisie* which preserved—for good or for evil—the leading traits of Greek city life and bequeathed them, with the sanction of their own support, to posterity.

The proletariat.

A concomitant of the creation and consolidation of the urban *bourgeoisie* was the formation of the class of working men. Some of these were in comfortable circumstances, enjoying a modest but secure and steady income, sufficient to support themselves and their families. But the majority lived in great poverty and may be styled the proletariat of the cities as opposed to the *bourgeoisie*. I have already more than once dealt with this class, and need only remind the reader of some salient facts.

The proletariat of the Greek cities of continental Greece, of the islands, and of the coasts of the Euxine, consisted chiefly of wage-earners and of slaves, who characteristically are sometimes styled in our literary sources 'hirelings for life' (*perpetuus mercenarius*).* As regards free labour, work was scarce and

* Chrysippus *ap.* Seneca, *De benef.* iii. 22.

became ever scarcer and increasingly irregular. Unemployment both temporary and protracted grew rapidly. The more numerous the idle hands, the lower the wages. We must also take into account the competition of slave labour. I have shown above, when speaking of the Achaean and of the first Mithridatic wars, how large was the number of slaves in continental Greece in the late second and early first centuries B.C. Their number in the third and early second centuries must likewise not be underestimated (above, Ch. IV, p. 207 and Ch. V, p. 626). The situation was probably not different in the islands, and certainly not in Asia Minor (above, p. 670). We may suppose that in continental Greece and in the ancient Greek cities in general the greater part of them were domestic slaves owned by well-to-do *bourgeois*. Wages being low, the competition of slaves with free labour in workshops and in the fields could not be very keen; indeed slave labour in general was less efficient and probably more expensive than free labour. But our information on this point is scanty, and the methods of exploiting slave labour were various. Even if the majority were domestic slaves, we must bear in mind that their work, as applied in Greek domestic economy, was in itself a rival of free labour. It was, for example, domestic slaves who produced most of the clothing of *bourgeois* families, and flour and common bread were made by them in the houses of well-to-do Greeks.

The problem of labour became especially acute in the Greek cities when the great period of civil and military emigration to the new regions of the Greek world came to an end, when the armies of the Hellenistic monarchies ceased to absorb the same large numbers of mercenaries as before, and when the civil settlement of the new territories was almost completed, while on the other hand the political situation grew steadily more disturbed and economic difficulties increased. Greece reacted to the stress by restriction of families, exposure of children, and so forth. But the depopulation of Greece was a slow process and the growth of the proletariat was not arrested by it.

It is not surprising if, in these conditions, the social atmosphere in the Greek cities became ever stormier. There was a crying lack of harmony in these cities between their political and their social and economic structure. On the one hand, in the economic sphere, there was a rapid decline in the demand for free labour, while in the social sphere the *bourgeoisie* was becoming increasingly exclusive and endeavouring to shape the life of the city to suit its own interests, without due regard for the needs of the proletariat. On the other hand, politically, the part played by the proletariat in the affairs of the city remained as important as before. No wonder that they constantly strove to get the upper hand in the political management of the cities, and having once obtained it made strenuous efforts to bring into effect the social and economic reforms most coveted by them—cancellation of debts and redistribution of land. If this programme was never realized with enduring effect, even on a small scale,* the reason lay chiefly, as I have pointed out, in the resistance of the *bourgeoisie* and in intervention from above. In the few cases where social revolution was successful, this was the result of political conjunctures which prompted the leaders of the day to lend their support to the social aspirations of the proletariat. Such was the motive that actuated Cleomenes and Nabis in Sparta, Philip and the Romans during the short periods when they made use of the proletariat to frighten the *bourgeoisie* of the Greek cities, and Aristonicus and Mithridates (see Chs. IV, V, VI, and VII).

Thus no solution of the paramount antinomy in Greek city life, that of wealth and poverty, luxury and indigence, the *bourgeoisie* and the proletariat, was ever seriously attempted either by the individual cities on their own initiative, or by a great reformer seeking to impose a sweeping reform on the whole of Greece. City government was too conservative and too fearful of any violent change to undertake any experiment in this field. The case of Rhodes, very little known, is a rare exception. Few cities were rich enough to follow her example and to feed the proletariat systematically at the expense of the city and of the *bourgeoisie*. As regards possible reformers,

* I may remind the reader, however, of the activity of Nabis of Sparta and of the conditions in Boeotia, Thessaly, and other parts of Greece at the beginning of the second century B.C. discussed above, Ch. V, pp. 611 ff.

from without, we have seen that in itself the problem of the distribution of wealth and of the antagonism between *bourgeoisie* and proletariat excited very little interest in the political masters of the day.

Nor was a theoretical solution suggested by the philosophy of the time. The leading Hellenistic schools were of course aware of the existence and importance of the problem. But they took it up and treated it from their own point of view according to their general philosophical tenets. It must be remembered that Hellenistic philosophy was not interested in social and economic problems as such. Sociological studies died in their infancy after their first brilliant appearance under the auspices of Plato and especially of Aristotle. The main concern of the Hellenistic schools was to guide the individual in his inner life, to show him how to live, as an individual and to a certain extent as a member of society, in accordance with the law of nature, so as to achieve internal peace and undisturbed balance, that is to say, individual perfection equivalent to wisdom. Such being their chief aim, they viewed the problem of πενία and πλοῦτος, not as an important social and economic issue, but as a question of individual morals.

This subject cannot be discussed at length in the present work. The material relating to it is abundant and scattered and has never been completely assembled and studied, though various scholars have devoted some attention to it. A few remarks will suffice to illustrate the general statement made above.[61]

The school that took most interest in wealth and poverty was that of the Cynics. I have referred above (Ch. IV, p. 210 and n. 34) to the meliamb of Cercidas containing a violent attack on the αἰσχροκέρδεια, the greed of the rich, on the accumulation of wealth in a few hands, and on the protection given to it by gods and men. But the frequent and violent attacks of the Cynics, the advocates of life according to nature and of poverty, and the great enemies of civilized observances, were mere outbursts of bad temper. They had no remedies to suggest, and even if they had, they would not propound them. Nor would they advise the poor to unite and to organize a social revolution. Their philosophy was too individualistic to permit of this, and their indignation was of a purely moral character. For them the rich were not, as for some of their modern successors, criminals, but fools.

Milder but again purely moral and individualistic was the approach of the Stoics and the Epicureans to the problem. Both regarded wealth as 'irrelevant', but neither classed it as an evil or was opposed to a moderate accumulation of wealth in the hands of wise men, since such an accumulation guaranteed to the σοφός that amount of freedom and leisure which was required for other and higher purposes. Of the two schools, the Stoics were (from the point of view of the *bourgeoisie*) more conservative, the Epicureans a little more radical. It is not improbable that the attitude of both schools towards wealth was in part dictated to them by their regard for their pupils and followers, who mostly belonged to the circle of intellectuals and to the *bourgeoisie*. In illustration of the Stoic and Epicurean point of view two short remarks may be quoted, one of Chrysippus, another of Epicurus. Chrysippus* says emphatically: 'crazy are those who deem of no account, and do not strive to secure, wealth, health, leisure, and complete soundness of body'; and the same point of view is expressed in many other fragments of his various works.[62] Different in several respects, but essentially similar, was the point of view of Epicurus. References to the problem of wealth will be found in many of his fragments. One of the most interesting is that in fragment A, 67 (Bailey): 'Free life does not tolerate the accumulation of goods in large quantities, since this is difficult without serving mobs or rulers, but the free man (as such) possesses all things in unfailing abundance; and if by chance he acquires large means (in addition), he will readily give a share of them to those near to him in order to win their benevolence'.[63]†

---

* *Stoic. Vet. Fr.* iii, p. 33, fr. 138, von Arnim: μαίνεσθαι τοὺς τὸν πλοῦτον καὶ τὴν ὑγίειαν καὶ τὴν ἀπονίαν καὶ τὴν ὁλοκληρίαν τοῦ σώματος ἐν μηδενὶ ποιουμένους, μηδ' ἀντεχομένους τῶν τοιούτων.

† ἐλεύθερος βίος οὐ δύναται κτήσασθαι χρήματα πολλὰ διὰ τὸ πρᾶγμα ⟨μὴ⟩ ῥᾴδιον εἶναι χωρὶς θητείας ὄχλων ἢ δυναστῶν, ἀλλὰ σὺν συνεχεῖ δαψιλείᾳ πάντα κέκτηται· ἂν δέ που καὶ τύχῃ χρημάτων πολλῶν καὶ ταῦτα ῥᾳδίως ἂν εἰς τὴν τοῦ πλησίον εὔνοιαν διαμετρήσαι.

I may note in passing that in dealing with the philosopher, the σοφός, as an economic being, both the Epicureans and the Stoics look upon philosophy as a special τέχνη and the philosophers as *technitai*. When speaking of wealth occasionally acquired by the philosophers, they regard it as derived not from profitable business in the field of agriculture, industry, or trade, but from the exercise of their special 'craft'. I have just quoted the remark of Epicurus. The attitude of Chrysippus is the same. In his treatise *De quaestu** he says that the σοφός acquires wealth either from 'kingship' in a direct or indirect way, being himself a king, or having in some way (probably as adviser of the kings) a share in μοναρχικὰ κτήματα, or deriving his means from the city and friends in high position, leaders of the city (again probably as their adviser), or even from a more direct exercise of his τέχνη, by receiving, like the sophists, fees from his pupils (ἀπὸ σοφιστείας εὐπορήσειν). These passages serve to corroborate the evidence which I have adduced about philosophers acting as advisers to men prominent in political life.

Yet neither in their writings nor in their capacity as personal advisers did the Stoics and Epicureans ever deal seriously with the problem of the distribution of wealth. They were interested in it, they studied it from the metaphysical and moral point of view, but their discussion never treated it as an economic and social question, but as one of the personal moral problems which faced those individuals who endeavoured to attain εὐδαιμονία and ἀταραξία.

Some of the philosophers, as private persons, had a share in the counsels of certain reformers, and perhaps advised the adoption of sweeping reforms. We hear of Sphaerus and Cleomenes (above, Ch. IV, n. 34), of Blossius and Aristonicus on the one hand, and of Tiberius Gracchus on the other (above, Ch. VI, p. 808). We know of several philosophers who assisted kings, and who may have recommended to them a radical policy by adapting certain general principles of their creed to actual life. But we never find such topics discussed or radical measures of a general character advocated in their theoretical treatises.

* S.V.F. iii. frs. 685 and 686, cf. Diog. L. vii. 189.

The only departures from this practice were the many Utopias of the time, such as those of Zenon, Hecataeus of Abdera, Euhemerus, and Iambulus. But, again, these Utopias were mere products of theoretical speculation and brilliant imagination, and had no relation to or influence on practical politics. The one possible exception, that of the influence of Iambulus on Aristonicus, is very doubtful (see Ch. VI, p. 808).[64]

Nor did the principal philosophical schools approach in a more progressive spirit some of the other cardinal problems of the social system. We may disregard the Cynics and their extravagant suggestions, for their utterances were never taken quite seriously. The other schools were very moderate in their social views. Even the Stoics, in spite of their doctrine of the equality of all human beings, never advocated, for example, the emancipation of all women and a general improvement of their status. They regarded some exceptional women as capable of becoming 'wise', but in the main they treated them as beings much inferior to men and destined to work and toil for them. In this respect Aristotle professed much deeper and more liberal views in his excellent sociological studies of the family. The Stoic attitude in respect of slavery was more favourable to reform. The early Stoa stood firm for the equality of slaves and free men and for their equal capacity to achieve wisdom. Here again, however, their discussion of the question was purely theoretical and ethical. They never inculcated the wholesale emancipation of slaves, and the Middle Stoa—perhaps under the pressure of its followers—reverted temporarily to the Aristotelian idea that slavery was a natural institution based on the inferiority of certain men and certain races.[65]

In general none of the philosophical schools, except the Cynics, took social and economic questions very seriously. And none, not even the Cynics, ever urged a general and thoroughgoing solution of them. They kept strictly to theoretical discussions and showed in the main a far-reaching conservatism, radical as they were in their theoretical postulates. It is interesting to see, for example, how conservatively the 'economic' treatises of the Neo-Pythagoreans of late Hellen istic times clung to the old-fashioned spirit of the urban *bourgeoisie*: I refer to those of Bryson (Οἰκονομικός), of Callicratidas (Περὶ οἴκου εὐδαιμονίας), of Perictione (Περὶ γυναικὸς ἁρμονίας), and of Phintys (Περὶ γυναικὸς σωφροσύνης). These eclectic treatises are typical representatives of the ethics of the period. Their moral standard is fairly high, and there is no suggestion of any moral decay in the family, to which their admonitions relate. They abhor luxury and the accumulation of wealth. But none of the great economic and social questions affect or interest them. These they never mention.[66]

Yet we cannot say that philosophy did not exert a certain influence on the attitude of the intellectual classes towards many vital economic and social problems of the day. The new philosophical conceptions were in the air. Those who never read any philosophical work and never listened to philosophers got their ideas through the medium of contemporary literature, especially through the drama. The New Comedy, without following one or other school of philosophy, is full of maxims and utterances borrowed from them. It contains, for example, frequent allusion to the problem of πενία and πλοῦτος, as also did Hellenistic poetry and prose in general, from which the Romans inherited the problem.[67]

It was therefore natural that many persons, and even kings and cities, should adapt their conduct to the more liberal and more humane ideas of contemporary philosophy. I have cited the liberal policy of certain individuals and cities towards slaves, the principles of conduct of certain doctors and bankers. The reader need hardly be reminded in this connexion of the influence of contemporary philosophy on some of the Hellenistic kings.

All this, however, brought only a partial improvement. Philosophy never saw the need of sweeping and general reforms on a large scale, or it was unwilling to advocate them. It was and remained in this respect also individualistic.

It is astonishing how limited is our knowledge of the life, ideals, and mode of thought of the Greek city proletariat in Hellenistic times. Even Menander and the other authors of the New Comedy tell us very little, and Herondas and Theocritus not much more, offering little beyond semi-conventional figures of slaves, cooks, and parasites. It is evident that they were not interested in the psychology of the lower classes as such. Few of the titles of comedies or mimes (which often treated the same subjects as comedies) refer to the working classes. And even those works which dealt with them may have had as their leading characters members of the *bourgeois* class. Unfortunately we have no substantial fragments of any of them and we are wholly ignorant of their contents. It must I fear, be assumed that even in these lost dramas members of the lower classes were presented in the same light as in those which survive.[68]

We may form some estimate of the miserable economic situation of the proletariat in general from a comparison of their wages with the range of prices, and from their occasional outbursts of indignation in times of social and political revolution; but this gives us very little help towards forming an idea of their mental outlook, of their mode of life, of their morals or even of their religious aspirations.

II. SOME FEATURES OF ECONOMIC LIFE

It is not easy to give in a few pages a short systematic survey of the more important economic features that distinguished the Hellenistic world of the period between Alexander and Augustus. The evidence at our disposal is very scanty and throws but little light on such fundamental matters as population and capital, new sources of wealth, and the influence of science and technique on the development of economic life. Moreover, we are no better informed about the economic structure of the Greek and Oriental world in the pre-Hellenistic than in the subsequent age, and it is often impossible to say whether some feature of economic life, first mentioned in the Hellenistic period, was in fact unknown in the fifth and fourth centuries B.C. It is even more difficult to discriminate between Hellenistic times and those, much better known, of the early Roman Empire. For example, some instances of progress in technique first mentioned by writers of the Roman Empire may have been inventions of the first centuries A.D., but they may equally well go back to Hellenistic days, and have been adopted and perhaps improved subsequently. All the statements that follow, based mostly on the evidence adduced and discussed in the preceding chapters, must therefore be taken for what they are—tentative suggestions founded on scattered and more or less well-ascertained facts.

1. POPULATION AND CAPITAL

Among the essential prerequisites for understanding the economic life of any region of the world in any period is a more or less exact knowledge, on the one hand, of the density of the population in that region and of its decrease or increase, and on the other of the amount of capital accumulated by its population through the exploitation of its natural sources of wealth.

I must admit at the outset that as regards the Hellenistic world our knowledge in this respect is scanty and defective. Statistical data which were available to contemporaries are very rarely mentioned in our texts and, if they are, they are given in a form which makes their interpretation difficult and disputable. Modern science has carefully collected all the data that we possess, and has attempted with the help of modern methods of research to apply them to the building up of a statistical skeleton as the basis of an economic investigation of the ancient world in general, including the Hellenistic portion. These endeavours, however, valuable as they are, have yielded only meagre, inadequate, and highly speculative and controversial results. I have previously referred to various problems connected with the extant statistical data. In the following pages I shall try to summarize these scattered remarks.

Population. I may begin by setting forth the little evidence that we have regarding the population of the Hellenistic world.[69] For GREECE and the islands no statistics are available. General considerations and some figures concerning the population of part of the Peloponnese and notably of Athens in the time of Demetrius of Phalerum suggest that in the early years of the Hellenistic era the population of Greece and the islands remained static and may even have increased in some places. Many Greeks emigrated to the new monarchies (no figures are available), but the loss may have been compensated by the increasing number of resident aliens, slaves and freedmen, especially in the larger cities, and by the natural increase of that part of the original population which remained at home, an increase promoted chiefly by general prosperity. But, as I have explained, the situation was gradually changing. Continuous war in Greece, general insecurity, economic decline were factors unfavourable to any steady increase in population, and our authorities are unanimous (without of course furnishing figures in support of their view) in insisting upon the gradual depopulation of Greece, which became acute at the end of the third and the beginning of the second century B.C. This process, with some local and temporary fluctuations persisted until the time of Augustus.[70]

Not much more is known of MACEDONIA. It is probable from general considerations that in the days of Philip II and Alexander the Great Macedonia was drained to the utmost of her man-power. Thousands of adult male Macedonians left their native country never to return. A large part of the Macedonian army of Alexander was never demobilized after Alexander's death; on the contrary, it was from time to time reinforced by fresh Macedonian recruits. Many of them, and of the children whom they reared while on active service remained in the East as settlers in the colonies of Alexander and of his successors.

Under Antigonus Gonatas and his immediate successors the man-power of Macedonia—a rural country—was probably restored to its former, pre-Alexandrian standard, and remained high until the wars of Philip and Perseus. I have cited above (Ch. V, p. 632) evidence of Philip's desire, after the wars of the early part of his reign, to increase the population both rural and urban of his kingdom. This suffered renewed losses at the time of Andriscus. For the later period we have no means of estimating the inroads on the population caused by the continuous wars on the northern frontier of Macedonia and the frequent incursions of her northern neighbours.[71]

Of the eastern Hellenistic monarchies we are best informed about the population of EGYPT. Our texts have preserved several figures which make it possible to form an approximate idea of the size and density of the population of Ptolemaic Egypt in the various periods of its history. These figures have been more than once discussed in the light of recent papyrological discoveries, the classical treatment being that of U. Wilcken.[72] The basic text is Diodorus i. 31. 6–8. In his reference to the unusually large population of Egypt in the past and in his own day he is repeating, as regards the former, the data of Hecataeus of Abdera, a contemporary of Ptolemy Soter; for his own time he probably relied upon information (from official and semi-official sources) which he received himself during his stay in Egypt in 60 B.C. Unfortunately the text of Diodorus' statement as it stands appears to be corrupt, but it has been convincingly emended.[73]

According to his statement, official sources (ἱεραὶ ἀναγραφαί) attested the existence of 18,000 towns and villages in pre-Ptolemaic times, while in the reign of Soter the number of towns and villages had risen to 30,000, which number remained unchanged until his own days (the numbers may be corrupt, but the relation between the smaller and the larger figure is probably correct). The difference in the number of villages in Ptolemaic and pre-Ptolemaic times may be attributed to the increase in the number of settlements in Egypt after Alexander, but it is more probable that in pre-Ptolemaic sources larger villages only were taken into account, while in the Ptolemaic official lists all the κῶμαι, both large and small, were recorded. It is, however, surprising that the number remained the same until 60 B.C. We know that a multitude of new settlements were created by the first Ptolemies, especially by Philadelphus, many of them large and populous. It may be suggested either that the number of villages increased between Soter and Philopator and then reverted to approximately the number under Soter (the figures of Diodorus are round figures), or that the new foundations of Philadelphus were really pre-existing villages rebuilt and enlarged (cf. the case of Alexandria and Racotis). In the same passage Diodorus adds that the total number of the λαός in Egypt was seven millions, both τὸ παλαιόν and in his own time. The expression τὸ παλαιόν as a definition of time is vague. In all probability he means by it the pre-Ptolemaic period. If so, the figure he gives relates to the population of the χώρα only, not including that of Alexandria, and was the same in the pre-Ptolemaic period and in his own day. We may suppose, therefore, that between these two dates the population may have been and probably was much larger. The accuracy of the figures of Diodorus is confirmed by the well-known statement of Fl. Josephus (*B.J.* ii. 16. 4, parag. 385), who estimates the total population of Egypt in the reign of Nero at seven and a half millions, not including Alexandria. He adduces in support of his statement data relating to the poll-tax which had probably been quoted to him in general terms by the authority on whom he relies. The number of inhabited centres and the total population of Ptolemaic Egypt in its most brilliant phase we have no means of estimating. The density of the population of Egypt has been calculated by A. Segré with some probability at 280 inhabitants per square kilometre.

In the figures mentioned above the population of Alexandria is probably not included. But some reliable data regarding it are on record. Diodorus (xvii. 52. 6), basing his statement on information received from those who 'kept the registers of the population', says that the total number of the free inhabitants of Alexandria was at this time more than 300,000 (it appears that a special register was kept for the slaves).[74] A little later, in the reign of Augustus, this number according to Strabo (see below on Antioch and Seleuceia) grew to about 500,000, and still later, about A.D. 37 it may, according to some modern scholars, have risen to more than a million.

The last figure is derived from an interesting document of Egyptian origin recently published, the so-called 'gerusia acts', a section of the well-known collection of the 'acts of martyrs' of Alexandria.[75] This document, in the course of a report on the audience granted to representatives of Alexandria by Caligula, mentions a body of 173 gerontes of Alexandria recently elected by a citizen body of 180,000.[76] Since such a body of adult males implies the existence of a total Greek population of Alexandria of about 500,000, while Alexandrian documents of the time of Augustus (published in *B.G.U.* iv)[77] make it probable that the non-Greek and slave inhabitants of the city at least equalled the Greeks in number, the total population of Alexandria in the time of Caligula must be estimated at one million at least.

So rapid a growth of the population of Alexandria while that of the *chora* remained unchanged is surprising. I cannot here enter into a detailed discussion of the degree of reliance to be placed on the data supplied by the 'gerusia acts'. But I must draw the attention of my readers to two considerations. The existence of a *numerus clausus* of 180,000 citizens of Alexandria is never mentioned in the evidence we possess concerning this city, not even in the other sections of the 'acts of martyrs'. It may therefore have been an invention of the author of the 'gerusia acts', intended to give an impressive idea of the large size of the body in whose name the deputation was speaking to the emperor. Moreover, the existence of so large a body of citizens could only be the result of the transformation by Caligula of the aristocratic constitution of Alexandria, as it existed in the times of the Ptolemies and of Augustus and Tiberius, into a full-fledged democracy, whereby the tumultuous Alexandrian proletariat had been granted the citizenship, and such a transformation especially at a time of unrest appears to me more than doubtful.

The evidence cited above with regard to the population of Alexandria raises afresh the question previously discussed (Ch. IV, p. 331 f.) of the size of the Greek population of Egypt. How did the number of immigrants, and in particular of Greeks, compare with the number of natives in Egypt? If Alexandria really had in 60 B.C. a population of 300,000 free inhabitants, then, if we take into consideration the information about the proportion of Greeks to foreigners in the time of Augustus supplied by the Alexandrian documents mentioned above, there must have been in 60 B.C. more than 150,000 'Greeks' resident in Alexandria. The number of Greeks in Alexandria in earlier times may have been larger or smaller. We may suppose that it was reduced by the persecutions of Euergetes II, but on the other hand among the 'Greeks' of the second and first centuries B.C. there were probably many hellenized natives. We may therefore take 150,000 as perhaps the average number of the Greeks in Alexandria in the Ptolemaic period in general. We must add to these the Greeks of Ptolemais and Naucratis (no figures are known to us) and the Greeks settled in the *chora*. As regards these last we know that the 'Greeks' of the Fayûm formed in the time of Nero and later a political body, a *numerus clausus* of 6,475.* But in what sense the 'Hellenes' of the Fayûm numbered 6,475 is controversial, and this number, moreover, relates to the Fayûm alone. No general estimate is therefore possible of the number of Greeks in Egypt in early and late Ptolemaic times.[78]

We have no evidence about the SELEUCID EMPIRE similar to that relating to Egypt. We do not know the total number or the average density of its population. The latter certainly varied very much from place to place, the most densely populated parts (after the loss of India, Bactria, and the best-cultivated and most populous parts of the eastern Iranian satrapies) being without doubt Babylonia and the kernel of Seleucid Syria, and later Phoenicia and Palestine. But even for these parts we have no data. The sole exceptions are Antioch on the Orontes and Seleuceia on the Tigris. Strabo (xvi. 2. 5, p. 750) says that the population of Antioch (probably in his own day, not in the time of Artemidorus of Ephesus) was a little smaller than that of Alexandria or Seleuceia on the Tigris. Now in the time of Pliny (*N.H.* vi. 122) Seleuceia was reported to have a population of 600,000 (an approximate estimate of which the ultimate source is unknown), and it is not improbable that Alexandria may have had a population of the same size in the reign of Augustus.[79] But these two figures do not help us to estimate the total of the population of the Seleucid Empire or even that of Babylonia and Seleucid Syria. No similar figures are at our disposal for the certainly prosperous and growing cities of Phoenicia and Palestine. Beloch's estimate of thirty millions, with a density of 9 to 12 inhabitants per square kilometre in the time of Antiochus I, is a pure guess.† Nor do we know anything positive about the number of Macedonians and Greeks settled in the Seleucid Empire, the calculations of A. Segré being highly speculative

* *O.G.I.* 668; *I.G.R.* i. 1124.

† On some data concerning Seleucid Syria see above, Ch. IV, p. 497, and n. 276.

(above, Ch. IV, p. 497, and n. 275). One point is certain. The early Seleucids certainly had in view a rapid increase of the Macedonian and Greek population settled in the many cities founded by them. This is proved by the ruins of Dura-Europus. The city was planned on a very large scale with ambitious fortifications, wide streets, a spacious *agora*, and a considerable citadel. It is more than probable that many other Seleucid colonies were laid out on the same scale. But the plan of the founder of Dura was never carried out. The fortifications, the *agora*, and the citadel remained unfinished. Some wards of the city lay unoccupied or half-occupied. The founder probably regarded the early colonists of Dura-Europus as no more than a nucleus of the future city. But this nucleus apparently never grew in size. Was the history of Dura typical of that of other Seleucid colonies, or was it an exception? Did other cities, especially those of Seleucid Syria, grow as rapidly as Antioch on the Orontes and Seleuceia on the Tigris? And if they did, was it by the addition of new groups of Greek colonists to the old stock or by a rapid infiltration into the cities of native elements, as appears to have happened at Dura in later times?[80]

It would be useless to try to recalculate after Beloch, in the light of a few new data, the population of the rest of the Hellenistic world in the period between Alexander and Augustus, especially that of ASIA MINOR. An approximate calculation is indeed possible for some cities, especially those which have been carefully excavated, such as Priene and Miletus. We may for example tentatively determine the size of the population of Miletus in the time of Eumenes II from the amount of his donation of corn to the city. From the numbers of the Galatians who fought against Manlius Vulso we may derive some information about the population of Galatia. But this does not help us to form an adequate idea of the population of the various Hellenistic kingdoms and cities of Asia Minor in the various periods of their existence.[81]

From the few known figures and from the general development of the Seleucid Empire and of those parts of Asia Minor which did not belong to it we derive the impression that, as in Egypt in the third and early second centuries B.C., there was no decrease of population in the Asiatic Hellenistic monarchies, but, on the contrary, a steady and rapid increase. This may be inferred with certainty from the facts collected above (Ch. IV) relating to the early Seleucid Empire; it is highly probable as regards the reigns of Antiochus III, Seleucus IV, and Antiochus IV, and appears to be true even for the period of the decay of the Seleucid monarchy in respect of those territories which still remained in the hands of the descendants of Seleucus. For Pergamon and the other monarchies of Asia Minor a steady increase of population may also be taken for granted. Some of the ancient Greek cities of Asia Minor, such as Miletus, may have shared the fate of the cities of continental Greece and have become gradually depopulated; we know how the Milesians tried to attract foreigners to their city in order probably to check this process (above, Ch. IV, p. 666), but the cumulative weight of the evidence shows that for the greater part of Asia Minor the tendency was in the opposite direction. I may quote for example the part taken by the Ionian cities of Asia Minor (for instance Magnesia on the Maeander) in colonizing certain parts of the Seleucid Empire.[82] They certainly had a surplus of population. And this continued to be the case, apart from temporary and local fluctuations, until the end of the Hellenistic period. I may cite after Beloch* the instances of Alexandria Troas, which was able to put a force of 4,000 men in the field against the Galatians in 216 B.C.† and of some cities of southern Asia Minor such as Aspendus and the town and tribe of Etenna, which were able to contribute to the army of Achaeus in 218 B.C. 4,000 and 8,000 hoplites respectively;‡ Cibyra, too, found no difficulty in mobilizing for its tyrants 30,000 foot and 2,000 horse.§ I may also remind the reader of the staunch resistance which the local militia of the Carian cities offered to Labienus and the Parthians (see Ch. VII).

Such being the evidence at our disposal, we must admit that it does not allow us to form even an approximate idea of the density of the population of the Hellenistic world, of its fluctuations, or of the relative size of the various elements in the

* *Bevölkerung*, pp. 236 ff.   † Polyb. v. 111. 4.
‡ Ibid. 73. 3.   § Strabo, xiii. 4. 17, p. 631.

population, such as the proportion of free citizens to metics and slaves in the cities, and of natives to immigrants in the eastern monarchies.

Accumulated Wealth. No less sparse and inadequate is our information about the accumulated wealth of the Hellenistic world, the proportions of its component parts, and its distribution among the various classes of the population.

It is evident that the inhabitants of continental GREECE, of the ISLANDS, and of the ancient GREEK COLONIES in Asia Minor, on the northern coast of the Aegean, and on the coasts of the Euxine, had by hard work and unrivalled inventiveness and ingenuity accumulated much wealth in pre-Hellenistic times. The comparatively poor natural resources of continental Greece and the islands, and the more abundant wealth of the colonized territories, had been thoroughly exploited by the numerous population. Agriculture had reached a high standard, cattle were being reared in large numbers, the mineral resources were well known and actively developed. Greek industry, moreover, was flourishing, and its products, owing to their technical and artistic qualities, enjoyed a world-wide reputation, while works of Greek art had attained an unparalleled renown. Commerce was fairly well developed and connected the various regions and cities of the Greek world among themselves and with their neighbours. A large part of the accumulated capital had been invested in public and religious buildings, so that the cities of Greece were the most beautiful and the best-planned in the civilized world. There was not a city in the Greek world but could boast of beautiful temples, theatres, gymnasia and palaestrae, halls and porticoes, most of them adorned with exquisite statues and paintings by local and foreign artists. Not less impressive were the cities of the dead, which were real museums of art. The great sanctuaries of the Hellenic world vied in splendour with the cities. I need only remind the reader, on the one hand, of Athens with the Piraeus, of Corinth, of such minor cities of the Peloponnese as Phigalia and Lycosura with their famous temples, of Miletus, Ephesus, Magnesia on the Maeander, and the small city of Priene in Asia Minor, of Rhodes, Lindus, Samos, Thasos, Cos, and the other cities of the islands, of

Olynthus in Chalcidice, of Olbia and Panticapaeum on the northern shore of the Euxine, not to speak of the glorious cities of South Italy and Sicily; and on the other, of the great sanctuaries of Olympia, Delphi, Epidaurus, Eleusis, Delos, and minor shrines such as the Ptôion of Boeotia.

The ruins of these and other cities and sanctuaries, some of which have been excavated, are a testimony, not only to the unfettered and unlimited creative genius of the Greeks, but also to the large amount of wealth accumulated by them in the Archaic and the so-called Classical periods of their existence. We cannot estimate in figures the capital invested in the profusion of buildings—at least no one has tried to do so, though the building accounts of some of the great edifices might be used as a starting-point for such an estimate—but it is certain that it reflects great prosperity.

Some of this wealth was destroyed during the Peloponnesian war and in the subsequent period of political anarchy, but the bulk of it was inherited by the Hellenistic world. In some cities it probably increased in the time of Alexander and the Successors. This may have been the case in the great commercial cities of the time, rivals of Athens, such as Rhodes, Miletus, and Ephesus on the one hand, and on the other Cyzicus, Byzantium, and the other centres of the Euxine trade. The well-known fact that the revenue of Rhodes from customs duties amounted in the early second century B.C. to one million drachmas illuminates the sources of its wealth. I may also recall that the losses of Athens, despite its political vicissitudes and the competition of the cities named above, were not so heavy as we should have expected. We know that under the rule of Demetrius of Phalerum the revenue of the city amounted to 1,200 talents.*[83] The amount of the accumulated capital of Greece as a whole may have remained constant, with local fluctuations.

The situation was no longer the same in the second half of the third century B.C. and later. Under the pressure of war and the changed economic conditions in general, Greece began to spend its capital and never ceased to do so until the end of the Hellenistic period. I have described this process above

* Duris of Samos, Fr. 10, *F. Gr. Hist.* 76.

and need only refer to what I have said on the subject in Chs. IV (concerning, for example, Mantinea and Megalopolis, pp. 194 ff.), V, VI, and VII, to indicate how large a portion of the accumulated wealth of Greece was destroyed during the times of war and anarchy in the late third, the second, and the first centuries B.C., and how much of it was exported to Italy by the Romans. The extent of this export cannot be illustrated by figures, even with the help of data concerning the booty carried off and the sums paid by Greece as war indemnities, but the fact is well known and must be taken for certain. In the last two centuries B.C. there was a heavy drain on the accumulated wealth of Greece, her regular income being insufficient to cover the cost of wars.

But care must be taken to avoid too general a statement. In some parts of Greece at certain periods wealth did not cease to accumulate, or its accumulation was resumed. The former was the case in the great commercial cities, especially Rhodes and Delos, the islands connected with them, and the cities of the Straits and the Propontis; the latter, at Athens during the second and the early first century B.C. (see above, Chs. V and VI).

Of the distribution of wealth in Hellenistic Greece we know very little. We cannot estimate how much of it was in the possession of corporative bodies—the cities, the temples, and the associations. As regards private persons, I have shown in the preceding chapters and in the first part of this chapter that the bulk of the accumulated wealth was concentrated in the hands of the urban *bourgeoisie*. When discussing evidence supplied mostly by the New Comedy I have suggested that among the members of this class in the early Hellenistic period very few, if any, were exceedingly rich. Their income was modest and their daily life simple. A few *parvenus* who had enriched themselves during Alexander's conquest of the East were exceptions. Certain foreign merchants, such as Zenon the Cypriote, the founder of the Stoic school, imported large fortunes from their homes (gossip estimated the fortune of Zenon at more than 1,000 talents, which were invested in bottomry loans).* But Zenon was certainly an exception. The coin hoards of this time found in Greece (described above,

* Diog. L. vii. 13.

Ch. III, n. 38) are much poorer than those of the East and of Macedonia.

Some modern scholars, speaking of the great wealth accumulated in the hands of private persons, quote the instances of the Athenians Euthycrates (60 talents), Diphilus (160 talents), and Epicrates (300 talents). But these men belong to the middle of the fourth century B.C. and became rich in peculiar circumstances by exploiting the silver mines. They are products of different times and of a different economic situation. Another instance quoted is Crates, who is supposed to have had 200 talents before his conversion. But it is evident that this figure is not trustworthy; for our authorities wished to emphasize the greatness of the sacrifice made by Crates. Much more instructive is the evidence of the dramatists of the New Comedy, and especially Menander, regarding the dowries which well-to-do *bourgeois* of Athens were in the habit of giving their daughters,* and the well-known wills of the heads of the Peripatos preserved by Diogenes Laertius. These men, Aristotle,† Theophrastus,‡ Straton,§ Lycon‖ were all of them well-to-do. Their wills unfortunately give no figures regarding the total value of their fortunes. But the fact that Aristotle, a favourite of Philip II and Alexander, bequeathed to his concubine no more than one talent (in addition to his previous gifts), shows that his fortune cannot be estimated at many hundreds of talents. The same impression is conveyed by the number of slaves owned by the heads of the Lyceum. We must therefore accept as certainly correct the general statement of Plutarch quoted above (Ch. IV, p. 205), which asserts that the wealth even of the rich kings of Sparta, of Agis and Cleomenes, was no more than a trifle if compared with that of the slaves of Oriental satraps and the stewards of Ptolemy and Seleucus.[84]

For the later period an illustration of the standard of wealth prevailing among the *bourgeoisie* of continental Greece may be seen in the well-known statement of Polybius, who was thoroughly familiar with the Greece of his own time, that the richest man in Greece about 200 B.C. was Alexander Isius,

---

* Above, Ch. III, p. 163 f., and n. 37.   † Diog. L. v. 12 ff.
‡ Ibid. 51 ff.   § Ibid. 61 ff.   ‖ Ibid. 69 ff.

 one of the political leaders of Aetolia. His fortune, which may have been acquired at least in part by robbery, was estimated at more than 200 talents.* But we must compare this with the fortunes of the wealthy *bourgeois* of Asia Minor of a slightly later period—for example Chaeremon and his son Pythodorus of Nysa (who was possessed of a fortune of 2,000 talents), Hieron of Laodicea (2,000 talents), and several others who are mentioned as very rich men,† in order to realize how low was the standard of *bourgeois* wealth in continental Greece by the side of that of Asia Minor and certainly of that of the rich merchants in the great commercial cities of the Aegean, the Propontis, and the Euxine.

Another illustration of the magnitude of the accumulated wealth of cities and individuals may be drawn from the inscriptions of Messene of the late second or the early first century B.C., discussed above (Ch. VI, pp. 750 ff.). The total wealth of Messene subject to an extraordinary levy (ὀκτώβολος εἰσφορά) was 1,256 talents. As with all the statistics in our texts, the interpretation of this figure is difficult and controversial. Does it represent landed property alone or does it also include houses and movable property? Does it represent the value of the accumulated wealth of the city of Messene and its territory only or of the whole of Messenia? Was all the wealth taxed or only part of it, the *timema* being the portion subject to the tax? I have indicated my opinion tentatively above (loc. cit.), but the interpretation of the inscription remains open to dispute. In any case the sum, if compared with other similar estimates, though it conveys the idea of a certain recovery in Messene, testifies to the very low general standard of wealth then prevailing in Greece. The same is true of the average wealth of individuals at that time as it may be inferred from the inscriptions of Messene. One talent appears to have been the minimum property required to qualify a citizen for certain offices. The sum is rather low and to my mind attests a low standard of wealth among the *bourgeois* of Messene, probably lower than that which prevailed at Athens in the time of Menander. Our evidence is meagre and

---

* Polyb. xxi. 26. 14.
† Above, Ch. VI, p. 820 f. and n. 98; cf. p. 805 f. and n. 75.

ambiguous, but it seems fairly clear that the standard of wealth in continental Greece was not rising or even stable in the late third and the second centuries B.C.[85]

While the prosperity of the middle class in Greece was declining, a few members of that class acquired large fortunes much larger than before. This phenomenon cannot be regarded as a sign of increasing prosperity. In some cases and in some periods it may be so, but here its significance is precisely the contrary. In times of war and devastation some shrewd and unscrupulous individuals profited by the disturbed conditions and amassed much property at the expense of the rest of the population. This certainly happened in the second century B.C. in continental Greece. It is characteristic of the period that many of these rich men were not Greeks but Italian immigrants, who settled all over Greece in increasing numbers in the second and first centuries.* We cannot estimate their fortunes in figures, but some of them were certainly very rich and towered high in wealth and influence over the mass of the native population. We cannot say, however, that they had a monopoly of large fortunes, for there were many Greeks who were as rich as the Italians (Ch. VI, p. 766 f.). It is interesting to notice that they appear mostly on the periphery of continental Greece and in the cities of the Euxine, which were much affected by wars and inroads of barbarian neighbours. As regards the region forming the kernel of Greece I may again remind the reader of the inscriptions of Messene, in which some wealthy men (among them Italians) figure among the payers of extraordinary taxes. I may cite also the picture of Athenian society at the very end of the second century B.C. drawn by W. S. Ferguson.† Here the political power was at that time concentrated in the hands of a few rich men, who held it solely in virtue of their wealth.

We have no means of estimating what proportion of the wealth of the *bourgeois* class was in the hands of full citizens and metics respectively. It must be remembered that the Greek cities were no longer so strict as they had been in reserving the right to acquire land to citizens alone, and I may mention the well-known part that metics played in the business

* See above Ch. VI, pp. 762 ff, and n. 29.   † *Hell. Ath.*, p. 435.

life of Athens in the fourth century B.C. and probably continued to play in Hellenistic times. In this connexion a very interesting example is afforded by the city of Rhodes. Here the citizen body was very small. At the time of the siege by Demetrius the adult citizens able to defend the city numbered no more than 6,000, which indicates a citizen body (including women and children) of 24,000.* The bulk of the population consisted, as I have pointed out (Ch. V, p. 688 f.), of foreign residents of various types and of slaves. We may conjecture that the citizens were chiefly landowners, and that business was to a large extent in the hands of metics, freedmen, and slaves. But Rhodes was probably an exception.

The proportion of the wealth of Greece owned by members of the lower classes was very small. Throughout the Hellenistic age their material situation remained the same, with some fluctuations. The large majority of the working class lived in indigence, with no savings and very little property of their own. They lived on what they earned by their manual labour as peasant landowners mostly overburdened with debts, as tenants of parcels of land owned by the cities, the temples, various corporations, and private persons, or as hired hands in agriculture and industry. The only difference between them and the slaves was their personal freedom and their more precarious situation as regards work and food. Slaves were at least sure of receiving their regular food and the minimum of clothing from their masters.

Much larger was the capital accumulated in MACEDONIA and in the EASTERN MONARCHIES. The Greeks always looked on the wealth of these countries with admiration and envy. They regarded the eastern kings as the great holders and distributors of riches. It is not surprising that they repeatedly begged for subsidies and gifts, often successfully. The accumulated capital of the Greek cities as expressed in their buildings and adornments was increased in the Hellenistic period chiefly by gorgeous and imposing temples, porticoes, markets, &c., bestowed upon them by the Hellenistic monarchs. A catalogue of these and of other royal gifts to the Greek cities, which cannot be compiled here, would certainly be very

* Diod. xx. 84. 2.

impressive. I have referred to them several times in the preceding chapters.

We can form no estimate in figures of the accumulated wealth of Macedonia and the eastern monarchies. But an approximate idea of the possessions of some of the kings may be derived from casual evidence relating to the amount of their yearly revenues. We have, in the first place, some reliable figures concerning the revenues of the PTOLEMIES. Hieronymus (*in Dan.* xi. 5, p. 560, Migne) reports that the yearly income of Philadelphus from Egypt alone (not including the foreign dominions) amounted to 14,800 talents of silver and 1,500,000 *artabae* of corn. These figures have been variously interpreted by modern scholars. Some of them regard the figure of the income in silver as grossly exaggerated. I see no reason to question the accuracy of the figure, which Hieronymus certainly did not invent, but derived from some source. His sources are mostly reliable and the case under consideration is no exception. The *basilikon* of Philadelphus kept careful accounts of the royal revenue, and Philadelphus had no reason to keep these accounts secret. The historians of the period were deeply interested in this aspect of his rule, and would use the information regarding it which they gathered in Alexandria. In itself, if we take into consideration all that we know of the financial and economic system of the Ptolemies, the sum is not very large. The income in money derived by the Ptolemies from their property in Egypt (the gold-mines, the fisheries, the monopolized branches of industry, and so forth) and from taxes paid in money, including the customs-duties, must have been enormous. Of the money which was put into circulation by the Ptolemaic mints a large part certainly returned to the royal treasury.

Nor is there a manifest incompatibility between the figure given by Hieronymus and what Herodotus says about the tribute which Egypt, Libya, and Cyrenaica paid to Darius— 700 talents (Babylonian) of silver and 120,000 *artabae* of corn, the latter for the maintenance of the army of occupation.* His statement is not quite clear and has been variously interpreted. But it is evident, on the one hand, that the tribute in

* Herod. iii. 91.

silver represented only part of the personal income that the Persian kings derived from Egypt; for Herodotus also says that, in addition, the fisheries of Lake Moeris yielded them a substantial income in silver, and this may have been only part of the revenues drawn from the private property of the kings in Egypt, for example from quarries and mines. On the other hand, the 120,000 *artabae* of corn mentioned by Herodotus certainly did not represent the whole cost of the maintenance of the army of occupation. The rest was apparently supplied by the satrap, and so was the cost of administration. The means to cover this expense, which Philadelphus defrayed from his general income, the satrap certainly derived from taxation, of which only part was used for the payment of the royal tribute.

The figure of the yearly revenue in corn presents greater difficulty. Modern calculations of the total production of corn in Egypt and of the part thereof paid by the producers to the king, based on the study of various documents, show, in spite of the problems involved, that the revenue of the king in corn was certainly larger than the amount mentioned by Hieronymus. But it is evident that only part of the gross revenue formed the net income of the king. Large quantities of grain were expended on the spot or kept in the royal granaries for emergency. *P. Teb.* 703. 70 ff., in the passage dealing with the transport of corn to Alexandria contains this explicit injunction: 'Take care that the corn in the nomes, with the exception of that expended on the spot for seed and of that which cannot be transported by water (ἀπλώτου, the reading is uncertain), be brought down'. Of the corn shipped to Alexandria much was applied to the needs of the king's household, including the Museum, of the garrison of Alexandria, and of some of the garrisons abroad. It is therefore possible that when Hieronymus spoke of one and a half million *artabae*, he referred to corn not expended by the king in the *chora* and in Alexandria, that is to say, the net income of the king in corn which he could sell abroad or lay up in his Alexandrian storehouses. But even so the figure appears to be rather small, at least certainly not exaggerated.

The figures of Hieronymus, especially that of the income in

silver, would be invaluable for calculating the income in money of the whole of the population of Egypt if we knew what proportion of this income it represented. The fiscal pressure of the Ptolemaic system of taxation was high, and the methods of extracting money from the population were numerous, but our information is insufficient to permit of any general estimate. As regards corn, A. Segré has calculated with some probability that the income of the king formed about one-third of the total production.

The sums mentioned by Hieronymus probably did not include the revenue of the first Ptolemies from their foreign trade (in corn and certain products of Egypt partly or wholly monopolized by the kings, such as papyrus, *aromata*, linen stuffs), which was certainly important, and that from their foreign dominions in Palestine, Phoenicia, Ptolemaic Syria, Asia Minor, and Thrace. Some figures of the revenue from the provinces preserved in official documents (see Ch. IV, p. 335 f.) show that it was large and regular. The sum of 8,000 talents a year recorded by Flavius Josephus (*A.J.* xii, paragr. 175) as derived from the Syrian dominions in general may after all be not so far from the truth.

How much of it was put aside by the first Ptolemies and constituted their reserve, their treasure, is difficult to say. The expenditure entailed by their foreign policy and their wars was heavy and was very seldom compensated by the booty they obtained. It appears surprising, therefore, to find in Appian (*Prooem.* 10) the figure of 740,000 talents of silver as representing the amount of money accumulated by Philadelphus. But I must agree with Wilcken that we are unable to reject or to accept this figure or to substitute another for it, in view of the inadequacy of our information. One point, however, is certain: Appian (or his source) certainly wished to impress on his readers how enormous was the wealth accumulated by Philadelphus and may have exaggerated the figure. But we must not forget that Cleomenes of Naucratis during his brief rule over Egypt, built up a reserve fund of 8,000 talents.*

For the later period, when a process of decay and impover-

* Diod. xviii. 14. 1.

shment had set in, we have two figures, both of which refer to the reign of Auletes. Cicero in one of his lost orations (probably *de rege Alexandrino*) mentions 12,500 talents as being the yearly income of the king,* while Diodorus (xvii. 52. 6) speaks of 6,000 talents, probably as the same total income. This discrepancy cannot be discussed here. Many interpretations of the two figures have been suggested by modern scholars. Perhaps the most satisfactory explanation is that which regards the sum mentioned by Cicero as derived from official data where the income was given in the debased Ptolemaic currency of the time, while Diodorus may have calculated the same income according to its real value.[86]

The distribution of wealth in Egypt in Ptolemaic times cannot be illustrated by figures. I may remind the reader of what I have said on this subject in the sections of Chs. IV, V, and VI which deal with Egypt. There were many exceedingly rich persons in Egypt in the last three centuries B.C. But it is evident that all those of whom we have knowledge were sharing the wealth of the king, to use the expression of Chrysippus (see above, p. 1131). They were rich by the king's favour. We have types of these men in Apollonius, the *dioecetes*, and the other holders of various kinds of *doreai*. Their fortunes were part of the fortune of the king conferred on them as a revocable gift. But, no doubt, in the course of exploiting the gifts that the kings entrusted to them, they may have put aside large sums and acquired possession of houses, land, cattle, and so on, which were their private property. The same is true of those who were their assistants of various grades. A typical figure is that of Zenon, the steward of Apollonius on his Philadelphian estate. At the end of his life his correspondence shows him no longer in the service of Apollonius, but a rich man engaged in various economic pursuits. The same was certainly true of the functionaries who in various grades and capacities helped the king or other magnates in the administration of their great οἶκοι. We must suppose that some of the holders of military *cleroi* were in the same case, such for example as Horus of the Pathyrites nome of the late second century B.C., whose business

* Strabo, xvii. i. 13, p. 798.

career has been revealed to us by the recently published Adler papyri.[87] We may also include in the same category many priests of the flourishing Egyptian temples.

Thus was gradually formed the peculiar *bourgeoisie* of Egypt, whose prosperity endured until the end of the Ptolemaic régime. Of its history very little is known. Under the pressure of the government many of its members were ruined and became proletarians. But the class as a whole appears as strong in late Ptolemaic times as it had been under Philadelphus and Euergetes. We have many proofs of this, for example the growth in the later period of the γεοῦχοι, and the development of a gay club life, chiefly, it appears, among the more or less prosperous members of the *bourgeoisie*, both Greek and native.[88]

It is a pity that we know so little of the economic life of the residents of Alexandria. In Roman times the *bourgeoisie* of Alexandria was wealthy, proud, quarrelsome, and influential. It was probably so in the Ptolemaic period. Unfortunately we know nothing of the sources of its wealth. Commerce may have contributed to it in an important degree.[89]

The situation of the labouring classes was different. Our information on this subject is defective, but it is certain that most of the royal tenants had very little property: a house or part of a house in a village, a few agricultural implements, some cattle.* The same is true of the artisans. The greater part of what they earned by their labour was absorbed by the State and the powerful bureaucracy. What remained was probably just sufficient to support the family and feed its live stock. Such is the impression produced by the documentary evidence. The situation of the *laoi* may have varied from time to time, but such fluctuations were insignificant. A very small part of the accumulated wealth of Egypt was in their hands, and their main capital was their capacity for labour.[90] Finally, I may remind the reader of what I have said above (Ch. IV, p. 321 f.) about the part played by the slaves in the economic life of Egypt. It was certainly insignificant in the *chora* but it may have been much more important in Alexandria.

We have much less information about the revenue of the

---

* *Teb.* 5, 231 ff.; Hunt–Edgar, *Sel. Pap.* 210.

SELEUCIDS.[91] Justin (xiii. 1. 9) says that the general revenue of Alexander amounted to 30,000 talents. This sum is generally regarded as exaggerated, but in my opinion without good grounds. Though it is much larger than the income that the Persian kings derived from the tribute of the satrapies, it must be remembered that in Persian times the satrapies had to bear in addition the cost of the army of occupation and of the administration.[92] It may have been otherwise under Alexander. In the time of Antigonus (315 B.C.), who held almost the whole of the Asiatic part of Alexander's empire, the total revenue from his kingdom according to Diodorus (xix. 56. 5, based on Hieronymus of Cardia) was 11,000 talents. This appears to be more than accrued from it in Persian times, but less than under Alexander. We may conjecture that in the days of Antigonus his satrapies defrayed their own expenditure and that the contributions of the individual satrapies were increased.

For the subsequent period we have no data. But general considerations set forth in the previous chapters suggest that the revenue of the Seleucids—after making due allowance for that previously derived from the lost satrapies—rather increased than decreased until the death of Antiochus IV, with some fluctuations due mostly to wars, especially in the calamitous years that followed the death of Antiochus II. A decline set in under the successors of Antiochus IV. But the prosperity of the kernel of the Seleucid monarchy and the income from the caravan trade guaranteed a steady revenue to the late Seleucids. In the times of complete disintegration and anarchy this revenue certainly diminished catastrophically. It is no wonder, therefore, that after their annexation by Pompey the three new Asiatic provinces of Pontus, Bithynia, and Syria yielded to Rome no more than approximately 6,000 talents of silver.

We know no more of the distribution of property in the Seleucid kingdom than of its total revenue. There is no doubt that, as in Egypt, several persons—his generals and high officials—shared in the wealth of the king. I have mentioned the frequent references in our scanty texts to large _doreai_ granted by the kings in Asia Minor, Syria, and Babylonia.

We do not know how wealthy the holders of the *doreai* were. Mnesimachus' Sardian estate was valued at 1,325 gold staters. But we do not know whether this estate was his only source of revenue.[93] A certain idea of the size of fortunes accumulated by some of the magnates may be derived from such casual mentions in our literary sources as the statement of Polybius (v. 50. 2) about Hermeias, the prime minister of Antiochus III, who (about 200 B.C.) was able to advance the pay of the royal army from his own funds, or about Dionysius, one of the assistants of Antiochus IV, who owned silver plate, which was displayed in the *pompe* of Antiochus IV, to the value of one million drachmas.* Some other examples have been mentioned in the preceding chapters.

These opulent officials were rivalled in wealth by groups of rich citizens of the ancient Phoenician, Palestinian, Syrian, Mesopotamian, Babylonian, and Elamitic cities of the kingdom, their secular and priestly aristocracy. I have cited above instances of rich Phoenicians, and I may remind the reader of the wealthy aristocracy of hellenized Jews, headed by the high priest, as it appears in the books of the Maccabees, and of the rich native families of Uruk in Babylonia. The sources of their wealth are not known, but it is fair to suggest that many of them were enriched by commerce, while some were owners of large estates.

Next came the middle class, the *bourgeoisie*, composed partly of the immigrants settled in the new cities of the Seleucids, such as the citizens of Dura-Europus and others who took up their residence in the ancient Oriental towns, partly of well-to-do native inhabitants of these towns, who gradually coalesced with the former. As I have said, we can form no estimate of the numbers of this class, which formed the backbone of the Seleucid Empire. But it is certain that they owned the greater part of the accumulated capital of the Seleucid kingdom.

Finally, we come to the working classes. Their history, as I have remarked, was not exactly the same in the Seleucid and the Ptolemaic Empires. There was certainly a tendency under the Seleucids gradually to transform larger and smaller groups

* Polyb. xxx. 25. 16.

of *laoi* resident in villages and hamlets, bondsmen bound to their villages, into more or less free peasants, owners of their land, houses, cattle, and agricultural implements. Our information about this process is defective, as it is also about the legal and economic situation of the former bondsmen. But the gradual formation of a class of free peasants in the Seleucid Empire appears very probable. We know much less of the situation of the 'sacred slaves' in the large and powerful Oriental temples, some of them tillers of the soil and others temple servants and temple artisans. And practically nothing can be gathered from the scanty evidence regarding the lower strata of the population of the Oriental cities and of the new Greek cities in the Seleucid dominions. Nor are we able to say how large was the capital invested in slaves in the various parts thereof.

A few words will suffice to give an approximate idea of the capital accumulated in the monarchies of Asia Minor. The best known is PERGAMON. Here again the greater part of the wealth was concentrated in the hands of the kings. We have no figures, except for the treasure of 9,000 talents deposited by Lysimachus in Pergamon and appropriated by Philetaerus; but the cumulative evidence makes it certain that a large amount of capital was gradually amassed by the Attalids and that this steadily increased. The Attalids were owners of large tracts of land, of forests and mines, of lakes and fisheries, of industrial undertakings carried on by numerous slaves of both sexes; they exported a good deal of the produce of their property and they derived a large income from the tribute and taxes paid by their direct subjects and by the inhabitants of the Greek cities of their kingdom.

The distribution of wealth among the various elements of the population was similar to that which we observed in the kingdoms of the Ptolemies and the Seleucids. We find in Pergamon a group of rich men who assisted the king in the management of his kingdom. Some of them appear to have been rich citizens of the Greek cities, who increased their wealth by royal grants. A new feature, characteristic of the Pergamene kingdom and less so of the dominions of the Ptolemies and Seleucids, was the rapid accumulation of great wealth in the hands of the urban *bourgeoisie*, especially in the richer districts of that kingdom. The evidence, which I have collected above (Ch. VI, pp. 805 f., 820 f.), refers mostly to the period after the transformation of the Pergamene kingdom into the Roman province of Asia. But it is evident that the large fortunes owned at that time by the inhabitants of the cities were not acquired in the Roman period. They went back to the days of the independence of Pergamon and the other Hellenistic kingdoms of Asia Minor. Fortunes of 2,000 talents were regarded as very large but not exceptional. There is no doubt, therefore, that much wealth was accumulated, or was added to pre-existing capital, especially in the second and even in the first century B.C., for during the third century the greater part of Asia Minor had suffered severely. This accumulation of wealth in the hands of the urban *bourgeoisie* explains, as I have previously pointed out, their ability to satisfy the greed of their Roman masters in the first century B.C.

There is no doubt that, alongside of the plutocracy of the Pergamene kingdom and of the cities of Asia Minor which were not subject to the Pergamene kings, there was a large and well-to-do middle class, both in the ancient Greek cities of Anatolia and in those first founded there by the Seleucids and Attalids. It was this class which, with the help of the kings and of some persons of great wealth, laid the foundations of the splendour of most of the Anatolian cities as revealed by their extant ruins, a splendour inherited and increased by the Roman Empire. I may name once more such cities as Miletus, Ephesus, Smyrna, Magnesia on the Maeander, Priene, Teos, and several in Caria, which in the second century B.C. developed a feverish building activity and enhanced their beauty by the construction of fine and costly edifices.

The working classes had in all probability a very modest share in the wealth of the Pergamene kingdom. The situation of the tillers of the soil is not illuminated by any documents, but one thing may be noted: that while in the Ptolemaic and Seleucid monarchies slave labour was very little used in agriculture, agricultural slaves are frequently mentioned in Asia Minor. The traditions and habits of the motherland were apparently strong in the cities of that region, and the Pergamene kings adopted them from the Greek cities. Slaves also played an important part in the industrial enterprises owned by the kings, and similar conditions probably prevailed in some Greek cities of Asia Minor. I have cited examples of this in the previous chapters of this book.

It is highly probable that the above sketch of the Pergamene kingdom would apply equally to the other Hellenistic monarchies of Asia Minor—Bithynia, Pontus, Cappadocia, Armenia—to the kingdom of Bosporus and to the free commercial cities of the Straits, the Sea of Marmora, and the southern, western, and northern coasts of the Euxine. The wealth of the Pontic kingdom of the Mithridatids, as revealed by the activity of several of its kings and especially of Mithridates the Great, was largely concentrated in the hands of the king, his assistants, and the prosperous *bourgeoisie* of the cities. It is incorrect to affirm that most of it was the result of the pillage of Asia Minor. Unless we assume the existence of a strong economic foundation constituted by the accumulated wealth of the Pontic kingdom itself, the career of Mithridates cannot be explained.

2. New Sources of Wealth

There is, I think, no occasion for a detailed survey of the sources of wealth of the Hellenistic world as an introduction to this section. I have mentioned the most important of them in my previous chapters when dealing with the various Hellenistic territories. For more detailed lists and tabulations I may refer to surveys compiled by modern scholars for the regions in question in pre-Hellenistic and post-Hellenistic, that is to say Roman, times. I have enumerated the first in Chapter II; the second will be found in a handy form for Egypt, Syria, and Asia Minor in the corresponding sections of T. Frank's *Economic Survey*. It is to be regretted that no such lists have been compiled for Greece and Macedonia in the appropriate section of Frank's *Survey*, while Thrace, the Danube lands, and the western and northern coasts of the Euxine have not been included in it at all.[94]

A corresponding list for the Hellenistic period would in the main be a repetition of the above-mentioned tabulations, since naturally most of the sources of wealth remained the same in the Hellenistic period as they had previously been and as they are known to have remained in the subsequent period. I have therefore thought it more useful and more illuminating to indicate in brief outline the new sources of wealth which were first developed in the Hellenistic period and bequeathed by it to Roman times. No complete list of such accessions can be given here. The evidence on the subject is scanty and ambiguous, and has certainly not been collected in full by myself. But the general lines of evolution are discernible.

Reclaimed land. I have frequently mentioned, and shall have occasion to return to the point, that the most important source of wealth of the ancient world in all periods of its history was agriculture, with its subsidiary branches and cattle-breeding. The Hellenistic period was no exception. GREECE and the islands, the kernel of the Hellenistic world, were at this time cultivated with great skill, energy, and perseverance. Very little could be added to the cultivated territory of Greece by efforts of individuals. But there were in many parts of the country stretches of potentially fertile land covered with shallow lakes or forming swamps and marshes. Attempts to drain these areas were made from time to time, perhaps from the earliest days of Greek history. It is characteristic of the state of prosperity of the Hellenistic world and especially of Greece, and of the buoyant spirit of the population during and immediately after the reign of Alexander, that we hear repeatedly of attempts made at this time to drain lakes and swamps and thus to increase the cultivated area of Greece. The most famous case is that of Lake Copais in Boeotia. We learn from Strabo* and from Diogenes Laertius† that Crates, one of the μεταλλευταί or ταφρωρύχοι (that is to say, sappers, miners, and hydraulic engineers) of Alexander, carried out at the bidding of the king extensive though unfinished works for the drainage of this lake. Some modern scholars believe that the important remains of constructions of this character to be seen in this region must be ascribed in

* ix. 2. 18, p. 407.   † iv. 23.

part or in whole to the activity of Crates.⁹⁵ Similar work, probably at about the same time, was done according to Theophrastus* in the region round Larissa in Thessaly. And finally a long inscription found at Eretria in Euboea†—a contract (συνθῆκαι) between this city and a group of private capitalists headed by Chaerephanes—speaks in detail of the projected drainage of a lake. The fertile land to be recovered by the hydraulic works of Chaerephanes and his associates was in case of success to be leased to him for ten years for a payment of 60 talents. The inscription is assigned with great probability to the time between 322 and 309 B.C. It is tempting to suggest further that Chaerephanes may have learned his craft and acquired his means in the service of Alexander. We have, however, no evidence of any works of the same kind during the later period, which may not be an accident.

The same class of work was carried out in MACEDONIA and THRACE by Philip and Alexander, and probably by their successors also. The planting of Macedonian colonies in Thrace naturally involved not only the introduction of new agricultural methods but also the improved cultivation of land which had hitherto been only primitively tilled and the reclamation of waste land. I may remind the reader of the inscription at Philippi (Ch. V, n. 38), which refers to efforts made by Alexander to increase the cultivated area in the territory of the city and to improve its irrigation.

We have evidence of similar operations, on a larger scale and more systematically conducted, in the eastern Hellenistic monarchies. I have previously mentioned (Ch. IV, pp. 360 ff.) the important achievements in this respect by the first Ptolemies in EGYPT. The improvement and extension of irrigation works, the reclamation of dry land by means of irrigation, and the drainage of marshy land in the Fayûm and probably in the Delta, especially in the nomes around Alexandria, are well known and need not detain us here. The same work was started in BABYLONIA by Alexander,⁹⁶ and it is certain that his successors Seleucus and the Seleucids did much in the same direction. I have quoted‡ the inscriptions at Susa which

* *C. P.* v. 14, 2.   † *I.G.* xii. 9. 191; *Inscr. jur. gr.* ix.
‡ Ch. IV, p. 489 f., and n. 270; Ch. VI, p. 858, and n. 140.

speak of the restoration of the system of canals around that city in Parthian times, a system which certainly was in operation in Hellenistic times, though probably of earlier origin. The same activity was in all probability displayed by the Seleucids in the neighbourhood of their new colonies in Syria, Mesopotamia, and elsewhere, whether in the form of the restoration of ancient irrigation works, or of the addition of new canals and reservoirs. It is highly probable that the agricultural territory of Dura-Europus, including the lower Khabur region, was as well irrigated in Hellenistic times as before, if not better.

Plants and Animals. We may regard as additions to the natural resources of a country the introduction and cultivation of new plants or new kinds of plants already in cultivation and the acclimatization and breeding of new races of domestic animals, often produced by cross-breeding.[97] This was no novelty in the Greek world. From early times interchanges in this respect between the various centres of Greek life, and the introduction of new plants and animals from foreign countries, especially from the East, were a common feature of Greek economic life. Sometimes the infiltration was sporadic and casual, but in some cases experiments in this field were carried out on a large scale. We know of the activity in this respect shown by the Greek tyrants, the best-known example being Polycrates, the tyrant of Samos, who made so strong an impression on his contemporaries and remains an important figure in the literature of the fourth and third centuries. We are told by well-informed authorities that he imported dogs from Epirus and Lacedaemon, goats from Scyros and Naxos, sheep from Miletus and Attica, pigs from Sicily,* an instance of interchange between the various Greek cities. We learn also that Dionysius the Elder planted a plane-tree in Rhegium,† and that the Bosporans (probably the Spartocids) anticipated Harpalus and the first Ptolemies in trying (vainly) to acclimatize at Panticapaeum the laurel and the myrtle, attempts subsequently repeated by Mithridates.‡

* Ath. xii. 540 c–d, quoting Clytus the 'Aristotelian' and the Σάμιοι Ὧροι of Alexis.   † Theophr. *H.P.* iv. 5. 6; Plin. *N.H.* xii. 7.
‡ Theophr. *H.P.* iv. 5. 3; Plin. *N.H.* xvi. 137.

We have in the well-known letter of Darius to his satrap Gadates evidence of the transfer of Oriental plants to Asia Minor and Syria as part of the economic policy of the Persian kings:* 'I praise your intentions', says the king, 'in that you are improving my land by transplanting fruit-bearing plants from beyond the Euphrates into the lower parts of Asia, and great gratitude for it is in store for you in the royal house (ll. 8 ff.).' It is to be regretted that we do not know what plants Gadates was acclimatizing: whether it was new types of corn and vegetables, or various fruit trees, the glory of Iranian lands. These experiments were certainly carried out by Gadates not as a private hobby but in order to please the king; and they were not exceptional. We know that the Persians made an attempt to plant Chalybonian vines, of which the produce was so highly esteemed at the Persian court, in the territory of Damascus,† and that it was Darius who first introduced lucern into Greece,‡ probably in order to provide the horses of his cavalry with their accustomed fodder. We may suppose that the pistachio tree was first planted in Syria near Aleppo by the Persians, and that the famous Pontic walnut trees were first cultivated in Greece at the same time.[98]

The Hellenistic kings inherited the policy of the Greek tyrants and the Achaemenids, as we know in regard to almost all of them. I may quote some examples without aiming at completeness. In Aristotle's *History of Animals* there are two references, in passages inserted later by editors of the treatise, to measures of this kind taken by the famous Pyrrhus, king of Epirus. He was reputed to have produced special breeds of cows (Πυρρικαὶ βόες) and sheep (Πυρρικὰ πρόβατα) of exceedingly large size, which aroused the admiration of his contemporaries. Attempts were made to acclimatize these new breeds in other countries, but without success. I may mention in passing that the cattle-breeding estates of the Aeacids in Epirus were organized on model lines. We are told that

---

* Copy on stone of the first–second century A.D. found at Magnesia on the Maeander, of a document of the early fifth century, *S.I.G.*³ 22.

† Posidonius *ap.* Athen. i. 28 d; Fr. 68, *F. Gr. Hist.* 87.

‡ Plin. *N.H.* xviii. 144.

Neoptolemus, the predecessor of Pyrrhus, employed a special manager of the royal herds of oxen and sheep.[99]

I have set forth above evidence of the interest taken by the PERGAMENE KINGS in such matters; but the best-known experiments in this field are those of the PTOLEMIES (see above, Ch. IV, pp. 352 ff.). They keenly desired to improve the quality of corn produced in their kingdom by acclimatizing new types of wheat (Syrian and various kinds of Greek wheat). They intensified the planting of vines and olive-trees and introduced new and better sorts. They endeavoured to cultivate on Egyptian soil new kinds of oleaginous plants (probably sesame), vegetables, and fruit-trees. They introduced new or little-used domestic animals (for instance camels), new breeds of sheep (Milesian and Arabian) and of dogs and poultry. In doing so they had recourse especially to the experience ($\dot{\epsilon}\mu\pi\epsilon\iota\rho\dot{\iota}a$) of the new settlers in their kingdom, both Orientals and Greeks. I may refer in this connexion to Apollonius and Zenon and their agricultural staff. But they certainly did not neglect the treatises on botany, agriculture, viticulture, gardening, bee-keeping, &c., of which I shall have more to say in the following section. Their aim was not only to increase the prosperity of their kingdom and their own revenue by placing better wheat and larger quantities of it on the Greek market, but also to supply the new population of Egypt with products to which they were accustomed and, as it were, to provide them with congenial surroundings (by planting decorative trees without any economic value) which would make them feel at home in their new country.[100]

The same was done by the SELEUCIDS in Syria, Mesopotamia, and probably in the Iranian satrapies also. It is surprising to learn from Strabo* that it was the Macedonians who first planted vines (he mentions expressly that it had not been done before) in Susiana and in Babylon; and he adds some perfectly reliable details as regards the mode of planting the vines. Now we know with certainty that vines were cultivated in Babylonia and Assyria (and probably in Susiana also) since Sumerian times with excellent results. It is probable, therefore, that Strabo misunderstood his good and trustworthy source.

* xv. 3. 11, p. 731.

We may suppose that exactly the same occurred here as in Egypt. The Macedonian colonists planted vines extensively on the plots assigned to them in Babylon and Susiana, and applied their own methods in doing so. I may quote as a parallel the similar proceedings of the Macedonians in Dura-Europus. In any case Strabo attests an interesting fact, characteristic of the new settlements of both the Seleucids and the Ptolemies. We find the same similarity between Egypt and the Seleucid kingdom as regards the extensive acclimatization of European plants in the new Macedonian settlements. The famous attempts of Harpalus to plant Greek trees and shrubs in the parks of Babylon, which Theophrastus reports and discusses so carefully, resemble the experiments of Apollonius on his Philadelphian estate.[101] The introduction of some typically Egyptian plants into Palestine, and perhaps later into Syria and Babylonia, such as Egyptian beans, lentils, mustard, gourds, may have been effected at the time when Palestine and a part of Syria were provinces of the Ptolemies, or later in Roman times.[102]

The Seleucids, as heirs of the Persian kings, were not satisfied with hellenizing the vegetation of their kingdom, but also sought to introduce plants from the farther East into their various satrapies. A casual notice by Pliny* speaks of attempts made by Seleucus (probably Seleucus I) to acclimatize in his kingdom the Indian *amomum* and *nardum*, which had been brought from India by sea.† The terms in which Pliny in the same paragraph speaks of cinnamon ('non habet vires frutex cinnami in Syriae vicina perveniendi') suggest that similar experiments were tried with this Cingalese plant also. Pliny likewise mentions,‡ when treating of frankincense, that 'Asiae reges' had planted frankincense trees in their kingdom. By 'Asiae reges' he may mean the Seleucids. It is therefore probable that the Seleucids made many attempts to produce in their own kingdom some of the Indian and Arabian goods which were so eagerly bought by their own subjects and by

---

* *N.H.* xvi. 135.

† 'Non ferunt amomi nardique deliciae, ne in Arabiam quidem, ex India et nave peregrinari; temptavit enim Seleucus rex.'

‡ Ibid. xii. 57.

their European customers. Similar attempts may be ascribed with confidence to the Ptolemies, for Pliny mentions their efforts, as true successors of Hatchepsut, to plant in Egypt frankincense trees* and to acclimatize the *ladanum* (mastic-shrub).† But these attempts remained sporadic and were unsuccessful, herein differing completely from those which aimed at europeanizing the agricultural life of the Near East. In fact, nothing essential, nothing which would change considerably the economic life of the eastern monarchies was achieved by these efforts at acclimatization. Much could have been done with ease, but was never even attempted. By way of example I may quote some typical instances.

Some Iranian fruit-trees such as the apricot, peach, and cherry were probably never seen in Egypt in Ptolemaic times (our knowledge is of course defective and some of the evidence is variously interpreted). They appear to have been first acclimatized in Italy by the Romans and were transferred thence to the Hellenistic East.[103] The same was probably the case with oranges and lemons. The *citrus medica Risso*, the only kind of *agrumi* ever planted in large quantities in the classical world, was apparently first acclimatized in Italy by the Romans.[104] Banana-trees, well known to the botanists of Alexander, remained entirely foreign to the Hellenistic world. Still more striking is the fact that cotton, though known in Egypt from a very early date and familiar to the classical world in general, grown on the Bahrein Islands in the Persian Gulf and in Meroe and used there for making textiles, was never cultivated on a large scale in the Hellenistic monarchies, and cotton stuffs, both cheap and expensive, were mostly imported.[105] The same is true of rice. In the time of Alexander and the Successors, rice was cultivated not only in Bactria but also in Babylonia and Susiana,‡ but it appears not to have penetrated into Egypt until late in the Roman Empire and never became a rival to the traditional grain plants of the ancient world. This neglect of rice in the Mediterranean countries is not confined to antiquity. It must be explained by the difficulties which its cultivation presents there.[106]

* Plin. *N.H.* xii. 56. † Ibid. xii. 76.
‡ Strabo (Aristobulus), xv. 1. 18, p. 692; Diod. xix. 13. 6.

It is a well-known fact that the part which sugar plays in modern times was reserved in the ancient world exclusively to honey. The production of honey was of course limited, and some substitute or supplement to it was highly desirable. Such a substitute existed in India and was known, though imperfectly, to Hellenistic visitors to that country.* And yet no attempt was made in Hellenistic or in Roman times to learn more about it or to acclimatize any of the sugar-yielding plants in the Greco-Roman world, though sugar (σάκχαρον) was occasionally imported from India, certainly in the Roman but perhaps also in the Hellenistic age.†[107] Nor was any attempt made to produce real silk. Inferior raw silk known as Assyrian and Coan (perhaps also made in the island of Amorgos), extracted from cocoons produced in the Near East, remained for a long time the only material for the home-made Greek silk stuffs. The real Chinese silk was imported.[108]

Our information about the acclimatization of new plants and animals by the cities of GREECE is very meagre. We certainly should know more about it if we had at our disposal the many treatises on agriculture written in Hellenistic times in Greece and in the Greek islands. But these treatises are irretrievably lost. We are reduced, therefore, to some occasional references. As regards fruit-trees, a passage of the *Geoponica* (x. 12. 3–4) derived from Paxamus, a writer on agriculture probably of the first century B.C., indicates that this author was the first to describe the way of planting the pistachio tree in Greece. The tree was probably first imported from Syria to Greece in the lifetime of Paxamus. I may also mention the experiments in the planting of palm-trees in Greece in the time of Theophrastus‡ and the attempt made by the Rhodians, friends of the Ptolemies and their associates in trade, to plant the Egyptian persea tree in Rhodes. As for domestic animals, it is probable that domestic ducks were first raised in Greece in Hellenistic times.[109]

In the aggregate, the measures taken by the Hellenistic kings

* See, for example, Nearchus in Strabo, xv. 1. 20, p. 693–4.

† Diod. xix. 94. 10.

‡ Theophr. *H.P.* ii. 2. 10; iii. 3. 5, cf. *C.P.* ii. 3. 7, and Plin. *N.H.* xvi. 111 and 135.

added a large number of new plants of great economic value to those previously cultivated in their kingdoms. The agricultural aspect of large parts of Egypt, for example, was considerably changed. It was no longer so monotonous as it had been. In many respects, for instance in the cultivation of wheat, changes of great economic importance were made to the advantage of the population and of the rulers. Nevertheless, nothing comparable to the later activity of the Arabs was carried out or aimed at. The agricultural aspect of Egypt was hellenized to a certain extent, but its chief features remained the same as before. And the same was probably true of the other parts of the Hellenistic world.

Forests. Next in economic importance to agriculture (in the broad sense of the word, including the culture of the vine and olive and of oleaginous plants, besides grazing and bee-keeping), came forestry and mining (including the quarrying of stone). These provided the ancient world with lumber and firewood, and with metal and stone for building and other purposes. We know little of the exploitation of forests by the Hellenistic rulers. It should be noticed that all the chief Hellenistic monarchies possessed valuable forests, which supplied them not only with timber and firewood but also with pitch and tar. The wealth of Macedonia in this respect is well known; there was no lack of excellent timber in the principal territories of Asia Minor (except Galatia), certain regions such as Mount Ida, the Mysian Olympus, Pontus, Lycia, and Cilicia being exceptionally rich; the Seleucids had at their disposal the woodlands of northern Syria and Mesopotamia, besides controlling in the early period of their rule some of the above-mentioned regions of Asia Minor, and in the later period the cedar woods of the Lebanon; finally, the Ptolemies, though possessing very little wood in their own land of Egypt, drew an abundant supply of timber from Cyprus and, in their earlier days, from the Lebanon and from Lycia and Cilicia. Greece was an exception. Large parts of it had, by Hellenistic times, been denuded of their forests. Other parts, especially some of the islands, never had forests. These areas depended therefore on imported timber, pitch and tar. The classical example is Delos, which, as there is much evidence to show, had to import these commodities besides firewood and charcoal. However, there still remained in Greece certain areas rich in and celebrated for their beautiful forests. Some parts of Elis and Laconia, Mounts Taygetus, Parnassus, Olympus, Pelion, and Ossa, and especially Arcadia with Mount Cyllene, are mentioned by Theophrastus and others as still covered with woods and forests. Among the islands Crete still abounded in native woods, which the Cretans used for building their piratical fleets.[110]

It is evident that the great demand for wood for building houses and ships, for wagons and carts, for weapons and engines of war, for tools, and for fuel led the Hellenistic rulers to exploit their forests more intensively than had been customary.

We learn from casual mention that Antigonus the One-eyed and his son Demetrius, for the purposes of their own ship-building and that of their allies, cut large quantities of timber in the forests of Cyprus, which had been protected and sparingly used by the local kings of the time. There is no doubt that the successors of Antigonus and Demetrius in Cyprus, the Ptolemies, acted in the same way. We may safely assume that the same intensive exploitation of forests was carried on by all the Hellenistic monarchs: the Seleucids, the Attalids, the kings of Bithynia and of Pontus.[111]

How this intensive exploitation was effected we do not know. The cutting of trees may have been conducted with more method than in the past. The kings now had at their disposal an exact knowledge and scientific classification of wild trees, a careful description of the most important varieties, and valuable information about the market value of different kinds of wood and the technical processes used by professional lumbermen (ὑλοτόμοι) and carpenters in Greece, Macedonia, Asia Minor, Syria, and Egypt. Theophrastus' admirable treatises on the *History of Plants* and on the *Causae plantarum* were certainly published either in his lifetime or perhaps shortly after his death, which occurred probably about 285 B.C.[112]

It is to be regretted that the policy of the Hellenistic kings with regard to deforestation, the most vital problem of forestry in general and the natural result of intensive exploitation, is unknown to us. The forests that they inherited from their predecessors were not virgin forests, but had been systematically and, as a rule, ruthlessly despoiled in the past. How this was done we may learn from a highly illuminating passage of Eratosthenes* relating to Cyprus, which I may give verbatim: 'Eratosthenes says that in the older times the plains of the island were so thickly overgrown with wood that they were covered with continuous forests and were not cultivated at all. Some help was afforded by the working of mines, since trees were felled to smelt the copper and silver ores, and further help came from the building of fleets as soon as navigation became safe and naval forces sailed the sea. But as no complete victory [over the forests] was won in this way, everyone who was willing and able was permitted to cut the trees and to own the land thus cleared as private and tax-free property.'

Whether the Seleucids and Ptolemies took steps not only to exploit their forests more intensively but also to prevent complete deforestation, we unfortunately do not know. I have said that in Cyprus the native kings who preceded the Macedonian rulers had already protected their forests. We may suspect that some system of protection and of methodical felling was applied, in Roman times at least, to the famous cedars of the Lebanon. Whether or not the Ptolemies learned something from the Cyprian kings, whether or not the measures taken by the Romans in Syria went back to the Ptolemies and the Seleucids, in any case the importance of the problem was realized by the Ptolemies so far as concerned Egypt. I have mentioned above their provident management of the trees of Egypt, the steps which they took to protect such as there were and to plant the dikes and embankments systematically with trees and shrubs. This may point to a similar policy in their dominions.[113]

Mines. Of even more importance to the Hellenistic States were the mines. The demand for metals was rapidly increasing in the Hellenistic world. Gold, silver, and copper were needed for the abundant and ever-increasing coinage of the time. Precious metals in coined form, in ingots, but mostly in the

* Quoted by Strabo, xiv. 6. 5, p. 684.

form of silver and gold plate, were hoarded as reserve capital by all the monarchs. The same was done by several of the richer temples. Silver and gold plate, silver and gold jewels were extensively used by private persons, and also formed their savings and reserve capital. Copper was still in large demand for plate, statues and statuettes, furniture, toilet articles, tools, surgical instruments, and weapons. Still more important was iron. There was no department of life which did not need an abundant supply of iron: war, agriculture and industry, transport and navigation absorbed it in ever-increasing quantities. For many çountries like Egypt the real iron age did not begin until the Hellenistic period.

The modern mineral resources of what used to be the Hellenistic world are little known and have been unequally investigated. Greece, Macedonia, and Egypt, thoroughly explored as they have been, are exceptions. Over the greater part of the former Hellenistic world—Asia Minor, Syria, Mesopotamia, the Iranian lands, Arabia—very little has been done in this respect. Nor is our evidence regarding ancient times—literary, epigraphical, and archaeological—any better. Mines are mentioned by our literary texts sporadically. Even Strabo, who was much interested in the subject, does not deal exhaustively even with the parts of the Hellenistic world that he knew best, viz. Asia Minor, to say nothing of those regions which were known to him from his literary sources only. Epigraphical evidence (except as regards Laurium in Attica) and papyrological evidence are very meagre. Nor have the archaeologists contributed much except for Greece and Macedonia, and for Egypt.[114]

In these circumstances, it is very difficult to estimate the activity of the Hellenistic rulers in the field of prospecting and mining, to say how many new mines were opened by them, and how much more intensively the old mines were worked than before. There are *a priori* reasons for supposing that great efforts were made by all the Hellenistic States in this respect. An abundant supply of metals was of such vital importance to them all that it must be assumed that they did their best to develop all the available mineral resources of their respective territories. We know how greatly the success of Philip II depended on his systematic endeavours to increase by conquest and prospecting the output of base and precious metals from his territories. The policy of Philip was inherited by Alexander, and was pursued by the latter in Macedonia and later in his new Asiatic empire. We learn from a chance reference* that he had a special mining engineer and prospector (μεταλλευτής) on his staff during his great expedition. The engineer—Gorgus by name—investigated the mineral resources of the kingdom of Sopeithes (between Hyarotis and Hyphasis, near modern Lahore) and found, besides salt mines, rich veins of silver and gold very primitively exploited by the Indians. He presented his report to Alexander and later published it in book form. There is no doubt that Alexander organized a more systematic exploitation of these mines and that Gorgus was not the only *metalleutes* in Alexander's army who met with success in his prospecting operations.[115]

It is evident that all the successors of Alexander acted in the same way. Very little could be done in GREECE.[116] The Greeks were excellent prospectors, and the mineral wealth of Greece and the islands was well known to them. All the existing mines were carefully worked long before the Hellenistic period and some of them (very few were rich) were exhausted. Many of the Greek cities of the Hellenistic period depended therefore for their supply of metals chiefly on the import of semi-finished products. In MACEDONIA the situation was different.[117] Here the mineral wealth was very large and far from being exhausted. It is certain that the successors of Alexander in Macedonia paid as much attention to their mines as did Philip and Alexander. We may infer, for instance, that under Perseus much prospecting was done and that the existing mines of his country were worked extensively.† By these means and by increasing the burden of taxation he accumulated large quantities of gold and silver, part of which ultimately came into the hands of the Romans.‡ I may also note that, according to modern investigations, the comparatively

---

* Strabo, xv. i. 30, p. 700.   † Liv. xlv. 40.

‡ Diod. xxx. 9 and 19; xxxi, 14 (on his mercenaries and allies), and Liv. xlv. 40. 1, cf. 29; Vell. Pat. i. 9. 6; Plin. *N.H.* xxxiii. 56 (booty taken by the Romans).

rich silver and gold mines of Chalcidice were first discovered in the time of Philip II and then actively developed in Hellenistic times. The same seems to be true of the copper mines of Othrys in Thessaly.

In EGYPT much energy was shown by the Ptolemies in prospecting and mining. Modern investigations in the eastern Desert of Egypt show that in this region: 'the ancients . . . left little of value; near Umm Hat they tested every blue stain for argentiferous copper'.[118] The Ptolemies certainly inherited the knowledge of their predecessors and were not behind them in applying it both in Egypt and in their other dominions. I have mentioned above how intensively they exploited the gold mines of Nubia and the mines (gold, copper, iron) of the eastern Arabian desert.[119] So long as the rule of the Ptolemies lasted, these mines (perhaps with short interruptions) were in operation and probably yielded substantial returns. Next to Egypt in importance and richer in copper, silver, and iron was Cyprus.[120] There is no doubt that the Ptolemies intensified mining in that island and received thence all the copper that they needed, besides some silver and iron. The wealth of Cyprus in copper explains, in my opinion, the abandonment by the Ptolemies of the copper mines of Sinai, which were difficult to exploit and whose output was probably small. To the mineral resources they possessed in Egypt and Cyprus the Ptolemies probably added those of their possessions in Asia Minor and in Syria, Phoenicia, and Palestine. How much silver and iron they received from Asia Minor and what mines were here under their control, it is impossible to say. South-western Asia Minor has been little explored in this respect in modern times and we are poorly informed about the extent of the Ptolemaic territory behind the line of coastal cities. We may conjecture, for example, that they had access to the iron mines from which Cibyra received its supply of iron.*[121] The wealth in copper and iron of Palestine and especially Idumaea (ancient Edom) and the adjoining districts of Arabia has recently been revealed. These deposits were apparently extensively worked in pre-Hellenistic times. One of the centres of smelting and refining copper and iron from the

* Strabo, xiii. 4. 17, p. 631.

eleventh to the seventh century B.C. was the famous industrial and commercial city of Ezion-Geber on the Gulf of
Akabah, which has recently been excavated. According to
the letter of Ps.-Aristeas the working of the Idumean mines
was suspended under the Persian domination.[122] It may have
been resumed by the Nabataeans, who controlled Idumaea,
and the metals may have been used by them and exported to
Ptolemaic Palestine and later to the Seleucid kingdom. But
we have no positive evidence to this effect. The copper and
iron mines were certainly not exhausted and were capable of
a large output. It is therefore puzzling to find it stated by
Strabo* that the Nabataeans, while rich in native gold and
silver, imported their supply of iron and copper. Were the
Nabataean kings forced to abandon the production of these
metals either by political pressure (which is highly improbable,
especially during the late Seleucid and early Roman times, a
period of great political expansion for the Nabataeans) or by
lack of fuel? Further archaeological exploration of the Nabataean region, so splendidly begun by Dr. N. Glueck, will
probably solve this problem. The Ptolemies may also have
exploited certain other mines in Palestine and the copper and
iron mines of the Lebanon.[123] All these sources of supply in
Asia Minor and in Palestine were of course lost to them after
the battle of Panium.

On the activity of the SELEUCIDS in respect of prospecting
and mining we know practically nothing. In their early days
they were self-sufficient as regards the basic metals—gold,
silver, copper, iron, tin, lead, &c.[124] Mines of these metals
were scattered all over the huge empire of the early Seleucids.
Its poorest part was the central kernel. Copper and iron mines
were situated especially in the Lebanon (which was under the
control of the Ptolemies in early Seleucid times) and in the
upper Euphrates and Tigris regions, some of them comparatively rich (the copper mines of Arghana near Diarbekr,
ancient Amida). To these we may add the copper mines of
the Persian Gulf, especially those of Oman and the Bahrein
Islands. There were some much richer mines in Iran, especially
those of Carmania (Luristan), which is described by Strabo†

* xvi. 4. 26, p. 784. † xv. 2. 14, p. 726.

as possessing an abundance of all sorts of metals, including gold and silver. Strabo further mentions the tin mines of Drangiana.* India was also praised by the Greeks for its wealth in various metals. I have mentioned the mines of the Cathaeans and I may add that allusions to the mineral wealth of India in general are comparatively frequent in our literary texts.† Nearer to the centre of the early Seleucid kingdom and probably under the control of the early Seleucids were the rich silver and iron mines of the southern Caucasus, Armenia, and the celebrated region of the Chalybes between Amisus and Trapezus. We know the reputation that their iron mines and iron works enjoyed throughout the Greek world. The wealth of this mining region and the skill of the Chalybian smiths were a common topic in Greek literature from the early fifth century B.C. It was generally believed by the Greeks, who probably from early times drew their main supply of iron from this region and perhaps also from South Russia, that iron and iron weapons were a Scythian discovery. The mines were still in full operation in early‡ and late§ Hellenistic times.[125] Finally, the Seleucids possessed some of the rich iron and silver mines of the Taurus mountains, such as the silver mines of the modern Bulghar Maaden (Cilicia).

The situation of the Seleucids in respect of the supply of metals changed greatly for the worse in the later period, when they lost one part of their empire after another, both in the East and in the West. Especially disastrous were the losses in the West. Almost all the rich mining districts of Asia Minor now fell into the hands of the independent Anatolian kings. Central Asia Minor and its mineral wealth became the property of the Pergamene kings, while the Mithridatids of Pontus controlled the rich mining districts of the south-eastern Euxine coast, those of the southern Caucasus and of Armenia, and some of those of the Taurus. Finally the whole of Asia Minor was severed from the Seleucid kingdom by the treaty of Apamea. The Seleucids of the second century B.C. were thus

---

* Ibid. 10, p. 724.

† Ctesias, *ap.* Phot. *Bibl.*, ed. I. Bekker, 1824, p. 46 B. 25; Diod. ii. 36. 2, and Plin. *N.H.* vi. 67.

‡ Apoll. Rh. *Argon.* ii. 1002 ff.   § Strabo, xii. 3. 19, p. 549.

confined to the kernel of their kingdom, including Phoenicia and Palestine. Whether they made the best of this situation and endeavoured to develop the output of the mines of their reduced territory and to increase their number by systematic prospecting we do not know.

In speaking of the mineral resources of the Seleucid kingdom I may briefly mention bitumen and petroleum. These products were well known and extensively used for various purposes in the pre-Hellenistic period. When the Macedonians and Greeks took possession of the rich oilfields of Mesopotamia and the bitumen of the Dead Sea they showed great interest in them and carefully registered all the known sources of supply. But they never made any serious efforts to utilize these materials. They stuck to pitch and tar, and never thought of replacing them by bitumen. They never endeavoured to make use of petroleum for military purposes, as fuel, or as a possible substitute for vegetable oils as illuminants. The use of bitumen and petroleum in the Hellenistic and Roman times remained very limited.[126]

It is unnecessary to repeat here the little that we know of the mining operations of the lesser kings of the Hellenistic world. It may be supposed that they showed no less interest in developing the mineral resources of their respective countries than did the Antigonids, the Ptolemies, and the Seleucids.

Quarries. Closely connected with mining was the quarrying of various kinds of stone, both common building material and the rare and more expensive qualities, such as varieties of marble, the glory of Greece and Asia Minor, and the famous alabaster, granite, diorite, basalt, porphyry, &c., of Egypt. We know little about the subject either in general or as regards the Hellenistic period in particular. It is evident that active work must have been carried on in Hellenistic times in most of the quarries, for the extensive building operations in all the Hellenistic States gave rise to an increasing demand for stone. Yet it must be noted that the quarries in many of these States were worked on a much more limited scale than later in the Roman period. I may mention for example that the quarries of Docimium–Synnada, which yielded an excellent kind of variegated marble, appear to have been much less

actively developed in Hellenistic than in Roman times,* and
that in Egypt many rich quarries of the best and rarest stone
were probably first opened by the Romans.[127]

I cannot here review all the other sources of wealth of the
Hellenistic world. As regards these the general picture will be
approximately the same: great efforts made in the Hellenistic
period to intensify their exploitation in order to supply the
needs of the respective States and to export the surplus.

Fishing. I may, however, make one exception and say a few
words about fishing. We must bear in mind that this industry
played a very important part in the economy of the ancient
world in general, in all periods of its evolution, a part perhaps
even more important than it plays in modern times. Bread
and fish, with the addition of olive-oil and wine, formed in
ancient times the most substantial parts of the diet of the people,
rich and poor. Fish, fresh and salted, pickled and dried, was
consumed in large quantities, the poorer classes being almost
entirely dependent for their *opson* on the cheaper qualities
and especially on salted and dried fish. This was so in Greece
from a very early time and also in the Near East. The needs
of the latter region were supplied by the rich fisheries of its
great rivers—the Tigris and the Euphrates in Mesopotamia
with the adjacent parts of the Persian Gulf, and the Nile with
the lake of the Fayûm in Egypt. Sea fish, except along the
Syrian and Phoenician coast, played a secondary part, the
main yield being that of the rivers. The Greek cities supplied
their needs partly by extensive local fishing along the coast
of the Aegean and in certain rivers and lakes (for instance
Lake Copais in Boeotia), but in great part by the import of
fish from the rich and flourishing fisheries of the Euxine, the
Straits, and the Propontis, and of the great northern rivers,
the Danube, Dniester, Bug, Dnieper, Don, and Kuban.[128]

The popularity of fishing and the keen interest in fish throughout the Greek world are reflected in the frequent mentions of
this subject in the Greek literature of Classical and Hellenistic
times. In the hands of Aristotle and his successors ichthyology
became a science, while the many authors of *Halieutica*, chiefly
of the Hellenistic and Roman periods, made of fishing a τέχνη

* Strabo, xii. 8. 14, p. 577; cf. ix. 5. 16, p. 437.

based on reports collected from fishermen of the methods they followed. Athenaeus, himself keenly interested in fish from various points of view, gives an interesting list of these methods (i. 13). The only example of the *Halieutica* still extant, that of Oppian of Anazarbus in Cilicia, a contemporary of Athenaeus, probably gives a fair idea of what the earlier *Halieutica* were like: a combination of a *catalogue raisonné* of various kinds of fish, based on ichthyological studies, with detailed descriptions of the various ways of fishing. The same popularity of everything connected with fish and fishing is attested by the abundance of monuments of art on which these are represented. I may remind the reader of the South Italian red-figured 'fish-dishes', distributed all over the Greek world,* and continued in the Italian fish mosaics of the Hellenistic period, of which the examples at Pompeii are well known. These in their turn were imitated in the later fish mosaics of Italy and of the western and eastern Roman provinces. I may cite also in this connexion the many painted vases of the Classical period and the still more numerous mosaics and paintings of Roman times, the latter derived from Hellenistic originals which display the various ways of fishing, and the Hellenistic statues and statuettes representing typical figures of fishermen.[129]

Our information about fishing and fisheries in Hellenistic times is defective. New fisheries can hardly have been discovered in this period. The habits of the river fish of the great Oriental rivers were well known to the local population from very early times. The same may be said of Greece. The art of Aegean and Mycenean Greece shows how thoroughly acquainted the inhabitants of Greece were in those days with the various kinds of fish in the Aegean waters. This knowledge was inherited and extended by the Greeks. Aristotle's masterly descriptions of various fish were based on this accumulated knowledge and they were in all probability the source of most of the data about fish and fishing collected by the late Hellenistic authorities on whom Aelian, Pliny, and Oppian relied. There is, for example, not the slightest doubt that the Greeks of Panticapaeum, Chersonesus, Olbia, Byzantium,

* A fragment has been found even in Uruk, see p. 90, n. 22.

Cyzicus, Sinope, and so on, who had applied themselves energetically to fishing since the foundation of these cities, were thoroughly familiar before the Hellenistic period with the seasonal migrations of the tunnies and the *pelamydes* (one-year-old tunnies), and with the best places and devices for catching them. What could be added to this knowledge in Hellenistic times was probably very slight. New and important methods may, however, have been introduced in the organization of the fishing industry, especially as regards the preparation of fish for the market and its preservation. But precisely in this respect our evidence is very meagre and does not permit us to discriminate between new and traditional methods. I may say a few words on the subject here, to avoid recurring to it in the following section.

Fishing proper, that is to say, the catching of fish by various methods carefully described in our texts, had from time immemorial been carried on by individual fishermen or by groups, and this probably remained the custom in the Hellenistic period both in the East and in Greece. There was more complexity, from the economic standpoint, in the preparation of salted, pickled, and dried fish, and the organization of export. These required capital and planning, which were probably supplied in Greece by cities and individual capitalists. We have some scattered evidence on the subject. For example, the city of Sinope constructed θαυμαστὰ πηλαμυδεῖα, as conspicuous and admirable as its famous ναύσταθμα and probably contiguous to them.* Unfortunately we do not know the date of this construction. In Cos in the second century B.C. and elsewhere there were public as well as private σκοπαί (watchtowers for tunnies).† There is occasional mention of rich exporters of fish, who perhaps at the same time organized the preparation of fish for export. I may quote the famous instance of Chaerephilus, the dealer in τάριχος, a contemporary of Demosthenes, who received the franchise for his services to the city.‡ He had certainly successors in the Hellenistic period. For the Hellenistic monarchies the evidence with which I have dealt above is a little better. Here I may cite again (Ch. IV, p. 297) certain papyri from Tebtunis which convey a fair idea of the

* Strabo, xii. 3. 11, p. 545.   † *S.I.G.*³ 1000.   ‡ Athen. iii. 119 f.

organization of the catching and sale of fish on an extensive scale in some large fisheries of the Fayûm, which belonged either to the king or to the holder of a gift-estate. Whether all was new in the skilful organization of this great undertaking cannot be ascertained.

3. EXPLOITATION OF THE NATURAL SOURCES OF WEALTH

As a consequence of the eastward extension of the Greek world, the Greeks of the Hellenistic age, both in their native lands and in the new kingdoms, were confronted with many new factors in their social and economic life. It was inevitable therefore, that they should change to some extent their ancestral methods of exploiting the ample natural resources at their disposal. Some of these were new; others, though known before, were first placed within their reach by Alexander. The same is true of the native population of the East, which after Alexander's time entered upon a new phase of its age-long economic and social evolution.

We should accordingly expect, *a priori*, to find various innovations in the methods of agriculture, industry, and commerce designed to meet the gradually increasing demand for more and better goods which resulted from more diversified and ever more refined requirements. We may accept, for instance the view of many modern scholars, that the brilliant development of exact science in the Hellenistic period contributed largely to the improvement of methods of production and exchange, by the invention of new technical devices in the economic spheres in question.

The aim of this section will therefore be to promote a clear understanding of the subject by summarizing the material related to it, of which the greater part has been set out in the previous chapters. The reader will thus be enabled to realize the number and importance of the innovations in this field first introduced in the Hellenistic period, and the great changes they effected in the economic aspect of the Hellenistic world.

A. AGRICULTURE

Agriculture remained during the Hellenistic age what it had previously been—the chief industry of all the States that formed the Hellenistic world. According to Greek ideas agriculture was the natural occupation of a free man, of a citizen of one of the cities; a craft (τέχνη) that was lucrative, healthy, respectable, and easy to learn. Such is at least the philosophy of agriculture formulated by Xenophon* for a gentleman-farmer, a typical figure of his own time. The same *mutatis mutandis* is true of the Oriental world.

I may therefore begin my economic survey with a few remarks on this industry, dealing first with the GREEK cities,† then with the Hellenistic monarchies.

Land tenure. The main features of land tenure in the Greek city system are little known. We have no statistical data, even approximate, concerning the distribution of land among the various classes of the population. It is certain, however, that substantial changes in this respect were taking place. Peasant-owned land, characteristic of Greece in the fifth century, was gradually declining in importance. Land was passing from the hands of small farmers or peasants into those of various corporative bodies: cities, subdivisions of cities (such as *phylae*, phratries, and demes), temples, and various corporations, and into those of landowners residing in the cities or living on their farms but exploiting their property not by applying the farm produce to the support of themselves and their families, but by drawing a steady though modest income from the sale of that produce or by renting the land to tenants.[130]

This process of concentration of landed property began early. It was a typical feature of the fourth century B.C. (above, Chs. II and III, pp. 96, 162). The gentlemen-farmers for whom Xenophon wrote his books on οἰκονομία are well known to us from various sources of that century, especially from the orators and the authors of the Middle and New Comedies. We have a characteristic example in the estate of Phaenippus, a contemporary of Demosthenes, a medium-sized area of about 750 acres (300 hectares). Its barley, wine,

---

* *Oec.* v. 1 and 17, cf. 3 on cattle breeding.

† As I have had no occasion in the preceding chapters to deal in detail with land tenure and agriculture in the cities of continental Greece and the islands, I devote some pages to the subject here.

and firewood yielded the owner in years of good harvest and high prices an income of more than five talents.[131] Such or smaller estates were probably owned by many of his contemporaries, as depicted in the comedies of Menander and other dramatists. Even more common were estates which consisted of small farms scattered over a wide region. While we find several mentions of medium-sized estates of these two types, cultivated either by slaves and hired hands or by tenants, we seldom hear of peasant proprietors and of owners of large *latifundia*. The typical land tenure of the fourth century B.C. was therefore probably *bourgeois* ownership.

For the later period, the third and the subsequent centuries, our evidence is very meagre. We may assume, however, that there were no substantial changes in this respect until the troubled times of the second and first centuries B.C., when many members of the middle class were ruined, and from these ruins a few magnates emerged, who may have invested their capital in large estates. The ruling aristocracy of Athens of the second and first centuries B.C. may have belonged to this small group.[132]

System of Cultivation. Of the system of turning land to account during this period we know very little. It appears, however, that the traditional, old-fashioned peasant land economy gradually gave place to new methods inspired by the desire to produce the best qualities of the most marketable goods in the largest possible quantity, so as to obtain the maximum return.* Agriculture in the hands of the landowners of the new type appears to have become a τέχνη, and many manuals were written to help landowners in the management of their property. Such manuals were known to Plato (?) and Aristotle, and were used by Theophrastus. With them we may class Xenophon's books on οἰκονομία and the most ancient sources of the Roman *scriptores rei rusticae*, so far as these ancient manuals were authentic and not *pseudepigrapha*, that is to say, later works circulated under famous names.[133]

Of their character we may form some idea by studying the botanical treatises of Theophrastus. They appear to have been collections of maxims of practical farmers, the results of their

* Arist. *Pol.* i. 11. 1258[b], 1259[a].

ἐμπειρία, systematically classified and logically interpreted. Theophrastus in his botanical works endeavoured to combine this ἐμπειρία with his theoretical and scientific study of plants, but his attempt was never repeated or extended by other writers, and his own work was rejected by later practical agriculturists as too scientific and theoretical. Varro* when quoting the works of Theophrastus among those concerned with agriculture remarks that they were 'non tam idonei iis qui agrum colere volunt quam qui scholas philosophorum'.[134]

It is evident that post-Theophrastian agricultural treatises reverted to the old type and developed it extensively. There were many of them.[135] It is regrettable that though we know many names of authors of such works (Varro speaks of there being fifty and names forty-nine, *R.R.* i. 1. 8), not one of the manuals of the Hellenistic period has survived or can be reconstructed from the few quotations by the *scriptores rei rusticae* of Roman times, except perhaps the frequently quoted and very popular manual (Γεωργικά) of Bolus Democritus of Mendes in Egypt. This manual has recently been ingeniously reconstructed by M. Wellmann. It may be noted that Bolus assumed his second name in order to present himself to the reader as a kind of second Democritus, the famous philosopher of Abdera who gradually became a half-mythical person, a source of the most important wisdom.[136]

Of the fifty Greek writers on agriculture mentioned by Varro (in his 'bibliography', repeated by Columella and Pliny) no direct use was made by Varro himself and his successors (with perhaps a few exceptions). But they were read and studied by Cassius Dionysius and incorporated in his work on agriculture, a translation of the famous agricultural handbook of Mago, the Carthaginian, who likewise had made ample use of Greek sources, as did Cato in Rome.[137] Now Cassius Dionysius' treatise, either in the original or in the abbreviation by Diophanes of Bithynia, was the chief source of all the Roman writers on agriculture. It follows that the Latin books on agriculture (and the late Greek *Geoponica*) contained a large amount of Greek material and may be regarded in many respects as a continuation of Greek agricultural literature.

* *R.R.* i. 5. 1-2.

It is to be regretted that we are so poorly informed about the Greek agronomical writers. Not only are we unable to reconstruct their works, but we do not even know the dates of the individual authors nor, in all cases, their places of origin. Among those whose place of origin was known to Varro, the large majority, it may be noted, were inhabitants of the islands and Asia Minor. Very few were natives of continental Greece, and all these were Athenians.

The relation between the Greek and the Roman agronomical literature which I have indicated above, and which is reflected in the Greek terminology adopted (in Latin form) by the Roman writers on agriculture,[138] as in other ways, may suggest that not only were certain technical processes borrowed by the Latins from the Greeks, but also that the general spirit of the Roman agricultural τέχνη was not very different from that of their Greek predecessors and contemporaries. The Romans, like the pre-Hellenistic and Hellenistic Greeks, treated their subject as a systematic science, based on experience and logic, and having as its object the extraction from the soil of the largest possible amount of produce. Their own system they sharply contrasted with that of the old-fashioned peasantry, based exclusively on tradition and suspicious of any innovations.

To illustrate this point I may refer to the famous passage in Varro* where, speaking of the labour used in agriculture, he contrasts the peasants with the modern cultivators, a passage, I may add, apparently borrowed by Varro in one way or another from his ultimately Hellenistic sources. In the course of this passage Varro says: 'all the fields are cultivated either by slaves or free men, or both: by free men when they work on their [own] land with their own hands [the Greek αὐτουργοί], such as the many poor people (*pauperculi*) with their families, or when they are employed as hired hands . . . or those whom Romans called *obaerarii* and who still exist in large numbers in Asia, Egypt, and Illyricum'.

The casual remark of Varro is very interesting. His mention of peasants and serfs shows that the land economy based on peasant labour and that based on serf labour were known to

* *R.R.* i. 17. 2.

him, but were regarded by him as survivals not worth special study, and without interest or relevance from the point of view of a progressive farmer. It is noteworthy that he regards the peasants as a feature of Italian land economy, while the serfs have a certain importance in the economic system of Asia and Egypt (observe the omission of Syria) and of some barbarian tribes of the Balkan peninsula. Greece is not mentioned as a home either of peasant economy or of serf economy (Sparta, Thessaly, Crete), nor is there any mention of Carthage. It appears that Varro's statement is derived partly from a Hellenistic source unfamiliar with Greece and Africa, and partly from personal observation.

Though of no interest to the progressive farmer, peasant and serf cultivators were nevertheless still important elements of agricultural life in the time of the Hellenistic writer on whom Varro drew and in his own day. This we know not only from Varro but from other sources also. Widely adopted as it had been, the systematic land economy of the agricultural writers was not completely dominant in the Hellenistic period. Peasant economy and serf economy still survived and retained some importance. I shall speak of the Hellenistic monarchies later in this section. Here I may say a few words about Greece.

In continental Greece serf economy, though very little known, certainly existed in some places. It lost its importance in Sparta after the time of Nabis, but it may have retained comparative vitality in Thessaly and in Crete.[139] Nor was peasant economy completely eliminated by the concentration of land in the hands of corporative bodies and of the urban *bourgeoisie*. The bulk of our information about land tenure and methods of cultivation is derived from the numerous contracts of lease of land engraved on stone and found in various parts of Greece and Asia Minor. The parties to these leases are various corporative bodies on the one hand, and private persons on the other. No contracts between private landowners and their tenants are extant. This does not mean, of course, that private landowners never leased their land. The absence of private contracts of lease engraved on stone must be explained otherwise: either the contracts were oral or more probably they were never recorded on stone, an expensive procedure not needed in private transactions. A careful study of the above-mentioned leases may perhaps reveal the standing of the tenants and their methods of cultivation, and may show whether they were for the greater part small peasants or men of wealth who invested their capital in leases of this kind. My impression is that both were represented and that it was the former who prevailed at Thespiae, while the latter were characteristic of Delos. But without minute study, no final conclusions can be drawn.[140]

It is not easy to ascertain what progress was achieved in agriculture in general in Hellenistic Greece. Our evidence on the point is very poor and the opinions of modern scholars differ widely. Jardé, for instance, sees no progress, while Heichelheim takes a much more favourable view. I am inclined to side with the former rather than with the latter. I may adduce some facts, and first as regards the production of corn.

Agricultural Implements and Methods. To begin with agricultural implements: these appear to have remained in Hellenistic Greece the same as they had been in the Classical period. We have some evidence about the plough.[141] It would seem from representations of it on vases and coins and from the few existing descriptions that no essential changes had been made in its design and construction since the days of Hesiod. There is evidence of some partial improvements for the first time in the late Hellenistic period in Italy. It is interesting to note that the iron ploughshare (ὖνις, *vomer*), the only part of the plough that was not made of wood, is not mentioned by Hesiod and very rarely in later authors, and it appears highly probable that it was not in common use in Greece even in Hellenistic times. In Italy, I may observe, it was the essential feature in the plough, but in the light soil of Greece it would seem not to have been indispensable. Nor can we record any progress or important change in the methods of cultivation. The biennial system—sown and fallow land alternating (in Greek ἀροῦν τὴν γῆν ἐναλλάξ), the fallow land being sometimes sown with light leguminous crops—remained the traditional and general system of cultivation. The triennial system, the so-called 'three-fields' system, with rotation of crops, was not in common use and is not mentioned in our texts, except perhaps by Xenophon.*[142] Nor were there notable changes in the methods of preparing the land for sowing, in the traditional system of manuring (though the importance of the matter was discussed by Theophrastus and improvements in it were possible and desirable), or in the reaping and threshing of corn. More attention may have been paid by progressive farmers to seed corn (selection of the best grain and use of foreign varieties), and to the cultivation of new plants (for example lucern, above, p. 1163). In some fertile parts of Greece even the 'two crops a year' system ($\delta\iota\sigma\pi\iota\rho\epsilon\hat{\iota}\nu$) was practised. But this was exceptional.[143]

No general conclusions, however, are justified. Improvements in agricultural technique and in the methods of growing annual crops may have been adopted in the richer parts of Greece and on estates of the more progressive farmers. But the general character of agriculture can hardly have been essentially changed by these partial improvements. It was dictated by the nature of the land, to which the Greeks adapted themselves with great skill. Primitive as the methods were, they were the best possible, and the Greeks applied them with patience and tenacity.

Corn-growing. A large part of the territory of Greece was sown with corn (barley and wheat). Next in importance to corn were the vines and the olive plantations. We are unable to say whether the area planted with vines and olive-trees increased or decreased in the Hellenistic period. It could not be extended indefinitely. The market for wine and olive-oil was limited, for local production both in Greece and in the monarchies of the East competed with imported supplies. Moreover, it was natural that corn production should always remain the principal concern of peasants who sought in the first place to satisfy the needs of their families and live-stock. Nor was corn production unprofitable on larger estates: the market for oil and wine was unstable, while there always was a local demand for wheat and barley. At moments of food shortage and of scanty imports such as occurred frequently in Greek history, when prices of home-grown corn were very

* *Oec.* xvi. 12–15.

high, the production of corn was much more profitable than that of wine and oil.

Viticulture. The cultivation of vines was highly elaborate. It would be very instructive to compare the casual remarks on their cultivation made by Theophrastus in his two treatises with the stipulations imposed by landowners on tenants in certain leases of vineyards chiefly of the fourth century B.C., such as the contract regarding the sacred land of Arcesine, which contains an enumeration of various processes which had to be carried out by the lessee in the vineyard.* No less valuable would be a careful study of the terminology of viticulture in the fourth century and of the character of various operations performed in the vineyards at that time, in the light of the much more elaborate suggestions made in this regard by the Roman agronomists and the *Geoponica,* and of the operations required of certain lessees of vineyards (or contractors for work done in the vineyards, μισθωταὶ ἔργων) in contracts of Roman times found in Egypt.† No such comparisons are here possible. In perusing the documents cited above, I have found a striking coincidence between Theophrastus and the contracts of his time, and between the practice of the fourth century B.C. and that of later times. These coincidences cannot be accounted for unless we assume that the elaborate system of vine culture as it appears in late Hellenistic and Roman times had in all essentials been worked out by the vine planters of Classical Greece and had been substantially adopted, with only partial changes and improvements, by the viticulturists of Greece, Italy, and Egypt in Hellenistic and Roman times. How much precisely was added to the original practice in these later periods we are unable to say. We know the names of many authors of the Hellenistic period who published special treatises on viticulture or dealt with it in their general manuals of agriculture, but we know nothing of the contents of their works. We may conjecture that while collecting information about viticulture and its methods in various parts of the Hellenistic world they may have advised

---

* *S.I.G.*³ 963, cf. the contract of lease of the demos of Aexone of 346/5 B.C., ibid. 966.

† The most elaborate are *Oxyr.* 1631 and 1692.

their readers to introduce certain improvements in the existing practice and that their readers may have done so. I may quote, for example, the instance of Chaereas, the Athenian, who was apparently well acquainted with the peculiar methods practised in Babylonia and with some innovations made by the vine-growers of that country, for he mentions a specially delectable kind of Babylonian wine which he calls nectar;* Bolus Democritus of Mendes was probably well acquainted with the Egyptian practice, and so forth. The Roman successors of Hellenistic agronomists, who were familiar (through Cassius Dionysius) with the practice of the Hellenistic vine-growers, may have taken due notice of their new contributions and may have added some further innovations practised in Italy and Punic Africa. But all this is pure conjecture. For fuller knowledge we must await fresh evidence, which may be furnished by the discovery in Greece, Asia Minor, the Seleucid kingdom, or more probably Egypt, of new contracts of lease with detailed prescriptions regarding the cultivation of vines.[144]

Culture of Olives, &c. We have less information about the culture of olives, figs, and other fruit-trees and the management of kitchen-gardens. I need not insist on the importance of oil production in the Greek economy. Nor should we underestimate the part played by figs in Greek diet. The ancient agronomists were as explicit on these subjects as they were on viticulture. We know of several writers later than Theophrastus who had much to say about olive-trees in general, and dealt in particular with the methods of treating them. We hear also of special manuals relating to gardening (κηπου-ρικά). It is unnecessary to remind the reader of the importance of olive culture in the Italian economy of Republican and Imperial times, for a glance at the treatises of Cato, Varro, Columella, and Pliny will suffice. But the evidence at our disposal does not enable us to determine what improvement was made in this field in Hellenistic times. We have no elaborate contracts of lease of olive plantations in that period, and the contracts of Roman times found in Egypt are few and contain hardly any technical details.[145]

* Athen. i. 32 b.

I may add in conclusion that little is known about the implements used in vineyards and olive plantations. It may be conjectured that those found in Pompeii were in use not only in Italy but also in the Hellenistic world.[146] The slow development of oil- and wine-presses in the Hellenistic period has already been noticed (Ch. IV, p. 364 and n. 158).

Cattle-breeding. The rearing of oxen, sheep, and goats, and of draught animals—donkeys, horses, and mules—was from the earliest times one of the main occupations of the Greeks in continental Greece and in the islands. Certain parts of Greece were naturally adapted to it. Epirus, Acarnania, Thessaly, Boeotia and Euboea, and some parts of the Peloponnese, especially Arcadia, were always areas of large flocks and of cattle-breeding. Moreover, no agriculture was possible without live-stock, especially oxen and mules, which were required even in the primitive peasant economy. So it was in Homeric times and in the days of Hesiod, and so it remained later; and the Hellenistic period was no exception. I may cite as evidence of the importance of cattle-breeding in Hellenistic times the famous XXVth Idyll of Theocritus, his vivid description of the 'fleecy flocks' of Augeas, king of the Epeians in Elis, and of his large cattle-breeding estate. This was no fancy picture, but reflected real life. No doubt it was not the life of the Greek cities and of the farmers of Greek city-territories in the author's day. What Theocritus describes are the large and well-organized 'dairies' of Hellenistic times, especially those of the kings. He certainly had seen in the Sicily of Hiero II and the Egypt of the Ptolemies some such great royal estates where cattle-breeding was the main concern, while corn- and vine-growing were subsidiary. He was not attempting to describe a particular estate. He gives a composite picture, an impressionistic vision, under a veil of myth, of a large cattle-breeding estate in general. It might apply as well to Sicily and Egypt as to Epirus, Thessaly, Macedonia, or Pergamon. Perhaps even some large estates of private landowners in Acarnania, Arcadia, and Euboea resembled it in their main features.

It is rare to find in the scanty texts that have come down to us such a charmingly romantic and at the same time realistic and exact description of one aspect of economic life in Hellenistic times. The royal dairy is shown in full operation. We see the cattle on the land, moving from one pasture to another according to seasons;* a large staff of herdsmen and supervisors,† bondsmen of the king; their living quarters; the fierce dogs, guardians of the herds; the king himself inspecting his property; thousands of cows with their calves and hundreds of proud bulls. Then the return of the lowing cows to their elaborate folds of solid stone; the milking, done in a manner foreign to Greece, which Theocritus may have observed in Egypt; the admission of the calves to their mothers, the curdling of the milk 'for a good fat cheese'. All this is not pure imagination but a beautiful presentation of impressions familiar to Theocritus and to many of his readers. I may note in passing that in v. 117 f. we may even detect an allusion to the estates of some rich landowners, connected with the kings, perhaps the royal gift-estates of the Hellenistic world.

In such large model estates many experiments were carried out and many results achieved. I have mentioned above what was done in this way by the Aeacids in Epirus, by the Attalids in Pergamon (whose lead was later followed by Amyntas), and by the Ptolemies in Egypt. Similar experiments were certainly carried out in the Greek cities also. We learn for example from Aeschylides, author of Γεωργικά in which he appears to have dealt chiefly with agriculture in his native Ceos, that its inhabitants, by selecting special food for their sheep, overcame the difficulties which sheep-breeding presented in their rocky island, where there was no pasture and the soil was very thin, and produced a brand of cheese which vied successfully with the famous cheese of their neighbours the Cythnians and, like the animals themselves, fetched a very high price.‡ It must be remembered that cheese was a very important part of Greek diet, especially among the poorer classes.[147]

Bee-keeping. An important element in Greek agriculture was bee-keeping. Honey was for the ancient world what sugar is for the modern. Wax was used extensively and for many purposes. It is not surprising that bee-keeping was one of the

---

* Cf. above, n. 29, on the herds of Pyrrhus.

† Cf. the same note.   ‡ Aelian, *N. An.* xvi. 32.

most lucrative occupations of ancient land-owners, and large and small apiaries were a prominent feature of Greek country life. Its rational organization was therefore an important matter. It was based on minute research into the life, habits, and activity of bees. It is well known that this subject had received attention in Greece from very ancient times. The best study of bees from a zoological standpoint is that of Aristotle, supplemented by the discussion of bee-keeping, chiefly from the practical point of view, by the author of the IXth book of [Aristotle's] *Historia animalium*, a peripatetic philosopher and probably a bee-keeper of the third century B.C. Among his contemporaries were the authors of didactic poems on bee-keeping such as Menecrates, the teacher of Aratus, and the famous Nicander of Colophon (end of the third century B.C.), a prolific poet who among other things wrote a poem on bee-keeping (Μελισσουργικά). To the same time probably belong two enthusiastic bee-keepers and students of bees, Aristomachus of Soli (in Cilicia or Cyprus), who devoted fifty-eight years of his life exclusively to the study of bees, and perhaps Philiscus of Thasos 'in desertis apes colentem' (Plin. *N.H.* xi. 19). To these we may add a certain Neoptolemus. They were the source (through Cassius Dionysius) of most of what we read in the detailed descriptions of bees and bee-keeping in Varro, Virgil, Columella, Pliny, Palladius, and the *Geoponica*, which exhibit a vast amount of knowledge and a rational and practical organization of the craft. The mere enumeration of names given above shows that there was much interest in bee-keeping and that probably much progress was achieved in Hellenistic times; to the Hellenistic stock of knowledge very little was added later. The organization of this craft in Ptolemaic Egypt (where it was traditional) was certainly influenced by Greek experience, through the medium of expert bee-keepers from Caria and probably other parts of Greece and Greek Asia Minor (above, p. 295 f.) It is to be regretted that the correspondence of Zenon gives us only glimpses of his methods and does not allow us to determine how far they were based on Egyptian practice or on Greek innovations.[148]

Poultry. The breeding of poultry, chiefly pigeons and

chickens—geese and ducks (above, p. 1167) were much rarer—was certainly a common feature in farm life in Greece. Some of the poultry reared on the farms, perhaps the greater part, were sold by the farmers in the city market. I may remind the reader of several statues and statuettes of Hellenistic times representing sturdy peasants and old peasant women bringing to market, on donkey or muleback, or in their hands, baskets containing chickens, vegetables, probably eggs, cheese, and other produce of their farms (Pls. XXXII and XXXIII). But it appears that poultry-breeding was organized on a much larger scale in some parts of the Hellenistic world. Varro* refers to the flourishing *villatica pastio* of his time, that is to say, to the rearing of geese, chickens, pigeons, cranes, peacocks, fish, and certain wild animals such as hares, dormice (*glires*), and wild boars, which were kept respectively in chicken runs (*ornithones*), pens for hares (*leporaria*), and fish-tanks (*piscinae*); he speaks of this as a new venture of certain progressive farmers of his day, the pioneer being Seius. In this connexion he mentions that useful instructions on the subject of the *villatica pastio* were to be found in Mago and Cassius Dionysius, 'et alii quae-d⟨am⟩ separatim ac dispersim in libris reliquerunt, quae Seius legisse videtur et ideo ex iis pastionibus ex una villa maiores fructus capere quam alii faciunt ex toto fundo'. The 'et alii' are certainly the Greek sources of Cassius Dionysius, the Greek writers on agriculture. It was therefore probably in the Hellenistic world (and perhaps in Carthage also) that *villatica pastio* was first organized and described in detail—where precisely we do not know. The neighbourhood of the Hellenistic capitals suggests itself, of Alexandria, Antioch, Pergamon, and also Carthage, with their luxurious life and great demand for delicacies, rather than that of Greek cities of continental Greece, the islands, and Asia Minor, where a simpler life prevailed. I may remind the reader of the pheasants and guinea-fowls bred by Ptolemy Euergetes II in his palace in Alexandria. He kept there many of these birds, the pheasants being imported, and produced a cross-breed of pheasants and guinea-hens which was served at his table as a special delicacy.†

In the course of my discussion of agriculture and the con-

* *R.R.* iii. 2. 13 ff.   † Athen. xiv. 654 c.

nected branches of production in the Hellenistic cities of continental Greece and the islands, I have more than once referred to certain features which were characteristic not of this part of the Hellenistic world, but of the HELLENISTIC MONARCHIES. Agriculture was as vital a concern to the latter as it was to Greece. The main revenue of the Hellenistic kings was derived from agriculture in one form or another: from the direct exploitation of their estates, from rents of tenants of the royal land, and from taxation of royal and private land.

It was natural that all the Hellenistic kings should pay much attention to the development of agriculture in their respective kingdoms. They were all interested in its progress, and not only read and studied agricultural manuals, but consulted and patronized agricultural experts, and even themselves contributed to the literature of the subject. Among the authors on agricultural subjects used by Cassius Dionysius in his translation of Mago, and quoted by Varro, Columella, and Pliny, appear Hiero II and Attalus III, whose interest in agriculture is attested by other evidence; moreover, Pliny, in his XVIIIth book devoted to agriculture,* quotes Archelaus, king of Cappadocia (by appointment of M. Antony), who may accordingly be supposed to have written a special book on the subject or may have dealt with it in his chorographic work. We hear further that a certain Archibius dedicated a book, apparently on agriculture, to one of the Seleucids,† and that Diophanes of Bithynia made an abbreviation of Cassius Dionysius' translation of Mago for King Deiotarus of Galatia.‡ I may add that in Varro's list of agricultural writers, the great majority of those writers whose place of origin was known to him came either from the large fertile islands,§ or from Thrace and Macedonia,‖ or from Asia Minor.¶ It is evident that at least some of these authors, such as Aeschylides of Ceos quoted above, endeavoured to enrich

* Plin. *N.H.* xviii. 22; and in the catalogue of sources.   † Ibid.294.
‡ Varro, *R.R.* i. 1. 10; Colum. i. 1. 10.
§ Chios (1), Rhodes (2), and Thasos (2).
‖ Maronea (2) and Amphipolis (1).
¶ Pergamon (1), Miletus (1), Cyme (1), Priene (2), Colophon (1), Mallus and Soli in Cilicia (2), Nicaea in Bithynia (1) and Heraclea (Pontica?) (1).

the stock of knowledge collected by their predecessors with new observations derived from their own local experience and to adapt the general science to local conditions. The same may be true of Bolus Democritus of Mendes (for Egypt) and of Archibius (for Syria).

We cannot say precisely what innovations were introduced into the ancient Greek practice and into the traditional agriculture of the East by the efforts of progressive Greek farmers in Asia and Syria: by the kings on their large domains, by the holders of gift-estates, by the large and small landowners in the city territories, and by the military colonists in their κατοικίαι. The evidence on this subject is extremely poor. I have mentioned the endeavours of the kings to introduce new plants and domestic animals, to improve the local breeds of the latter, to devise new methods of viticulture, to organize the royal dairies on systematic lines, and to start the rearing of poultry for the market on a large scale. But all the evidence on these points is vague and allows us only to infer the general direction in which progressive farmers, and especially the kings, were moving in their attempts to increase the agricultural production of Asia Minor and the Seleucid Empire.

But the main question remains unanswered: to what extent was the agricultural practice of pre-Hellenistic times modified in the regions in question by the efforts I have described? It must be remembered that the little we know of the royal estates and their management by the Seleucids shows that the income from them consisted mainly of the rents paid by the *laoi*. Did the kings, besides collecting these rents from the *laoi*, also try to improve their methods of cultivating the royal land? Similarly as regards the gift-estates, which consisted of villages inhabited by the *laoi*. How far did the holders of these estates interfere with the agricultural methods of their bondsmen? When some of these *laoi* became πάροικοι of the Greek cities, did it follow that their methods of cultivation were altered? Assuming that the policy of the Seleucid kings was directed to the transformation of former bondsmen (*laoi*) into small farmers, owners or hereditary tenants of their land, are we to suppose that their change of status was accompanied by a change in their agricultural methods? To these questions no satisfactory answer can be given. No direct evidence is available.

It is, however, certain that some of the landowners in the Seleucid Empire and in Asia Minor instead of renting their estates, large or small, in parcels to local farmers, cultivated them by means of slave labour and hired hands. We may conjecture that this was the method of cultivation adopted by the Attalids on some of their estates. There is evidence of the same practice on the estates of some rich landholders in the city territories (for example Priene), and it may be assumed to have prevailed on the holdings—*cleroi*—of foreign settlers in the κατοικίαι and cities created by the Hellenistic kings, when these *cleroi* were not rented to local tenants. Such was apparently the practice of Mnesimachus and his fellow cleruchs near Sardis. Here no doubt the landowners cultivated part of their land according to the accumulated experience of Greek farmers, adapted to local conditions of soil and climate. What was the influence of these progressive farms on their surroundings, on the peasant economy of their neighbours? No answer can be given to this question. The general impression left on the student is that the estates managed in the Greek manner remained scattered islands in the Oriental sea of small peasant holdings and larger estates, whose native owners had their own traditional methods of exploitation or cultivation. And it is questionable whether the methods of the peasants and native landowners were much inferior to those introduced by the new settlers.[149]

Egypt is the only part of the Hellenistic world where the method of agricultural exploitation adopted by the new masters of the land is the subject of trustworthy and comparatively abundant information. The evidence that we possess about its agricultural transformation at the hands of the Ptolemies has been discussed in the fourth chapter of this book and in the previous sections of the present chapter, and I need therefore only summarize briefly what has been said. The changes introduced by the first Ptolemies in the administration of the royal domain were many and important. In their planned economy they were at great pains to organize the agricultural work of the royal peasants on lines which appeared to them rational and profitable, and which promised to increase production. They insisted upon systematic irrigation and careful ploughing, they enforced upon the peasants the use of the best possible seed-corn (including some foreign varieties) which they chose themselves, they prescribed the crops to be sown by the individual peasants, they regularized the rotations, they provided the peasants with oxen for field-work, they may have supplied them in case of necessity with better agricultural implements, they saw to it that weeding, harvesting, and threshing were properly carried out. Their main object was not so much a radical change in the traditional system of agriculture in Egypt—it was too deeply rooted and well adapted to the conditions of the land—as its partial improvement (for example by rotation of crops, better seed-corn, and so forth) and its systematic organization.

Very few changes, for example, were introduced in the Ptolemaic period in agricultural implements. The Egyptian plough was never replaced by the Greek model, and no wonder, for the Greek plough was very primitive and ill-adapted to the soil of Egypt. Several ploughs of the Roman period have been found at Caranis, all of the traditional Egyptian type. It is to be noted in this connexion that iron ploughshares or shoes, known to Pharaonic Egypt, were occasionally employed on the Philadelphian estate of Apollonius, but never came into general use. No iron ploughshares have been found at Caranis. On the other hand iron hoes and probably an iron pick were discovered there. The iron ploughshare appears not to have been regarded as very suitable for Egyptian land.[150] I have noticed above certain other innovations in irrigation and agricultural machinery.*

Next in importance to the great royal agricultural οἶκος, which comprised the whole of the royal land of Egypt, were the smaller οἶκοι of the principal assistants and friends of the kings, the gift-estates granted to them by the kings. We know the names of many holders of these estates (Ch. V, p. 731), but we are acquainted with their management in one case only, that of the *dorea* or *doreai* of Apollonius, so frequently referred to in previous chapters. The Philadelphian gift-estate

* Ch. IV, pp. 359 ff., and notes 155–7.

of Apollonius consisted of 10,000 *arourae* of recently reclaimed land, virgin soil which could be exploited as desired. Its holder was not, like the king, bound by a time-honoured tradition transmitted by the hereditary tenants of the king, the 'royal folk'. And in fact Apollonius, in the name of his royal master Philadelphus, carried out on his virgin land many experiments which were impossible on the rest of the royal domain.

It appears that the land used for sowing corn and other annual crops was managed in various ways. The evidence on the matter is scattered over many documents of Zenon's correspondence. Since I dealt with this subject in my *Large Estate* many new documents have come to light, and the text and interpretation of others have been amended. No one has since discussed the subject in detail, and no such study can be attempted here. A few words on the matter must suffice.

The main question is as follows. Philadelphia was a new creation and most at least of the 10,000 *arourae* of Apollonius consisted of recently reclaimed land. But there were old Egyptian villages with their peasant population in the neighbourhood of Philadelphia, and many peasants belonging to the Memphite nome and the Delta settled in Philadelphia. In what relation did these peasants, old residents and newcomers, stand to the estate of Apollonius in respect of the cultivation of the land? Did the old villages with their territories form part of the estate? Were these territories cultivated in the traditional manner after the creation of the estate? Were the new-comers to Philadelphia temporary or permanent residents? Did they receive land for cultivation from the estate for an indefinite term of years or were these new-comers individually or in groups granted annual leases of the *dorea* land, to be sown with special crops on conditions similar to those governing tenants of royal land managed directly by the crown? No certain answer can be given to these questions. As regards the new settlers, I am inclined to think that the practice was that last suggested, and that the *laoi* who took up temporary residence in Philadelphia had no definite rights in respect of the land of the *dorea*. They went to Philadelphia looking for employment and were treated accordingly. But this is no more than my impression.

But cultivation by *laoi* after the old-fashioned system, with slight modifications, was only one of the methods adopted by Apollonius. Much of the cornland was exploited directly by the holder of the estate by means of hired and perhaps occasionally slave labour, under the supervision of Greek superintendents, subordinates of Zenon. Further, certain parcels, large and small, were rented to individual tenants (γεωργοί)— Macedonians, Greeks, and natives. These parcels belonged chiefly to the class of land which, though irrigated, was not yet entirely ready for cultivation. It is evident that on land managed directly by Apollonius and his staff, and on that rented to Macedonians and Greeks, new methods of cultivation could be used more freely. Whether this was done or not is doubtful. The Macedonian, Greek, and native tenants may have been no more than middlemen who sublet parcels of their land to small native farmers.

The situation was different as regards vines, olive-trees, orchards, and gardens. The planting of vines, olive-trees, and the like was one of the main concerns of Zenon (above, pp. 353 ff.). It is reasonable to suppose that here Zenon himself and his subordinates chiefly applied Greek methods. We know that most of the vine-dressers who worked for Apollonius, as hired hands, or tenants, or a combination of both, were Greeks. But, as I have said, nothing precise is known about the methods of cultivation that they used, except for the coincidences previously mentioned between Theophrastus and the leases of vineyards of the second and third centuries A.D. found in Egypt in respect of the terminology of the craft and of the various operations performed by the vine-dressers. The same is true of orchards and gardens. I have already pointed out that, except palm-trees, most of the fruit-trees were not native to Egypt. The κηπουροί naturally were Greeks and would employ methods familiar to themselves.[151]

What I have said about the estate of Apollonius applies also to the larger and smaller κλῆροι assigned by the Ptolemies to civil officials, officers, and settled soldiers. Most of the holders of these *cleroi* were foreigners, chiefly Greek. Those who did not lease their land to native farmers but were interested in developing it and in increasing its productivity would naturally adopt Greek methods and deal with the land in Greek fashion. I have noted elsewhere how popular among them was the planting of vines and olive-trees, and we must assume that the class of γεοῦχοι of which I have spoken in the fifth chapter showed a similar partiality.

But the chief point, how far the new methods and the new spirit penetrated into the core of the Egyptian population, remains a crucial question which cannot be answered with the evidence at our disposal. The land which was held by the temples, and, especially in the south, was in the hands of hereditary tenants or owners, some of whom belonged to the higher and lower clergy, probably escaped the pressure of the government and was cultivated in the old-fashioned way. The same may be assumed of the numerous *cleroi* held by the Egyptian *machimoi*. It must be borne in mind that our information relates chiefly to the Fayûm, the creation of the Ptolemies. To what extent the Ptolemies were able and desirous to break the traditional routine of agriculture in other parts of Egypt, where it was more deeply rooted, remains unknown. Nor do we know whether the progressive methods of the first Ptolemies in respect of agriculture were carried on by their successors.

B. INDUSTRY

It would be interesting to know the importance of the part played by industry in the economic life of the Hellenistic period, what technical innovations were introduced in the methods previously known and applied in Greece and in the Oriental monarchies, to what extent industrial production was intensified by the new conditions of life and by the technical innovations, whether it ever came to resemble modern mass production for an indefinite market, and finally how far the organization of industrial production differed from that, more or less familiar to us, of earlier times, both in the East and in Greece.

I am afraid that no conclusive answers can be given to any of these questions. The literary evidence about the development of industry is much scantier than that which concerns agriculture. We have nothing comparable to the treatises of the Roman writers on agriculture. Some chapters in Pliny's

Naturalis Historia referring chiefly to metallurgy and the
dyeing of textiles are a very inadequate substitute, especially
as we are unable to discriminate between such of Pliny's
statements as are derived from his Hellenistic and pre-Hellenistic sources, and those which represent the progress made
in Italy in the late republican and early imperial times. I do
not mean that no technical treatises of the Hellenistic period
are extant. We have many of them, but they are all of a
peculiar character. They will be discussed later in this
chapter.

The archaeological material, if collected in full and properly
studied, may be of great assistance. But it must be borne
in mind that for the Hellenistic period there exist practically
no remains of industrial establishments, such as workshops
with their equipment, in cities and villages, or of mines and
mining settlements and the implements employed, in country
districts. Much of our material as regards the former is derived
chiefly from Pompeii, Herculaneum, and Ostia, and illustrates
the somewhat different trend of evolution of Italy; while as
regards the latter, with the exception of Laurium, most of
the extant remains of exploitation belong to the late Roman
period.

Nor are we better supplied with representations of craftsmen
working in their shops. Pre-Ptolemaic Egypt (including the
grave of Petosiris) has yielded many of these—invaluable
material for the study of the various crafts; some instructive
pictures of the same type have been found in Babylonia, and
the Greek vases, *pinakes*, and early terracotta figurines, in
their beautiful illustrations of Greek life of the Archaic and
Classical periods, never neglect the various crafts in which the
Greeks were engaged.* Then comes a gap. Hellenistic secular
and religious art—both in the motherland and in the East—
was not interested in scenes of real life. It devotes its attention
chiefly to mythological subjects on the one hand and to ornamental motifs on the other. The only exceptions are some
painted and carved funeral *stelae* (which, however, never
represent craftsmen at work in their shops or with instruments

* The latest Greek potters who occasionally give representations of industrial scenes are those who made the early Megarian bowls, see Pls. xxv f

in their hands) and the terracotta figurines. But the latter mostly illustrate life as seen on the stage—in comedies and mimes, and even so, though they often depict peasants and occasionally fishermen, never show any interest in artisans (see Pls. XXII ff. and XXX ff.).

We are left with the products of the various crafts, including their tools, the thousands of objects found in ruins and graves. I have frequently discussed these in the previous chapters and have pointed out how incompletely and disconnectedly they have been studied, especially for the purpose of dating them exactly and understanding them from the economic and technical standpoints. The only notable exception is pottery. But even in this field more problems have been raised than solved. Moreover, among the products of Hellenistic crafts-manship much more attention has been and still is paid by students to those of art and artistic industry than to·those which, though without artistic value, are nevertheless of great economic significance, such as various tools and implements and the common articles produced by the various industries.

Such being the character of the evidence, it is manifest that the task of modern students of Hellenistic industry is a very difficult one. It is not surprising that most of those who have studied ancient industry in general from the economic stand-point* should have devoted their attention chiefly to the better known Classical period of Greece, and that the few who have treated the economic development of the Hellenistic period† should have very little to say on the subject with which we are concerned. The only exception is F. M. Heichel-heim, who has devoted a substantial section of his *Wirtshafts-geschichte* to the development of industry in the Hellenistic world.

To understand that development an essential prerequisite is a knowledge of the evolution of industrial technique in the period. Much useful work has been done in this field. Several specialists in modern technique and science and many classical philologists familiar with technical matters have made valu-able contributions to the study of ancient technique in general and of industrial technique in particular. But these contribu-

* See Ch. II, notes 25 and 35. † See Ch. III, note 1.

tions are of little assistance to the student of Hellenistic economic history. One group of writers—most of them engineers and scientists—treat the industry and technique of the ancient world as a whole, without discriminating between various countries and various periods. Historical method is foreign to them. Another group devote their attention chiefly to the various technical treatises of antiquity, of which an important section belongs to the Hellenistic period. These treatises, however, as I have said, are of a peculiar character. Some of them are either purely theoretical or refer exclusively to architecture and military industries, especially the construction of military engines. Others are more concerned with pseudo-philosophical questions, and their references to industry are connected with experiments bearing on the 'philosophical' tenets of their respective creeds. I shall speak of these two groups in greater detail later in this section.

In view of the character of the evidence, it would be a waste of time to discuss all the crafts of the Hellenistic period one after another. It will be preferable to concentrate our attention on certain basic and better-known industries such as pottery, metal-working, textiles, building, and engineering. The picture we shall draw of them may be applied to other less known branches of industry.[152]

In dealing with the development of industry in the Hellenistic period we must bear in mind certain fundamental facts already discussed. To begin with, the mode of life remained as simple as it had previously been. Articles of clothing continued to be few and plain: nightgowns, socks, and stockings, elaborate forms of shoes and hats were still either unknown or very little used. House furniture was very scanty: it consisted of a few couches, chairs, tables, and chests of various forms. In rich houses, couches for example—the best known pieces of furniture—were real products of art, being adorned with bronze sculptures (on the legs, backs, and side-supports), inlaid with ivory and coloured glass, and covered with fine mattresses, rugs, and pillows (above, Ch. IV, n. 177 and Pl. XLVI). But in the average houses all the articles of furniture were of plain design and cheap material. Table and domestic utensils, including lamps, were mostly of clay and of comparatively few shapes and plainly made (see below on pottery). Rich people could indulge in kitchen utensils and lamps of bronze and copper, in bronze candelabra and in gold and silver plate, the last serving at the same time as the reserve capital of a richer household. Women of course were fond of perfumes and cosmetics, and of jewellery. Of the latter there were different qualities, cheap and expensive. The purchase of better and more expensive jewels was another mode of accumulating reserve capital in a family.

The large majority of the population, as I have said, had very modest incomes. Most of the working classes lived from hand to mouth and their purchasing power was very low. What they bought on the market was mostly foodstuffs and a few products of industry of the cheapest sort: clothing, furniture, table and kitchen utensils. And so it was with their few tools and instruments: poor peasants and artisans could not afford to buy expensive tools. We have seen how important a part in agricultural production was played by the small farmers, and we shall see in this section how much of the industrial production was in the hands of poor artisans.

The purchasing power of the *bourgeoisie* was greater. But, even here (as I have endeavoured to show), the standard of wealth of the average *bourgeois*, even in the periods of general prosperity, was not very high. Rich people among them were an exception. And I have tried to prove that in all parts of the Hellenistic world, after a longer or shorter period of prosperity, there set in a phase of comparative decline, more rapid in some regions, comparatively slow but steady in others. The middle *bourgeoisie* became gradually poorer. The rapid growth of wealth in the hands of a few members of the class did not compensate for its impoverishment as a whole. In consequence the standard of life of the *bourgeois*, with some exceptions, remained modest and their buying capacity rather low. We may compare for example, among the few residences of the urban *bourgeoisie* that have been excavated, those of Hellenistic with those of Roman date in the same cities, or the general aspect of these cities, as an illustration of the wealth of that class in the two periods.

Much greater was the purchasing power of the few rich

people of the Hellenistic world: the various kings, their wealthy assistants and associates, the few opulent members of the urban middle class. But we know little of their life. The anecdotes that I have quoted about the luxury of this small group mostly refer to public display of wealth for purposes of propaganda. Even among the kings there were many who lived a modest *bourgeois* life. I need only refer again to the instance of the Attalids and their small palaces on the *acra* of Pergamon. But even as regards the Ptolemies and the Seleucids, I am convinced that although their palaces and villas (Pl. xxxviii) and their general trend of life may have been more artistic and more refined than those of the Roman emperors and the Roman magnates, they could not vie with the latter in the dimensions of their buildings and in the ostentatious display of luxury.

The task with which the industry of the time was confronted was therefore as follows. To meet the requirements of the working classes it had to produce the cheapest and plainest goods, not in very large or steadily increasing quantities. For the *bourgeoisie* it had to supply better goods and in large but fluctuating amount. Here again it was mostly cheap goods that were in demand, inexpensive but pretentious, imitations in cheap materials of the luxury products used by the rich. And finally the best and finest goods were made for the few wealthy folk. The demand for these was intermittent, and we must not forget that the wealthiest households may have had among their slaves specialists in various crafts, who according to ancient tradition worked for their master, the head of a large and opulent οἶκος. Moreover in Egypt, where industry was under State control, the requirements of the royal οἶκος were probably supplied, not only by royal *ergasteria*, but also by the artisans of the country, who worked at the command, and under the directions, of the king and his officials.

With these preliminary remarks I may pass on to review certain branches of industry.

Pottery. The industry of the Hellenistic world that is best known and has been most thoroughly studied is pottery. Here I need only remind the reader of certain basic features of its history. The cheapest pottery, of which our knowledge is very slight and to which very little study has been given, was certainly produced locally or imported from the neighbourhood. This was the case, according to H. A. Thompson, at Athens, where the common ware was perhaps imported from Aegina, and it was the same in other Greek cities of the Hellenistic period, of which very few have been studied from this point of view.[153]

The types of Hellenistic pottery that predominate in our museums are the better qualities, the ware that was produced for the needs of the *bourgeoisie*. The aspect of this pottery, if compared with that of previous times, showed considerable changes. It may be divided into two classes. One consists of the types of ceramic ware, of one and the same form, technique, and decoration, that are found all over the Hellenistic world; we may call it Panhellenistic pottery. Side by side with this class there were special types of pottery which had a narrower market and were confined to a single larger or smaller region; we may call this group local pottery.

For a time, in the early Hellenistic age, Attic ware still dominated the market. During this period Attic black-glazed vases may be called the chief Panhellenistic ware. We have seen that all kinds of this Attic pottery were soon imitated in various places (e.g. in Asia Minor, Alexandria, and Italy) and made locally. Especially popular (in the Seleucid monarchy and elsewhere) was the common black-glazed pottery of Attic shapes without ornaments or with impressed ornaments.[154]

This last pottery was soon superseded in the East by a special type of red ware with a fine brilliant red glaze, called generally the 'Pergamene' or 'Samian' ware. It met with striking success. Introduced during the second century, it soon took the place of its black-glazed predecessor and became the most common ware of better quality (though not luxury ware) throughout the Hellenistic world.[155]

The finer and more artistic Attic black-glazed pottery and its imitations found rivals, early in the Hellenistic period, in various new kinds of pottery which may all be called Panhellenistic.[156] Here I need only remind the reader of those which were most popular, without aiming at completeness. In the field of painted pottery the leading part was taken by the various types of ware covered with a white glaze or left without any coating and adorned with designs of various character. Most popular were the so-called *lagynoi*, with their impressionistic monochrome designs of various shades of brown, mostly geometric ornaments or plants and implements characteristic of the Dionysiac cult. The *lagynoi* were wine bottles and were adorned accordingly. Similar were the vases of various types with white glaze adorned with polychrome designs. Some of these brands were Panhellenistic, others local, the last especially popular in Italy (for example the famous Centuripae ware in Sicily and the Canosa ware, both being blends of relief and painted pottery). Somewhat different was a very popular Italic pottery (the so-called Gnathia ware), black-glazed and adorned with designs mostly in white but also pink and yellow, an Italian counterpart to a certain extent of the Attic 'West slope' ware. It started in Apulia in the fourth century B.C. and had great success and a long life in Italy. But it penetrated also into the East, where it vied with the eastern brands of painted pottery. It may also be classed as Panhellenistic.[157]

Much more popular and much more widely distributed than the painted ware were the relief vases, imitations of metal ware. Such were, for example, the vases with *appliqué* reliefs well known in Pergamon and Ptolemaic Egypt, and especially the highly esteemed Megarian bowls and related types of pottery of which I have spoken so often in the preceding chapters. To these we may add the well-known plastic vases. The latest offspring of the Hellenistic relief vases were the vases of various forms imitating metal ware covered with a vitreous glaze. They became very popular in the first century B.C.[158]

Side by side with these types of Panhellenistic pottery there existed in various parts of the Hellenistic world local products of a better, more artistic make than the common ware. Some of them spread over a wide area, others were confined to the region of some particular city. I have mentioned above the various brands of pottery that originated in Egypt in Hellenistic times and were used almost exclusively in that country (specimens of it found outside of Egypt are rare). In the field of painted vases I may recall the Hadra *hydriae* (used mostly as funerary urns and made in a technique similar to that of the *lagynoi*), and in that of relief pottery, the many types of Egyptian faience, a combination of the plain faience of the Egyptian past with the fashionable painted vases and relief pottery.[159] Another important centre of Hellenistic faience ware was Mesopotamia. Here again faience was developing into a peculiar brand of relief pottery. This Mesopotamian ware was characteristic of the whole extent of the Parthian kingdom at the time of its greatest expansion, and found its counterpart further East in the Chinese faience of the Han period.[160] Other brands of pottery were limited to a more restricted area. I may mention for example the Pontic pottery of the Hellenistic age known from finds in Amisus (see description of Pls. LXIV and LXV).

This rapid survey indicates the many novelties that were placed on the pottery market in the Hellenistic period. The forms of the vases varied considerably. But they all go back, in the Aegean region, to forms well known in the past. Some of them were continuations of these forms, others were revivals of archaic designs (*lagynoi*, Megarian bowls). In the local brands of eastern pottery we notice a combination of eastern and Greek forms. The decoration shows the same features. In the Aegean region and in Italy it reflects in painted vases the new designs and the new style of painting prevalent in Hellenistic times, and in the relief vases it follows closely its metallic originals. In the East ornamentation participates in the artistic development of the various regions of the eastern Hellenistic world. Greek in its origin, it gradually becomes slightly orientalized.

It is interesting to note in this connexion that, from the point of view of technique, no new and revolutionary devices were introduced into the potter's craft in the Hellenistic period. Not being a specialist in technical matters, I have consulted Miss Gisela M. A. Richter of the Metropolitan Museum and Prof. R. Zahn of Berlin, and what follows is a combination of the information they have given me with my own observations. I may add that my advisers and myself found ourselves in complete agreement on all the points set forth below.

It is evident that vases ornamented with monochrome (*lagynoi*) or polychrome painting were a continuation of similar Attic vases on the one hand, and on the other of certain ceramic products of insular and western Asiatic workshops. For the last I may cite with Leroux (*Lagynos*, 1913) some archaic vases from Cyprus and refer to the Hellenistic pottery of Amisus (for the monochrome ornaments, Pl. LXVI, 2.). The Gnathia ware (black glaze) has also its prototypes in Attica.

As regards the relief vases, *appliqué* relief and other types of relief were used commonly in earlier Greek ware. Not less common in Greece, from the sixth to the fourth century, were the plastic vases made in moulds. 'However', Miss Richter remarks, 'in the earlier times the clay was always *pressed* into the mould, while in the Hellenistic times it was sometimes poured into the mould in slip form.'

And finally the faience ware both in Egypt and Mesopotamia was produced by the same technical methods as in ancient times. The bodies of the vessels were made of the same siliceous material, the 'glaze' was of the same type—a coat of pure glass.[161] The 'Anatolian' faience of the first century B.C. presents a problem in itself. If the 'glaze' be lead glaze (otherwise unknown in the ancient world, except in China), the appearance of this pottery was as great an innovation as was the production of blown glass (see above, n. 158).

Very interesting, though not entirely new, was the method of producing the Megarian bowls. Combining the observations of H. A. Thompson and of Miss Richter, I may describe the technical .process as follows. A mould for the bowl was centred on the wheel, the clay was pressed into the mould, the shape was made, and 'the holes on the inside made by pressing the clay into the mould were filled with soft clay while the bowl was thrown' (Miss Richter). In this way 'the bowl and its rim were wheel-made, its lower surface moulded. The negative impressions in the mould itself were produced either by shaping the mould on another vessel of metal and terracotta, or, more commonly, by pressing into its still soft clay stamps bearing the individual scenes, leaves, flowers, etc. in any desired combination. . . . Such methods permitted of almost infinite variety' (Thompson). The result was that duplicates are almost unknown among the Megarian bowls, since the moulds were naturally short-lived.

From the economic standpoint the above outlines of some of the technical devices used by the Hellenistic potters, besides showing that no basic innovations, but only modifications in technique, were introduced into the craft, indicate that, though there was a certain tendency among the Hellenistic potters to make the work more mechanical and more speedy by standardizing the ware produced, the method of manufacture was not that of a factory, was not a mass production of the same types of vases from the same forms by purely mechanical devices. The craft was still to a very large extent individualistic, especially in the field of painted pottery. For example, no exact duplicates of *lagynoi* are in existence. But the tendency towards mass production is noticeable. This is why the more mechanically produced relief pottery finally ousted the painted brands and why the mould triumphed over the potter's wheel.

Still more important from the economic point of view is the distribution of the Panhellenistic pottery and its local peculiarities, of which I have frequently spoken. All the commonest types of Panhellenistic pottery probably started each in one place. For a time its production was concentrated there. But as soon as a certain type of local pottery became fashionable and popular with foreign buyers, it was produced by local potters wherever the demand for it was keen. Decentralization of production became the tendency of the day, and local, not centralized, production became the dominating feature of the ceramic industry. I have shown this as regards the Megarian bowls, and the same is true of all the other Panhellenistic kinds of pottery for which there was a large demand. This, together with the character of the technique, was another reason why mass production never became a leading feature in the ceramic industry.

How the ceramic industry in its many centres was organized we do not know. It may be suggested that larger factory-like undertakings were created for the production of the ceramic containers employed in the transport of goods and in store-houses, the well-known large jars so characteristic of the ancient world. We may see evidence of this in the great quantities of such jars that are found all over the Hellenistic countries, and in the depot(?) of such jars at Villanova in Rhodes (Pl. CXII, 2). Moreover, some special brands of pottery, such as the Attic pottery of the early Hellenistic period, some types of Megarian bowls of early and late Hellenistic times (for example the so-called Delian type), some braziers and cooking-vessels of special forms, clay, and make, and the ubiquitous fusiform *unguentaria*, are known to have been exported in great quantities and must therefore have been produced in large numbers. We may suppose that for this production establishments resembling factories were organized by enterprising business men. Ariston may have been one of these. Lamps made in moulds, pitchers in relief ware, and jars, all stamped with his name, are found in comparatively large quantities in the second century B.C. in màny parts of the Hellenistic world. The location of his 'factory' is unknown. It may have been Rhodes. But on the whole our evidence is inconclusive and these articles may have been produced not in large factory-like establishments but by single artisans or in small *ergasteria* to the order of an enterprising dealer.

I may mention in conclusion that no manuals on the ceramic craft are extant and none are mentioned in our literary texts.

Lamps and terracottas. Part of the potter's craft was the production of lamps and terracotta statuettes. The terracottas, while mostly repeating the same types, were for the greater part produced locally (see Index under 'Terracottas'). The same is true of the lamps. These, it is interesting to note, from the second century B.C. were no longer wheel-made, but produced in moulds.

Glass. As regards glass, a few words will suffice (see Index, s.v.). Glass was used extensively in Egypt and in Phoenicia for various purposes. It was certainly known in Greece, but did not play any important part in its economy. Of the glass vessels—objects of luxury—mentioned in our literary and epigraphical sources in connexion with Greece the great majority were probably imported from the East. It was not until the late first century B.C. that the glass industry was revolutionized by the invention of blown glass.

Metal industry. The second branch of ancient industry, more important even than pottery and the related crafts, was that of metals and metal-working. Our information about it is of the same kind as that regarding the other crafts. The literary evidence is very poor. Pliny in his *Natural History*, in the books in which he deals with metals (xxxiii and xxxiv), gives a brief but substantial account of the technical aspect of his subject. He is much more informative with regard to the medical use of metals, their history (with moral background), and the artistic products of metal-working. This is most probably due to the character of his sources, of which none apparently dealt with technical subjects, with the exception perhaps of Theophrastus and Bolus Democritus (on the latter see below). From other sources we know that in addition to Theophrastus (Περὶ μετάλλων),* Straton, the physicist, successor of Theophrastus, wrote Περὶ μεταλλικῶν μηχανημάτων† and a certain Philon‡ a work with the title Μεταλλικόν. It is probable that Pliny's main source was Theophrastus' treatise, which very probably was similar to his Περὶ λίθων (in part extant). He may also have obtained some information from mining contractors and imperial officials connected with the rich mines of Spain. This may indicate that, after Theophrastus, the scientific study of metals made very little progress.[162]

The archaeological material is much richer. Metal objects of various kinds are as common in our museums as pieces of pottery, for instance tools and implements, parts of machines, of vehicles and ships, and of furniture, armour and weapons, horse-trappings, artistic products (statues, bas-reliefs, &c.), various types of vessels of gold, silver, and bronze, used as table plate or as votive offerings to the gods, lamps and candelabra, toilet articles, jewels of various kinds, and so forth. Some of these objects—especially the products of art and of artistic industry—have been carefully studied. The other material has been somewhat neglected. But in general much

---

* Diog. L. v. 44.　　　　　　　　† Ibid. 59 (on mining machinery).
‡ Pupil of Aristotle (?), ibid. 38, mentioned by Athenaeus vii. 322 a.

less attention has been paid to metal-work than to pottery. In this short summary no detailed study of Hellenistic metallurgy can be offered to the reader, but I may say a few words on the subject, especially as regards technique and organization.

Mining. I have already spoken of the mines that were worked by the rulers of the various parts of the Hellenistic world. A mining settlement was a familiar sight to the Hellenistic Greeks. I have referred to the description by Agatharchides of the Nubian gold-mines, and to our extensive knowledge of the silver-mines of Laurium from literary, epigraphical, and archaeological sources. I may remind the reader again of the Pontic σανδαρακουργεῖα near Pompeiopolis and the Pontic castle Pimolisa, as described by Strabo.* A fine short impressionistic picture of a mining settlement will be found in Apollonius Rhodius' vision, probably inspired by personal acquaintance with one of the Hellenistic mining settlements, of the city of the Chalybes, who know nothing of agriculture and cattle-breeding, 'but they cleave the hard iron-bearing land and exchange their wages for daily sustenance; never does the morn rise for them without toil, but amid black sooty flames and smoke they endure heavy labour'.†163

The technique of mining, and of smelting and refining the ore of various metals, is comparatively well known from a study of the evidence (mostly fourth century B.C.) relating to Laurium and of that relating to the Roman mines. This evidence has been repeatedly collected and discussed by specialists.164 Their conclusions need not be repeated here. The main question before us, to what extent the technique of mining, smelting, and refining advanced in Hellenistic times, can hardly be solved with the help of the material at our disposal. The general impression is that the basic principles on which these processes were carried on, and the chief tools and implements used in the mines and furnaces, were all well known in the fourth century B.C. at Laurium, and that only partial improvements were achieved later. A comparison, for example, of the reliable description by Agatharchides of the Nubian gold-mines with what we know about Laurium is instructive

* xii. 3. 40, p. 562.
† Apoll. Rh. *Arg.* ii. 1002 ff. (Loeb Libr., transl. by R. C. Seaton).

as indicating the similarity of the various operations in the two places.

Even more interesting is a comparison of the technical methods followed at Laurium and in the Roman mines. The most important features in the two places, as they have been minutely described by many scholars, the last being O. Davies, are nearly the same, with some differences attributable to local conditions (for instance the more extensive use of water in the Roman mines in the West) and to some partial improvements, probably of Roman invention. For example, the essential mining-tools and implements, such as iron picks, gads, and hammers, crowbars, spades, and hoes, commonly found in and around the ancient mines, show approximately the same forms, and were used for the same purposes at Laurium, in Egypt in Hellenistic times, and in the western provinces of the Roman Empire.

Some improvements in the management of the mines may, however, be ascribed to the Hellenistic period: for instance the machines used by the Romans in their mines for drainage, the water-wheels and the Archimedean pump (*coclea*, Ch. IV, n. 156). Though not proved to have been in use in the Hellenistic mines, they were both inventions of the Hellenistic period and certainly would have been used not only for the irrigation of fields and gardens but also for the drainage of mines, if needed. Further, it has been suggested by competent modern scholars that certain optical geodetic instruments of the type of the *dioptra* of Heron (the precursor of the modern theodolite) may have been used for surveying at Laurium and later in Spain.[165]

The main operations after the extraction of the ore as summarized by Pliny* quod effossum est, tunditur, lavatur, uritur, mollitur (*v.l.* molitur),' or in the *lex metalli Vipascensis* 'purgare, tundere, ure]re, expedire, frangere, cernere, lavare,'† were all, as far as my information goes, known in the Greek world and were carried out by the same means both in Greece (in the Classical and the Hellenistic periods) and in Rome. There was the same similarity in the processes of crushing the ore in hand-mills of various forms, washing it in an elaborate system of basins and canals well known in the Laurium mines, roasting,

* *N.H.* xxxiii. 69.　　　　　　　† Dessau, *I.L.S.* 6891, 1. 46 f.

smelting, and cupellating the ore in furnaces of various types, of which the most perfected—the shaft furnace—was in common use at Laurium and earlier in other Greek mines. In the process of smelting and cupellating, blow-pipes and bellows of the same design were commonly used throughout the ancient world from a very early period. The best known type of bellows was a skin with a hole closed by the heel of the operator and a cord to inflate it. Less common, if known at all, was the modern type of bellows with boards and a valve, of which there are perhaps reproductions on Roman lamps (if these lamps be genuine). It may have been first invented either in Hellenistic or in Roman times, but it appears never to have been used extensively.[166]

Metal-working: (a) *Gold, silver, bronze.* Nor were there many innovations in the methods of metal-working. There is very little doubt that the manipulation of gold and silver was highly developed both in the East and in Greece long before the Hellenistic period, and it is more than probable that the latter added very little to the methods in common use in the fourth century B.C. I may quote for example the statement of so competent a scholar as A. Lucas regarding Egypt:* 'Gold was shaped both by hammering and casting; it was engraved and embossed; it was made into thin sheets for decorating furniture, wooden coffins, and other objects, for plating copper and for cutting into thin strips to make wire; it was beaten into still thinner leaf for gilding; it was coloured and it was soldered; in fact there are few of the modern practices of working gold that were not known and employed in ancient Egypt.' I may add that a glance at the Greek jewellery of the fifth and the fourth centuries B.C. will show that Greece was not behind Egypt in this respect. The same is true of the other branches of artistic metal industry in the East and in Greece, for example the toreutic art and the bronze industry. In addition to what has been said on this subject by several capable scholars in modern times, I may quote one striking instance. The plaster casts used as models by ancient toreutic artists which have been found at Athens and assigned to the sixth, fifth, and fourth centuries B.C. have exactly the same aspect

* *Ancient Egyptian Materials and Industries*, 1934, p. 188.

and were used for the same purposes as those of the third and second centuries B.C. found in the workshops of Mit-Rahineh. The same is true of the moulds. In this field therefore nothing could be added, and nothing was in fact added, in the Hellenistic and Roman periods to the knowledge previously acquired by the ancient world. Minute study may perhaps detect some minor innovations, but I have been unable to discover any, nor has Miss Chr. Alexander of the Metropolitan Museum, whom I have consulted on this subject.[167]

No doubt in the bronze, silver, and gold industry there may be observed the same changes in style, design, and type of production as we have noticed in respect of pottery. There were in circulation some 'Panhellenistic' products of standardized forms and ornamentation found all over the Hellenistic world. There may therefore have been some important centres of production and export. But the outstanding feature was differentiation and local production both of Panhellenistic objects and of those which show local designs and continued local traditions. Change in taste and fashion is noticeable and common to the whole of the Hellenistic world. I may remind the reader of what I said in Ch. III about the tendency to produce polychrome jewellery and plate by means of inset stones, enamel, and niello. In addition to the characteristics mentioned above we may notice the general tendency to produce cheaper ware, and in larger quantities, for the use of poorer customers, to standardize the forms and decoration, and to use more mechanical and time-saving methods of manufacture. I may mention, for instance, the pseudo-granulation of the Hellenistic and Roman times as compared with the genuine granulation of the previous periods, and the more common use of moulding. As in the case of pottery, there was therefore a tendency towards mass production. But, in the main, metal-working never became mechanized to any large extent. The production of the goldsmiths and silversmiths and of the bronze workers, though it tended to become an industry rather than an art, remained nevertheless individualistic, and exact repetitions of pieces of jewellery and silver and bronze plate, except of the commonest quality, are very rare in our Museums.

(*b*) *Iron*. The most important metal from the economic point of view was iron. It was the last which came into common use in the ancient world and the most difficult to work. Though iron weapons, tools, and instruments rapidly replaced those of copper and bronze, and though antiquity in Hellenistic times became more and more 'iron-minded', the methods of manipulating this metal remained rather primitive. Wrought and forged iron were known and extensively used, but cast iron remained unknown to antiquity, though the welding of iron was commonly practised. The crucial problem of the ancient world was the production of hard iron and steel. It is well known that iron extracted from the ore by methods used for the other metals contains too little carbon and is therefore little harder than copper and bronze. It is natural therefore that early in the history of iron attempts should have been made to produce a harder quality, that is to say, to carburize it. This was achieved at an early date by very simple methods. A careful analysis of Egyptian iron tools has shown that carburization, heat treatment, and quenching, were well known in Egypt in 1200–800 B.C.[168] What was known in Egypt became certainly familiar to the rest of the ancient world. It was by this method that carburized iron, or steel, of a better or worse quality, depending mainly on the quality of the ore, was produced all over the Roman Empire.* In the Greek and Hellenistic periods the problem of steel was as acute as it was later in the Roman Empire. It is interesting to note that the best steel used in Greece and the Hellenistic monarchies in Classical and Hellenistic times was produced in the East. For the Greeks of the Classical period iron and steel were always associated with the Scythians and the Chalybes of the Pontic coast (above, p. 1175), and continued to be so in Hellenistic times. Daimachus, a writer of the early Hellenistic period (not identical, in the opinion of C. Jacoby, with the man of the same name who was a contemporary of Seleucus Nicator and author of *Indica*), in his Πολιορκητικὰ Ὑπομνήματα, probably a technical treatise on military affairs, says† that the best steel of his time was that produced by the Chalybes, at Sinope, in Lydia, and in Laconia.

* Plin. *N.H.* xxxiv. 145.   † Fr. 4, *F. Gr. Hist.* 65.

It is unfortunate that we do not know by what methods this superior steel of the Greek and Hellenistic world was made and the extent to which it was used. A careful comparative analysis of the few iron weapons from the Scythian graves, and excavations in Pontus and especially in the country of the Chalybes, may help us to clearer knowledge. It is for instance not impossible that the technique employed in some parts of Asia Minor for producing steel (perhaps borrowed by the Laconians) was superior to that commonly used in ancient times in the rest of the Near East, in Greece, and in the West. It may have been derived ultimately from the Far East and from India.

It is well known that in the Roman Empire steel produced by the Seres and the Parthians was regarded as far superior to that made in the Roman Empire and was imported.* And in fact we know that both China and India produced excellent steel in ancient times. The primacy probably belonged to India, which was certainly the country of origin of the famous Damascene steel of the Middle Ages and modern times, a subject of recent careful study by specialists. In all likelihood the later Damascene steel was produced by the same methods as the excellent steel of which were made a bar 'found at the bottom of the Khan Baba stone pillar' (before 125 B.C. according to Sir Robert Hadfield) and the famous Delhi pillar of about A.D. 300, a solid piece of steel 24 feet in length and weighing 6½ tons. This steel was probably made, like the later Damascene steel, by melting in a crucible pure black magnetite ore of Hyderabad with an admixture of the best kind of charcoal. From this Indian method was derived that of the Persians (inherited by them from the Parthians?), the charge of the crucible being soft iron and graphite.[169]

The method employed by the Chalybes and by the Lydians for the manufacture of their steel may have been the same or similar. It has been suggested recently by Mr. Richardson that the mention of the Chalybes by pseudo-Aristotle† implies the use by them of the crucible process.[170]

In any case, and the fact is important, the Hellenistic world had at its disposal certain products of superior technique and

* Plin. *N.H.* xxxiv. 145.   † *De mirab. auscult.* 48.

of better quality than those commonly used in the Greek and Oriental world. Some Hellenistic craftsmen were probably acquainted with the methods by which these superior products were made. But there is no evidence that this superior technique was extensively adopted in Hellenistic times, even by the Seleucid kings, who were for a time masters and then neighbours of India and Parthia. Was this because the technique was applicable to some special ores only and was not suitable for ores of inferior or different quality? Or is it another testimony to the conservative spirit of the Hellenistic period in regard to technical innovations in the field of industry? Or is it perhaps the case that the Seleucids and the Anatolian kings did use the better methods for producing steel, and that these were subsequently lost in the times of anarchy and of the early Roman domination?

The organization of the metal industry in Hellenistic times is as little known as that of pottery. It is certain *a priori* that the Hellenistic world did all it could to obtain the maximum output from the mines at its disposal, for metals were in great demand and the supply was inadequate. Its methods of intensifying the production of raw metals were peculiar. No effort was made to improve the conditions of work in the mines, to make them more sanitary and safer for the workmen. Progress in technical devices was slow. The only way to increase output was to employ large quantities of cheap labour. Free labour could hardly be used extensively in the ancient mines, for no free man, if he could help it, would commit slow suicide in this way. It is not surprising therefore that whenever we hear of the exploitation of mines and quarries we find slaves and criminals, or sometimes the forced labour of free men, employed in the work. Such was the case in the Nubian gold-mines of the Ptolemies, in their quarries, and in the σανδαρακουργεῖα of Pontus on the one hand, and in the mines of Laurium and those of the Roman Republic in Spain on the other. Mass production of metals could not be organized in any other way. No doubt side by side with these great undertakings there may have existed single pits worked with the labour of their owners or lessees. But we have no direct evidence of this except at Laurium. In some cases certain tribes may have carried on the collection and smelting of ore in a primitive way. Here and there this method may have been developed and perfected, for instance in the region of the Chalybes. But it appears from our meagre evidence that the typical mine was a large one owned by the State and worked on a large scale by slaves and criminals.

Once extracted and smelted, the metals passed into the hands of artisans. We should expect to find in the Hellenistic monarchies mass production of certain articles, in the first place of defensive and offensive weapons. It is highly probable that factories for the manufacture of weapons, of various implements used by soldiers, of military engines, of military equipment for troops and horses, existed in the Roman Empire and were distributed all over it. It may be assumed that the same method, to a smaller extent, was adopted to meet the requirements of the Hellenistic armies. Scattered references in our literary texts suggest that Alexander during his expedition supplied his regular army with defensive and offensive weapons, while his 'allies' and mercenaries relied upon themselves to satisfy their needs in this respect (except in emergency). It is probable that the soldiers of the Ptolemaic regular army, when first enrolled, received their military equipment from the king. It then became their private property (had they to pay for it?) and was bequeathed by them to their sons. The mercenaries of course brought with them their own equipment. In case of emergency or of a difficult war, the royal arsenals were able to provide the mobilized armies with uniform equipment of good quality and with a sufficient number of military engines. We learn for example from Polybius (v. 64) that Sosibius and Agathocles before Raphia rearmed their forces completely by providing each soldier 'with suitable arms and accoutrements, taking no account of those they had used before'. This appears to refer chiefly to the mercenaries, but there is every reason to suppose that the same system was applied to the mobilized 'Macedonians' and certainly to the Egyptian μάχιμοι. This however, was an emergency measure, and is reported by Polybius as such. In general the soldiers, when mobilized, on garrison duty, or on police service, appeared in their own uniforms and with their own weapons. The same was probably true of the Seleucid army. I may remind the reader of the account given by Posidonius of the war between Larissa and Apamea, in which the soldiers of the Syrian territorial army took the field with their own rusty arms and helmets.[171]

There is no doubt therefore that the arsenals of all the Hellenistic States—monarchies and cities—were well equipped with weapons and military engines. Appian* mentions that reserve weapons for 300,000 men were stored by Philadelphus. I have mentioned that the ruins of the Pergamene arsenals are still extant,† and that those of Cyzicus, Sinope, Rhodes, and other large and wealthy city-states were famous in the ancient world. The stock of weapons and engines had to be replenished and repaired from time to time. It is therefore probable that many metal-workers, carpenters, and specialists in leather-work were in the permanent service of the Hellenistic States, while in time of emergency their numbers increased considerably. In Ptolemaic Egypt, as I have indicated above, although there never existed a complete State monopoly of the metal-industry, metal-workers, like textile-workers, belonged in all probability to the ἐπιπεπλεγμένοι ταῖς προσόδοις, were carefully registered, and were expected to give priority to the orders of the king. In case of emergency they could be mobilized and put on State work with the greatest ease. A similar organization may have existed in the other Hellenistic monarchies and similar measures may have been taken by Greek city-states in case of war. In time of peace, however, there was no mass production of war equipment in the Hellenistic world, the needs of the small standing armies being easily supplied. I may mention in this connexion that no systematic study has been made of the abundant material relating to the various types of war equipment used in the Hellenistic armies. It is a fascinating and promising subject, which merits attention (cf. my remarks on Pls. xvii, xix, xxxvii and lvii). In the absence of such a study it is difficult to say how far the equipment of the Hellenistic regular armies was uniform and standardized‡ as compared with the very varied equipment of the soldiers of

* *Prooem.* 10.   † Note 38 to this chapter and Pl. lxxi.
‡ The contingents of 'allied' troops in the Seleucid kingdom were of course armed each in its own way.

the Greek city-states. The Sidonian funeral *stelae* which represent mercenaries show a far-reaching uniformity in this respect.

Metal-working was highly diversified in pre-Hellenistic times both in the East and in Greece, and so it remained during the period under consideration. There were specialists who confined themselves to the manufacture of a single article. In the production of larger metal objects, such as candelabra or large bronze statues, several specialists would co-operate. There was, however, nothing new in this organization. Though we have no direct evidence, the general impression derived from our sources of information is that metal-working was in the main concentrated in small shops, in the hands of single artisans assisted by their families, apprentices, and a few slaves. The output of each shop was sold to customers as a rule in the shop. In general the organization was the same as that prevailing for example in the shoe industry, as described by Herondas (*Mim.* vii—Σκυτεύς), or in the types of industry which are so well illustrated in Pompeii and Herculaneum. Larger undertakings, employing more labour, may have existed, as they had existed previously at Athens, but they certainly were exceptions. To purchase metal ware a customer went to the producer direct. I may recall what I have said about the shops of Memphis and the bronze models found in the shop at Galjub in Egypt.* A portion cf the artisan's output might be bought up by merchants and sold by them to customers either in foreign countries or in the larger cities of the same country.

Textile industry. The textile industry reached a high stage of perfection in the ancient world long before the Hellenistic period. We have evidence of this, as regards Egypt, in several specimens of linen stuffs found in the graves of Pharaonic times, and we are acquainted with the technical methods of their production from numerous painted bas-reliefs, paintings, and models representing weavers at work. Nor was Babylonia less famous than Egypt for its woollen and linen stuffs, and Persia did not fall short of Babylonia. I need hardly recall the dyed stuffs of Phoenicia and the flourishing and famous textile industry of Cyprus and of Asia

* Ch. IV, notes 169 and 173.

Minor, especially Phrygia and Lydia, from which countries it was taken over and developed by several Greek cities of the Anatolian coast, notably Miletus, and of the Anatolian mainland. Not less widely distributed but technically less perfect was the textile industry in Greece. Some centres of production were famous. I may mention the fabrics made of the so-called wild silk in Cos and perhaps in Amorgos also (above, n. 108).

The primacy in the textile industry belonged throughout to the Near East, both in pre-Hellenistic and in Hellenistic times. For example, as regards the former period, a comparison of the fragments of textiles of the fifth to fourth centuries B.C. found in South Russia with Egyptian fabrics of a slightly earlier date tells all in favour of Egypt.[172]

Our information about the textile industry in Hellenistic times is very defective. For this period we have no representations of textile-workers at work similar to the beautiful vase-paintings of Classical Greece or to those of the Roman age, especially the paintings of Pompeii and the funeral bas-reliefs of the Roman provinces. Nor have there been found in the ruins of Hellenistic cities remains of establishments used for the production of textiles similar to those of Pompeii, Herculaneum, and other cities of the Roman Empire. And finally, while fragments of woollen, linen, and even cotton and silk materials of the Pharaonic, Classical Greek, and Roman times are known, fabrics of the Hellenistic period have never been found. The only exception is the woollen stuffs found at Noin-Ula in Mongolia, which, though their date is about the beginning of the Christian era, certainly represent Hellenistic traditions either of Syria, as I am inclined to believe, or of South Russia.[173]

In these circumstances it is impossible to say what progress was made in the textile industry in Hellenistic times. Valuable light might be thrown on this question by a careful investigation and comparison of the textiles of various dates found in different places, such as the Egyptian fabrics of Pharaonic times, the specimens of Greek woollen stuffs found in South Russia (both common and refined qualities), even the numerous fabrics of Roman date found mostly in Egypt (the so-called Coptic stuffs), Mesopotamia, and Syria (at Dura-Europus,

Palmyra, Halibiyeh), Central Asia (in Mongolia, the Altai mountains, and Lu-lan), South Russia, and also in Italy and in the Western provinces. But no such comparative analysis has ever been made.[174]

The general impression produced by the poor material at our disposal suggests that spinning, weaving, cleaning, dyeing, milling, bleaching, and dressing were carried on in the Hellenistic period, both in Egypt and the Asiatic monarchies and in Greece, by the same methods and with the same instruments as in pre-Hellenistic times.

Some innovations, however, in the textile craft of the West were first introduced in Hellenistic times. We may conjecture that the unity of the Hellenistic world favoured the transmission of certain improved Eastern methods to the western and northern Hellenistic countries. In Egypt, for example, looms of various types were in use. The horizontal loom had been known from time immemorial; then during the New Kingdom the vertical loom came into use for the production of finer textiles of the Gobelin type. This vertical loom was gradually improved and became more and more adapted to the weaving of the finest fabrics. In Greece the horizontal loom seems to have been completely unknown, and the vertical loom prevailed. For a long time it retained there its primitive form, inherited from prehistoric times. Looms of this kind are alone represented on Greek vases of the fifth century, our main source of information. But, some time between the fifth century B.C. and the early Roman Empire, the improved vertical loom of Egyptian design (and perhaps the horizontal loom also) appeared in Greece and Italy. It is fair to suggest that this was the result of the technical interpenetration of the two parts of the ancient world in Hellenistic times.[175]

Certain other innovations, which may be ascribed to the Hellenistic period and attributed to the progress of Hellenistic science, can be detected, for example the cloth press known from a painting in Pompeii and from a well-preserved specimen found in Herculaneum. Since it is based, like the wine- and oil-presses of about the same time, on the use of the Archimedean screw, it cannot be earlier than the third century B.C. But it may be much later.

Great attention in the Hellenistic period was paid to the problem of dyeing in general and to that of dyeing textiles in particular. Our information on this subject is of a peculiar character. A well-known philosopher, writer, and encyclopaedist of the early second century B.C., Bolus Democritus of Mendes, a Greco-Egyptian, whom I have already mentioned above in connexion with his *Georgica*, compiled several books on dyeing, perhaps as part of his great Encyclopaedia. The exact title of this work is unknown: Φυσικαὶ βαφαί, Βίβλοι φυσικῶν βαφῶν or Βαφικά. These books had an interesting destiny. They were extensively used by a certain Anaxilaus of Larissa (first century A.D.), a philosopher and magician, author of a book similar in contents to that of Bolus, and they were excerpted probably for various purposes in still later times. And finally they gave rise to the famous pseudo-science of alchemy which began to develop in the second and third centuries A.D.

We may form an idea of the contents of the Βαφικά of Bolus from a book of excerpts from them (of the third century A.D.) found in Egypt in two fragments, one now in Leyden (*P. Leid.* x), another in Uppsala (*P. Holmiensis*), and from the alchemistic treatises of various times. These suggest that a substantial part of Bolus' work consisted of recipes for the imitation of gold and silver, pearls, precious stones, and purple-dyed stuffs. I cannot enter here into the keenly debated question of the purpose of the Βαφικά and of the excerpts in question. It is probable that Bolus collected experiments in the process of dyeing carried out by professional βαφεῖς in Egypt, and himself, with the help of his pupils and colleagues, made experiments of the same kind chiefly in order to prove and to illustrate the basic principle of his creed (he was a Neo-Pythagorean), cosmic sympathy and antipathy: 'one nature enjoys the other, one nature violates the other, and one nature conquers the other'.* On the other hand, the author of the third-century recipes may have had a purely practical object: to compile a vade-mecum for the imitation of precious materials.[176]

* ἡ φύσις τῇ φύσει τέρπεται καὶ ἡ φύσις τὴν φύσιν κρατεῖ καὶ ἡ φύσις τὴν φύσιν νικᾷ, H. Diels, *Fr. d. Vorsokr.* ii, ed. 3, 131. 6 f.

However this may be, the recipes of Bolus and of his excerptors, though not of much technical value*[177] and the remarks of Pliny on the dyeing of stuffs, partly derived from Bolus Democritus,† indicate that there was some activity in the textile and especially the dyeing craft in the Hellenistic period, that various experiments were carried out, and that there was a tendency to create a branch of learning more or less similar to our applied chemistry.‡ The trend of this activity is characteristic of the time. The main endeavour was to produce, as in pottery, cheap substitutes for costly goods inaccessible to the small *bourgeois*, who, as I have said, had great pretensions but little money. It was to them that the 'chemists' offered their various 'substitutes': synthetic gold, coloured glass and cheap stones simulating precious stones, imitation pearls, and cheap substitutes for purple-dyed stuffs.[178]

The little we know of the textile industry in the Hellenistic period, apart from the data set out above, shows that it prospered in the new world and continued to produce excellent fabrics. Our information relates naturally to exceptional products, chiefly luxury goods; it will suffice to mention the popularity of Babylonian and Egyptian rugs in Rome in imperial times,§ certainly inherited from the Hellenistic period. I may mention again *exempli causa* the careful description by Callixeinus of rugs in the banqueting tent of Philadelphus,‖ where side by side with elegant local materials were displayed those of Phoenicia and Persia, and I may remind the reader of the well-known Alexandrian *beluata tonsilia tapetia* of Plautus.¶

To the ancient centres of production were added new ones: I need only mention the *aulaea*** and *vestes* of Pergamon, all called by the name of Attalus (cf. Ch. IV, p. 563 f.).

---

* R. Pfister thinks that most of them are not utilizable and that the dyes recommended for textiles are very poor.

† Pliny, *N.H.* ix. 125 ff.; xix. 47.

‡ It was called χημεία or χυμεία in our ancient texts; the meaning of these terms is disputed.

§ Mart. xiv. 150: 'haec tibi Memphitis tellus dat munera; victa est pectine Niliaco iam Babylonos acus'; cf. ii. 16. 3.

‖ Athen. v. 196 and 197.

¶ *Ps.* i. 2. 14.

** Plin. *N.H.* viii. 196; Propert. ii. 32. 12; *tori*, ibid. 13, 22.

It is certain that Alexandrian, Babylonian, Borsippan,*
Phoenician, and Anatolian workshops continued their production on the same lines as before. Their technique remained
the same, but they certainly modified the designs and ornamentation of the goods they produced to suit the taste of their
new customers. I have cited and in some instances repro-
duced† some paintings and mosaics of Alexandria, Syria, and
Pergamon, which give a fair idea of the general aspect of the
products of their looms. A cursory inspection will show how
greatly they had been hellenized. I may mention again the
'tunics inwoven with gold and exquisite cloaks, some having
likenesses of the kings inwrought, others mythical scenes'‡
displayed by Philadelphus (cf. Ch. IV, nn. 177–179).

But side by side with luxury goods, we hear occasionally of
the manufacture and export of plain articles of clothing. A
casual remark by Theophrastus§ is interesting in this connexion. Speaking of gypsum he mentions that a ship carrying
some gypsum and a cargo of *himatia* caught fire, when the
latter were drenched with water.

But we must not exaggerate the extent of the production of
textiles for the market in the Hellenistic world. We must bear
in mind that in this field, more than in that of pottery and
metal-work, domestic industry competed with professional
artisans working in their larger or smaller *ergasteria*. It is
evident that in Greek cities the women of the house and the
female domestic slaves, especially in *bourgeois* families, were
actively occupied, and provided the household with its plain
daily clothing. The classical example is that of Gorgo in
Theocritus' *Adoniazusae* (vv. 18 ff., where her husband brings
home five πόκοι of worthless wool). The same is true of the
larger and richer households. The numerous girl-slaves must
have been kept busy. It was of course different with the proletariat, which probably bought chiefly in the market the
little that it needed. The luxury articles were naturally

* Linen, Strabo, xvi. 7, p. 739.   † pp. 376 ff. and Pls. XXXV, XLVI,
LXXIV and LXXXIX.

‡ χιτῶνες χρυσοϋφεῖς ἐφαπτίδες τε κάλλισται, τινὲς μὲν εἰκόνας ἔχουσαι τῶν
βασιλέων ἐνυφασμένας, αἱ δὲ μυθικὰς διαθέσεις, Callixeinus *apud* Athen. v.
196 f.   § *Lap.* 68.

purchased in the shops and were partly imported, as we learn from Menander. In the market also were bought the raw materials, coloured and plain, to be spun and woven in the houses. Nor was it possible in private households of no great wealth to mill and felt the woven fabrics and to dye them. This required special treatment and a certain amount of machinery, well illustrated in the numerous *fullonicae* of Pompeii. The same may be true of the furnishings of beds and couches, such as mattresses, pillows, and coverings, known to us from the painted couches of Hellenistic Alexandria and from the correspondence of Zenon (above, pp. 376 ff.).

In these conditions we are hardly justified in speaking of mass production in the textile industry. The craft was certainly more diversified and more specialized than before, as we may infer from the many new terms used to describe various classes of textile workers, as collected and tabulated by Blümner, Chwostow, and Heichelheim. This suggests that workshops played a larger part than before in the production of textiles, but does not imply a highly specialized mass production. I may quote one instance. In *Teb.* 703, ll. 91 ff. the weavers (ὑφάνται or λίννφοι) are supposed also to embroider or to make stuffs with inwoven coloured ornaments or figures (ποικιλία), and are therefore at the same time ποικιλεῖς or ποικιλταί (broiderers). The evidence, taken as a whole, makes it more than probable that in the Greek cities the typical form of production was by artisans, working in larger and smaller *ergasteria* with apprentices, hired hands, and slaves, while great factories were unknown. Even in places where special types of stuffs were produced, for example the Coan silk stuffs, we have no evidence of the existence of anything like factories.

Nor was the situation very different in the eastern Hellenistic monarchies. It is much to be regretted that we know nothing of the organization by the Attalids of the textile industry of Pergamon. It is certain that slave labour, especially of women, was extensively used by them, but this is all that we know. The same remark applies to the royal *textrinum* in Alexandria (Ch. IV, n. 332).

We have more information as regards Egypt. The organization of the textile industry in the χώρα, as illustrated by several documents, makes it certain that the makers of various textile specialities were small artisans residing in their own houses and owning their implements. No concentration of workmen in large *ergasteria*, with many looms and elaborate machinery, is ever mentioned. A passage in *Teb.* 703, ll. 99 ff., suggests that the washing also was done by the λινεψοί in their own establishments (ἐψητήρια), kiki-oil and nitre being supplied to them by the government. These artisans, distributed all over Egypt, worked in part for the king, and executed his special orders. But they may also have worked for the market. Whether home production of linen stuffs was tolerated by the kings is unknown. I have pointed out that the situation may have been different in the woollen industry, which gave more opportunities for home production. Alongside of the artisans in the χώρα and the royal *ergasteria* and small artisans in Alexandria,* the temples were still producing linen, probably in considerable quantities, for the use of the gods, the priests, the population of the temple itself and of the temple estates, and perhaps also for the dead, the mummies. Apart from certain features in their relation to the crown as producers of textiles, we know very little of the organization of the textile industry in the temples. But it is reasonable to suppose that it was not different from that which prevailed in the χώρα in general.

In this respect the *doreai* resembled the temples. It is certain that some textiles were made by artisans residing on these estates and working for their owners. But the relation of these artisans to the owners of the *doreai* and to the government, the type and the yield of their production and its destination, whether for the use of the owners and of the personnel of their οἶκος only or for sale by them in the open market, also remain controversial. The evidence, recently much increased, remains inconclusive and may be variously interpreted. The existence of large factories in the *doreai* managed by the owners and their assistants, which I was inclined to assume in my *Large Estate*, appears to me now to be highly problematic (above, Ch. IV, n. 176).

* The last are several times mentioned in the papyri of Abusir, *B.G.U.* iv.

The slight sketch which I have given of the development of the three basic industries, pottery, metal-working, and textiles, in the Hellenistic period will enable the reader of this short summary to grasp the leading features of Hellenistic industry in general: its slow technical progress and its restricted range of output, never reaching the stage of mass production concentrated in a few industrial centres. The causes of these limitations are chiefly to be found, on the one hand in local production of manufactured goods and the arrest of the development of large industrial centres, and on the other in the low buying capacity and the restricted number of customers. An enumeration of the little evidence which we possess about the development of other branches of industry would hardly add anything fresh to the picture I have drawn above.

I must add, however, that the characteristics above described do not apply to two important branches of Hellenistic industry, in which technical progress was much more rapid and achievements much more remarkable. I refer to the building and the military industries, the sphere of architects and engineers.

Building and military industries. I have frequently mentioned how actively building was carried on in the Hellenistic world. While in continental Greece few additions were made to the existing edifices in most of the chief cities, and these few were due chiefly to the munificence of rich donors, especially the kings of the period of the balance of power, in the principal islands, the great commercial cities of the coasts of Asia Minor, the Straits, and the Propontis, much building was in progress. The degree of activity displayed depended on the changing political conditions of the time, as I have adduced some evidence to show. I have mentioned the remodelling of the greater and lesser harbours (above, n. 8), the re-planning and rebuilding of Miletus, Ephesus, and Smyrna, the great building activity that reigned in these cities in the early and late Hellenistic period. Nor was it otherwise in the less important cities of the islands and Asia Minor.

In this connexion I may mention that the description by Vitruvius (vi, ch. 7) of a private Greek house of palatial character refers apparently to houses typical of the large commercial cities of the islands and Asia Minor (best known in Delos), and I may add that the names of some of the imposing rooms in such houses as recorded by the same author are all derived from the leading commercial cities of continental Greece, of the islands, of Asia Minor, and of Egypt. Such are the Corinthian *atrium*;* the various reception and dining-rooms styled οἶκοι, viz. the Corinthian, the Egyptian (i.e. Alexandrian) and the Cyzicene οἶκοι,† the Cyzicene *triclinium*,‡ the Rhodian peristyle.§[179]

Still more spectacular was the zeal shown in this direction by the Hellenistic kings. New cities, all of them fortified on the most modern principles, were built in all parts of their dominions in early Hellenistic times; in Macedonia, in the Anatolian kingdoms, in Seleucid Syria, Mesopotamia, and Asia Minor, and in Ptolemaic Egypt. Some of them—capitals of the new monarchies and other large cities—developed into vast, beautiful, and well-planned centres of urban life, and grew steadily in size and splendour. In the capitals arose royal palaces, whose magnificence was rivalled by that of the imposing sanctuaries, public buildings, and suburban villas. From time to time the kings would erect splendid temporary buildings for impressive celebrations and manifestations of their power (Pl. XLIX. 2). Moreover, they certainly built all over the Hellenistic world stupendous mausolea for themselves and their ancestors, in the style of the mausoleum of Halicarnassus. As examples I need only mention the mausoleum of Alexander and the Ptolemies in Alexandria, the funeral monument of the Seleucids near Antioch, and that of Antiochus II near Ephesus (Behlevi) (Pl. LII. 1), and the majestic shrine of the dynasty of Commagene. Not content with building new cities and temples, the Hellenistic kings applied themselves to rebuilding those which already existed, mostly on Greek lines. I have given many instances of this (for example Damascus).

While actively engaged in building, the kings and the Greek cities were also (as I have said) improving the road systems of their territories, and making life easy and comfortable in the cities by keeping the streets in good repair, by constructing

* Vitr. vi. 3. 1.·   † Ibid. 3, 9 f.   ‡ Ibid. 7. 3.   § Ibid.

excellent aqueducts, and by devising efficient drainage systems. But very little remains of what they effected. The Roman Empire with its still grander constructions obliterated most of the achievements of Hellenistic times. But the little that survives and the literary and epigraphical evidence referring to what has disappeared, enable us to visualize the feverish activity in building that reigned throughout the Hellenistic world, almost without interruption, but shifting from place to place according to political vicissitudes. I may adduce two instances—the history of the building of Philadelphia, the modest village in the Fayûm, as reflected in Zenon's correspondence, and the well-known history of Pergamon and its great royal *acra*. The economic importance of this activity must not be minimized. Hundreds of architects (in which term the ancients included engineers) and thousands—probably scores of thousands—of skilled and unskilled workers were employed by the cities and the kings. We have some records on this point in the literary evidence and in the inscriptions of Miletus and Delos. Vast sums were spent on building materials and labour. The exploitation of mines, of quarries, and of forests, the metal industry, the carpenters' craft, the work of sculptors, painters, and mosaicists, and so forth, were all stimulated by it.

The same *mutatis mutandis* may be said of the war industry of Hellenistic times. The Hellenistic kings were incessantly struggling for hegemony or for independence, the Greek independent cities were making strenuous efforts to preserve their political liberty. Success depended not only on man-power, on the military training of the armies, and on skilful leadership; it was closely connected also with the improvement of the technical side of warfare, with the adoption of new devices in the military art. I may recall the role of elephants in the Hellenistic armies, those 'tanks' of antiquity, the revival by the Seleucids of 'armoured cars', scythed war-chariots, the incorporation in their cavalry of mailed horsemen, *cataphractarii*, borrowed from the Persians by the Seleucids. These innovations were accompanied by efforts to improve offensive and defensive weapons, and especially to perfect so far as possible the siege-engines and the artillery inherited from their predecessors. All this of course stimulated war industry. Money was spent as lavishly on war preparations as on building. Scores of military engineers were occupied in designing and constructing new types of military engines, and many workmen were employed for the purpose. The same *mutatis mutandis* applied to the navies of the period.

The kings and cities naturally did their utmost to secure the services of the best specialists available and certainly did not hesitate to remunerate them correspondingly. This stimulated the 'architects', who vied with each other in inventing ever new devices and in constructing engines of ever greater efficiency. In this respect the history of the siege of Rhodes by Demetrius Poliorcetes, as related by Vitruvius, is very instructive. He tells of the competition during the siege between Callias of Aradus and Diognetus of Rhodes, the architect of the city, 'who received from the State as honorarium a fixed salary proportionate to his professional skill'.* Callias temporarily defeated his rival and secured his post from the city by demonstrating in a public lecture a new type of revolving crane intended to lift the enemy's siege engines and remove them within the city.

It is accordingly not surprising that the two crafts of architecture and engineering and their representatives occupied a special position among the other crafts and craftsmen, that there existed a much closer collaboration between science and technique in these crafts than in other branches of industry, and that progress in their technical devices was more rapid and more continuous. A few words may be said on these three points.

A vivid picture of an ideal architect and engineer has been drawn by Vitruvius, one of the greatest men of this profession. He was a contemporary of the Roman civil wars, who in his old age, after a long life spent as a practical architect and engineer in the service of the State, wrote his books on architecture and dedicated them to C. Caesar (Augustus), probably some time before 27 B.C. In this work he set a very high standard for a man of his craft, as high as that set by his contemporary Cicero for an orator. According to Vitruvius

* Vitr. x. 16. 3f.

an architect, in addition to a wide experience of his own craft, should possess a good general education and especially a thorough grasp of certain branches of learning closely related to that craft. Such, according to him, were philosophy, law, and exact science, chiefly mathematics, mechanics, astronomy, physical science, and medicine. Moreover he required from the ideal architect a high moral standard and a lofty conception of his task.

Was this ideal architect of Vitruvius a creation of the author's imagination, and was the social position of an architect in fact much lower than he would lead us to suppose? In view of what has been said above, I am inclined to think that the profession of an architect was in fact regarded as much higher than that of an ordinary craftsman, and that his responsibility and the qualities required of him were accordingly of quite a different standard. I am moreover of opinion that Vitruvius did not create his picture of an ideal architect, but inherited it from the Hellenistic period; in other words, that the profession of an architect ranked as high in Hellenistic as in Roman times.

One of the most salient features in the picture drawn by Vitruvius is his insistence on a harmonious co-operation, in the exercise of the architect's functions, between science and learning on the one hand and his practical craft on the other. This I regard again as borrowed by him from his Hellenistic predecessors. In Hellenistic times such a co-operation was a fact, not a *pium desiderium*. It must be remembered that many of the greatest scientists of this age were at the same time ingenious inventors of various machines, most of them designed for use in building and in military engineering. I need only mention the names of a few leading men in this sphere: Ctesibius of Alexandria, a contemporary of Philadelphus, his successor and contemporary Philon of Byzantium, and Archimedes of Syracuse, one of the greatest mathematicians of all time. By their theoretical research they prepared the ground for the invention of new, and the improvement of old, machines. But they were also inventors themselves. Their theoretical studies in the field of mechanics, air and steam pressure, and torsion led them to the construction of various engines, some of which never went beyond the stage of models, while others rendered great services to their contemporaries and to posterity: besides siege and other military engines may be mentioned the screw of Archimedes, which was adapted to divers purposes (already described), the force-pump, the water-clock, the water-organ, the hodometer, automata of certain kinds, and so on.

The tradition established by these great scientists was kept alive by their contemporaries and successors, some of them professional constructors of machines and architects. To the Hellenistic period certainly belongs Biton of Pergamon, a constructor of catapults and a contemporary of Attalus I; while Heron of Alexandria, Vitruvius, Athenaeus, and Apollodorus lived in the time of the Roman Empire (the dates of Heron and Athenaeus are controversial).[180]

Architects and engineers were very popular in the Hellenistic world. Not only did they enjoy the protection of the State, but they were stimulated by a constant contact with theoretical science, were employed on great constructions (some of them included among the 'marvels of the world'), and were connected with spectacular and famous events. Many of them took care to secure the eternity of their fame by describing their achievements in their own writings.

As regards architects proper, Vitruvius in his seventh book (Preface, 11 ff.) enumerates twenty-four authors of the Classical and Hellenistic periods whose works he has read and used. All of them were practical architects. The majority described their own celebrated buildings, some dealt with the art of architecture in general and with certain theoretical questions. Of those of the Hellenistic period the best known are Pytheus (late fourth century B.C.) and Hermogenes (second century B.C.),* both associated with famous buildings of Asia Minor, in part still extant.

Some other great architects were not writers. Nevertheless their names were widely known and were recorded in contemporary literature and documents. Such for example were the two great architects connected with the early days of Alexandria: Deinocrates, who laid out the city, and Sostratus,

* Above, pp. 179 and 824.

who built its glorious Pharos.* I may add Archias of Corinth, the resourceful builder of the giant ship Syracosia-Alexandris of Hieron II, who carried out his work under the supervision of Archimedes.† But the names of many great architects whose work we know and admire have not been handed down to us, such as those who planned the hundreds of new cities in the Hellenistic world, those who covered the *acra* of Pergamon with noble buildings and erected various other great edifices of Asia Minor.

Nor were the military engineers less celebrated. Of these again some were also authors, and I have named above those whose works are extant. To them we may add the twelve authors of works styled περὶ μηχανημάτων enumerated by Vitruvius in his seventh book. All of them were famous practical engineers. With some of them Vitruvius deals in greater detail in his history of military engineering (Bk. x), and their names reappear in the so-called *Laterculi Alexandrini*.¹⁸¹ These are mostly connected with the famous sieges of the Hellenistic period: those of Byzantium by Philip (Polyeidus), of Tyre and other fortified cities by Alexander (Diades and Charias),‡ of Rhodes by Demetrius Poliorcetes (Diognetus and Callias on the side of Rhodes, Epimachus and Epicrates (?) on that of Demetrius), of Chios, of Apollonia (Tryphon), of Massilia.§ But here again how many names of eminent engineers are unknown to us, though we know their works! I may mention for example the fine aqueducts of various Greek cities, of which the best known and most thoroughly studied is the recently excavated aqueduct of Pergamon.¹⁸²

I cannot enter into an analysis of the technical achievements of the Hellenistic architects and engineers. This has been done repeatedly by competent modern scholars, whose conclusions I am unable to set forth intelligently for lack of special knowledge of mechanics. The technical facilities at the disposal of ancient engineers and architects were not very numerous. Steam pressure though theoretically known was never, and air pressure very seldom, utilized in the machines that they constructed. Electricity was unknown.

* Above, p. 398, fig. 3.   † Athen. v. 206 d and f.
‡ Vitr. x. 13, 1 ff.   § Ibid. 16, 1 ff.

And yet by skilful combination of lever, balance, steelyard, winch, roller, wheels (including the toothed and the tread-wheel), pulley, screw, inclined plane, capstan, &c., they achieved, by ingenuity and careful calculation, remarkable results.

It is interesting again to note the striking difference between the building and military engineering crafts and the other τέχναι discussed above. While in the former the combination of science and τέχνη was taken for granted and yielded striking results, in the latter it was experience, not scientifically conducted experiments, that governed practice. It is sufficient to compare the attitude of Varro to the beginnings of scientific agriculture, as represented by the works of Theophrastus, with that of his contemporary Vitruvius to theoretical mechanics, though perhaps as regards the craft of architecture they may have been in complete agreement. Are we to attribute this difference to the brilliant progress made by theoretical mechanics in Hellenistic times, while biological science was neglected and sterile after Theophrastus' day and chemistry was not even born? Or are we to suppose that mechanics was stimulated by the demand for improved methods in the building and engineering crafts, whereas there was no similar incentive in the field of agriculture and industry? Modern technical improvements in agriculture and industry are due to the steadily growing demand for agricultural products and the consequent need for mass production. I have shown above that no such steady increase in consumption is to be observed in the Hellenistic world. Nor was the labour problem ever really acute. The supply of cheap labour alike of free men, serfs, and slaves, was plentiful, with a few local exceptions. It was not slavery that made it abundant and cheap. It was the general conditions of the labouring classes as I have described them in previous pages. In such conditions no urgent need was felt for machinery and other technical improvements either in agriculture or in industry. Production, primitive and limited as it was, met the needs of the population and yielded a satisfactory return to the producers. We hear nothing of over-production or of keen competition in agriculture and industry during the Hellenistic period. But the situation was quite different, as we have seen, in the building and engineering crafts. Here demand was active and steady, and competition was keen.[183]

C. TRADE AND BANKING

When we speak of the trade of the Hellenistic world[184] we must distinguish between two kinds of trade. One was the internal trade of the Hellenistic system of States, whether local trade, trade between different parts of the same State, or trade between different States belonging to that system. The other was that of the Hellenistic world with States and regions outside that system; this we may call foreign trade.

As regards the latter a few preliminary remarks are required, for the subject is variously understood by modern scholars. The most important foreign trade of the Hellenistic world was carried on with the highly civilized States, its neighbours in the east and south, and in the west. They were all politically independent and all had their own peculiar religion, constitution, civilization, and social and economic structure. On the other hand, they were all subject to Hellenistic influence in varying degrees. Some modern scholars therefore are inclined to include these States, especially from an economic standpoint, in the Hellenistic world, and to treat them in this respect as constituent parts of it. I cannot share their view.

In my opinion trade with India, Parthia, and the south Arabian States was foreign trade for the Hellenistic world no less than trade with the Illyrians, Thracians, Celts, Sarmatians, and Scythians in Europe, or with the Libyans, Nubians, and Ethiopians in Africa. It was trade with States and nations of a quite different, though more or less hellenized, civilization and political, economic, and social structure.

Somewhat different and exceptional were the trade relations of the Greek Hellenistic States with the Italians, their neighbours and later their masters. While in the fourth and third centuries B.C. the relations between Italy and the Greek States were much less close than they had been, and the economic structure of Italy diverged ever more widely from that of the Greek and Hellenistic world, in the second and first centuries B.C. Italy, though retaining its original and peculiar social and economic structure, remodelled certain branches of its economy on Hellenistic patterns, so that in some respects Italian economic organization may appear to the observer as Hellenistic. But this remodelling never went very far and never affected the traditional foundations of Italian economic life. On the other hand, the political connexion between Italy and the Hellenistic world became increasingly close, and more and more tracts of Hellenistic territory came under the direct control of Roman magistrates. In consequence the Hellenistic world gradually became, from a political standpoint, a constituent part of the Roman Empire, and the two were bound together by ever faster economic ties. In this period, therefore, we may regard the trade between Italy and the Hellenistic world as a trade within one and the same system of States, of which States one was the protector and master of the others.

Besides distinguishing between internal and foreign trade, we may further classify it according to its character, organization, and means of transport. We may accordingly subdivide it into sea-trade, land-trade, and river-trade. The most important was that carried by sea, primarily in the Mediterranean, subordinately in the Black Sea, the Persian Gulf, and the Red Sea. Much less developed was the land-trade. Its most considerable and peculiar branch was the caravan trade of Syria, Mesopotamia, Arabia, and the Iranian lands. River-trade played a minor part and had almost exclusively a local character. Of the rivers that carried trade the most important was the Nile, the main highway for the internal trade of Egypt and for the goods of India, Arabia, and eastern Africa in course of transit to the Mediterranean. Similar, though less important, was the role of the Euphrates. In the rest of the Hellenistic world navigable rivers were few. The system of central European and Russian rivers remained outside the range of the Hellenistic merchants, though these rivers were extensively used to supply goods to the markets of certain Hellenistic cities.

I have dealt with the development of Hellenistic trade in the preceding chapters, where I have explained its character and its importance in Hellenistic economy. The few pages that I shall here devote to it will be more in the nature of a summary and repetition than were those which I have given to agriculture and industry. A few remarks of a general character on the scope of the Hellenistic trade may not be out of place.

The activity of commerce in general and of Greek commerce in particular certainly increased in the Hellenistic period. To this many factors contributed. I have drawn attention to the unity of the Hellenistic world, achieved by Alexander and his successors. The vast regions of the East became much better known and much more easily accessible than they had been. The connexion between its various parts, in spite of the political differences between them, was closer than in the days of the Persian Empire as a consequence chiefly of the uniform Greek superstructure that extended to them all. This is true of the Hellenistic world in general and even more so of its component parts, especially of that medley of nations and civilizations which constituted the Seleucid Empire. Trade relations within the various Hellenistic kingdoms and between them were made much easier not only by the improvement of the system of roads but also by the general extension of the use of money as the medium of exchange, to which the abundant, reliable, and in the main uniform coinage of these kingdoms greatly contributed. This was accompanied by the diffusion all over the Hellenistic world of one common language, the Greek κοινή, which much facilitated commercial intercourse between its various parts, and the parallel diffusion of a uniform Greek law and of identical forms of business transactions.

It is of course impossible to estimate the volume of Hellenistic trade. No statistics are available, except as regards the transit trade of Rhodes in 170 B.C., a subject which has been discussed above (Ch. V, n. 96). But general considerations suggest that the commercial turnover of Hellenistic times was more considerable than that of the preceding period. The Greek market at the end of the fourth and in the early third century B.C. showed an increased power of absorption. This was due to an increasing though shortlived prosperity, which raised the standard of life of the Greek urban *bourgeoisie* and perhaps of a portion of the working classes.

Macedonia shared in the prosperity of Greece. The new settlers in the East were for the most part well-to-do, while the change in political conditions did not bring ruin to the class of wealthy natives of the previous age. A mixed native and Greek *bourgeoisie* was gradually formed in the eastern kingdoms and probably increased steadily in numbers.

The gradual impoverishment of Greece at the end of the third century B.C. and the decline of prosperity in Macedonia, Egypt, and perhaps in Syria also, in the second century, as a consequence of political events, was compensated by the steadily increasing prosperity of Asia Minor, which persisted until the time of the Mithridatic war. Side by side with it grew the prosperity of Italy, which gradually became the richest country of the Mediterranean world. Its commercial requirements were peculiar, and Hellenistic trade had to adapt itself to them, but this involved readjustment only, not decay. At the same time, although the impoverishment of the Hellenistic territories that I have named reduced their buying capacity, it did not change their general economic situation. Their need for foreign goods continued, and they had to import, regularly or from time to time, a larger or smaller portion of their daily supply of foodstuffs and industrial goods.

Trade was therefore thriving in Hellenistic times. It had its periods of expansion and decline in this or that region of the Hellenistic world and in one or other of its branches, but on the whole this department of Hellenistic economy showed great vigour and activity.

There were, however, from the outset serious obstacles to a free, steady, and rapid development of trade in the Hellenistic world which retarded its growth and reduced its volume more than is generally admitted by modern scholars. I have repeatedly pointed out that the chief of these obstacles was the otherwise legitimate tendency of all the States of the Hellenistic balance of power, whether cities or kingdoms, to achieve by any means in their power the highest possible degree of self-sufficiency, so that the needs of each might be met out of its own resources. I have stressed this point in connexion with the Greek cities, but especially with Egypt.

This tendency gravely affected the expansion of trade.

Although, in the international atmosphere of the time, trade was free and the prices of commodities were, with few exceptions, determined by the law of demand and supply, the pursuit of self-sufficiency interfered with its freedom and required repeated readjustments of its methods. I may mention for example the planned economy and State control of the Ptolemies in Egypt. I shall discuss presently its influence on the development of both internal and external trade (through protective tariffs, the prohibition of certain classes of exports, for example slaves, perhaps the registration and compulsory employment of such merchants as were at the same time shipowners). Of minor importance but not without some influence were certain features in the monetary policy of the Hellenistic States, such as the rigid monetary monopoly of the Ptolemies with its complete exclusion of foreign currencies from circulation in Egypt and the similar exclusion of Ptolemaic coins by the Seleucids.* Such measures had been common in the Greek city-states in pre-Hellenistic times, but they were a retrograde step in comparison with the monetary policy of Alexander, whose ideas were still alive and operative in Hellenistic times. Even more disturbing and more detrimental to the steady growth and the regularity of trade, though unconnected with the policy of isolation followed by the Hellenistic States, were certain drastic political measures adopted by the Romans. They were not directed at trade, but caused violent dislocations in its development. I refer to such acts as the destruction of Carthage and Corinth and the proclamation of Delos as a free port.

A factor that contributed no less to check the growth of trade in all its branches was the general political insecurity characteristic of the Hellenistic world. I have repeatedly discussed the detrimental effect on its economic development of the almost incessant wars both among the Hellenistic States and with foreign Powers. Trade was affected by them no less than industry and other activities. To the general insecurity caused by war must be added that arising from piracy on the sea and brigandage on land. I have endeavoured to show the grave consequences to the economic life of the Hellenistic

* Above, Ch. IV, pp. 198, 656 ff., Ch. V, p. 866 f.

world of a well-organized piracy, which was never entirely suppressed, and it is unnecessary to dwell further on this subject. Finally, I may mention the frequent political and social revolutions in the Greek cities and the internal wars within the monarchies. The mercantile profession therefore involved risk and anxiety. Besides the dangers of war, piracy, and brigandage there were those due to the elements. More ships probably perished as a result of storms, difficulties of navigation, and lack of good maps than at the hands of enemies and pirates. I have pointed out that there was no progress in nautical science sufficient to mitigate these dangers. Sea transport remained slow and insecure, while transport by land was even slower.

Foreign Trade

I may now review the various branches of trade as classified above, beginning with foreign trade. The trade with India, Arabia, and eastern Africa was carried on in part by sea and in part by caravan. I have described its general evolution and the routes which it followed.[185] A portion of it was under the control of the Seleucids, another under that of the Ptolemies. The routes controlled by the Seleucids terminated, in the early Hellenistic period, in the Syrian and Anatolian ports, and those under the control of the Ptolemies either in the Palestinian and Phoenician ports or in Alexandria. The only route that was not in the hands of these two dynasties was one of the later Chinese silk routes, which skirted the northern shore of the Caspian Sea and ended in the Bosporan kingdom (Tanais and Panticapaeum). In the early Hellenistic period it was of little importance. The situation changed considerably in the course of the second century B.C. The eastern sections of the Asiatic and Indian caravan routes now ran through the Parthian kingdom. The Parthians also controlled the Caspian Sea and the Persian Gulf. In the West the Palestinian and Phoenician outlets of the south Arabian trade were, after Panium, in the hands of the Seleucids. The Ptolemies retained their control over the Red Sea routes of the Indian and south Arabian trade. The western and the eastern caravan routes from South Arabia were never in the sphere of influence either of the

Seleucids or the Ptolemies. The northern sections of these route were in the hands of the Gerrhaeans in the East and of the Nabataeans in the West.

In early Hellenistic times the Seleucids and the Ptolemies organized with efficiency their respective portions of the Indian, south Arabian, and east African trade. Our information on the subject is scanty and chiefly concerns the measures adopted by the early Ptolemies. But it is evident that the early Seleucids were not less active and took appropriate steps to safeguard the trade which passed through their kingdom.

The situation was more complicated in the late Hellenistic period. We may suppose that the eastern sections of the Indian and Asiatic trade routes were efficiently protected by the Parthians. But the western section was in confusion. Political chaos reigned in the Syrian desert and in Upper Mesopotamia. The caravans that had to cross these regions in order to reach the Phoenician, Syrian, and Anatolian harbours were exposed to great risks. I have explained how this anarchy brought into existence the Palmyrene caravan State, which gradually concentrated in its own hands the control of the caravan routes of the Syrian desert.* The same role was played in the West by the Nabataean caravan State, which grew rapidly in size and importance and became the chief clearing-house for the Indian and south Arabian caravan trade, directing the goods which passed through the northern Arabian desert either to Alexandria or to the Palestinian and Phoenician ports.†

Meanwhile Egypt, whose trade with eastern Africa, Arabia, and India under the later Ptolemies had been disorganized by internal troubles, endeavoured to restore it to order by developing her maritime connexions with those countries. I have described the measures taken by the Ptolemies in Ch. VI‡ and discussed the important results that they attained. The most remarkable achievement was the advantage taken of the monsoons to establish direct relations between the Egyptian ports on the west coast of the Red Sea and India.

* Above, Ch. VI, p. 866, and n. 152.
† Ibid., p. 867 and n. 153.
‡ pp. v. 923 ff., and notes 203 ff.

The purpose of this rapid sketch of the history of the eastern and southern trade is to remind the reader of the vicissitudes to which it was exposed in Hellenistic times, as described in greater detail in the preceding chapters, especially in Chs. IV, V, and VI, and to indicate its importance. In the most troubled periods of the history of the Seleucids and Ptolemies the trade adapted itself, sometimes with the help of those rulers, but often by its own efforts, to the changing political conditions, and never, even for a brief period, suffered interruption on any of its routes. Neither dangers, privations, nor the exorbitant exactions of greedy potentates could daunt the merchants or deter them from their business. The demand for the goods that they imported appears to have been steady, and even the highest prices did not discourage the customers. This is the more remarkable as the commodities to which I refer were from our point of view articles of luxury, not of the first necessity: frankincense for the gods, unguents, perfumes, and cosmetics for men and women, some dyeing materials (such as indigo), spices for gourmets, precious stones and pearls, expensive silk and cotton fabrics, and so forth. It is obvious, however, that in the conception of the ancient Orientals and Greeks these articles were not strictly luxuries, but almost necessaries of life, for which no equivalent substitutes, in spite of every effort to devise such, could be found in the Hellenistic world.

We know very little of the organization of this trade in Hellenistic and pre-Hellenistic times, that is to say, of the way these goods were dealt with by merchants before reaching the Mediterranean ports, when they became one among the many classes of commodities which were exchanged between States and were disposed of in the same way as the rest.

The merchandise which the southern and eastern foreign trade brought to the Hellenistic world was transported from its places of origin to the Seleucid and Ptolemaic centres of export either by caravan or by sea. We know nothing of the organization of the maritime traffic except that the Seleucids created some Greek harbours for it on the eastern coast of the Persian Gulf, and the Ptolemies a group of landing-places on the western or Egyptian coast of the Red Sea. As regards the

Ptolemaic sea-trade with India we know that in early Hellenistic times it was chiefly in the hands of south Arabian merchants, as was also for a time the trade with Somaliland. What part was taken in this trade by Greek merchants of the Ptolemaic kingdom we do not know. In the late Hellenistic period both the direct trade which Egypt carried on with India with the help of the monsoons, and the sea traffic between Somaliland and the ports of the Red Sea appear to have passed into the hands of international merchants who resided at Alexandria. I have mentioned the Berlin papyrus which throws a vivid light on the proceedings of a temporary company of such merchants of various nationalities.* As for the coastal maritime trade along the shores of the Persian Gulf, the eastern route may have been from the outset chiefly in the hands of Greek and Babylonian merchants of the Seleucid Empire, while the western was managed by the Gerrhaean Arabs.†

No less meagre is our information about the overland caravan trade in pre-Hellenistic and Hellenistic times. It is not until the Partho-Roman period that we learn more about it. The main caravan roads in the Mesopotamian and Syrian desert, with their wells and khans, which have recently been mapped and studied by Père Poidebard and Sir Aurel Stein with the help of aerial surveys, belong to this period; as do also the few inscriptions from Palmyra, Dura, and Petra which throw some light on the organization of the caravans, and the building at Dura which was used as a club-house by the caravan merchants of Palmyra residing there. Of the same date are the few bas-reliefs and drawings from Dura and Palmyra which represent caravans, men of the desert mounted police, and the gods who protected the caravans and who are shown in some cases on horseback or on camels and armed.[186]

From this information and from what we read in later Oriental texts and can gather from a study of modern caravans[187] we may derive a fair idea of the caravan traffic of the Hellenistic period. For the East is very conservative and the caravan trade certainly had its origin in very early times and persisted without essential change for many centuries. The

* Ch. VI, p. 922, and n. 202.   † Ch. IV, p. 457 ff., and n. 253.

Oriental caravan was a complicated and well-organized institution. It was a travelling State ruled by a monarch—the
chief of the caravan. It advanced slowly from its starting-
point along well-known roads, provided with wells and guarded
between one resting-place and another. The great caravan
cities, such as Seleuceia on the Tigris in Mesopotamia, Palmyra in Syria, and Petra and Gerrha in Arabia, were not only
resting-places but also great clearing-houses. In these centres
resided wealthy merchants and bankers who organized the
caravans and financed them. Their range of activity was
sometimes very wide and may have often extended to the
Mediterranean ports. But one and the same caravan, that is
to say, the same men and beasts of burden, never travelled
very far: as a rule no farther than from one great clearing-
house to another. In each of these new caravans were formed
and very often the merchandise carried by the caravans
changed hands. I cannot enter into greater detail in this
summary. What is of importance for our present purpose is
that large sums of money were invested by many persons in a
caravan, and that, in spite of various dangers and great risk,
the investors, rich and poor, probably found the caravan trade
a profitable business. What proportion of them were Greeks
we do not know. In Roman times, at Palmyra and Petra, the
chiefs of the caravans and probably the majority of investors
were native business men. It may have been otherwise in the
Hellenistic age. I may, however, remind the reader of the
many Semitic merchants whom we find in that period in Greek
commercial cities, especially at Delos (Ch. V, p. 702, and
n. 124). But this may be due to a resumption by the caravan
trade of its Oriental character in the later part of that period
and to the growing political and commercial importance of the
Nabataean kingdom and the Palmyrene State.

What the Hellenistic world offered in exchange for Oriental
and southern merchandise is imperfectly known. Early Roman
sources furnish a little information on the subject, and it may
be suggested, not without hesitation, that it applies also to
the Hellenistic period. In Somaliland the trade was by barter.
Egyptian merchants offered products of Egypt for the Somali
goods. Trade may have been similar, though on a less

primitive basis, with the Arabs of South Arabia and with the Indians. In any case, no large quantities of Ptolemaic coined silver or gold have been found in India, at least nothing comparable to the abundance of Roman coins. On the other hand, while products of Hellenistic industry have been found occasionally in South Arabia, none are known to have come from central and southern India. This may suggest that in the period that followed the secession of Bactria and the formation of Parthia, it was Bactria and Parthia that paid for Indian merchandise with their money and products, and reexported it to the Seleucid kingdom against payment in money or goods; while the Ptolemies until the end of the second century received their Indian wares from Arabia, which paid for them with its own products and resold them to the Ptolemaic merchants for money and goods.

Trade Between the Hellenistic States

Of vital consequence to the well-being, even to the existence, of several parts of the Hellenistic world was their mutual trade in foodstuffs, raw materials, semi-finished goods, and industrial products. Our information about this trade, its volume, and the demand for various commodities in one country or another, is very meagre. Practically the only branch of trade about which we have some, though insufficient, information is the corn trade. The character of this information is, however, peculiar: decrees of the Greek cities in honour of donors of corn (on a large or small scale), or of merchants who had supplied corn and sold it at a reasonable price in times of foodshortage and famine, supplemented by some literary evidence about gifts of corn by the kings to certain cities, decrees in honour of magistrates who had dealt successfully with the difficult problem of corn supply and distribution, records of measures taken by the cities to secure a regular corn supply, and other similar documents. I have quoted many of them above and drawn from them conclusions regarding the economic structure and the vicissitudes of the Greek cities. To this evidence concerning Greece we may add some Egyptian documents which furnish us with miscellaneous information about the Egyptian corn trade. About other branches of trade we have here and there a stray notice in our literary texts, in inscriptions, and especially in papyri, but from these scanty materials we can form no adequate idea of the importance of the business in question or of the countries between which it was transacted.

It is natural, therefore, that modern studies of Hellenistic trade are lacking in positive results, and nothing further, I fear, can be done with the evidence available. I shall therefore, in the following pages, summarize what I have said about the development and character of the trade between the Hellenistic States, general and conjectural as my conclusions may be.[188]

Corn trade. To begin with the highly important corn trade, I have frequently insisted on the dependence of many Greek cities, including some of those situated in Asia Minor, on imported corn, and in this respect few Greek cities were self-sufficient. They offered therefore a steady and capacious market for foreign corn, though the demand fluctuated with the quality of the crops in the city territories. The situation of the Hellenistic kingdoms was different. In normal times they produced enough corn to feed their own populations, and in addition a surplus, varying in amount, for export. This was the position in Macedonia, Thrace, the Anatolian kingdoms, the Seleucid Empire, Ptolemaic Egypt, the Bosporan kingdom, and the Sicilian kingdom of Hieron II. I may cite in support of this statement the passage in Polybius (v. 88 f.) regarding the assistance given to Rhodes after the earthquake of 227/6 B.C. by the principal monarchs of the time. All the kings mentioned by Polybius—Hieron and Gelon, Ptolemy Euergetes I, Antigonus Doson, and Seleucus Callinicus—were able, in a greater or less measure, to help Rhodes with gifts of corn (above, p. 230). The countries richest in corn and therefore able (in normal years) to export it regularly and in comparatively large quantities, were Egypt, the Bosporan kingdom, and Thrace. But it may be emphasized that in South Russia and Thrace the harvest depended entirely on the rainfall and in Egypt on inundation. When these failed, those countries were themselves in need of imported corn. The same is true of Asia Minor and the Seleucid kingdom. We must realize further that wars on a large scale sometimes made it necessary to import corn. It may be added that Italy and Carthage in the early Hellenistic period, when faced with the necessity of conducting vast and perilous wars, were unable to export any corn, though they produced it in large quantities, and were forced from time to time to buy it in Sicily and even in the East. The demand for corn in the Hellenistic world and especially in the Greek cities of the Aegean was therefore very large and irregular, as was also the supply. It is no matter for surprise that in these conditions the corn trade was subject occasionally, even in time of peace, not to speak of periods of war, to spasmodic convulsions which led to acute shortage and even famine. The intensity of these phenomena varied of course with the general political and economic situation.

I need only briefly recapitulate a few of the examples I have already given. Famines in the early Hellenistic period were frequent, widespread, and serious. Two of them have left many traces in our records, one in 331–323 B.C.[*] and another in 289/8–282/1 B.C.[†] These terrible calamities were probably due to a combination of factors—bad crops, war, the economic readjustment of Greece, and the disorganization of the established trade. The supply was apparently insufficient to meet the growing requirements of the Greek world, whose purchasing power was never so high as in the time of Alexander and the Successors. We must bear in mind that Egypt and Syria were in the course of reorganization, that Asia Minor was greatly affected by disastrous wars, and that Thrace after the time of Lysimachus experienced all the calamities of the Celtic invasion. The most abundant source of supply was therefore South Russia. It is no wonder that the closing of the Straits had the immediate effect of raising prices, and that Greek relations with the Bosporan kingdom were of such vital importance.[189]

After these stormy times the Hellenistic world enjoyed a few decades of comparative calm and order. In spite of some wars, of the never-ceasing activity of the pirates, of the gradual economic decline of continental Greece, and of occasional food shortages in the countries of production, for instance in Egypt in the reigns of Philadelphus[‡] and Euergetes I,[§] the Ptolemies

---

[*] Above, p. 95, and n. 29.   [†] Above, p. 168, and n. 41.

[‡] Relieved by Hiero II, Athen. v. 209 b.   [§] Canopus decree.

in collaboration with Rhodes,* and the kings of the Bosporus †
were able, during the period of the Ptolemaic hegemony in the
Aegean, to provide the Greek cities with a regular and comparatively cheap supply of corn. In addition to Egypt, whose
production of corn had been intensified, and the kingdom of
Bosporus, whose prosperity was very high, the fertile territories of Asia Minor, especially Bithynia and Pergamon, contributed their share to this supply as did also Macedonia and
the Seleucid kingdom. It is natural therefore that we should
hear little of food shortages and famines in the Greek cities
during this period.‡

The situation changed for the worse in the last years of the
third century, before and after the Roman intervention.
Disastrous wars, especially those started by Philip V and
Antiochus III and those of the Roman intervention, reduced
the supply, while the anarchy in the Aegean gave a new impe-
tus to piracy. Egypt's production was falling, the resources
of Syria were absorbed by Antiochus III for his wars, Asia
Minor was attacked and pillaged by Philip V, the kingdom of
Bosporus was disorganized, and the condition of Thrace was
no better. Moreover, the buying capacity not only of continental Greece but also of the islands was gradually declining. It is no wonder that we again hear of famines and
scarcity in the Aegean countries, and that complaints about
piracy become bitter (above, Ch. V). The acuteness of the
crisis should not, however, be exaggerated. Egypt's production was diminishing, but there is no reason to suppose that
there was no surplus available for export. The troubles in the
Bosporus and Thrace were intermittent, and some corn may
have come from the West, especially from Carthage.§

The corn market once disorganized never recovered. The
corn problem remained acute in the Hellenistic world throughout the second and first centuries B.C., until its incorporation
in the Roman Empire. In some periods, however, we may
detect temporary improvements; for instance after the first
Roman victories in the East, in the heyday of Rhodes and
Pergamon, and at the time of the renascence of Athens (above,

* Above, Ch. IV, pp. 225 ff.   † Ibid., pp. 595 ff.
‡ Above, Ch. IV, n. 42.   § Above, Ch. V, pp. 618 ff., and n. 20.

pp. 628 ff.), when the steadily growing and well-organized kingdom of the Attalids was making a considerable addition to the supply of corn available from other lands, and when Rhodes was policing the sea and organizing the market. This improvement persisted, with a slight change for the worse after Pydna, until the first Mithridatic war. I may remind the reader that, though Egypt was steadily losing its importance in the corn market, the supply derived from Asia Minor, which remained prosperous even after the death of Attalus III, was at this time supplemented by the Bosporan corn, which was seen once more in the Aegean,* and by that of Numidia, which now made its first appearance in the eastern Mediterranean. In respect of the period of the Mithridatic wars and that which followed, our information is very slight, but it is evident that during these miserable times the corn supply and corn trade grievously deteriorated.

This rapid historical survey will indicate the vital importance of the corn trade to the Hellenistic world. It was to some extent the backbone of Hellenistic economic life. For the consumers a sufficient import of corn was often a matter of life and death, for the producers a sufficient export was one of the chief sources of their revenue; that is why we hear so much about it. The volume of this trade cannot be estimated in figures, but it must have been very large, probably much larger than in pre-Hellenistic times. Hundreds if not thousands of ships were engaged in carrying corn from one part of the Hellenistic world to another, and a corresponding number of merchants and their clerks, of seamen and dock hands, were occupied with the operations of the trade.

Wine and olive-oil. For the corn it imported Greece had to pay. For a time it did so chiefly by exporting wine and olive-oil. In the early Hellenistic period one of the most important consumers of these Greek products was Egypt. It is interesting to see how large a proportion of the shipments to Apollonius in the reign of Philadelphus consists of them, and this notwithstanding the high tariff imposed on their import.†
Later, after Egypt had developed its own viticulture on a large

* Above, Ch. V, notes 87 and 89.
† Above, p. 227, and notes 53 and 55.

scale, the import of wine from Greece fell considerably. It was also affected by the competition of Syria (see further below). It was otherwise, however, with olive-oil. The oil produced in Egypt was of inferior quality, and all efforts to improve it failed. Most of the olive-oil consumed in Egypt was consequently imported from Syria and Greece both in early and in late Ptolemaic times.* We have no direct evidence about the import of Greek wine and oil into Syria, but general considerations make it improbable that the quantity was considerable. Syria produced excellent wine from very early times and it was famous for its olive-oil. In Zenon's correspondence and other papyri we hear repeatedly of Syrian oil imported into Egypt, and I have mentioned that during the period of Syria's dependence on Egypt in late Hellenistic times Laodicea-on-the-sea sent large quantities of wine to Alexandria.† If, therefore, Greek wine and olive-oil were imported into Syria it must have been the finest qualities, luxury commodities. The export of Greek wine and olive-oil to the Pontic regions and the Danube lands was considerable; it had been so in pre-Hellenistic times and so it remained in the Hellenistic period. As regards the southern coast of the Euxine, I may remind the reader‡ of the purchase by Sinope (about 220 B.C.), while it was besieged by Mithridates IV of Pontus, of ten thousand *keramia* of wine from Rhodes, money for the purpose being borrowed from the latter. As to the northern coast, I may mention the large quantities of stamped Greek jars of the Hellenistic period found in these regions, some of which at least had contained wine and oil. Maronea and Thasos (above, Ch. VI, n. 30) were the chief producers of the wine exported to Thrace and to the Celtic lands; this had a rival in the wines sent to the north-east by Rhodes (not necessarily Rhodian). Finally, Italy in the second and first centuries B.C. consumed large quantities of Greek wine and olive-oil. Even in the first century, when the production of wine in Italy was considerable and certain qualities had won a high reputation, Greek wine was still preferred by the population of that country.[190] In return for this import Italy appears

---

* See Ch. VI, n. 196.   † Ibid., n. 142.
‡ See Ch. V, p. 677, and n. 92.

to have exported some of its own wine and olive-oil to Greece. But the presence of Italian oil and wine merchants at Delos in the first century B.C. and the discovery there of some Italian stamped jars do not necessarily imply that there was a demand in Greece for Italian wine and oil. The merchants may have been exporters of Greek products, while the *amphorae* with Latin stamps may indicate no more than an import into Delos for the consumption of the many Italian residents there, perhaps mainly those of the lower classes.*

Fish and other foodstuffs. Salted, dried, and pickled fish, the staple food of the Greeks, was imported in large quantities into Greece, Egypt, and probably Syria from the Pontic regions and from Sicily. Some of these imports—the finer kinds of pickled fish and fish-sauces—were luxury articles, but the bulk was intended for the poorer households. The situation in this respect has not changed much in modern times, except that the Pontic territory is now replaced by Norway. I may recall that in spite of the large quantities of native fish consumed in Egypt (pp. 296 ff.), Hieron II in a period of food shortage exported to Alexandria, in addition to corn, ten thousand *keramia* of Sicilian τάριχος.† Of much less importance—if of any—was the trade in meat. This was a luxury in Greek diet, and we very seldom hear of salted or dried meat.[191] Salt, I may add, a universal need, was not produced in large quantities and of good quality in every part of the Hellenistic world, and many cities and regions had to import it. The trade by sea in salt was therefore comparatively important. I may note that in the *Cercidea* a moralizing poet, speaking of the instability of wealth, uses the simile, 'the salt cargo returns whence it came'.‡ Finally an active interchange of the finer kinds of various foodstuffs—honey, vegetables, dried fruit (especially figs), and nuts—was carried on in the Hellenistic world. I draw attention again to the lists of goods imported by or sent to Apollonius (above, p. 228).

Raw materials: (*a*) *timber*. Next to foodstuffs in importance was the trade in raw materials and half-finished products for the various branches of industry, such as building and the

---

* Above, Ch. VI, p. 790, and n. 57.   † Athen. v. 209 a.
‡ *Cercidea*, v. 106, in A. D. Knox's *Herodes, Cercidas, &c.*, p. 239.

military crafts. We know little of the volume of exchange in these goods, but the indirect evidence shows that it was very considerable. As regards timber the monarchies were self-sufficient, and some of them had a large surplus of it. I have mentioned the gift made by Antigonus and Demetrius to Athens of Cyprian timber for shipbuilding. The account by Polybius (v. 88 f.) of the gifts to Rhodes after the great earthquake of 227/6 B.C. is also instructive. Besides money, the kings of the day gave assistance in the form of building materials and war equipment. Among these timber for building ships and for other uses plays an important part. Ptolemy Euergetes I supplied Rhodes with timber (from his foreign dominions) to build ten quinqueremes and ten triremes, and gave in addition 'forty thousand cubits (good measure) of squared deal planking'. Even more lavish, being richer in wood, was Antigonus Doson: 'ten thousand pieces of timber ranging from eight to sixteen cubits in length to be used as rafters, five thousand beams of seven cubits long, a thousand talents of pitch, and a thousand *amphorae* of raw pitch'.* Even Seleucus Callinicus was able to present Rhodes with ten quinqueremes fully equipped, with ten thousand cubits of timber, and with a thousand talents of hair and resin. Similar gifts, says Polybius, were made by Prusias I of Bithynia and Mithridates II of Pontus, both of them owners of rich forests. No mention is made of Attalus I.

The foregoing enumeration of gifts of timber shows not only how great was the quantity of it at the disposal of all the Hellenistic monarchs at the end of the third century, but also the extent of the demand for it in the Greek commercial cities and their dependence on foreign supplies. It must be remembered that timber was of vital consequence to them: ancient ships were shortlived and the building activity of the period was considerable, especially in the rich commercial cities. Many other less important cities were in the same position. The Delian accounts, for example, show that the city and temple imported all the wood they required for building and for fuel, as well as all the pitch and tar they needed, chiefly from Macedonia. It has been shown by modern scholars how

* The translations are those of W. R. Paton, Loeb Library.

greatly the prices of these commodities fluctuated, and how irregular was the supply, for these depended, as is natural, on the political conditions of the time.

To the Greek cities which were consumers of imported timber we must in all probability add Egypt in the late Hellenistic period. By this time it may be supposed that the forests of Cyprus were in great measure exhausted, while the other Egyptian dominions rich in forests had been lost. Yet the demand for timber was urgent, for Egypt needed a strong navy for its protection even in the period of its political decay, and its sea and river commerce was still considerable. From what countries timber was imported into Egypt at this time we are unable to say. One of the sources may have been the forests of Sila in South Italy.

(b) *Metals.* What I have said about timber applies also to metals. I have shown that here again most of the Hellenistic kingdoms supplied their needs from their own resources. An exception, to some extent, was Egypt (including Cyprus), which possessed very little, if any, indigenous iron. On the other hand most of the Greek cities relied on imports for their supply of metals. A typical instance is again Rhodes. In the passage of Polybius quoted above metals figure largely among the royal gifts to her. Hieron and Gelon, besides coined money, sent silver cauldrons and *hydriae*; Ptolemy gave three hundred talents of silver, one thousand talents of coined copper, and, for the re-erection of the Colossus, another three thousand talents, apparently of copper or bronze (ingots or coins ?); and finally Antigonus Doson, who had the greatest abundance of metals, bestowed on Rhodes one hundred talents of silver (coined ?) and three thousand talents of iron, and his wife Chryseis added the same amount of lead. It should be noticed that Seleucus was unable to vie with his fellow kings in this respect.

An enumeration of other raw materials would serve no purpose, for our evidence about them is very meagre. But the volume of trade in these goods must not for that reason be underestimated. Much of the raw material, for example, needed for the textile industry was of course produced in the immediate neighbourhood of the places where it was spun and woven; but some was imported. Flax was not grown in very many regions, and the wool of certain parts of the Hellenistic world was of inferior quality. I have mentioned the efforts made by the early Ptolemies to improve Egyptian wool (by importing Arabian and Milesian sheep, pp. 357 f.). Meanwhile a superior quality for the use of the Greeks of Alexandria and of the χώρα was brought to Egypt from abroad. It is not surprising therefore to learn that Hieron II sent 'twenty thousand talents of wool' to Philadelphus in his 'Syracosia'. In many Hellenistic countries the supply of hemp (and its substitutes) and of hides was insufficient to meet local requirements.

Finally I should mention that of the goods exported from India, Arabia, and east Africa, some reached the Aegean and Italian markets as finished industrial products (unguents, perfumes, cosmetics, jewels), but others were sold in Greece and Italy in the form in which they were exported from their places of origin.

Manufactured articles. A few words about the trade in manufactured goods will suffice. It was never important in Hellenistic times. The need for these in any given place, as I have shown, was met either by production in the home or by local artisans. A few things were imported from the immediate neighbourhood and from more distant places within the territory of the State.

There were of course some exceptions to this rule. Certain products of industry were peculiar to a given place or region and no equivalent substitutes for them were available. Such were, among goods in common use, the Egyptian papyrus and its rival the parchment of Syria and Pergamon; and there were likewise certain special luxury products. Among these I may name, as examples, the purple-dyed stuffs of Phoenicia; the rugs and carpets of Persia, Babylonia, Lydia, and Egypt; hangings, pillows, and dresses of special make produced in Pergamon; special kinds of dyed woollens from Asia Minor; Coan and perhaps Amorgan silk dresses; fine woollen frocks of Tarentine manufacture; and so forth. To these we may add Egyptian and Syrian (?) glass and faience, certain special types of silver and gold plate, of jewels, and of furniture, and several articles made chiefly in Syria and Egypt from raw materials imported from foreign countries, especially from India, Persia, south Arabia, and east Africa: unguents, perfumes, cosmetics, objects manufactured from rare woods and ivory, jewels and plate ornamented with precious stones, gems, silk and cotton stuffs, &c. A few articles actually manufactured in India and Persia were also brought to Greece and Italy, probably as curiosities.[192]

Finally, from time to time, as we have seen, new types of manufactured products, such as new kinds of pottery, were started in some industrial centre, became fashionable in other Hellenistic States, and were exported to these. But no sooner were these articles placed on the market than they were everywhere imitated and produced locally. The trade in manufactured goods between the Hellenistic States was therefore comparatively little developed. It was chiefly a trade in luxury articles for which the demand was small and irregular.

Slaves. Much more important was the traffic in slaves both among the Hellenistic States and with other countries. Modern scholars, recoiling from the grossly exaggerated and untenable Marxian doctrine regarding the role of slavery in ancient times, are inclined to minimize the numbers of slaves and the part played by them in pre-Hellenistic Greek economy. It must be emphasized, however, that antiquity was unanimous in believing that slaves were very numerous in the ancient city-states of Greece, though the figures which they occasionally give of the slave population of some of the larger Greek cities in the fifth and fourth centuries are, in all cases, probably exaggerated; but this question cannot be discussed here. Nor was slavery of various kinds unknown in the East. The number of slaves in the Persian kingdom cannot even be conjectured.

In any case the Hellenistic States, whether city-states or kingdoms, inherited large numbers of slaves from the past. These numbers did not decline in the early Hellenistic times. War and piracy, though the former was more humane than it had been, supplied the slave market with a multitude of prisoners of war and victims of kidnapping,* and the trade in slaves with the North certainly continued as active as in earlier days.

* See Ch. IV, pp. 195 f., 202 ff., and notes 24 ff.

There may have been some diminution in the number of human beings sold in the slave markets during the period of the balance of power, when wars were conducted with the same relative humanity as in the time of the Successors; and piracy, though it survived, was to a certain extent checked by the efforts of the Ptolemies and the Rhodians.* But with the end of the third century, when warfare became once more as cruel and ruthless as ever, when the practice was resumed of selling the entire population of cities and regions into slavery, and when piracy flourished as never before, slaves appeared again on the market in vast numbers.†

In the early part of our period the supply of slaves offered on the Hellenistic markets was absorbed chiefly by the Greek city-states and by the new kingdoms. With the intervention of Rome in the affairs of the East, a new buyer appeared in the eastern part of the Mediterranean. Rome in the second half of the second and in the first century B.C. reorganized her economic life. Labour was scarce in Italy after the Punic wars, and the more systematic and more modern organization of agriculture, grazing, and industry (especially mining) now introduced by Roman and Italian capitalists, as well as the more luxurious character which Italian domestic life now assumed, called for a large amount of labour, both skilled and unskilled. The demand for slaves in the West became therefore considerable. Part of the supply came from the West, but the best, the more civilized and more docile slaves, were shipped to Italy from the East.

These conditions naturally led to a rapid increase in the second and especially in the first century B.C. in the demand and supply of slaves. Greece, especially the large trading cities, was still in need of slaves, though its buying capacity was declining; Asia Minor and particularly the Pergamene monarchy absorbed large numbers of them; and in addition there came the large and ever-growing demand of the West. This spurred the enterprise of slave merchants, and made the traffic in slaves one of the chief features of the international trade of the late Hellenistic world (see Ch. VI).

* Ch. IV, p. 207, n. 32; and Ch. V, notes 23, 27, and 30.
† Ibid., notes 23, 27, and 30; cf. Ch. VI, n. 49.

The slave trade was thus a prominent element in Hellenistic economy at all periods of its development. The demand for slaves varied in intensity from time to time and from place to place, but it was always large in the Hellenistic countries. I may be a little more specific on this subject.

In the Greek cities slaves were an important factor in all departments of economic life. The cities employed large numbers of them as public servants of various kinds (δημόσιοι) and as labourers in their mines, their building operations, their mints, and so forth. The temples also owned slaves. Slaves furnished the domestic labour in all the richer households. Every artisan and shopkeeper employed slaves if he could afford to buy them, and landowners did the same.

In the Hellenistic monarchies the Greek portion of the population—the kings, the aristocracy and bureaucracy, the plain *bourgeois* and the craftsmen of all kinds—owned slaves. I may mention by way of example the large number of slaves in the household of Apollonius, the *dioecetes*, in Alexandria, and those whom he and his assistants purchased in Syria and Palestine. I may also refer again to the painted funeral *stelae* of soldiers of early Hellenistic times found in Alexandria and Sidon (Pls. XIX and XXXVII), which constantly show the deceased on foot or on horseback accompanied by a servant, in all probability a slave. We may infer that the mercenaries, and probably also the soldiers of the territorial army, had each of them at least one slave attendant. In addition, all the Hellenistic kings made extensive use of servile labour in certain departments of their economic activity, for example the mines.

But the importance of slave labour and the policy of the Hellenistic monarchs in regard to it varied from country to country. The Ptolemies never favoured slavery. They checked the importation of slaves by special regulations and imposed heavy taxes on slave-owners.* Moreover, the peculiar organization of agriculture and industry in Ptolemaic Egypt almost excluded slave labour, and the Ptolemies had no wish to see foreign slaves competing with native labour in these spheres. The situation may have been somewhat different in the

* p. 321 f., and n. 119.

Seleucid Empire. Slavery was an established institution in Babylonia in pre-Hellenistic times and remained so under the Seleucids, as shown by a special tax (ἀνδραποδική) levied in Babylonia, whatever the character and the scope of this tax may have been.* It is reasonable to suppose that the same was true of the large Phoenician cities. But apparently in the rest of the Seleucid Empire, as in Ptolemaic Egypt, servile labour, at least in the field of agriculture, was unable to compete successfully with native peasant labour. There is no doubt, however, that the Greek immigrants employed domestic slave labour as extensively as they did in their own country.

Slavery played a much more considerable role in the economic life of Asia Minor in general and of the Pergamene kingdom in particular. Slave labour was used on a large scale by the *bourgeoisie* of the Greek Anatolian cities, probably even more so than in continental Greece and on the islands,† and it is certain that the Pergamene kings owned many slaves, of both sexes, whom they employed in the management of their large estates and various industrial *ergasteria*.‡

Finally in the West, both in the Carthaginian Empire and in Italy, and after the third Punic war in the growing Roman Empire, slave labour was always used, more extensively in Carthage, in the other Phoenician cities, and in the Carthaginian provinces, less so in Italy. But with the reorganization of Italian economic life as described above, servile labour became one of its dominating features. The facts are well known and need not be dealt with here at any length. A striking example may be seen in the number of slaves at Minturnae.§

The supply of slaves on the Hellenistic markets came from various sources. The home-bred slaves (οἰκογενεῖς and παράτρο-φοι)‖ formed a large part of the slave population of the Greek cities and also of the monarchies. The exposure of children and the institution of θρεπτοί increased this home supply, at least in Greece and Asia Minor. But the most abundant

* Ch. IV, p. 471, n. 260.
† This is decisively shown by the important part taken by the slaves in the war of Aristonicus.
‡ See Ch. IV, p. 564 f., and Ch. VI, p. 806 f., n. 76.   § Above, Ch. VI, n. 47.
‖ Polyb. xl. 2. 3 (xxxviii. 15. 3); cf. above, p. 207, n. 32.

sources of supply were war, piracy, and brigandage, and the regular traffic in slaves carried on by professional merchants with the northern neighbours of Greece (Thracians, Illyrians, Dardanians, Celts, Scythians, and Sarmatians) and with some of the Hellenistic kingdoms of the East. I have quoted the evidence of the Delphian manumissions of 201 to 50 B.C. (Ch. VI, n. 49): less than one-third of the slaves concerned came from Greece, a little more from the north, but the majority came from Asia Minor, Syria, and Palestine. In Rhodes, where slaves played an important part in the economic and social life of the city, the picture is approximately the same. No statistical data similar to those of Delphi are available. The evidence has never been collected in full, but the large majority of Rhodian slaves appear to have come from Asia (Asia Minor, Syria, Armenia, Media) and a few from Thrace and from South Russia.* It is to be regretted that our information about Delos is so meagre. It is highly probable that here again the majority of the slaves sold and of those who were employed there came from Asia. And the same inference may be drawn as regards Alexandria and Egypt from the correspondence of Zenon. We know that the situation was exactly the same in Italy in the second and first centuries B.C.†

There is reason to suppose that few of these northern and Asiatic slaves were prisoners of war, sold directly by their captors. A larger number may have been brought to the international slave markets by the pirates directly. But the majority were conveyed to the Greek and Italian world by professional slave-dealers. Their supply of slaves was acquired partly in the train of the fighting armies and partly from pirates and brigands. But I am confident that many of the slaves sold on these markets were former bondsmen whom their masters (in the North and in the East) sold to slave-dealers under some cloak of legality. It is worthy of note that hardly any Egyptians appear among the slaves of the Hellenistic world. I am inclined to think that this was due to the strict measures taken by the Ptolemies against the 'enslavement of free persons' in their kingdom. I may further remind the reader that the Ptolemies, probably with the same

* Ch. V, p. 675, and n. 87, cf. 692.   † Ch. VI, n. 76.

object of safeguarding the liberty of the _laoi_, forbade completely the export of slaves from Egypt or subjected it to
restrictive measures (pp. 321 ff.).[193]

Organization of the trade between the Hellenistic States.
The organization of the trade between the Hellenistic States,
a wholesale traffic carried on for the greater part by sea, is but
imperfectly known. Its centres were naturally the ports of
the Hellenistic world. Some of these were no more than the
outlets to the sea of the region that lay behind them, whether
this was the territory of a city or a part or the whole of the
realm of a larger or smaller monarchy. Others might possess
greater importance from being also the terminus of one or
more of the great trade routes that passed through several
States and brought goods of foreign origin to the sea. Finally
some of them, besides serving the above purposes or even without doing so, were prominent as centres of a considerable transit
trade and at the same time as clearing-houses in which goods
coming from various countries were sorted out and reshipped
according to the orders placed with the merchants who resided
at the ports.

To the first class belonged the majority of the ports of the
Aegean. These numbered hundreds, and it would serve no
purpose to enumerate some of them.

Of the second class I may give a few examples, without
any attempt at a completeness which is unattainable in the
state of our information. Panticapaeum in the Crimea was not
only one of the outlets (with Theodosia and Chersonesus) for
the goods produced in that peninsula, but also the centre of
export for merchandise from the Sea of Azov (fish) and from
part of the south Russian steppes. In addition it was the
terminus of the caravan road which came from central Asia,
a role which it shared probably with Tanais and perhaps
Phanagoria. Olbia at the mouth of the Bug and the Dnieper
played a similar part. It forwarded to Greece both the products of the somewhat hellenized territories on the shores of
these rivers and those of central Russia which were shipped
down the rivers. Less important were Tyras at the mouth of
the Dniester and the many cities of the western coast of the
Black Sea; among these Istrus, the terminus of the great

trading routes which converged on the Danube, was the most conspicuous. In Macedonia a corresponding position was occupied by Thessalonice and Demetrias. In Asia Minor I may name, to begin with, Sinope on the southern coast of the Black Sea, one of the outlets (with Amisus) for the products of the kingdom of Pontus and at the same time the chief distributor of the metals mined on the Pontic coast and in the southern Caucasus. It was at the same time one of the termini (with Heraclea Pontica) of sea routes which came from the East and the North and probably of a land road which ran from the East and skirted the southern coast of the Euxine. More important than Sinope, Amisus, and Heraclea were Smyrna, Ephesus, and Miletus, the most active export harbours of Asia Minor and termini of the great royal roads of Anatolia that carried the eastern trade. Similar was the role of the Syrian ports (Seleuceia in Pieria and Laodicea-on-the-sea and the Phoenician ports (Aradus, Sidon, and Tyre, to name only the most important), and of Alexandria in Egypt. Of all these I have spoken in previous chapters.

Of the third class, the transit ports and clearing-houses, I may name as regards the maritime trade Byzantium, the great *entrepôt* of the Pontic trade; Cyzicus, a place of call for ships and a clearing-house for goods of the same trade; Corinth, the chief transit port for the western trade (chiefly with Italy); and above all Rhodes, the most important clearing-house in the Aegean for the eastern sea trade and the trade of Egypt. Delos late in the Hellenistic period played for a time more or less the same role as Rhodes, and in the Seleucid kingdom Seleuceia on the Tigris played a similar part for the Indian, Asiatic, and south Arabian trade.

Hellenistic trade, like Hellenistic industry, was decentralized. No Power was in a position to dictate to the great and wealthy maritime cities, unless they lay within the territory of some powerful Hellenistic State. There was nothing in the Hellenistic Age comparable to the Athenian hegemony of the sea (*thalassocracy*). The Ptolemies for a while exercised a political control over the Aegean, but this was never complete and unchallenged. After its collapse nothing similar came into being. Rhodes endeavoured, with the help of other Powers, to police the sea and curb piracy, but it never aimed at any kind of political and commercial domination. Its watchword was free trade on safe seas. Commercially, as politically, the Hellenistic world was a balance of power.

In early Hellenistic times the part formerly taken by Athens as the chief clearing-house for Aegean trade, especially in corn, was distributed among several Aegean ports. Rhodes became the chief agent of the Ptolemies; it was an ideal *entrepôt* for the merchandise that came by sea from the Ptolemaic dominions in Asia and perhaps also, to a certain extent, for that shipped from the harbours of Seleuceia in Pieria and the Syrian Laodicea. Smyrna, Ephesus, and Miletus were the chief distributors of the goods that were conveyed by land from Asia Minor and the rest of the Seleucid kingdom. At the same time Miletus tried to renew its relations with the Pontic cities and to attract to itself a portion of the corn exported by them. The Pergamene kingdom made use of its own harbour of Elaea for the dispatch of its products to the Aegean. The Pontic Hanse remained in control of the Pontic trade. Macedonia had Thessalonice and Demetrias. Both the Pontic Hanse and the Macedonian kings (and perhaps the Attalids also) seem to have preferred Delos to Rhodes as an *entrepôt* in the Aegean for their wares, though the Delian merchants were financially dependent on their much richer Rhodian partners and friends.*

After the downfall of the Ptolemaic sea-power the part played by Rhodes in the Aegean trade became increasingly important. By the tacit consent of the Powers interested, it was recognized as the chief commercial centre in the Hellenistic world. The facts which support this statement have been set out in Ch. V, pp. 680 ff. The most eloquent of them is the unanimity of almost all the States that participated in the Aegean trade, and, with them, the rulers of Sicily, in helping Rhodes after the earthquake of 227/6 B.C. No less eloquent is the distribution of the Rhodian stamped jars over the Hellenistic world, which shows that the services of Rhodes were indispensable to the Pontic traders and at the same time

* See Chs. III, pp. 169 ff., IV, pp. 225 ff. (Rhodes); pp. 230 ff. (Delos); pp. 591 ff. (the Pontic cities).

PLATE CXII

1. View of the commercial harbour of Cnidus. Restoration by Prof. F. Krischen. Prof. Krischen has kindly allowed me to reproduce his admirable unpublished drawing and has placed at my disposal the following description of it (translated from the German). 'The drawing represents the harbour of Cnidus, a typical harbour of Hellenistic times, and is based on the study of the site carried out by the author of the drawing in 1913, probably in more favourable conditions than would now prevail. A plan [of the harbours and city] will be found in A. von Gerkan, *Griechische Städteanlagen*, 1924, p. 113 f. and fig. 10. Prof. von Gerkan was with the author in Cnidus in 1913. One sees in the drawing an island in front of the harbour, connected with the mainland by a dam. The island cuts the bay into two parts: a smaller section—the military harbour (not seen in the drawing), and a larger one—the commercial harbour. The commercial harbour is situated, so to speak, outside the city and is surrounded by fortifications, while the military harbour lies inside the city-wall; it is reached through a protected inlet as if through a gate (see F. Krischen, *Die griechische Stadt*, pl. 2). The entrance to the commercial harbour is formed by two moles which consist of large blocks of limestone and are still effective. Of the surrounding defensive wall several layers of stone are still extant. On its southern side outlets for water and many heavy stone rings for fastening the ships are still to be seen. The wall on the slope to the east of the city (shown in the foreground of the drawing) is better preserved, and some important details of its construction could be ascertained. Since the steeply ascending slope would allow a view from above on to the 'chemin de ronde', the strong wall, four and a half metres thick, rising in steps, was surmounted on both sides by narrower walls, which were doubtless roofed, as we know the walls of Athens to have been. The towers are in part well preserved to a height of as much as 8·5 metres. Since the extant parts formed the bases of the towers and are massively constructed of very large blocks (each layer about o·80 m. high), the towers must have been of considerable height. According to the Hellenistic practice we must suppose the existence of at least two stories, one with loopholes and another, above it, with windows, and a roof. In the plain and near the water the towers were probably still higher. The line of fortifications and their structural peculiarities are thus sufficiently ascertained, while as regards the city we know only the general direction of the streets.'

2. Deposit (?) of large Rhodian jars excavated at Villanova (Rhodes). About one thousand jars were found. The stamps on the handles permit us to date the deposit (or perhaps a wall built of jars) *c.* 200–180 B.C. *Clara Rhodos*, i (1928), pp. 84 ff. Photograph supplied by Prof. L. Laurenzi, Director of the Archaeological Service at Rhodes.

PLATE CXII

1. Commercial harbour of Cnidus

2. Deposit of jars at Rhodes

HELLENISTIC COMMERCE

to those of the West (comprising Sicily and Carthage), for the disposal of their wares in the Hellenistic countries and the delivery in return of the Hellenistic goods that they needed. Byzantium (pp. 673 and 677) and later Eumenes II and Prusias II* tried to interfere with the freedom of trade of which Rhodes was the champion, but were forced to submission and co-operation.[194]

The position of Rhodes and its role in the trade of the Aegean, or rather of the Mediterranean, was at first consolidated by the part which it took in the political events connected with the Roman intervention. As a staunch partisan of Rome, she enjoyed for a time the full support and confidence of the great western power. But this was the beginning of the end. After the Persean war her commercial influence began rapidly to decline. Suspicious of the Rhodian power, Rome made Delos a free port and her principal agent in her growing commercial relations with the East. It was at Delos that the merchants of Rome provided themselves with the goods that were in demand in Italy: slaves and the commodities imported into the Greek world from China, India, Parthia, South Arabia, and east Africa. As a free port and the main centre of Italian trade, Delos naturally attracted many former clients of Rhodes, who preferred to dispose of their goods without paying any customs duties. But I have endeavoured to show that Delos never completely replaced Rhodes and that the latter, by reason of its commercial experience and accumulated wealth, remained an important centre of Aegean trade even in the time of Roman protectorate and domination.†

How the transit trade concentrated in the harbour of Rhodes was conducted is imperfectly known. It is probable that the Rhodian merchants and bankers developed a considerable practice of granting credits to foreign merchants and acting as commission agents and that they themselves took an active part in commercial operations, by buying goods consigned to Rhodes, sorting them in their storehouses, and distributing them among their clients in the Aegean, Pontic, south Mediterranean, and west Mediterranean regions. It

* Above, Ch. VI, p. 772 f., and n. 38.   † Ibid., pp. 771 ff., and n. 36.

appears to me very probable that the Rhodian jars bearing the official stamps (whatever the meaning of these stamps may be) were used not only to export Rhodian goods, that is to say, goods produced in the island, but also goods of various origin bought by the Rhodian merchants and reshipped by them in new containers to their customers. We do not know what were the contents of the Rhodian jars exported in such large numbers. But it is difficult to suppose that they all contained wine, olive-oil, dried fruit, and so on, of Rhodian production. To my mind they are a testimony to the activity of Rhodian merchants as buyers and distributors both of Rhodian and of foreign produce.[195]

The business of the Delian bankers and merchants of various nationalities was probably of a similar kind. They were known, according to a long-established terminology, as τραπεζῖται on the one hand, and as ἔμποροι, ναύκληροι, and ἐκδοχεῖς on the other. It is highly probable that in Hellenistic times the last three terms were used for distinct professions within the merchant craft: wholesale merchants, ship-owners who may have been at the same time merchants, and thirdly, it may be, distributors of goods, owners of large warehouses, though the true meaning of ἐκδοχεῖς is a difficult question. The three types of business may have been combined, although no certain instance of this is known. The profession of an ἔμπορος was probably sometimes differentiated, one ἔμπορος specializing in one class of goods, another in a different class. But as a rule ἔμπορος means 'wholesale dealer' in general. More doubtful is the meaning of the terms προπράτωρ, προπωλητής, προπώλης, which have been explained as 'intermediary', the German 'Makler'.[196]

It is hardly necessary to repeat that the activity of Rhodes and Delos did not interfere with that of the other great trade centres of the Hellenistic world. The Pontic Hanse was as active as before, Athens regained at least part of her former trade, Ephesus in the hands of the Attalids replaced Elaea as the centre of Pergamene export, Thessalonice was steadily gaining in importance. Nor were the Phoenician and Syrian ports less active than they had been. The same is, of course, true to a certain extent of Alexandria.

The business of merchants of the Hellenistic period retained its earlier individualistic character. No trading companies are known to have existed. From time to time groups of men would undertake a trading venture and would act as a company. I have mentioned in this section the international group of merchants of the second century B.C. which was formed to organize a trading expedition to Somaliland. The caravans of the Oriental world may have had a similar organization. But trading firms comprising a number of partners appear to have been foreign to the ancient world.

The various, mostly national, associations of merchants, of which we hear at Athens, in Samos, Thasos, and especially Delos, were quite different. Their character was religious and social, though they consisted of men of the same profession. Their premises were chiefly centres for the performance of certain religious acts, and club-houses for social intercourse. In these club-houses, the discussion of professional affairs, business transactions involving the production of samples stored in the club-house, were no doubt of common occurrence. Thus the associations played an important part in the business life of the Hellenistic world.[197]

The part taken by the Hellenistic States themselves in trade is little known. The cities were certainly important buyers of foodstuffs, which were then sold to the population. I have dealt above (Ch. V) with their purchasing agents: *sitonai* and *elaionai*. These were often seen in the great clearing-houses of Hellenistic trade and probably also in other exporting centres. We know even less of the transactions of the kings of States with a large exportable surplus, of which the kings themselves were to a large extent the owners. In Egypt Cleomenes carried out commercial operations on a large scale. But it is not certain that the Ptolemies acted in the same way and undertook such operations through their own agents. We have no evidence that they did so. On the other hand, the presence of foreign merchants in Alexandria, their transactions in the country to which the letter of Demetrius (Ch. IV, n. 201) bears witness, and the frequent mention in the 'Revenue Laws' of ἔμποροι, probably both natives and foreigners, who dealt in foreign goods, suggest that it was not agents of the king who went to foreign ports to sell his goods and buy other merchandise, but foreign merchants who came to Alexandria to sell their goods and buy those of the king. They had the co-operation of the native wholesale merchants, ship-owners, and owners of warehouses, who may have acted both in an independent capacity and as royal agents. In order to know exactly who they were and the facilities at their disposal, the kings may have allowed or required them to form professional associations.

Among these dealers in foreign goods and exporters of Egyptian produce, whether belonging to the king or to private persons, may have been the owners of the large gift estates, most of them men of influence in the royal counsels. The correspondence of Zenon makes it clear that Apollonius was in the habit of buying and selling various goods both in Egypt and in the Egyptian dominions. But it is not certain that he extended his commercial operations (of whatever character they may have been) to foreign countries, and competed with the foreign merchants and with the professional native traders engaged in this business. Before we speculate about a new class of merchants who were at the same time owners of large estates and important officials, and about their role in external trade, we must await conclusive evidence that Apollonius did take an active part not only in the internal but also in the foreign trade of Egypt. The parallel drawn by F. M. Heichelheim between Apollonius and Cato the Elder in this respect is far-fetched and unconvincing.[198]

What I have said of the Ptolemies is probably true of the other rulers who had merchandise to dispose of. There is every reason to think that the Spartocids had no commercial fleet of their own, but sold most of their goods to foreign merchants who came to Panticapaeum, and to merchants who were their own subjects. We have no evidence concerning the other kings, and conjectures as to the part they took in international trade are idle.[199]

I may add in conclusion that the social role of wholesale merchants in the Hellenistic world constantly increased in importance. It is reasonable to suppose that the richest men

in the cities—and concentration of wealth in the hands of a
few people was one of the leading features of the second and
first centuries—were either merchants or landowners or a combination of both. And in all probability commerce came first,
able men acquiring their fortunes by it and later investing
their money in land. Another social phenomenon connected
with commerce was the increasingly international character of
the merchant class in all the great trading centres. The company, established in Alexandria, of the traders with Somaliland, to which I have referred, is one instance; another is
Delos with its Greek, Syrian, Italian, and Arab merchants.
I must remind the reader that among the merchants residing
at Delos there were many very slightly hellenized Semites.

Internal and local trade. A few words will suffice on internal
and local trade. When speaking of agriculture and industry I
mentioned that the inhabitant of an ordinary Greek city provided himself as a rule with the necessities of life—foodstuffs
and industrial products—in the market and in the shops,
home-production gradually losing its importance except perhaps in the richer households. Bread was prepared in bakeries
(Pl. xxv) and sold by dealers; wine, oil, fish, vegetables, and
fruit were bought in their appropriate shops; domestic utensils,
whether of pottery or metal ware, furniture, tools, &c., likewise. The only exception was clothing, which was still made
in part by the housewives, their daughters, and their maids.
All the above were bought for cash and usually in small quantities. The abundance of copper coins, small change, found in
the ruins of almost all the Hellenistic cities testifies to this
practice.

So it had been in the homeland and so it was in the new
centres of urban life throughout the Hellenistic world. We
have evidence of this in the spacious Hellenistic *agorai* of the
Macedonian colonies of the East, surrounded by shops, as at
Dura-Europus, and in the large quantities of small change
found in all the excavations of this region, for example at
Dura-Europus and in the cities of Palestine.

The retail trade of the Greek cities of the Hellenistic world
was in the hands of small dealers who sometimes traded in a
variety of goods (παντοπῶλαι and κάπηλοι(?)) but as a rule

specialized in a particular commodity, of artisans who sold the products of their own craft, of pedlars, and of the farmers who brought their produce to market and sold it to customers direct. The picture which is presented by Pompeii and Herculaneum in respect of the early first century A.D., with hundreds of shops along the streets, with many *thermopolia* (note the Greek term), with pedlars and artisans displaying their wares in the *forum*, may with confidence be applied to the Hellenistic cities of the third and second centuries B.C. In this connexion I may again remind the reader of the many terracotta and bronze statuettes of the Hellenistic period which show fishermen and peasants (men and women) bringing their goods to the city, and pedlars selling, for example, cakes and sweets.* The Oriental counterpart of a medium-sized town such as Pompeii, which does not differ greatly from the modern medium-sized towns of the East, is best represented by Dura-Europus of the Parthian period, with its hundreds of shops grouped so as to form extensive streets, the precursors of the modern *sûks*.

The goods sold to the people of an average small or medium town in continental Greece and the islands in Hellenistic times were mostly produced in its territory (foodstuffs) and in its workshops (industrial goods). A few articles were imported from the immediate neighbourhood. Exchange of goods among the cities of the Aegean was one of the leading features of the economic life of that region from very ancient times and remained so in the Hellenistic period. Some of these goods were brought by ships, others by roads connecting the territories of neighbouring cities. I have already referred to cheap common pottery as an example. In general the aspect of the market of a Greek town of this type and period did not differ very much from that of the Athenian market in the fifth century as described by Aristophanes. The same may be assumed to apply to the Greek cities, old and new, of Asia Minor and of the Seleucid kingdom. Commercial intercourse between neighbouring towns is, for example, suggested by the coins found in Priene and Pergamon. In such small and medium-sized towns there was no great abundance of goods imported from other States and from beyond the Hellenistic

* See the beautiful table service in bronze found at Pompeii.

world. These were as a rule expensive luxury articles which found few buyers. From time to time, at moments of crisis and famine, large quantities of foreign corn, oil, wine, and fish would be sold by the city to the starving population.[200]

Somewhat different in this last respect was the aspect of the great new cities of the the Hellenistic world: royal capitals, large industrial and commercial centres, important administrative and military headquarters. In most cases even in normal times their territories were unable to feed their numerous population. Foodstuffs therefore were certainly imported in larger or smaller quantities from more distant places. In Alexandria, for example, the bulk of them was shipped down the Nile, while some of finer quality came from the dominions and from abroad. In Antioch the situation may have been similar, the produce of its large and fertile territory being supplemented by imports from other parts of Syria. Of the great trading cities, those which possessed a large area of fertile land may have been almost self-sufficient, such as Rhodes, Cyzicus, Heraclea Pontica, Amisus, Sinope, Smyrna, Ephesus, and Miletus; while Corinth, Athens, and Delos were very dependent on imports. The situation as regards manufactured goods was similar. Each of the large cities was of course an important industrial centre. Its artisans not only supplied the population of the city with their products, but also produced to meet the needs of the remainder of the State's territory and of foreign customers. At the same time the wealthy part of the population of such cities, not being content with the products of their own city and country, would naturally absorb large quantities of imported manufactured goods of finer quality.

Though the character of the supply was thus different in the larger cities I do not think that the method of its distribution greatly differed from that prevailing in the small and medium towns. The shops of the retail dealers in the former may have been larger and better stocked, the shopkeepers themselves may have been richer and may have had several assistants, the owners of workshops (*ergasteria*) may have employed a certain number of slaves, but the general character of retail trade even in the largest cities did not differ from that of the smaller towns. In the Near East up to 1914 there was no organic difference between business in the bazaars of Smyrna, Aleppo, Beirut, Baghdad, and Constantinople and that transacted in the more modest *sûks* of the smaller cities. The turnover was larger but the type of trade was the same. Individual retailers sold foodstuffs, small restaurants and cafés supplied the needs of their clients, the artisan-tradesman was the typical producer and seller of manufactured goods.

I may conclude with some remarks on the peculiar organization of commerce within Ptolemaic Egypt. Alexandria in its external aspect probably resembled the other capitals of the Hellenistic world. To what extent free trade was restricted there by the existence of royal monopolies and State control is hard to say. Monopolized goods were certainly sold in Alexandria in the same way as in the *chora*, that is to say, by concessionaires of the State. In the *chora* retail trade was in the hands of licensed merchants and was carried on probably in small shops. The prices of many articles were fixed by the State and the merchants were practically its agents. In the case of others the retail merchants, though not strictly bound by fixed prices, were under State control. I may quote again the general direction in this respect given by the *dioecetes* to the *oeconomi* of the *chora* :* 'See to it, too, that the goods for sale be not sold at prices higher than those prescribed. Make also careful investigation of those goods which have no fixed prices and on which the dealers may put what prices they like; and after having put a fair surplus [that is, a fair addition to the cost of production] on the wares being sold, make the (dealers?) dispose of them.' Whatever the meaning of the last incomplete sentence may be, 'it is evident that even in those branches of trade for which no fixed prices were officially dictated trade was by no means free, since the prices were thus subject to control'.†

The system of monopolies and of State control of production and trade, whereby local commerce was effectively promoted and the population relieved of any cash which taxation left at its disposal, was, however, neither complete nor general. Whatever surplus of production the landlords and the artisans

* *Teb.* 703 (Hunt and Edgar, *Sel. Pap.* 204), 174–82.   † Ibid., p. 97.

may have had after satisfying the demands of the government (and there certainly was such a surplus in the non-monopolized branches of agriculture and industry), this surplus, in so far as it was not consumed or used by the producers themselves, was sold in the open market. State control of the prices of non-monopolized goods, which probably did not extend to the wholesale traders, appears to have left a fair and not strictly limited margin of profit to the retailers. In any case there was a lively exchange of goods in the *chora* of Egypt both in the early and in the late Ptolemaic period.

This is proved by many documents, about which I may say a few words. As regards wholesale trade we have a mine of information in those letters of Zenon's correspondence which refer to the sale and purchase of goods by Apollonius and by Zenon himself. I have already described their transactions,* and need only remind the reader of the flotilla of merchant-men owned by Apollonius and commanded by Criton the στολάρχης, and of the many commercial agents of the former who bought and sold various commodities in different parts of Egypt.

Apollonius was not exceptional in his commercial activity. Not only the other owners of large gift-estates, but also pro-fessional wholesale dealers, both foreigners and natives, were engaged in the same kind of business. I have mentioned above (Ch. IV, n. 201) the letter of Demetrius† in which, referring to the results of the royal order that foreign and certain local coins should be re-minted, the writer says that the wholesale traders (ἔμποροι) and the owners of warehouses (ἐγδοχεῖς), most of them probably residents in Alexandria, and the 'foreigners who are sailing in' (ξένοι οἱ εἰσπλέοντες), were indignant because the mismanagement of the operation had made it impossible for them 'to send (their money) into the country for the pur-chase of goods' (l. 23 f.). A large proportion of these goods were shipped to Alexandria and part of them probably ex-ported. But the ἔμποροι certainly sold some of them in the country to private persons and to the numerous retail dealers. The same methods, though on a smaller scale, were followed

* Ch. IV, p. 384 f. with n. 184, and p. 397 with n. 200.

† Hunt and Edgar, *Sel. Pap.* 409.

by other private owners of goods for sale. We still possess many deeds of sale and other documents dealing with such transactions between private individuals. They testify to a lively traffic in foodstuffs, raw materials, manufactured goods, domestic animals, slaves, &c. A list of these documents would be too long to give here. Nor can I enumerate the many classes of retail traders, to whom large quantities of these goods were sold and by them resold to consumers. They included dealers who sold a variety of unspecified goods (παντοπῶλαι(?)), and also those who specialized in a particular commodity (such as σιτοκάπηλοι, &c., ὀθονιοπῶλαι, ἐριοπῶλαι, &c.); some of them were at the same time artisans who produced articles of one kind or another.[201]

Of such commercial dealings between persons other than traders, and of the business of the retail dealers, a fair idea may be derived from the private contracts mentioned above, and from many documents in Zenon's correspondence bearing on transactions of this kind in Philadelphia. I have dealt with these last elsewhere* and I need not repeat what is there said. An excellent picture of this side of Egyptian life is further supplied by a fragmentary document found at Tebtunis and recently published (*Teb.* 890, second century B.C.). A careful study of the document in the light of the Zenon correspondence and the various private contracts, &c., of the Ptolemaic period will convey a much more vivid idea of the actual conditions than any tabulation or so-called statistics.

The document in question contains fragments of the daily accounts of a country bank of the Heracleopolite nome, in which were recorded, not the transactions of the bank as a department of the royal treasury, but the payments it made to the order of its depositors, including officials of the government. It is surprising how many of the villagers other than agriculturists (who appear to have conducted their affairs largely through the State corn banks, the θησαυροί) had a deposit or current account in the bank and made use of it to effect their payments (ἀπὸ τραπέζης, *Teb.* 891, 36, second century B.C.).

The bank had many clients, of various classes. Conspicuous among them were the business aristocracy. In the first place

* *Large Estate*, pp. 118 ff.

may be mentioned the merchants (ἔμποροι), all of them Greeks; one—Megalleus, son of Apollonius—was especially active.* He was in relations with the retailers and apparently dealt in various goods, for example oxen. Next comes a shipowner and freighter (ναύκληρος), again a Greek (l. 80). There are several mentions of a banker, Apollonius (ll. 82, 90, 132). A dealer in honey, a Greek 'from the city', appears to be a wholesale dealer (μελιτοπώλης, l. 36f.). A trierarch in charge of a war-ship policing the river and his crew frequently draw money from the bank.† And many State officials receive their salaries and money for their expenses from the bank. Comparatively rich men, however, are few. The bulk of the clients of the bank are the native retail dealers and artisans. The chief business of the place appears to have been in textiles and clothes. Dealers in linen (ὀθονιοπῶλαι), in *himatia* (ἱματιοπῶλαι), in flax fibre (λινέμποροι: one was a native woman, l. 23, another a Greek, l. 32), and in wool (ἐριέμπορος, again a Greek, l. 169), fullers (γναφεῖς), weavers of byssos (βυσσουργοί), tailors (ἡπηταί), appear repeatedly in the accounts. A brisk business was carried on by silversmiths and goldsmiths (χρυσοχόοι) and by a coppersmith (χαλκεύς). It is interesting to find that one of the former, by name Opus, pays his debts in uncoined (ἄσημος) silver and gold according to the ancient Egyptian tradition.[202] A leather-worker (σκυτεύς) and an architect (οἰκοδόμος) may also be mentioned. Nor are traders in foodstuffs absent: dealers in grain (σιτοκάπηλοι), in oil (ἐλαιοπώλης), in calves (μοσχοπώλης), a butcher (μάγειρος), and many innkeepers (κάπηλοι); cf. above, n. 196.

All these native dealers carried out various business operations through the bank, mostly payments for goods and liquidation of private (not bank) loans. They often specify for what purpose their payments are made: for the purchase of hemp fibre (στυππεία), of a *himation* and *sindon*, of a *chiton*, of linen, of a bag, of copper, of oxen, and so on.

About the other monarchies of the Hellenistic world we have no information comparable to that concerning Egypt. We do not know therefore how retail trade was organized in those

* ll. 94, 164–5, 225; cf. 116 and 174.
† ll. 20 (?), 34, 93; cf. above, Ch. V, p. 715, and n. 134.

parts of the Seleucid Empire which were not dependent on some Greek or Macedonian city. In Babylonia there appears to have been no notable change in this respect in the pre-Hellenistic methods. As regards the great urban centres of Eastern life, which had retained their ancient constitution and economic structure, we have no information.

Banking. Banking operations[203] were as ancient in the Greek world as the use of a coinage issued and guaranteed by the State. Since coins of different standards and of varying weight and quality were minted in divers cities and in Lydia and Persia (see Pl. XI), money-changing became from early times a profession in the hands of skilful and experienced specialists. The earliest bankers—the money-changers—sat behind their tables (τράπεζαι) in the streets and market-places, like their successors in the modern East. They were therefore called *trapezitai* and the banking concerns *trapezai*. They played an increasingly important part in the economic life of Greek cities in the Classical period; their business constantly expanded and its machinery became more and more compli-cated. Being honest, skilful, trustworthy, and rich, the *trape-zitai* not only helped the population and especially the mer-chants of a city in their dealings in foreign currency, but accepted the custody of their savings and acted as partners, assistants, and intermediaries in all sorts of transactions car-ried out by their clients.

Large quantities of coined money were accumulating in the treasuries of the temples, as offerings, donations, and founda-tions. States, corporations, and private individuals in posses-sion of surplus funds were naturally desirous to deposit their reserves in the temples as places of safety. The custody of deposits of various kinds would therefore tend to become a usual feature in the affairs of a temple. Temples would naturally invest their own funds in one way or another, chiefly in loans, and with the consent of the owners of deposits and subject to payment of interest they may have employed in the same way the money of which they were the custodians. Thus temples gradually developed into regular banks.

Finally certain cities, which issued large quantities of cur-rency and disposed of reserves of capital, besides the sums given to them as donations and foundations, would require the assistance of specialists in their money transactions, and instead of having recourse to private bankers or temples would create city banks, where their funds were managed by experts in co-operation with the mints and the various financial departments of the administration. A further step was to concentrate all banking operations in the hands of the city bank, that is to say, to establish a city banking monopoly.

Thus in the Greek cities various types of banks were taking part in the custody and investment of money: temple banks, city banks, and private banks. The natural money operations of any bank would be: transactions in foreign money, especially the exchange of foreign into local currency and vice versa; care of deposits of various kinds, such as those for simple safe-keeping, current deposits without interest, and the so-called *depositum irregulare* subject to interest; what is known as *giro* or *incasso*, i.e. various types of transfer operations; credit operations of various sorts—loans on collateral security, pledges and mortgages, and a special very popular type—bottomry loans.

We find the banking business well developed on all these lines in many Greek cities of the fourth century B.C. The greatest centre of banking was naturally Athens, and we have good literary and epigraphical evidence regarding some private banks of that city.

The Hellenistic cities inherited the banks from the past. One of the principal new features of this period was the rapid spread of city banks, which appear comparatively often even in our scanty epigraphical evidence: the best known are those of Cos and Miletus, but they are mentioned occasionally in many other cities. It is to be noted, however, that the majority of them belong to the time after 200 B.C.[204]

Another conspicuous phenomenon of the Hellenistic period was the further development of temples as banking institutions and of private banks. As regards the former, we know a little of the money transactions of the temples at Delos. We hear of cities keeping deposits there, and of loans granted by the temples to cities and private persons. I have referred above*

* Ch. IV, pp. 139, 231, with n. 57; cf. 233 ff.

to the help given by Philadelphus to Delos in collecting its debts from several cities. An interesting feature in the affairs of the temples of Delos is their co-operation with private bankers resident in the island. While keeping the money of their clients on deposit, the temples themselves deposited their own money with private bankers. There is no evidence of a city bank at Delos before the second Attic domination.[205]

Other temples as rich as those of Delos, perhaps richer, probably followed the same practice. Prominent among these were the Anatolian temples of Oriental origin affiliated to Greek cities, such as the temples of Ephesus and Sardis. Of Ephesus we know that in the time of the Lydians and Persians the temple was pre-eminently the place of safety, where kings, cities, and private persons kept their money. It is highly improbable that this practice was discontinued in the Hellenistic period. We have no direct information, but all our evidence about Hellenistic Ephesus is very poor. It is, however, certain that even in the difficult times of Mithridates its temple possessed large revenues and granted many loans at interest. The decree or law of Ephesus of 85 B.C., several times referred to above (Ch. VII, p. 943, n. 14), mentions the insolvent debtors of the temple* and the loans of various kinds granted from the sacred funds.† There is comparatively good evidence that the temple still continued the same financial operations in the Roman period.[206] As regards Sardis we know that, probably in the second half of the third century B.C., the temple was lending money to rich landowners on mortgage of their estates.‡ Even minor temples of Asia Minor, such as those of Caria, conducted, on a smaller scale, the same business as the temples of Ephesus and Sardis.§ I see no evidence of any decrease in the banking activity of the temples in Hellenistic times.

But temple banks were of minor importance as compared with private banks, especially those in the larger commercial cities. When speaking of Rhodes I mentioned the loans ‖

* *S.I.G.*³ 742, ll. 29 ff. (cf. J. H. Oliver, *A.J. Phil.* lx (1939), pp. 468 ff.).
† Ibid., ll. 38 ff.
‡ See Ch. IV, p. 495, and n. 274; cf. p. 467, and n. 255.
§ Above, Ch. V, p. 672, and n. 82.   ‖ See above, p. 172; and Index s.v.

granted by wealthy Rhodians to various cities, and discussed the funeral inscription of one of the Rhodian bankers.* It is very regrettable that we know so little of the dealings of the Rhodian bankers. About Delos our information is more abundant. Delian inscriptions tell us the names of several bankers in every period of the island's history. The majority of them came from other places, like the Athenian bankers of the fourth century B.C. Certain groups of them formed associations like the merchants. We have some indications of the character of their operations, which, as might be expected, were mainly connected with the steadily growing trade of Delos.† There is no doubt that there were private bankers in all the large Hellenistic cities, though they are not frequently mentioned.‡ It is unfortunate that information about their business, the volume of their transactions, the management of the various branches of banking, and their technique, is so meagre, indeed almost entirely lacking. The cumulative evidence, such as it is, points to a steady and almost uninterrupted development of banking business, its chief centres shifting from place to place with the vicissitudes of international trade.[207]

The banks of the Hellenistic period, though a typical feature of the economic life of the Greek cities of continental Greece, of the islands, and of the Greek colonies in the West and East, were not confined to these localities. With the Greeks they migrated to the Oriental monarchies. We have no positive evidence of the existence of private and city banks in the Greek settlements in the East. But there is no reason to affirm the contrary, at least in the larger Greek and Macedonian centres of the Seleucid Empire.

We do not know what happened to the rich and well-organized private banks of Oriental type which are well known to have existed in Babylonia in the Neo-Babylonian period and probably existed also in pre-Hellenistic times in the larger trading cities of Syria, Phoenicia, and Palestine. Nor are we well informed regarding the financial business in the Hellenistic

* Ch. V, p. 680, with n. 95, and p. 689, with n. 106.
† Above, Chs. IV, p. 233, with n. 62, and VI, p. 798, with n. 64.
‡ See n. 204 to this chapter.

age of the great Oriental temples, which retained their wealth and importance.

It is certain, however, that the temples were not deprived under the Seleucids of a certain political and economic autonomy, and were highly respected by them, at least in the early times of the dynasty.* I have mentioned that some of the temples in the eastern parts of the Seleucid Empire continued probably to issue their own money, and that all of them were very rich until temporary financial difficulties forced Antiochus III, Seleucus IV, and Antiochus IV to require the surrender of a substantial part of their wealth.† Not only did they possess accumulated capital in the form of estates, cattle, slaves, gold and silver vessels and sacred utensils, and coined money, but they also held private deposits of gold, silver, and money. This was the case at least in Jerusalem, in the reign of Seleucus IV, when, hard pressed by his financial difficulties, he attempted to confiscate the treasury of the temple. The attempt aroused the indignation of the priests and the population, not only because of its sacrilegious character in their eyes, but also because the bulk of the money consisted of private deposits, in part the property of widows and orphans. I do not discuss the authenticity of the story as told in the books of the Maccabees,‡ but it is evident that the statement about the private deposits in the temple cannot have been invented. It is supported by what we know of the similar business undertaken by the temple of Jerusalem in Roman times.§[208] We hear of other kinds of banking operations, for example by the hellenized Oriental temple of Sardis mentioned above. It is highly probable that the acceptance of such business by the temple was no innovation but was in conformity with an old Oriental tradition.

In Egypt banking assumed a peculiar and unique character. We know the Ptolemaic banking system comparatively well both from contemporary evidence and from documents of the Roman period. I have briefly summarized our knowledge of it.‖ Its chief novelty was the centralization of banking, that

---

* Ch. IV, pp. 435 ff., and notes 233 ff.   † Ch. V, p. 695 f., and n. 115.
‡ 2 Macc. iii. 3, 10 and 15, and iv. 4 and 7.
§ Fl. Jos. *Bell. Jud.* vi. 282.   ‖ Ch. IV, pp. 404 ff., with n. 203.

is to say, the creation of a central State bank in Alexandria, with branch banks in the capitals of the nomes and sub-branches in all the more important villages. Private banks, in so far as they existed, played a secondary part in the economic life of the country.

The State bank of the Ptolemies was organized on Greek lines. The terminology, the accounting, the operations were Greek. No local influence is perceptible, except in the peculiar organization of that department of the system which dealt with corn (the θησαυροί, with their managers the σιτολόγοι). In general the Ptolemaic βασιλικὴ τράπεζα was not very different from a regular city bank. In all probability its operations were designed on a much larger scale, the management was more elaborate, the personnel more diversified, the accounting much more detailed, and the book-keeping more accurate, but on the whole the Ptolemaic State banks had the same general functions and were organized on the same lines as the Greek city banks.

Like these, the Egyptian royal bank was a State institution and its main purpose was to serve the interests of the State. In fact it was both a department of the financial administration of the country and a State bank concerned chiefly with the custody and investment of the State's money. The management of private funds and the interests of the bank's private clients were of secondary concern to it. As a department of the treasury, it co-operated with the royal officials and the tax-farmers in collecting the revenue, so far as this took the form of money, and it had the duty of effecting, again with the co-operation and under the control of the royal officials, all payments by the State to official and private persons. It had the custody of the money collected by it and invested in some way on behalf of the State such funds as were not expended.

It is to be regretted that while we know much of the activity of the royal bank as a department of the treasury, our information about its methods of investing State money is very meagre. We know from the 'Revenue Laws' of Philadelphus (coll. 77–8) that loans were the usual form of such investment. Unfortunately we know nothing of the conditions on which such loans were granted. In one document (*Teb.* 766, of 136

B.C. (?)) we have a private individual asking the bank for a short-term loan to enable him to pay a debt to the crown. Otherwise, so far as my knowledge goes, there is no evidence of bank loans to private persons. This is hardly an accident. The State in all probability required various guarantees from those who sought to borrow from it and made the procedure complicated and cumbersome. Persons in need of money therefore had recourse to private money-lenders, not excluding the professional usurers. I shall return to this presently.

As a consequence of their good management and the security they offered (thanks to royal control and the support of the State's authority), the royal banks of Egypt naturally offered attractions to private owners of money, for the deposit of their savings and liquid capital, and as a means of effecting and receiving payments. The kings were not opposed to this extension of the bank's functions, since it meant an increase in their income and involved very little risk. The banks therefore became great deposit institutions and developed an extensive business of this kind, receiving money from their clients, keeping it on deposit, and making payments from these deposits.

It is on this aspect of the activity of the banks, that concerned with the affairs of their private clients, that we are best informed. The Zenon correspondence is highly instructive. Apollonius, the head of the central bank of Alexandria, had deposits, in his private capacity, in various branches of the royal bank. From time to time he would pay in money to one branch or another, and his commercial agents and other subordinates would draw on these deposits. We have instances of his subordinates' paying various obligations on his behalf through the bank, besides using it extensively for their own private affairs.[209] Even more important, because it is more explicit, is the evidence supplied by the accounts mentioned above, of one of the small banks of the Heracleopolite nome in the second century B.C. (*Teb.* 890). These show how widely the bank was used by private persons for the deposit of money and for effecting payments.

The accounting of the Heracleopolite bank is comparatively simple. Two types of entries may be distinguished: those appended to a name in the genitive, and those appended to a name in the dative. According to the editors 'the datives are apparently names of persons to whom, or to the debit of whom, payments were made from the bank, whereas the genitives are the names of those by whom the sums entered were paid in or to whom they were credited'. In many instances it is evident that the payments were effected by transfer from one account to another without money passing. Such are evidently the entries in ll. 5 and 6, 7 and 9, 179 and 181. In ll. 21–3 is recorded 'an indirect payment from Ptolemaeus to Thabis of 5,100 dr.; of this sum she receives 2,000, leaving a credit of 3,100'. I have mentioned this detail in the bank procedure, familiar in modern times, because many eminent scholars have thought it improbable that such transfers were made in ancient times. Whether or not it was an innovation of Ptolemaic banking (used also in corn transactions) cannot be ascertained.[210]

The accounts of the bank are especially interesting because they show how popular recourse to the banks became with the people of Egypt. It was so already in early Ptolemaic times, and the habit became even more firmly established in the later Ptolemaic period, as is proved by these accounts. It must be remembered that the majority of the clients of the bank were natives—retail dealers, artisans, subordinate officials. The Ptolemaic organization of Egypt was certainly successful in promoting the use of money and in helping the people to deal in this medium. Convenient in itself, the system of paying one's debts through the bank had the additional advantage of officially recording the transactions and thus providing important evidence in case of litigation.

The existence of banking facilities did not, however, altogether eliminate private business transactions in which money passed from hand to hand (διὰ χειρός or similar expression), in particular private loans of money, as contrasted with payments through the bank (δι[ά τε] χειρὸς καὶ τῆς Κάστορος κολλυβιστι[κῆς] τραπ[έζ]ης).* This procedure was less cumbersome and more elastic, permitting the parties to disregard certain annoying restrictions on the freedom of contract, such

* *B.G.U.* 1156, 8–9, first century B.C.

as the maximum rate of interest (24 per cent.) prescribed by a royal *diagramma* early in the third century B.C. and subsequently valid throughout Egypt, a rate of interest much higher than prevailed in the rest of the Hellenistic world (8 to 10 per cent. with some exceptions). This high rate of interest shows that money was scarce in Egypt. This was due in part to the fact that the Ptolemies ingeniously extracted people's money by means of monopolies and taxation, employing it to meet their expenditure abroad, the cost of wars and the pay of their mercenaries, and to accumulate large reserves. It may be regarded as probable that another reason for the scarcity of money was the endeavour of the Ptolemies to exclude foreign capital from the Egyptian money market. A striking illustration of this scarcity which led to usury and blackmail, and of the restricted scope of the bank's operations in the matter of private loans, will be found in one of the Zenon Papyri in the possession of Columbia University (Inv. 272); this is soon to be published by Prof. W. L. Westermann, who has been kind enough to allow me to quote it in this connexion. It is a petition (ἔντευξις) to Philadelphus by Antipater, a Greek of Philadelphia, concerning a loan which his wife had contracted with another Greek (of Heracleopolis?), Nicon by name, perhaps a professional usurer, who demanded an exorbitant rate of interest (6 per cent. a month, i.e. 72 per cent. a year). The affair is obscure and the real facts escape us, but it is evident that loans of this kind, though probably illegal (Antipater quotes in ll. 15–16 the royal *diagramma* concerning the rate of interest), were of frequent occurrence and that the usurers occasionally had recourse to violent but apparently not entirely illegal methods of collecting their money (detention of the debtor as ἐνέχυρον or pledge in private custody).²¹¹

Popular as the use of money became under the patronage of the kings and the administration, and thanks to the facilities provided by the development of the banks, it was not intended (as I have often said) to oust completely the traditional corn economy of Egypt. Corn in Egypt was almost an equivalent of money. It was natural therefore that banking should not be confined to transactions in money but should be extended to dealings in corn. The government's granaries ($\theta\eta\sigma\alpha\nu\rho o\iota$), scattered all over the country and inherited by the Ptolemies, were transformed by them into a network of corn banks with their centre in Alexandria. They were managed by a special staff ($\sigma\iota\tau o\lambda\acute{o}\gamma o\iota$ and their subordinates), who had the same functions as the bankers; that is to say, they received taxes and rents paid in kind and effected payments in corn from the government granaries on behalf of the State. At the same time, like the bankers, they acted as agents for private persons. They kept their corn on deposit and effected payments in corn on their behalf. The evidence about these transactions is more abundant than that about the banks. It has been frequently discussed,* and I cannot enter here into details.

In conclusion I may mention one important problem in connexion with the Ptolemaic banking system. I have pointed out that it was Greek in essence and that its organization did not differ from that of the Greek State banks. Are we to ascribe to the Ptolemies the idea of making the banks a State institution, with the king as the sole banker and all the banking business of the country concentrated in his hands, or was it borrowed by the Ptolemies from certain Greek city-states? The meagre evidence relating to the fourth and early third centuries B.C. does not indicate any city where private banking was eliminated and banking business made a government monopoly. This certainly was not done at Athens, the greatest banking centre of the Greek world in the fourth century. But a partial monopoly of banking is recorded in some Greek cities which were centres of international trade. At Byzantium a monopoly of exchange was introduced in the late fourth century,† as it was also at Olbia.‡ But the existence of such a monopoly was natural, inasmuch as the cities of Greece, which coined their own money, would be inclined to protect their currency by a measure of this kind. A monopoly of exchange does not mean, however, the complete elimination of private banking. As things stand, it seems probable that the Ptolemies were the first to make banking a government undertaking. It may have been under their influence, either

* See Ch. IV, n. 204.
† Ps.-Aristotle, *Oecon.* ii, p. 1346^{b}24.   ‡ *S.I.G.*^{3} 218.

direct or indirect (perhaps exerted through the Pergamene kingdom, which may have adopted the Ptolemaic banking system), that after 200 B.C. certain Greek cities, chiefly of Asia Minor, created the State banks mentioned above. This, however, is no more than a conjecture.

The Ptolemaic banking system did not disappear with the rule of the Ptolemies. It was retained with some modifications by the Roman administration of Egypt and it influenced the Roman system of tax and rent collection.* It is interesting to note that even the idea of a central State bank survived. Cassius Dio (in the famous speech of Maecenas) suggested the organization of such a bank as a credit institution for the whole of the Roman Empire (lii. 28 ff.).[212]

Coinage. Trade and banking were closely connected with coinage and the monetary policy of the Hellenistic States. I have sketched the outlines of the evolution of coinage and discussed its local peculiarities, illustrating these with reproductions of several coins, and I need only touch briefly on the subject here. A more comprehensive survey of Hellenistic coinage would require much space and is beyond my competence. Numismatics in recent decades has become a highly specialized branch of learning, based on minute technical observations. Moreover, the close study of Hellenistic coinage is in its earliest stages and no substantial general survey yet exists.[213]

The use of money became in the Hellenistic age an economic factor of great importance. It was already well established in the Greek city-states of the fourth century B.C. and was a comparatively prominent feature of the Persian Empire. In the Hellenistic period it took firm root in the East and to a very large extent replaced barter in the economic life of what had been that Empire. It was inherited from the Seleucids by the Greek Bactrian kingdom and by the Parthians, and became dominant, under Hellenistic influence, in India. The Sacians and later the Kushans continued the Hellenistic tradition in Bactria and northern India. In the same way it was inherited by the Arabs, especially the Nabataeans, and by

---

* The Roman *mensae* (τράπεζαι) were distributed all over the Roman Empire.

several minor native States which seceded from the Seleucid Empire, such as Palestine, Armenia, &c. In the North the use of money was widely adopted in the northern Balkan peninsula, among the Thracians and the Celts. These from early Hellenistic times (see Pl. LXVII. 4) made large issues of currency, in which coins of Philip II, Alexander, and later of Thasos and Maronea were imitated. I need hardly add that the use of money, which had long been familiar to the Greek cities of the West, made conspicuous progress in Italy and Carthage in Hellenistic times.

There was therefore a large demand for coined money in the whole of the Hellenistic world and beyond it: to some extent for gold, but chiefly for silver and copper. Money was more and more extensively used in all classes of trade, internal and external. A large proportion of the metals mined in the Hellenistic world was transformed into coinage, which circulated far and wide in all parts of it. The volume of coins in circulation depended of course on many factors—political circumstances, the monetary policy of the various States, and the supply of metal in each.

In the early Hellenistic age money was abundant and cheap. Violent fluctuations of prices in the days of the Successors were temporary and must be attributed to the political chaos of the time. When political stability was achieved, the money market became regular and steady, and so to a certain extent did prices and the rate of interest, though these were naturally not uniform in the various parts of the Hellenistic world. The situation changed in the late Hellenistic times. The supply of metal was reduced by various causes, such as the exhaustion of certain mines, which the discovery of new mines did not fully compensate ;* the diminished area of some of the Hellenistic kingdoms, which involved the loss of rich mines; and political measures such as the temporary suspension by the Romans of the exploitation of the very productive Macedonian mines. The practice of hoarding money adopted, as a rule for political reasons, by States (especially the Hellenistic kings

---

* I may mention as a probable instance of new supplies of metal the case of the coinage of Histiaea in Euboea in the early second century B.C., which was for a time of exceptional abundance.

and Rome), by temples, and by individuals, immobilized for longer or shorter periods some of the currency which had previously been in circulation; trade with foreign countries absorbed a certain proportion of it; and finally the drainage by the Romans of coined money and precious metals from the East increased the stringency of the situation.

But the demand for money remained active and probably tended to increase rather than diminish. We have no means of estimating the volume and value of the money coined in the late Hellenistic period. But general considerations rather point to a comparative scarcity of coinage at the end of the second century B.C. and in the first. We know little of prices in this troubled period. Nor do we know exactly the rate of interest then prevailing. The little we know suggests that the money market was disorganized and unstable. This disorganization and the scarcity of gold and silver in circulation may explain the important role played by copper during this period in business transactions, and the temporary adulteration of silver coins, of which there are indications in certain countries. But, apart from Egypt (see below), there is no sign in any of the Hellenistic States of a real and enduring inflation. But our general information about this period, it must be added, is inadequate and inconclusive. One point is certain. The only State that possessed an ample and steadily increasing supply of gold and silver was Rome. This supply came in part from the Spanish mines and in part from the pillage and exploitation of the East. It is not surprising that Roman currency began gradually to replace the Hellenistic currencies, and that the latter, for example that of Athens, were forced to adapt themselves to it. Moreover, it was now the Roman capitalists who dominated the money market and carried on an active business in money-lending, often at exorbitant rates of interest.[214]

After these general remarks a few words may be said about the monetary policy of the individual Hellenistic States. It varied from time to time and from place to place. But at all times and in all parts of the Hellenistic world it was dominated by certain basic ideas, which are manifest in Greek political, social, and economic life in general. I refer to the two deeply rooted tendencies of the Greek world, contradictory and conflicting as they were, one towards a unity to be effected by imposing the will of one State on the others, and the other towards particularism and isolation, expressed in the pursuit of political liberty at any cost and economic self-sufficiency.

Alexander was the chief active promoter of the idea of the unity of the civilized world. This idea directed his monetary policy. He designed to establish in his Empire one currency, which by its abundance, reliability, and cheapness, and with the help of certain political measures, should put an end to the monetary chaos and anarchy that then prevailed. The efforts of Alexander were successful. His money became pre-eminently the currency of his empire. His successors continued his coinage, but each for himself and in his own name: coinage was one of the signs and symbols of political independence, it was a powerful instrument of political influence and propaganda, and it yielded a substantial revenue. With the further disintegration of his empire, coinage became ever more diversified, each sovereign State, whether a monarchy or a city, minting its own money. The result was that after Apamea the currencies of the ancient world presented almost the same aspect as in the late fourth century B.C.

A few somewhat more specific observations may be added about the monetary development of the chief Hellenistic States. Particularism in monetary policy was especially strong in the Greek city-states, the same particularism that we have noticed in the other fields of their economic life. As was natural, such cities as Athens, Rhodes, and the other large commercial centres, so long as they remained independent, never closed their mints; nor did the powerful Achaean and Aetolian Leagues, and the minor leagues such as the Acarnanian, Boeotian, Arcadian, Euboean, Thessalian, and Epirote in continental Greece, and the Lycian in Asia Minor. Those Greek cities which were under the domination of kings were forced to discontinue their coinage. But as soon as, by one means or another, they recovered their liberty, they at once resumed their coinage. We see this in the case of cities liberated by Rome in 197 and 189 B.C. and of the Syrian cities which received liberty and autonomy from the hands of their own kings.

Coinage in the Greek cities was the monopoly of the State, and the use of the local coinage was compulsory in the territory of a given city. This exclusiveness led in some cases to very strict measures, such as the monopolizing by the State of the exchange of foreign coins (above, p. 1287). Every Greek State endeavoured to secure the largest possible circulation for its currency, adopting various means for the purpose. Of these we know little, but we have some idea of their results. We know that Rhodes secured a wide circulation for its drachmas, that Athens maintained the ancient reputation of its currency, that Thasos and Maronea secured a wide circulation for their silver tetradrachms in the north-east, and that Apollonia and Dyrrhachium did the same for their silver coins in the north-west. I have discussed above the attempt made by Athens in the early first century B.C. to obtain predominance for its coins in the Greek market by an Amphictionic decree.

The Greek cities, though their monetary policy was inspired by particularism and self-sufficiency, nevertheless made some important concessions to the principle of monetary unity which was recommended by economic and political considerations. I may adduce a few facts taken at random. The minting of the Greek Leagues was guided by this idea of unity, that is to say, of a unity within each League. More important and more general was the extension of the Attic standard over the Hellenistic world. It was never accepted by all the cities, for many retained their old standards or introduced new ones, as for example did Rhodes. But the outstanding feature was the adoption of the Attic standard, which greatly facilitated trade between the States. It was the same considerations that dictated the issue on a large scale of posthumous Alexanders and Lysimachi. Such issues were made by many cities before 197 and 189 B.C., and subsequently by many more. This was a legacy of Alexander's monetary unity and an attempt to create some kind of partial substitute for an international currency. The same principle, on a minor scale, may be detected in the minting by some cities of the so-called 'Ausgleichsmünzen', that is to say, coins adapted to two different standards. This was done for example at Ephesus and Priene in respect of coins of small denomination.[215]

The same general tendencies determined the monetary policy of the Hellenistic monarchies. In all of them the predominant trend was towards isolation and self-sufficiency. All the monarchies, as soon as established, minted their own royal coins. Minting was from the outset and remained throughout the exclusive prerogative of the kings. They never tolerated any competition in this field and never gave the right of minting to any of their subject cities. The use of the royal money in each kingdom was compulsory, and no foreign money, *de jure*, was allowed to circulate in it.

Some of the kings were more consistent than others in giving effect to these principles. The Seleucids, for example, made many concessions to the idea of monetary unity on the one hand and to the particularism of the Greek city-states on the other. I have mentioned how from the first they tolerated the circulation in their empire of foreign coins of their own Attic standard. This was certainly a concession to the needs of international commerce. When, after the reign of Antiochus III, there was an acute shortage of silver, they opened wide the doors of their empire to the silver tetradrachms of various Anatolian mints, including those of the Pergamene kings, probably as the result of an understanding with the Attalids. Some of these coins were authenticated as legal currency by Seleucid countermarks. Among these coins of foreign mintage there were, as before, posthumous Alexanders and Lysimachi.

On the other hand, though they insisted on their monopoly of coinage, the Seleucids did not object to the minting of small silver and copper coins by their subject cities, including some of their colonies. It was a wise measure dictated by the needs of local commerce, needs which the royal mints were hardly able to satisfy. They went even further. Antiochus IV granted the right of coinage, of minting royal coins, to many cities of his kingdom, and his successors were willing to grant the same right to several of those cities in conjunction with the privilege of autonomy.[216]

The monetary policy of the Attalids was in many respects similar. Their own coinage was sound and abundant. Like the Seleucids they insisted on their monetary prerogative. But Eumenes II, in order to increase the issue of coined silver and thus to promote commerce, did not hesitate to grant to several cities of his kingdom the right of minting under his control special uniform coins, the so-called *cistophori*, which soon became a Pan-Anatolian currency and circulated in large quantities both in Asia Minor and abroad. Nor did the Attalids differ from the Seleucids in their policy of allowing the local minting of small change.[217]

I cannot discuss the monetary policy of the other kings of the eastern part of the Hellenistic world, for this would require much space and a minute study. But I am convinced that the principal measures adopted by them resembled those of the Seleucids and Attalids. I may remind the reader of what I have said, for example, of the coinage of Philip and Perseus.*

The Ptolemies were far more consistent than the Seleucids in their adoption of monetary monopoly and self-sufficiency. They made no concessions either to the tendency towards monetary unity or to the particularism of their subject cities. Their monetary policy was guided almost exclusively by their own, chiefly fiscal and to a certain extent national, interests.

Many points, no doubt, in that policy remain obscure and controversial. But the chief tendencies may perhaps be perceived. I have dealt with the subject above,† and I may therefore be brief.

The Ptolemies pursued from the outset their own monetary policy regardless of what happened in this respect in the rest of the world. For reasons unknown to us, but probably dictated chiefly by economic rather than political considerations, they separated themselves and their kingdom sharply from the rest of the Hellenistic world: they dropped the Attic standard and adopted, after some experiments, their own standard, which is generally called Phoenician, but may be better styled Ptolemaic.

Within the territory of Egypt they established a rigid monopoly of coinage. The circulation of foreign coins of whatever standard was prohibited, probably in the whole of the Ptolemaic Empire, but certainly in Egypt proper. Foreign coins

* Ch. V, p. 633.

† See Ch. IV, pp. 398 ff.; and cf. the Excursus by E. S. G. Robinson at the end of this book.

brought to Egypt by foreign and native merchants had to be
re-minted and transformed into Ptolemaic currency in order
to be used in that country. It is very probable that a concomitant of this monopoly of currency was the exclusion of
foreign capital from the Egyptian money-market.

The next step towards isolation and self-sufficiency may be
seen in the policy of the Ptolemies with regard to copper. As
a concession to the ancestral habits of the native population
copper, of which the Ptolemies had an abundant supply, was
minted in large quantities and was dealt with in the same way
as silver and gold. A trimetallic system, unknown to the Hellenistic world, was thus introduced. This step was followed
by another of even greater consequence. At some moment in
the reign of Philopator copper was made the standard currency
of Egypt and a fixed ratio was established between copper and
silver (1 to 60). The policy of the early Ptolemies with regard
to copper, as with regard to the standard of coinage, was a
local measure intended to achieve some of their aims. On the
one hand it was a concession to the habits of the natives, on
the other a powerful means of concentrating gold and silver
in their own hands. These metals they needed for wars, diplomatic subsidies, payment of mercenaries, and foreign purchases. A large part of it was stored in the treasury of the
kings as a reserve. I draw attention to what I have said
above (p. 1152) of the reserves accumulated by Philadelphus.

The monetary policy of the early Ptolemies as sketched
above had important consequences. Whether or not they
thought of making their currency a universal, or at least a
Panhellenistic, currency is difficult to say; it is not very
probable that they had such a design but, if they had, they
never achieved it. The result of their adoption of a standard
of their own was first to split the Hellenistic world into two
monetary sections—one comprising Ptolemaic Egypt, another
the rest of that world—and ultimately, with the political
decline of the Ptolemies, to isolate Egypt with its copper
standard from the rest of the Hellenistic world.

The effect on the economic life of Egypt proper was less
important. We do not know how actively the Ptolemies carried on minting. The general impression is that the currency

issued by the various Ptolemaic mints was abundant. Ptolemaic gold and silver coins figure largely in our numismatic collections and much copper is found in the Egyptian hoards. If money was scarce and of high value in early Ptolemaic Egypt, if the prices of commodities were low and the rate of interest high (above, p. 1286), it was not because little currency was minted. The reasons for this state of things, which I have already discussed, were of a more general character, viz. the accumulation of money by the kings and the extraction of money from the population by means of monopolies and taxation.

Nor was it the monetary policy of the Ptolemies which caused the catastrophic decline of the purchasing power of money in the second and first centuries B.C., or what is called the Ptolemaic inflation. It was the general political and economic evolution which involved the currency in the general ruin. Commodities became expensive in Egypt because the quantity produced was small, and this diminished output was due to internal wars and revolutions and the passive and active opposition of the working classes to the government. Silver rose in price and was adulterated by the kings because little of it was imported from abroad, while none came into Egypt from the lost foreign dominions. I need not repeat here what has been said on this subject in my fifth and sixth chapters.

The monetary policy of the Ptolemies was certainly peculiar. But there was nothing new in the devices they adopted. Their policy was in fact an adaptation to the peculiar economic conditions of Egypt of the ideas that then prevailed in the Hellenistic world, an adaptation carried out rigidly and consistently.

Weights and measures. Closely connected with the coinage of the various States of the Hellenistic world and of great importance to their economic life was their management of weights and measures. The history of the various systems of weights and measures and the problems of their interrelations cannot be treated here, for the subject is difficult and highly controversial. Nor can I enter into a discussion of the measures by which civilized States maintained a certain order in this field by establishing officially recognized and well-devised metrological systems within their boundaries, and by preventing the use of false weights and measures by their agents and private citizens. While the former subject has been frequently treated, very little study has been given to the latter.[218]

In these conditions it is not easy to indicate the innovations that were introduced in this connexion in Hellenistic times. I have more than once referred to the subject in previous chapters, and I need only add here some general remarks.

We find indeed very little that was new in this respect in the life of the Hellenistic cities. As before, each city had its own weights and measures and magistrates in charge of them. We are comparatively well informed about their functions at Athens in the late second century B.C. from an Athenian decree (*I.G.* ii², 1013), already referred to (Ch. VI, n. 9), which contains several regulations on the subject. Similar laws and decrees certainly existed in many of the Hellenistic cities.[219] Some idea of the activity of the Greek cities in this matter, of their endeavours to induce or even to force the population to use weights and measures conforming to the city's approved standards and certified by the city authorities, may be derived, not only from the above-mentioned inscription, but also from the hundreds of weights and a number of other measures of stone, bronze, and lead which have been found in the ruins of ancient cities and which were in daily use. The abundant set of Attic weights of various denominations, uniform and officially certified, is especially instructive.[220]

What changes were first introduced in Hellenistic times in the various systems of weights and measures used by the Greek cities we do not know; nor whether any attempt was made by these (after the failure of Athens to enforce its own system of weights and measures on the Greek world) to effect some kind of unification in this respect, similar to attempts at unification of coinage. Certain adjustments were natural, and of these we have some information. But more importance attaches to the question of the policy adopted in this connexion by the new overlords of the Greek cities, the Hellenistic monarchs. Did they endeavour to substitute a single well-conceived royal system of weights and measures for the variety of systems that prevailed in the cities? Though we have no evidence on this point, I much doubt whether the Hellenistic kings ever made such an attempt or encroached in this way on the liberty of the ancient Greek cities now included in their respective dominions.

This brings us to the question of the general policy of the Hellenistic monarchs with regard to the weights and measures in use in their territories. It appears that in this the monarchies (with the exception of Macedonia) inherited from the Persian Empire a certain dualism. It may be conjectured that, while for their coinage and for the purposes of the central administration the Persian kings used a single royal standard of weights and measures, they never interfered with the systems customarily used in the various satrapies. In Egypt, for example, they found in existence an admirable, well-balanced, and stable system of weights and measures. They do not seem ever to have thought of replacing it by their own system. On the contrary, they based their relations with the population of Egypt on the local, not on the 'federal', system of weights and measures. The same is true, *mutatis mutandis*, of the other civilized satrapies and their constituent parts, especially Babylonia. I cannot enter into a detailed discussion of this subject, and in particular of the relations between the fine Babylonian system of weights and measures and the above-mentioned official system of the Persian Empire.[221]

Such being the pre-Hellenistic conditions, the question arises: how did the Hellenistic kings—the Seleucids, the Ptolemies, the Attalids—act in regard to them? Did they retain them as they inherited them from the Persians, or did they radically change them? The situation in their kingdoms was even more complicated than under the Persians, inasmuch as the Greeks now formed the leading element in the political, social, and economic life of those kingdoms and brought with them their own systems of weights and measures.

This question has never been treated exhaustively by modern scholars. The few who have dealt at all with the weights and measures in use in the various monarchies have limited themselves to collecting the material: the names of the weights and measures, the meaning of these names, the equivalents of the weights and measures, and their relation to those previously used in one country or another.[222]

Not being a specialist in metrology, I cannot here take up the subject in its entirety. I may, however, raise certain points and offer a few random remarks regarding them. It is interesting to note, for example, that the so-called *Scriptores metrologici* of Roman times, when tabulating the various systems of weights and measures, mention standards which they call Ptolemaic, Philetaeric, and royal. Does this mean that in Egypt and in Pergamon the Romans inherited special official systems of weights and measures to which they gave the royal names just mentioned, systems which had existed in the Hellenistic monarchies before the Roman conquest? If so, a natural suggestion would be that these systems were a continuation of those previously in force, in the time of the Persian domination, that is to say, a continuation of the ancestral metrological systems of the several countries slightly modified first by the Persian satraps and again by the Hellenistic monarchs.[223]

The documentary evidence which we have on the subject, scanty and difficult to interpret as it is, does not contradict this suggestion. In Egypt we are aware of no changes in the metrological system. All the weights and measures in use in Ptolemaic times, despite the Persian and Greek names by which some of them were designated, are traditional and go back to the native Egyptian system. Moreover, it appears that the Ptolemies never tried to introduce complete uniformity in this respect. Though they probably prescribed the use of certain measures in the various departments of their financial administration, these measures were not uniform. Thus for instance *artabae* of different capacity were used for different types of dry goods, and so it was with the *metretai* and *keramia* used for measuring wine, oil, and other liquids. It would appear that the Ptolemies inherited this rather complicated system from the past and never changed it. Nor can we affirm that they required from their subjects the exclusive use of royal weights and measures. Several *artabae* of different capacity besides the official measures were in use in Egypt in private transactions in the Ptolemaic and later in the Roman period. We have no evidence of any attempt made by the Ptolemies to introduce uniformity in this matter. The same is true of the Greek measures. In the customs tariffs the customs duties on imported wine and other goods were calculated according to the foreign containers, equivalent to foreign metrical units, in which the goods were imported. Even in Egypt itself these foreign units remained in use both in Ptolemaic and Roman times.[224]

It appears that the same policy was adopted by the Seleucids in their empire. I have referred above to the royal and royal-municipal weights found in large numbers in Syria.* These weights have never been fully collected and comprehensively studied, and until such a collection and study are available no general conclusions can be drawn. But it seems reasonable to infer, with A. Segré, from those which have been published that the royal weights of Syria go back to one and the same standard, to a sort of blend of the Attic *drachma* with the *siclus* of the Persian *mina*. At the same time, alongside of the royal weights, local weights were freely recognized and were probably in common use in private business transactions.[225]

Flexible and liberal as it was, the policy of the Hellenistic kings with regard to weights and measures was nevertheless animated by the desire to keep this department of economic life under strict control. We have little information on the subject, but certain documents attest how careful the Ptolemies were to prevent their own officers from cheating the population by using arbitrary measures, larger than those prescribed, in collecting taxes and rents in kind. For this offence the penalty was death (*Teb.* 5, 91 f.). I may also mention the detailed character of the directions given, and the efficiency of the measures taken, to prevent the men engaged in the transport of corn from defrauding the government by the use of false measures.[226]

In general, although we have no exact information, it appears that weights and measures were a matter of great concern to

* Ch. IV, pp. 451 ff., and Pls. LIV and LV.

the Hellenistic royal governments, and it is probable that both in Egypt and in the Seleucid kingdom special officers were placed in charge of this department of the royal administration.

III. CONCLUSION

THE LEGACY OF THE HELLENISTIC PERIOD

I need not speak of the legacy of the Hellenistic world in the fields of literature, art, religion, philosophy, and science. The subject and the problems that it involves are familiar to all who are interested in ancient history, and a book devoted to social and economic history is not the appropriate place for their discussion. But a few words on the social and economic heritage that the Hellenistic world transmitted to the Roman Empire will form a natural conclusion to the present work. By the word heritage I do not, of course, mean to imply that the Romans borrowed consciously from their Hellenistic predecessors, that they imitated or reproduced some of their institutions; I use the word to signify the continued development of certain features of Hellenistic social and economic life in the atmosphere of the Roman Empire.

One of the most important of these was the unity of the Hellenistic world of which I have so frequently spoken. This unity, though shaken and jeopardized by political vicissitudes, never ceased to act as a potent factor in Hellenistic life. I have shown how the group of highly civilized city-states in Italy—Greek, Samnite, Etruscan, Umbrian, and Latin—absorbed in its peculiar development many Hellenistic features and came into ever closer connexion with the Hellenistic countries. This process ended in a political union of the two parts of the civilized world, in which the western part was politically dominant. With political union cultural, social, and economic interpenetration became more rapid. In this process the 'romanization' of the Hellenistic world was slight, the 'hellenization' of the steadily expanding Latin world much more conspicuous. The social and economic structure of the West gradually assumed a striking resemblance to that of the East. After Augustus and especially in the second century A.D. there was in this respect, so far at least as the city-states were concerned, little difference between a Latin-speaking city community in Italy and the western provinces, and the Greek-speaking communities of the East.

Certain aspects of this process may be mentioned more specifically. In the economic field Greek genius in the Hellenistic period evolved no new conceptions of a revolutionary kind. But some notable improvements and partial changes were effected. Among them may be noted some technical innovations in agriculture, industry, and commerce, based partly on scientific discoveries and partly on the interchange of long-established methods between the constituent parts of the Hellenistic world. This interchange was facilitated by the tabulation and systematic classification made by Greek technical science of the results of an experience which had accumulated during centuries in the various Hellenistic countries. Italy and the West adopted the new devices and used them freely in reshaping their economic system. They added thereto the experience of the West—of Italy, Carthage, and the western provinces of the Roman Empire—and summarized the results in technical treatises modelled on Greek originals. We may still follow this process if we read attentively the Roman treatises on agriculture and architecture, and the encyclopaedia of Pliny the Elder. A study of certain products of industrial activity, such as pottery, will illustrate it further.

We may notice a similar process in the organization of various branches of economic life. In this no revolutionary changes were made, but the recasting and rearrangement of methods of the past led to improvements. Such were the more skilful and systematic management of agricultural estates large and small, which were exploited mainly with the object, not of supplying the owner and his family, but of obtaining the largest possible amount of the best products for sale. Various new methods were adopted for this purpose: increase of production by improved methods of cultivation, the employment of a better qualified and more specialized staff of supervisors on the large estates, the solution of the labour problem in accordance with the varying conditions of locality and period. I may mention as an instance the use of slave labour in different countries and at different times.

Similar though less progressive was the development of industry. Here again no radical innovations were introduced in the organization of various crafts. But in all branches of industry one may notice a general tendency towards standardization and the production of larger quantities of standardized goods. Mass production according to modern conceptions was not attained, but there was a step towards it.

The evolution of commerce and banking was similar. These developed on old lines, but their scope was much extended, and the interchange of goods, assisted by the better-organized operations of the banks, became easier and smoother than before. If general conclusions may be drawn from the scanty and dispersed evidence, I may suggest that fuller information about commerce and banking would reveal the introduction in Hellenistic times of more new features in these enterprises than in agriculture and certainly in industry.

The innovations in the organization of economic life, all of which tended towards what, with all reserve, we may call 'capitalism' (I hesitate to use a term whose meaning is so much disputed), certainly did not remain confined to the Hellenistic world. They soon became familiar in the West. How far the economic organization of the West in the second and first centuries B.C. resembled that of the East is difficult to say. But its development was certainly in the same direction, and it may be not too hazardous to suggest that this was due to the incorporation of the West in the economic οἰκουμένη; for within this οἰκουμένη the interchange of methods was a natural phenomenon. I may remind the reader of what I have said with regard to agriculture, and I may add that the production of such types of pottery as the Arretine ware and the lead-glazed vessels, probably introduced into Italy by immigrants from the East, must have been organized, more or less closely, on lines with which these men were familiar.

In the later stage of the history of the ancient world the process which began in the second and first centuries led to a far-reaching assimilation. I doubt very much whether in the Roman Empire there were important differences between West and East in the management of a progressive farm, of a branch of industry, or of a commercial business, other than those attributable to climate, geophysical conditions, and national peculiarities. Commerce certainly was organized in the same way and remained as complicated and highly developed and as international, oecumenical, as it had been in Hellenistic times. I see no signs of any simplification of forms in comparison with the Hellenistic period.

The most important inheritance of the Roman world was, however, the incorporation of the Greek city-states in the fabric of the Roman Empire. The process began early in Roman history but did not assume large proportions until the second half of the second century B.C.

I have shown in the preceding chapters and in the first part of this chapter that the Greek city-state underwent no important changes in its political, economic, and social structure in Hellenistic times. The Greek city constitutions, the Greek financial and economic organization, the Greek life remained the same in the last three centuries before Christ as they had previously been.

It is unnecessary to stress this point. As regards their economic structure the Greek cities in the Hellenistic period remained as self-centred as in the past. Some innovations may have been introduced in taxation, in the management of city mints, in financial administration, in the organization of food supply, in the regulation of liturgies, in banking. But the general character of the city economy remained the·same, both in the cities which remained independent or retained a semblance of political independence, and in the cities, old and new, that were subject to the Hellenistic kings. The Hellenistic monarchs (with few exceptions) never showed any desire to change the economic structure of the cities which were constituent parts of their respective kingdoms.

But certain momentous developments in the life of the Greek cities took place in this period. The most important was the consolidation of the Greek *bourgeoisie*, which gradually became the pivot of their social system. I have dealt with the *bourgeoisie* earlier in this chapter. I have shown how it became the leading class in all the cities of the Hellenistic world, and assumed responsibility for the city administration and for the welfare and comfort of the population. Finally, it was this class which, by gifts and donations, contributed lavishly to the embellishment of the cities and to the maintenance of the temples and religious ceremonies, of games, *agones*, and similar institutions.

Moreover in those cities, both old and new, which were under the direct control of the Hellenistic kings, the *bourgeoisie* stood in direct relations with the central power, and served as intermediary between the king and his bureaucracy on the one hand and the inhabitants in general on the other. As holders of the administrative offices, as members of the city councils, and in virtue of their influence in the popular assembly, the *bourgeoisie* bore the responsibility for all the demands of the central power in respect of regular tribute, extraordinary taxes, billeting of troops, deliveries in kind to the army, transportation of military forces, maintenance of roads in the city territory, mobilization of soldiers and equipment of ships for the royal army and navy, expense connected with royal visits, and other like charges. Our information about this side of the life of the cities is imperfect, but we know how deeply they were affected by the εἰσφοραί, the ἐπισταθμίαι, the παρουσίαι, the ἀγγαρεῖαι, &c. There is no doubt that it was the urban administration which, in collaboration with the royal officials, had to organize these services and to collect, or help to collect, the contributions, and that it was the *bourgeoisie* who had to bear the greater part of the financial burden.

Last but not least, the elected magistrates and senates and the popular assemblies of the several cities, though they had little connexion with each other (and that of the sort resulting, in Asia Minor, from membership of the religious κοινά) or none at all, nevertheless, taken all together, formed a kind of subordinate representative government, which carried out important administrative and financial functions in that part of the monarchies which consisted of the cities and their territories. This was the position, to a greater or less extent, in all the Hellenistic monarchies except Egypt. The significance of the part thus played by the cities, that is to say, chiefly by the *bourgeoisie*, must not be underestimated. It was local government, a government controlled and closely watched by the central power, but exercising a decisive influence on many aspects of the life of a large and prominent part of the population of a Hellenistic kingdom. It is even more important to bear in mind that it was the population not only of the capital but of all the Greek cities of a kingdom that formed its public opinion, on which the general popularity of the king in great measure depended, and which often determined his success or failure.

In spite of the great hardships caused by wars, of bitter internal struggles, and of heavy material burdens, the *bourgeoisie* firmly established itself in the old cities of Greece in the early Hellenistic period and constantly grew in wealth and importance. In the same period it took firm root in the new cities of the Hellenistic kingdoms and steadily increased in numbers by assimilating the upper strata of the native population. This was why it was able to survive the ordeals of the second and first centuries B.C., which decimated, humiliated, and demoralized its members, and caused their gradual impoverishment and in some instances their utter ruin. Prostrated but subsisting, the *bourgeoisie* and with it the city-state (or vice versa) were inherited by their new masters, the Romans, who, after treating them with harshness for a time, finally became reconciled with the cities and their dominant middle class. They not only supported and protected the latter against the lower classes, but maintained it in all the functions which it discharged in the city and State systems, and made it the pillar of their rule over the eastern provinces, except of course in Egypt.

I cannot dwell on the part played by the city *bourgeoisie* under the Roman domination in what had been the Hellenistic world. I have discussed this vital feature in the life of the Roman Empire in my volume dealing with its social and economic history. The only point of interest here is that the *bourgeoisie* of the Hellenistic part of the Roman Empire was not created by Rome, and it was not Rome that devised and worked out its functions in the machinery of the Roman State. These were a legacy of the Hellenistic period.

It is even more important to recall that the role of the cities and of the *bourgeoisie* was not confined to the eastern part of the Roman Empire. The urbanization of its western section, which I have discussed at length in my Roman volume, was a complicated process in which many factors co-operated, the policy of the Roman emperors being only one of these. The same is true of the formation of the western city *bourgeoisie*. But the role which was assigned by the Roman government to the cities and the *bourgeoisie* in the West, and which was almost exactly the same as that played by them in the East, was a deliberate creation of the Roman emperors and was thus another legacy of the Hellenistic world.

Besides the Greek cities with their territories, the Hellenistic kingdoms comprised large tracts of land which never formed part of city territories and were subdivided into villages with their respective districts. I have discussed their status several times above, and need only here remind the reader of its chief features. Most of the villages depended directly on the kings and tilled the soil at first as royal bondsmen and serfs, later probably as 'king's tenants' or 'king's folk' (λαοὶ or γεωργοὶ βασιλικοί). This was the position in Egypt, where they formed a large part of the population, and likewise in almost all the Asiatic monarchies. To the same class belonged the sacred slaves of the gods and temples, both in Egypt and in the rest of the Hellenistic world, and also the tenants of the large estates which the kings bestowed as revocable gifts on members of the royal family or influential members of their staff. It is probable that the status of the royal tenants, both on the royal and on the gift estates, was gradually improved by their masters and lords, so that the former bondsmen or serfs came to be treated as free hereditary tenants of the king or of the State, almost as landowners, though still subject to some restrictions on their personal and economic freedom. As regards the status of tenants of the temples during Hellenistic times we have hardly any information, so far as concerns the more progressive kingdoms, Egypt, the Seleucid monarchy, and Pergamon.

In Egypt the 'royal tenants' were inherited by the Romans and became hereditary State tenants, their position being slightly modified as compared with that which they held under the Ptolemies. Their fate under Roman rule in the former Hellenistic monarchies of Asia is little known and is matter of controversy. The problem has been dealt with in the preceding and the present chapter. Even if we assume with some modern scholars that most or all of the royal tenants became free landholders, owners of their parcels of land, under the Romans, which to me seems highly improbable, they still remained in their own conception the royal or State tenants of the past. Their status was changed only externally. When in the course of the economic development of the eastern provinces they became in one way or another hereditary tenants of the emperors, of members of the imperial family, or of owners of large exterritorial estates, they certainly did not feel themselves degraded or cheated. They reverted to their traditional status which they had probably never forgotten. But there is reason to think that the evolution was different. In many regions of Asia the former royal tenants never changed their status. As in Egypt, they became tenants of the Roman State instead of being tenants of the king. Some of them, in ways unknown to us, may have changed their status to that of free landowners. But many in all probability became later, after vicissitudes about which we have no direct information, hereditary leaseholders of the Roman emperors or of private landowners. I am still convinced, as I was thirty years ago, that the roots of the Roman colonate as it existed in the East must be looked for in the Hellenistic period.

This does not mean that the colonate in the West was formed consciously by the emperors as a counterpart of its eastern branch. In the West the history of the colonate is even more complicated than in the East and differs from place to place. It was a result of many political, social, and economic processes, both general and local. Nor is it clear how far the establishment of the legal and economic status of tenants of the State or emperor in the West which we find well attested under the later Roman Empire was influenced by the immemorial relations between such tenants and their landlords in the East. This influence deserves careful study and cannot be discarded offhand as improbable.

Egypt occupied a special position in the Hellenistic world. I have discussed its economic and social structure and traced its evolution, and need only add a few words here. In Ptolemaic Egypt, in contrast with the other Hellenistic kingdoms, we find two classes confronting one another, and standing entirely apart from those few cities which formed a foreign enclave in the country's homogeneous structure. I mean the *bourgeoisie* of foreign origin, which for the greater part was employed in the service of the State and always retained its Greek identity, and the labouring mass of the native population. The whole of Egypt was the οἶκος of the king, his private household, which he owned in his character of a living god. Parts of this οἶκος he might entrust to the management of the priests for the maintenance of the worship of the gods, or might bestow on members of his household—generals or other military officers and men, officials, members of his family, or favourites. But the whole of Egypt remained nevertheless his οἶκος, partly subdivided into smaller and less important οἶκοι.

The chief task of the Ptolemies, men of Macedonian descent and Greek mentality, was to organize the exploitation of this Oriental οἶκος with the help of assistants, most of them Greek or hellenized, who, from the social and economic standpoint, may be called the *bourgeoisie* of Egypt. They effected their purpose by creating an ingenious bureaucratic machinery to conduct their elaborately planned and State-controlled economy.

Such, in bare outline, was the structure of Egypt as established by the early Ptolemies and only slightly modified by their successors. It was their elaborate οἶκος that the Romans inherited and the only changes that the latter ever made in its structure were devised in the spirit of the late Ptolemies and were of no fundamental importance.

It was as a foreign body of this kind that Egypt remained for centuries one of the provinces of the Roman Empire. The Roman emperors understood its structure thoroughly, since Egypt was one of their main sources of revenue. Did they try to apply their knowledge to the organization of the rest of their empire? Did they introduce into the structure of the latter some of the methods of the bureaucracy and State-controlled economy of the Ptolemies? These questions have been frequently discussed by modern scholars and among them by myself, and cannot be dealt with here. Some features in the organization of the city of Rome may have been inspired by that of Alexandria. The increasingly elaborate central financial administration of the early emperors, which in fact was originally an administration of the imperial οἶκος (an οἶκος utterly different in character, origin, and evolution from the Oriental οἶκοι in general and from the Ptolemaic in particular), may have been of Hellenistic, though not necessarily of Ptolemaic origin. The strict State control to which the tax-farmers were gradually subjected, and the ultimate transition to direct tax-collection by agents of the State, may have been suggested to the Roman emperors by the financial organization of Egypt. The organization of direct tax-collection by State collectors responsible to the emperor in person and property, through *mensae* (τράπεζαι) with their elaborate accounting and book-keeping, was probably an extension to the other Roman provinces of the Egyptian system of tax-collection. Some other features of administration may perhaps be added to the above. But the distinctive element in the Ptolemaic economy, control and planning by the State, was never transferred from Egypt to the other provinces. These provinces were characterized by a city economy directed by the imperial administration in a manner which recalls rather the Seleucid and Attalid kingdoms than that of the Ptolemies.

Not until the time of Diocletian did State control and planned economy become the pivot of the life of the Roman Empire. But that emperor's system had no connexion with the refined and highly elaborate methods of the Ptolemies.

A few words in conclusion. The reader of the present work may derive the impression that I have minimized the achievements of the Hellenistic period in the social and economic field. My intention has been neither to minimize nor to exaggerate these achievements, but to collect the few facts known about them, to classify and to interpret them and to draw from them the conclusions that they suggest. I hope that my readers will realize the difficulty of this task and the paucity of our information. But that information is sufficient to manifest the importance of the Hellenistic period in the evolution of antiquity. The Hellenistic world in itself was a stupendous creation of the Greek genius, and it had a far-reaching influence on the future. This influence lay chiefly in the field of literature, art, religion, philosophy, science, and learning, but it was considerable also in the social and economic sphere. It is vain to attempt to compare the achievements of the Hellenistic period with those of the Roman Empire, to speak of the former having reached heights in social and economic development which the latter never attained. We have no standards for such comparison. In many respects the Roman Empire created institutions and devised methods which have survived it and still subsist, but were unknown or little developed in the Hellenistic period. In our special field the Roman peace brought about conditions which the Hellenistic world never enjoyed, and led to results which it never achieved, results which may be described and whose evolution may be understood but which cannot be measured.

One thing, however, is certain. The Hellenistic genius might have created more than in effect it did. Its generative force was undermined too early in its development. Though it never became sterile and senile, at least in the Hellenistic period, it was handicapped in its natural development by external causes. After about a century of intensive creation, the peculiar evolution of its political life and certain political ideas inherent in the Greek mind put an early end to progress in almost all the fields of Greek activity. It was those political conditions and also incessant wars that debarred the Hellenistic world from even greater achievements. The blame should not be laid on individuals. The desire for political independence and domination, jealousy, and the tendency ruthlessly to suppress the weak were salient characteristics of the Greek no less than his indomitable creative impulse.

It was these peculiarities of the Greek mind that first weakened the Hellenistic world and then opened the door to Roman intervention, and so brought about Roman domination. By their political rivalry and jealousy the Greeks gave the Romans a pretext for active interference in their political affairs, and the same rivalry and jealousy prevented them from uniting to check the rapid progress of the intruders. These failings were fatal to Greece. Roman destruction was radical. But the Romans alone cannot be blamed for it: they accelerated the process of disintegration and destruction, but they did not initiate it.

It is idle to speculate how the Hellenistic world would have fared without Roman interference in its affairs. Rome existed on the political horizon, a civilized, united, and excellently organized body politic, conscious of its strength and imbued with the desire for domination, while Greece was split into hundreds of States, each prepared to achieve its own political ends by any means. In these conditions Roman intervention sooner or later was inevitable. And Roman intervention, as we now know, meant for her political opponents destruction, humiliation, and demoralization.

It is another melancholy instance in the history of mankind of the antinomy of destructive and creative forces within one and the same great people.

PRINTED IN GREAT BRITAIN
AT THE UNIVERSITY PRESS, OXFORD
BY VIVIAN RIDLER
PRINTER TO THE UNIVERSITY